SQL
FUNDAMENTALS
Second Edition

John J. Patrick

Prentice Hall PTR
One Lake Street
Upper Saddle River, NJ 07458

ISBN 0-13-066947-4

90000

9 780130 669476

Library of Congress Cataloging-in-Publication Data

Patrick, John J.
    SQL fundamentals / John J. Patrick.--2nd ed.
        p. cm.
    ISBN 0-13-066947-4
        I. SQL (Computer program language) I. Title.

    QA76.73.S67 P38 2002
    005.75'65--dc21
                                            2002025186

Production Editor and Compositor: *Vanessa Moore*
Acquisitions Editor: *Victoria Jones*
Editorial Assistant: *Michelle Vincenti*
Marketing Manager: *Debby Van Dijk*
Manufacturing Buyer: *Maura Zaldivar*
Cover Design: *Nina Scuderi*
Cover Design Director: *Jerry Votta*
Series Interior Design: *Meg Van Arsdale*
Project Coordinator: *Anne R. Garcia*

Prentice Hall books are widely used by corporations and government agencies for training, marketing, and resale.

For information regarding corporate and government
bulk discounts, please contact:
Corporate and Government Sales
Phone: 800-382-3419; E-mail: corpsales@pearsontechgroup.com

Other company and product names mentioned herein are the trademarks or registered trademarks of their respective owners.

ISBN 0-13-066947-4

Pearson Education Ltd.
Pearson Education Australia PTY, Limited
Pearson Education Singapore, Pte. Ltd
Pearson Education North Asia Ltd
Pearson Education Canada, Ltd.
Pearson Educación de Mexico, S.A. de C.V.
Pearson Education — Japan
Pearson Education Malaysia, Pte. Ltd

Dedicated to four wonderful teachers

Seymour Hayden, who taught me mathematics
Stanley Sultan, who taught me Irish literature
Jim Seibolt, who taught me computers
Scot Stoney, who taught me databases

and to all my students.

CONTENTS AT A GLANCE

Contents

PREFACE

SQL is now one of the most important computer languages. It is used in over 100 software products, and new ones are being added all the time. This book shows you how to get the most out of your database. It explains how to use SQL to solve practical problems, using the most widely used SQL products Oracle and Microsoft Access. Oracle and Access are both widely used, easily available and run on personal computers. By learning these two products in detail, you will have all the basic skills to use any of the many products based on SQL.

Every concept in this book is illustrated with an example of SQL code. In most cases, a *task* is set, then the SQL code is given to complete that task. The *beginning* and *result* tables of data are also shown. There are more than 200 of these examples. Each part stands on its own. You can read this book sequentially or skip around to find the parts that you need.

Be sure to look at the appendices for practical tips on how to run Oracle and Access. The CD-ROM contains the database files and the code for all the examples.

In several places throughout this book, I have expressed opinions about computer technology, something that many other technical books avoid doing. These opinions are my own and I take full responsibility for them. I also reserve the right to change my mind. If I do so, I will put my revised opinion and the reasons that have caused me to change my thinking on the Web site for this book,

www.sqlfun.com

Acknowledgments

Many people contributed greatly to this book. I would like to thank them for all the support they have given me during the time I was writing it. Their ideas and feedback have improved the quality of the material and the way I present it. In particular, I want to thank the following people:

Anila Manning, for her help in all aspects of writing this second edition.

Paul Reavis, who teaches this course with me at UC Berkeley Extension.

Todd Matson, who reviewed the Access material.

Faysal Shaarani and Bill Allaway, who reviewed the Oracle material.

Spencer Brucker and UC Berkeley Extension, who have supported me in teaching the SQL Fundamentals course and developing the material in this book.

All the folks at Prentice Hall PTR, especially Vanessa Moore, production editor; Anne Garcia, project coordinator; Victoria Jones, acquisitions editor; and the many other people with whom I never worked directly.

Thanks especially to my mom, Jean Praninskas, and to my son, Richard Watts, who also reviewed this book.

chapter 1

STORING INFORMATION IN TABLES

In relational databases, all the data is stored in tables and all the results are expressed in tables. In this chapter we examine tables in detail.

Introduction

1-1   What is SQL?

The name SQL stands for Structured Query Language. It is pronounced "S-Q-L" and can also be pronounced "sequel."

SQL is a computer language designed to get information from data that is stored in a relational database. In a moment, I discuss what a relational database is. For now, you can think of it as one method of organizing a large amount of data on a computer. SQL allows you to find the information you want from a vast collection of data. The purpose of this book is to show you how to get the information you want from a database.

SQL is different from most other computer languages. With SQL, you describe the type of information you want. The computer then determines the best procedure to use to obtain it and runs that procedure. This is called a *declarative* computer language because the focus is on the result: You specify what the result should look like. The computer is allowed to use any method of processing as long as it obtains the correct result.

Most other computer languages are *procedural*. These are languages like C, Cobol, Java, Assembler, Fortran, Visual Basic, and others. In these languages, you describe the procedure that will be applied to the data; you do not describe the result. The result is whatever emerges from applying the procedure to the data.

Let me use an analogy to compare these two approaches. Suppose I go to a coffee shop in the morning. With the declarative approach, used by SQL, I can say *what* I want: "I would like a cup of coffee and a donut." With the procedural approach, I cannot say that. I have to say *how* the result can be obtained and give a specific procedure for it. That is, I have to say how to make a cup of coffee and how to make a donut. So, for the coffee, I have to say, "Grind up some roasted coffee beans, add boiling water to them, allow the coffee to brew, pour it into a cup, and give it to me." For the donut, I will have to read from a cookbook. Clearly, the declarative approach is much closer to the way we usually speak and it is much easier for most people to use.

The fact that SQL is easy to use, relative to most other computer languages, is the main reason it is so popular and important. The claim is often made that anyone can learn SQL in a day or two. I think that claim is more a wish than a reality. After all, SQL is a computer language, and computers are not as easy to use as telephones — at least not yet.

Nonetheless, SQL is easy to use. With one day of training, most people can learn to obtain a lot of useful information. That includes people who are not programmers. People throughout an organization, from secretaries to vice presidents, can use SQL to obtain the information they need to make business decisions. That is the hope and, to a large extent, it has been shown to be true.

Information is not powerful by itself. It only becomes powerful when it is available to people throughout an organization when they need to use it. SQL is a tool for delivering that information.

Notes: About SQL

- SQL is the designated language for getting information from a relational database.

- SQL says *what* information to get, rather than *how* to get it.

- Basic SQL is easy to learn.

- SQL empowers people by giving them control over information.

- SQL allows people to handle information in new ways.

- SQL makes information powerful by bringing it to people when they need it.

1-2   What is a relational database and why would you use one?

A *relational database* is one way to organize data in a computer. There are other ways to organize it, but in this book, we do not discuss these other ways, except to say that each method has some strengths and some drawbacks. For now, we look only at the strengths that a relational database has to offer.

SQL is one of the main reasons to organize data into a relational database. Using SQL, information can be obtained from the data fairly easily by people throughout the organization. That is very important.

Another reason is that data in a relational database can be used by many people at the same time. Sometimes hundreds or thousands of people can all share the data in a database. All the people can see the data and all the people can change the data (if they have the authority to do so). From a business perspective, this provides a way to coordinate all the employees and have everybody working from the same body of information.

A third reason is that a relational database is designed with the expectation that your information requirements may change over time. You might need to reorganize the information you have or add new pieces of information to it. Relational databases are designed to make this type of change easy. Most other computer systems are difficult to change. They assume that you know what all the requirements will be before you start to construct them. My experience is that people are not very good at predicting the future, even when they say they can. But here I am showing my own bias toward using relational databases.

From the perspective of a computer programmer, the flexibility of a relational database and the availability of SQL make it possible to develop new computer applications much more rapidly than with traditional techniques. Some organizations take advantage of this. Others do not.

The idea of a relational database was first developed in the early 1970s to handle very large amounts of data — millions of records. At first, the relational database was thought of as a back-end processor that would provide information to a computer application written in a procedural language such as C or Cobol. Even now, relational databases bear some of the birthmarks of that heritage.

Today, however, the ideas have been so successful that entire information systems are often constructed as relational databases, without much need for procedural code (except to support input forms). That is, the ideas that were originally developed to play a supporting role for procedural code have now taken center stage. Much of the procedural code is no longer needed.

In relational databases all the data is kept in tables, which are two-dimensional structures with columns and rows. I describe tables in detail later in this chapter. After you work with them for a while, you will find that tables provide a very nice structure for handling data. They adapt easily to changes, they share data with all users at the same time, and SQL can be run on the data in a table. Many people start thinking of their data in terms of tables. Tables have become the metaphor of choice when working with data.

Today, people use small personal databases to keep their address books, catalog their music tapes, organize their libraries, or track their finances. Business applications are also built as relational databases. Many people prefer to have their data in a database, even if it has only a few records in it.

The beginning of relational databases

- Relational databases were originally developed in the 1970s to organize large amounts of information in a consistent and coherent manner.

- They allowed thousands of people to work with the same information at the same time.

- They kept the information current and consistent at all times.

- They made information easily available to people at all levels of an organization, from secretaries to vice presidents. They used SQL, forms, standardized reports, and ad-hoc reports to deliver information to people in a timely manner.

- They were designed to work as an information server back end. This means that most people would not work directly with the database; instead, they would work with another layer of software. This other software would get the information from the database and then adapt it to the needs of the person.

- They empowered people by making current information available to them when they needed to use it.

Today — How relational databases have changed

- In addition to the large databases described already, now there are also many smaller databases that handle much smaller amounts of information. These databases can be used by a single person or shared by a few people.

- Databases have been so successful and are so easy to use that they are now employed for a wider range of applications than they were originally designed for.

- Many people now work directly with a database instead of through a layer of software.

- Many people prefer to keep their data in databases. They feel that relational databases provide a useful and efficient framework for handling all types of data.

1-3   Why learn SQL?

SQL is used in more than 100 software products. Once you learn SQL, you will be able to use all of these products. Of course, each one will require a little study of its special features, but you will soon feel at home with it and know how to use it. You can use this one set of skills over and over again.

There are reasons SQL is used so much. One reason is that it is easy to learn, relative to many other computer languages. Another reason is that it opens the door to relational databases and the many advantages they offer. Some people say that SQL is the best feature of relational databases and it is what makes them successful. Other people say that relational databases make SQL successful. Most people agree that together they are a winning team.

SQL is the most successful declarative computer language — a language with which you say what you want rather than how to get it. There are some other declarative languages and report-generation tools, but most of them are much more limited in what they can do. SQL is more powerful and can be applied in more situations.

SQL can help you get information from a database that may not be available to people who do not know SQL. It can help you learn and understand the many products that are based on it.

Finally (don't tell your boss), learning SQL can be enjoyable and fun. It can stretch your mind and give you new tools to think with. You might start to view some things from a new perspective.

Major SQL Products	Other SQL Products (and products based on SQL)
Oracle	MYSQL
Microsoft Access	SQLBase
DB2	Cold Fusion
Microsoft SQL Server	SAP
Informix	Business Objects
SQL Windows	ODBC
Sybase	Ingres
SAS sql procedure	Ocelot SQL
FoxPro	OsloData
dBase	PostgreSQL
Tandem SQL	Rapid SQL
	XDB
	SQL/DS
	Mini SQL
	Empress
	Interbase
	Progress
	Supra
	SQL Report Writer
	Paradox
	Delphi
	VAX SQL
	Essbase
	Beagle SQL
	GNU SQL Server
	Just Logic/SQL
	PrimeBase
	Altera SQL Server
	DataScope
	PowerBuilder
	(and many more)

1-4   What is in this book?

The subject of this book

This book shows you how to use SQL to get information from a relational database. It begins with simple queries that retrieve selected data from a single table. It progresses step by step to advanced queries that summarize the data, combine it with data from other tables, or display the data in specialized ways. It goes beyond the basics and shows you how to get the information you need from the databases you have.

Who should read this book?

Everyone with an interest in getting information from a database can read this book. It can be a first book about databases for people who are new to the subject. You do not need to be a computer programmer. The discussion begins at the beginning and it does not assume any prior knowledge about databases. The only thing you need is the persistence to work through the examples and a little prior experience working with your own computer.

Professional programmers can also use this book. The techniques shown here can help them find the solutions to many problems. Whether you are a novice or a professional, an end user or a manager, the SQL skills you learn will be useful to you over and over again.

Organization of this book

This book discusses the practical realities of getting information from a database. A series of specific tasks are accomplished and discussed. Each concept is presented with an example.

The tasks are designed and arranged to show the most important aspects of the subject. Each topic is discussed thoroughly and in an organized manner. All the major features and surprising aspects of each topic are shown.

Why compare two different implementations of SQL — Oracle and Access?

If a book discusses only the theory of SQL, and no particular product that implements it, then the reader will be left with no practical skills. He or she will be able to think about the concepts, but might have difficulty writing code that works.

If a book discusses only one implementation of SQL, then it is easy to get distracted by the quirks and special features it has. You also lose sight of the fact that SQL is used in many products, although in slightly different ways.

This book compares Oracle and Access because they are two of the most widely used SQL products and because they both run on a PC. They are somewhat different. You will see them side by side. Oracle is used mostly for larger business applications. Access is used mostly for personal database applications and smaller business applications.

The Parts of a Table

SQL always deals with data that is in tables. You probably understand tables already on an informal level. The tables used in a relational database have a few unusual features. Because computers need precise definitions, the description of a table must be formalized. In this section, I define what a table is and what its parts are.

1-5   Data is stored in tables

In a relational database, all the data is stored in tables. A table is a two-dimensional structure that has *columns* and *rows*. Using more traditional computer terminology, the columns are called *fields* and the rows are called *records*. You can use either terminology.

Most people are familiar with seeing information in tables. Bus schedules are usually presented in tables. Newspapers use tables to list stock values. We all know how to use these tables. They are a good way to present a lot of information in a very condensed format. The tables in a relational database are very similar to these tables, which we all understand and use every day.

All the information in a relational database is kept in tables. There is no other type of container to keep it in — there are no other data structures. Even the most complex information is stored in tables. Someone once said that there are three types of data structures in a relational database: tables, tables, and tables. In a relational database, we have nothing but tables; there are no numbers, no words, no letters, and no dates unless they are stored in a table.

You might think that this restricts what a relational database can do and the data it can represent. Is it a limitation? The answer is no. All data is capable of being represented in this format. Sometimes you have to do some work to put it in this format. It doesn't always just fall into this format by itself. But you can always succeed at putting data into tables, no matter how complex that data is. This has been proven in mathematics. The proof is long and complex and I do not show it to you here. However, you can have confidence that tables are versatile enough to handle all types of data.

The following two depictions show a basic table structure and how a table might store information.

A conceptual picture of a table.

First Name	Last Name	Age	Gender	Favorite Game
Nancy	Jones	1	F	Peek-a-boo
Paula	Jacobs	5	F	Acting
Deborah	Kahn	4	F	Dolls
Howard	Green	7	M	Baseball
Jack	Lee	5	M	Trucks
Cathy	Rider	6	F	Monsters

An example of a table: A table of information about children.

Each row contains information about one child. Each column contains one type of information for all the children. As always, this table contains only a limited amount of information about each child. It does not say, for instance, how much each child weighs.

Notes

- In a relational database, all the data is stored in tables.
- A table has two dimensions called columns and rows.
- Tables can hold even the most complex information.
- All operations begin with tables and end with tables. All the data is represented in tables.

1-6   A row represents an object and the information about it

Each row of a table represents one object, event, or relationship. I call them all objects for now, so I do not have to keep repeating the phrase "object, event, or relationship."

All the rows within a table represent the same type of object. If you have 100 doctors in a hospital, you might keep all the information about them in a single table. If you also want to keep information about 1,000 patients who are in the hospital, you would use a separate table for that information.

The tables in a relational database may contain hundreds or thousands of rows. Some tables even contain many millions of rows. In theory, there is no limit to the number of rows a table can have. In practice, your computer will limit the number of rows you can have. Today, business databases running on large computers sometimes reach billions of rows.

There are also some tables with only one row of data. You can even have an empty table with no rows of data in it. This is something like an empty box. Usually, a table is only empty when you first build it. After it is created, you start to put rows of data into it.

In a relational database, the rows of a table are considered to be in no particular order so they are an unordered set. This is different from the tables most people are familiar with. In a bus schedule, the rows are in a definite and logical order. They are not scrambled in a random order.

Database administrators (DBAs) are allowed to change the order of the rows in a table to make the computer more efficient. In some products, such as Access, this can be done automatically by the computer. As a result, you, the end user seeking information, cannot count on the rows being in a particular order.

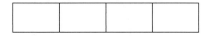

A conceptual picture of a row.

Notes

- A row contains data for one object, event, or relationship.

- All the rows in a table contain data for similar objects, events, or relationships.

- A table may contain hundreds or thousands of rows.

- The rows of a table are not in a predictable order.

1-7   A column represents one type of information

A column contains one particular type of information that is kept about all the rows in the table. A column cannot, or should not, contain one type of information for one row and another type for another row. Each column usually contains a separate type of information.

Each column has a name, for instance "favorite game," and a datatype. We discuss datatypes in chapter 4, but for now let's keep it simple. There are three main datatypes: text, numbers, and dates. This means that there are three types of columns: columns containing text, columns containing numbers, and columns containing dates.

Some columns allow nulls, which are unknown values. Other columns do not allow them. If a column does not allow nulls, then data is required in the column for every row of the table. This means it is a required field. When a column does allow nulls, the field is optional.

Most tables contain 5 to 40 columns. A table can contain more columns, 250 or more, depending on the relational database product you are using, but this is unusual.

Each column has a position within the table. That is, the columns are an ordered set. This contrasts with the rows, which have no fixed order.

Information about the columns — their names, datatypes, positions, and whether they accept nulls — is all considered to be part of the definition of the table itself. In contrast, information about the rows is considered to be part of the data and not part of the definition of the table.

A conceptual picture of a column.

Notes

- A column contains one type of data about each row of the table.

- Each column has a name.

- Each column has a datatype. The most important datatypes are:

    text

    numbers

    dates with times

- Some columns accept nulls, and others do not. A null is an unknown value.

■ Each column has a position within the table. In contrast to rows, the columns of a table form an ordered set. There is a first column and a last column.

■ Most tables have 40 columns or fewer.

1-8   A cell is the smallest part of a table

A *cell* occurs where one row meets with one column. It is the smallest part of a table and it cannot be broken down into smaller parts.

A cell contains one single piece of data, a single unit of information. At least that is the way it is in theory, and this is how you should begin to think about it. In practice, sometimes a cell can contain several pieces of information. For now, we consider that a cell can contain an entire sentence, a paragraph, or more. A cell can contain one of the following:

■ One word

■ One letter

■ One number

■ One date, which includes the time

■ A null, which indicates that there is no data in the cell

For the first few chapters of this book, we consider the information in a cell to be *atomic*, which means that it is a single indivisible unit of information. We gather and arrange information from a table by manipulating its cells. We either use all the information within a cell or we do not use that cell at all. Later, when we discuss row functions, you will see how to use only part of the data from a cell.

A column is a collection of cells. These cells have the same datatype and represent the same type of information. A row is a collection of cells. Together, they represent information about the same object, event, or relationship.

A conceptual picture of a cell.

Notes

- A cell contains a single piece of data, a single unit of information.

- Usually a cell contains one of the following types of data:

    text — sometimes one word, or sometimes a one-letter code, such as M for male and F for female

    a number

    a date and time

    a null, which is an unknown value (some people call this an empty cell, or missing data)

- All the cells in a column contain the same type of information.

- All the cells in a row contain data about the same object, event, or relationship.

1-9　Each cell should express just one thing

Each cell expresses just one thing — one piece of information. That is the intent of the theory of relational databases. In practice, it is not always clear what this means. The problem, partly, is that English and other spoken languages do not always express information clearly. Another part of the problem is that information does not always come in separate units.

Let's examine one case in detail. A person in America usually has two names — a first name and a last name. Now that is a bit of a problem to me when I want to put information in the computer. There is one person, but there are two names. How should I identify the person? Should I put both names together in one cell? Should I put the names into two separate cells? The answer is not clear.

Both methods are valid. The designers of the database usually decide questions like this. If the database designers think that both names will always be used together, then they will usually put both names in a single cell. But if they think that we will sometimes use the names separately, then they will put each name in a separate cell.

The problem with this is that the way a database is used may change over time. So, even if a decision is correct when it is made, it might become incorrect later on.

Full Name
Susan Riley

(A)

First Name	Last Name
Susan	Riley

(B)

Two ways to show the name of a person in a table. (A) One column for the name. Both the first and last names are put in a single cell. (B) Two separate columns: one for the first name and another for the last name. Each cell contains a single word.

Notes

- Both methods are equally valid.

- The first method emphasizes that Susan Riley is one person, even though the English language uses two separate words to express her name. It implies that we will usually call her "Susan Riley," using both her names together as a single unit.

- The second method emphasizes the English words. It implies that we will want to use several different variations of her name, calling her "Susan" or "Susan Riley" or "Miss Riley." The words "Susan" or "Riley" can come from the table in the database. Any other words must be supplied by some other means.

- The database design intends each cell to be used in whole or not used at all. In theory, you should not need to subdivide the data in a cell. However, in practice that is sometimes required.

1-10 Primary key columns identify each row

Most tables contain a *primary key* that identifies each row in the table and gives it a name. Each row must have its own identity so no two rows are allowed to have the same primary key.

The primary key consists of several columns of the table. By convention, these are usually the first few columns. The primary key may be one column or more than one. We say that there is only one primary key, even when it consists of several columns, so it is the collection of these columns, taken as a single unit, that is the primary key and serves to identify each row.

The primary key is like a noun because it names the object of each row. The other columns are like adjectives because they give additional information about the object.

A table can only contain a single primary key, even if it consists of several columns. This makes sense because there is no point in identifying a row twice — those identities could conflict with each other. Suppose, for example, that we have a table of employees. Each employee can be identified by an employee number or by a Social Security number. The database designers would need to choose which column to make the primary key of the table. They could choose either one to be the primary key of the table, or they could choose to use both together to make a primary key. However, they are not allowed to say that each column by itself is a primary key.

The name of a column is considered to be part of the definition of the table. In contrast, the name of a row, which is the primary key of the row, is considered to be part of the data in the table.

There are two rules that regulate the columns of the primary key of a table:

1. None of the columns of the primary key can contain a null. This makes sense because a null is an unknown value. Therefore, a null in any part of the primary key would mean we do not know the identity of the object or the row. In databases, we do not want to enter information about unidentified rows.

2. Each row must have an identity that is different from every other row in the table. That is, no two rows can have the same identity — the same values in all the columns of the primary key. For any two rows of the table, there must be at least one column of the primary key where their values are different.

Primary Key

A			
B			
C			
D			

The first column is usually the primary key of the table.

Primary Key

A	1		
A	2		
B	1		
B	2		

Sometimes the primary key is the first several columns of the table.

Notes

- Most tables have primary keys.

- Usually, the primary key consists of the first column or the first several columns of the table.

- The primary key names the object, event, or relationship the row represents. In grammatical terms, it is a noun because it is the subject of all the information in the row.

- The other columns of the table make statements about the primary key. In grammatical terms, they are adjectives or adverbs that describe the object named by the primary key and give additional information about it.

1-11 Most tables are tall and thin

Many books on SQL give the impression that tables are usually square —
that they have about the same number of rows as they have columns. This
false impression is left because the tables in most SQL books are approximately square. In any book, the tables must be kept small. In a book, when
you run SQL code you must be able to examine the results in full detail.

However, the tables that are used in real production systems usually have a
different shape. They are tall and thin. They may have 30 columns, but
1,000,000 rows.

Not all tables have this shape, but most do. Some tables have only one
row.

I tell you this because I am one of the people who like to visualize the data
and the tables I am working with. If you like to visualize them too, then at
least I have provided you with the correct picture. If you are not inclined to
visualize these things, then do not worry about it. Just go on to the next
page.

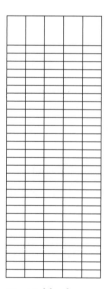

Most tables have many more rows than columns.

Examples of Tables

Up to now, we have discussed the theory of tables, but you have not seen any real ones. In the following sections you will see some actual tables. We look at a table to see how it looks in both Oracle and Access. We discuss some of the design decisions that are used in constructing many tables. And we examine the tables of the Lunches database, which is used in many of the examples throughout this book.

1-12 An example of a table in Oracle and Access

This section shows the same table in both Oracle and in Access. This is our first opportunity to examine how Oracle and Access compare.

You will have to decide for yourself how similar they are and how different they are. To me, this example shows that they are about 90% similar and about 10% different. Of course, this is just one example. You might ask yourself which percentages you would use to describe this.

1_employees table: Oracle format

```
EMPLOYEE                         DEPT                  CREDIT  PHONE   MANAGER
      ID FIRST_NAME LAST_NAME  CODE  HIRE_DATE         LIMIT  NUMBER       ID
-------- ---------- ---------  ----  -----------       ------ ------  -------
     201 SUSAN      BROWN      EXE   01-JUN-1998       $30.00 3484     (null)
     202 JIM        KERN       SAL   16-AUG-1999       $25.00 8722        201
     203 MARTHA     WOODS      SHP   02-FEB-2004       $25.00 7591        201
     204 ELLEN      OWENS      SAL   01-JUL-2003       $15.00 6830        202
     205 HENRY      PERKINS    SAL   01-MAR-2000       $25.00 5286        202
     206 CAROL      ROSE       ACT   (null)            (null) (null)   (null)
     207 DAN        SMITH      SHP   01-DEC-2004       $25.00 2259        203
     208 FRED       CAMPBELL   SHP   01-APR-2003       $25.00 1752        203
     209 PAULA      JACOBS     MKT   17-MAR-1999       $15.00 3357        201
     210 NANCY      HOFFMAN    SAL   16-FEB-2004       $25.00 2974        203
```

1_employees table: Access format

Employee_id	First_name	Last_name	Dept_code	Hire_date	Credit_limit	Phone_number	Manager_id
201	Susan	Brown	Exe	6/1/1998	$30.00	3484	
202	Jim	Kern	Sal	8/16/1999	$25.00	8722	201
203	Martha	Woods	Shp	2/1/2004	$25.00	7591	201
204	Ellen	Owens	Sal	7/1/2003	$15.00	6830	202
205	Henry	Perkins	Sal	3/1/2000	$25.00	5286	202
206	Carol	Rose	Act				
207	Dan	Smith	Shp	12/1/2004	$25.00	2259	203
208	Fred	Campbell	Shp	4/1/2003	$25.00	1752	203
209	Paula	Jacobs	Mkt	3/17/1999	$15.00	3357	201
210	Nancy	Hoffman	Sal	2/16/2004	$25.00	2974	203
					$0.00		0

Record: 11 of 11

Similarities between Oracle and Access

- Column names are printed at the top of the column. The column names are part of the structure of the table, not part of the data in the table.

- Sometimes the column names shown in the column headings are truncated.

- Columns containing text data are justified to the left.

- Columns containing numbers are justified to the right.

- Columns containing dates often display only the date. The format for displaying the date is not part of the data. The value of the date is stored in the table, but the format of the date is specified separately. The date actually contains both a date and a time, but the time is often not displayed.

- Columns displaying currency amounts are actually stored as numbers, and use a format to put in the dollar signs and decimal points.

Differences between Oracle and Access

- **Display framework:** Oracle displays lines of character data. Access uses graphical techniques to display the data in a grid and color the borders of the grid.

- **Case:** The Oracle table is shown all in uppercase. The Access table uses uppercase only for the first letter. It is a common convention to set the databases up this way. Mixed-case data can be put into an Oracle table, but this makes the data more difficult to handle, so Oracle data is usually either all uppercase or all lowercase. Access data is handled as if it were all uppercase, although it is displayed in mixed case. This makes it look nicer, but sometimes it can also be deceiving. In Access, the data appears to be mixed case, but the data behaves as if it were in uppercase. For instance, John and jOhn appear different in Access, but they are handled as if they are the same.

- **Column headings:** Oracle can use several lines for a column heading. Access displays the heading on a single line.

- **Date formats:** The dates are shown in different formats.

    Oracle date format: 16-AUG-1999

    Access date format: 8/16/1999

    Oracle and Access can both display dates in a variety of formats, but these are the default formats that are used when no other format is specified.

- **Date alignment:** Oracle aligns dates to the left, whereas Access aligns them to the right.

- **Nulls:** In this book, I have set up Oracle to always display nulls as (null) in all the columns of every table. This cannot easily be done in Access.

- **Position pointer:** The Access table contains a record selector and a pointer to a particular field within that record, which allows you to modify the data. The Oracle table does not contain these.

- **Ability to add data:** In Access, a blank row at the bottom of a table indicates that new rows of data can be entered into the table. This is not done in Oracle.

Notes

Oracle has another format available to display tables, which is similar to the dynamic, screen-oriented format used by Access. However, it is packaged as part of the Developer Toolkit and it is not included as part of Personal Oracle, so I do not deal with it in this book.

1-13 Some design decisions in the `1_employees` table

The `1_employees` table contains some design decisions that I want to point out to you because they reflect some common practices within relational databases. Like all design decisions, they could have been made in other ways. This is not the only way to design the table. It may not even be the best way. But you may often encounter these design decisions and you need to be aware of them.

`1_employees` table

EMPLOYEE ID	FIRST_NAME	LAST_NAME	DEPT CODE	HIRE_DATE	CREDIT LIMIT	PHONE NUMBER	MANAGER ID
201	SUSAN	BROWN	EXE	01-JUN-1998	$30.00	3484	(null)
202	JIM	KERN	SAL	16-AUG-1999	$25.00	8722	201
203	MARTHA	WOODS	SHP	02-FEB-2004	$25.00	7591	201
204	ELLEN	OWENS	SAL	01-JUL-2003	$15.00	6830	202
205	HENRY	PERKINS	SAL	01-MAR-2000	$25.00	5286	202
206	CAROL	ROSE	ACT	(null)	(null)	(null)	(null)
207	DAN	SMITH	SHP	01-DEC-2004	$25.00	2259	203
208	FRED	CAMPBELL	SHP	01-APR-2003	$25.00	1752	203
209	PAULA	JACOBS	MKT	17-MAR-1999	$15.00	3357	201
210	NANCY	HOFFMAN	SAL	16-FEB-2004	$25.00	2974	203

Design decisions to be aware of

- The `phone_number` column contains text data, not numbers. Although the data look like numbers, and the column name says number, it actually has a text datatype. You can tell this by its alignment, which is to the left. The reason the table is set up this way is that the phone number data will never be used for arithmetic. You never add two phone numbers together or multiply them. You only use them the way they are, as a text field. So this table stores them as text.

- The `employee_id` column contains numbers. You can tell this by its alignment, which is to the right. Now, we do not do arithmetic with employee IDs, we never add them together, so why isn't this a text field too? The answer is that numbers are often used for primary key columns even when no arithmetic will be performed on them. This can make the computer handle the table more quickly.

- The `manager_id` column contains numbers, but it is not a primary key column. So why doesn't it contain text? This column is intended to match with the `employee_id` column, so it has been given the same datatype as that column. This improves the speed of matching the two columns.

- The name of the table, `1_employees`, might seem strange. The `1` indicates that this table is part of a group of tables. The names of all the tables in the group start with the same letter(s). In this case it shows that the table is part of the `Lunches` database. (Here I use the term *database* to mean a collection of related tables.)

- The people who design databases put a considerable amount of work into the consistent naming of objects, using standard prefixes, suffixes, abbreviations, and column names. This makes the whole model easier to understand and more usable for the code that is developed for each database.

1-14 The `Lunches` **database**

Most of the examples of SQL code in this book are based on the `Lunches` database. The CD-ROM contains a complete listing of this database. To read this book, you will need to understand the story and the data. Here is the basic story.

There is a small company with 10 employees. This company will serve lunch to its employees on three occasions. Each employee can attend as many of these lunches as his or her schedule permits. When employees register to attend a lunch, they get to pick what they want to eat. They may choose from among the 10 foods available to them. They can decide to have a single portion or a double portion of any of these foods. The Lunches database keeps track of all this information.

That is the story. Now let's look at the data. When I call this a database, I mean that it is a collection of related tables. The set of tables, taken together, tell the story. There are seven tables in this database:

- Employees (1_employees)

- Departments (1_departments)

- Constants (1_constants)

- Lunches (1_lunches)

- Foods (1_foods)

- Suppliers (1_suppliers)

- Lunch Items (1_lunch_items)

To show that these tables are all related to each other and to distinguish them from other tables we may use, the names of these tables are all pre-fixed with the letter 1. When there are multiple words, such as lunch_items, the spaces are replaced with underscore characters. This helps the computer understand that the two words together are a single name.

1_employees table

EMPLOYEE ID	FIRST_NAME	LAST_NAME	DEPT CODE	HIRE_DATE	CREDIT LIMIT	PHONE NUMBER	MANAGER ID
201	SUSAN	BROWN	EXE	01-JUN-1998	$30.00	3484	(null)
202	JIM	KERN	SAL	16-AUG-1999	$25.00	8722	201
203	MARTHA	WOODS	SHP	02-FEB-2004	$25.00	7591	201
204	ELLEN	OWENS	SAL	01-JUL-2003	$15.00	6830	202
205	HENRY	PERKINS	SAL	01-MAR-2000	$25.00	5286	202
206	CAROL	ROSE	ACT	(null)	(null)	(null)	(null)
207	DAN	SMITH	SHP	01-DEC-2004	$25.00	2259	203
208	FRED	CAMPBELL	SHP	01-APR-2003	$25.00	1752	203
209	PAULA	JACOBS	MKT	17-MAR-1999	$15.00	3357	201
210	NANCY	HOFFMAN	SAL	16-FEB-2004	$25.00	2974	203

The `1_employees` table lists all the employees. Each employee can be identified by an employee ID, which is a number assigned to them. This allows the company to hire two people with the same name. The primary key is the `employee_id` column.

Each employee has a manager, who is also an employee of the company. The manager is identified by their employee ID. For instance, the `manager_id` column shows that Jim Kern is managed by employee 201. Employee 201 is Susan Brown.

Susan Brown is the only employee without a manager. You can tell this because there is a null in her `manager_id` column. This is because she is the head of the company. The null in this case does not mean that we do not know who her manager is. Rather, it means that she does not have a manager.

1_departments table

```
DEPT
CODE  DEPARTMENT_NAME
----  ------------------------------
ACT   ACCOUNTING
EXE   EXECUTIVE
MKT   MARKETING
PER   PERSONNEL
SAL   SALES
SHP   SHIPPING
```

Each employee works for one department. The department code is shown in the `1_employees` table. The full name of each department is shown in the `1_departments` table. The primary key of this table is `dept_code`.

These tables can be linked together by matching the `dept_code` columns. For example, the `1_employees` table shows us that employee 202, Jim Kern, has a department code of `SAL`. The `1_departments` table says that the sales department uses the department code `SAL`. This tells us that Jim Kern works in the sales department.

1_constants table

BUSINESS_NAME	BUSINESS START_DATE	LUNCH_BUDGET	OWNER_NAME
CITYWIDE UNIFORMS	01-JUN-1998	$200.00	SUSAN BROWN

The 1_constants table contains some constant values and has only one row. We use these values with the other tables of the database. These values are expected to change infrequently, if at all. Storing them in a separate table keeps the SQL code flexible by providing an alternative to hard-coding these values into SQL. Because the table of constants has only one row, it does not need a primary key.

1_lunches table

LUNCH_ID	LUNCH_DATE	EMPLOYEE_ID	DATE_ENTERE
1	16-NOV-2005	201	13-OCT-2005
2	16-NOV-2005	207	13-OCT-2005
3	16-NOV-2005	203	13-OCT-2005
4	16-NOV-2005	204	13-OCT-2005
6	16-NOV-2005	202	13-OCT-2005
7	16-NOV-2005	210	13-OCT-2005
8	25-NOV-2005	201	14-OCT-2005
9	25-NOV-2005	208	14-OCT-2005
12	25-NOV-2005	204	14-OCT-2005
13	25-NOV-2005	207	18-OCT-2005
15	25-NOV-2005	205	21-OCT-2005
16	05-DEC-2005	201	21-OCT-2005
17	05-DEC-2005	210	21-OCT-2005
20	05-DEC-2005	205	24-OCT-2005
21	05-DEC-2005	203	24-OCT-2005
22	05-DEC-2005	208	24-OCT-2005

The 1_lunches table registers an employee to attend a lunch. It assigns a lunch ID to each lunch that will be served. For example, employee 207, Dan Smith, will attend a lunch on November 16, 2005. His lunch is identified as lunch_id = 2.

The lunch_id column is the primary key of this table. This is an example of a *surrogate key*, which is also called a *meaningless primary key*. Each row is assigned a unique number, but there is no intrinsic meaning to that number. It is just a convenient name to use for the row, or the object that the row represents — in this case, a lunch.

The 1_lunches table shows the most common way to use a surrogate key. Usually a single column is the primary key. That column has a different value in every row.

Some database designers like to use surrogate keys because they can improve the efficiency of queries within the database. Surrogate keys are used especially to replace a primary key that would have many columns, and when a table is often joined to many other tables.

Other designers do not like surrogate keys because they prefer to have each column contain meaningful data. This is an area of debate among database designers, with many pros and cons on each side. People who use databases need only be aware that these columns are meaningless numbers used to join one table to another.

1_foods table

SUPPLIER ID	PRODUCT CODE	MENU ITEM	DESCRIPTION	PRICE	PRICE INCREASE
ASP	FS	1	FRESH SALAD	$2.00	$0.25
ASP	SP	2	SOUP OF THE DAY	$1.50	(null)
ASP	SW	3	SANDWICH	$3.50	$0.40
CBC	GS	4	GRILLED STEAK	$6.00	$0.70
CBC	SW	5	HAMBURGER	$2.50	$0.30
FRV	BR	6	BROCCOLI	$1.00	$0.05
FRV	FF	7	FRENCH FRIES	$1.50	(null)
JBR	AS	8	SODA	$1.25	$0.25
JBR	VR	9	COFFEE	$0.85	$0.15
VSB	AS	10	DESSERT	$3.00	$0.50

The 1_foods table lists the foods an employee can choose for his or her lunch. Each food is identified by a supplier ID and a product code. Together, these two columns form the primary key. The product codes belong to the suppliers. It is possible for two suppliers to use the same product code for different foods. In fact, the product code AS has two different meanings. Supplier JBR uses this product code for soda, but supplier VSB uses it for dessert.

The price increases are proposed, but are not yet in effect. The nulls in the `price_increase` column mean that there will not be a price increase for this food item.

1_suppliers table

```
SUPPLIER
ID        SUPPLIER_NAME
--------  -----------------------------
ARR       ALICE & RAY'S RESTAURANT
ASP       A SOUP PLACE
CBC       CERTIFIED BEEF COMPANY
FRV       FRANK REED'S VEGETABLES
FSN       FRANK & SONS
JBR       JUST BEVERAGES
JPS       JIM PARKER'S SHOP
VSB       VIRGINIA STREET BAKERY
```

The `1_suppliers` table shows the full names for the suppliers of the foods. For example, the `1_foods` table shows that french fries will be obtained from supplier ID FRV. The `1_suppliers` table shows that Frank Reed's Vegetables is the full name of this supplier. The primary key of these tables is the supplier ID.

1_lunch_items table

```
                         SUPPLIER PRODUCT
LUNCH_ID ITEM_NUMBER ID       CODE    QUANTITY
--------- ----------- -------- ------- ---------
        1           1 ASP      FS             1
        1           2 ASP      SW             2
        1           3 JBR      VR             2
        2           1 ASP      SW             2
        2           2 FRV      FF             1
        2           3 JBR      VR             2
        2           4 VSB      AS             1
        3           1 ASP      FS             1
        3           2 CBC      GS             1
        3           3 FRV      FF             1
        3           4 JBR      VR             1
        3           5 JBR      AS             1
(and many more rows)
```

When you look at the `l_lunch_items` table you need to be aware that the data in the `item_number` column is aligned to the right because it is a column of numbers. The data in the `supplier_id` column is aligned to the left because it is a column of text. So when you look at the first row, `1 ASP` is not a single piece of data. Instead, the `item_number` value is `1` and the `supplier_id` value is `ASP`.

The `l_lunch_items` table shows which foods each employee has chosen for his or her lunch. It also shows whether they want a single or a double portion. For example, look at `lunch_id 2`, which we already know to be Dan Smith's lunch on November 16. It consists of four items. The first item is identified as `ASP-SW`. Here I am putting the `supplier_id` and the `product_code` column data together separated by a hyphen. Looking in the `l_foods` table, we find this is a sandwich. The `l_lunch_items` table says he wants two of them, which is shown in the `quantity` column. See if you can figure out all the foods he wants for his lunch.

The correct answer is

   2 sandwiches

   1 order of french fries

   2 cups of coffee

   1 dessert

The primary key of this table consists of the first two columns of the table, `lunch_id` and `item_number`. The `item_number` column is a *tie-breaker column*, which is another type of meaningless primary key. In this design, I wanted to use the lunch ID to identify each food within a lunch. However, most lunches have several foods. So I cannot use the lunch ID by itself as a primary key, because that would create several rows in the table having the same value in the primary key, which is not allowed. I needed a way for each row to have a different value in the primary key. That is what a tie-breaker column does. The `item_number` column numbers the items within each lunch. Therefore, the combination of lunch ID and item number provides a unique identity for each row of the table and can serve as the primary key. A primary key of this sort, containing more than one column, is sometimes called a *composite key*.

Challenging features of the Lunches database

Most SQL books have you work with a database that is tame and contains no challenges. This book is different. I have intentionally put some features in the Lunches database that could cause you to get the wrong result if you do not handle them properly. I show you how to become aware of these situations and how to deal with them. Many real business databases contain similar challenges. Here are a few of them — a more complete list of the challenges is on the Web site, *www.sqlfun.com.*

- Two employees are not attending any of the lunches — employee 209, Paula Jacobs, and employee 206, Carol Rose.

- One food has not been ordered in any of the lunches — broccoli.

- One of the departments is not yet staffed with any employees — the personnel department.

Summary

In this chapter we discussed SQL as a language to get information from relational databases. You learned the parts of a table: rows, columns, cells, and primary keys. We looked at a table in Oracle and the same table in Access, which gave us our first comparison of these two SQL products. We also discussed each of the tables in the Lunches database, which is the database used in most of the sections of this book.

chapter 2

GETTING INFORMATION FROM A TABLE

This chapter explains the basic technique for getting the information you want from a table when you do not want to make any changes to the data and when all the information is in one table. The table may be very large and you might only want a small amount of data from it.

The Select Statement

In SQL, the `select` statement is used to get information from a table. Much of this book is concerned with the `select` statement. This chapter explains its four basic clauses and the options available for three of these clauses.

2-1 The goal: Get a few columns and rows from a table

Our goal is to get the data we want from a table. The table may be large and contain a lot of data. We only want a small part of it and we do not want to change the data in any way. The `select` statement allows us to retrieve a few columns and a few rows of data from the table.

Let's put some numbers on this. The particular numbers are not important, but they draw the picture more clearly. Suppose that printing all the data in the table would take 1,000 pages, and suppose we want only two pages of data from it. The `select` statement allows us to get just the two pages of data we want.

It is as if we want to read an article on redwood trees from an encyclopedia. We only want to see that one article. We do not want to read the entire encyclopedia from the beginning to the end. The `select` statement allows us to find the particular article we want to read.

The following diagram shows a large table of data. A small amount of that data is being retrieved into the result of the `select` statement. In this diagram, the data we want is scattered throughout the table in various columns and rows. It is collected together by the `select` statement.

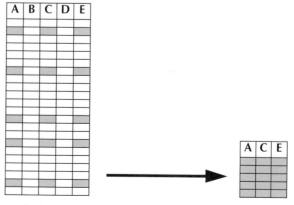

Beginning table.   Result table.

Handling small tables of data

If a table of data is small, there might not be much reason to write a `select` statement. For instance, if we can print the entire table in two pages, then why not print it completely and let people work to find the information they want? In many situations, this approach makes sense.

In this book, we use small tables as learning tools. With tables this size, there is not much reason to use `select` statements. However, these tables are being used as examples to show how the `select` statement works when it is used with larger tables.

2-2   Overview of the `select` statement

The `select` statement is used to get some of the data from a table. It has six clauses.

`select`	Which columns of data to get
`from`	Which table has the data
`where`	Which rows of data to get
`group by`	Described in chapter 12
`having`	Described in chapter 12
`order by`	Which columns are used to sort the result

They must be written in this order. `Group by` and `having` are used in summarizing data, and we examine them later.

This chapter discusses the options available for the `select`, `where`, and `order by` clauses. For now, the `from` clause will always list only one table.

A `select` statement is often called a *query*. These two terms are used interchangeably. The term "`select` statement" emphasizes the syntax of the SQL command. The term "query" emphasizes the purpose of the command.

Task

Show an example of a `select` statement that uses all of the clauses listed above. Show the `employee_id`, `last_name`, and `credit_limit` columns from the `1_employees` table of the `Lunches` database. Show only the employees who have a credit limit greater than $20.00. Sort the rows of the result by the last name of the employee.

Oracle & Access SQL

```
select employee_id, ❶
       last_name,
       credit_limit
from 1_employees ❷
where credit_limit > 20.00 ❸
order by last_name; ❹
```

Beginning table (1_employees table)

EMPLOYEE ID	FIRST_NAME	LAST_NAME	DEPT CODE	HIRE_DATE	CREDIT LIMIT	PHONE NUMBER	MANAGER ID
201	SUSAN	BROWN	EXE	01-JUN-1998	$30.00	3484	(null)
202	JIM	KERN	SAL	16-AUG-1999	$25.00	8722	201
203	MARTHA	WOODS	SHP	02-FEB-2004	$25.00	7591	201
204	ELLEN	OWENS	SAL	01-JUL-2003	$15.00	6830	202
205	HENRY	PERKINS	SAL	01-MAR-2000	$25.00	5286	202
206	CAROL	ROSE	ACT	(null)	(null)	(null)	(null)
207	DAN	SMITH	SHP	01-DEC-2004	$25.00	2259	203
208	FRED	CAMPBELL	SHP	01-APR-2003	$25.00	1752	203
209	PAULA	JACOBS	MKT	17-MAR-1999	$15.00	3357	201
210	NANCY	HOFFMAN	SAL	16-FEB-2004	$25.00	2974	203

Result table ❺

EMPLOYEE ID	LAST_NAME	CREDIT LIMIT
201	BROWN	$30.00
208	CAMPBELL	$25.00
210	HOFFMAN	$25.00
202	KERN	$25.00
205	PERKINS	$25.00
207	SMITH	$25.00
203	WOODS	$25.00

Notes

❶ The `select` clause lists the columns you want to show in the result table. They can be listed in any order. Their order in the `select` clause determines their order within the result table. When the computer sees a column name that is not followed by a comma it expects to see the next clause, the `from` clause.

Also, note that the names of these columns do not contain spaces. Access allows this, but I do not recommend it because a space is usually used as a delimiter. The underscore character (_) is usually used instead of a space to separate the words in the name of each column. By typing `last_name` with an underscore, you are telling the computer that this is the name of a single column. If you typed `last name` with a space, the computer would try to find a column named `last` and it would not find any column with that name. This would cause an error and the computer would not process the `select` statement. Chapter 3 discusses the issue of using spaces in column names in more detail.

❷ The `from` clause names the table that the data comes from — the `l_employees` table of the `Lunches` database. In the naming scheme used here, the prefix "`l_`" indicates that the `employees` table is part of the `Lunches` database. This table is shown as the beginning table.

❸ The `where` clause indicates which rows to show in the result table. The condition `where credit_limit > 20.00` eliminates the rows for employees 204 and 209 because they have a $15.00 credit limit, and employee 206, which has a null value.

Note that the dollar amount is written without the dollar sign. It must also be written without any commas. The decimal point is acceptable, but not required. The condition could also be written as follows: `where credit_limit > 20`. In this SQL code, two zeros are put after the decimal point to make it look more like a currency value. This does not format the results.

❹ The `order by` clause specifies that the rows of the result table should be sorted in alphabetical order by the `last_name` column. A semicolon marks the end of the SQL statement. In Oracle, this statement will not run without the semicolon. In Access, it is optional. In Oracle, you could put a slash (/) on the next line as an alternative to the semicolon. Because using a semicolon is valid within both products, in this book I use a semicolon at the end of every SQL statement.

❺ Some people would call this a *query result listing*. This name has some merit, because it is not a table. It is the result of running a query, also known as a `select` statement. In Oracle, these results are shown on the screen as if they are printed out on paper. In Access, they are shown on the screen as if they are in a table, with some interactive elements, in datasheet view. In other books you may find the terms *derived table* and *virtual table*.

I call this a *result table* because according to relational database theory, tables are the only database structure. The input to a query is a table, and the output of a query is a table. This result table appears only on the screen. It is not stored on the disk.

The Select Clause

The select clause is the first part of a query. The select clause says which columns of information you want, what order you want them in, and what you want them to be called. Do not confuse the select clause with the select statement.

2-3   Overview of the select clause

There are three forms of the select clause. The following pages show an example of each of these.

select *a list of columns*

- Get only the columns listed.
- Put them in the order they are listed.
- You can rename them.

select *

or select *table_name.**

- Get all the columns of the table.
- Put them in the same order they are in the table.
- You cannot rename them in SQL. (Within some products, you can rename them in other ways.)
- When any additional columns are listed, besides those of one table, the table name is required before the asterisk. A period is placed between the table name and the asterisk, so the command reads as follows: select *table_name.**

select distinct *a list of columns*

- Get only the columns listed.
- Put them in the order they are listed.
- You can rename them.
- Eliminate duplicate rows from the result.

The first form, select *a list of columns*, gets only the columns that are listed. It can rename these columns, giving them a *column alias*. It also specifies the order in which the columns are to be listed.

The second form, `select *`, gets all the columns of a table. This does not list the columns individually, so it cannot give the columns an alias or specify an order for the columns. The columns are listed in the order in which they appear in the table.

The third form, `select distinct` *a list of columns*, is similar to the first form, but it includes the word `distinct`. This eliminates all the duplicate rows from the result table. Two rows are duplicates if they have identical values in every column of the result table. If even one column is different, then they do not match and they are not duplicates.

The only required clauses are the `select` clause and the `from` clause. You can write a `select` statement with only these two clauses. The following query lists all the columns and all the rows of the `l_employees` table.

```
select *
from l_employees;
```

2-4   Using the `select` clause to get a list of some of the columns

This section shows an example of a `select` clause that is used to get a list of columns. Only the columns listed in the `select` clause appear in the result table. The other columns of the beginning table are omitted.

The order of the columns within the `select` clause determines their order within the result table. This can be different from their order within the beginning table.

It is possible for the same column to be listed two or more times. This is sometimes useful when different formatting or functions are applied to the column. Chapters 6 and 7 discuss formatting. Functions are covered in chapters 9, 10, and 11.

A literal value can be included in the `select` clause. That value will then appear in every row of the result table. If the literal value is text or a date, it must be enclosed in single quotes. If it is a number, no quotes are used.

A column can be renamed by giving it a column alias. This changes the heading that appears in the result table. It does not have any permanent effect on the table or the database. To assign a column alias, use this syntax:

```
column_name AS alias_name
```

The `AS` is optional in Oracle and required in Access. I recommend that you use it because it makes the `select` statement easier to read and understand. Usually you should avoid having spaces within the name of the column alias. A common convention is to replace the spaces with underscore characters.

Sometimes the column heading is truncated in the result table to save space. Instead of showing the full column name or column alias, only the beginning part is shown. This is done in both Oracle and Access.

In Access, if you want to see the full column heading, use the mouse to make the column wider. This can be done after SQL has been run.

In Oracle, you must use a command to the SQLplus environment to set the column width. This must be done before SQL is run. The syntax of this command is

```
COLUMN <column name or column alias> FORMAT  A <maximum width> ;
```

So in the following example, for Oracle, I used the SQLplus commands

```
column employee_number format 9999;
column extension format a10;
```

`Employee_number` is a numeric column because it comes from `employee_id`, a number column. Each 9 in the format for this column stands for one digit, so the format for this column says that it will be formatted as a four-digit number.

`Extension` is a text column because it comes from `phone_number`, a text column. "A" in the format means that this is an alphanumeric column, consisting of letters and numbers. Alphanumeric is another word for a text column. The 10 after the A makes the column ten characters wide.

I have already set up for you most of these column formats you will need in this book. Oracle does not retain them from one session to another, so each time you log on to Oracle, you should refresh them by entering the command

```
start c:\temp\sqlfun_login.sql
```

Replace `c:temp\` with your own path name. This Oracle script is explained further in appendix B.

Task

Get three columns from the `1_employees` table:

```
employee_id
phone_number
last_name
```

Display them in that order. Change the name of the `employee_id` column to `employee_number` and the name of the `phone_number` column to `extension`. Also create two new columns: `evaluation` and `rating`. Give every employee an evaluation of "excellent worker" and a rating of 10.

Oracle & Access SQL

```
select employee_id as employee_number, ❶
       phone_number as extension,
       last_name,
       'excellent worker' as evaluation, ❷
       10 as rating ❸
from 1_employees;
```

Beginning table (`1_employees` table)

EMPLOYEE ID	FIRST_NAME	LAST_NAME	DEPT CODE	HIRE_DATE	CREDIT LIMIT	PHONE NUMBER	MANAGER ID
201	SUSAN	BROWN	EXE	01-JUN-1998	$30.00	3484	(null)
202	JIM	KERN	SAL	16-AUG-1999	$25.00	8722	201
203	MARTHA	WOODS	SHP	02-FEB-2004	$25.00	7591	201
204	ELLEN	OWENS	SAL	01-JUL-2003	$15.00	6830	202
205	HENRY	PERKINS	SAL	01-MAR-2000	$25.00	5286	202
206	CAROL	ROSE	ACT	(null)	(null)	(null)	(null)
207	DAN	SMITH	SHP	01-DEC-2004	$25.00	2259	203
208	FRED	CAMPBELL	SHP	01-APR-2003	$25.00	1752	203
209	PAULA	JACOBS	MKT	17-MAR-1999	$15.00	3357	201
210	NANCY	HOFFMAN	SAL	16-FEB-2004	$25.00	2974	203

Result table

```
EMPLOYEE_NUMBER EXTENSION   LAST_NAME   EVALUATION            RATING
--------------- ----------  ----------  -----------------  ----------
            201 3484        BROWN       EXCELLENT WORKER          10
            202 8722        KERN        EXCELLENT WORKER          10
            203 7591        WOODS       EXCELLENT WORKER          10
            204 6830        OWENS       EXCELLENT WORKER          10
            205 5286        PERKINS     EXCELLENT WORKER          10
            206 (null)      ROSE        EXCELLENT WORKER          10
            207 2259        SMITH       EXCELLENT WORKER          10
            208 1752        CAMPBELL    EXCELLENT WORKER          10
            209 3357        JACOBS      EXCELLENT WORKER          10
            210 2974        HOFFMAN     EXCELLENT WORKER          10
```

Notes

❶ The `employee_id` column is being renamed `employee_number`. This new name, the column alias, is the column heading in the result table. An underscore character is used to join the words "employee" and "number." This makes the column alias a single word, as it contains no spaces. The reason for doing this is that Oracle and Access SQL are the same as long as the column alias does not contain spaces.

Both Oracle and Access allow spaces in the column alias. However, the code is written with a slight difference. In Oracle, *double quotes* must be used around a column alias that contains a space, while in Access, *square brackets* are used:

```
Oracle:  select employee_id as "employee number"
Access:  select employee_id as [employee number]
```

❷ The text `'excellent worker'` is added to every row of the result table in a column called `evaluation`. This is an example of placing a literal value in a `select` statement. In this case, the literal value is text, so it is enclosed in single quotes.

❸ Here the literal value is a number, so it is not enclosed in quotes.

2-5   Using the `select` clause to get a list of all of the columns

Here is an example of a `select` clause that gets all the columns of a table and lists them in the same order in which they occur within the beginning table. In this example, there is no `where` clause, so the result table contains all the columns and all the rows of the beginning table. This means that the beginning table and the result table are identical.

This is the simplest `select` statement that you can write. The `select` clause and the `from` clause are required in any `select` statement. All other clauses are optional.

Task

Get the entire `1_employees` table, all the columns and all the rows. Display all the columns in the same order as they are defined in the table.

Oracle & Access SQL

```
select *
from 1_employees;
```

Beginning table (`1_employees` table)

EMPLOYEE ID	FIRST_NAME	LAST_NAME	DEPT CODE	HIRE_DATE	CREDIT LIMIT	PHONE NUMBER	MANAGER ID
201	SUSAN	BROWN	EXE	01-JUN-1998	$30.00	3484	(null)
202	JIM	KERN	SAL	16-AUG-1999	$25.00	8722	201
203	MARTHA	WOODS	SHP	02-FEB-2004	$25.00	7591	201
204	ELLEN	OWENS	SAL	01-JUL-2003	$15.00	6830	202
205	HENRY	PERKINS	SAL	01-MAR-2000	$25.00	5286	202
206	CAROL	ROSE	ACT	(null)	(null)	(null)	(null)
207	DAN	SMITH	SHP	01-DEC-2004	$25.00	2259	203
208	FRED	CAMPBELL	SHP	01-APR-2003	$25.00	1752	203
209	PAULA	JACOBS	MKT	17-MAR-1999	$15.00	3357	201
210	NANCY	HOFFMAN	SAL	16-FEB-2004	$25.00	2974	203

Result table ❶

EMPLOYEE ID	FIRST_NAME	LAST_NAME	DEPT CODE	HIRE_DATE	CREDIT LIMIT	PHONE NUMBER	MANAGER ID
201	SUSAN	BROWN	EXE	01-JUN-1998	$30.00	3484	(null)
202	JIM	KERN	SAL	16-AUG-1999	$25.00	8722	201
203	MARTHA	WOODS	SHP	02-FEB-2004	$25.00	7591	201
204	ELLEN	OWENS	SAL	01-JUL-2003	$15.00	6830	202
205	HENRY	PERKINS	SAL	01-MAR-2000	$25.00	5286	202
206	CAROL	ROSE	ACT	(null)	(null)	(null)	(null)
207	DAN	SMITH	SHP	01-DEC-2004	$25.00	2259	203
208	FRED	CAMPBELL	SHP	01-APR-2003	$25.00	1752	203
209	PAULA	JACOBS	MKT	17-MAR-1999	$15.00	3357	201
210	NANCY	HOFFMAN	SAL	16-FEB-2004	$25.00	2974	203

Notes

❶ The result table is identical to the beginning table, except possibly for the order of the rows. In the listings here, the rows are in exactly the same order. I did this to make the example easy to understand. In theory, however, the rows of both tables are unordered sets, so the rows in the result table could appear in a different order.

Oracle & Access SQL: Variation 1 — Adding a where clause

If a where clause is added to the select statement, the result table can contain only some of the rows of the beginning table. For example:

```
select *
from l_employees
where manager_id is null;
```

This lists the two rows for employees 201 and 206.

Variation 1: Result table

EMPLOYEE ID	FIRST_NAME	LAST_NAME	DEPT CODE	HIRE_DATE	CREDIT LIMIT	PHONE NUMBER	MANAGER ID
201	SUSAN	BROWN	EXE	01-JUN-1998	$30.00	3484	(null)
206	CAROL	ROSE	ACT	(null)	(null)	(null)	(null)

Oracle & Access SQL: Variation 2 — Adding an order by clause

If an order by clause is added to the select statement, the rows of the result table may be sorted in a different order. For example, you could sort them by hire_date. When there is no order by clause, the computer is allowed to list the rows of the result table in any order. To control the order and ensure that the rows are sorted by the value in the employee_id column, it is necessary to write:

```
select *
from l_employees
order by employee_id;
```

Result table — Same as the result table on page 44

Displaying the data in any table

If you know the name of any table, you can display all the data in it with the `select` statement

```
select *
from table_name;
```

You replace `table_name` with the name of your table. In Oracle, if the table contains many rows, the screen may start to scroll. To stop the scrolling, you can use

```
      CTRL + C
or    File -> Cancel
```

In Access, this problem does not occur. The screen scrolls only in response to your input.

2-6   Using the `select` statement to get the distinct values in one column

This section shows an example of using `select distinct` on one column to find all of its values and list each of them only once. This is particularly useful when you are working with a column that contains codes, such as the `dept_code` column. In this example, we apply `select distinct` to the `manager_id` column. In the result table, manager ID 201 is displayed only once, even though there are three rows of the beginning table with this value. The duplicate values are removed.

Notice that the null value does appear in the result table. Here we see that `select distinct` treats nulls as it treats any other data in the table. If there were several nulls in the `manager_id` column of the beginning table, the result table would still contain only a single null.

Task

Get a list of all the different values in the manager_id column of the l_employees table.

Oracle & Access SQL

```
select distinct manager_id
from l_employees;
```

Beginning table (l_employees table)

EMPLOYEE ID	FIRST_NAME	LAST_NAME	DEPT CODE	HIRE_DATE	CREDIT LIMIT	PHONE NUMBER	MANAGER ID
201	SUSAN	BROWN	EXE	01-JUN-1998	$30.00	3484	(null)
202	JIM	KERN	SAL	16-AUG-1999	$25.00	8722	201
203	MARTHA	WOODS	SHP	02-FEB-2004	$25.00	7591	201
204	ELLEN	OWENS	SAL	01-JUL-2003	$15.00	6830	202
205	HENRY	PERKINS	SAL	01-MAR-2000	$25.00	5286	202
206	CAROL	ROSE	ACT	(null)	(null)	(null)	(null)
207	DAN	SMITH	SHP	01-DEC-2004	$25.00	2259	203
208	FRED	CAMPBELL	SHP	01-APR-2003	$25.00	1752	203
209	PAULA	JACOBS	MKT	17-MAR-1999	$15.00	3357	201
210	NANCY	HOFFMAN	SAL	16-FEB-2004	$25.00	2974	203

Result table

MANAGER ID
201
202
203
(null)

Where nulls are placed in the sort order —
A difference between Oracle and Access

In Oracle, nulls are placed at the bottom of the sort order. In Access they are placed at the top. This is not a big difference. It causes a slight difference in the appearance of the result, although the rows in the result are the same in both cases.

Everyone agrees on the sort order for the numbers 0 to 9 and for the letters A to Z. However, there is no such agreement about how nulls fit into the sort order. In the absence of a common agreement, the developers of Oracle decided to resolve the issue one way and the developers of Access decided to resolve it another way.

The result table shown next shows the null at the bottom. This is the Oracle method. People using Access will find the null at the top. In Access, the null appears as a blank.

In this example, one could argue that because the `select` statement contains no `order by` clause, the rows of the result table are allowed to be in any order. In theory, the null can appear in any position within the result table. In practice, when `select distinct` is used, a sort is performed as part of the process of eliminating duplicates. Therefore, the rows of the result table are presented in sorted order, even though no `order by` clause is used. In this case, the sort is performed on the `manager_id` column.

Oracle & Access SQL:
Variation 1 — Adding a `where` clause to `select distinct`

Select distinct may be used with a `where` clause to limit the number of rows in the result table. The `where` clause is processed first, which removes some rows from the beginning table. Then the `select distinct` clause is processed. Here is an example:

```
select distinct manager_id
from l_employees
where employee_id in (201, 208, 210);
```

Variation 1: Result table

```
MANAGER
     ID
-------
    203
(null)
```

Oracle & Access SQL:
Variation 2 — Adding an `order by` clause to `select distinct`

`Select distinct` may be used with an `order by` clause to sort the rows of the result table in either an ascending or a descending order.

```
select distinct manager_id
from l_employees
order by manager_id desc;
```

Variation 2: Result table

```
MANAGER
     ID
-------
(null)
    203
    202
    201
```

Oracle & Access SQL:
Variation 3 — What happens if you eliminate the word `distinct`?

If the word `distinct` is removed from the `select` statement, then the result table will be the same as the `manager_id` column of the beginning table. The value 201 will appear three times. No duplicate values will be removed, nor will any sort occur. The rows might appear in the same order as in the beginning table, or they could appear in some completely different order. Here is an example:

```
select manager_id
from l_employees;
```

Variation 3: Result table

```
MANAGER
     ID
-------
(null)
    201
    201
    202
    202
(null)
    203
    203
    201
    203
```

2-7   Using the `select` clause to get the distinct values of several columns

This section shows an example of using `select distinct` with two columns. The SQL code is similar to the code in the previous section. Here a second column is added to the `select distinct` clause, the `credit_limit` column. The result table shows all the different combinations of values in the two columns, `manager_id` and `credit_limit`.

When `select distinct` is used with several columns, the result table shows a single instance of each valid combination of the columns. In other words, no two rows of the result table are the same. Every two rows differ in the values of at least one of the columns.

Task

Get a list of all the different values in the `manager_id` and `credit_limit` columns of the `1_employees` table.

Oracle & Access SQL

```
select distinct manager_id,
                credit_limit
from 1_employees;
```

Beginning table (`1_employees` table)

EMPLOYEE ID	FIRST_NAME	LAST_NAME	DEPT CODE	HIRE_DATE	CREDIT LIMIT	PHONE NUMBER	MANAGER ID
201	SUSAN	BROWN	EXE	01-JUN-1998	$30.00	3484	(null)
202	JIM	KERN	SAL	16-AUG-1999	$25.00	8722	201
203	MARTHA	WOODS	SHP	02-FEB-2004	$25.00	7591	201
204	ELLEN	OWENS	SAL	01-JUL-2003	$15.00	6830	202
205	HENRY	PERKINS	SAL	01-MAR-2000	$25.00	5286	202
206	CAROL	ROSE	ACT	(null)	(null)	(null)	(null)
207	DAN	SMITH	SHP	01-DEC-2004	$25.00	2259	203
208	FRED	CAMPBELL	SHP	01-APR-2003	$25.00	1752	203
209	PAULA	JACOBS	MKT	17-MAR-1999	$15.00	3357	201
210	NANCY	HOFFMAN	SAL	16-FEB-2004	$25.00	2974	203

Result table

```
MANAGER   CREDIT
     ID    LIMIT
-------   -------
    201   $15.00
    201   $25.00
    202   $15.00
    202   $25.00
    203   $25.00
 (null)   $30.00
 (null)   (null)
```

What it means to eliminate duplicate rows from the result

The result table here contains two rows with a manager ID of 201. In section 2-6, there was only one such row. What is the difference?

There is another column in the result, the `credit_limit` column. The two rows in which manager ID equals 201 have different values in the `credit_limit` column, $15.00 and $25.00. Two *rows* of the result are distinct as long as there is at least one column in which they differ. In section 2-6, the credit limit was not part of the result, so the difference between these rows is not in the result. That is why these two occurrences of 201 are condensed into a single row.

The beginning table contains three rows with a manager ID of 201. Two rows have a $25.00 credit limit and one has a $15.00 credit limit. The result table shows only one row for each of these combinations.

In the result table, each *row* is distinct. You can think of this as a three-step process. First, all the columns in each row of the result table are concatenated together into a single unit of data, then these units are sorted. Last, all the duplicate units are removed.

The Where Clause

The `where` clause is used to choose which rows of data you want to retrieve. Because a table can have thousands of rows, this clause must be flexible enough to specify many different conditions. This makes it more complex than the other clauses we examine in this chapter.

2-8 Overview of the `where` clause

The `where` clause specifies a condition that is true for all the rows you want in the result table. For all other rows the condition is false or unknown. The following table summarizes the conditions you can use. All of these conditions can be used with any of the main types of data — text, numbers, and dates.

Each condition has both a positive form and a negative form. The negative form is always the exact opposite of the positive form. For example, the `is not null` condition is true for every row for which the `is null` condition is false. And the `not between` condition is true for every row where the `between` condition is false.

Comparison conditions that can be used in the `where` clause.

Condition	Meaning	Examples
EQUAL — and other comparison tests		
`=`	equal	with numbers: `credit_limit = 25.00`
		with text: `first_name = 'sue'`
		with dates: `hire_date = '01-jun-2010'`
`<`	less than	`credit_limit < 25.00`
`<=`	less than or equal	`first_name <= 'm'`
`>`	greater than	`hire_date > '01-jan-2010'`
`>=`	greater than or equal	`credit_limit >= 30.00`
`<>` and others	not equal	`first_name <> 'alice'`
SET INCLUSION TEST — a list of specific values		
`in`	in a set	`credit_limit in (15.00, 25.00)`
`not in`	not in a set	`dept_code not in ('exe', 'mkt', 'act')`
RANGE TEST — anywhere between two values		
`between`	in a range	`credit_limit between 21.00 and 27.00`
`not between`	not within a range	`dept_code not between 'act' and 'sal'`
PATTERN MATCHING TEST — using wildcard characters		
`like`	matches a pattern	`phone_number like '%48%'`
`not like`	does not match a pattern	`dept_code not like '%a%'`
NULL TEST — find nulls		
`is null`	is a null value	`manager_id is null`
`is not null`	is not a null value	`manager_id is not null`
BOOLEAN CONNECTORS — joining simple conditions together		
`and`	both of the conditions are true	`(credit_limit = 25.00)` `and (first_name = 'sue')`
`or`	one of the conditions is true	`(credit_limit = 25.00)` `or (first_name = 'sue')`
`not`	the condition is false	`not (credit_limit = 25.00)`

2-9   Using an Equal condition in the `where` clause

This section shows a query in which the `where` clause uses an Equal (=) condition. All the rows from the beginning table that have `manager_id` values equal to 203 are shown in the result table.

Note that the employees who have a null value in the `manager_id` column are not shown. This affects employees 201 and 206. The null value means that the value is missing in the database. The value could be equal to 203, but we do not know this, so the row for the employee is not shown in the result table.

Task

For all employees who report to employee 203, Martha Woods, list the following:

```
employee_id
first_name
last_name
manager_id
```

Oracle & Access SQL

```
select employee_id, ❶
       first_name,
       last_name,
       manager_id
from l_employees
where manager_id = 203; ❷
```

Beginning table (`1_employees` table)

```
EMPLOYEE                          DEPT                CREDIT  PHONE   MANAGER
      ID FIRST_NAME LAST_NAME CODE HIRE_DATE           LIMIT NUMBER        ID
-------- ---------- --------- ---- ------------      ------- ------   -------
     201 SUSAN      BROWN     EXE  01-JUN-1998        $30.00 3484     (null)
     202 JIM        KERN      SAL  16-AUG-1999        $25.00 8722        201
     203 MARTHA     WOODS     SHP  02-FEB-2004        $25.00 7591        201
     204 ELLEN      OWENS     SAL  01-JUL-2003        $15.00 6830        202
     205 HENRY      PERKINS   SAL  01-MAR-2000        $25.00 5286        202
     206 CAROL      ROSE      ACT  (null)            (null) (null)    (null)
     207 DAN        SMITH     SHP  01-DEC-2004        $25.00 2259        203
     208 FRED       CAMPBELL  SHP  01-APR-2003        $25.00 1752        203
     209 PAULA      JACOBS    MKT  17-MAR-1999        $15.00 3357        201
     210 NANCY      HOFFMAN   SAL  16-FEB-2004        $25.00 2974        203
```

Result table

```
EMPLOYEE                        MANAGER
      ID FIRST_NAME LAST_NAME        ID
-------- ---------- ---------- -------
     207 DAN        SMITH          203
     208 FRED       CAMPBELL       203
     210 NANCY      HOFFMAN        203
```

Notes

❶ The `select` clause lists four columns, and the result table shows these four columns.

❷ The `where` clause contains only one condition:

`manager_id = 203`

Three rows of the beginning table satisfy this condition, and the result table shows all these rows.

Task: Variation

The task is the same as the preceding one, except include the rows for employees 201 and 206, which have a null value in the manager_id column.

Oracle & Access SQL: Variation — Include nulls

```
select employee_id,
       first_name,
       last_name,
       manager_id
from l_employees
where manager_id = 203
    or manager_id is null; ❸
```

Result table: Variation

```
EMPLOYEE                          MANAGER
      ID FIRST_NAME LAST_NAME          ID
-------- ---------- ---------- -------
     201 SUSAN      BROWN      (null)
     206 CAROL      ROSE       (null)
     207 DAN        SMITH         203
     208 FRED       CAMPBELL      203
     210 NANCY      HOFFMAN       203
```

Notes

❸ Adding this line includes the rows that have a null value in the manager_id column.

2-10 Using a Less Than condition in the `where` clause

This section shows an example of a query that uses a Less Than (<) condition in the `where` clause. If there were rows with a null value in the `credit_limit` column, they would not be included in the result table.

Task

List all employees who have a credit limit less than $17.50. Show the columns:
```
employee_id
first_name
last_name
credit_limit
```

Oracle & Access SQL

```
select employee_id,
       first_name,
       last_name,
       credit_limit
from 1_employees
where credit_limit < 17.50; ❶
```

Beginning table (1_employees table)

```
EMPLOYEE                          DEPT              CREDIT PHONE  MANAGER
      ID FIRST_NAME LAST_NAME CODE HIRE_DATE         LIMIT NUMBER      ID
-------- ---------- --------- ---- ----------- ------- ------ -------
     201 SUSAN      BROWN     EXE  01-JUN-1998 $30.00 3484   (null)
     202 JIM        KERN      SAL  16-AUG-1999 $25.00 8722      201
     203 MARTHA     WOODS     SHP  02-FEB-2004 $25.00 7591      201
     204 ELLEN      OWENS     SAL  01-JUL-2003 $15.00 6830      202
     205 HENRY      PERKINS   SAL  01-MAR-2000 $25.00 5286      202
     206 CAROL      ROSE      ACT  (null)      (null) (null) (null)
     207 DAN        SMITH     SHP  01-DEC-2004 $25.00 2259      203
     208 FRED       CAMPBELL  SHP  01-APR-2003 $25.00 1752      203
     209 PAULA      JACOBS    MKT  17-MAR-1999 $15.00 3357      201
     210 NANCY      HOFFMAN   SAL  16-FEB-2004 $25.00 2974      203
```

Result table

```
EMPLOYEE                     CREDIT
      ID FIRST_NAME LAST_NAME  LIMIT
-------- ---------- ---------- -------
     204 ELLEN      OWENS      $15.00
     209 PAULA      JACOBS     $15.00
```

Notes

❶ The where clause contains only one condition:

```
where credit_limit < 17.50
```

This condition uses the less than (<) sign. The numeric value in the SQL code, 17.50, cannot contain a dollar sign or a comma. This can be confusing because often dollar signs and commas are displayed when you see the data in a table. The beginning table has two rows that satisfy this condition. The result table shows those two rows.

Task: Variation

Show another way to write this query, using the greater than or equal to (>=) sign and negating the condition with a Boolean not.

Oracle & Access SQL: Variation

```
select employee_id,
       first_name,
       last_name,
       credit_limit
from l_employees
where not (credit_limit >= 17.50); ❷
```

Result table: Variation — Same as above

Notes

❷ This is another way to write the Less Than condition.

2-11 Using a Not Equal condition
in the where clause

This section shows an example of a query that uses a Not Equal condition in its where clause.

Most SQL products support several ways to write the Not Equal condition. Unfortunately, some of the ways that work in one product may not work in another product. I prefer the method shown here because it works in all products and it is easy for both people and computers to understand.

When possible, it is best to avoid using a Not Equal condition because it is much less efficient for the computer to process than conditions such as Equal (=) or between.

Task

List all employees who do not report to employee 203, Martha Woods. Show the following columns:

```
employee_id
first_name
last_name
manager_id
```

Oracle & Access SQL

```
select employee_id,
       first_name,
       last_name,
       manager_id
from l_employees
where not (manager_id = 203);  ❶
```

Beginning table (1_employees table)

```
EMPLOYEE                          DEPT                      CREDIT  PHONE   MANAGER
      ID FIRST_NAME  LAST_NAME    CODE  HIRE_DATE           LIMIT   NUMBER       ID
-------- ----------  ---------    ----  ------------        -------  ------  -------
     201 SUSAN       BROWN        EXE   01-JUN-1998         $30.00  3484    (null)
     202 JIM         KERN         SAL   16-AUG-1999         $25.00  8722       201
     203 MARTHA      WOODS        SHP   02-FEB-2004         $25.00  7591       201
     204 ELLEN       OWENS        SAL   01-JUL-2003         $15.00  6830       202
     205 HENRY       PERKINS      SAL   01-MAR-2000         $25.00  5286       202
     206 CAROL       ROSE         ACT   (null)              (null)  (null)  (null)
     207 DAN         SMITH        SHP   01-DEC-2004         $25.00  2259       203
     208 FRED        CAMPBELL     SHP   01-APR-2003         $25.00  1752       203
     209 PAULA       JACOBS       MKT   17-MAR-1999         $15.00  3357       201
     210 NANCY       HOFFMAN      SAL   16-FEB-2004         $25.00  2974       203
```

Result table

```
EMPLOYEE                         MANAGER
      ID FIRST_NAME  LAST_NAME        ID
-------- ----------  ----------   -------
     202 JIM         KERN             201
     203 MARTHA      WOODS            201
     204 ELLEN       OWENS            202
     205 HENRY       PERKINS          202
     209 PAULA       JACOBS           201
```

Notes

❶ The Boolean not reverses the meaning of the condition that follows it. It only applies to that one condition. Here it changes the Equal condition into the Not Equal condition.

Variations

Some other ways to write the Not Equal condition are

```
where manager_id <> 203
where not manager_id = 203
where manager_id != 203
where manager_id ^= 203
```

You might find these variations in code you inherit, or you might prefer to use some of them yourself.

SQL uses 3-valued logic

The result table in this section does not show the rows that have a null value in the `manager_id` column. To show all the rows from the beginning table, we need to consider three different conditions:

```
where manager_id = 203
where not (manager_id = 203)
where manager_id is null
```

This is an example of what is meant when people say SQL uses 3-valued logic.

2-12 Using the `in` condition in the `where` clause

This section shows an example of a query that uses an `in` condition in its `where` clause. The `in` condition is used to show membership in a set. It is used when there is a list of discrete values that satisfy the condition. The set of all these valid values is placed in parentheses as a comma-delimited list.

All the values must have the same datatype — numbers, text, or dates. All the values can be numbers, or they can all be text, or they can all be dates. It does not make sense to mix these categories. More specifically, the values must have the same datatype as the column being tested.

It would not make sense to include null in the list of valid values because the `in` condition is never satisfied by a null in the data.

Sometimes in production code an `in` condition checks for 10 to 50 different values. In this situation it is much more efficient to write the code using an `in` condition rather than many Equal conditions. The examples in this book do not show this efficiency because they check for only two or three values.

Task

List all employees who report to employees 202 or 203, Jim Kern or Martha Woods. Show the following columns:

```
employee_id
first_name
last_name
manager_id
```

Oracle & Access SQL

```
select employee_id,
       first_name,
       last_name,
       manager_id
from 1_employees
where manager_id in (202, 203);  ❶
```

Beginning table (1_employees table)

EMPLOYEE ID	FIRST_NAME	LAST_NAME	DEPT CODE	HIRE_DATE	CREDIT LIMIT	PHONE NUMBER	MANAGER ID
201	SUSAN	BROWN	EXE	01-JUN-1998	$30.00	3484	(null)
202	JIM	KERN	SAL	16-AUG-1999	$25.00	8722	201
203	MARTHA	WOODS	SHP	02-FEB-2004	$25.00	7591	201
204	ELLEN	OWENS	SAL	01-JUL-2003	$15.00	6830	202
205	HENRY	PERKINS	SAL	01-MAR-2000	$25.00	5286	202
206	CAROL	ROSE	ACT	(null)	(null)	(null)	(null)
207	DAN	SMITH	SHP	01-DEC-2004	$25.00	2259	203
208	FRED	CAMPBELL	SHP	01-APR-2003	$25.00	1752	203
209	PAULA	JACOBS	MKT	17-MAR-1999	$15.00	3357	201
210	NANCY	HOFFMAN	SAL	16-FEB-2004	$25.00	2974	203

Result table

```
EMPLOYEE                            MANAGER
      ID FIRST_NAME LAST_NAME         ID
-------- ---------- ---------- -------
     204 ELLEN      OWENS          202
     205 HENRY      PERKINS        202
     207 DAN        SMITH          203
     208 FRED       CAMPBELL       203
     210 NANCY      HOFFMAN        203
```

Notes

❶ This condition means that the manager_id column is equal to either 202 or 203.

Oracle & Access variation: Using Equal conditions

Show another way to write the same query. Use two Equal conditions combined together with a Boolean or.

```
select employee_id,
       first_name,
       last_name,
       manager_id
from l_employees
where manager_id = 202
      or manager_id = 203;❷
```

Notes

❷ You must repeat the column name, manager_id, within each Equal condition.

Result table: Variation — Same as above

2-13 Using the between condition in the where clause

This section shows an example of a query that uses the between condition in its where clause. Note that the end points, August 16, 1999, and July 1, 2003, are both included in the result table. Some people prefer not to use the between condition with dates because a date can also contain a time, which can create some confusion.

The between condition can be applied to numbers, text, and dates. In this example, it is applied to dates. In Oracle, dates must be enclosed in single quotes (' '). In Access, they must be enclosed in pound signs (##). That is the only difference between the Oracle SQL and the Access SQL in this example.

Task

List all employees hired between August 16, 1999, and July 1, 2003. Show the following columns:

```
employee_id
first_name
last_name
hire_date
```

Oracle SQL

```
select employee_id,
       first_name,
       last_name,
       hire_date
from l_employees
where hire_date between '16-aug-1999'
                and '01-jul-2003';
```

Access SQL

```
select employee_id,
       first_name,
       last_name,
       hire_date
from l_employees
where hire_date between #16-aug-1999#
                and #01-jul-2003#;
```

Beginning table (`1_employees` table)

```
EMPLOYEE                          DEPT                    CREDIT PHONE   MANAGER
      ID FIRST_NAME LAST_NAME CODE HIRE_DATE         LIMIT NUMBER      ID
-------- ---------- --------- ---- ------------     ------- ------  -------
     201 SUSAN      BROWN     EXE  01-JUN-1998      $30.00 3484    (null)
     202 JIM        KERN      SAL  16-AUG-1999      $25.00 8722       201
     203 MARTHA     WOODS     SHP  02-FEB-2004      $25.00 7591       201
     204 ELLEN      OWENS     SAL  01-JUL-2003      $15.00 6830       202
     205 HENRY      PERKINS   SAL  01-MAR-2000      $25.00 5286       202
     206 CAROL      ROSE      ACT  (null)           (null) (null)  (null)
     207 DAN        SMITH     SHP  01-DEC-2004      $25.00 2259       203
     208 FRED       CAMPBELL  SHP  01-APR-2003      $25.00 1752       203
     209 PAULA      JACOBS    MKT  17-MAR-1999      $15.00 3357       201
     210 NANCY      HOFFMAN   SAL  16-FEB-2004      $25.00 2974       203
```

Result table

```
EMPLOYEE
      ID FIRST_NAME LAST_NAME  HIRE_DATE
-------- ---------- ---------- ------------
     202 JIM        KERN       16-AUG-1999
     204 ELLEN      OWENS      01-JUL-2003
     205 HENRY      PERKINS    01-MAR-2000
     208 FRED       CAMPBELL   01-APR-2003
```

Variation: Using an `in` condition

Write the same query as in the preceding task with an `in` condition. This requires you to write about 1,400 dates and demonstrates the usefulness of the `between` condition. Even when the code can be written in another way, the code is more compact and less prone to errors when the `between` condition is used.

Oracle SQL

```
select employee_id,
       first_name,
       last_name,
       hire_date
from l_employees
where hire_date in ('16-aug-1999',
                    '17-aug-1999',
                    '18-aug-1999',
```
(about 1,400 more dates)
```
                    '29-jun-2003',
                    '30-jun-2003',
                    '01-jul-2003');
```

Access SQL

```
select employee_id,
       first_name,
       last_name,
       hire_date
from l_employees
where hire_date in (#16-aug-1999#,
                    #17-aug-1999#,
                    #18-aug-1999#,
```
(about 1,400 more dates)
```
                    #29-jun-2003#,
                    #30-jun-2003#,
                    #01-jul-2003#);
```

Result table: Variation — Same as above

Notes on the dates in this variation

Actually, these two methods of writing the code are not quite equivalent. A date in SQL always includes a time, although often the time is not shown when the data is displayed. With the SQL code using the `between` condition, all the times of all the dates are included. But with the code using the `in` condition, the time must be midnight on the dates listed. `Between` always specifies a range and `in` always specifies a series of points.

2-14 Using the `like` condition in the `where` clause

This section shows an example of a query that uses the `like` condition in its `where` clause. The `like` condition is used for finding patterns in the data. Patterns are specified using wildcard characters, which are used only with the `like` condition. When the same characters are used with another condition, such as the `between` condition, they are no longer wildcards. A column of any of the major datatypes — text, number, or date — can be searched with a pattern. Case sensitivity is often an issue, but here I have turned it off. For details, see section 3-13.

In both Oracle and Access SQL, the pattern specification should be enclosed in single quotes. Patterns are specified differently in Oracle than they are in Access. Access allows a greater variety of patterns than Oracle. The wildcard characters are different. These wildcard characters are shown in the following table.

Wildcard characters and their meanings.

Oracle	Access	Meaning
% (percent sign)	* (asterisk)	A string of characters of any length, or possibly no characters at all (a zero-length string).
_ (underscore)	? (question mark)	One character.
(not available)	# (pound sign)	One digit (numeric character).
(not available) ❶	[c-m] (square brackets with a dash)	Range of characters.
(not available) ❷	[!c-m]	Outside a range of characters.
\% or _ (backslash) ❸	[*] or [?] or [#] (square brackets)	In Access, putting a character in square brackets means to take it literally, rather than using it as a wildcard character.

The following table shows some examples of patterns.

Examples of wildcard patterns.

Pattern	Oracle	Access	Examples

Text string beginning with an n	`'n%'`	`'n*'`	`'none'`
			`'n123'`
			`'No credit'`
			`'n'`

Four characters ending with an e	`'_ _ _ e'`	`'???e'`	`'none'`
			`'123e'`
			`'1  3e'`

Starting with a letter between a and g, followed by two digits	(not available)	`'[a-g]##'`	`'a47'` `'b82'`

Notes

❶ Sometimes this code can be used: `'c' <= value and 'm' > value`

❷ Sometimes this code can be used: `'c' > value or 'm' <= value`

❸ In Oracle, you can set up the backslash to be an Escape character. Any character placed after it is treated as a literal value rather than given a special meaning. To activate the backslash as an Escape character, use the SQLplus command

```
set escape \;
```

Task

List all employees who have the letter n in their last name. Show the following columns:

```
employee_id
first_name
last_name
```

Oracle SQL

```
select employee_id,
       first_name,
       last_name
from l_employees
where last_name like '%n%';
```

Access SQL

```
select employee_id,
       first_name,
       last_name
from l_employees
where last_name like '*n*';
```

Beginning table (1_employees table)

```
EMPLOYEE                        DEPT                    CREDIT PHONE   MANAGER
      ID FIRST_NAME LAST_NAME  CODE HIRE_DATE           LIMIT NUMBER       ID
-------- ---------- ---------- ---- ----------------- ------- ------  -------
     201 SUSAN      BROWN      EXE  01-JUN-1998       $30.00 3484    (null)
     202 JIM        KERN       SAL  16-AUG-1999       $25.00 8722       201
     203 MARTHA     WOODS      SHP  02-FEB-2004       $25.00 7591       201
     204 ELLEN      OWENS      SAL  01-JUL-2003       $15.00 6830       202
     205 HENRY      PERKINS    SAL  01-MAR-2000       $25.00 5286       202
     206 CAROL      ROSE       ACT  (null)            (null) (null)  (null)
     207 DAN        SMITH      SHP  01-DEC-2004       $25.00 2259       203
     208 FRED       CAMPBELL   SHP  01-APR-2003       $25.00 1752       203
     209 PAULA      JACOBS     MKT  17-MAR-1999       $15.00 3357       201
     210 NANCY      HOFFMAN    SAL  16-FEB-2004       $25.00 2974       203
```

Result table

```
EMPLOYEE
      ID FIRST_NAME LAST_NAME
-------- ---------- ----------
     201 SUSAN      BROWN
     202 JIM        KERN
     204 ELLEN      OWENS
     205 HENRY      PERKINS
     210 NANCY      HOFFMAN
```

2-15 Using the `is null` condition in the `where` clause

This section shows an example of a query that uses an `is null` condition in its `where` clause. A null value is used to show where data is missing in the database tables.

Note that you must write this condition "is null," rather than "= null." This is to remind you that a null is missing data and it is not like any other value in the table, because it does not have a particular value.

Nulls receive special treatment in several situations within a database. Throughout this book I point out when they are treated differently from other data.

Task

List all employees who have a null in the `manager_id` column. Show the following columns:

```
employee_id
first_name
last_name
manager_id
```

Oracle & Access SQL

```
select employee_id,
       first_name,
       last_name,
       manager_id
from l_employees
where manager_id is null;
```

Beginning table (`1_employees` table)

```
EMPLOYEE                          DEPT                   CREDIT PHONE  MANAGER
      ID FIRST_NAME LAST_NAME CODE HIRE_DATE             LIMIT NUMBER      ID
-------- ---------- --------- ---- ------------         ------- ------ -------
     201 SUSAN      BROWN     EXE  01-JUN-1998          $30.00 3484   (null)
     202 JIM        KERN      SAL  16-AUG-1999          $25.00 8722      201
     203 MARTHA     WOODS     SHP  02-FEB-2004          $25.00 7591      201
     204 ELLEN      OWENS     SAL  01-JUL-2003          $15.00 6830      202
     205 HENRY      PERKINS   SAL  01-MAR-2000          $25.00 5286      202
     206 CAROL      ROSE      ACT  (null)               (null) (null) (null)
     207 DAN        SMITH     SHP  01-DEC-2004          $25.00 2259      203
     208 FRED       CAMPBELL  SHP  01-APR-2003          $25.00 1752      203
     209 PAULA      JACOBS    MKT  17-MAR-1999          $15.00 3357      201
     210 NANCY      HOFFMAN   SAL  16-FEB-2004          $25.00 2974      203
```

Result table

```
EMPLOYEE                         MANAGER
      ID FIRST_NAME LAST_NAME        ID
-------- ---------- ---------- -------
     201 SUSAN      BROWN      (null)
     206 CAROL      ROSE       (null)
```

Why databases use nulls

Before nulls were invented, computer systems often used spaces or special values, such as 99, to designate that data was missing. This caused two problems.

One problem was a lack of uniformity. Each computer system used different values to designate missing data. Often a single application used three of these special values: one for numbers, one for text, and one for date fields.

The special values for numbers were often all 9s, but one application might use 999, whereas another used 999999. Sometimes the various fields within a single application would use different numbers of digits.

The special values for text were often spaces. However, some applications used a single space. Others would fill the field with spaces. The computer would not always consider these to be equal. Some applications even used a zero-length string, which just confused things even more.

For date fields, January 1, 1900, often designated missing data, but some applications used other dates.

The second problem was that these special data values were sometimes processed as if they were actual data. This could lead to errors that were difficult to detect, particularly if some calculation was done that changed the values of these fields.

To solve these problems, nulls were created to designate missing data. A rigid distinction is made between nulls and other types of data. Nulls do not have datatypes, meaning there is no distinction between a null in a numeric column and one in a text or date column.

The Order By Clause

The `order by` clause determines how the rows of the result table are sorted when they are printed or displayed on the screen. If you leave out the `order by` clause, you are saying that you do not care about this order and you are giving the computer permission to display the rows of the result in any order.

2-16 Overview of the `order by` clause

In working with most of the tables in this book, you can get acceptable results even if you do not write an `order by` clause because most of the tables are small. They contain only a few rows. However, when you work with larger tables, it is essential to use an `order by` clause.

This section shows the syntax of the `order by` clause and a few examples of it. The clause contains a list of columns and a specification for each of these columns to sort them in either ascending order or descending order.

The first column listed in the `order by` clause is the primary sort order. The columns that are listed after the first one are used only when two rows have identical values in the first column. This rule applies to all the columns. For example, the third column is only used to sort the rows that have identical values in the first two columns of the `order by` clause.

Ascending order is the default. It is usually not specified. To sort on a column in descending order, `desc` must always be specified.

Columns are usually specified by their names. Another method is to specify a number — this is the position of the column within the `select` clause. This is an older method that is being phased out. Some brands of SQL allow you to use a column alias in an `order by` clause. Oracle allows this, but Access does not.

A column can sometimes be listed in the `order by` clause without listing it in the `select` clause. However, it is good programming practice to list in the `select` clause all the columns used in the `order by` clause.

In Oracle, nulls are sorted at the bottom. In Access, they are sorted at the top. Other slight differences in the sort order can occur depending on a variety of factors, such as

- Which SQL product you are using
- Whether you are using a small computer or a large computer
- Whether you are using a special alphabet
- Options set by your database administrator (DBA)

Syntax of the `order by` clause

`order by` *a list of column names*	- You may specify a sort order for each column. (see below)
`order by` *a list of numbers*	- You may specify a sort order for each column. (see below)

Sort order options for each column

`asc`	- Means ascending order (default)
`desc`	- Means descending order

Examples

```
order by employee_id

order by last_name, first_name

order by hire_date desc,
         last_name,
         first_name
```

2-17 Sorting the rows by several columns in ascending order

This section shows a query with two columns in its order by clause, both of which are sorted in ascending order.

Task

List the department codes and last names of all the employees, except for employee 209. Sort the rows of the result table on both columns in ascending order.

Oracle & Access SQL

```
select dept_code,
       last_name
from l_employees
where not (employee_id = 209)
order by dept_code, ❶
         last_name; ❷
```

Beginning table (l_employees table)

EMPLOYEE ID	FIRST_NAME	LAST_NAME	DEPT CODE	HIRE_DATE	CREDIT LIMIT	PHONE NUMBER	MANAGER ID
201	SUSAN	BROWN	EXE	01-JUN-1998	$30.00	3484	(null)
202	JIM	KERN	SAL	16-AUG-1999	$25.00	8722	201
203	MARTHA	WOODS	SHP	02-FEB-2004	$25.00	7591	201
204	ELLEN	OWENS	SAL	01-JUL-2003	$15.00	6830	202
205	HENRY	PERKINS	SAL	01-MAR-2000	$25.00	5286	202
206	CAROL	ROSE	ACT	(null)	(null)	(null)	(null)
207	DAN	SMITH	SHP	01-DEC-2004	$25.00	2259	203
208	FRED	CAMPBELL	SHP	01-APR-2003	$25.00	1752	203
209	PAULA	JACOBS	MKT	17-MAR-1999	$15.00	3357	201
210	NANCY	HOFFMAN	SAL	16-FEB-2004	$25.00	2974	203

Result table

```
DEPT
CODE  LAST_NAME
----  ----------
ACT   ROSE
EXE   BROWN
SAL   HOFFMAN
SAL   KERN
SAL   OWENS
SAL   PERKINS
SHP   CAMPBELL  ❸
SHP   SMITH  ❸
SHP   WOODS  ❸
```

Notes

❶ The rows of the result table are sorted first and primarily on the dept_code column. For instance, all four rows with a dept_code of SAL are sorted before the three rows with SHP.

❷ The rows with identical values in the dept_code column are then sorted on the last_name column. Within the SAL department code, the last names are put in ascending alphabetic order. Within the SHP department code, the names are put in a separate ascending alphabetic order.

❸ Note the order of these rows in the result table. Here, for the employees within any particular department, the last names are in ascending order. In the next section, we change the order and place the last names in descending order.

2-18 Sorting the rows by several columns in various orders

This shows the same query as in the previous section, except that the sort on the last_name column is in descending order. The contrast with the result table in the previous section shows the difference.

Task

List the department codes and last names of all the employees, except for employee 209. Sort the rows of the result table in ascending order on the dept_code column and in descending order on the last_name column.

Oracle & Access SQL

```
select dept_code,
       last_name
from l_employees
where not (employee_id = 209)
order by dept_code, ❶
         last_name desc; ❷
```

Beginning table (`1_employees` table)

```
EMPLOYEE                       DEPT                 CREDIT PHONE   MANAGER
      ID FIRST_NAME LAST_NAME  CODE HIRE_DATE        LIMIT NUMBER      ID
-------- ---------- ---------  ---- -----------     ------- ------ -------
     201 SUSAN      BROWN      EXE  01-JUN-1998     $30.00 3484    (null)
     202 JIM        KERN       SAL  16-AUG-1999     $25.00 8722       201
     203 MARTHA     WOODS      SHP  02-FEB-2004     $25.00 7591       201
     204 ELLEN      OWENS      SAL  01-JUL-2003     $15.00 6830       202
     205 HENRY      PERKINS    SAL  01-MAR-2000     $25.00 5286       202
     206 CAROL      ROSE       ACT  (null)          (null) (null)  (null)
     207 DAN        SMITH      SHP  01-DEC-2004     $25.00 2259       203
     208 FRED       CAMPBELL   SHP  01-APR-2003     $25.00 1752       203
     209 PAULA      JACOBS     MKT  17-MAR-1999     $15.00 3357       201
     210 NANCY      HOFFMAN    SAL  16-FEB-2004     $25.00 2974       203
```

Result table

```
DEPT
CODE LAST_NAME
---- ----------
ACT  ROSE
EXE  BROWN
SAL  PERKINS
SAL  OWENS
SAL  KERN
SAL  HOFFMAN
SHP  WOODS    ❸
SHP  SMITH    ❸
SHP  CAMPBELL ❸
```

Notes

❶ The rows of the result table are sorted first and primarily on the `dept_code` column.

❷ All the rows with the same value in the `dept_code` column are sorted on the `last_name` column in descending order. This is applied twice, once with the SAL department codes and again with the SHP ones.

❸ Note the order of these rows. Compare the order here with the order shown in the previous result table.

2-19 The whole process so far

Here is a quick summary of the process a `select` statement describes. Note that clauses of the `select` statement are processed in a different order than they are written.

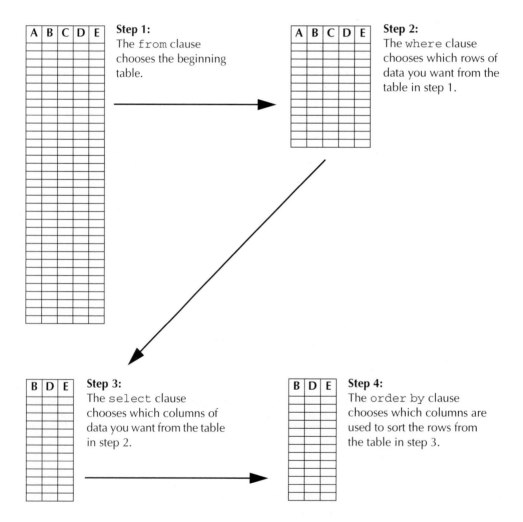

Step 1:
The `from` clause chooses the beginning table.

Step 2:
The `where` clause chooses which rows of data you want from the table in step 1.

Step 3:
The `select` clause chooses which columns of data you want from the table in step 2.

Step 4:
The `order by` clause chooses which columns are used to sort the rows from the table in step 3.

Summary

In this chapter you learned to get information from a table using the `select` statement. You learned the four main clauses of the `select` statement:

- `select`

- `from`

- `where`

- `order by`

We also explored many details about these clauses. Along the way, I have discussed nulls, the 3-valued logic used in SQL, and several other database issues.

You also saw that most of the time, the same SQL code that works in Oracle also works in Access.

Exercises

How the exercises are organized throughout this book

Most chapters have four exercises that give you practice using some of the most important material in the chapter. You can decide how many of these exercises you want to do. For most of the exercises there are several correct ways to write the SQL code. The exercises can be done using either Oracle or Access.

Each exercise has at least a part A and a part B. There is also sometimes a part C and a part D. The answer for part A is given to you within the exercise. It provides a model for solving the other parts of the exercise. Be sure to study part A carefully if you have difficulty with any other part of the exercise.

You can verify that your answer is correct by checking the result table. The result tables for most of the exercises in this book are available on the Web site, *www.sqlfun.com.*

How to do the exercises on the computer

There are several methods you can use to enter SQL commands. The recommended way is to type your commands into Notepad or some other text editor, then copy the whole command and paste it into Oracle SQLplus or Access. This gives you the maximum amount of control over your code. It is easy to make changes to your code, save it, and print it.

Another way is to type your commands directly into SQLplus or Access. If you use this technique, you will have less control over your code and you will need to use some tricks. See appendices B and C for information about these tricks.

In Oracle, you must run the SQLFUN_LOGIN.SQL script before you work these exercises. It sets up the environment in many ways. For example, it turns off case sensitivity.

Exercises for chapter 2

    1. Goal: List all the columns and all the rows of a table. (Section 2-5)

        a. List all the columns and rows of the `l_employees` table.

Oracle & Access SQL

```
select  *
from l_employees;
```

        b. List all the columns and rows of the `l_foods` table.

        c. List all the columns and rows of the `l_lunches` table.

2. Goal: Use all four main clauses of the `select` statement. Get a subset of the columns and rows of a table. Rename a column. (Section 2-4)

   a. List the following columns of the `1_employees` table in this order:

   ```
   last_name
   hire_date
   phone_number
   employee_id
   dept_code
   ```

   Change the name of the `hire_date` column to `start_date` within the result table. List only the rows for employees from the sales department. Sort the rows of the result table by the `last_name` column in ascending order.

   ## Oracle & Access SQL

   ```
   select last_name,
          hire_date as start_date,
          phone_number,
          employee_id,
          dept_code
   from 1_employees
   where dept_code = 'sal'
   order by last_name;
   ```

   b. List the same columns as in part 2a from the `1_employees` table. Also change the name of the `dept_code` column to `department_code` within the result table. List all the employees hired in 2003 and 2004. Sort the rows of the result table on the `hire_date` column in descending order.

   Hint: You want all the employees hired from January 1, 2003, to December 31, 2004. Oracle dates are enclosed in single quotes and Access dates are enclosed in pound signs.

   c. List the same columns as in part 2a from the `1_employees` table, except use the `manager_id` column in place of the `dept_code` column. List all the employees with a null value in the `manager_id` column. Sort the rows of the result table on the `employee_id` column in reverse order.

3. Goal: List all the distinct values in one column. (Section 2-6)

   a. List all the distinct `lunch_date` values in the `l_lunches` table. Sort these dates in descending date order.

Oracle & Access SQL

```
select distinct lunch_date
from l_lunches
order by lunch_date desc;
```

   b. List all the distinct `employee_id` values in the `l_lunches` table. Sort these IDs in ascending numerical order.

   c. List all the distinct values in the `date_entered` column of the `l_lunches` table. Sort these in ascending date order.
   How does this result differ from the results you got in parts 3a and 3b? Why is it different?

4. Goal: List all the distinct combinations of values in two or more columns. Exclude some rows of the beginning table from the result. (Section 2-7)

   a. List all the distinct combinations of `dept_code` and `credit_limit` values from the `l_employees` table. Exclude the employees whose manager is unknown. Sort the rows of the result table first on `dept_code` in ascending order and then on `credit_limit` in descending order.

Oracle & Access SQL

```
select distinct dept_code,
                credit_limit
from l_employees
where not (manager_id is null)
order by dept_code,
         credit_limit desc;
```

   b. List all the distinct combinations of `supplier_id` and `product_code` from the `l_lunch_items` table. Exclude the data for lunch 17. Sort the result on both columns in ascending order.

5. Goal: Sort the rows on more than one column. Put the columns in a particular order. (Section 2-18)

a. Using the `1_employees` table, list the following columns:
```
dept_code
credit_limit
last_name
first_name
```

Place the columns in that order. Sort the rows by:
`dept_code` in ascending order
`credit_limit` in descending order
`last_name` in ascending order

Oracle & Access SQL

```
select dept_code,
       credit_limit,
       last_name,
       first_name
from 1_employees
order by dept_code,
         credit_limit desc,
         last_name;
```

b. Using the `1_foods` table, place the columns in this order:
```
menu_item
description
price_increase
price
supplier_id
product_code
```

Sort the rows by:
`product_code` in ascending order
`supplier_id` in descending order

6. Goal: Get one specific row with a `where` condition that uses equality (=). (Section 2-9)

   a. From the `1_employees` table, get the row for Susan.

Oracle & Access SQL

```
select   *
from 1_employees
where first_name = 'susan';
```

   b. From the `1_foods` table, get the price of a grilled steak.

   c. From the `1_employees` table, get the hire date and phone number for Paula Jacobs.

7. Goal: Get several specific rows with a `where` condition that uses Less Than (`<`) or Greater Than (`>`). (Section 2-10)

   a. From the `1_employees` table, list the employee ID, first name, last name, and credit limits of the employees with a credit limit over $20.00. Sort them by the size of the credit limit.

Oracle & Access SQL

```
select employee_id,
       first_name,
       last_name,
       credit_limit
from 1_employees
where credit_limit > 20
order by credit_limit;
```

   b. List the foods costing less than $2.00. Show the description and price of each food. Sort the rows by the description of the food.

   c. List the employees hired before 2002. Show the `employee_id`, `first_name`, `last_name`, and `hire_date` columns. Sort the rows by the `employee_id`.

8. Goal: Get specific rows, using the `in` condition to specify a particular set of values. (Section 2-12)

a. From the `l_employees` table, list the `employee_id`, `first_name`, `last_name`, and `credit_limit` columns for employees with the last names:
Brown
Woods
Owens

Sort the rows by the `last_name`.

Oracle & Access SQL

```
select employee_id,
       first_name,
       last_name,
       credit_limit
from l_employees
where last_name in ('brown', 'woods', 'owens')
order by last_name;
```

b. From the `l_foods` table, list the `description` and `price` values of the following foods:
Hamburger
French fries
Soda

Sort the rows by the `description`.

c. From the `l_departments` table, list the `dept_code` and `department_name` of the following departments:
MKT
SAL

Sort the rows by the `dept_code`.

9. Goal: Get specific rows, using the `between` condition to specify a particular range of values. (Section 2-13)

a. List the employees hired in 2003. Show the `employee_id`, `first_name`, `last_name`, and `hire_date`. Sort the rows by the `hire_date`.

Oracle SQL

```
select employee_id,
       first_name,
       last_name,
       hire_date
from l_employees
where hire_date between '01-jan-2003'
                   and '31-dec-2003'
order by hire_date;
```

Access SQL

```
select employee_id,
       first_name,
       last_name,
       hire_date
from l_employees
where hire_date between #01-jan-2003#
                   and #31-dec-2003#
order by hire_date;
```

b. List the foods priced between $1.00 and $2.00. Show the `description` and the `price`. Sort the rows by `description`.

c. List the employees with last names starting with H through P. Show the `employee_id`, `first_name`, and `last_name`. Sort the rows by the `employee_id`. (This is a little tricky. My solution is given in section 3-14, but you can try it yourself first.)

10. Goal: Get several specific rows. Use a `like` condition in the `where` clause for pattern matching. (Section 2-14)

   a. From the `l_employees` table, list the `last_name` values that contain the letter n. Sort the rows in ascending order.

Oracle SQL

```
select last_name
from l_employees
where last_name like '%n%'
order by last_name;
```

Access SQL

```
select last_name
from l_employees
where last_name like '*n*'
order by last_name;
```

   b. From the `l_foods` table, list the foods that have "fresh" in their descriptions. Sort these rows in ascending order.

   c. List the employees that have a phone number ending with 4. Show the `employee_id`, `first_name`, `last_name`, and `phone_number`. Sort the rows by the `employee_id`.

11. Goal: Get specific rows, using the `is null` condition. (Section 2-15.)

   a. List the employees who do not have a manager. Show the `employee_id`, `first_name`, and `last_name`. Sort the rows by the `employee_id`.

Oracle & Access SQL

```
select employee_id,
       first_name,
       last_name
from l_employees
where manager_id is null
order by employee_id;
```

b. List the employees who do not have a phone number. Show the `employee_id`, `first_name`, and `last_name`. Sort the rows by the `employee_id`.

c. List the foods for which no price increase has been specified. Show the `description` of the foods and sort them in ascending order.

chapter 3

COMPOUND CONDITIONS IN THE WHERE CLAUSE

In chapter 2 we used fairly simple conditions in the `where` clause. In this chapter we discuss how to combine several of these simple conditions into a compound condition. This is particularly important when we are handling tables with many rows. It allows us to specify the particular set of rows we want.

This chapter also discusses tables of constant values and punctuation. Constant values can be put into a one-row table. This is an alternative to hard-coding the values into our code. Punctuation is always a crucial matter in all computer languages.

Compound Conditions in the Where Clause

This group of sections deals with the Boolean connectors and, or, and not. It shows how to place complex conditions in the where clause into standard form. Along the way, it shows you the rules you need to know to work with these Boolean connectors.

If you handle large tables, with a million or more rows, you may need to use very complex conditions in the where clause to specify the set of rows you want in the result. To keep this complexity down to a reasonable level, these conditions are often put into standard form.

The standard form is discussed in sections 3-3 to 3-8. You should read these sections over once, but do not worry if you have difficulty with them. This material is not needed in the rest of the book, but the details are here if you need them later when you are working with very large tables.

3-1   Using a compound condition in the where clause

Compound conditions can be formed using the three Boolean connectors: and, or, and not. And and or combine two conditions to form a single compound condition. They can be applied repeatedly, thus combining many conditions into a single compound condition. Not is applied to a single condition and reverses its meaning.

Definition of and

The statement "A and B" is true only when both A and B are true.

Definition of or

The statement "A or B" is true when either A or B is true.

Definition of not

The statement "not A" is true when A is false.

In the preceding definitions, A and B stand for any statement, such as employee_id < 500 or first_name = 'Mary'.

Within a complex condition, when several Boolean connectors are being used, parentheses should be used liberally. Even if you think they are not needed by the computer, they are needed to make the statement easy for people to read and understand. If you leave out some of the parentheses, the computer may understand the statement one way, but most people will interpret the statement in another way.

The example in this section shows a query that has a `where` clause that uses a compound condition. It shows how to include the null values when using a Not Equal condition. You must explicitly ask for the nulls if you want them to appear in the result table.

Task

List all employees who do not report to employee 203, Martha Woods. Include rows with a null value in the `manager_id` column. Show the following columns: `employee_id`, `first_name`, `last_name`, and `manager_id`.

Oracle & Access SQL

```
select employee_id,
       first_name,
       last_name,
       manager_id
from l_employees
where not (manager_id = 203) ❶
   or manager_id is null; ❷
```

Beginning table (l_employees table)

EMPLOYEE ID	FIRST_NAME	LAST_NAME	DEPT CODE	HIRE_DATE	CREDIT LIMIT	PHONE NUMBER	MANAGER ID
201	SUSAN	BROWN	EXE	01-JUN-1998	$30.00	3484	(null)
202	JIM	KERN	SAL	16-AUG-1999	$25.00	8722	201
203	MARTHA	WOODS	SHP	02-FEB-2004	$25.00	7591	201
204	ELLEN	OWENS	SAL	01-JUL-2003	$15.00	6830	202
205	HENRY	PERKINS	SAL	01-MAR-2000	$25.00	5286	202
206	CAROL	ROSE	ACT	(null)	(null)	(null)	(null)
207	DAN	SMITH	SHP	01-DEC-2004	$25.00	2259	203
208	FRED	CAMPBELL	SHP	01-APR-2003	$25.00	1752	203
209	PAULA	JACOBS	MKT	17-MAR-1999	$15.00	3357	201
210	NANCY	HOFFMAN	SAL	16-FEB-2004	$25.00	2974	203

Result table

EMPLOYEE ID	FIRST_NAME	LAST_NAME	MANAGER ID
201	SUSAN	BROWN	(null)
202	JIM	KERN	201
203	MARTHA	WOODS	201
204	ELLEN	OWENS	202
205	HENRY	PERKINS	202
206	CAROL	ROSE	(null)
209	PAULA	JACOBS	201

Notes

❶ Not is used to reverse the meaning of "manager_id = 203" to create the meaning "manager_id is not equal to 203." The parentheses are optional. I used them here to make the meaning more clear to people who read the SQL code.

❷ Or is used to combine the two conditions

```
not (manager_id = 203)
```

and

```
manager_id is null
```

to form a single compound condition

```
not (manager_id = 203)  or  manager_id is null
```

3-2   Using not with in, betweeen, like, and is null

This section shows the word not can be used in two different ways with the following conditions: in, between, like, and is null. The meanings are exactly the same.

Version 1 will show the word not used as part of the condition test. There is one condition test called in and there is another condition test called not in. The same applies to all these conditions:

```
in                    not in
between               not between
like                  not like
is null               is not null
```

Version 2 will show the word not used as a Boolean connector modifying an entire condition. In the first line of the where clause, not is applied to the condition

```
dept_code in ('act', 'mkt')
```

This condition is then written with an additional set of parentheses:

```
not (dept_code in ('act', 'mkt'))
```

The computer also understands this without the additional set of parentheses:

```
not dept_code in ('act', 'mkt')
```

However, this can be more confusing to most people, so I do not recommend it.

In the following code, you will notice that the patterns used with the `like` condition differ in Oracle and in Access. We discussed this in section 2-14.

Task

Show the `employee_id`, `first_name`, `last_name`, and `manager_id` of the employees having all of the following conditions:

dept_code is not act or mkt

last_name does not begin with any letter from J to M

last_name does not end with S

manager_id is not a null value

Oracle & Access SQL:
Version 1 — Using not within the condition

```
select employee_id,
       first_name,
       last_name,
       manager_id
from l_employees
where dept_code not in ('act', 'mkt')
  and last_name not between 'j' and 'm'
  and last_name not like '%s'          (Oracle)
  and last_name not like '*s'          (Access)
  and manager_id is not null;
```

Oracle & Access SQL: Version 2 — Using a Boolean not

```
select employee_id,
       first_name,
       last_name,
       manager_id
from 1_employees
where not (dept_code in ('act', 'mkt'))
  and not (last_name between 'j' and 'm')
  and not (last_name like '%s')       (Oracle)
  and not (last_name like '*s')       (Access)
  and not (manager_id is null);
```

Beginning table (1_employees table)

EMPLOYEE ID	FIRST_NAME	LAST_NAME	DEPT CODE	HIRE_DATE	CREDIT LIMIT	PHONE NUMBER	MANAGER ID
201	SUSAN	BROWN	EXE	01-JUN-1998	$30.00	3484	(null)
202	JIM	KERN	SAL	16-AUG-1999	$25.00	8722	201
203	MARTHA	WOODS	SHP	02-FEB-2004	$25.00	7591	201
204	ELLEN	OWENS	SAL	01-JUL-2003	$15.00	6830	202
205	HENRY	PERKINS	SAL	01-MAR-2000	$25.00	5286	202
206	CAROL	ROSE	ACT	(null)	(null)	(null)	(null)
207	DAN	SMITH	SHP	01-DEC-2004	$25.00	2259	203
208	FRED	CAMPBELL	SHP	01-APR-2003	$25.00	1752	203
209	PAULA	JACOBS	MKT	17-MAR-1999	$15.00	3357	201
210	NANCY	HOFFMAN	SAL	16-FEB-2004	$25.00	2974	203

Result table

EMPLOYEE ID	FIRST_NAME	LAST_NAME	MANAGER ID
207	DAN	SMITH	203
208	FRED	CAMPBELL	203
210	NANCY	HOFFMAN	203

3-3 The standard form of a complex condition in the `where` clause

This section shows an example of a query with a very complex condition in its `where` clause. You might need to use a condition of this sort when you are dealing with a large table that has many millions of rows. As a general rule, as a table gets larger the `where` clause gets more complex. Additional conditions are required to select the rows you want. Also, sometimes the logic within a query needs to be quite complex.

The purpose of this example is to show a condition in the `where` clause that is organized in the standard form of a Boolean expression. With a little effort, any complex condition can be written in this form. Writing a condition in this way can make it easy for people to read, understand, and work with. Complex conditions that are not in standard form are prone to errors. So, part of the debugging effort of a `select` statement can be working with the condition in the `where` clause to put it into standard form. Here I am using the term *standard form* to mean that the expression is placed in a standardized format.

The example in this section is a bit contrived. You really do not need complexity on this scale when you are dealing with tables as small and simple as the ones in this book. However, I want to show you the principle.

Definition of standard form in the `where` clause

The three Boolean connectors `and`, `or`, and `not` are strictly controlled.
- `Not` is applied only to simple conditions. It is not applied to compound conditions that include an `and` or an `or`.
- `And` is used to combine simple conditions and conditions involving `not`. None of these conditions are allowed to contain an `or`. Many conditions can be combined together with `and`. If there is more than one `and`, the conditions can be combined in any order and no parentheses are required. Each of these compound conditions is usually enclosed in parentheses.
- `Or` is the top-level connector. It combines all the compound conditions using `and` and `not`. If there is more than one `or`, the compound conditions can be combined in any order and no parentheses are required

Task

Show an example of a `select` statement that has a `where` clause in standard form. The following example shows the format. It does run, but it is not intended to make much sense.

Oracle & Access SQL

```
select employee_id,
       first_name,
       last_name
from l_employees
where (manager_id is null ❶
       and first_name = 'susan'
       and credit_limit = 30.00)
    or ❷
      (not (hire_date is null) ❸
       and credit_limit between 10.00 and 50.00 ❹
       and last_name in ('smith', 'jacobs', 'patrick')
       and not (dept_code = 'shp'))
    or
      (credit_limit > 22.00
       and hire_date is null)
    or
      (employee_id > 700
       and dept_code in ('sal', 'mkt')
       and manager_id = 400);
```

Beginning table (`l_employees` table)

EMPLOYEE ID	FIRST_NAME	LAST_NAME	DEPT CODE	HIRE_DATE	CREDIT LIMIT	PHONE NUMBER	MANAGER ID
201	SUSAN	BROWN	EXE	01-JUN-1998	$30.00	3484	(null)
202	JIM	KERN	SAL	16-AUG-1999	$25.00	8722	201
203	MARTHA	WOODS	SHP	02-FEB-2004	$25.00	7591	201
204	ELLEN	OWENS	SAL	01-JUL-2003	$15.00	6830	202
205	HENRY	PERKINS	SAL	01-MAR-2000	$25.00	5286	202
206	CAROL	ROSE	ACT	(null)	(null)	(null)	(null)
207	DAN	SMITH	SHP	01-DEC-2004	$25.00	2259	203
208	FRED	CAMPBELL	SHP	01-APR-2003	$25.00	1752	203
209	PAULA	JACOBS	MKT	17-MAR-1999	$15.00	3357	201
210	NANCY	HOFFMAN	SAL	16-FEB-2004	$25.00	2974	203

Result table ❺

EMPLOYEE ID	FIRST_NAME	LAST_NAME
201	SUSAN	BROWN
209	PAULA	JACOBS

Notes

❶ This line and the next two lines are a compound condition joined together with and. The parentheses enclosing these three lines are optional, but makes the condition easier to read.

❷ This is an or joining together the compound conditions formed with and.

❸ This shows a Boolean not applied to a simple condition that does not contain any and or or.

❹ The and on this line is part of the between condition. It is not a Boolean and connector.

❺ The result table shows that this code actually runs. In this example, it is not important to follow the precise logic.

3-4   How to put a complex condition into standard form

When you have a complex Boolean condition in a where clause, the procedure to put it into standard form is straightforward and mechanical. It requires some work, but it is often worth the effort. This procedure has two parts.

Part 1

First, you work with all the instances of the Boolean not. The goal is to have a not apply only to a simple condition, which is a condition without an and or or. To achieve this, you apply these three rules:

```
1.  not (A and B) = (not A) or (not B)
2.  not (A or B) = (not A) and (not B)
3.  not (not A) = A
```

Rule 1 shows how to transform a not that is applied to an and condition. The not is applied to all the individual conditions joined by and and the and becomes an or.

Rule 2 shows how to transform a not that is applied to an or condition. The not is applied to all the individual conditions joined by or and the or becomes an and.

Rule 3 is familiar to most people. A not cancels out another not. A double negative is the same as a positive.

In these rules, A and B stand for any conditions in the where clause. They may even be compound conditions involving and and or. Some examples are as follows:

```
manager_id is not null
employee_id between 200 and 400
manager_id is not null and credit_limit > 50.00
manager_id is not null or not (credit_limit > 50.00)
```

Rules 1 and 2 can also be written in a more general form, which shows the left side having more than two conditions joined by and or or:

1. not (A and B and C) = (not A) or (not B) or (not C)
2. not (A or B or C) = (not A) and (not B) and (not C)

Part 2

Next, you need to unscramble the ands and ors. The goal is to have clusters of conditions joined with and and to use or only in joining these clusters. To achieve this, you apply the following rule:

4. (A or B) and C = (A and C) or (B and C)

Rule 4 shows how to transform a situation where an and is applied to an or. On the left side, the or is not on the top level. On the right side, it is on the top level and that is the way you want it to be.

3-5   Example of rules 1 and 3

This section shows an example of rules 1 and 3 from section 3-4. Both SQL statements give exactly the same result. Before rule 1 is applied, the not modifies a compound condition joined with and. After it is applied, not modifies three simple conditions that are joined with or.

Rule 3 is shown in the third condition within the where clause. Before rule 1 is applied, this condition is

```
hire_date is not null
```

After rule 1 is applied, this condition becomes

```
not (hire_date is not null)
```

Then, applying rule 3, the two `not`s cancel each other. So then the condition can be written

```
hire_date is null
```

You might ask, "Do nulls in the data affect these rules?" No, the rules are not affected by nulls in the data because nulls are ignored by all of the `where` clause conditions except the `is null` condition. They are ignored in the same way before and after these rules are applied.

Task

Show an example of rules 1 and 3 from section 3-4.

Oracle & Access SQL: Before rules 1 and 3 are applied

```
select employee_id,
       dept_code,
       hire_date
from l_employees
where not (dept_code in ('sal', 'shp') ❶
           and employee_id between 202 and 205
           and hire_date is not null)
order by employee_id;
```

Oracle & Access SQL: After rules 1 and 3 are applied

```
select employee_id,
       dept_code,
       hire_date
from l_employees
where not (dept_code in ('sal', 'shp')) ❷
   or not (employee_id between 202 and 205)
   or hire_date is null ❸
order by employee_id;
```

Beginning table (`1_employees` table)

```
EMPLOYEE                         DEPT                CREDIT  PHONE   MANAGER
      ID FIRST_NAME LAST_NAME  CODE HIRE_DATE        LIMIT  NUMBER      ID
-------- ---------- ---------  ---- ------------    -------  ------  -------
     201 SUSAN      BROWN      EXE  01-JUN-1998     $30.00  3484    (null)
     202 JIM        KERN       SAL  16-AUG-1999     $25.00  8722       201
     203 MARTHA     WOODS      SHP  02-FEB-2004     $25.00  7591       201
     204 ELLEN      OWENS      SAL  01-JUL-2003     $15.00  6830       202
     205 HENRY      PERKINS    SAL  01-MAR-2000     $25.00  5286       202
     206 CAROL      ROSE       ACT  (null)          (null)  (null)  (null)
     207 DAN        SMITH      SHP  01-DEC-2004     $25.00  2259       203
     208 FRED       CAMPBELL   SHP  01-APR-2003     $25.00  1752       203
     209 PAULA      JACOBS     MKT  17-MAR-1999     $15.00  3357       201
     210 NANCY      HOFFMAN    SAL  16-FEB-2004     $25.00  2974       203
```

Result table

```
EMPLOYEE DEPT
      ID CODE HIRE_DATE
-------- ---- ------------
     201 EXE  01-JUN-1998
     206 ACT  (null)
     207 SHP  01-DEC-2004
     208 SHP  01-APR-2003
     209 MKT  17-MAR-1999
     210 SAL  16-FEB-2004
```

Notes

❶ The `not` here modifies a compound condition of the form (A and B and C).

❷ Rule 1 changes the position of the `not` so that it now modifies the individual components. We now have (not A) or (not B) or (not C).

❸ Rule 3 eliminates a double `not`. After I apply rule 1, I get the condition

`not (hire_date is not null)`

The two `not`s cancel each other out and I end up with

`hire_date is null`

3-6   Example of rule 2

This section shows an example of rule 2 from section 3-4. Both SQL statements give the same result. Before the rule is applied, the `not` modifies a compound condition joined with an `or`. After the rule is applied, `not` modifies two simple conditions and these two conditions are joined with an `and`.

Task

Show an example of rule 2 from section 3-4.

Oracle & Access SQL: Before rules 2 and 3 are applied

```
select employee_id,
       dept_code,
       hire_date
from 1_employees
where not (dept_code in ('sal', 'shp') ❶
           or employee_id between 202 and 205
           or hire_date is not null)
order by employee_id;
```

Oracle & Access SQL: After rules 2 and 3 are applied

```
select employee_id,
       dept_code,
       hire_date
from 1_employees
where not (dept_code in ('sal', 'shp')) ❷
  and not (employee_id between 202 and 205)
  and hire_date is null
order by employee_id;
```

Beginning table (`1_employees` table)

EMPLOYEE ID	FIRST_NAME	LAST_NAME	DEPT CODE	HIRE_DATE	CREDIT LIMIT	PHONE NUMBER	MANAGER ID
201	SUSAN	BROWN	EXE	01-JUN-1998	$30.00	3484	(null)
202	JIM	KERN	SAL	16-AUG-1999	$25.00	8722	201
203	MARTHA	WOODS	SHP	02-FEB-2004	$25.00	7591	201
204	ELLEN	OWENS	SAL	01-JUL-2003	$15.00	6830	202
205	HENRY	PERKINS	SAL	01-MAR-2000	$25.00	5286	202
206	CAROL	ROSE	ACT	(null)	(null)	(null)	(null)
207	DAN	SMITH	SHP	01-DEC-2004	$25.00	2259	203
208	FRED	CAMPBELL	SHP	01-APR-2003	$25.00	1752	203
209	PAULA	JACOBS	MKT	17-MAR-1999	$15.00	3357	201
210	NANCY	HOFFMAN	SAL	16-FEB-2004	$25.00	2974	203

Result table

EMPLOYEE ID	DEPT CODE	HIRE_DATE
206	ACT	(null)

Notes

❶ The `not` here modifies a compound condition of the form (A or B or C).

❷ Rule 1 changes the position of the `not` so that it now modifies the individual components. We now have (not A) and (not B) and (not C).

3-7   Example of rule 4

This section shows an example of rule 4 from section 3-4. Both SQL statements give the same result. Before the rule is applied, the `and` is forced by the parentheses to be at a higher level than the `or`. After the rule is applied, the `or` is the highest-level connector and the `where` clause is in standard form.

Task

Show an example of rule 4 from section 3-4.

Oracle & Access SQL: Before rule 4 is applied

```
select employee_id,
       dept_code,
       hire_date,
       manager_id
from l_employees
where (dept_code in ('sal', 'shp') ❶
       or employee_id between 202 and 205
       or hire_date is null)
   and manager_id = 203
order by employee_id;
```

Oracle & Access SQL: After rule 4 is applied

```
select employee_id,
       dept_code,
       hire_date,
       manager_id
from l_employees
where (dept_code in ('sal', 'shp') ❷
       and manager_id = 203)
    or
       (employee_id between 202 and 205
        and manager_id = 203)
    or
       (hire_date is null
        and manager_id = 203)
order by employee_id;
```

Beginning table (`1_employees` table)

```
EMPLOYEE                            DEPT                     CREDIT PHONE  MANAGER
      ID FIRST_NAME LAST_NAME  CODE HIRE_DATE         LIMIT NUMBER     ID
-------- ---------- ---------- ---- ------------     ------- ------  -------
     201 SUSAN      BROWN      EXE  01-JUN-1998      $30.00 3484    (null)
     202 JIM        KERN       SAL  16-AUG-1999      $25.00 8722       201
     203 MARTHA     WOODS      SHP  02-FEB-2004      $25.00 7591       201
     204 ELLEN      OWENS      SAL  01-JUL-2003      $15.00 6830       202
     205 HENRY      PERKINS    SAL  01-MAR-2000      $25.00 5286       202
     206 CAROL      ROSE       ACT  (null)           (null) (null)  (null)
     207 DAN        SMITH      SHP  01-DEC-2004      $25.00 2259       203
     208 FRED       CAMPBELL   SHP  01-APR-2003      $25.00 1752       203
     209 PAULA      JACOBS     MKT  17-MAR-1999      $15.00 3357       201
     210 NANCY      HOFFMAN    SAL  16-FEB-2004      $25.00 2974       203
```

Result table

```
EMPLOYEE DEPT                    MANAGER
      ID CODE HIRE_DATE              ID
-------- ---- ------------     -------
     207 SHP  01-DEC-2004          203
     208 SHP  01-APR-2003          203
     210 SAL  16-FEB-2004          203
```

Notes

❶ The statement here is in the form (A or B or C) and D.

❷ Rule 4 changes it to a statement in the form (A and D) or (B and D) or (C and D).

3-8   A common mistake

This section shows a common mistake that people make when they write a complex condition in the `where` clause and they do not specify enough parentheses. In this example, most people understand that the first three conditions of the `where` clause are related because they all involve the same column, `employee_id`. So placing a pair of parentheses around the first three conditions can represent the understanding that most people have.

To a computer, however, `or` is always a higher-level connector than `and` when parentheses do not say otherwise. So the computer understands the statement differently. To the computer, there are three clusters joined together by `or`.

Task

Of the employees whose employee IDs are 203, 204, or 205, list only the ones in the sales department.

Beginning table (`1_employees` table)

```
EMPLOYEE                         DEPT                  CREDIT PHONE   MANAGER
      ID FIRST_NAME LAST_NAME    CODE HIRE_DATE         LIMIT NUMBER       ID
-------- ---------- ---------    ---- -----------      ------- ------  -------
     201 SUSAN      BROWN        EXE  01-JUN-1998      $30.00 3484    (null)
     202 JIM        KERN         SAL  16-AUG-1999      $25.00 8722       201
     203 MARTHA     WOODS        SHP  02-FEB-2004      $25.00 7591       201
     204 ELLEN      OWENS        SAL  01-JUL-2003      $15.00 6830       202
     205 HENRY      PERKINS      SAL  01-MAR-2000      $25.00 5286       202
     206 CAROL      ROSE         ACT  (null)          (null)  (null)  (null)
     207 DAN        SMITH        SHP  01-DEC-2004      $25.00 2259       203
     208 FRED       CAMPBELL     SHP  01-APR-2003      $25.00 1752       203
     209 PAULA      JACOBS       MKT  17-MAR-1999      $15.00 3357       201
     210 NANCY      HOFFMAN      SAL  16-FEB-2004      $25.00 2974       203
```

Oracle & Access SQL: Parentheses are missing — A common mistake

```
select *
from 1_employees
where employee_id = 203 ❶
   or employee_id = 204
   or employee_id = 205
  and dept_code = 'sal';
```

Notes

❶ This where clause does not contain enough parentheses to control the way that the individual conditions are combined. Most people will understand it to mean one thing, but the computer will understand it to mean something else.

Oracle & Access SQL: How people often misunderstand this code

```
select *
from 1_employees
where (    employee_id = 203 ❷
        or employee_id = 204
        or employee_id = 205)
  and dept_code = 'sal';
```

Result table that people often expect from this code

EMPLOYEE ID	FIRST_NAME	LAST_NAME	DEPT CODE	HIRE_DATE	CREDIT LIMIT	PHONE NUMBER	MANAGER ID
204	ELLEN	OWENS	SAL	01-JUL-2003	$15.00	6830	202
205	HENRY	PERKINS	SAL	01-MAR-2000	$25.00	5286	202

Notes

❷ The pair of parentheses here shows how most people understand the code in ❶.

Oracle & Access SQL: How a computer understands this code

```
select *
from l_employees
where (employee_id = 203) ❸
    or
        (employee_id = 204)
    or
        (employee_id = 205
        and dept_code = 'sal');
```

Result table that the computer produces ❹

EMPLOYEE ID	FIRST_NAME	LAST_NAME	DEPT CODE	HIRE_DATE	CREDIT LIMIT	PHONE NUMBER	MANAGER ID
203	MARTHA	WOODS	SHP	02-FEB-2004	$25.00	7591	201
204	ELLEN	OWENS	SAL	01-JUL-2003	$15.00	6830	202
205	HENRY	PERKINS	SAL	01-MAR-2000	$25.00	5286	202

Notes

❸ The pairs of parentheses here show the way that the computer understands the code in ❶. The computer combines phrases with and before combining phrases with or.

❹ This table contains the row from employee_id 203, Martha Woods, who is in the shipping department. This occurred because a mistake was made when writing the code in ❶. The mistake was in leaving out a pair of parentheses. If you don't want this row in your result table, you must write the code in ❷.

Constant Values

On the level of data in a table, a *constant value* is a column that contains the same value in every row. Usually there is no reason to place a column like this in a table. Two other techniques can be used instead. One technique places a literal value into the `select` clause as a hard-coded value. This works well when you have only a few `select` statements. However, when you have a large number of `select` statements, this technique can make the code inflexible. This means that the code cannot easily be changed to adapt to changing requirements.

The other technique places the constant values in a separate table, which I call a *table of constants*. This is defined as a table that has only one row. It has a separate column for each distinct constant value. The names of these columns are usually designed so they are unique and are not identical to the column names in any other table. After this table has been created, it can be used in coding `select` statements with any other table.

This technique is used primarily when you have 20 or more `select` statements that all use the same set of constants. For instance, I once became responsible for a set of quarterly reports someone else had written. The beginning date and ending date of the quarter was hard-coded into each `select` statement. Each time I wanted to run these reports I had to change the beginning date and ending date in all of the code. This took most of a day, and there would always be some errors to find and correct, so the whole process took about two days. After doing this a few times, I got tired of it and I changed the code to get the dates from a table of constants. It would then take me only a few minutes to run all the reports.

3-9   Using a constant value in the `select` clause

This section shows constant values hard-coded within a `select` clause. This example shows all the different types of data that can be coded as constant values — text, numbers, and nulls. The column that appears to be a date is actually a text field, where the text represents a date.

You will understand this comment about dates better when we discuss the Date datatype and the formatting of dates in chapters 6 and 7. Data with a Date datatype can be stored in a table, but cannot be printed directly.

Dates must be printed as text. So when a date appears in a `select` clause, it must appear as text.

The following diagram shows what happens on a conceptual level when a constant value is used within a `select` clause. It is as if a new column was added to the beginning table. This new column contains the same value in every row and it can be given a column alias, a temporary name, just like any other column. The syntax is the same here as it is for a column. The syntax is

```
constant_value AS column_alias
```

This is parallel to

```
column_name AS column_alias
```

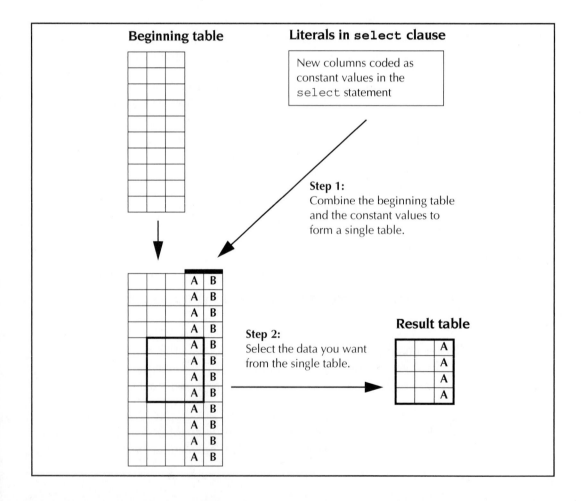

Task

Show a query that contains hard-coded values in the `select` clause. Show a text value, a numeric value, a date value, and a null value.

Oracle & Access SQL

```
select employee_id,
       last_name,
       'excellent worker' as evaluation, ❶
       10 as rating, ❷
       '01-jan-2005' as eval_date, ❸
       null as next_eval ❹
from l_employees
order by employee_id;
```

Beginning table (`l_employees` table)

```
EMPLOYEE                         DEPT                CREDIT PHONE  MANAGER
      ID FIRST_NAME LAST_NAME CODE HIRE_DATE          LIMIT NUMBER      ID
-------- ---------- --------- ---- -----------       ------- ------ -------
     201 SUSAN      BROWN     EXE  01-JUN-1998       $30.00 3484   (null)
     202 JIM        KERN      SAL  16-AUG-1999       $25.00 8722      201
     203 MARTHA     WOODS     SHP  02-FEB-2004       $25.00 7591      201
     204 ELLEN      OWENS     SAL  01-JUL-2003       $15.00 6830      202
     205 HENRY      PERKINS   SAL  01-MAR-2000       $25.00 5286      202
     206 CAROL      ROSE      ACT  (null)            (null) (null) (null)
     207 DAN        SMITH     SHP  01-DEC-2004       $25.00 2259      203
     208 FRED       CAMPBELL  SHP  01-APR-2003       $25.00 1752      203
     209 PAULA      JACOBS    MKT  17-MAR-1999       $15.00 3357      201
     210 NANCY      HOFFMAN   SAL  16-FEB-2004       $25.00 2974      203
```

Result table

```
EMPLOYEE                                              NEXT
      ID LAST_NAME  EVALUATION          RATING EVAL_DATE  EVAL
-------- ---------- ---------------- --------- ---------- ------
     201 BROWN      EXCELLENT WORKER         10 01-JAN-2005 (null)
     202 KERN       EXCELLENT WORKER         10 01-JAN-2005 (null)
     203 WOODS      EXCELLENT WORKER         10 01-JAN-2005 (null)
     204 OWENS      EXCELLENT WORKER         10 01-JAN-2005 (null)
     205 PERKINS    EXCELLENT WORKER         10 01-JAN-2005 (null)
     206 ROSE       EXCELLENT WORKER         10 01-JAN-2005 (null)
     207 SMITH      EXCELLENT WORKER         10 01-JAN-2005 (null)
     208 CAMPBELL   EXCELLENT WORKER         10 01-JAN-2005 (null)
     209 JACOBS     EXCELLENT WORKER         10 01-JAN-2005 (null)
     210 HOFFMAN    EXCELLENT WORKER         10 01-JAN-2005 (null)
```

Notes

❶ This constant value is a text field. Although it is a hard-coded literal within the `select` clause, it behaves as if it had created a new column within the beginning table.

❷ This constant value is a numeric field.

❸ This constant value is a text field that represents a date.

❹ This constant value is a null. You must not put quotes around the word "null".

3-10 Using a table of constants

Here are some of the benefits of using a table of constants:

1. It adds flexibility to your SQL code. Your `select` statements can change easily if the value of any of these constants ever changes.

2. It guarantees consistency. You are sure that all the `select` statements are using the same values for these constants.

This section shows an example of a `select` statement that uses a table of constants. To do this, the `from` clause needs to list two tables: the table of constants and another table of data. All the other clauses of the `select` statement can refer to the columns of either table. No relationship between the two tables is required. The fact that a table of constants has only one row ensures that all the constant values will be copied into every row of the other table.

For this technique to work, the names of the columns in the table of constants must all be different from any column name in the other table. When this is not true, you need to use other techniques discussed in chapter 13.

The following diagram shows what happens on a conceptual level when a table of constants is used with another table in a `select` statement. It is as if new columns have been added to the other table. These new columns contain the same value in every row.

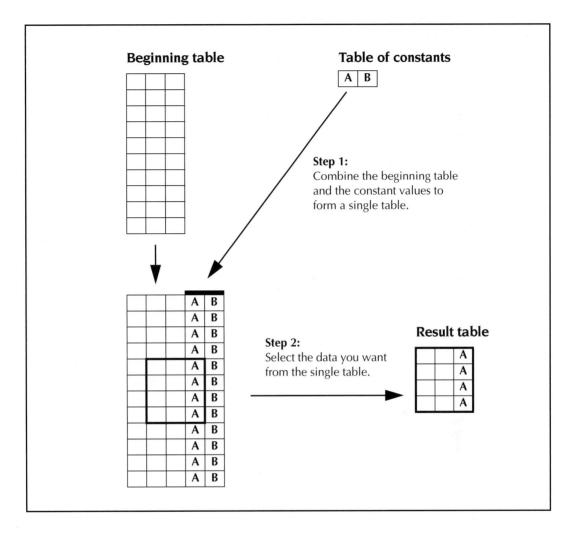

Task

Code the select statement from the previous section using a table of constants instead of hard-coded literals.

Oracle & Access SQL

```
select employee_id,
       last_name,
       evaluation, ❶
       rating, ❶
       eval_date, ❶
       next_eval ❶
from   l_employees,
       sec0310_constants
order by employee_id;
```

Beginning table 1 (1_employees table)

EMPLOYEE ID	FIRST_NAME	LAST_NAME	DEPT CODE	HIRE_DATE	CREDIT LIMIT	PHONE NUMBER	MANAGER ID
201	SUSAN	BROWN	EXE	01-JUN-1998	$30.00	3484	(null)
202	JIM	KERN	SAL	16-AUG-1999	$25.00	8722	201
203	MARTHA	WOODS	SHP	02-FEB-2004	$25.00	7591	201
204	ELLEN	OWENS	SAL	01-JUL-2003	$15.00	6830	202
205	HENRY	PERKINS	SAL	01-MAR-2000	$25.00	5286	202
206	CAROL	ROSE	ACT	(null)	(null)	(null)	(null)
207	DAN	SMITH	SHP	01-DEC-2004	$25.00	2259	203
208	FRED	CAMPBELL	SHP	01-APR-2003	$25.00	1752	203
209	PAULA	JACOBS	MKT	17-MAR-1999	$15.00	3357	201
210	NANCY	HOFFMAN	SAL	16-FEB-2004	$25.00	2974	203

Beginning table 2 (sec0310_constants table)

EVALUATION	RATING	EVAL_DATE	NEXT EVAL
EXCELLENT WORKER	10	01-JAN-2005	(null)

Result table

```
EMPLOYEE LAST                                              NEXT
      ID NAME     EVALUATION        RATING EVAL_DATE       EVAL
-------- -------- ----------------- ---------- ----------- ------
     201 BROWN    EXCELLENT WORKER          10 01-JAN-2005 (null)
     202 KERN     EXCELLENT WORKER          10 01-JAN-2005 (null)
     203 WOODS    EXCELLENT WORKER          10 01-JAN-2005 (null)
     204 OWENS    EXCELLENT WORKER          10 01-JAN-2005 (null)
     205 PERKINS  EXCELLENT WORKER          10 01-JAN-2005 (null)
     206 ROSE     EXCELLENT WORKER          10 01-JAN-2005 (null)
     207 SMITH    EXCELLENT WORKER          10 01-JAN-2005 (null)
     208 CAMPBELL EXCELLENT WORKER          10 01-JAN-2005 (null)
     209 JACOBS   EXCELLENT WORKER          10 01-JAN-2005 (null)
     210 HOFFMAN  EXCELLENT WORKER          10 01-JAN-2005 (null)
```

Notes

❶ This column now comes from the table of constants instead of being hard-coded as a literal into the `select` clause.

Punctuation Matters

It is almost embarrassing to talk in detail about punctuation . Small problems, like the one in the previous sentence, are often ignored. (Did you notice that there is a space before the period?) People usually focus on the words first and then expect the punctuation to be easy. However, computers focus on the punctuation first and then look at the words. Any mistake in punctuation can completely confuse the computer. More than half the errors most people make while learning SQL are errors in punctuation.

This is made more difficult because punctuation has additional meanings in SQL that it does not have in English or any other spoken language. Also, Oracle and Access use punctuation somewhat differently.

Section 3-11 contains the minimum you need to know about punctuation. Section 3-12 contains a more detailed discussion of punctuation. You might want to skim this section for now and refer to it later. Section 3-13 discusses case sensitivity in databases, when it matters if you use uppercase or lowercase letters.

3-11 Punctuation you need to know right now

This section contains short explanations about punctuation. I only tell you enough here to keep you out of trouble and tell you about the best practices. More detailed explanations are presented in the next section.

Spaces in names — Avoid them when you can

It is best to avoid using a space in any name — table names, column names, and the names of any other database objects. Use an underscore character instead of a space. For example, do not name a column `hire date`, which has a space between the e of hire and the d of date. Name it `hire_date`.

Comma

Commas separate the items of a list. A list cannot end with a comma. If the last item of a list is removed, the comma preceding it must also be removed. The following example shows a common error:

```
select first_name,
       last_name,
from l_employees;
```

Do not use commas or dollar signs when entering numbers. Decimal points are the only punctuation allowed within numbers.

Single quotes

In Oracle, you should use only single quotes to surround text strings and dates. Do not use quotes around numbers. See the following examples.

Oracle SQL:

```
select *
from l_employees
where dept_code in ('sal', 'shp')
   or hire_date > '01-jan-2003'
   or employee_id = 201;
```

In Access, like in Oracle, text strings must be enclosed in quotes and numbers must not be enclosed in them. However, dates are punctuated differently in Access than they are in Oracle. In Access, dates are enclosed in pound signs, not in quotes.

Access SQL:

```
select *
from l_employees
where dept_code in ('sal', 'shp')
   or hire_date > #01-jan-2003#
   or employee_id = 201;
```

Double quotes

In Oracle, single quotes and double quotes have different meanings. You should almost always use single quotes, except in two special situations, which are explained in the next section.

In Access, single quotes and double quotes have the same meaning, so you can use double quotes anywhere you can use single quotes. In this book I mostly use single quotes because I want the same code to work in both Oracle and Access.

Pound sign

Access uses the pound sign to enclose dates. See the previous example.

Semicolon

A semicolon marks the end of an SQL statement.

Reserved words — Avoid them

SQL uses some reserved words. In general, you should avoid using any word you think might be reserved. For example, do not try to name a column `from` or `date`. Few reserved words contain an underscore, so adding an underscore is a way to avoid using a reserved word. In the example, it would be okay to name a column `from_` or `date_`.

3-12 Punctuation reference section

This is a reference for the most common types of punctuation required by Oracle and Access. It includes the previous section. This section covers punctuation you can learn later. You do not need to read it now.

How to avoid having spaces in names

It is best to avoid using spaces in the names of database objects or column names. Traditionally with computers, spaces have been used as a separator character and you are simply asking for trouble if you start to use a space in any other way.

There are two methods that are often used to eliminate spaces. One method replaces the spaces with underscore characters. The other method uses mostly lowercase letters, except each word begins with one uppercase letter. The spaces are removed. Here is an example of both methods:

```
Name with spaces:   hire date
Method 1:           hire_date
Method 2:           HireDate
```

In this book I use the first method. To me, this makes the code easier to read, but this is a matter of taste, so you can use the other method if you prefer it.

How to handle spaces in names

Sometimes you cannot avoid having spaces in names, usually because the system is already set up before you arrive. Then you just have to deal with them. Both Oracle and Access provide a way to handle this situation. In Oracle, you enclose the name in double quotes. In Access, you enclose the name in square brackets. For example:

```
Name with spaces:   hire date
Oracle method:      "hire date"
Access method:      [hire date]
```

Comma

Commas separate the items of a list. A list cannot end with a comma. If the last item of a list is removed, the comma preceding it must also be removed.

This example shows a common error:

```
select first_name,
       last_name,
from l_employees;
```

Do not use commas or dollar signs when entering numbers. Decimal points are the only punctuation allowed within numbers.

Single quotes

In Oracle, character strings and dates must be enclosed in single quotes. The terms *character string* and *text string* mean the same thing. In Access, they can be enclosed in either single quotes or double quotes.

Two single quotes next to each other can be use to code an apostrophe. For details, see the discussion of apostrophes.

Double quotes

In Access, double quotes and single quotes mean the same thing, so text strings can be enclosed in either single quotes or double quotes.

In Oracle, double quotes are used around a column alias that contains a special character or a space. For example:

```
select first_name as "first name"
from l_employees
order by "first name";
```

In Oracle, double quotes are also used to put text into date formats. We discuss date formats in chapter 7. Here is an example:

```
select employee_id,
to_char(hire_date, '"hired in the year " yyyy')
from l_employees;
```

Apostrophe

An apostrophe can be written as two single quotes next to each other. To find the names of all the suppliers with an apostrophe in their names, you can write:

Oracle SQL:

```
select *
from l_suppliers
where supplier_name like '%''%';
```

Access SQL: Method 1

```
select *
from l_suppliers
where supplier_name like '*''*';
```

An easier method to write an apostrophe in Access encloses a single quote in a pair of double quotes:

Access SQL: Method 2

```
select *
from l_suppliers
where supplier_name like "*'*";
```

Pound sign

Access uses the pound sign to enclose dates:

```
select *
from l_employees
where hire_date = #16-feb-2004#;
```

Oracle encloses dates in single quotes:

```
where hire_date = '16-feb-2004';
```

SQL can be written in free format

Most of the SQL in this book is written in a highly structured way. I recommend using this format. However, this formatting is not required. The code can all be written on one line, or you can get creative and write it in some fancy shape.

The clauses of the `select` statement must always be written in a specified order. However, you can run the lines together in any way you wish. You can write

```
select *
from l_employees;
```

or

```
select * from l_employees;
```

or

```
select
  *   from
            l_employees
  ;
```

There are two exceptions to this. Oracle usually does not allow any completely blank lines in the middle of an SQL statement. You can set an option in SQLplus to allow them.

Access allows blank lines, but it does not allow any characters after the semicolon that marks the end of the SQL statement.

Double dash (comment line)

In Oracle and most other SQL products, any text written after two dashes is a comment. The dashes can be written at the beginning of the line or in the middle:

```
-- This is a comment line
```

or

```
select first_name, last_name  -- this is a comment
```

Access does not allow comments in the SQL window. So, when you write SQL for both Oracle and Access, you cannot put comments into it.

Period (and exclamation mark)

A period is often used between a table name and a column name to indicate that the column is part of that particular table:

```
select l_employees.first_name
from l_employees;
```

In Access, an exclamation mark is sometime used to mean the same:

```
select l_employees!first_name
from l_employees;
```

Access cannot include a period in a column alias.

Ampersand

In Oracle, the ampersand is often used to indicate a variable. For instance, `&fox` could be a variable. A slightly different type of variable is `&&fox`. You will be asked to supply a value for `&fox` each time it occurs in Oracle script. With `&&fox` you will only be asked to supply a value the first time it occurs.

If you want to use an ampersand as an ordinary character, you should turn this feature off. To do this you run the following command:

```
set define off
```

This is an SQLplus command, not an SQL command. It sets the environment in which SQL runs in Oracle.

In Access, an ampersand is used for concatenation. For example:

"sweet" & "heart" = "sweetheart"

Double bar

The double bar is the uppercase symbol above the backslash. The key usually shows two short lines, one above the other. However, many printers display it as a single line. Oracle uses it to make two or more lines in a column heading within the `column` command. For example:

```
column first_name heading 'FIRST | NAME'
```

Oracle uses two consecutive double bars for the concatenation function. For example:

```
'sun' || 'shine' = 'sunshine'
```

Semicolon

A semicolon marks the end of an SQL statement. This tells the computer that the statement is complete and may now be processed. Oracle requires a semicolon to end a statement. Oracle also accepts a forward slash as another method of statement termination. In Access, the semicolon is optional.

Numbers — Commas, decimal points, and dollar signs

When you are using a number within SQL code, do not use commas or dollar signs. Decimal points may be used.

Square brackets

In Access, square brackets are used to enclose names that contain spaces.

Asterisk

In both Oracle and Access, `select *` means "select all the columns." `Count(*)` means "count all the rows." An asterisk is also used as a sign for multiplication. In Access patterns, it is a wildcard character meaning "any number of characters, or possibly no characters at all."

Forward slash

In Oracle, a forward slash can be used to terminate an SQL statement. More precisely it means "run the SQL code that is now in the buffer." In both Oracle and Access, a forward slash is used for division.

Multi-line comment

In Oracle, you can enter a multi-line comment by beginning it with `/*` and putting `*/` at the end. For example:

```
/*
this is the beginning of the comment,
then you add as many lines as you want
and you end the comment this way
*/
```

Not Equal

The Not Equal condition is shown in several ways. To exclude `employee_id` 201, you can write any of the following:

```
where employee_id != 201          Oracle only
where employee_id ^= 201          Oracle only
where employee_id <> 201          Oracle & Access
where not employee_id = 201       Oracle & Access
where not (employee_id = 201)     Oracle & Access
```

Wildcards

Wildcards are used in a `where` clause with a `like` condition.

In Oracle:

% (percent)	is used to mean any number of characters, or possibly no characters at all.
_ (underscore)	is used to mean exactly one unknown character.

In Access:

* (asterisk)	is used to mean any number of characters, or possibly no characters at all.
? (question mark)	is used to mean exactly one unknown character.
# (pound sign)	is used to mean exactly one digit, 0 to 9.
[a-d] (square brackets)	are used to mean a range of characters, in this case from a to d.
[*] (square brackets around a wildcard character)	means the character itself, without its wildcard properties.

3-13 Case sensitivity

Some people like to run their databases with case-sensitive data, because they want to make a distinction between uppercase and lowercase letters. For example, between "John" and "john". This is done particularly in Oracle databases run under the UNIX operating system. The UNIX operating system itself is case sensitive, and so it seems natural to carry that over to the databases.

Some other people want to run their databases with case sensitivity turned off. When they search or sort the data, they do not want case to be an issue. This controversy has been going on for years, and people on both sides feel strongly that they are right. As an application programmer, you will have to go along with the shop you are working for.

Access turns off case sensitivity automatically, by default. Oracle requires a bit more work, because by default it is case sensitive. In this book I have decided to run the databases with case sensitivity turned off because I think that is easier to handle when people are first learning SQL.

In Oracle, to turn off the case sensitivity I have stored all the data in upper-case letters. This is how it is frequently done. Usually when you do this, it affects the SQL code. Any text within quotes would need to be in upper-case. For example:

```
select *
from l_employees
where dept_code in ('SAL', 'SHP');
```

However, you may have noticed that the code in this book is written with `sal` and `shp` in lowercase letters. The reason I can get away with that is because SQLplus has the command

```
set sqlcase upper;
```

SQLplus is the environment in which Oracle SQL is run. This command causes SQLplus to translate every SQL command into all uppercase letters before it runs. So, in effect, `sal` and `shp` and everything else in the `select` statement are translated into uppercase letters before the code executes.

This command is issued when the Oracle login script is run, which sets up the SQLplus environment in a standard way. You should run this script each time you log onto Oracle. However, if you forget to run it, this command will not be issued and you will find that your SQL queries will only work if the text within quotes is placed in uppercase letters.

In Access, there are actually two separate issues: preserving the case in which the data was entered, and using case-sensitive comparisons. Access always preserves the case in which the data was entered. Comparisons in Access are not case sensitive.

Some Exercises Solved for You

Here are some exercises I have solved for you. The problems might look simple, but they are actually a bit tricky. I chose to solve these exercises because they illustrate many of the fine points in the topics we have already discussed.

3-14 Exercise 1

Task

List the employees who have last names starting with H through P.

Oracle & Access SQL: First attempt — INCORRECT

```
select employee_id,
       first_name,
       last_name
from l_employees
where last_name between 'h' and 'p'
order by employee_id;
```

Beginning table (l_employees table)

EMPLOYEE ID	FIRST_NAME	LAST_NAME	DEPT CODE	HIRE_DATE	CREDIT LIMIT	PHONE NUMBER	MANAGER ID
201	SUSAN	BROWN	EXE	01-JUN-1998	$30.00	3484	(null)
202	JIM	KERN	SAL	16-AUG-1999	$25.00	8722	201
203	MARTHA	WOODS	SHP	02-FEB-2004	$25.00	7591	201
204	ELLEN	OWENS	SAL	01-JUL-2003	$15.00	6830	202
205	HENRY	PERKINS	SAL	01-MAR-2000	$25.00	5286	202
206	CAROL	ROSE	ACT	(null)	(null)	(null)	(null)
207	DAN	SMITH	SHP	01-DEC-2004	$25.00	2259	203
208	FRED	CAMPBELL	SHP	01-APR-2003	$25.00	1752	203
209	PAULA	JACOBS	MKT	17-MAR-1999	$15.00	3357	201
210	NANCY	HOFFMAN	SAL	16-FEB-2004	$25.00	2974	203

Result table ❶

```
EMPLOYEE
      ID FIRST_NAME LAST_NAME
-------- ---------- ----------
     202 JIM        KERN
     204 ELLEN      OWENS
     209 PAULA      JACOBS
     210 NANCY      HOFFMAN
```

Notes

❶ Henry Perkins is not listed in the result table. The problem is that P means "P followed by a space" in this context, and PE comes after P followed by a space.

Oracle SQL: Second attempt — INCORRECT

```
select employee_id,
       first_name,
       last_name
from l_employees
where last_name between 'h' and 'p%' ❷
order by employee_id;
```

Access SQL: Second attempt — INCORRECT

```
select employee_id,
       first_name,
       last_name
from l_employees
where last_name between 'h' and 'p*' ❷
order by employee_id;
```

Result table

```
EMPLOYEE
      ID FIRST_NAME LAST_NAME
-------- ---------- ----------
     202 JIM        KERN
     204 ELLEN      OWENS
     209 PAULA      JACOBS
     210 NANCY      HOFFMAN
```

Notes

❷ Here we are trying to use a wildcard character after the P to mean "P followed by any other character." The code runs, but Henry Perkins is still missing from the result.

Only the like condition supports wildcard characters. When these characters are used with the between condition, they are considered to be regular characters instead of wildcard characters. So here the percent sign and the asterisk are regular characters. PE comes after P% and P*, so Perkins is not included in the result.

Oracle & Access SQL: Third attempt — CORRECT

```
select  employee_id,
        first_name,
        last_name
from 1_employees
where last_name between 'h' and 'pz' ❸
order by employee_id;
```

Result table

```
EMPLOYEE
      ID FIRST_NAME LAST_NAME
-------- ---------- ----------
     202 JIM        KERN
     204 ELLEN      OWENS
     205 HENRY      PERKINS
     209 PAULA      JACOBS
     210 NANCY      HOFFMAN
```

Notes

❸ This stretches the between condition to the end of the Ps.

Oracle & Access SQL: Fourth attempt — CORRECT

```
select employee_id,
       first_name,
       last_name
from l_employees
where last_name between 'h' and 'q'  ❹
order by employee_id;
```

Notes

❹ This is another way to stretch the range of the between condition to include all words beginning with P.

Access SQL: Fifth attempt — CORRECT

```
select employee_id,
       first_name,
       last_name
from l_employees
where last_name like '[h-p]*'  ❺
order by employee_id;
```

Notes

❺ In this solution we are using the like condition instead of the between condition. We can do this in Access, but not in Oracle, because Access supports a greater variety of patterns than Oracle does.

Oracle & Access SQL: Sixth attempt — CORRECT (the best solution)

```
select employee_id,
       first_name,
       last_name
from l_employees
where last_name >= 'h'
  and last_name < 'q'
order by employee_id;
```

3-15 Exercise 2

In the 1_suppliers table, list the row for Alice & Ray's Restaurant.

Oracle & Access SQL: First attempt — INCORRECT

```
select *
from 1_suppliers
where supplier_name = 'alice & ray's restaurant'; ❶
```

Result — We get an error message

Oracle & Access SQL: Second attempt — CORRECT

```
select *
from 1_suppliers
where supplier_name = 'alice & ray''s restaurant'; ❷
```

Access SQL: Third attempt — CORRECT

```
select *
from 1_suppliers
where supplier_name = "alice & ray's restaurant"; ❸
```

Beginning table (1_suppliers table)

```
SUPPLIER
ID        SUPPLIER_NAME
--------  --------------------------
ARR       ALICE & RAY'S RESTAURANT
ASP       A SOUP PLACE
CBC       CERTIFIED BEEF COMPANY
FRV       FRANK REED'S VEGETABLES
FSN       FRANK & SONS
JBR       JUST BEVERAGES
JPS       JIM PARKER'S SHOP
VSB       VIRGINIA STREET BAKERY
```

Result table

```
SUPPLIER
ID        SUPPLIER_NAME
--------  ---------------------------
ARR       ALICE & RAY'S RESTAURANT
```

Notes

❶ The name of this supplier contains an apostrophe, which confuses the computer.

❷ Use two consecutive single quotes to code an apostrophe in a text string that is enclosed in single quotes.

❸ In Access, we can enclose a text string in double quotes. When we do this, the apostrophe in the name does not cause a problem.

3-16 Exercise 3

List the `employee_id`, `first_name`, `last_name`, and `hire_date` of all the employees hired in the year 2004.

Oracle & Access SQL: First attempt — INCORRECT

```
select employee_id,
       first_name,
       last_name,
       hire_date
from l_employees
where hire_date = '2004';        (Oracle) ❶

where hire_date = #2004#;        (Access)
```

Result — We get an error message

Oracle & Access SQL: Second attempt — CORRECT

```
select employee_id,
       first_name,
       last_name,
       hire_date
from 1_employees
where hire_date between '01-jan-2004'        (Oracle) ❷
                  and '31-dec-2004';         (Oracle)

where hire_date between #01-jan-2004#        (Access)
                  and #31-dec-2004#;         (Access)
```

Beginning table (1_employees table)

EMPLOYEE ID	FIRST_NAME	LAST_NAME	DEPT CODE	HIRE_DATE	CREDIT LIMIT	PHONE NUMBER	MANAGER ID
201	SUSAN	BROWN	EXE	01-JUN-1998	$30.00	3484	(null)
202	JIM	KERN	SAL	16-AUG-1999	$25.00	8722	201
203	MARTHA	WOODS	SHP	02-FEB-2004	$25.00	7591	201
204	ELLEN	OWENS	SAL	01-JUL-2003	$15.00	6830	202
205	HENRY	PERKINS	SAL	01-MAR-2000	$25.00	5286	202
206	CAROL	ROSE	ACT	(null)	(null)	(null)	(null)
207	DAN	SMITH	SHP	01-DEC-2004	$25.00	2259	203
208	FRED	CAMPBELL	SHP	01-APR-2003	$25.00	1752	203
209	PAULA	JACOBS	MKT	17-MAR-1999	$15.00	3357	201
210	NANCY	HOFFMAN	SAL	16-FEB-2004	$25.00	2974	203

Result table

EMPLOYEE ID	FIRST_NAME	LAST_NAME	HIRE_DATE
203	MARTHA	WOODS	02-FEB-2004
207	DAN	SMITH	01-DEC-2004
210	NANCY	HOFFMAN	16-FEB-2004

Notes

❶ When we specify a date, we cannot only give the year.

❷ To specify a year, we must say that the date is between January 1 and December 31 of that year.

Oracle SQL: Another solution, using features we have not covered yet

```
select employee_id,
       first_name,
       last_name,
       hire_date
from l_employees
where to_char(hire_date, 'yyyy') = '2004'; ❸
```

Access SQL: Another solution, using features we have not covered yet

```
select employee_id,
       first_name,
       last_name,
       hire_date
from l_employees
where year(hire_date) = 2004; ❹
```

Notes

❸ In Oracle, the `to_char` function can specify the format of a date. For more details, see section 7-2.

❹ In Access, the year function shows only the year part of a date, and it shows this as an integer. Here the `hire_date` is 2004, which is an integer and not a date so it is not enclosed within pound signs.

Summary

In this chapter we discussed how to use Boolean expressions to form compound conditions in the `where` clause. I showed you how to put a complex compound condition into standard form. I also showed you how to use a table of constants.

The chapter has a reference section on punctuation. Everybody makes mistakes in punctuation, even me!

Exercises

1. Goal: Show how to work with `not`.

   a. Modify the following SQL code so that the `not` applies directly to the simple conditions in the `where` clause. In other words, bring the `and` or `or` outside the scope of the `not`. (Section 3-5)

   Beginning SQL

   ```
   select *
   from l_employees
   where not (dept_code = 'sal'
              and manager_id = 202);
   ```

   Another way to ask this question: We want to make the following code have the same meaning as the preceding code. In the following code, should xxx be the word `and` or should it be the word `or`?

   ```
   select *
   from l_employees
   where not (dept_code = 'sal')
     XXX not (manager_id = 202);
   ```

   Oracle & Access SQL

   ```
   select *
   from l_employees
   where not (dept_code = 'sal')
      or not (manager_id = 202);
   ```

   b. Perform the same exercise as 1a, using the following beginning code.

   Beginning SQL

   ```
   select *
   from l_employees
   where not (dept_code = 'sal'
              or manager_id = 202);
   ```

c. Perform the same exercise as 1a. Also resolve any double negatives.

Beginning SQL

```
select *
from l_employees
where not (dept_code = 'sal'
           or manager_id is not null);
```

2. Goal: Show how to work with a table of constant values.

a. Modify the following SQL code to replace the hard-coded values with columns from a table of constants. (Section 3-10)

Beginning SQL

```
select employee_id,
       first_name,
       last_name,
       'citywide uniforms' as company
from l_employees
where not (dept_code = 'sal')
   or not (manager_id = 202);
```

Table of constants (ex302a table)

```
Company = 'citywide uniforms'
Excluded_dept = 'sal'
Excluded_manager = 202
```

Oracle & Access SQL

```
select employee_id,
       first_name,
       last_name,
       company
from l_employees,
     ex0302a
where not (dept_code = excluded_dept)
   or not (manager_id = excluded_manager);
```

b. Perform the same exercise as 2a, using the following beginning SQL and table of constants.

Beginning SQL

```
select employee_id,
       first_name,
       last_name,
       'citywide uniforms' as company,
       '415-643-6904' as company_phone
from 1_employees
where (dept_code = 'sal'
       and manager_id = 202)
   or (dept_code = 'exe'
       and manager_id is null)
   or (dept_code = 'shp'
       and manager_id = 201);
```

Table of constants (ex0302b table)

```
Company = 'citywide uniforms'
Company_phone = '415-643-6904'
Dept_1 = 'sal'
Manager_1 = 202
Dept_2 = 'exe'
Dept_3 = 'shp'
Manager_3 = 201
```

3. Goal: Include an apostrophe in SQL code. (Section 3-15)

   a. In the 1_suppliers table, list the row for Alice & Ray's Restaurant.

Oracle & Access SQL

```
select *
from 1_suppliers
where supplier_name = 'alice & ray''s restaurant';
```

   b. In the 1_suppliers table, list the row for Jim Parker's Shop.

4. Goal: Get specific rows using the Boolean connectors (and, or, not) to combine several conditions together. (Section 3-1)

   a. List the employees in the sales or marketing departments who were hired in 2003 or 2004. Show the first_name, last_name, dept_code, and hire_date columns. Sort the rows by the last_name.

   ## Oracle SQL

   ```
   select first_name,
          last_name,
          dept_code,
          hire_date
   from l_employees
   where (dept_code = 'sal'
          or dept_code = 'mkt')
     and hire_date >= '01-jan-2003'
     and hire_date <= '31-dec-2004'
   order by last_name;
   ```

   ## Access SQL

   ```
   select first_name,
          last_name,
          dept_code,
          hire_date
   from l_employees
   where (dept_code = 'sal'
          or dept_code = 'mkt')
     and hire_date >= #01-jan-2003#
     and hire_date <= #31-dec-2004#
   order by last_name;
   ```

   b. From the l_lunch_items table, list the rows having a supplier_id of cbc and product_code of gs (these are the grilled steaks). Sort the rows by the lunch_id.

chapter 4

SAVING YOUR RESULTS

The table of results of a query has columns and rows. It is a table and it can be handled like any other table. This chapter shows you how to save the results of a query in a new table and make modifications to the data.

Saving Your Results in a New Table or View

All the queries you have written so far display their results on the screen. After the computer is turned off, the results are gone. This chapter shows how to save the results in a table. Alternatively, they can be saved in a view, which is similar to a table.

To see the data in your table or view, you must use

```
select * from new_table or view;
```

4-1 Creating a new table from the results of a `select` statement

This section shows how to create a new table from the results of a `select` statement. Both Oracle and Access can perform this operation, but they specify it with different syntax. Oracle follows the SQL standard, but Access has created its own nonstandard expression.

You are the owner of the new table and have complete control over it. The new table is private and can only be seen and used by you unless you decide to share it with other people. You can modify the data in this table by adding new rows, changing rows, or deleting rows.

Description of the process

Begin with any `select` statement. In Oracle, one new line is added before the `select` clause. This line says `create table`, and then gives the name of the new table, followed by the word `as`. In Access, a new clause is added right after the `select` clause. This clause says `into` followed by the name of the new table. Except for this one change, the original `select` statement does not need to be changed. However, there are some special considerations about an `order by` clause.

Until recently, you could not include an `order by` clause. If the original `select` statement included this clause, you had to delete it. The reasoning was that the rows of a table are, in theory, an unordered set. So when you created a new table, you were not allowed to specify an order for its rows.

Now this has changed. The newest versions of Oracle and Access do allow you to use an `order by` clause in a `create table` statement. However, this is a very new feature, and many readers may not have it available, so I do not use it in this book.

In both Oracle and Access, I recommend that the name of the new table should be a new name that is not already used by any object in the database. Both Oracle and Access allow some exceptions to this rule, but you are inviting confusion if you have two objects with the same name. Each table must have a unique name. If the name is already being used, you will receive an error message and your SQL statement will not be processed.

Task

Save the result table of the following `select` statement. Create a new permanent table. Show how to change a `select` statement so that the result is saved in a new table, instead of being displayed on the screen. Name the new table `sales_staff`.

```
select employee_id, ❶
       first_name,
       last_name,
       dept_code
from l_employees
where dept_code = 'sal'
order by employee_id; ❷
```

Oracle SQL: Modified `select` statement — Save results in a table

```
create table sales_staff as ❸
select employee_id,
       first_name,
       last_name,
       dept_code
from l_employees
where dept_code = 'sal';
```

Access SQL: Modified `select` statement — Save results in a table

```
select employee_id,
       first_name,
       last_name,
       dept_code
into sales_staff ❹
from l_employees
where dept_code = 'sal';
```

Oracle & Access SQL: Show the table you created ❺

```
select *
from sales_staff ❻
order by employee_id; ❼
```

Beginning table (`1_employees` table)

EMPLOYEE ID	FIRST_NAME	LAST_NAME	DEPT CODE	HIRE_DATE	CREDIT LIMIT	PHONE NUMBER	MANAGER ID
201	SUSAN	BROWN	EXE	01-JUN-1998	$30.00	3484	(null)
202	JIM	KERN	SAL	16-AUG-1999	$25.00	8722	201
203	MARTHA	WOODS	SHP	02-FEB-2004	$25.00	7591	201
204	ELLEN	OWENS	SAL	01-JUL-2003	$15.00	6830	202
205	HENRY	PERKINS	SAL	01-MAR-2000	$25.00	5286	202
206	CAROL	ROSE	ACT	(null)	(null)	(null)	(null)
207	DAN	SMITH	SHP	01-DEC-2004	$25.00	2259	203
208	FRED	CAMPBELL	SHP	01-APR-2003	$25.00	1752	203
209	PAULA	JACOBS	MKT	17-MAR-1999	$15.00	3357	201
210	NANCY	HOFFMAN	SAL	16-FEB-2004	$25.00	2974	203

Result table

EMPLOYEE ID	FIRST_NAME	LAST_NAME	DEPT CODE
202	JIM	KERN	SAL
204	ELLEN	OWENS	SAL
205	HENRY	PERKINS	SAL
210	NANCY	HOFFMAN	SAL

Notes

❶ You can begin with any `select` statement.

❷ If there is an `order by` clause you must remove it. You can put it back in later.

❸ In Oracle, you add a `create table` clause before the `select` clause.

❹ In Access, you add an `into` clause after the end of the `select` clause and before the `from` clause.

❺ After you create a new table, you can write any `select` statement using the data from the new table. To see the data in the new table you created, you need to use the following:

```
select * from sales_staff;
```

❻ The `from` clause here names the new table.

❼ The `order by` clause here restores the order specified in the original `select` statement.

4-2   Creating a new view from the results of a `select` statement

This section shows another way to save the results of a query. Here the results are saved in a view rather than a table. A view is very much like a table. The next two sections discuss the similarities and differences between a view and a table, but for now, you can think of a view as a special type of table.

Access uses the term *saved query* instead of the term *view*. However, they both mean the same thing. Standard SQL calls it a view.

After the new view is created, it can be used like a table. It can be used in the `from` clause of any `select` statement. You are the owner of this view and have complete control over it. You are the only person who can use it, unless you decide to share it with other people.

Description of the process

Begin with any `select` statement. In Oracle, one new line is added before the `select` clause. This line says `create view`, and then gives the name of the new view, followed by the word `as`. Access uses a graphical user interface (GUI) method to create a saved query. The name of the view, just like the name of a table, must be unique.

Within standard SQL, the `order by` clause must be dropped when you are creating a view. However, both Oracle and Access allow you to use an `order by` clause. Even though this is a nonstandard feature, because both Oracle and Access support it, we use it in this book.

Task

Save the result table of the following `select` statement. Create a new view from this `select` statement and name it `sales_staff_view`.

```
select employee_id, ❶
       first_name,
       last_name,
       dept_code
from l_employees
where dept_code = 'sal'
order by employee_id; ❷
```

Oracle SQL:
Modified `select` statement — Save the results in a view

```
create view sales_staff_view as ❸
select employee_id,
       first_name,
       last_name,
       dept_code
from l_employees
where dept_code = 'sal'
order by employee_id; ❹

select * from sales_staff_view; ❺
```

■ This is not available in Access as an SQL command.

Access GUI method — Save the results in a saved query ❻

Step 1: Enter the `select` statement in the SQL window:

```
select employee_id,
       first_name,
       last_name,
       dept_code
from l_employees
where dept_code = 'sal'
order by employee_id;
```

Step 2: Run the query by pressing the toolbar button with the red exclamation point.
Step 3: Save the `select` statement.
Step 4: Enter a name for the query, as shown below.

The beginning table and result table are the same as in the previous section.

Notes

❶ Begin with any `select` statement.

❷ The `order by` clause is allowed in Oracle and Access.

❸ In Oracle, you add a `create view` clause before the `select` clause. I cannot use the name `sales_staff` for this view because I have already created a table with that name.

❹ A recent change to Oracle allows an `order by` clause to be used within a `create view` statement. This feature was introduced in Oracle8i.

❺ You can always use a `select *` to see the view you have created.

❻ Access does not have an SQL command to create a view, at least not on the SQL window level. Instead, it uses a GUI method to create a saved query.

4-3   Similarities between tables and views

Tables and views are very similar. They look alike. They both are two-dimensional structures that can contain the same types of data. They both have columns, rows, and cells. They can both be used as a source of data in the `from` clause of a `select` statement.

Most of the time there is no need to distinguish between them. Often when we use the word *table* we mean a view or a table. When we want to differentiate a table from a view, we usually call the table a *base table* or a *data table*.

4-4   Differences between tables and views

A table stores data directly on the disk. A view stores a `select` statement on the disk, but does not store any data. When SQL uses a view in the `from` clause of a query, it runs the `select` statement that defines the view. The result table of this `select` statement is the data of the view. On a basic level, tables store the data that is in a database. A view displays a presentation of the data that is already in the tables.

A table always requires much more disk space than a view. A table can contain thousands or even millions of rows, which can require a substantial amount of disk space. A view needs very little disk space because it is only storing a `select` statement.

A table is static, but a view is dynamic. If you want stability to be sure the data will not change unless you explicitly make changes to it, then you should store your data in a table. On the other hand, if you want the latest information that shows all the recent changes to the data in the database, then you should use a view.

Whenever you use a view, SQL runs the `select` statement that defines the view. The data is drawn from the underlying tables at that time. So the data in a view can change although no commands have been issued to explicitly change it.

The differences between a table and a view.

Table	View
Stores the data in the database on the disk drive.	Stores the `select` statement that defines the view. It has no data of its own.
Uses a lot of disk space for a large table.	Uses very little disk space.
The data belongs to the table.	The data does not belong to the view. It belongs to the tables used in the `select` statement that defines the view.
The data in a table is stable and does not change by itself.	The data in a view is dynamic and changes when the data in the underlying tables is changed.

Which one should you use?

Use a table when you want to store data that does not exist anywhere else in the database. Use a view when you want to present the data in a new way. The underlying data must already be present in the tables of the database.

4-5   Deleting a table

Now that you know how to create new tables, you also need to know how to delete them. Otherwise, you will eventually have more of them than you want.

In both Oracle and Access, you can delete a table with the SQL command `drop table`, followed by the name of the table. This gets rid of the table entirely. It deletes the data in the table, the table structure, and the definitions of the columns. The name of the table is no longer reserved.

Task

Delete the table named `sales_staff` created in section 4-1.

Oracle & Access SQL

```
drop table sales_staff;
```

Access alternative: GUI method

In Access, you can also use a GUI method to delete a table.

Step 1: Click the Tables tab.
Step 2: Highlight the name of the table, as shown below.

Step 3: Press the Delete key.

Beginning table (`sales_staff` table)

```
EMPLOYEE                           DEPT
      ID FIRST_NAME LAST_NAME      CODE
-------- ---------- ----------     ----
     202 JIM        KERN           SAL
     204 ELLEN      OWENS          SAL
     205 HENRY      PERKINS        SAL
     210 NANCY      HOFFMAN        SAL
```

Result — No table

4-6   Deleting a view

In Oracle, there is an SQL command to delete a view. In Access, you must use a GUI method. Except for this difference, deleting a view is like deleting a table.

Task

Delete the view named `sales_staff_view` created in section 4-2.

Oracle SQL

```
drop view sales_staff_view;
```

Access GUI method

Step 1: Highlight the name of the saved query, as shown below.

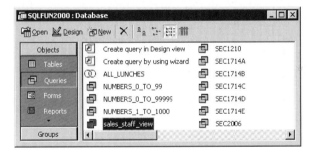

Step 2: Press the Delete key.

Beginning view (`sales_staff_view`)

```
EMPLOYEE                              DEPT
      ID  FIRST_NAME  LAST_NAME       CODE
--------  ----------  ----------      ----
     202  JIM         KERN            SAL
     204  ELLEN       OWENS           SAL
     205  HENRY       PERKINS         SAL
     210  NANCY       HOFFMAN         SAL
```

Result — No view

4-7   One view can be built on top of another view

A view can be defined from another view. This is similar to defining a view from a base table. In the `select` statement that defines a view, the `from` clause can name either a base table or another view.

Why would you want to do this? Why not just define each view directly from base tables? There are two reasons. One reason is to control complexity. A very complex query can often be replaced by a series of simple queries built on top of each other. This produces code that is easier for people to understand. The code can be verified and debugged more easily, and it is more likely to be correct.

The other reason is to coordinate two parts of a computer application. This can tie the parts together, so that if one part is changed, the other part is changed automatically to maintain a specific relationship with the first part.

There are layers of views

Circular definitions are not allowed. When one view is built from another view, care must be taken to ensure that there are no *circles* in the definition. A circle would occur if `view_1` depended on `view_2` and `view_2` depended on `view_1`. The computer must be able to find the base tables for every view. It could not do this if circles were allowed in the definitions.

Because of this, the views can be thought of as being organized into layers. Views built directly from base tables are the first layer, views built from these are the second layer, and so on.

What happens when an underlying base table or view is deleted?

If the view `sales_staff_1` is deleted, then the view `sales_staff_2` becomes invalid and cannot work. However, in both Oracle and Access, the `select` statement defining `sales_staff_2` is retained. If the underlying view, `sales_staff_1`, is restored, then the `sales_staff_2` view works again.

In some SQL products, all the views are deleted that are built on top of a base table or view that is being deleted. This is a cascaded delete. Dropping a base table or view can automatically trigger the dropping of many other views that are built on top of them. In this situation, you must be cautious before you drop any base table or view.

An example

The following example illustrates the principle just explained and shows the technique of defining one view from another view. I wanted to keep this example clear and simple, so I avoided any complexity. That is why this example does not show the level of complexity being reduced.

Here the `sales_staff_2` view could have been defined directly from the `1_employees` table, which is the base table. In this case, the view is so simple that there is no particular reason to define it in two steps, except to show the technique.

Task

Create a view, named `sales_staff_1`, that lists the employees in the sales department. Show the following columns: `employee_id`, `first_name`, `last_name`, and `dept_code`.

Then create another view, named `sales_staff_2`, from the first view. Use all the rows from the `sales_staff_1` view, except the ones with `employee_id` greater than 208. Use all the columns from the `sales_staff_1` view except `dept_code`.

Oracle SQL: Step 1 — Create the first view from a base table ❶

```
create view sales_staff_1 as
select employee_id,
       first_name,
       last_name,
       dept_code
from 1_employees
where dept_code = 'sal';
```

Access GUI method: Step 1 — Create the first view from a base table ❶

Step 1, Part 1: Enter this query in the SQL window:

```
select employee_id,
       first_name,
       last_name,
       dept_code
from 1_employees
where dept_code = 'sal';
```

Step 1, Part 2: Save the query. Name it `sales_staff_1`.

Result of Step 1 — `sales_staff_1` view

```
EMPLOYEE                              DEPT
      ID FIRST_NAME LAST_NAME    CODE
-------- ---------- ----------   ----
     202 JIM        KERN         SAL
     204 ELLEN      OWENS        SAL
     205 HENRY      PERKINS      SAL
     210 NANCY      HOFFMAN      SAL
```

Oracle SQL: Step 2 — Create a second view from the first one ❷

```
create view sales_staff_2 as
select employee_id,
       first_name,
       last_name
from sales_staff_1 ❸
where employee_id < 208;
```

Access GUI method: Step 2 — Create a second view from the first one ❷

Step 2, Part 1: Enter this query in the SQL window:

```
select employee_id,
       first_name,
       last_name
from sales_staff_1 ❸
where employee_id < 208;
```

Step 2, Part 2: Save the query. Name it `sales_staff_2`.

Result of Step 2 — `sales_staff_2` view

```
EMPLOYEE
      ID FIRST_NAME LAST_NAME
-------- ---------- ----------
     202 JIM        KERN
     204 ELLEN      OWENS
     205 HENRY      PERKINS
```

Notes

❶ This shows how the view `sales_staff_1` is created. In the `select` statement that defines this view, the `from` clause refers to a base table, `l_employees`.

❷ This shows how the view `sales_staff_2` is created. It is built on top of the `sales_staff_1` view.

❸ The `from` clause refers to the first view, `sales_staff_1`, rather than to a base table.

4-8   Preventative delete

A *preventative delete* drops the previous version of a table or view before it creates the new version. This ensures that the name will be available within the database. People use this coding technique when they are in the process of developing new code, and they need to try several versions before they get it correct. Preventative deletes are also used to ensure that the following `create table` or `create view` statement will run.

It is called a preventative delete because it prevents an error from occurring if the name of the table or view is already being used. Sometimes, we do not expect that anything will actually be deleted. There may be no such object to delete. The delete is done to prevent a possible problem.

Coding a preventative delete

For tables, a preventative delete can be coded by putting a `drop table` statement before a `create table` statement. In Oracle this is usually done within a script file, where several commands are run as a single unit. If the object does not currently exist, the `drop` command will fail and issue an error message. However, the Oracle script will continue to run.

For views, Oracle has a special option to support preventative deletes. You can say `create or replace view`, instead of `create view`. This is not part of standard SQL. It is an extension to the standard that is special to Oracle. Oracle does not have a similar feature for tables. This is probably because it would be too "dangerous" to encourage the use of preventative deletes with tables.

In Access, you get a warning message if the table or view already exists. You are given the option to replace the previous object. This makes preventative deletes less important in Access than they are in Oracle.

Task

Show how to code a preventative delete.

Oracle SQL: A preventative delete for a table

```
drop table sales_staff; ❶
create table sales_staff as
select employee_id,
       first_name,
       last_name,
       dept_code
from l_employees
where dept_code = 'sal';
```

- Access issues a warning message if you try to use the same name twice in the database.

Oracle SQL: Method 1 — A preventative delete for a view

```
drop view sales_staff_view; ❷
create view sales_staff_view as
select employee_id,
       first_name,
       last_name,
       dept_code
from l_employees
where dept_code = 'sal';
```

- Access issues a warning message if you try to use the same name twice in the database.

Oracle SQL: Method 2 — A preventative delete for a view

```
create or replace view sales_staff_view as ❸
select employee_id,
       first_name,
       last_name,
       dept_code
from l_employees
where dept_code = 'sal';
```

- This feature is not available in Access.

> ### Notes
>
> ❶ This `drop table` statement is a preventative delete. It is placed directly before the table is created.
>
> ❷ This `drop view` statement is a preventative delete.
>
> ❸ `Create or replace view` is a special feature available in Oracle to support preventative deletes.

Modifying the Data in a Table

After you have created a new table, you may want to put some rows of data in it. For tables that already contain data, you may want to add new rows, change the data in a few columns of an existing row, or delete some rows entirely. This section shows you how to do these things.

4-9   Adding one new row to a table

This section shows how to add a single new row to a table. There are two methods to do this. Both are versions of the `insert` statement, and begin with `insert into` followed by the name of the table. They both have the word `values` followed by a list of values in parentheses. The value put into any column must always match the datatype of that column: text, number, or date.

Method 1 specifies a value for each column of the table. The list of values must contain an entry for every column of the table and be listed in the same order as the columns of the table. The columns of a table always have a specific order. The information in the table is not affected by the order of the columns. However, the order of the columns does affect the syntax of some SQL statements, such as this one.

If you want to put a null in a column using this method, you must code the value `null` without quotes. SQL does not allow you to code two commas in a row to produce a null.

Method 2 puts values in only some of the columns of the table. These columns are listed after the name of the table in the SQL command. Nulls are placed in all the columns that are not listed. The list of values must contain an entry for each column in the list. The values must be listed in the same order as the columns.

When you use this method, you must include every column of the primary key in the list of columns. Otherwise, nulls would be entered in the columns of the primary key, which is not allowed. You receive an error message if you forget to list any of the columns of the primary key.

Method 2 is the standard in many shops. It is more specific even if it is a little more trouble to write. If a new column is added to a table, code written using the first method will no longer work, but code written using the second method will run.

Task

Add two new rows to the 1_foods table of the Lunches database. Show the two methods of adding a single row.

Oracle & Access SQL:
Method 1 — Putting data in all the columns

```
insert into 1_foods ❶
values ('arr', 'ap', 11, 'apple pie', 1.50, null); ❷
```

Oracle & Access SQL:
Method 2 — Putting data in only some columns

```
insert into 1_foods
(product_code, description, supplier_id, price) ❸
values ('bp', 'blueberry pie', 'arr', 1.60); ❹
```

Table before the changes (`1_foods` table)

SUPPLIER ID	PRODUCT CODE	MENU ITEM	DESCRIPTION	PRICE	PRICE INCREASE
ASP	FS	1	FRESH SALAD	$2.00	$0.25
ASP	SP	2	SOUP OF THE DAY	$1.50	(null)
ASP	SW	3	SANDWICH	$3.50	$0.40
CBC	GS	4	GRILLED STEAK	$6.00	$0.70
CBC	SW	5	HAMBURGER	$2.50	$0.30
FRV	BR	6	BROCCOLI	$1.00	$0.05
FRV	FF	7	FRENCH FRIES	$1.50	(null)
JBR	AS	8	SODA	$1.25	$0.25
JBR	VR	9	COFFEE	$0.85	$0.15
VSB	AS	10	DESSERT	$3.00	$0.50

Table after the changes

SUPPLIER ID	PRODUCT CODE	MENU ITEM	DESCRIPTION	PRICE	PRICE INCREASE	
ASP	FS	1	FRESH SALAD	$2.00	$0.25	
ASP	SP	2	SOUP OF THE DAY	$1.50	(null)	
ASP	SW	3	SANDWICH	$3.50	$0.40	
CBC	GS	4	GRILLED STEAK	$6.00	$0.70	
CBC	SW	5	HAMBURGER	$2.50	$0.30	
FRV	BR	6	BROCCOLI	$1.00	$0.05	
FRV	FF	7	FRENCH FRIES	$1.50	(null)	
JBR	AS	8	SODA	$1.25	$0.25	
JBR	VR	9	COFFEE	$0.85	$0.15	
VSB	AS	10	DESSERT	$3.00	$0.50	
ARR	AP	11	APPLE PIE	$1.50	(null)	❺
ARR	BP	(null)	BLUEBERRY PIE	$1.60	(null)	❻

Notes

❶ There is no list of columns following the table name. This means that values will be entered in all the columns of the table.

❷ A value is given for every column of the table. The last column contains a null, and this must be coded as `null` without quotes.

❸ The four columns listed after the table name are the only columns in which data can be entered. All other columns will be null.

❹ The values must be listed in the same order as the columns are listed in ❸. If any of these columns is null, the word `null`, without quotes, must be coded in the list of values.

❺ The first `insert` statement, using method 1, added this row.

❻ The second `insert` statement, using method 2, added this row.

4-10 `Commit` **and** `rollback`

Before we go any further with modifying the data in a table, I need to explain the basics about two commands: `commit` and `rollback`. In Oracle, we use `rollback` at the end of every section where we have made changes to the data in a table. This restores the table back to its original condition.

When you make a change to the data in a table, at first the change is made in a temporary way. Later, you can make the change permanent or reverse it. `Commit` makes the change permanent. It is a save command on the SQL level. `Rollback` throws out the changes. It is an undo command on the SQL level. `Rollback` goes back to the last `commit` point.

As an analogy, when you make changes to a word processing document, at first your changes are only held in memory. To make them permanent you must save them. That is like doing a `commit`. To throw out your changes, you close the document without saving the changes. That is like doing a `rollback`.

Oracle supports `commit` and `rollback`, so `commit` and `rollback` are actual commands within Oracle. Most other SQL products also support `commit` and `rollback`. However, Access does not support them. Access uses a different mechanism to provide the same ability — the UseTransaction Property. Because this property is used primarily on the Visual Basic level within Access, I do not discuss it further. To keep this book to a reasonable size, I am not discussing the Visual Basic level of Access.

That is as much as you need to know right now regarding `commit` and `rollback`. We expand on this discussion later. Section 4-15 discusses `autocommit` and section 5-1 discusses transactions.

Task

Reverse the changes you made in section 4-9. In section 4-9, we added two new rows to the l_foods table. We now want to delete these two rows and return the table to the way it originally was.

Then show how to permanently save changes to a table. In this example, there are no changes to be saved, but this shows the command you would use.

Oracle SQL: To clean up from section 4-9

```
rollback;
```

In Access, dete the rows you added in section 4-9. To do this, highlight them and press the Delete key.

Oracle SQL: To save changes permanently

```
commit;
```

- Access does not support this feature on the level of the SQL window.

4-11 Adding many new rows to a table with a `select` statement

This section shows you how to add several new rows to a table using a `select` statement. This can only be done when the data is already in the database in some form. You cannot enter data that is completely new using this method.

This is another variation on the command to enter a single row of data. The format of the SQL statement is as follows:

Method 1:

```
INSERT INTO table_name
select_statement;
```

Method 2:

```
INSERT INTO table_name (list_of_columns)
select_statement;
```

It is best to write the `select` statement that creates the new rows without an `order by` clause. If it does contain an `order by` clause, the statement will still run, but the ordering will be ignored.

The result table from the `select` statement must have the correct number of columns, in the correct order, and those columns must have the correct datatypes. It is as if each row of the result table provides a list of values to be inserted into the table (see section 4-9).

Task

In the `1_foods` table, duplicate all the rows from supplier ASP and change the supplier to ARR. Put nulls in the `price` and `price_increase` columns of the new rows.

You might do this if you are unhappy with supplier ASP and you are now going to get all those products from supplier ARR. This task would be the first step. The next step would delete all the rows for supplier ASP.

Oracle SQL: Method 1 — Putting data in all the columns

```
insert into 1_foods ❶
select 'arr', ❷
       product_code,
       menu_item,
       description,
       null,
       null
from 1_foods ❸
where supplier_id = 'asp'; ❹
❺
```

■ Access does not support this syntax. Use method 2 instead.

Oracle & Access SQL: Method 2 — Putting data in only some columns

```
insert into l_foods
(supplier_id, product_code, menu_item, description) ❻
select 'arr', ❼
        product_code,
        menu_item,
        description
from l_foods
where supplier_id = 'asp';
```

If you ran the code for method 1, you must do a `rollback` before you can run the code for method 2. Both SQL statements produce the same three new rows. These rows would be duplicates if you ran both statements. Duplicate rows are not allowed in this table, so the second SQL statement would fail.

Table after the changes

SUPPLIER ID	PRODUCT CODE	MENU ITEM	DESCRIPTION	PRICE	PRICE INCREASE	
ASP	FS	1	FRESH SALAD	$2.00	$0.25	
ASP	SP	2	SOUP OF THE DAY	$1.50	(null)	
ASP	SW	3	SANDWICH	$3.50	$0.40	
CBC	GS	4	GRILLED STEAK	$6.00	$0.70	
CBC	HB	5	HAMBURGER	$2.50	$0.30	
FRV	BR	6	BROCCOLI	$1.00	$0.05	
FRV	FF	7	FRENCH FRIES	$1.50	(null)	
JBR	AS	8	SODA	$1.25	$0.25	
JBR	VR	9	COFFEE	$0.85	$0.15	
VSB	AS	10	DESSERT	$3.00	$0.50	
ARR	FS	1	FRESH SALAD	(null)	(null)	❽
ARR	SP	2	SOUP OF THE DAY	(null)	(null)	❽
ARR	SW	3	SANDWICH	(null)	(null)	❽

Notes

❶ The l_foods table will receive the new rows of data. Because no columns are listed after the table name, the select statement must create a value for every column of the table.

❷ There are six columns in the table receiving the data, so there must be six columns listed in the select clause. Note that the last two columns are explicitly coded as the word null, without quotes. The 'arr' is a literal that is hard-coded into this select statement. Here it sets the supplier_id column to the value ARR in all the new rows of the result table.

❸ The data will be retrieved from the l_foods table. This is the same table that is receiving the new rows of data. This is an unusual situation, but it works without any problems.

❹ The where clause limits the data that is taken from the table named in the from clause in ❸.

❺ The select statement does not contain an order by clause.

❻ A list of columns follows the name of the table receiving the data. Only these columns can receive data. All the other columns will be null.

❼ Four columns are listed after the table name in ❻, so the select clause must contain four columns in the same order.

❽ These three rows have been added to the table by a single insert statement. Either the method 1 or the method 2 SQL statement can add all three of these rows.

To restore the data to its original form

In Oracle:

```
rollback;
```

In Access, delete the rows you added in section 4-11. To do this, highlight them and press the Delete key.

4-12 Changing data in the rows already in a table

This section shows you how to change data in rows that are already in the table. You can modify the values in one column or several columns. Usually, the data in only a few columns are modified at a time. If you want to modify the data in all the columns, it might be easier to add a new row to the table and delete the old row.

The format of the SQL statement is

```
UPDATE table_name
SET column_1 = value_1,
    column_2 = value_2
WHERE condition;
```

The values of any number of columns can be changed in one statement.

The syntax here is easier to read and work with than in the `insert` command. The name of the column is aligned with its value. You do not need to correlate two separate lists. However, this comes at a price. The names of the columns must be explicitly stated in each `update` statement.

The value can be a fixed value, a function, an expression, or even a subquery. In later chapters we discuss row functions and subqueries in detail.

Some people would call the functions in this example *expressions* because of the form in which they are written, with the plus sign in the middle, like "price + .10". They would call it a function if the plus sign were written first, like "+(price, .10)". I do not find this distinction to be very significant and I call them both functions.

The `where` clause is critical, because it indicates which rows of the table should be changed. Without it, all the rows of the table are changed. Data is changed only in the rows that satifsy the `where` condition. Other rows remain unchanged.

If you want to change the data in a single row, it is best to specify the values of the primary key columns in the `where` clause.

Task

Add 10 cents to both the price and the price increases for all the foods supplied by
JBR and FRV.

Oracle & Access SQL

```
update 1_foods ❶
set price = price + 0.10, ❷
    price_increase = price_increase + 0.10 ❸
where supplier_id in ('jbr', 'frv'); ❹
```

Table before the changes (1_foods table)

SUPPLIER ID	PRODUCT CODE	MENU ITEM	DESCRIPTION	PRICE	PRICE INCREASE
ASP	FS	1	FRESH SALAD	$2.00	$0.25
ASP	SP	2	SOUP OF THE DAY	$1.50	(null)
ASP	SW	3	SANDWICH	$3.50	$0.40
CBC	GS	4	GRILLED STEAK	$6.00	$0.70
CBC	SW	5	HAMBURGER	$2.50	$0.30
FRV	BR	6	BROCCOLI	$1.00	$0.05
FRV	FF	7	FRENCH FRIES	$1.50	(null)
JBR	AS	8	SODA	$1.25	$0.25
JBR	VR	9	COFFEE	$0.85	$0.15
VSB	AS	10	DESSERT	$3.00	$0.50

Table after the changes

SUPPLIER ID	PRODUCT CODE	MENU ITEM	DESCRIPTION	PRICE	PRICE INCREASE	
ASP	FS	1	FRESH SALAD	$2.00	$0.25	
ASP	SP	2	SOUP OF THE DAY	$1.50	(null)	
ASP	SW	3	SANDWICH	$3.50	$0.40	
CBC	GS	4	GRILLED STEAK	$6.00	$0.70	
CBC	SW	5	HAMBURGER	$2.50	$0.30	
FRV	BR	6	BROCCOLI	$1.10	$0.15	❹
FRV	FF	7	FRENCH FRIES	$1.60	(null)	❹❺
JBR	AS	8	SODA	$1.35	$0.35	❹
JBR	VR	9	COFFEE	$0.95	$0.25	❹
VSB	AS	10	DESSERT	$3.00	$0.50	

Notes

❶ The data will be changed in the `l_foods` table.

❷ Ten cents is added to the `price` column, then the result is placed back in the `price` column. The comma at the end of the line shows that there is another column with a value that will be changed.

❸ Ten cents is added to the `price_increase` column, then the result is placed in the `price_increase` column. Because there is no comma at the end of this line, there are no more columns being changed. Also note that there is no `from` clause.

❹ The `where` clause limits the rows that are changed. There are only four rows that satisfy the condition

```
supplier_id in ('jbr', 'frv')
```

These are the only rows that are changed.

❺ The price increase value is null in the result table because it is null in the beginning table.

To restore the data to its original form

In Oracle:

```
rollback;
```

In Access, answer "No" to the message "You are about to update 2 rows." The data can also be restored to the original values by typing over the values you want to change.

4-13 Deleting rows from a table

This section shows how to delete rows from a table. You can delete one row or several rows. The SQL statement format is

```
DELETE FROM table_name
WHERE condition;
```

The `where` condition is critical here, as in the `update` statement. Without it, all the rows of the table are deleted. The table structure remains and the table itself still exists, but it has no data in it.

The `where` clause controls which rows are deleted. It sets a condition that can be like any of the ones we used in the `where` clause of a `select` statement. All the rows for which the condition is true are deleted.

Task

Delete all the rows with `supplier_id` values of `cbc` and `jbr` from the `l_foods` table.

Oracle & Access SQL

```
delete from l_foods ❶
where supplier_id in ('cbc', 'jbr'); ❷
```

Table before the changes (`l_foods` table)

SUPPLIER ID	PRODUCT CODE	MENU ITEM	DESCRIPTION	PRICE	PRICE INCREASE	
ASP	FS	1	FRESH SALAD	$2.00	$0.25	
ASP	SP	2	SOUP OF THE DAY	$1.50	(null)	
ASP	SW	3	SANDWICH	$3.50	$0.40	
CBC	GS	4	GRILLED STEAK	$6.00	$0.70	❸
CBC	SW	5	HAMBURGER	$2.50	$0.30	❸
FRV	BR	6	BROCCOLI	$1.00	$0.05	
FRV	FF	7	FRENCH FRIES	$1.50	(null)	
JBR	AS	8	SODA	$1.25	$0.25	❸
JBR	VR	9	COFFEE	$0.85	$0.15	❸
VSB	AS	10	DESSERT	$3.00	$0.50	

Table after the changes

SUPPLIER ID	PRODUCT CODE	MENU ITEM	DESCRIPTION	PRICE	PRICE INCREASE
ASP	FS	1	FRESH SALAD	$2.00	$0.25
ASP	SP	2	SOUP OF THE DAY	$1.50	(null)
ASP	SW	3	SANDWICH	$3.50	$0.40
FRV	BR	6	BROCCOLI	$1.00	$0.05
FRV	FF	7	FRENCH FRIES	$1.50	(null)
VSB	AS	10	DESSERT	$3.00	$0.50

Notes

❶ Rows of data will be deleted from the l_foods table.

❷ Delete all the rows where the supplier_id value is cbc or jbr.

❸ These rows will be deleted.

To restore the data to its original form

In Oracle:

```
rollback;
```

In Access, answer "No" to the message "You are about to delete 4 rows from the specified table." You can also restore the deleted rows by inserting them again.

4-14 Constraints with insert, update, and delete

Sometimes you can enter a perfectly correct insert, update, or delete statement and it will not work, resulting in an error message. Many tables have restrictions on what data can be put into the table. These restrictions are called *constraints*. We discuss them further in chapter 8.

For instance, when a table has a primary key, this restricts the data that can be placed in that table. There cannot be nulls in the columns of the primary key. No two rows can have the same values in all the columns of the primary key. You will receive an error message if you try to put data that violates these constraints into the table.

Task

Show that you cannot add a new row to the `1_foods` table if that row has the same primary key as a row already in the table.

Oracle & Access SQL — INCORRECT

```
insert into 1_foods (supplier_id, product_code)
values ('cbc', 'sw');
```

Beginning table (1_foods table)

```
SUPPLIER PRODUCT    MENU                                      PRICE
ID       CODE       ITEM DESCRIPTION             PRICE INCREASE
-------- --------   -------  --------------------  -------- --------
ASP      FS            1 FRESH SALAD              $2.00    $0.25
ASP      SP            2 SOUP OF THE DAY          $1.50   (null)
ASP      SW            3 SANDWICH                 $3.50    $0.40
CBC      GS            4 GRILLED STEAK            $6.00    $0.70
CBC      SW            5 HAMBURGER                $2.50    $0.30
FRV      BR            6 BROCCOLI                 $1.00    $0.05
FRV      FF            7 FRENCH FRIES             $1.50   (null)
JBR      AS            8 SODA                     $1.25    $0.25
JBR      VR            9 COFFEE                   $0.85    $0.15
VSB      AS           10 DESSERT                  $3.00    $0.50
```

Oracle result — An error message (Access shows a different error message)

```
INSERT INTO L_FOODS (SUPPLIER_ID, PRODUCT_CODE)
*
ERROR at line 1:
ORA-00001: unique constraint (SQLFUN_2ED.PK_L_FOODS) violated ❶
```

Notes

❶ The word "constraint" in this error message tells us there is a rule restricting the data that can be placed in this table. That rule caused this `insert` statement to be rejected.

4-15 `Autocommit`

In Oracle, sometimes a `commit` command is issued automatically. This is called an `autocommit`. It is done at the following times:

1. When you exit Oracle.

2. When you create a new table or database object.

Within SQLplus, the environment in which Oracle is run, there is a command to set the `autocommit` property:

```
set autocommit on;
```

or

```
set autocommit off;
```

When the `autocommit` property is on, a `commit` command is issued whenever data is changed in any table by an `insert`, `update`, or `delete`.

4-16 Using the Access GUI environment to change the data in a table

Access is oriented to using the GUI environment to change the data in a table. The `insert`, `update`, and `delete` commands work in Access, but the GUI environment is the easiest way to work with the data. This is great for quick interactive changes that do not require an audit trail.

If you do want an audit trail, you should use the `insert`, `update`, and `delete` commands rather than the GUI method of changing data. Then save all these statements in a Notepad file. Do not rely on Access to keep track of your SQL statements, because it is not designed to do this well. The Notepad file is your audit trail.

Beginning table

▦ L_SUPPLIERS : Table	_ □ ×
SUPPLIER_ID	**SUPPLIER_NAME**
Arr	Alice & Ray's Restaurant
Asp	A Soup Place
Cbc	Certified Beef Company
Frv	Frank Reed's Vegetables
Fsn	Frank & Sons
Jbr	Just Beverages
Jps	Jim Parker's Shop
Vsb	Virginia Street Bakery
▶	

Record: ◄◄ ◄ 9 ► ►► ►✱ of 9

Inserting new rows

To add new rows, type the data into the blank row at the bottom of the table — the one with the asterisk beside it. As soon as you start to enter data in one new row, another blank row is added at the bottom of the table.

▦ L_SUPPLIERS : Table	_ □ ×
SUPPLIER_ID	**SUPPLIER_NAME**
Arr	Alice & Ray's Restaurant
Asp	A Soup Place
Cbc	Certified Beef Company
Frv	Frank Reed's Vegetables
Fsn	Frank & Sons
Jbr	Just Beverages
Jps	Jim Parker's Shop
Vsb	Virginia Street Bakery
⌿ NEW	ROW
✱	

Record: ◄◄ ◄ 9 ► ►► ►✱ of 9

Updating the data

To change data in rows already in the table, type over the value that is there.

SUPPLIER_ID	SUPPLIER_NAME
Arr	Alice & Ray's Restaurant
Asp	A Soup Place
Cbc	NEW VALUE
Frv	Frank Reed's Vegetables
Fsn	Frank & Sons
Jbr	Just Beverages
Jps	Jim Parker's Shop
Vsb	Virginia Street Bakery

L_SUPPLIERS : Table

Record: 3 of 8

Deleting rows

To delete a row of data, highlight the row by clicking on the left margin, then press the Delete key.

SUPPLIER_ID	SUPPLIER_NAME
Arr	Alice & Ray's Restaurant
Asp	A Soup Place
Cbc	Certified Beef Company
Frv	Frank Reed's Vegetables
Fsn	Frank & Sons
Jbr	Just Beverages
Jps	Jim Parker's Shop
Vsb	Virginia Street Bakery

L_SUPPLIERS : Table

Record: 5 of 8

Summary

In this chapter we discussed

1. How to create a new table using a `select` statement.

2. How to create a view.

3. The contrast between a table and a view.

4. How to control the data in a table by inserting, updating, and deleting rows.

In later chapters, we use the ability to create tables and views to solve problems in a series of steps. The next step(s) will be `select` statements that operate on the new tables or views. Many problems that would be complex to solve with a single `select` statement can be solved easily using a series of `select` statements.

You can now create many of your own tables and control the data in them. In chapter 6, you will learn about tables in even more detail.

Exercises

1. Goal: Create a new table by saving the results of a `select` statement. (Section 4-1)

   a. Create a new table containing the following columns: `employee_id`, `first_name`, `last_name`, and `dept_code`, in that order. Change the name of the `dept_code` column from `dept_code` to `department_code`. Include all the employees working in the sales and marketing departments.

   Oracle SQL: Step 1

   ```
   drop table ex0401a;
   create table ex0401a as
   select employee_id,
          first_name,
          last_name,
          dept_code as department_code
   from l_employees
   where dept_code in ('sal', 'mkt');
   ```

   Access SQL: Step 1

   ```
   select employee_id,
          first_name,
          last_name,
          dept_code as department_code
   into ex0401a
   from l_employees
   where dept_code in ('sal', 'mkt');
   ```

   Oracle & Access: Step 2

   ```
   select * from ex0401a;
   ```

   b. Create a new table containing the following columns from the `l_foods` table: `menu_item`, `description`, and `price`. Change the name of the `description` column to `food`. Include all the foods that cost less than $5.00.

2. Goal: Create a new view. (Section 4-2)

    a. Create a view similar to the table we created in exercise 1a. Right now, this view is very similar to the table you created in exercise 1a. Exercises 4, 5, and 6 show you how the view differs from the table.

Oracle SQL

```
create or replace view ex0402a as
select employee_id,
       first_name,
       last_name,
       dept_code as department_code
from l_employees
where dept_code in ('sal', 'mkt');
```

Access SQL

Step 1: Enter the following query in the SQL window:

```
select employee_id,
       first_name,
       last_name,
       dept_code as department_code
from l_employees
where dept_code in ('sal', 'mkt');
```

Step 2: Save this query. Name it ex0402a.

    b. Create a view similar to the table you created in exercise 1b.

3. Goal: Show that you can use the new table and view to write queries.

    a. List the last name of all the people in the sales department. Sort this list on the `last_name` column. Use the table you created in exercise 1a.

Oracle & Access SQL

```
select last_name
from ex0401a
where department_code = 'sal'
order by last_name;
```

b. Use the table you created in exercise 1b to list the `food` and `price` columns. Sort this list alphabetically on the name of the food.

c. Perform the same task as exercise 3b, except use the view you created in exercise 2b.

4. Goal: Add a new row to the `l_employees` table. Show the effect on the table created in exercise 1a and the view created in exercise 2a. (Section 4-9)

a. Add yourself to the `l_employees` table. Put yourself in the sales department as `employee_id 950`, with `manager_id 201`. Make up data for all the other columns. Check the effect on the `l_employees` table, `ex0401a` table, and `ex0402a` view.

Oracle & Access SQL

```
insert into l_employees
values (950, 'john', 'patrick', 'sal',
        '01-apr-2005', 25, null, 201);

select * from l_employees;
select * from ex0401a;
select * from ex0402a;
```

b. Add one of your friends to the `l_employees` table. Put your friend in the marketing department as `employee_id  951`, with `manager_id  201`. Add data for the other columns and use at least one null. Check the effect on the tables and view, similar to exercise 4a.

5. Goal: Change a row already in the `1_employees` table. Show the effect of this change as we did in exercise 4. (Section 4-12)

    a. Change yourself from the sales department to the marketing department. Show the effect of this change.

Oracle & Access SQL

```
update 1_employees
  set dept_code = 'mkt'
where employee_id = 950;

select * from 1_employees;
select * from ex0401a;
select * from ex0402a;
```

    b. Change your friend from the marketing department to the accounting department. Show the effect of this change.

6. Goal: Delete a row from the `1_employees` table. Show the effect of this change as we did in exercise 4. (Section 4-13)

    a. Delete yourself from the `1_employees` table. Show the effect of this change.

Oracle & Access SQL

```
delete from 1_employees
where employee_id = 950;

select * from 1_employees;
select * from ex0401a;
select * from ex0402a;
```

    b. Delete your friend from the `1_employees` table. Show the effect of this change.

chapter 5

MODIFYING DATA THROUGH A VIEW

This chapter expands on the topics we discussed in chapter 4. In this chapter we discuss transactions and modifying data through a view. We also discuss SQLplus, the environment in which Oracle SQL is run. You learn how to find information about the tables and views we have created and the ones that have already been created for us.

Transactions

This discussion of transactions continues our discussion of `commit` and `rollback`. A *transaction* is a way to package together several changes to the data in one or more tables. These changes are made using `insert`, `update`, and `delete` statements. When several changes to the data are put into a transaction, they will either all process successfully or they will all fail. Another way to say this is that if any one of the changes fails, then they will all fail.

A transaction is used to ensure that the data in the database stays consistent. Sometimes the data in several tables needs to be changed in a coordinated way. By placing all these changes within a transaction, you can be sure that the tables will not become corrupted if some of the changes succeed and others fail.

5-1   An example of a transaction

Suppose you have been saving to buy a new car. You have been putting money in your savings account and now you have $5,000 to put a down payment on the car you want. You need to transfer the money from your savings account to your checking account so you can write a check to the car dealer.

The bank keeps information about its savings accounts in one table and information about its checking accounts in another table. Both of these tables need to be changed in a coordinated way. You want to take $5,000 out of your savings account and put $5,000 into your checking account. These two changes should be put into a transaction so they both succeed or they both fail. The code to do this follows.

A transaction occurs between two `commit` points. You create a transaction by issuing the SQL command `commit` or `rollback`. The transaction consists of all the `insert`, `update`, and `delete` statements done after one `commit` or `rollback` and before the next `commit` or `rollback`. If any of your changes fail, you receive an error message. It is then up to you to issue the `rollback` command. If they all succeed, it is up to you to issue the `commit` command at the end of the process.

The following example does not include Access because Access does not support `commit` at the level of the SQL window. For further details, see section 4-10.

Task

Take $5,000 from the savings account of Amy Johnson and put $5,000 into her checking account. Wrap these two changes in a single transaction.

Oracle SQL

```
commit; ❶

update sec0501_savings_accounts ❷
  set balance = balance - 5000
where customer = 'amy johnson';
```

If you get an error message, do a rollback and stop entering this transaction.

```
update sec0501_checking_accounts ❸
  set balance = balance + 5000
where customer = 'amy johnson';
```

If you get an error message, do a rollback and stop entering this transaction.

```
commit; ❹
```

Table before changes 1 (sec0501_savings_accounts table)

S_ACCOUNT_ID	CUSTOMER	BALANCE
5926	FRED BOYD	15642.33
6197	AMY JOHNSON	5280.25
5926	VALERIE SHAW	35159.64

Table before changes 2 (sec0501_checking_accounts table)

C_ACCOUNT_ID	CUSTOMER	BALANCE
2741	BOB WILKINS	1567.35
3852	AMY JOHNSON	357.26
8954	JUDY SPENCER	6296.54

Commit happens . . .

Table after changes 1 (`sec0501_saving_accounts` table)

S_ACCOUNT_ID	CUSTOMER	BALANCE
5926	FRED BOYD	15642.33
6197	AMY JOHNSON	280.25
5926	VALERIE SHAW	35159.64

Table after changes 2 (`sec0501_checking_accounts` table)

C_ACCOUNT_ID	CUSTOMER	BALANCE
2741	BOB WILKINS	1567.35
3852	AMY JOHNSON	5357.26
8954	JUDY SPENCER	6296.54

Notes

❶ The first `commit` saves any changes you have already made. If you do a `roll-back`, you can return to this point.

❷ The first statement to modify the data begins the transaction.

❸ All subsequent statements that modify the data are part of the transaction.

❹ The final `commit` statement ends the transaction.

Modifying Data Through a View

Up to now, when we used an `insert`, `update`, or `delete` statement, that statement always named the table in which the data would be changed. For example, the word `insert` is followed by the name of the table that will receive the new row.

It is also possible to follow the word `insert` with the name of a view, instead of a table. You might wonder what this means because a view is only a `select` statement and it does not contain any data. It means to add a new row to the underlying table on which the view is based.

Here is an analogy: Picture yourself standing outside a house in the garden. Inside the house there is a large table with many things on it. You can reach through an open window to manipulate some of the things on the table. Other things on the table are beyond your reach. In this analogy, the view is the open window. You can manipulate the data in the table by reaching through the view.

If you are the only person using a database, you will probably change the data directly in a table, rather than using a view. It is simpler to do it that way. However, it is a common practice to change the data through a view when you are working with a large database that many people are using at the same time.

This is partly a matter of how large databases are managed and administered. Usually, only the DBAs are allowed to work directly with the tables. Everyone else who changes the data must use a view. The purpose of this rule is to allow the DBAs to make changes to the tables, such as adding a new column, at the same time that other people are modifying the data. DBAs and the other users are separated so they have a minimal impact on each other. Each can work separately without concern about what the other person is doing.

A view can also be used for security. It can limit the data a user can change, allowing changes to only certain columns and rows.

5-2   Changing data through a view

When you change data through a view, only some of the data in the table can be changed. In general, you can only change the data that can be seen through the view. Here are two exceptions to this rule:

1. You can only delete rows that can be seen through the view. When you delete a row, you delete the entire row, which includes all the columns, even those that cannot be seen through the view.

2. You can insert a new row even if it cannot be seen through the view. If the view is defined With Check Option, then you can only insert rows that can be seen through the view. See section 5-4 for details.

The following table summarizes these exceptions.

	Rows restricted to the ones in the view	Columns restricted to the ones in the view
Insert	No	Yes
Update	Yes	Yes
Delete	Yes	No

Only certain views can be used for changing data. These are called *updateable views*. A view is updateable when

1. It only contains data from one table.

2. It contains some or all of the columns and rows from the table.

3. It does not summarize the data or condense it by using `select distinct`. The data in each cell of the view comes from the data in only one cell of the table.

Both Oracle and Access allow a few more views to be updateable. However, this is the usual set of updateable views within most SQL products. In Access, it is easy to tell whether a view is updateable. If it is, a blank row is shown at the bottom of the view where you can enter new rows of data.

The following diagram shows a conceptual picture of a view and its underlying table.

Conceptual drawing of a view and its underlying table.

5-3   Example of changing data through a view

This section shows how to change the data in a table, using a process that changes it through a view. Part 1 shows all the components of this process. Parts 2 and 3 show data actually being changed.

This looks more complicated than changing the data directly in the table. However, from the user's perspective, the difference is very small. The user issues the same `insert`, `update`, and `delete` commands. The only difference is that these commands name a view instead of naming a base table.

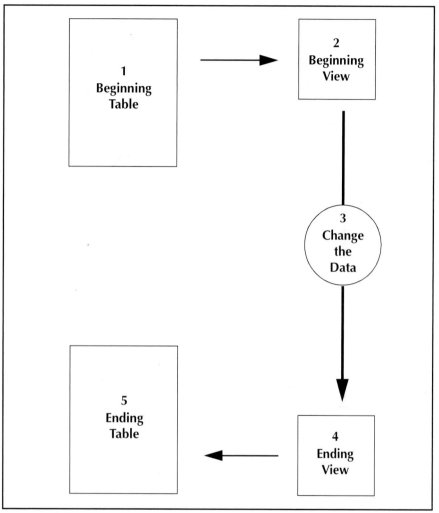

Conceptual drawing of changing data through a view.

The components of the process in the conceptual drawing

1. The first component is the beginning table. This is where the data is actually stored.

2. The second component is the beginning view. This is derived from the beginning table by applying the `select` statement that defines the view. The view definition is not shown separately in this diagram.

3. The data is changed through the view using an `insert`, `update`, or `delete` command. An `update` command can only work on the data that appears in the beginning view. It cannot change the data in any column or row that does not appear in the beginning view.

    The `insert` command can add rows to the table that do not appear in the view, but it can only place data in the columns that appear in the view. All other columns are set to null.

    The `delete` command can only delete rows from the table if they appear in the view. However, it deletes entire rows from the table, including columns that do not appear in the view.

4. The fourth component is the ending view. The drawing shows this from the user's perspective. From the computer's perspective, the changes are made directly to the ending table. The ending view is then derived from the ending table.

5. The last component is the ending table. This shows all the changes made to the data, regardless of whether they appear in the ending view.

In Access, if you are changing the data using the GUI environment, the ending view does not appear immediately. Access provides a stable working environment for making the changes. It shows you the beginning view and your changes as a working document called a *datasheet*. To see the ending view, you must close the view and then open it again.

This section shows two examples of changing data through a view. Here is the definition of that view:

Oracle SQL: `shipping_dept` view

```
create or replace view shipping_dept as
select employee_id,
       first_name,
       last_name,
       dept_code,
       credit_limit
from l_employees
where dept_code = 'shp';
```

Access SQL: `shipping_dept` view

Step 1: Delete the saved query `shipping_dept` if it already exists.
Step 2: Enter this query in the SQL window:

```
select employee_id,
       first_name,
       last_name,
       dept_code,
       credit_limit
from l_employees
where dept_code = 'shp';
```

Step 3: Save the query. Name it `shipping_dept`.

Beginning table (`1_employees` table)

```
EMPLOYEE                           DEPT                     CREDIT  PHONE   MANAGER
     ID  FIRST_NAME  LAST_NAME   CODE  HIRE_DATE         LIMIT  NUMBER       ID
--------  ----------  ----------  ----  ------------     -------  ------  -------
    201  SUSAN       BROWN        EXE   01-JUN-1998      $30.00  3484    (null)
    202  JIM         KERN         SAL   16-AUG-1999      $25.00  8722       201
    203  MARTHA      WOODS        SHP   02-FEB-2004      $25.00  7591       201
    204  ELLEN       OWENS        SAL   01-JUL-2003      $15.00  6830       202
    205  HENRY       PERKINS      SAL   01-MAR-2000      $25.00  5286       202
    206  CAROL       ROSE         ACT   (null)          (null)  (null)  (null)
    207  DAN         SMITH        SHP   01-DEC-2004      $25.00  2259       203
    208  FRED        CAMPBELL     SHP   01-APR-2003      $25.00  1752       203
    209  PAULA       JACOBS       MKT   17-MAR-1999      $15.00  3357       201
    210  NANCY       HOFFMAN      SAL   16-FEB-2004      $25.00  2974       203
```

Task 1

Add a new employee, John Patrick, with a credit limit of $25.00, to the shipping department. Increase Martha Woods' credit limit to $35.00 and delete the row for Fred Campbell. Make these changes through the `shipping_dept` view. You would be required to make these changes by updating a view if the `1_employees` table were part of a large database used by many people at the same time. The code to create the `shipping_dept` view is shown earlier in this section.

Notice that all these changes to the data show up in the ending view. For this reason, these are examples of changes that would continue to be allowed even if the view were defined With Check Option. See section 5-4 for a further discussion of this topic.

Before you go on to task 2, enter this command: `rollback;`

Notes

❶ You can make changes to any of the data that appears in the columns and rows of this view.
❷ All these commands make changes through the `shipping_dept` view.
❸ All the changes are reflected in the ending view.
❹ All the changes are reflected in the ending table.

Ending table (`1_employees` table) ❹

```
EMPLOYEE                           DEPT                     CREDIT  PHONE   MANAGER
     ID  FIRST_NAME  LAST_NAME   CODE  HIRE_DATE         LIMIT  NUMBER       ID
--------  ----------  ----------  ----  ------------     -------  ------  -------
    201  SUSAN       BROWN        EXE   01-JUN-1998      $30.00  3484    (null)
    202  JIM         KERN         SAL   16-AUG-1999      $25.00  8722       201
    203  MARTHA      WOODS        SHP   02-FEB-2004      $35.00  7591       201
    204  ELLEN       OWENS        SAL   01-JUL-2003      $15.00  6830       202
    205  HENRY       PERKINS      SAL   01-MAR-2000      $25.00  5286       202
    206  CAROL       ROSE         ACT   (null)          (null)  (null)  (null)
    207  DAN         SMITH        SHP   01-DEC-2004      $25.00  2259       203
    209  PAULA       JACOBS       MKT   17-MAR-1999      $15.00  3357       201
    210  NANCY       HOFFMAN      SAL   16-FEB-2004      $25.00  2974       203
    212  JOHN        PATRICK      SHP   (null)          $25.00  (null)  (null)
```

Beginning view (`shipping_dept` view) ❶

```
EMPLOYEE                          DEPT   CREDIT
      ID FIRST_NAME LAST_NAME     CODE   LIMIT
-------- ---------- ----------    ----   -------
     203 MARTHA     WOODS         SHP    $25.00
     207 DAN        SMITH         SHP    $25.00
     208 FRED       CAMPBELL      SHP    $25.00
```

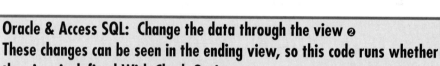

Oracle & Access SQL: Change the data through the view ❷
These changes can be seen in the ending view, so this code runs whether or not the view is defined With Check Option.

```
insert into shipping_dept
values (212, 'john', 'patrick', 'shp', 25.00);

update shipping_dept
  set credit_limit = 35.00
where employee_id = 203;

delete from shipping_dept
where employee_id = 208;
```

Ending view (`shipping_dept` view) ❸

```
EMPLOYEE                          DEPT   CREDIT
      ID FIRST_NAME LAST_NAME     CODE   LIMIT
-------- ---------- ----------    ----   -------
     203 MARTHA     WOODS         SHP    $35.00
     207 DAN        SMITH         SHP    $25.00
     212 JOHN       PATRICK       SHP    $25.00
```

Beginning table (1_employees table) ❶

EMPLOYEE ID	FIRST_NAME	LAST_NAME	DEPT CODE	HIRE_DATE	CREDIT LIMIT	PHONE NUMBER	MANAGER ID
201	SUSAN	BROWN	EXE	01-JUN-1998	$30.00	3484	(null)
202	JIM	KERN	SAL	16-AUG-1999	$25.00	8722	201
203	MARTHA	WOODS	SHP	02-FEB-2004	$25.00	7591	201
204	ELLEN	OWENS	SAL	01-JUL-2003	$15.00	6830	202
205	HENRY	PERKINS	SAL	01-MAR-2000	$25.00	5286	202
206	CAROL	ROSE	ACT	(null)	(null)	(null)	(null)
207	DAN	SMITH	SHP	01-DEC-2004	$25.00	2259	203
208	FRED	CAMPBELL	SHP	01-APR-2003	$25.00	1752	203
209	PAULA	JACOBS	MKT	17-MAR-1999	$15.00	3357	201
210	NANCY	HOFFMAN	SAL	16-FEB-2004	$25.00	2974	203

Task 2

Transfer Dan Smith from the shipping department to the marketing department and add Susan Manning as a new executive.

These changes do not show up in the ending view. You must look in the ending table to verify that the changes have been made. For this reason, these changes would not be allowed if the view were defined With Check Option.

Notes

❶ The beginning table shows Dan Smith in the shipping department, and there is no row for Susan Manning.

❷ You can make changes to any of the data that appear in the columns and rows of this view.

❸ The update and insert statements make changes through the shipping_dept view.

❹ You cannot verify that the changes were made correctly. The ending view does not contain a record for either Dan Smith or Susan Manning.

❺ In the ending table, the 1_employees table, you can verify that Dan Smith is now in the marketing department and Susan Manning is now an executive.

Ending table (1_employees table) ❺

EMPLOYEE ID	FIRST_NAME	LAST_NAME	DEPT CODE	HIRE_DATE	CREDIT LIMIT	PHONE NUMBER	MANAGER ID
201	SUSAN	BROWN	EXE	01-JUN-1998	$30.00	3484	(null)
202	JIM	KERN	SAL	16-AUG-1999	$25.00	8722	201
203	MARTHA	WOODS	SHP	02-FEB-2004	$25.00	7591	201
204	ELLEN	OWENS	SAL	01-JUL-2003	$15.00	6830	202
205	HENRY	PERKINS	SAL	01-MAR-2000	$25.00	5286	202
206	CAROL	ROSE	ACT	(null)	(null)	(null)	(null)
207	DAN	SMITH	MKT	01-DEC-2004	$25.00	2259	203
208	FRED	CAMPBELL	SHP	01-APR-2003	$25.00	1752	203
209	PAULA	JACOBS	MKT	17-MAR-1999	$15.00	3357	201
210	NANCY	HOFFMAN	SAL	16-FEB-2004	$25.00	2974	203
211	SUSAN	MANNING	EXE	(null)	$50.00	(null)	(null)

Beginning view (`shipping_dept` view) ❷

```
EMPLOYEE                          DEPT   CREDIT
      ID  FIRST_NAME  LAST_NAME   CODE   LIMIT
--------  ----------  ----------  ----   -------
     203  MARTHA      WOODS       SHP    $25.00
     207  DAN         SMITH       SHP    $25.00    ❷
     208  FRED        CAMPBELL    SHP    $25.00
```

Oracle & Access SQL: Change the data through the view ❸
These changes can only be seen in the ending table, not in the ending view,
so this code runs only if the view is not defined With Check Option.

```
update shipping_dept
set dept_code = 'mkt'
where employee_id = 207;

insert into shipping_dept
values (211, 'susan', 'manning', 'exe', 50.00);
```

Ending view (`shipping_dept` view) ❹

```
EMPLOYEE                          DEPT   CREDIT
      ID  FIRST_NAME  LAST_NAME   CODE   LIMIT
--------  ----------  ----------  ----   -------
     203  MARTHA      WOODS       SHP    $25.00
     208  FRED        CAMPBELL    SHP    $25.00
```

To clean up from section 5-3

In Oracle:

```
rollback;
```

In Access, delete the rows you added in this section. To do this, highlight them and press the Delete key.

5-4   Views using With Check Option

In the previous section we saw that a change can be made to the data through a view, even if the new or modified row does not appear in the ending view. In particular, an `insert` command can insert a new row even if that row does not appear in the ending view. Also, an `update` command can make a change to a row so that it does not appear in the ending view.

Sometimes we do not want to allow such changes. We can prevent them by defining the view With Check Option. This can be done in Oracle and most other types of SQL. However, Access does not support this option.

When the view is defined With Check Option, you are only permitted to use `insert` or `update` when the resulting row will appear in the ending view. You can still delete any row that appears in the beginning view. In effect, this says that you can only make changes when you can see the result of those changes and verify that they are correct. You are not allowed to make changes you cannot see.

In the example of the previous section, we would not be allowed to change the department for Dan Smith. We would also not be allowed to add Susan Manning, because she will not work in the shipping department.

Task

Show how to add With Check Option to the `shipping_dept` view.

Oracle SQL: Create the `shipping_dept` view not using With Check Option

```
create or replace view shipping_dept as
select employee_id,
       first_name,
       last_name,
       dept_code,
       credit_limit
from l_employees
where dept_code = 'shp';
```

Oracle SQL: Create the `shipping_dept` view using With Check Option

```
create or replace view shipping_dept as
select employee_id,
       first_name,
       last_name,
       dept_code,
       credit_limit
from l_employees
where dept_code = 'shp'
with check option; ❶
```

- Access does not support With Check Option.

Notes

❶ To code With Check Option, place it at the end of the `select` statement that defines the view.

Oracle SQLplus

SQLplus is the environment in which you run Oracle SQL. You can set many parameters to specify how you want it to operate. It also contains a set of simple utility programs that enhance the features of Oracle SQL.

When you type in a command, such as `select *`, you enter the command into the SQLplus environment. The environment makes some changes, such as changing all the letters to uppercase, and passes it to the SQL level. That level processes the statement and outputs a result table that you do not see directly. This table is passed back to the SQLplus environment, which makes a few modifications and then displays it.

The following sections discuss some of the most important features of SQLplus. A full discussion of SQLplus is available in the Oracle documentation.

5-5   How to set column formats and headings using SQLplus

When you run a `select` statement, you can use SQLplus to set the headings and formats of the columns of the result table. This is the feature of SQLplus that you will use most often.

The first part is the word `column` followed by the name of the column. This is the name of the column in the SQL output. It can be either the name of the column in the beginning table or a column alias.

The name of the table is not included with the name of the column. Changes are made to the formats and headings of all the columns with a particular name, no matter what table they are part of. This is an example of the simplicity of the SQLplus environment. It does not always support all the distinctions you might want to make.

The second part is the word `format` followed by a specification of a format for the data. If column contains text data, also called *character* or *alphanumeric* data, then the format specifies the width of the column. The letter a is followed by a number. This specifies the format. The number is the maximum number of letters the column can contain on one line. Usually this is used to ensure that there is enough room for the heading of the column, so that the heading does not get truncated. If a width is not specified for a text column, then the width is determined by the width of the column in the definition of the table, although this may truncate the column heading.

If the column contains numbers, then the format specifies the number of digits displayed, whether leading zeros are displayed or suppressed, and the use of commas, decimal points, and dollar signs. To Oracle SQL, a number is simply a number. If the number has a special format such as a dollar amount, it must get its formatting from SQLplus. If a data element does not fit within the number of digits specified in the format, then pound signs (##) are displayed in place of the data. The following code shows several examples of numeric formats. The elements of these formats are as follows:

- 9   is a digit

- 0   is a digit that is a leading zero

- $ is a floating dollar sign

- .   is a decimal point

- ,   is a comma

If a data element does not fit within the number of digits specified in the format, then pound signs (##) are displayed in place of the data.

The third part is the word `heading` followed by the heading for the column. This heading is case sensitive, so uppercase and lowercase letters are shown just the way you enter them. To form a multiline heading, use the double bar symbol, also called a pipe symbol (|), wherever you want a line break to occur. On most keyboards, this is Shift + Backslash. The quotes around the heading are optional, but I recommend using them. The semicolon at the end of the statement is also optional and I recommend it. Both of these options make the statement easier for most people to read.

To replace one format or heading with another, just issue another `column` command for that column name. The new format and heading replace the old ones.

Task

Show the most frequently used forms of the `column` command in SQLplus.

Oracle SQLplus: Set the format and heading of a text column

```
column column_alias_2 format a15; ❷
column column_alias_3 heading 'COLUMN|ALIAS|3'; ❸
column column_alias_4 format a2 heading 'de|pt'; ❹

-- Oracle SQL to show the column formatting
select employee_id,
       dept_code as column_alias_1, ❶
       dept_code as column_alias_2, ❷
       dept_code as column_alias_3, ❸
       dept_code as column_alias_4 ❹
from l_employees
where employee_id < 204;
```

Result table

```
                                        ❸
                                       COL   ❹
                  ❶        ❷          ALI  de
EMPLOYEE_ID  COL  COLUMN_ALIAS_2      3    pt
-----------  ---  ---------------     ---  --
        201  EXE  EXE                 EXE  EX
                                           E

        202  SAL  SAL                 SAL  SA
                                           L

        203  SHP  SHP                 SHP  SH
                                           P
```

Notes

❶ The heading of this column is `column_alias_1`. It is truncated to three characters because the data in this column is only three characters wide and no format has been specified.

❷ The heading of this column is `column_alias_2`. It is not truncated because the format, `a15`, specifies that it is 15 characters wide.

❸ The heading of this column is `column_alias_3` which is written on three different lines because of the pipe symbols in the specification of the heading. Each of these words is truncated to 3 characters because that is the width of the data and no format is specified.

❹ The heading of this column is `de` and `pt`, written on two separate lines. The format of this column specifies that it is 2 characters wide. The data is 3 characters wide so it will not fit in this format. Several options are possible to handle this situation. Here, the remaining data wraps to the next line.

Oracle SQLplus: Set the format and heading of a numeric column

```
column price_alias_1 format 99.99; ❻
column price_alias_2 format $0,999.99; ❼
column price_alias_3 format 9; ❽
column price_alias_4 format $90.99; ❾

-- Oracle SQL to show the column formatting
select description,
       price as price_alias_1, ❻
       price as price_alias_2, ❼
       price as price_alias_3, ❽
       price as price_alias_4 ❾
from l_foods;
```

Result table ❺

	❻	❼	❽	❾
DESCRIPTION	PRICE_ALIAS_1	PRICE_ALIAS_2	PRICE_ALIAS_3	PRICE_ALIAS_4
FRESH SALAD	2.00	$0,002.00	2	$2.00
SOUP OF THE DAY	1.50	$0,001.50	2	$1.50
SANDWICH	3.50	$0,003.50	4	$3.50
GRILLED STEAK	6.00	$0,006.00	6	$6.00
HAMBURGER	2.50	$0,002.50	3	$2.50
BROCCOLI	1.00	$0,001.00	1	$1.00
FRENCH FRIES	1.50	$0,001.50	2	$1.50
SODA	1.25	$0,001.25	1	$1.25
COFFEE	.85	$0,000.85	1	$0.85
DESSERT	3.00	$0,003.00	3	$3.00

Notes

❺ The headings of these columns are not truncated because they contain numbers.

❻ The format of this column is `99.99`. This means that there are 2 digits before the decimal point and 2 digits after the decimal point. Note that zeros are supplied in positions after the decimal place, but not in positions before the decimal place. For example, coffee in this column is .85.

❼ The format of this column is `$0,999.99`. This means that there are 4 digits before the decimal point and 2 digits after the decimal point. A dollar sign precedes the number. A comma is placed between the leading digit and the next digit. The leading zero in the format says that a zero will be supplied in that position if needed, and in all the positions from there to the decimal point.

❽ The format of this column is `9`. This means that there is 1 digit before the decimal point and no digits after the decimal point. The data is rounded to fit in this format. For example, coffee actually costs $.85, but in this column it is rounded to $1. In another example, a hamburger actually costs $2.50, but in this column it is rounded to $3.

❾ The format of this column is `$90.99`. This means that there can be 2 digits before the decimal point and 2 digits after it. The position of the zero in the format indicates this is the first position where a zero will be supplied if the data requires it. For example, coffee in this column is $0.85.

Oracle SQLplus:
Find the format and heading setting of one column name

```
column price;
```

Oracle SQLplus response

```
COLUMN   price ON
FORMAT   $990.99
```

Oracle SQLplus:
Find the format and heading settings of all the column names

```
column;
```

Oracle SQLplus response

```
COLUMN    lunch_date ON
HEADING   'LUNCH|DATE' headsep '|'  ❶
FORMAT    a12

COLUMN    manager_id ON
HEADING   'MANAGER|ID' headsep '|'
FORMAT    999

COLUMN    phone_number ON
HEADING   'PHONE|NUMBER' headsep '|'
FORMAT    a6

COLUMN    credit_limit ON
HEADING   'CREDIT|LIMIT' headsep '|'
FORMAT    $999.99

(and many more)
```

Notes

❶ Headsep is the heading separator. This shows that the pipe symbol is used to create multiline headings.

Oracle SQLplus:
Delete the format and heading settings of one column name

```
column price_alias_1 clear;
```

Oracle SQLplus:
Delete the format and heading settings of all the column names

```
clear columns;
```

5-6   How to find the column names in a table or view using SQLplus

The describe command in SQLplus provides an easy way to find the names of all the columns in a table or view. It also tells us the datatypes of these columns. Often this datatype information is far to the right and we must use the bottom scrollbar to find it.

If your bottom scrollbar does not work, see the workaround in appendix B.

Task

Find the names of all the columns in the l_employees table.

Oracle SQLplus

```
describe l_employees;
```

Oracle SQLplus response ❶

```
Name                Null?     Type
----------------    --------  ------------
EMPLOYEE_ID         NOT NULL  NUMBER(3)
FIRST_NAME                    VARCHAR2(10)
LAST_NAME                     VARCHAR2(10)
DEPT_CODE                     VARCHAR2(3)
HIRE_DATE                     DATE
CREDIT_LIMIT                  NUMBER(4,2)
PHONE_NUMBER                  VARCHAR2(4)
MANAGER_ID                    NUMBER(3)
```

Notes

❶ The null and type columns are far to the right. You need to use the bottom scrollbar to find them.

5-7 How to use a spool file

We can create an audit trail of an Oracle session by using a spool file containing a record of all the commands we entered and all the results we got from Oracle. This is a convenient way to keep track of our work.

Another use for a spool file is in an Oracle script containing many SQL commands. When the script is run, the SQL commands may execute faster than we can see them. If there is an error, the message may go by quicker than we can see it. The spool file provides a way to check for errors after the script file has finished running.

Before we begin a spool file, we usually use the command `set echo on`. This tells SQLplus to show everything in the spool file.

When we start a spool file, the file is open and we can write to it. We will not be able to see everything written to this file until after we close it.

Task

Create a spool file.

Oracle SQLplus: Begin a spool file

```
set echo on;
spool c:\temp\Oracle_session_july14.txt;
```

Oracle SQLplus: Close a spool file

```
spool off;
```

5-8 How to get online help in SQLplus

We can get some online help in SQLplus by entering `help` followed by the name of the command we want help with. We can get a list of all the online help topics by entering `help index`. More information about these commands is contained in the documentation.

Task 1

Get a list of all the topics available with the `help` command.

Oracle SQLplus

```
help index;
```

Oracle SQLplus response

```
@               COPY            PAUSE                    SHUTDOWN
@@              DEFINE          PRINT                    SPOOL
/               DEL             PROMPT                   SQLPLUS
ACCEPT          DESCRIBE        QUIT                     START
APPEND          DISCONNECT      RECOVER                  STARTUP
ARCHIVE LOG     EDIT            REMARK                   STORE
ATTRIBUTE       EXECUTE         REPFOOTER                TIMING
BREAK           EXIT            REPHEADER                TTITLE
BTITLE          GET             RESERVED WORDS (SQL)     UNDEFINE
CHANGE          HELP            RESERVED WORDS (PL/SQL)  VARIABLE
CLEAR           HOST            RUN                      WHENEVER OSERROR
COLUMN          INPUT           SAVE                     WHENEVER SQLERROR
COMPUTE         LIST            SET
CONNECT         PASSWORD        SHOW
```

Task 2

Get help for the `spool` command.

Oracle SQLplus

```
help spool;
```

Oracle SQLplus response

```
SPOOL
-----

Stores query results in an operating system file, or sends the
file to a printer.

SPO[OL] [file_name[.ext] | OFF | OUT]
```

5-9   How to show the parameter settings for SQLplus

SQLplus has more than 50 parameters that you can set. These parameters control the way that this environment works. To see the value of any of these parameters, we use the `show` command, followed by the name of a parameter. To see the values of all of the parameters, we can use the `show all` command. Do not expect to immediately understand the meaning of all these parameters. Information about them is available in the documentation.

Task

List all the SQLplus parameters and their current values.

Oracle SQLplus

```
show all;
```

Oracle SQLplus response

```
appinfo is ON and set to "SQL*Plus"
arraysize 15
autocommit OFF
autoprint ON
autorecovery OFF
autotrace OFF
blockterminator "." (hex 2e)
btitle OFF and is the first few characters of the next SELECT statement
cmdsep OFF
colsep " "
compatibility version NATIVE
concat "." (hex 2e)
copycommit 0
COPYTYPECHECK is ON
define OFF

(and many more)
```

5-10 About the **SQLFUN_LOGIN** script

Every time you log on to Oracle, you should run the SQLFUN_LOGIN script file to set up the SQLplus environment. If you have installed this script file in the c:\temp directory, you can run it by entering the following:

```
start c:\temp\sqlfun_login.sql;
```

You can set this up to run automatically. For details, see appendix B.

This section explains what this script file does when you run it. Basically it sets up the environment to be like a giant sheet of paper for you to work on. You might want to look at the code as you read this section.

First, the script clears the environment and displays a message. When you press Enter, the script continues and opens a spool file. It sets up many column headings. It sets most of the SQLplus parameters to their default settings to be sure they have not been set to some other value.

Then it makes a few changes to customize the environment. Here are the highlights:

1. The default date format is changed to use a four-digit year.

2. The ampersand character (&) will be handled as an ordinary character instead of indicating a variable.

3. When we run a `select` statement, we will always get a message indicating how many rows are in the result table.

4. Our work area is 998 characters wide.

5. All nulls will be displayed as `(null)`.

6. After 50 lines of the result table are displayed, the column headings are shown again.

7. SQL statements are allowed to contain blank lines.

8. SQL statements are converted to uppercase letters before they are run. This includes text within quotes.

Task

Show the code to make the preceding changes to the SQLplus environment.

Oracle SQL

```
alter session set nls_date_format = 'DD-MON-YYYY';
```

Oracle SQLplus

```
set define off;
set feedback 1;
set linesize 998;
set null (null);
set pagesize 50;
set sqlblanklines on;
set sqlcase upper;
```

5-11 How to use the Oracle SQLplus documentation

The complete documentation of SQLplus is available on the Online Documentation CD-ROM. To use it, follow the directions given next. This method requires Microsoft Internet Explorer. The screens shown below are from Oracle9i. Each version of Oracle changes these screens a bit.

Task

Find the entry for the `column` command in the SQLplus documentation.

Oracle procedure

Step 1: Insert the CD-ROM, open the Doc folder and double-click on Index.htm. You will see the following screen. If you have Autorun turned on, click Browse Documentation on the initial screen.

Step 2: To find information about the `column` command follow these steps:

- Click List of Books.

- Click SQL within the Shortcuts to Book Titles.

- Go to the line for SQL*Plus Users Guide and Reference.

- Click Index within that line.

- Click the letter C in the Index and scroll down to Column.

- Click the number 1 after the Column command. You will see the following screen.

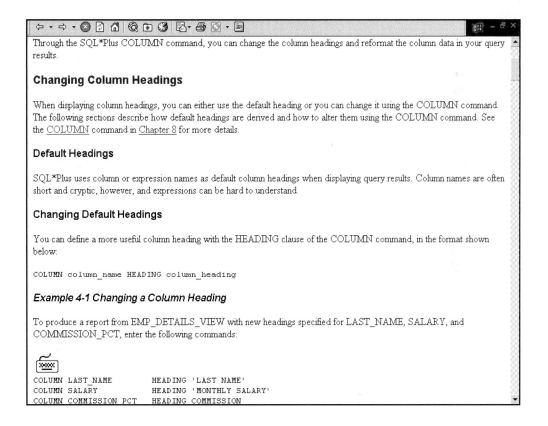

Through the SQL*Plus COLUMN command, you can change the column headings and reformat the column data in your query results.

Changing Column Headings

When displaying column headings, you can either use the default heading or you can change it using the COLUMN command. The following sections describe how default headings are derived and how to alter them using the COLUMN command. See the COLUMN command in Chapter 8 for more details.

Default Headings

SQL*Plus uses column or expression names as default column headings when displaying query results. Column names are often short and cryptic, however, and expressions can be hard to understand.

Changing Default Headings

You can define a more useful column heading with the HEADING clause of the COLUMN command, in the format shown below:

```
COLUMN column_name HEADING column_heading
```

Example 4-1 Changing a Column Heading

To produce a report from EMP_DETAILS_VIEW with new headings specified for LAST_NAME, SALARY, and COMMISSION_PCT, enter the following commands:

```
COLUMN LAST_NAME        HEADING 'LAST NAME'
COLUMN SALARY           HEADING 'MONTHLY SALARY'
COLUMN COMMISSION PCT   HEADING COMMISSION
```

Step 3: For further details, you can click on the hyperlink to Column and see the following screen.

COLUMN

Syntax

COL[UMN] [{*column|expr*} [*option* ...]]

where *option* represents one of the following clauses:

```
ALI[AS] alias
CLE[AR]
ENTMAP {ON|OFF}
FOLD_A[FTER]
FOLD_B[EFORE]
FOR[MAT] format
HEA[DING] text
JUS[TIFY] {L[EFT]|C[ENTER]|C[ENTRE]|R[IGHT]}
LIKE {expr|alias}
NEWL[INE]
NEW_V[ALUE] variable
NOPRI[NT]|PRI[NT]
NUL[L] text
OLD_V[ALUE] variable
ON|OFF
WRA[PPED]|WOR[D_WRAPPED]|TRU[NCATED]
```

Specifies display attributes for a given column, such as

- text for the column heading

Finding Information About Tables and Views

This section describes how to find information about the tables and views in a database. The database needs to keep track of all the tables and views for its own processing. This information is available to everyone who uses the database.

5-12 Overview of the Data Dictionary

The *Data Dictionary* is a set of tables that contains all the information about the structure of the database. It contains the names of all the tables, their columns, their primary keys, the names of the views, the `select` statements that define the views, and much more. The Data Dictionary is sometimes called the *System Catalog*. Most SQL products have a Data Dictionary.

These tables are created and maintained by the database system itself. They contain all the information the database system needs to support its own processing, its self-knowledge. Because this information is stored in tables, you can use `select` statements to get information from it. These tables are like any other tables. This may seem natural, but it is actually a big step forward. Often in software, the "inner knowledge" is in a completely different format than the "outer knowledge."

The details of the Data Dictionary differ for each SQL product. They even differ slightly from one version of a product to the next. The differences are in the names of the Data Dictionary tables, what columns they contain, and what codes are used.

These details are tied very closely to the inner workings of the database engine itself, the Database Management System (DBMS). When new capabilities are added to the DBMS, new information is often added to the Data Dictionary. Much of this information is meant only for the DBAs and can be ignored by other people. However, you can use a lot of the information that can be found there. Almost anything you might want to know about the database is contained in the Data Dictionary.

Oracle

Oracle has a data dictionary that is complete, and contains all the information about all the database objects. For now, we focus on obtaining information about tables and views from it.

Access

Access does not have a complete data dictionary. This is somewhat unusual for an SQL product. It has three approximations of a Data Dictionary. You can get to one of them with the following:

Tools → Options → View → System Objects

Another option is

Tools → Analyze → Documenter

Ordinarily this produces a hard-copy output, but you can save the data in a table using the command

File → Save as Table

Unfortunately this feature may not be supported in the newer versions of Access.

The third method that Access uses is to present the information using the GUI. I show you how to get information from Access using this method.

Having this information available via GUI is not always as good as having it in tables. If you simply want to look up the information by hand, the GUI method is fine, but if you want to write select statements that make use of this information, it is much better to have the information available in tables.

The Oracle Data Dictionary: Information about tables and views

Information to Get	Data Dictionary Table ❶	Data Dictionary Columns

Table names	`user_tables`
	or
	`all_tables`
		`table_name`

View names	`user_views`
	or
	`all_views`
		`view_name`

View definition	`user_views`
	or
	`all_views`
		`text`

Columns of tables and views	`user_tab_columns`
	or
	`all_tab_columns`
		`column_name`

Primary keys of tables	`user_constraints` and
	`user_cons_columns`
	or
	`all_constraints` and
	`all_cons_columns`
		(see section 5-17)

Notes

❶ `User_` tables are limited to information about the database objects that you own. `All_` tables may also include information about database objects that are owned by other people, but only if they have decided to share them with you.

5-13 How to find the names of all the tables

In working with any database, the names of the tables are the first thing you will want to know. All the data is contained in tables. They are the basic building blocks for everything else in the database. Once you know the name of a table, you can examine its data by using the following command:

```
SELECT *
FROM table_name;
```

In the Oracle Data Dictionary, the table named user_tables contains the names of all the tables you own. It has many columns and most of them will not interest you — they are for the DBAs. The column called table_name contains the name of every table.

In Oracle, the table names and the view names are contained in different Data Dictionary tables. In some other SQL products, the information about the tables and views is kept together in a single table.

Task 1

Find the names of all the tables you own.

Oracle SQL — List all the tables on your own userid

```
select table_name
from user_tables;
```

Oracle result table

```
TABLE_NAME
----------------
L_CONSTANTS
L_DEPARTMENTS
L_EMPLOYEES
L_FOODS
L_LUNCHES
L_LUNCH_ITEMS
L_SUPPLIERS
NUMBERS_0_TO_9

(and many others)
```

Task 2

Find the names of all the tables you are permitted to use.

Oracle SQL — List all the tables you are permitted to use

```
select table_name
from all_tables;
```

Access GUI method of finding all the tables

Click the Tables tab with the mouse. You will see the following screen.

5-14 How to find the names of all the views

This section shows how to find the names of all your views, which are another important part of a database. In the Oracle Data Dictionary, the table named user_views contains information about all the views owned by your userid. The view_name column is the only one you need right now.

Task

Find the names of all the views you own.

Oracle SQL

```
select view_name
from user_views;
```

Oracle result table ❶

```
VIEW_NAME
------------------
ALL_LUNCHES
NUMBERS_0_TO_99
SALES_STAFF_1
SALES_STAFF_2
SHIPPING_DEPT

(and many more)
```

Notes

❶ Your results may be different if you have not run all the Oracle SQL in the book so far.

Access GUI method

Click the Queries tab with the mouse. You will see the following screen.

5-15 How to find the `select` statement that defines a view

This section shows how to find the `select` statement that defines a particular view. You get the `text` column from the `user_views` table. You can use the `where` clause to specify which view definition you want.

Oracle retains the format of the `select` statement the way you enter it, but Access does not. Access uses its own formatting. Sometimes it rewrites the `select` statement entirely. In this example, the Access format is easy to read, but sometimes the format is difficult because it is written for computers and not for people.

Task

Find the `select` statement that defines the `shipping_dept` view.

Oracle SQL

```
select view_name,
       text
from user_views
where view_name = 'shipping_dept'; ❶
```

Oracle result table

```
VIEW_NAME                        TEXT
-------------------------------  --------------------------
SHIPPING_DEPT                    SELECT EMPLOYEE_ID,
                                        FIRST_NAME,
                                        LAST_NAME,
                                        DEPT_CODE,
                                        CREDIT_LIMIT
                                 FROM L_EMPLOYEES
                                 WHERE DEPT_CODE = 'SHP'
                                 WITH CHECK OPTION
```

Notes

❶ The `where` clause limits the information to a single view.

Access GUI method

Step 1: Click the Queries tab.
Step 2: Click once on the name of the query (view) you want information about.
Step 3: Click the Design button. You will see the following screen.

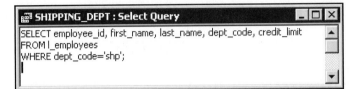

5-16 How to find the names of the columns in a table or view

This section shows you how to get the names of the columns to use in coding a `select` statement. When you look at a table, the column names seem to be displayed above each column. These names are meant to help a person read and understand the table, but they are not always the actual names you need to use to write a `select` statement. They can be truncated or they can be changed entirely by the SQLplus environment.

Oracle has two different methods to obtain this information. One method uses SQLplus, the environment in which Oracle SQL runs. In this method the command `describe` is followed by the name of the table. Sometimes the output is very wide and you will need to use the horizontal scrollbar to see the whole listing.

The other method uses the Oracle Data Dictionary. A Select statement gets the `column_name` column from the `user_tab_columns` table. This table contains information about the columns of both tables and views. The name of this table should be pronounced "User Table Columns," but in the spelling, the word "Table" is truncated.

A `where` clause is needed to limit the result to the columns of a single table or view. If you do not use a `where` clause you will get the names of all the columns of all your tables and views, which might be an overwhelming amount of information. In this `where` clause, `table_name` is set equal to the name of either a table or a view. The order of the columns within the table is contained in the `column_id` column.

Access has a GUI method to obtain this information. The *field names* are the names of the columns. Access is able to show the names of the columns for tables, but not for views.

Task

Find the full names of all the columns of the l_employees table. List these columns in their order within the table.

Oracle SQLplus command

```
describe l_employees;
```

Oracle SQLplus response

Name	Null?	Type
EMPLOYEE_ID	NOT NULL	NUMBER(3)
FIRST_NAME		VARCHAR2(10)
LAST_NAME		VARCHAR2(10)
DEPT_CODE		VARCHAR2(3)
HIRE_DATE		DATE
CREDIT_LIMIT		NUMBER(4,2)
PHONE_NUMBER		VARCHAR2(4)
MANAGER_ID		NUMBER(3)

Oracle SQL: Column names of tables and views

```
select table_name,
       column_name,
       column_id
from user_tab_columns
where table_name = 'l_employees'
order by column_id;
```

Result table

TABLE_NAME	COLUMN_NAME	COLUMN_ID
L_EMPLOYEES	EMPLOYEE_ID	1
L_EMPLOYEES	FIRST_NAME	2
L_EMPLOYEES	LAST_NAME	3
L_EMPLOYEES	DEPT_CODE	4
L_EMPLOYEES	HIRE_DATE	5
L_EMPLOYEES	CREDIT_LIMIT	6
L_EMPLOYEES	PHONE_NUMBER	7
L_EMPLOYEES	MANAGER_ID	8

Access GUI method: Column names for tables, but not for views

Step 1: Click the Tables tab.
Step 2: Click once on the name of the table you choose. The table name will be highlighted.
Step 3: Click the Design button. You will see the following screen.

Field Name	Data Type	Description
EMPLOYEE_ID	Number	
FIRST_NAME	Text	
LAST_NAME	Text	
DEPT_CODE	Text	
HIRE_DATE	Date/Time	
CREDIT_LIMIT	Number	
PHONE_NUMBER	Text	
MANAGER_ID	Number	

Field Properties

General | Lookup

Field Size	Decimal
Format	
Precision	3
Scale	0
Decimal Places	Auto
Input Mask	
Caption	
Default Value	
Validation Rule	
Validation Text	
Required	No
Indexed	Yes (No Duplicates)

A field name can be up to 64 characters long, including spaces. Press F1 for help on field names.

5-17 How to find the primary key of a table

This section shows how to find the primary key of a table. The primary key can consist of several columns, but is considered to be a single unit. A view does not have a primary key.

To find information about primary keys in the Oracle Data Dictionary, you need to know that a primary key is one type of constraint. A *constraint* is any rule that restricts the data that can be entered into a column. We will discuss constraints in more detail in chapter 8. A primary key is a constraint because the data that can be entered into its columns is restricted by the following rules:

1. Nulls are not allowed in primary key columns.

2. No two rows can have the same value in all the primary key columns.

For now, you must use a two-step process to find this information in the Oracle Data Dictionary. In section 13-18 I will show you how to combine these steps and get this information with a single `select` statement.

The goal of the first step is to find the exact name of the constraint from the `user_constraints` table. In the following example, the `select` statement lists all the constraints on the `l_foods` table. There are three of them. The primary key constraint is the one with a value of `P` in the `constraint_type` column, so the name of this constraint is `pk_l_foods`. If you have put `pk_` in the names of all the primary key constraints, this first step may not be necessary.

The second step finds all the columns involved with the constraint. It uses the `user_cons_columns` table. The name of this table is pronounced "User Constraint Columns," but in the spelling, the word "Constraint" is truncated. In the example, the `pk_l_foods` constraint is listed with two columns: `supplier_id` and `product_code`. You already know that this is the correct answer from the design of the `Lunches` database.

Task

Find all the columns in the primary key of the `l_foods` table.

Oracle SQL: Step 1

```
select table_name,
       constraint_type,
       constraint_name
from user_constraints
where table_name = 'l_foods'; ❶
```

Result table: Step 1 ❷

```
TABLE_NAME                         C CONSTRAINT_NAME
------------------------------     - -----------------

L_FOODS                            P PK_L_FOODS
L_FOODS                            R FK_FOODS_SUPPLIER_ID
L_FOODS                            C FOODS_MAX_PRICE
```

Oracle SQL: Step 2

```
select *
from user_cons_columns
where table_name = 'l_foods'; ❶
```

Result table: Step 2

OWNER	CONSTRAINT_NAME	TABLE_NAME	COLUMN_NAME	POSITION	
SQLFUN	FK_FOODS_SUPPLIER_ID	L_FOODS	SUPPLIER_ID	1	
SQLFUN	FOODS_MAX_PRICE	L_FOODS	PRICE	(null)	
SQLFUN	PK_L_FOODS	L_FOODS	SUPPLIER_ID	1	❸
SQLFUN	PK_L_FOODS	L_FOODS	PRODUCT_CODE	2	❸

Notes

❶ This `where` clause limits the result to the constraints on one table. This is what you want. Otherwise the result can become confusing to read.

❷ The constraint_type column contains the following codes:

P — Primary key
R — Referential Integrity, foreign key
C — Check constraint
U — Uniqueness constraint

Constraints are discussed in chapter 8.

❸ The constraint_name, pk_l_foods, shows you which rows you want from this table. The position says that supplier_id is the first column in the primary key, and product_code is the second column.

Access GUI method to find the primary key of a table ❹

Step 1: Click the Tables tab.
Step 2: Click once on the name of the table you choose. The table name will become highlighted.
Step 3: Click on the Design button. You will see the following screen.

Field Name	Data Type	Description
🔑 SUPPLIER_ID	Text	
🔑 PRODUCT_CODE	Text	
MENU_ITEM	Number	
DESCRIPTION	Text	
PRICE	Currency	
PRICE_INCREASE	Currency	

Field Properties

General | Lookup

Field Size	3
Format	
Input Mask	
Caption	
Default Value	
Validation Rule	
Validation Text	
Required	No
Allow Zero Length	No
Indexed	No
Unicode Compression	No

A field name can be up to 64 characters long, including spaces. Press F1 for help on field names.

Notes

❹ In Access, the columns of the primary key are shown with the key symbol to the left of the column names.

Summary

In this chapter we discussed:

1. Transactions

2. Modifying data in a table by working through a view

3. How to set up the SQLplus environment

4. How to use the Data Dictionary to find information about tables and views

Exercises

1. Goal: Use a transaction to add new rows to two tables at the same time. You must add a row into one table first, before the row can be added into the second table. (Section 5-1)

   a. Add yourself to the 1_employees table in a new department named DBA. The full name of this department is database administrator.

   You must first add a row to the 1_departments table before you add the row to the 1_employees table. Then look at the changes you have made. In Oracle, if you wanted to make these changes permanent you would do a commit after you have added both these rows. This is a transaction. In Access, you cannot use a transaction. At the end, I use a rollback rather than a commit because I do not want to make these changes permanent.

   As an experiment, try doing the insert into the 1_employees table first. You will get an error message because I created a rule that says, "When you insert a new row into the 1_employees table, the dept_code in the new row must already exist in the 1_departments table." The name of this rule in Oracle is fk_emp_dept_code. You will see this name used in the error message. This is because of business rules in this database, explained in chapter 8, which are enforced with Referential Integrity constraints.

Oracle & Access SQL

```
insert into 1_departments
values ('dba', 'database administrator');

insert into 1_employees
values (950, 'john', 'patrick', 'dba',
        '01-apr-2005', 25, null, 201);

-- View your changes
select * from 1_departments
select * from 1_employees

-- Finish the transaction
-- In Oracle, do a rollback
-- In Access, you must delete the rows individually
rollback;
```

b. Add a new food to the `1_foods` table from a new supplier. Add `Fresh Salmon` as menu item 11. The `supplier_id` is `CFF` and the `product_code` is `SA`. The `price` is $8.25 and there is no `price_increase` value.

First, add `CFF` to the `1_suppliers` table. The name of this supplier is `Cathy's Fresh Fish`. In Oracle, make these two inserts in a single transaction. You first need to add the row to the `1_suppliers` table because I have created a rule that says, "When a new row is added to the `1_foods` table, the `supplier_id` must already exist in the `1_suppliers` table."

In Oracle, do a `rollback` after you have inserted both rows and viewed your changes. In Access, delete the rows you have inserted. We do not want to make permanent changes to these tables at this time.

Hint: If you have trouble with the apostrophe, see section 3-15.

2. Goal: Change the data in a table by making changes to it through a view. (Section 5-3)

   a. Add Bob Miller to the 1_employees table as employee_id 952. Put him in the sales department. Use the view we created in chapter 4, exercise 2a to add this row. Check the table after you insert the new row.

   ### Oracle & Access SQL

   ```
   insert into ex0402a
   values (952, 'bob', 'miller', 'sal');

   select * from 1_employees;
   ```

   ---

   b. Change Bob Miller to the marketing department, MKT. Use the same view to make this change. Hint: Within the ex0402a view, the department code column is named department_code, not dept_code.

   c. Change Bob Miller to the accounting department, ACT. Use the same view to make this change.

   Note that you will not be able to make any more changes to the row for Bob Miller through this view. This view is only able to make changes to employees in the sales and marketing departments. If we had defined this view With Check Option, the change to the accounting department would not be allowed.

   d. In Oracle, do a rollback. In Access, delete the row for Bob Miller from the 1_employees table.

3. Goal: Find information about tables and views in the Oracle Data Dictionary.

   a. From the Oracle Data Dictionary, find the names of the tables you created in the exercises of chapter 4. Their names begin with ex04.

Oracle SQL

```
select table_name
from user_tables
where table_name like 'ex04%';
```

b. From the Oracle Data Dictionary, find the names of the views you created in the exercises of chapter 4. Their names begin with ex04. Also find the `select` statement that defines each of these views.

c. In the Oracle Data Dictionary, find the names of all the columns in the table ex0401a and the view ex0402a. Sort these column names into the order they have within the table and view.

Notice that column information about tables and views is kept together in the same table of the Data Dictionary. The name of the view is in a column called `table_name`.

4. Goal: Find information about the primary key columns in the Oracle Data Dictionary.

a. Find the primary key columns of the `1_employees` table. To do this you must look in two tables of the Oracle Data Dictionary and write your conclusion.

Oracle SQL

```
select table_name,
       constraint_type,
       constraint_name
from user_constraints
where table_name = '1_employees';

select *
from user_cons_columns
where table_name = '1_employees';
```

b. Find the primary key columns of the `1_departments` table. Write your conclusion.

c. Does the table `ex0401a` have a primary key?

d. Does the view `ex0402a` have a primary key?

chapter 6

CREATING YOUR
OWN TABLES

In this chapter, you learn how to create your own tables in a way that provides maximum control over every aspect of the table. In chapter 4, you created new tables from other tables. Here, you create tables from the beginning, without relying on other tables.

Creating Tables

A table can be created with an SQL command, giving you precise control over every part of the table.

6-1 The `create table` command

The `create table` statement creates a new table. When it is first created, this table will not have any rows of data in it. This command has the following format:

```
CREATE TABLE table_name
(column_name_1    data_type_1,
 column_name_2    data_type_2,
 ...);
```

This is the simplest form of the command. Many other options can be specified in this command or can be added later. All the columns of the table must be listed.

This method of creating a table allows the greatest control over all its elements. A table consists of

- A table name
- Names of the columns
- Datatypes of the columns
- A sequence to the columns

People sometimes think of a table as consisting of data, but this is incorrect. The table is a container, like a box. The data are held in a table.

The list of datatypes in Oracle is a little different from the one for Access. Each SQL product supports datatypes that differ slightly from other SQL products. Because the datatypes are named in this command, the SQL statement for Oracle is different from the one for Access.

Primary keys and many other options can be specified when the table is first created or they can be specified after it is already built. They can even be specified after the table has data in it. The `alter table` statement is used to add a primary key to a table after it has been created. We discuss this in section 6-6.

In the following example, the `create table` statements are the same for Oracle and Access, except for the names of the datatypes.

Task

Create a new table similar to the `l_foods` table by defining its columns with a `create table` statement. Move the position of the `menu_item` column to make it the first column.

Oracle SQL

```
drop table l_foods_2;

create table l_foods_2
(menu_item        number(2),
 supplier_id      varchar2(3),
 product_code     varchar2(2),
 description      varchar2(20),
 price            number(4,2),
 price_increase   number(4,2) );
```

Access SQL

```
drop table l_foods_2;

create table l_foods_2
(menu_item        byte,
 supplier_id      varchar(3),
 product_code     varchar(2),
 description      varchar(20),
 price            money,
 price_increase   money );
```

Result table

A new table is created. When a table is created, at first it does not contain any data, so you cannot see it. However, there is an entry for the table in the Data Dictionary, so you can see it if you look there.

6-2   Datatypes in Oracle and Access

Data are represented inside the computer as a pattern of 1s and 0s. Only certain patterns are meaningful — all others are nonsense. These meaningful patterns are called *datatypes*.

Oracle uses a different set of meaningful patterns than Access does. For instance, they use different patterns of 1s and 0s to represent the date January 1, 2010. The meaning of the data is the same, but the binary representation of it is different. In short, they use different datatypes. Each SQL product has its own set of datatypes. Each one assigns slightly different meanings to patterns of binary digits.

For the most part, the meanings are the same, even though they are represented differently on a binary level. The differences show up only at the extremes. Consider dates. Both Oracle and Access can handle dates between 100 AD and 9999 AD. That is a greater range of dates than I have ever needed to use.

However, Oracle dates and Access dates do have some differences because of the different patterns of 1s and 0s that represent them. In particular, Oracle can handle dates between 4712 BC and 100 AD, but Access cannot.

The main point here is that the datatypes for Oracle and Access are very similar, but they differ in the small details. The names of these datatypes are different, so the `create table` statements are different.

The next table shows the similarities and differences between the datatypes used in Oracle and Access. The datatypes for text, date/time, and storage are very similar. Access has a one-bit datatype for Yes/No and True/False, which Oracle does not have. Oracle might use an entire byte of data to represent this. Usually, that is acceptable.

Another difference is the numbers. Access uses many datatypes for numbers. This is the traditional approach and most computer products follow it. Oracle combines decimal numbers and floating-point numbers together in a single datatype.

The datatypes for storage are used for binary data such as pictures, sound clips, video clips, and compiled programs. These are not active elements within the database — you cannot search, sort, index, or apply functions to them.

The use of storage datatypes in databases is currently in the process of change. It is changing in two opposite directions at the same time. From one perspective, their use is being phased out in favor of storing files within the operating system, rather than in a database, and only placing a pointer to them in the database itself. From another perspective, their use is increasing to support object-oriented concepts.

The names of the datatypes given here are the *internal* names for the elements of the database engines. For Access they are the names used by the JET engine. The GUI graphical presentation layer of Access sometimes uses slightly different names.

Many of these datatypes also have synonyms or *external* names. These are intended to make one SQL product compatible with another. This is an attempt to map the datatypes of one product to the datatypes of another.

Main Oracle and Access datatypes.

Oracle	Access	Comments
CHARACTER DATATYPES		
`varchar2(Size)` (when size is 1 to 255)	`varchar(Size)` or `text(Size)`	Variable-length character string. `Size` is the maximum length of the column. `Size` can be from 1 to 255. In Oracle, the size can be larger but columns more than 255 bytes long are *long strings*. They have restricted capabilities and behave differently.
`char(Size)`	`char(Size)`	Fixed-length character strings. `Size` is the maximum length of the column. `Size` can be from 1 to 255.
DATE/TIME DATATYPES		
`date`	`datetime`	A date and time. Oracle: from 4712 BC to 9999 AD. Access: from 100 AD to 9999 AD.

Main Oracle and Access datatypes. *(continued)*

Oracle	Access	Comments
NUMERIC DATATYPES		
number(P,S)		Number: Either integers, decimals, or scientific notation (floating point) numbers. P: Precision, is the total number of digits other than zeros. From 1 to 38. S: Scale, is the number of digits to the right of the decimal point. From 0 to 130. Examples: 1234.56 has type number(6,2) 0.0000123 has type number(3,7) 1230000. has type number(7,0) Valid numbers: From .00...01 (129 zeros after the decimal point), which has type number(1,130) To 99...9900...00 (38 nines followed by 88 zeros), which has type number(38,0)
	byte	Integer, from 0 to 255.
	smallint	Integer, from about −32,000 to 32,000.
	integer or number	Integer, from about −2,000,000,000 to 2,000,000,000.
	money or currency	Integer and 4 decimal places. Plus or minus about 900,000,000,000,000 Automatically formatted as currency.
	real	Floating-point number (positive or negative). From about 1.4E−45 to 3.4E38.
	float	Floating-point number (positive or negative). From about 4.9E−324 to 1.8E308.

Additional Oracle and Access datatypes.

Oracle	Access	Comments
STORAGE DATATYPES (You cannot sort, search, or index them)		
`clob`	`memo`	Character data. CLOB is a Character Large OBject. Maximum length is 2 gigabytes or more.
`varchar2(Size)` (when size is 256 to 4,000)		Character data.
`raw(Size)`	`binary`	Binary data: pictures, sound. Oracle: up to 2000 bytes long Access: up to 255 bytes long.

`blob`	`image`
	 or
	 `OLE object`
		Binary data: pictures, video, sound, compiled programs, multimedia.
		 BLOB is a Binary Large OBject.
		 Maximum length is 2 gigabytes or more.

BIT DATATYPES		

	`bit`
	 or
	 `yesno`
		Any binary choice.
		 For instance: Yes or No. True or False.

PSEUDO DATATYPES		
	`counter`	Automatically numbers the rows in a table. Access GUI calls this `autonumber`.
`rowid`		Address of a row within its table. Each row has a different address.
`rownum`		Sequential number assigned to each row.
`bfile`	`OLE object`	Locator for a large binary file stored outside the database. This is a type of pointer. It points to a file, which is stored by the operating system.

Additional Oracle and Access datatypes. *(continued)*

Oracle	Access	Comments
SPECIALIZED TIME/DATE DATATYPES		
`timestamp(P)`		Point of time. Used to show the sequence of events within the computer. Year, month, day, hour, minute, second, and fraction of a second. P: Precision, is the number of digits in the fractional part of a second. From 0 to 9.
`interval year(P) to month`		Period of time in years and months. P: Precision, is the number of digits in the year.
`interval day(D) to second(S)`		Period of time in days, hours, minutes, and seconds. D: Number of digits in the day. S: Nnumber of digits in the fractional part of a second.

6-3   Two types of time

In English we have two concepts of time: point of time and duration of time. "The basketball game will be played on September 15 at 6:00 p.m." is an example of a point of time. "The song lasts 4 minutes and 35 seconds" is an example of duration of time. The main point here is that in English, these are both considered to be time.

Recently, Oracle has introduced a new datatype, `interval`, to handle durations of time. However, most databases still use a number to represent a lenth of time.

6-4   Putting data into the new `1_foods` table

Now that we have created a new version of the `1_foods` table, we will load the data into it. I am doing this now partly to continue the example and show you how a table is created. I am also doing it so that I can use it in other sections later in this chapter.

We have discussed two ways to put data in a table. One way uses an `insert` statement with literal values and adds one row at a time (see section 4-9). The other way uses an `insert` statement with a `select` statement and can add many rows at once (see section 4-11). In this example we use an `insert` with a `select` statement because all of the data is already in the original version of the table and it just needs to be copied into the new table.

Task

Copy all the data from the original version of the `1_foods` table to the new version of the table.

Oracle & Access SQL

```
insert into 1_foods_2
select menu_item,
       supplier_id,
       product_code,
       description,
       price,
       price_increase
from 1_foods;
```

Oracle only

```
commit;
```

The 1_foods_2 table with data loaded into it

MENU ITEM	SUPPLIER ID	PRODUCT CODE	DESCRIPTION	PRICE	PRICE INCREASE
1	ASP	FS	FRESH SALAD	$2.00	$0.25
2	ASP	SP	SOUP OF THE DAY	$1.50	(null)
3	ASP	SW	SANDWICH	$3.50	$0.40
4	CBC	GS	GRILLED STEAK	$6.00	$0.70
5	CBC	SW	HAMBURGER	$2.50	$0.30
6	FRV	BR	BROCCOLI	$1.00	$0.05
7	FRV	FF	FRENCH FRIES	$1.50	(null)
8	JBR	AS	SODA	$1.25	$0.25
9	JBR	VR	COFFEE	$0.85	$0.15
10	VSB	AS	DESSERT	$3.00	$0.50

6-5   Creating the 1_employees table in Oracle

It is time for you to look at some real code, instead of simplified examples. In this section I want to show you the Oracle code I wrote to create the 1_employees table of the Lunches database. The notes explain several features that I have not told you about until now, so I suggest that you read them carefully.

This code is from the SQLFUN_BUILD_TABLES.SQL script you ran to create the tables for this book. After you read this section, you might want to try to read the rest of this script to see how the other tables are built.

The stylized method of punctuation in the create table statement is intended to be an easy way to ensure that none of the punctuation is missing.

Task

Show the Oracle code that creates the `1_employee` table.

Oracle SQL

```
-- Create the l_employees table ❶
drop table l_employees cascade constraints; ❷
create table l_employees
(employee_id    number(3)
,first_name     varchar2(10)
,last_name      varchar2(10)
,dept_code      varchar2(3)
,hire_date      date
,credit_limit   number(4,2)
,phone_number   varchar2(4)
,manager_id     number(3))
)
storage (initial 2k next 2k pctincrease 0) ❸   -- optional
tablespace &users; ❹                           -- optional

alter table l_employees ❺
add constraint pk_l_employees
primary key (employee_id)
using index ❻                                  -- optional
storage (initial 2k next 2k pctincrease 0)     -- optional
tablespace &indx; ❼                            -- optional

insert into l_employees values
(201,'Susan','Brown','Exe','01-Jun-1998',30,'3484',null);
insert into l_employees values
(202,'Jim','Kern','Sal','16-Aug-1999',25,'8722',201);
insert into l_employees values
(203,'Martha','Woods','Shp','02-Feb-2004',25,'7591',201);
insert into l_employees values
(204,'Ellen','Owens','Sal','01-Jul-2003',15,'6830',202);
insert into l_employees values
(205,'Henry','Perkins','Sal','01-Mar-2000',25,'5286',202);
insert into l_employees values
(206,'Carol','Rose','Act',null,null,null,null);
insert into l_employees values
(207,'Dan','Smith','Shp','01-Dec-2004',25,'2259',203);
insert into l_employees values
(208,'Fred','Campbell','Shp','01-Apr-2003',25,'1752',203);
insert into l_employees values
(209,'Paula','Jacobs','Mkt','17-Mar-1999',15,'3357',201);
insert into l_employees values
(210,'Nancy','Hoffman','Sal','16-Feb-2004',25,'2974',203);
commit;
analyze table l_employees compute statistics; ❽
```

Notes

❶ This code begins with a brief comment that says what the code does. In Oracle and most other SQL products, a comment line begins with two dashes usually followed by a space.

❷ This is a preventative delete, discussed in section 4-8. The phrase `cascade constraints` ensures that the table will be dropped under all conditions. Without this phrase the table would not be dropped under certain conditions. We discuss Referential Integrity in chapter 8.

❸ The `storage` clause tells Oracle how much disk space to allocate to this table. Usually this is handled by the DBA and not by an application programmer. The database will use default values if this line and the other lines marked "optional" are omitted. In this `storage` clause, the `initial 2k` parameter tells Oracle to allocate 2 KB of disk space to the table when it is initially created. The `next 2k` parameter tells Oracle to allocate an additional 2 KB of disk space when the initial allocation is filled up. The `pctincrease 0` parameter, pronounced "percent increase," tells Oracle to keep any further allocations to 2 KB each. The alternative is to allocate ever-larger amounts of disk space. For example `pctincrease 50` would increase each successive allocation by 50%, so the next allocations would be 3 KB, then 4.5 KB. This parameter is sometimes used for tables that are growing rapidly.

❹ The `tablespace` clause tells Oracle in what tablespace the new table should be created. Here the new table will be created in the `users` tablespace, or in the tablespace you assigned to the `&users` variable.

A *tablespace* is a place to keep a table. It is an area of disk space that has a name. This is a DBA concept. A production database usually has many disk drives. The space on these drives is divided into tablespaces so it can be managed more easily. Usually an Oracle database has at least four tablespaces: `system`, `users`, `indx`, and `temp`. The `system` tablespace is used by the data dictionary and should not be used for anything else. The `users` tablespace is used to hold most tables. The `indx` tablespace is used to hold most indexes. The `temp` tablespace is used as an area to perform sorts. The DBA can create other tablespaces.

To find the names of the tablespaces, use a userid with DBA authority and enter:
```
select tablespace_name
from dba_tablespaces;
```

❺ This `alter table` command makes the `employee_id` column the primary key of the table (see section 6-6).

❻ When a primary key is created, an index is also created automatically. The `using index` clause sets the tablespace and disk space size for the index.

❼ The index for the primary key will be created in the `indx` tablespace, or in the tablespace you assigned to the `&indx` variable.

❽ You should run the `analyze table` command after you create a new table and load data into it. You should also run this command after you add a substantial amount of data to any table. The command puts information about the table, such as its size and other characteristics, into the Data Dictionary.

Changing Tables

The structure of a table is not cast in concrete and fixed forever. A table can be changed in many ways, even after it contains data. The `alter table` statement is especially designed to make changes to tables. It can make several types of changes. A few examples of this command are given in these sections.

6-6   Adding a primary key to a table

This section shows how to add a primary key to a table, even after the table contains many rows of data. The syntax is:

```
ALTER TABLE table_name
ADD CONSTRAINT name_of_the_constraint
PRIMARY KEY (list_of_columns_in_the_primary_key);
```

A primary key is one type of constraint, which is a rule that restricts the data that can be entered into the table. This is discussed in section 5-17. The preceding command adds a constraint to a table and the type of constraint it adds is a *primary key constraint*.

When you create a new table by saving the results of a `select` statement, as we did in chapter 4, the new table is created without a primary key. If you want to have a primary key on one of these tables, you must create it yourself.

If the table already contains data, that data must conform to the restrictions of a primary key. Otherwise, this command will fail and you will get an error message. A primary key cannot be put on a table if the data in the table does not support it. The data must not have two rows with the same values in all of the primary key columns, or nulls in any of the columns of the primary key.

A table is only allowed to have one primary key, although this key may consist of a combination of several columns.

It is not necessary to issue a `commit` command after an `alter table` command. Changes made by the `alter table` command are immediately made in a permanent way. Actually, a `commit` is never needed after a Data Definition Language (DDL) command, which creates a database object or changes the structure of an object. `commit` is only needed after the Data Modification Language (DML) commands, such as `insert`, `update`, and `delete`, which change the data in a table.

Task

Add a primary key to the new version of the `1_foods` table you created in section 6-1. The primary key of this table will consist of the two columns `supplier_id` and `product_code`.

Oracle & Access SQL: Add a primary key to a table

```
alter table 1_foods_2 ❶
add constraint pk_1_foods_2 ❷
primary key (supplier_id, product_code); ❸
```

Notes

❶ The new version of the `1_foods` table will be changed by this command.

❷ This gives a name to the constraint. Here the name is `pk_1_foods_2`. It combines `pk_`, meaning primary key, with the name of the table. This is my own naming convention. You can name it something else.

The name of the constraint is used mostly in error messages and in a few operations such as deleting the constraint or temporarily disabling it. It is not referred to directly in any `select` statement. The name should suggest the purpose of the constraint.

❸ The words, `primary key`, specify that this is a primary key constraint. The list of columns that follows contains the columns that will form the primary key. This list can contain any number of columns, even all the columns in the table, but it is usually limited to one or two columns.

6-7   Changing the primary key of a table

This section shows you how to change the primary key of a table. A table can have only one primary key, so you must delete the old primary key before you can create a new one. Often when you do this, the new primary key adds more columns to the old one.

Task

Change the primary key of the new version of the 1_foods table. Make the menu_item column the new primary key of this table. Show two ways to drop the primary key of a table.

Oracle & Access SQL:
Method 1 — Using the name of the constraint to drop it

```
alter table 1_foods_2
drop constraint pk_1_foods_2; ❶

alter table 1_foods_2
add constraint pk_1_foods_2
primary key (menu_item);
```

Oracle SQL:
Method 2 — Not using the name of the constraint to drop it

```
alter table 1_foods_2
drop primary key; ❷

alter table 1_foods_2
add constraint pk_1_foods_2
primary key (menu_item);
```

- Access does not support this syntax.

Notes

❶ On this line, `pk_1_foods_2` is the name of the constraint. The name of a constraint is easy to forget. You might need to find the name of the constraint in the Data Dictionary to delete the primary key.

❷ Using this format for the `alter table` statement, you do not need to know the name of the constraint to delete the primary key.

6-8   Adding a new column to a table

This section shows you how to add a new column to a table. The table may already have many rows of data in it. The new column is always positioned at the end of the table. Initially it contains only nulls. Later you will have the task of putting data into it.

The SQL code to add a new column is different in Oracle than it is in Access. This is partly because they must use their own datatypes in this command. Another reason is that Access uses the words `add column` where Oracle only uses `add`.

Task

Add a new column to the new version of the `1_foods` table. Name the new column `date_introduced` and give it a datatype of `date`.

Oracle SQL

```
alter table 1_foods_2
add date_introduced date;  ❶
```

Access SQL

```
alter table 1_foods_2
add column date_introduced datetime;  ❷
```

Beginning table (`1_foods_2` table)

```
 MENU  SUPPLIER  PRODUCT                                     PRICE
 ITEM  ID        CODE     DESCRIPTION           PRICE     INCREASE
-------  --------  -------  ------------------  --------  --------
     1  ASP       FS       FRESH SALAD           $2.00     $0.25
     2  ASP       SP       SOUP OF THE DAY       $1.50    (null)
     3  ASP       SW       SANDWICH              $3.50     $0.40
     4  CBC       GS       GRILLED STEAK         $6.00     $0.70
     5  CBC       SW       HAMBURGER             $2.50     $0.30
     6  FRV       BR       BROCCOLI              $1.00     $0.05
     7  FRV       FF       FRENCH FRIES          $1.50    (null)
     8  JBR       AS       SODA                  $1.25     $0.25
     9  JBR       VR       COFFEE                $0.85     $0.15
    10  VSB       AS       DESSERT               $3.00     $0.50
```

Ending table ❸

```
 MENU  SUPPLIER  PRODUCT                                     PRICE
 ITEM  ID        CODE     DESCRIPTION           PRICE     INCREASE  DATE_INTR
-------  --------  -------  ------------------  --------  --------  ---------
     1  ASP       FS       FRESH SALAD           $2.00     $0.25    (null)
     2  ASP       SP       SOUP OF THE DAY       $1.50    (null)    (null)
     3  ASP       SW       SANDWICH              $3.50     $0.40    (null)
     4  CBC       GS       GRILLED STEAK         $6.00     $0.70    (null)
     5  CBC       SW       HAMBURGER             $2.50     $0.30    (null)
     6  FRV       BR       BROCCOLI              $1.00     $0.05    (null)
     7  FRV       FF       FRENCH FRIES          $1.50    (null)    (null)
     8  JBR       AS       SODA                  $1.25     $0.25    (null)
     9  JBR       VR       COFFEE                $0.85     $0.15    (null)
    10  VSB       AS       DESSERT               $3.00     $0.50    (null)
```

Notes

❶ In Oracle, the `date_introduced` column is given the Oracle datatype `date`. Notice that the word `add` is followed by the column name. The implication is that a new column is being added.

❷ In Access, the `date_introduced` column is given the Access datatype `datetime`. Notice that the word `add` is followed by the word `column`.

❸ Initially, the new column contains nulls. After you define this column, you need to put data into it. The new column is always the last column in the table. Within most SQL products, you have no control over the placement of the column.

6-9   Expanding the length of a column

This section shows you how to expand the length of a column in Oracle by changing its datatype. A text column must remain a text column, but you can change its maximum length and switch between a fixed-length character string and a variable-length character string. A numeric column must remain a numeric column, but you can change the maximum number of digits it can contain or the number of digits after the decimal point. These changes are useful when you receive data that is too big to put into the columns you have defined.

All dates have the same datatype, so it does not make sense to change the datatype of a date column.

Task

Change the datatype of the `description` column of the new version of the `l_foods` table. It is currently defined as a variable-length character string with a maximum length of 20 characters. Change it to a character string with a length of 25 characters.

In Oracle, change the `price` column of this table. It is currently defined as a `number` with a maximum of four digits, two of which come after the decimal point. Change it to have a maximum of seven digits total — five before the decimal and two after. In Access, this change is not needed because the `price` column already has a datatype of `currency`, so it can already handle large numbers.

Oracle SQL

```
alter table l_foods_2
modify description varchar2(25);

alter table l_foods_2
modify price number(7,2);
```

Access SQL ❶

```
alter table l_foods_2
alter column description varchar(25);
```

Result table

The table does not show any difference.

Notes

❶ In Access you can make similar changes on the GUI level using the `Design` view of the table.

6-10 Deleting a column from a table

This section shows you how to delete a column from a table. Until recently Oracle did not support this option, but now it does. It is a new feature in Oracle8. New options continue to be added to the `alter table` command.

Task

Delete the `price_increase` column from the new version of the `1_foods` table.

Oracle & Access SQL

```
alter table 1_foods_2
drop column price_increase;
```

Beginning table (`1_foods_2` table)

MENU ITEM	SUPPLIER ID	PRODUCT CODE	DESCRIPTION	PRICE	PRICE INCREASE	DATE_INTR
1	ASP	FS	FRESH SALAD	$2.00	$0.25	(null)
2	ASP	SP	SOUP OF THE DAY	$1.50	(null)	(null)
3	ASP	SW	SANDWICH	$3.50	$0.40	(null)
4	CBC	GS	GRILLED STEAK	$6.00	$0.70	(null)
5	CBC	SW	HAMBURGER	$2.50	$0.30	(null)
6	FRV	BR	BROCCOLI	$1.00	$0.05	(null)
7	FRV	FF	FRENCH FRIES	$1.50	(null)	(null)
8	JBR	AS	SODA	$1.25	$0.25	(null)
9	JBR	VR	COFFEE	$0.85	$0.15	(null)
10	VSB	AS	DESSERT	$3.00	$0.50	(null)

Ending table

MENU ITEM	SUPPLIER ID	PRODUCT CODE	DESCRIPTION	PRICE	DATE_INTR
1	ASP	FS	FRESH SALAD	$2.00	(null)
2	ASP	SP	SOUP OF THE DAY	$1.50	(null)
3	ASP	SW	SANDWICH	$3.50	(null)
4	CBC	GS	GRILLED STEAK	$6.00	(null)
5	CBC	SW	HAMBURGER	$2.50	(null)
6	FRV	BR	BROCCOLI	$1.00	(null)
7	FRV	FF	FRENCH FRIES	$1.50	(null)
8	JBR	AS	SODA	$1.25	(null)
9	JBR	VR	COFFEE	$0.85	(null)
10	VSB	AS	DESSERT	$3.00	(null)

6-11 Making other changes to tables

This section shows a method of making changes to a table that does not use the `alter table` command. You already know this method, but I want to remind you of it here, in the context of the present discussion. This method can make almost any change you can think of. It is very flexible, but it is less efficient than the `alter table` command. Efficiency is usually important only when you are working with very large tables.

Here are some of the changes you can make to any table.

- Add new columns

- Delete columns

- Delete rows

- Rename columns

- Change the data in columns

- Change the datatype of columns

- Reorder columns

- Delete a primary key

This gives you nearly total control over every aspect of a table. Adding a primary key is the only change that requires the `alter table` command.

This technique uses a `create table` statement with a `select` statement, which we used in section 4-1.

Task

Create a `phone_list` table from the `l_employees` table. Include the columns `last_name`, `first_name`, and `phone_number`.

- Rename the `phone_number` column to `ext`.

- Change the order of the `first_name` and `last_name` columns.

- Delete many columns from the beginning table.

- Add a new column for `notes` and leave it blank.

- Change the phone number for Woods to 9408.

Oracle SQL ❶

```
drop table phone_list;
create table phone_list as
select last_name,
       first_name,
       phone_number as ext,
       '             ' as notes ❸
from 1_employees
where employee_id between 203 and 206;

update phone_list
set ext = '9408' ❹
where last_name = 'woods';
```

Access SQL ❷

```
select last_name,
       first_name,
       phone_number as ext,
       '             ' as notes ❸
into phone_list
from 1_employees
where employee_id between 203 and 206;

update phone_list
set ext = '9408'
where last_name = 'woods';
```

Beginning table (1_employees table)

EMPLOYEE ID	FIRST NAME	LAST NAME	DEPT CODE	HIRE_DATE	CREDIT LIMIT	PHONE NUMBER	MANAGER ID
201	SUSAN	BROWN	EXE	01-JUN-1998	$30.00	3484	(null)
202	JIM	KERN	SAL	16-AUG-1999	$25.00	8722	201
203	MARTHA	WOODS	SHP	02-FEB-2004	$25.00	7591	201
204	ELLEN	OWENS	SAL	01-JUL-2003	$15.00	6830	202
205	HENRY	PERKINS	SAL	01-MAR-2000	$25.00	5286	202
206	CAROL	ROSE	ACT	(null)	(null)	(null)	(null)
207	DAN	SMITH	SHP	01-DEC-2004	$25.00	2259	203
208	FRED	CAMPBELL	SHP	01-APR-2003	$25.00	1752	203
209	PAULA	JACOBS	MKT	17-MAR-1999	$15.00	3357	201
210	NANCY	HOFFMAN	SAL	16-FEB-2004	$25.00	2974	203

New table created in this section (`phone_list` table) ❺

```
LAST_NAME  FIRST_NAME EXT  NOTES
---------- ---------- ---- -------------
WOODS      MARTHA     9408
OWENS      ELLEN      6830
PERKINS    HENRY      5286
ROSE       CAROL      (nul ❻
                      l)
```

Notes

❶ In Oracle, the `create table` command and the `update` command can be put into a single script and run as a single unit.

❷ In Access, the `create table` command must be run first. Then the `update` command can be run. The SQL window in Access only allows us to run one command at a time.

❸ This adds a new column to the table and names it `notes`. There are 13 spaces between the beginning quote and the ending quote. In Oracle this makes the column a fixed-length character string with a length of 13 characters. In Access the 13 spaces are not needed, and you can use two quotes with one space between them. Spaces, not nulls, are put in this field.

❹ In the `update` statement, the `phone_number` must be referred to by its new name, `ext`.

❺ Here is the procedure you would follow if you wanted to name this new table `l_employees`, so that it would replace the beginning table. Do not do this now.

```
drop table l_employees;
create table l_employees as
select * from phone_list;
```

❻ Here (`null`) is wrapped to two lines. This is an Oracle listing. Access shows the null simply as a blank space, so this problem does not occur. In the Oracle SQLplus environment the (`null`) is wrapped to a second line because the column `ext` is only four characters wide. SQLplus puts the first four characters "(nul" on one line and puts the remaining characters "l)" on the next line. It does this because the command

```
set wrap on;
```

was issued. It would truncate the null to "(nul" if the command

```
set wrap off;
```

had been issued.

Tables with Duplicate Rows

In a relational database you are allowed to create tables with duplicate rows. That is, you can have two or more rows that have the same values in every column. Usually you want to avoid duplicate rows in your tables. When a table has a primary key, no duplicate rows are allowed. That is one of the purposes of a primary key.

6-12 The problem with duplicate rows

This section discusses when you may want to avoid duplicate rows and when you may want to allow them.

When to avoid duplicate rows

If you are going to share a table with someone else, or give it to them, then the table should have a primary key, which will ensure that it does not have any duplicate rows. Such rows are avoided because it is usually unclear what they mean. Two different interpretations are possible:

1. Each row represents a separate object.

2. These rows are redundant representations of the same object.

To prevent confusion, you should not allow duplicate rows in tables that are made public.

When to allow duplicate rows

If you are the only person using a table, then you might want to allow duplicate rows. You may allow them especially if the table is part of an intermediate step of some process, rather than a final result. The idea is that you will know what the duplicate rows mean in your own tables, even if nobody else knows.

Why duplicate rows are allowed in tables

Duplicate rows are allowed in tables for convenience. It is always better not to have duplicate rows in your tables, but it often requires extra effort to avoid them. You do not always have to make that effort.

For example, when you use a `select` statement to get a result table, two of the rows of the result table may be identical. That may or may not be a problem. It is a problem if you are showing the results to someone else and they do not know the meaning of these duplicate rows. It is not a problem if you are the only person seeing these results and you do know their meaning.

Example of duplicate rows that represent separate objects

In this example, the duplicate rows in a table represent distinct objects, events, or relationships. You are using a database to track your expenses. To keep things simple, you have decided to keep two pieces of data: the object you bought and the price. On Monday, you buy a hamburger for $2.00 and eat it. On Tuesday, you buy another hamburger for $2.00 and eat it. In your table of expenses these are duplicate rows. The duplicate row means that there is really another object. Together, the two rows mean that you bought two hamburgers and spent $4.00.

This example may seem artificial because if you also entered the date of the purchase, then the rows would not be duplicates. They are only duplicates because you have not recorded all the data. However, we are always in this situation, whether we are aware of it or not. Our tables contain what we consider to be the most significant pieces of information, but there is always some information that is left out.

The two duplicate rows are two different pieces of information (`sec0612a` table)

```
OBJECT_BOUGHT            PRICE
-------------------- --------
NEWSPAPER                $0.75
COFFEE                   $1.55
HAMBURGER                $2.00   ❶
FLOWERS                 $15.38
HAMBURGER                $2.00   ❶
BOOK                    $24.89
MOVIE TICKETS           $22.00
```

Example of duplicate rows that represent the same object

In this example, the duplicate rows in a table are redundant representations of a single object, event, or relationship. You are running an advertising campaign. You buy copies of several mailing lists and combine them into a single list. The duplicate rows have the same name and address. These duplicate rows are multiple representations of the same information. Here the duplicate row does not mean that there is another object. It only means that the same object is shown twice.

The two duplicate rows are a single piece of information (`sec0612b` table)

```
FIRST_NAME  LAST_NAME   ADDRESS
----------  ----------  -------------------
SUSAN       BROWN       512 ELM STREET    ❶
JIM         KERN        837-9TH AVENUE
MARTHA      WOODS       169 PARK AVENUE
SUSAN       BROWN       512 ELM STREET    ❶
ELLEN       OWENS       418 HENRY STREET
```

Notes

❶ These rows are duplicates.

6-13 How to eliminate duplicate rows

There are two ways to get rid of the duplicate rows in your tables. The method you use depends on the meaning you are giving to the duplicate rows. This section shows how to eliminate the duplicates if you consider them to be multiple representations of the same object. The next section shows how to add a new column that distinguishes between the duplicate rows. You use this method when you consider them to be representations of different objects.

If you want to keep only one row of each set of duplicate rows, you can create a new table using `select distinct`.

Task

Eliminate the duplicate rows from the `sec0612b` table. Keep only one copy of each row that has a duplicate.

Oracle SQL

```
drop table sec0613;
create table sec0613 as
select distinct *
from sec0612b;
```

Access SQL

```
select distinct *
into sec0613
from sec0612b;
```

Beginning table (`sec0612b` table)

```
FIRST_NAME LAST_NAME   ADDRESS
---------- ----------  -----------------
SUSAN      BROWN       512 ELM STREET   ❶
JIM        KERN        837-9TH AVENUE
MARTHA     WOODS       169 PARK AVENUE
SUSAN      BROWN       512 ELM STREET   ❶
ELLEN      OWENS       418 HENRY STREET
```

Result table (`sec0613` table)

```
FIRST_NAME LAST_NAME   ADDRESS
---------- ----------  -------------------
ELLEN      OWENS       418 HENRY STREET
JIM        KERN        837-9TH AVENUE
MARTHA     WOODS       169 PARK AVENUE
SUSAN      BROWN       512 ELM STREET   ❶
```

Notes

❶ The beginning table has a set of two duplicate rows. The result table contains just one of the rows from this set.

6-14 How to distinguish between duplicate rows

Suppose you have a table containing duplicate rows and you consider each of these rows to represent a separate object. You can change this table to distinguish between the duplicate rows by adding a new column of meaningful data to the table. For example, you could add a `date_purchased` column to the first table in section 6-12. This would show that the two hamburgers were purchased on different dates. The two rows for hamburgers would thus no longer be duplicates.

There are no duplicate rows in this table (`sec0614a` table)

```
OBJECT_BOUGHT              PRICE  DATE_PURCHA
--------------------    --------  -----------
NEWSPAPER                 $0.75   14-JUN-2010
COFFEE                    $1.55   14-JUN-2010
HAMBURGER                 $2.00   14-JUN-2010
FLOWERS                  $15.38   14-JUN-2010
HAMBURGER                 $2.00   15-JUN-2010
BOOK                     $24.89   15-JUN-2010
MOVIE TICKETS            $22.00   15-JUN-2010
```

Although it is best to add a new column of meaningful data, this may require a lot of work. Another method is commonly used, which adds a column of numbers to the table. Each row is given a distinct number, ensuring that there will no longer be any duplicate rows in the table. This method is shown next.

Why would you want to distinguish between duplicate rows? For example, you might have four rows that are identical, but you only want to have three of them.

Task

Distinguish between the duplicate rows of the `sec0612a` table by adding a column of numbers to the table. Make this the first column of the table.

Oracle SQL

```
drop table sec0614b;
create table sec0614b as ❶
select rownum as row_id, ❷
       object_bought,
       price
from sec0612a;
```

Access SQL

```
select *
into sec0614c ❸
from sec0612a;

alter table sec0614c
add column row_id counter; ❹

select row_id, ❺
       object_bought,
       price
into sec0614b
from sec0614c;
```

Beginning table (sec0612a table)

```
OBJECT_BOUGHT            PRICE
-------------------- --------
NEWSPAPER                $0.75
COFFEE                   $1.55
HAMBURGER                $2.00
FLOWERS                 $15.38
HAMBURGER                $2.00
BOOK                    $24.89
MOVIE TICKETS           $22.00
```

Ending table (sec0614b table)

```
  ROW_ID OBJECT_BOUGHT            PRICE
--------- -------------------- --------
        1 NEWSPAPER                $0.75
        2 COFFEE                   $1.55
        3 HAMBURGER                $2.00
        4 FLOWERS                 $15.38
        5 HAMBURGER                $2.00
        6 BOOK                    $24.89
        7 MOVIE TICKETS           $22.00
```

Notes

❶ In Oracle, when you add a column of numbers to a table, you can create either a new table or a new view.

❷ In Oracle, `rownum` generates the row numbers. It is a 0-parameter function that can be used within a `select` statement.

❸ In Access, when you add a column of numbers to a table, you must create a new table. You cannot create a new view because the `alter table` statement only works with tables.

❹ In Access, `counter` generates the row numbers. It is a sequence generator that is handled as a datatype. To add it to a table you must use an `alter table` statement, which will place the `row_id` column at the end of this table.

❺ This places the `row_id` column as the first column of the table, which is one of the requirements of this task.

Loading a Large Amount of Data from a Flat File

The `insert` statement is fine for adding a single row or even a moderate number of rows to a table. If you want to add a large number of rows to a table, this is easier to do if you put the data into a flat file. By a *flat file* I mean just an ordinary file with no special structure. You can create a flat file using Notepad or your favorite text editor.

It is also possible to place your data in a spreadsheet or in some other type of structured file, and then load the data into the table of your database. Many options are available. However, in my opinion, the most reliable method is putting your data into a flat file.

In Oracle, we use the Load utility to load data from a flat file. In Access, we use a wizard, which we can start with

File ➜ Get External Data ➜ Import

6-15 The SQL*Loader in Oracle

In Oracle we use a utility program called SQL*Loader to put data from a flat file into a table. This is called a *utility* because it is run from the operating system level, rather than from some Oracle environment, such as SQLplus. You can find additional information in the Oracle documentation, within the Utilities manual.

Two files are required to run the loader: a Control file and a BAT file. The Control file contains instructions about how to load the data and it also contains the data. In the following code, the data for each column is in a fixed position and the Control file specifies what those positions are. It specifies the format of the dates. It also indicates whether to add the data to the rows currently in the table or replace all of them. Those options are:

Append	Add the data to the rows already in the table.
Insert	Only add the data if there are no rows in the table.
Replace	Replace all the current data with the new data.

The BAT file is a DOS batch file that contains commands to the DOS level of the operating system. It invokes the SQL*Loader program and tells it to load the data in the Control file. It also specifies several output files. To the computer, this command is one long line of code. I have divided it into several lines using the ^ symbol, which is the line continuation sign within a BAT file.

The BAT file invokes the Load utility with the SQLLDR.EXE command. This is followed by several optional parameters:

Input files:

Control	The name of the Control file.

Output files:

Log	A report of the result of the load.
Bad	Records that could not be loaded.

Frequency of `commit` operations:

Rows	How many rows to `commit` at a time. For example, suppose you are loading 1,000 rows of data into a table. ROWS 50 means that a `commit` is performed each time 50 rows have been loaded.

There are many other options that can be set in the Control file and BAT file. For example, people often want to separate the data from the Control file. The documentation contains reference material for all the options and also many examples of load procedures. You can find this material on your online documentation CD-ROM. Follow the path:

Oracle Server → Oracle Utilities → SQL*Loader

In the following example, note that blank spaces in the data are automatically converted into nulls.

Task

Create a new copy of the 1_employees table and load data into it using SQL*Loader. Use data with fixed positions.
   I take you through this process step by step.

Oracle SQL:
Step 1 — Create a new table without any data in it

```
-- create a second copy of the employees table

drop table 1_employees_2 cascade constraints;

create table 1_employees_2
(employee_id      number(3)
,first_name       varchar2(10)
,last_name        varchar2(10)
,dept_code        varchar2(3)
,hire_date        date
,credit_limit     number(4,2)
,phone_number     varchar2(4)
,manager_id       number(3)
);
```

Result message

```
Table created.
```

Step 2 — Optional: Verify that the table has been created

```
select * from l_employees_2;
```

Result message

```
No rows selected.
```

Step 3 — Optional: Find the names of the columns in the new table

```
describe l_employees_2;
```

Result message

```
Name
-------------------
EMPLOYEE_ID
FIRST_NAME
LAST_NAME
DEPT_CODE
HIRE_DATE
CREDIT_LIMIT
PHONE_NUMBER
MANAGER_ID
```

Step 4 — Position the files that will load data into the table

The files to load the data are on the CD-ROM. Move them into your c:\temp directory. The code in these files is shown below. The files are

Sec0615.bat
Sec0615_load_data.ctl

Here is the Sec0615.bat file ❶:

```
sqlldr.exe ^ ❷
control = 'c:\temp\sec0615_load_data.ctl' ^ ❸
log = 'c:\temp\sec0615_log.txt' ^ ❹
bad = 'c:\temp\sec0615_bad.txt' ^ ❺
rows = 50 ❻
```

Here is the Sec0615_load_data.ctl file ❼:

```
load data
infile *
append

into table l_employees_2
(employee_id   position(01:03),
first_name     position(05:14),
last_name      position(16:25),
dept_code      position(27:29)  ,
hire_date      position(32:42) date(11)  "dd-mon-yyyy",❽
credit_limit   position(46:50),
phone_number   position(52:55),
manager_id     position(63:65))

BEGINDATA
201 SUSAN     BROWN     EXE   01-JUN-1998   30.00 3484      ❾
202 JIM       KERN      SAL   16-AUG-1999   25.00 8722   201
203 MARTHA    WOODS     SHP   02-FEB-2004   25.00 7591   201
204 ELLEN     OWENS     SAL   01-JUL-2003   15.00 6830   202
205 HENRY     PERKINS   SAL   01-MAR-2000   25.00 5286   202
206 CAROL     ROSE      ACT                                  ❾
207 DAN       SMITH     SHP   01-DEC-2004   25.00 2259   203
208 FRED      CAMPBELL  SHP   01-APR-2003   25.00 1752   203
209 PAULA     JACOBS    MKT   17-MAR-1999   15.00 3357   201
210 NANCY     HOFFMAN   SAL   16-FEB-2004   25.00 2974   203
```

Notes

❶ A BAT file is a command file within the DOS operating system.

❷ In a BAT file, ^ is used for line continuation. It means that the next line is a continuation of the present line. The computer looks at this entire BAT file as if it is a single line of code. If you do not use ^, you must write all the parameters on a single line.

SQLLDR.EXE is the name of the file for the Oracle SQL*Loader. This is the program that runs. Everything else in this BAT file is a parameter that is passed to the Loader program.

❸ The Control file contains the data and the instructions for loading the data. It is an input file.

❹ The Log file is an output file, and will contain messages from the load.

❺ The Bad file is an output file, and will contain any rejected data.

❻ This tells the loader to do a `commit` each time it has loaded 50 rows.

❼ This is the Control file. It contains the data and instructions to load the data.

❽ We must specify the format of the date in the data. `Date(11)` means that the date will be at most 11 characters long.

❾ To enter nulls, just leave blanks in the data.

Step 5 — Run the BAT file. This loads the data into the table.

1. In Windows:

   Start → Run

2. Enter the name of the BAT file, as shown in the following screen.

   `c:\temp\sec0615.bat`

3. Press OK.

4. You will be prompted to enter your Oracle userid and password, as seen in the following screen. This runs the BAT file, which starts the Oracle SQL*Loader and passes the Control file to it. Then this DOS window will close.

```
C:\WINDOWS\System32\cmd.exe                                              _ □ X

C:\temp>sqlldr.exe control = 'c:\temp\sec0615_load_data.ctl' log = 'c:\temp\sec0
615_log.txt' bad = 'c:\temp\sec0615_bad.txt' discard = 'c:\temp\sec0615_discard.
txt' rows = 50                                                        0
Username:sqlfun
Password:_
```

Result file

c:\temp\sec0615_log.txt

Step 6 — Check the messages in the Log file

Here is the part of the Log file that you need to check.

Sec0615_log file:

```
Table L_EMPLOYEES_2:
  10 Rows successfully loaded. ❶
  0 Rows not loaded due to data errors.
  0 Rows not loaded because all WHEN clauses were failed.
  0 Rows not loaded because all fields were null.


Total logical records skipped:          0
Total logical records read:             10 ❶
Total logical records rejected:          0
Total logical records discarded:         0
```

Notes

❶ This says that 10 rows of data were read and they all were loaded.

Oracle SQL: Step 7 — Examine the table

```
select * from l_employees_2;
```

Result table

EMPLOYEE ID	FIRST NAME	LAST NAME	DEPT CODE	HIRE_DATE	CREDIT LIMIT	PHONE NUMBER	MANAGER ID
201	SUSAN	BROWN	EXE	01-JUN-1998	$30.00	3484	(null)
202	JIM	KERN	SAL	16-AUG-1999	$25.00	8722	201
203	MARTHA	WOODS	SHP	02-FEB-2004	$25.00	7591	201
204	ELLEN	OWENS	SAL	01-JUL-2003	$15.00	6830	202
205	HENRY	PERKINS	SAL	01-MAR-2000	$25.00	5286	202
206	CAROL	ROSE	ACT	(null)	(null)	(null)	(null)
207	DAN	SMITH	SHP	01-DEC-2004	$25.00	2259	203
208	FRED	CAMPBELL	SHP	01-APR-2003	$25.00	1752	203
209	PAULA	JACOBS	MKT	17-MAR-1999	$15.00	3357	201
210	NANCY	HOFFMAN	SAL	16-FEB-2004	$25.00	2974	203

6-16 Loading delimited data in Oracle

In the previous section, the exact position of each field needed to be specified. Using delimited data is often more convenient because you do not have to keep the data perfectly aligned in the right columns. This section provides an example of that method. I show you just the files. All the steps of the procedure are the same as in the previous section.

We must choose some character that does not occur in the data to be the delimiter. Here we are using a comma, which is placed between every two fields. It marks the end of one field and the beginning of another. Usually the data is all pushed together with no blanks between the fields.

Task

Create a new copy of the `l_employees` table and load data into it using SQL*Loader. Use data delimited with commas.

Oracle SQL: Step 1 — Create the table without any data in it

```
-- create a third copy of the employees table

drop table l_employees_3 cascade constraints;

create table l_employees_3
(employee_id      number(3)
,first_name       varchar2(10)
,last_name        varchar2(10)
,dept_code        varchar2(3)
,hire_date        date
,credit_limit     number(4,2)
,phone_number     varchar2(4)
,manager_id       number(3)
);
```

Files for SQL*Loader

You can get these files from the CD-ROM and put them in the c:\temp directory. Or you can create these files yourself using Notepad.

Here is the Sec0616.bat file:

```
sqlldr.exe ^
control = 'c:\temp\sec0616_load_data.ctl' ^
log = 'c:\temp\sec0616_log.txt' ^
bad = 'c:\temp\sec0616_bad.txt' ^
rows = 50
```

Here is the Sec0616_load_data.ctl file:

```
load data
infile *
append

into table l_employees_3
fields terminated by "," optionally enclosed by '"'   ❶
(employee_id,   ❷
first_name,
last_name,
dept_code,
hire_date date(20)   "dd-mon-yyyy",
credit_limit,
phone_number,
manager_id)

BEGINDATA
201,SUSAN,BROWN,EXE,01-JUN-1998,30.00,3484,              ❸
202,JIM,KERN,SAL,16-AUG-1999,25.00,8722,201
203,MARTHA,WOODS,SHP,02-FEB-2004,25.00,7591,201
204,ELLEN,OWENS,SAL,01-JUL-2003,15.00,6830,202
205,HENRY,PERKINS,SAL,01-MAR-2000,25.00,5286,202
206,CAROL,ROSE,ACT,,,,                                   ❸
207,DAN,SMITH,SHP,01-DEC-2004,25.00,2259,203
208,FRED,CAMPBELL,SHP,01-APR-2003,25.00,1752,203
209,PAULA,JACOBS,MKT,17-MAR-1999,15.00,3357,201
210,NANCY,HOFFMAN,SAL,16-FEB-2004,25.00,2974,203
```

Ending table (`1_employees_3` table)

EMPLOYEE ID	FIRST_NAME	LAST_NAME	DEPT CODE	HIRE_DATE	CREDIT LIMIT	PHONE NUMBER	MANAGER ID
201	SUSAN	BROWN	EXE	01-JUN-1998	$30.00	3484	(null)
202	JIM	KERN	SAL	16-AUG-1999	$25.00	8722	201
203	MARTHA	WOODS	SHP	02-FEB-2004	$25.00	7591	201
204	ELLEN	OWENS	SAL	01-JUL-2003	$15.00	6830	202
205	HENRY	PERKINS	SAL	01-MAR-2000	$25.00	5286	202
206	CAROL	ROSE	ACT	(null)	(null)	(null)	(null)
207	DAN	SMITH	SHP	01-DEC-2004	$25.00	2259	203
208	FRED	CAMPBELL	SHP	01-APR-2003	$25.00	1752	203
209	PAULA	JACOBS	MKT	17-MAR-1999	$15.00	3357	201
210	NANCY	HOFFMAN	SAL	16-FEB-2004	$25.00	2974	203

Notes

❶ This line says that the delimiter between columns is a comma.

❷ You do not need to code exact positions for the data, which you had to do in section 6-15.

❸ Nulls are placed in the data here. All the commas are still required.

6-17 `Analyze table` in Oracle

After you load data into a table in Oracle, run the `analyze table` command. This tells the Data Dictionary how many rows are in the table and other information. This information is used by the Optimizer to improve the processing of your `select` statements. Without this information in the Data Dictionary, the processing will not be as efficient.

Task

Tell the Oracle Data Dictionary how many rows are in the `1_employees_2` table and also put other statistics about the table into the dictionary.

Oracle SQL

```
analyze table 1_employees_2 compute statistics;
```

6-18 File import in Access

Access is also able to load data from a flat file. It uses a wizard to gather much of the information that is contained in the Oracle Control file, so only the data is needed in the flat file. The following example shows the data fields in fixed positions. Delimited data can also be handled by Access. To start the wizard, use

File ➜ Get External Data ➜ Import

Create a new copy of the 1_employees table and load data into it using File Import. Use data with a fixed position.

Access SQL:
Step 1 — Create the table without any data in it

```
drop table l_employees_2 cascade;

create table l_employees_2
(employee_id        smallint
,first_name         varchar(10)
,last_name          varchar(10)
,dept_code          varchar(3)
,hire_date          datetime
,credit_limit       money
,phone_number       varchar(4)
,manager_id         smallint
);
```

Step 2 — Access data file

Create this file using Notepad. Name it c:\temp\sec0618_load_data.txt. Do not paste it into the SQL window in Access. This file is used by the wizard later. You can also find it on the CD-ROM in the file Access\Chapter6\sec0618_data_to_load.txt.

```
201 SUSAN    BROWN     EXE  01-JUN-1998  30.00 3484
202 JIM      KERN      SAL  16-AUG-1999  25.00 8722  201
203 MARTHA   WOODS     SHP  02-FEB-2004  25.00 7591  201
204 ELLEN    OWENS     SAL  01-JUL-2003  15.00 6830  202
205 HENRY    PERKINS   SAL  01-MAR-2000  25.00 5286  202
206 CAROL    ROSE      ACT
207 DAN      SMITH     SHP  01-DEC-2004  25.00 2259  203
208 FRED     CAMPBELL  SHP  01-APR-2003  25.00 1752  203
209 PAULA    JACOBS    MKT  17-MAR-1999  15.00 3357  201
210 NANCY    HOFFMAN   SAL  16-FEB-2004  25.00 2974  203
```

Access wizard procedure

Step 1:
> File → Get External Data → Import
> Choose the file containing the data.
> Click Import.
> This brings up the following screen.

Step 2:
Click Advanced.
Change the Date Format to DMY.
This brings up the following screen.

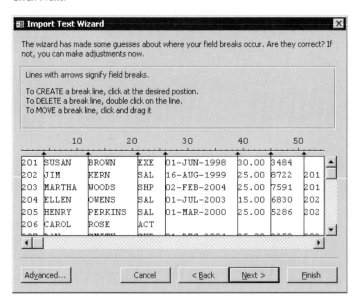

Step 3:
Click OK.
Click Next.

Step 4:
Click Next.
Select the name of the table.

Step 5:
Click Finish.
Click OK to the information message.
Open the table.

employee_id	first_name	last_name	dept_code	hire_date	credit_limit	phone_number	manager_id
201	SUSAN	BROWN	EXE	6/1/1998	$30.00	3484	
202	JIM	KERN	SAL	8/16/1999	$25.00	8722	201
203	MARTHA	WOODS	SHP	2/2/2004	$25.00	7591	201
204	ELLEN	OWENS	SAL	7/1/2003	$15.00	6830	202
205	HENRY	PERKINS	SAL	3/1/2000	$25.00	5286	202
206	CAROL	ROSE	ACT				
207	DAN	SMITH	SHP	12/1/2004	$25.00	2259	203
208	FRED	CAMPBELL	SHP	4/1/2003	$25.00	1752	203
209	PAULA	JACOBS	MKT	3/17/1999	$15.00	3357	201
210	NANCY	HOFFMAN	SAL	2/16/2004	$25.00	2974	203

Record: 11 of 11

Summary

In this chapter we got down to the nuts and bolts of how a table is constructed. We discussed how to build a table by naming each column and giving it a datatype. You are now able to construct any table you want and put data into it.

You saw ways of changing a table even after it has a lot of data in it. In a relational database, a table is a very flexible structure. It can adapt easily to changing requirements and keep pace with our evolving understanding of a problem we are trying to solve.

Primary keys are important in tables that are shared with other people. A primary key prevents the table from having duplicate rows that can make data unclear.

Data can be loaded from a flat file. This method is often preferred when a large number of rows are added to a table. There are many options and variations available with this technique.

Exercises

1. Goal: Create a new table. Define each of its columns. Include at least one text, date, and numeric column.

   a. Build a table to track the basketball games of the Boston Celtics.

   Oracle SQL

   ```
   drop table boston_celtics_games;
   create table boston_celtics_games
   (game_id         number,
   game_date        date,
   opponent         varchar2(30),
   celtics_score   number,
   opponent_score number,
   game_duration   number);
   ```

   Access SQL

   ```
   drop table boston_celtics_games;
   create table boston_celtics_games
   (game_id         smallint,
   game_date        datetime,
   opponent         varchar(30),
   celtics_score   byte,
   opponent_score byte,
   game_duration   smallint);
   ```

   b. Build a table of your favorite songs. Include a song ID, the name of the song, the performer, and the duration of the song. You may include other columns if you wish.

2. Goal: Load data into the table from a flat file.

    a. Load data into the table of basketball games we created in exercise 1a. Note that the opponents are enclosed in double quotes. This is a good practice whenever the data for a column contains spaces.

Oracle data file

```
load data
infile *
append

into table boston_celtics_games
fields terminated by "," optionally enclosed by '"'
(game_id,
game_date  date(20)   "dd-mon-yyyy",
opponent,
celtics_score,
opponent_score,
game_duration)

BEGINDATA
1, 03-NOV-2007, "NEW YORK KNICKS", 99, 98, 132
2, 07-NOV-2007, "LOS ANGELES LAKERS", 108, 101, 140
3, 12-NOV-2007, "GOLDEN STATE WARRIORS", 97, 94, 118
4, 17-NOV-2007, "MIAMI HEAT", 103, 99, 116
5, 23-NOV-2007, "CHICAGO BULLS", 107, 103, 145
6, 28-NOV-2007, "HOUSTON ROCKETS", 102, 99, 121
```

Oracle BAT file

```
sqlldr.exe ^
control = 'c:\temp\ex0602a_load_data.ctl' ^
log = 'c:\temp\ex0602a_log.txt' ^
bad = 'c:\temp\ex0602a_bad.txt' ^
rows = 50
```

Access data file

```
1, 03-NOV-2007, "NEW YORK KNICKS", 99, 98, 132
2, 07-NOV-2007, "LOS ANGELES LAKERS", 108, 101, 140
3, 12-NOV-2007, "GOLDEN STATE WARRIORS", 97, 94, 118
4, 17-NOV-2007, "MIAMI HEAT", 103, 99, 116
5, 23-NOV-2007, "CHICAGO BULLS", 107, 103, 145
6, 28-NOV-2007, "HOUSTON ROCKETS", 102, 99, 121
```

Note: To use this, change the Date Format to DMY, within Advanced Options.

b. Load data for at least five of your favorite songs into the table you created in exercise 1b.

3. Goal: Add a primary key to a table.

a. In the `boston_celtics_games` table, make the `game_id` column the primary key.

Oracle & Access SQL

```
alter table boston_celtics_games
add constraint pk_bc_games
primary key (game_id);
```

b. Make a primary key for your table of favorite songs.

4. Goal: Add a new column to the table.

    a. Add a new column of `game_comments` to the basketball table we created in exercise 1a. In Oracle, make it a variable-length text string with a maximum length of 2,000 characters. In Access, make it a `longtext` field.

Oracle SQL

```
alter table boston_celtics_games
add game_comments varchar2(2000);
```

Access SQL

```
alter table boston_celtics_games
add column game_comments longtext;
```

---

    b. Add a new column, `album_name`, to the table of favorite songs that you created in exercise 1a.

5. Goal: Put a value into the new column in one of the rows of the table.

    a. Add the game comment "This game was down to the wire." to row 3 of the `boston_celtics_games` table. In Oracle SQLplus, format the `game_comments` column to be 31 characters wide.

Oracle & Access SQL

```
update boston_celtics_games
set game_comments = 'This game was down to the wire.'
where game_id = 3;
```

---

    b. Add the `album_name` to two of the rows in your table of `favorite_songs`. Do this with two `update` statements.

    In Oracle SQLplus, format the `album_name` column to display a text string with a maximum length of 20 characters.

6. Goal: Add one new row to the table using an `insert` statement.

a. Add a new row to the `boston_celtics_games` table.

Oracle & Access SQL

```
insert into boston_celtics_games
values(7, '05-dec-2007', 'alaska huskies', 98,
105, 131, 'first game in alaska');
```

Note: This code works in Access, even though the date is enclosed within single quotes rather than pound signs. In some cases, this works in Access. However, at other times it can get you into trouble, so it is better to always write your code in Access with pound signs enclosing the dates.

Access SQL

```
insert into boston_celtics_games
values(7, #05-dec-2007#, 'alaska huskies', 98,
105, 131, 'first game in alaska');
```

---

b. Add a new row to your table of `favorite_songs`.

chapter 7

Formats, Sequences, and Indexes

You now know how to build your own tables and put data in them. This chapter discusses some other features you may want to add to your tables.

Formats affect the appearance of the data without changing its value. In Access, formats can be part of the definition of a table. In Oracle, they are used mostly within SQL statements to format dates. In Oracle, text fields and numeric fields are usually formatted on the SQLplus level, which we discussed in chapter 5.

Sequences provide a way to automatically number the rows of a table. Indexes are used mostly to speed up the processing of `select` statements within large databases.

This chapter also discusses the Data Dictionary, which shows you how to find information about the tables you create.

Formats

People often confuse formats with functions. A *format* refers to the way a value is presented. For instance, "01-jan-10" and "January 1, 2010" are two formats for the same date. A function makes a change to the value. For instance, "01-jan-10 + 1" is "January 2, 2010".

7-1   Formats of dates

In both Oracle and Access, dates and times are stored together within a single datatype. Whenever you see a date, there is always a time stored with it. Whenever you see a time, there is always a date stored with it.

Inside the database a date is stored in a very compressed manner. If you saw one directly, you would not know what it was. When a date is displayed in a result table, it is always translated into a character string, such as "Jan 1, 2010", so that you can understand it. Several different translations are available. Another one is "2010-01-01". The date format you specify tells the database how you want the dates to be displayed. If you do not specify a date format, the default date format is used.

In this section we discuss how to specify a format that is different than the default date format. In the following two sections, you will see how these formats can be applied to display dates in particular ways and how to enter times with dates.

The following table shows some of the most useful date formats. These can be combined together in any way you wish. These are used both for displaying dates and entering dates into tables.

In Oracle, there is one default format for dates. It is usually set to `dd-mon-yy`, which shows dates in the format 20-JAN-10 with a two-digit year. In the SQLFUN_LOGIN script, I change this default format to `dd-mon-yyyy` with a four-digit year. Whatever the default format is, if you want to display or enter dates in any other format, you must explicitly state what format you are using. In Oracle, dates and times are enclosed in single quotes. This is similar to text strings.

In Access, when you enter a date, you enclose it in pound signs (##) to set it apart from a text string. Access knows it is a date by the pound signs, and will attempt to automatically determine what format this date is in. Access can accept a date in many formats.

In Access, the default format for displaying a date is set by the Windows operating system, using the Regional Settings in the Windows Control Panel.

Oracle and Access date formats.

Oracle Format	Access Format	Example	Comment
YEAR			
yyyy	yyyy	1998	Four-digit year
yy	yy	98	Two-digit year
MONTH			
month	mmmm	October	Full name of the month
mon	mmm	Oct	Abbreviated name of the month
mm	mm	10	Number of the month, 01 to 12
DAY			
dd	dd	18	Date of the month, 01 to 31
day	dddd	Friday	Full name of the day
dy	ddd	Fri	Abbreviated name of the day
d	w	6	Numeric day of the week: 1 is Sunday, 2 is Monday, 7 is Saturday
TIME			
hh24	hh	14	24-hour time, 00 to 23
hh12	hh am/pm	02	12-hour time, 00 to 11
hh	hh am/pm	02	12-hour time, 00 to 11
mi	nn	30	Minute after the hour, 00 to 59
ss	ss	59	Second, 00 to 59
am	am/pm		AM or PM, whichever one applies
pm	am/pm		AM or PM, whichever one applies
OTHER			
q	q	4	Quarter of the year, 1 to 4
ww	ww	45	Week of the year, 1 to 54
JULIAN			
ddd	y	350	Number of days since January 1
j			Number of days since Dec 31, 4713 BC
sssss			Number of seconds since midnight Used to calculate with times

Some combinations of date formats.

mm-dd-yyyy hh:mi:ss am	mm-dd-yyyy hh:nn:ss am/pm	10-18-1998 05:36:45 PM
mm-dd-yyyy hh:mi am	mm-dd-yyyy hh:nn am/pm	10-18-1998 05:36 PM
day, month dd, yyyy	dddd, mmmm dd, yyyy	Sunday, October 18, 1998
dd-mon-yy	dd-mmm-yy	18-Oct-98
mm-dd-yyyy	mm-dd-yyyy	10-18-1998
hh:mi:ss am	hh:nn:ss am/pm	05:36:45 PM
hh:mi am	hh:nn am/pm	05:36 PM
hh24:mi	hh:nn	17:36

7-2   Displaying formatted dates

In Oracle, the `to_char` function specifies the format to use when displaying a date. `To_char` means that we are converting a date datatype into a character datatype so it can be displayed. In Access, the `format` function is used the same way.

These functions have two parameters. The first is the name of the column containing the dates. The second is the format to be used in displaying the date. The format specification must be enclosed in single quotes. It is possible to add text to the format, such as "In the year of". This text must be enclosed in double quotes.

Task

From the `l_employees` table, list the `employee_id`, `first_name`, and `hire_date` of all the employees. Add another column showing the hire date formatted in the form `mm-dd-yyyy` followed by the time. Sort the rows of the result by the `employee_id`.

Oracle SQL

```
column formatted_date format a20; ❶

select employee_id,
       first_name,
       hire_date,
       to_char(hire_date, 'mm-dd-yyyy hh:mi am') ❷
                          as formatted_date ❹
from l_employees
order by employee_id;
```

Access SQL

```
select employee_id,
       first_name,
       hire_date,
       format(hire_date, 'mm-dd-yyyy hh:nn am/pm') ❸
                          as formatted_date ❹
from l_employees
order by employee_id;
```

Beginning table (`l_employees` table)

EMPLOYEE ID	FIRST_NAME	LAST_NAME	DEPT CODE	HIRE_DATE	CREDIT LIMIT	PHONE NUMBER	MANAGER ID
201	SUSAN	BROWN	EXE	01-JUN-1998	$30.00	3484	(null)
202	JIM	KERN	SAL	16-AUG-1999	$25.00	8722	201
203	MARTHA	WOODS	SHP	02-FEB-2004	$25.00	7591	201
204	ELLEN	OWENS	SAL	01-JUL-2003	$15.00	6830	202
205	HENRY	PERKINS	SAL	01-MAR-2000	$25.00	5286	202
206	CAROL	ROSE	ACT	(null)	(null)	(null)	(null)
207	DAN	SMITH	SHP	01-DEC-2004	$25.00	2259	203
208	FRED	CAMPBELL	SHP	01-APR-2003	$25.00	1752	203
209	PAULA	JACOBS	MKT	17-MAR-1999	$15.00	3357	201
210	NANCY	HOFFMAN	SAL	16-FEB-2004	$25.00	2974	203

Result table ❺

```
EMPLOYEE
      ID FIRST_NAME HIRE_DATE     FORMATTED_DATE
-------- ---------- ------------- --------------------
     201 SUSAN      01-JUN-1998   06-01-1998 12:00 AM
     202 JIM        16-AUG-1999   08-16-1999 12:00 AM
     203 MARTHA     02-FEB-2004   02-02-2004 12:00 AM
     204 ELLEN      01-JUL-2003   07-01-2003 12:00 AM
     205 HENRY      01-MAR-2000   03-01-2000 12:00 AM
     206 CAROL      (null)        (null)
     207 DAN        01-DEC-2004   12-01-2004 12:00 AM
     208 FRED       01-APR-2003   04-01-2003 12:00 AM
     209 PAULA      17-MAR-1999   03-17-1999 12:00 AM
     210 NANCY      16-FEB-2004   02-16-2004 12:00 AM
```

Notes

❶ This is an SQLplus command that sets the format of the `formatted_date` column in Oracle. It sets the width of the column to 20 characters.

❷ In Oracle, the `to_char` function is used to control the format in which a date is displayed. The second parameter is the Oracle date format you want to use. It is enclosed in single quotes.

The `to_char` function is used, not the `to_date` function. When a date is stored in the database, it has a date datatype. You want to change the format to a text datatype, so that it can be displayed.

❸ In Access, the `format` function is used to control the format in which a date will be displayed. The second parameter is the Access date format you want to use. It is enclosed in single quotes.

❹ `as formatted_date` creates a column alias for the previous line. I would write it as part of that line if I had room to do so. I created the column alias on the next line and indented it to the far right to show that it is a continuation of the preceding line.

❺ The data in the table show that all the formatted dates have 12:00 a.m. (midnight) as their time. This is the default time that is set in Oracle and Access when no specific time is entered.

7-3   Entering formatted dates

This section shows you how to enter a time when you enter a date. All dates in SQL include a time, but the time is automatically set to midnight unless you enter a different time.

In Oracle, the DBAs have selected one default date format, which usually does not show the time. If you want to enter a time with a date, you must use the `to_date` function. It changes the text you enter for the date into a date datatype that can be stored in the database. This function has two parameters enclosed in single quotes. The first parameter is a character string, which expresses the date and the time. The second parameter tells Oracle how to format the first string into a date datatype. It gives the date format of the first parameter. The `to_date` function changes the character string you entered into a date with a time.

In Access the process is much simpler. You just enclose the date and time in pound signs, showing that what you enter is a date. Access will determine the format automatically.

Task

Insert a new row into the `1_lunches` table. Use the data:

```
lunch_id = 25
lunch_date = December 5, 2005 at 11:30 a.m.
employee_id = 202
date_entered = (use the current date and time)
```

Use a date format, if needed, to enter the date.

Oracle SQL

```
insert into 1_lunches
values (25,
to_date('12-05-2005 11:30 am','mm-dd-yyyy hh:mi am'), ❶
202, sysdate); ❷
```

Access SQL

```
insert into 1_lunches
values (25, #dec 5 2005 11:30 am#, ❸
202, now()); ❹
```

Beginning table (1_lunches table)

```
            LUNCH         EMPLOYEE
  LUNCH_ID  DATE                ID DATE_ENTERE
  --------- ------------- -------- -----------
         1  16-NOV-2005        201 13-OCT-2005
         2  16-NOV-2005        207 13-OCT-2005
         3  16-NOV-2005        203 13-OCT-2005
         4  16-NOV-2005        204 13-OCT-2005
         6  16-NOV-2005        202 13-OCT-2005
         7  16-NOV-2005        210 13-OCT-2005
         8  25-NOV-2005        201 14-OCT-2005
         9  25-NOV-2005        208 14-OCT-2005
        12  25-NOV-2005        204 14-OCT-2005
        13  25-NOV-2005        207 18-OCT-2005
        15  25-NOV-2005        205 21-OCT-2005
        16  05-DEC-2005        201 21-OCT-2005
        17  05-DEC-2005        210 21-OCT-2005
        20  05-DEC-2005        205 24-OCT-2005
        21  05-DEC-2005        203 24-OCT-2005
        22  05-DEC-2005        208 24-OCT-2005
```

New row ❺

```
        25  05-DEC-2005        202 17-JUN-2005
```

Notes

❶ In Oracle, we use the `to_date` function to enter dates into tables. The date you write in an SQL statement is text because it is enclosed in single quotes. You need to change the text string into a date datatype to store it in the table. The `to_date` function does this.

Dates can be entered in any format, but the specific format of the text data must be explicitly specified. A time can be entered along with a date if the format includes a time.

If a time is entered, it is permanently stored in the table. However, it will only be displayed when it is explicitly requested. Dates containing times can cause errors if the users are not aware that the times are contained in the data.

❷ In Oracle, `sysdate` gives you the current date and time.

❸ In Access, a date is surrounded by pound signs (##), indicating that you want to enter a date. Most date formats are recognized automatically by Access. Their format does not need to be explicitly declared.

It is best to avoid ambiguous date formats. For example, does #7/4/99# mean April 7 or July 4? The meaning in America is different from the meaning in Europe.

❹ In Access, now() gives you the current date and time.

❺ The time, 11:30 a.m., is present in the data, even though it is not displayed.

To restore the data to its original form

In Oracle:

```
rollback;
```

In Access, delete the rows you added in this section. To do this, highlight them and press the Delete key.

7-4   Other formats in Oracle

In Oracle, there are also formats for text and number fields. These are set within SQLplus, and not on the SQL level (see section 5-5).

7-5   Formats in Access

In Access, the format of a column is often specified in the field properties of the table design. It can also be specified within a select query using the format function. In addition to date formats, there are also formats for numbers, text, and yes/no datatypes.

Access offers a greater variety of formats than Oracle does. There are two types of formats: predefined formats, which are ready-made for you and have names, and custom formats, which you specify yourself. A reference to all these formats is available in the Format Property Help.

In the example below, I created a custom format for the phone_number column, which has a text datatype. The format is:

```
"(415) 643-"@@@@
```

The characters within double quotes will be added as a literal value to each phone number. The @ represents a single character from the data in the phone_number column.

Oracle can also display the phone numbers this way, but it uses a different method. In Oracle, we could code a literal into the select statement and concatenate it to the phone number. For more details see section 9-12.

Task

Format the phone_number column entries of the l_employees table. Give each phone number the area code (415) and the prefix 643-. Show two methods of doing this in Access: a GUI method and an SQL method. In the SQL, show the employee_id, first_name, last_name, and the formatted phone_number columns.

Access GUI: Set field properties in the table design ❶

🖽 L_Employees : Table			
Field Name	**Data Type**	**Description**	
🔑 Employee_id	Number		
First_name	Text		
Last_name	Text		
Dept_code	Text		
Hire_date	Date/Time		
Credit_limit	Currency		
Phone_number	Text		
Manager_id	Number		

Field Properties

General | Lookup |

Field Size	4
Format	"(415) 643-"@@@@
Input Mask	
Caption	
Default Value	
Validation Rule	
Validation Text	
Required	No
Allow Zero Length	No
Indexed	No
Unicode Compression	Yes

The display layout for the field. Select a pre-defined format or enter a custom format. Press F1 for help on formats.

Access SQL: Use the `format` function

```
select employee_id,
       first_name,
       last_name,
       format(a.phone_number, '"(415) 643-"@@@@') ❷
                                  as phone_number ❸

from 1_employees a; ❹
```

Result table

employee_id	first_name	last_name	phone_number
201	Susan	Brown	(415) 643-3484
202	Jim	Kern	(415) 643-8722
203	Martha	Woods	(415) 643-7591
204	Ellen	Owens	(415) 643-6830
205	Henry	Perkins	(415) 643-5286
206	Carol	Rose	
207	Dan	Smith	(415) 643-2259
208	Fred	Campbell	(415) 643-1752
209	Paula	Jacobs	(415) 643-3357
210	Nancy	Hoffman	(415) 643-2974

Record: 11 of 11

Notes

❶ This screen is the `Design` view of the `1_employees` table. First select the `phone_number` field, which will become highlighted. Then set the field properties in the bottom half on the screen.

❷ In Access SQL, the same format is used as in the Access GUI. The difference is that it is placed as the second parameter within the `format` function and enclosed in single quotes. See notes ❸ and ❹ for an explanation of the "a" before the `phone_number`.

❸ When the `format` function is applied to the `phone_number` column, the result is an expression and is no longer named `phone_number`. To name the formatted expression `phone_number` it is necessary to give it a column alias. In Access, to give this expression the alias `phone_number`, I had to put an "a" before the column name `phone_number`. This is a table reference, and specifies that this is a column of the `1_employees` table. In Oracle, this trick is not needed. The column alias can be `phone_number` without putting an "a" and a dot before the column name.

❹ This line assigns table alias "a" to the `1_employees` table.

Sequences

A *sequence* is used to generate numbers sequentially. After the numbers are generated, their value is fixed and they are only numbers — there is no dynamic quality to them at all. If a row is deleted, the sequence numbers in the remaining rows do not change. The column with data generated by a sequence must have a numeric datatype.

The idea is that each row will be given a different number. Sequences are used in several ways: They can be used to put the rows in a specific order or to make sure that no two rows are identical. Sometimes a sequence is used as a "meaningless" primary key for a table. When several people are entering data into a table at the same time, a sequence may be used to show which record was entered first. It is up to the application to determine the meaning of the numbers generated by the sequence.

In the `Lunches` database, a sequence is used as the primary key of the `l_lunches` table. In this case, each time a person signs up to attend a lunch, that lunch is assigned the next number. So far, the numbers 1 through 22 have been used. A few numbers are missing, just like they would be in real life. These numbers were actually generated in sequence, but their rows have been deleted. The next row in this table will be assigned the number 23.

Both Oracle and Access offer sequences, but they implement them in different ways. In Oracle, a sequence is a database object, similar to a table. Oracle also has the `rownum` function to generate sequences. In Access, a sequence is implemented as a datatype.

7-6   Creating sequences in Oracle

In Oracle, a sequence is a type of object in the database. This means that it exists within the database in the same way that a table or view exists. It can be created with the words `create sequence`, followed by the name of the new sequence. The starting number and the increment can be set in this command. I like to begin the names of all my sequences with `seq_` followed by an identification of the column it is used with.

A particular sequence is usually used to generate numbers for just one column, so if several columns in your tables use sequences, a separate sequence is set up for each one.

To delete a sequence enter `drop sequence`, followed by the name of the sequence.

Task

Create a sequence to use with the `lunch_id` column.

Oracle SQL: Create and drop a sequence

```
-- Delete command for a sequence ❶
-- This is a preventative delete for the sequence we
-- are about to create.
drop sequence seq_lunch_id; ❷

-- Create a new sequence
create sequence seq_lunch_id ❸
    start with 23
    increment by 1;
```

Result

After you create a sequence you can use it. See the next section.

Notes

❶ In Oracle and most other SQL products, a line that begins with two dashes is a comment line. In my opinion, all code should begin with at least one or two comment lines. In this book I usually do not include comment lines in the code because Access does not allow them and I am trying to write code that works in both Oracle and Access.

❷ This deletes the sequence, if it already exists. A preventative delete ensures that the name of the sequence is available for the `create sequence` command to use.

❸ This command creates the sequence.

7-7   Using sequences in Oracle

A sequence can do just two things: It can give you its current value or its next value. To get either of these you begin with the name of the sequence, followed by a period. Immediately after the period use `currval` to get the current value or `nextval` to get the next value. These can be used in a `select` statement, an `insert` statement, or any other SQL statement.

Task 1

Insert two rows into the l_lunches table using the seq_lunch sequence to assign the values in the lunch_id column.

Oracle SQL: Get the next value of a sequence

```
insert into l_lunches
values (seq_lunch_id.nextval, ❶
 '07-dec-2005', 202, sysdate); ❷

insert into l_lunches
values (seq_lunch_id.nextval, ❸
 '07-dec-2005', 204, sysdate);

select * from l_lunches;
rollback;
```

Result — The new rows

```
          LUNCH        EMPLOYEE
LUNCH_ID  DATE              ID  DATE_ENTERE
--------- ------------ --------- -----------
      23  07-DEC-2005      202  17-JUN-2005
      24  07-DEC-2005      204  17-JUN-2005
```

Task 2

Determine the most recent value that has been assigned by the seq_lunch sequence.

Oracle SQL: Get the current value of a sequence

```
select seq_lunch_id.currval ❹
from dual; ❺
```

Result table

```
CURRVAL
--------
      24
```

Notes

❶ This gets the next value from the sequence. We told it to start with 23 and that is the first value we get.

❷ In Oracle, `sysdate` supplies the current date and time.

❸ This gets the next value from the sequence. This time it gets the value 24.

❹ This gets the current value of the sequence.

❺ The `dual` table in Oracle is a dummy table used to print out values. For more details see section 9-7.

7-8 Sequences in Access

Access's way of generating sequences is called `autonumber` on the GUI level and `counter` on the JET engine level, and is treated as a datatype. It automatically assigns sequential numbers to new rows. If a new column is added to a table and that column is given the `counter` datatype, then all the rows currently in the table are assigned sequential numbers.

The JET engine level of Access is the level that processes the SQL. Access is a complex product with many levels. We are dealing with it on one particular level in this book — the level of the SQL view in the query mode.

Task

Add a new column to the `sec0708_suppliers2` table that numbers all the rows sequentially. Show two methods to accomplish this, one using Access SQL and the other using Access GUI.

Access SQL

```
alter table sec0708_suppliers2
add column new_num2 counter; ❶
```

Beginning table (`sec0708_suppliers2` table)

Supplier_id	Supplier_name
Arr	Alice & Ray's Restaurant
Asp	A Soup Place
Cbc	Certified Beef Company
Frv	Frank Reed's Vegetables
Fsn	Frank & Sons
Jbr	Just Beverages
Jps	Jim Parker's Shop
Vsb	Virginia Street Bakery

Record: 9 of 9

Ending table

Supplier_id	Supplier_name	new_num
Arr	Alice & Ray's Restaurant	1
Asp	A Soup Place	2
Cbc	Certified Beef Company	3
Frv	Frank Reed's Vegetables	4
Fsn	Frank & Sons	5
Jbr	Just Beverages	6
Jps	Jim Parker's Shop	7
Vsb	Virginia Street Bakery	8
		(AutoNumber)

Suppliers_2 : Table

Record: 9 of 9

Access GUI method ❷

Suppliers_2 : Table

Field Name	Data Type	Description
Supplier_id	Text	
Supplier_name	Text	
new_num	AutoNumber	

Field Properties

General | Lookup

Field Size	Long Integer
New Values	Increment
Format	
Caption	
Indexed	No

A field name can be up to 64 characters long, including spaces. Press F1 for help on field names.

Notes

❶ On the SQL level, Access uses `counter` as the name of the special datatype of a sequence.

❷ On the GUI level, Access uses `autonumber` as the name of the special datatype of a sequence. Note that the field size is shown as `long integer`, which is the actual datatype of the column.

Indexes

Indexes are mysterious in SQL. They lurk behind the scenes, and you rarely work with them directly. An index is used to make SQL process more efficiently. It can make a `select` statement run much faster. Indexes are usually created by the DBA, so I do not discuss them in detail here. Application programmers and end users only need to have a slight awareness of indexes. The most important things to know are that indexes exist and you can talk to your DBA about them.

An index is always formed on certain columns of a particular table. It is something like a table, but it has an additional layer of organization that enables it to find information quickly by finding the correct rows of the table to use. It contains pointers that go directly into the table. It is a database object, it contains data drawn from the table, and it requires disk space. An index for a large table may require a considerable amount of disk space. All the indexes on a set of tables may require as much disk space as the tables themselves, which can be a large amount.

An index is a double-edged sword. Although it will speed up your `select` statements, it may also slow down changes that are being made to the data. The reason is that indexes in SQL are updated dynamically at runtime. Whenever the data in a table is changed, all the indexes on that table also must be changed. If this causes an index to be reorganized, a delay can occur while the reorganization takes place.

One way of "tuning" a database is to add an index to it. When an index is added to a database, certain `select` statements will run much faster, but others will not run faster at all. When a database is fairly young and does not contain much data, all queries run quickly and the database has a lot of flexibility. However, when the database ages and contains much more data, indexes must be built to keep it performing well. Because of these indexes some specific queries will still run quickly, but all other queries will run slowly, perhaps taking an hour or more. Then we say that the database has lost much of its flexibility.

You have already created some indexes, although you might not have known it. When you add a primary key to a table, an index is automatically built on the primary key columns. This all happens behind the scenes, without any messages to you. That is how elusive indexes can be.

7-9   Creating indexes

It is very simple to create an index. The trick is to know which ones have more benefit than cost. Your DBA can help you determine this.

The command to create an index is

```
CREATE INDEX name_of_the_new_index
ON table_name (ordered_list_of_columns_in_the_index)
```

I like to name indexes "ix" followed by the name of the table and then some indicator of the columns in the index. An index can be created even if there are several rows with the same values in the index columns. In the following example, it would be acceptable if there were several employees with the same first and last names.

Another kind of index, called a *unique index*, prevents such duplicate values. We will discuss unique indexes in chapter 8. To delete an index, use the command `drop index` followed by the name of the index.

Task

Create an index on the names of the employees in the `l_employees` table. Include both the `last_name` and the `first_name` values in the index, in that order.

Oracle & Access SQL

```
create index ix_l_employees_name
on l_employees (last_name, first_name);
```

Result

An index is built, but you cannot see it. You can find entries for it in the Data Dictionary.

7-10 The Optimizer

You never use an index when you code a `select` statement. Instead, the Optimizer figures out the best way to process your `select` statement and it will make the best possible use of the indexes that have been built. The Optimizer is a very important component of database software.

Here is what goes on behind the scenes when you submit a `select` statement for a DBMS to run. First the statement is parsed. It is broken apart grammatically, so the computer understands what you want done. The next question is how to do it. This is where the Optimizer comes in.

The Optimizer makes a list of many different ways the `select` statement could be processed. It considers using many different indexes, searching and sorting the records in various ways. Then for each possible process it estimates how long it would take and how much computing power would be required. Then it decides which process is best, giving the fastest response and using the least amount of the computer's resources. This is the process the computer uses to create an answer to your `select` statement.

7-11 An example of how an index works

Here is an example of how an index works. This example is very simplified to show the basic principle. Many complexities have been removed. First you need some background about the way computers work. Here I am speaking about one computer that is not networked with other computers.

The slowest operation in a computer is its I/O (input and output), which is reading and writing to the disk drive. It is approximately 1,000 times slower than any operation in the computer's central processing unit (CPU), which handles all the complex logic. You can have a good idea of how long a process will take if you can estimate how much I/O it requires. That is, how many times it will need to read and write to the disk.

One way to measure the size of a table is by the number of I/O operations it takes to read the entire table. Each read from the disk may get 100 rows, depending on the size of the rows in the table and many other factors. If a table contains 1,000,000 rows, it might require 10,000 reads to get the entire table. This might take 10 or 20 minutes or even longer, depending on the speed of the computer and how many other people are using it.

As an example, suppose that this table is the `l_employees` table and it contains 1,000,000 rows. We are going to write a query to find all the people who were hired from 2009 to the end of 2010. First we examine how the query is processed if no indexes have been built on this table, or at least no indexes involving the `hire_date` column. Then we examine how it could be processed if an index has been created on that column. Here is the query:

```
select employee_id,
       last_name,
       first_name,
       hire_date
from l_employees
where hire_date >= '01-jan-2009'
  and hire_date <= '31-dec-2010'
order by last_name,
         hire_date,
         employee_id;
```

Before this query can be run, the Optimizer must determine how to process it. The primary factors are the `from` clause and the `where` clause, which indicate what table or tables the data will come from and which rows of those tables to use. This is what affects the amount of I/O. In this example, all the data comes from the `l_employees` table and only the `hire_date` column is used in the `where` clause.

If no indexes have been built on the `l_employees` table, then the only way the computer can process this query is to read the whole table and test each row to see if the condition in the `where` clause is satisfied. Testing 1,000,000 rows may seem like a lot of work to you, but to the computer that is the easy part — reading all the rows of the table from the disk is the hard part. This process may take 20 minutes or more as we discussed earlier.

The processing of this `select` statement will be very different if an index has already been built on the `hire_date` column of the `l_employees` table. The Optimizer will use this index to determine which rows of the table are needed. This can greatly reduce the number of rows that need to be read from the disk. Instead of 10,000 I/O operations, perhaps only 100 are needed for the data of the result table. Using the index might require 10 I/O operations. Therefore, the total might be 110 I/O instead of 10,000. This would produce the result table 100 times quicker and use less of the computer's resources.

Finding More Information in the Data Dictionary

In chapter 5 you learned to use the Oracle Data Dictionary. You found information in it about all the database elements studied up to that point. Since then you have learned about datatypes, sequences, and indexes. We now want to see how to find information about these things in the Data Dictionary. I also show you how to use the two indexes for the Dictionary.

7-12 How to find information about the datatype of a column

This section shows you how to find detailed information about the datatypes of the columns in a table or view. We will use the table in the Oracle Data Dictionary called User Table Columns, which is spelled

user_tab_columns

Note that this table contains information about the columns of both tables and views, even though its name mentions only tables. This table contains many columns of information, but we are only interested in a few of them. I have picked out the columns I want you to understand now. Here is a quick summary of what these columns mean:

Column	Meaning
column_id	Shows the order of the columns within the table or view — which column is first, second, etc.
column_name	Shows the name of the column.
data_type	Shows the datatype of the column. Of course, these are all Oracle datatypes.
data_length	For fixed-length datatypes, such as numbers and dates, this shows the number of bytes of disk space required to store one cell of the column. For variable-length datatypes, such as variable-length character strings (varchar2), this shows the maximum length of the column.
data_precision	Used only with number columns. This is the maximum number of digits allowed for the number — both the digits before the decimal point and those after it.
data_scale	Used only with number columns. This is the number of digits after the decimal point.
nullable	Shows Y if a null can be entered into the column. Shows N if a null cannot be entered into the column.

I want to point out some things from the result table in the following example. The first line in the result table shows the first column of the `l_employees` table, which is the `employee_id` column. Its datatype is `number` and it allows a maximum of three digits with no digits after the decimal point. Nulls are not allowed in this column. You can guess that the reason nulls are not allowed in this column is because it is the primary key, although its status as the primary key is not shown here. Within each row, this column requires 22 bytes of disk space even though this number can only contain three digits.

The second row of the result table shows a text column, the `first_name` column. It is the second column within the `l_employees` table. Its datatype is `varchar2`, which is a variable-length character string and it has a maximum length of 10 characters. Nulls are allowed in this column.

The fifth row of the result table shows a date column, the `hire_date` column. Nulls are allowed in this column. Within each row, this column requires 7 bytes of disk space.

The sixth row of the result table shows a number with some digits after the decimal point. This is the `credit_limit` column. It can contain only numbers with a maximum of four digits, two before the decimal and two after.

In Access, much of this information is available on the GUI level from the `Design` view of the table. When you select a column, the field properties in the bottom part of the screen show details about the exact definition of the column.

Task

Find information about the datatypes of all the columns of the `l_employees` table.

Oracle SQL

```
-- Find information about the datatypes of columns ❶
select column_id,
       column_name,
       data_type,
       data_length,
       data_precision,
       data_scale,
       nullable
from user_tab_columns
where table_name = 'l_employees' ❷
order by column_id; ❸
```

Result table

```
COLUMN_ID COLUMN_NAME   DATA_TYPE DATA_LENGTH DATA_PRECISION DATA_SCALE N
--------- ------------- --------- ----------- -------------- ---------- -
        1 EMPLOYEE_ID   NUMBER             22              3          0 N
        2 FIRST_NAME    VARCHAR2           10 (null)          (null)    Y
        3 LAST_NAME     VARCHAR2           10 (null)          (null)    Y
        4 DEPT_CODE     VARCHAR2            3 (null)          (null)    Y
        5 HIRE_DATE     DATE                7 (null)          (null)    Y
        6 CREDIT_LIMIT  NUMBER             22              4          2 Y
        7 PHONE_NUMBER  VARCHAR2            4 (null)          (null)    Y
        8 MANAGER_ID    NUMBER             22              3          0 Y
```

Notes

❶ This is a comment line. It may be omitted. Comment lines begin with two dashes.

❷ This where clause limits the result to showing the columns of a single table, the l_employees table.

❸ This order by clause sorts the columns into the same order they have within the l_employees table.

Access GUI

7-13 How to find information about sequences

In Oracle, we said that a sequence is a database object, so you should expect to find information about sequences in the Oracle Data Dictionary. The dictionary table to use is called `user_sequences`. By examining the columns in this table, you can learn exactly what an Oracle sequence is composed of. You can also make an educated guess about the options that are available when you create a sequence. The columns of this table are as follows:

Column	Meaning
`sequence_name`	Sequence name
`min_value`	Minimum value of the sequence
`max_value`	Maximum value of the sequence
`increment_by`	Value by which sequence is incremented
`cycle_flag`	Does sequence wrap around on reaching limit?
`order_flag`	Are sequence numbers generated in order?
`cache_size`	Number of sequence numbers to cache (hold in memory)
`last_number`	Last sequence number written to disk

In Access, sequences are handled as if they were datatypes, so information about them is available on the GUI level from the `Design` view of the table. When you select a column with the `autonumber` datatype, the field properties in the bottom part of the screen show details about the sequence.

Task

Find all the information about your sequences in Oracle.

Oracle SQL

```
select *
from user_sequences;
```

Result table

SEQUENCE_NAME	MIN_VAL	MAX_VALUE	INCREMENT_BY	C	O	CACHE_SIZE	LAST_NUMBER
SEQ_EMPLOYEE_ID	1	1.000E+27	1	N	N	20	211
SEQ_LUNCH_ID	1	1.000E+27	1	N	N	20	43
SEQ_MENU_ITEM	1	1.000E+27	1	N	N	20	11

Access GUI

7-14 How to find information about indexes

In Oracle, you need to look at two tables in the Data Dictionary to find information about the indexes that have been built. This is similar to the way you found information about primary keys in section 5-17. An index, like a primary key, is a single database structure that may involve many columns in a particular order. All the columns must come from a single table. The two dictionary tables with information about indexes are:

```
user_indexes
user_ind_columns
```

The `user_indexes` table contains one row for each index, even if several columns are involved in the index. This table has many columns, but we are only interested in a few of them. These columns are as follows:

Column	Meaning
index_name	Name of the index
table_name	Name of the table on which the index is formed
uniqueness	Whether two rows are allowed to have the same values in all of the columns of the index
tablespace_name	Name of the tablespace containing the index
status	Whether the index is valid or not

In the following example, you can see that there are two indexes on the `1_employees` table. They both are in the `indx` tablespace, which is where they should be. They are both valid, unique indexes.

The `user_ind_columns` table contains a row for every column involved with every index. This tells you all the columns involved with each index. We will not use the last two columns of this table, so you do not have to worry about what they mean. The columns of this table are as follows:

Column	Meaning
index_name	Name of the index
table_name	Name of the table on which the index is formed
column_name	Name of a column in the index
column_position	Position of the column within the index
column_length	Length of the column within the index
descend	Sort order — whether the index is in ascending or descending order

In Access, you can see the indexes on a table by opening the table in Design view. Then go to the View menu and choose Indexes. In the following example, you can see that there are two indexes on the l_employees table. Sometimes indexes are created automatically within Access as part of its "self-tuning" abilities.

Task

Find all the indexes on the l_employees table and which columns they contain.

Oracle SQL: Step 1

```
select index_name,
       table_name,
       uniqueness,
       tablespace_name,
       status
from user_indexes
where table_name = 'l_employees';
```

Result table

```
INDEX_NAME               TABLE_NAME      UNIQUENES  TABLESPACE_NAME   STATUS
--------------------     -------------   ---------  ---------------   ------
PK_L_EMPLOYEES           L_EMPLOYEES     UNIQUE     INDX              VALID
UNIQUE_EMP_PHONE_NUM     L_EMPLOYEES     UNIQUE     INDX              VALID
```

Oracle SQL: Step 2

```
select *
from user_ind_columns
where table_name = 'l_employees';
```

Result table

```
                                                     COLUMN    COLUMN
INDEX_NAME               TABLE_NAME      COLUMN_NAME  POSITION  LENGTH DESC
--------------------     ------------    -----------  --------  --------- ----
PK_L_EMPLOYEES           L_EMPLOYEES     EMPLOYEE_ID         1        22 ASC
UNIQUE_PHONE_NUM         L_EMPLOYEES     PHONE_NUMBER        1         4 ASC
```

Access GUI

Index Name	Field Name	Sort Order
▶ PHONE_NUMBER	PHONE_NUMBER	Ascending
🔑 pk_l_employees	EMPLOYEE_ID	Ascending

Index Properties

Primary	No	
Unique	Yes	The name for this index. Each index can use
Ignore Nulls	No	up to 10 fields.

7-15 How to find information about all your database objects in Oracle

Most of the tables of the Oracle Data Dictionary are concerned with only a single type of database object, but there is one table that lists all of the objects you own regardless of what type of object it is. In addition to listing all of your objects, it also tells you when each object was created and the last time each object was changed. Sometimes this is very handy information to know. The name of this table is User Objects. Its most interesting columns are as follows:

Column	Meaning
object_name	The name of the object
object_type	The type of database object (table, view, sequence, index, etc.)
created	The date and time that the object was created
last_DDL_time	The last date and time that the object was changed
status	Valid or Invalid

Task

List all the database objects you own in Oracle, the date each was created, and the most recent date each was changed.

Oracle SQL

```
select object_name,
       object_type,
       created,
       last_ddl_time,
       status
from user_objects;
```

Result table

```
OBJECT_NAME          OBJECT_TYPE CREATED     LAST_DDL_TI STATUS
-------------------- ----------- ----------- ----------- -------
L_CONSTANTS          TABLE       06-JUN-2001 06-JUN-2001 VALID
L_DEPARTMENTS        TABLE       06-JUN-2001 06-JUN-2001 VALID
L_EMPLOYEES          TABLE       06-JUN-2001 20-JUN-2001 VALID
L_FOODS              TABLE       06-JUN-2001 06-JUN-2001 VALID
L_LUNCHES            TABLE       06-JUN-2001 06-JUN-2001 VALID
L_LUNCH_ITEMS        TABLE       06-JUN-2001 06-JUN-2001 VALID
L_SUPPLIERS          TABLE       06-JUN-2001 06-JUN-2001 VALID
NUMBERS_0_TO_9       TABLE       06-JUN-2001 06-JUN-2001 VALID
NUMBERS_0_TO_99      VIEW        06-JUN-2001 06-JUN-2001 VALID
PK_L_DEPARTMENTS     INDEX       06-JUN-2001 06-JUN-2001 VALID
PK_L_EMPLOYEES       INDEX       06-JUN-2001 06-JUN-2001 VALID
PK_L_FOODS           INDEX       06-JUN-2001 06-JUN-2001 VALID
PK_L_LUNCHES         INDEX       06-JUN-2001 06-JUN-2001 VALID
PK_L_LUNCH_ITEMS     INDEX       06-JUN-2001 06-JUN-2001 VALID
PK_L_SUPPLIERS       INDEX       06-JUN-2001 06-JUN-2001 VALID
SEQ_EMPLOYEE_ID      SEQUENCE    19-JUN-2001 19-JUN-2001 VALID
SEQ_LUNCH_ID         SEQUENCE    17-JUN-2001 17-JUN-2001 VALID
SEQ_MENU_ITEM        SEQUENCE    19-JUN-2001 19-JUN-2001 VALID
UNIQUE_PHONE_NUM     INDEX       20-JUN-2001 20-JUN-2001 VALID

(and many more)
```

7-16 How to use the index of dictionary tables in Oracle

The Oracle Data Dictionary contains more than 200 tables. It can be difficult to determine which table contains the information you are looking for.
The Dictionary table solves this problem because it contains an entry for
each of these tables, so it functions as an index to all the other tables. It
contains two columns: `column_name` and `comments`. You can use `like` to
search for patterns of letters in either of these columns. The `comments`
column is very long and it is best to format it with the following SQLplus
command:

```
column comments format a40 word_wrap;
```

This is already done for you when you run the login script.

Task

Find all the tables in the Oracle Data Dictionary that contain information about
sequences. To do this, find the names of all the tables with the letters "SEQ" in
them. Also list the comments about these tables.

Oracle SQL

```
select *
from dictionary
where table_name like '%seq%';
```

Result table

TABLE_NAME	COMMENTS
ALL_SEQUENCES	Description of SEQUENCEs accessible to the user
USER_SEQUENCES	Description of the user's own SEQUENCEs
SEQ	Synonym for USER_SEQUENCES

7-17 How to use the index of dictionary columns in Oracle

After you know the name of the dictionary table you want to look at, often the next problem is to learn the meanings of its columns. The Dictionary Columns table can give you this information, as the example below shows. This table contains three columns: `table_name`, `column_name`, and `comments`. Of course, these columns can also be used with `like` to search for patterns of letters.

Task

Find the meaning of all the columns of the `all_sequences` table.

Oracle SQL

```
select *
from dict_columns
where table_name = 'all_sequences';
```

Result table

```
TABLE_NAME      COLUMN_NAME      COMMENTS
--------------  ---------------  -------------------------------------
ALL_SEQUENCES   SEQUENCE_OWNER   Name of the owner of the sequence
ALL_SEQUENCES   SEQUENCE_NAME    SEQUENCE name
ALL_SEQUENCES   MIN_VALUE        Minimum value of the sequence
ALL_SEQUENCES   MAX_VALUE        Maximum value of the sequence
ALL_SEQUENCES   INCREMENT_BY     Value by which sequence is incremented
ALL_SEQUENCES   CYCLE_FLAG       Does sequence wrap around on reaching
                                 limit?
ALL_SEQUENCES   ORDER_FLAG       Are sequence numbers generated in order?
ALL_SEQUENCES   CACHE_SIZE       Number of sequence numbers to cache
ALL_SEQUENCES   LAST_NUMBER      Last sequence number written to disk
```

An Exercise Solved for You

7-18 Creating a table of the days you want to celebrate

This section integrates the various topics we've discussed in this chapter. We create a table, put some data in it, and display it using a date format. I encourage you to make your own modifications to the following code and experiment with any variations that occur to you.

Task

Create a new table to keep track of events in your life you want to celebrate. Put three columns in the table: a sequence, a text column, and a date column. Put a primary key on the table using the sequence as a primary key. Put a few rows of data into the table and list them out, formatting the dates to show the day of the week, the full name of the month, and a four-digit year.

Oracle SQL

```
drop table my_days;
create table  my_days
(my_seq_id     number,
my_event       varchar2(25),
my_date        date);

alter table my_days
add constraint pk_my_days
primary key (my_seq_id);

drop sequence seq_my_days;
create sequence seq_my_days
start with 1
increment by 1;

insert into my_days
values (seq_my_days.nextval,
'birth date', '16-jan-1971');

insert into my_days
values (seq_my_days.nextval,
'college graduation', '24-jun-1993');

insert into my_days
values (seq_my_days.nextval,
'wedding', '14-feb-1994');
```

```
commit;

select my_seq_id,
       my_event,
       to_char(my_date, 'day month dd, yyyy') as my_date
from my_days
order by my_seq_id;
```

Access SQL

```
drop table my_days;

create table my_days
(my_seq_id     counter,
 my_event      text(25),
 my_date       datetime);

alter table my_days
add constraint pk_my_days
primary key (my_seq_id);

insert into my_days (my_event, my_date)
values ('birth date', #16-jan-1971#);

insert into my_days (my_event, my_date)
values ('college graduation', #24-jun-1993#);

insert into my_days (my_event, my_date)
values ('wedding', #14-feb-1994#);

select my_seq_id,
       my_event,
       format(my_date, 'dddd mmmm dd, yyyy') as my_date2
from my_days
order by my_seq_id;
```

Result table

```
MY_SEQ_ID MY_EVENT                    MY_DATE
--------- -------------------------   ----------------------------
        1 BIRTH DATE                  SATURDAY   JANUARY   16, 1971
        2 COLLEGE GRADUATION          THURSDAY   JUNE      24, 1993
        3 WEDDING                     MONDAY     FEBRUARY  14, 1994
```

Summary

In this chapter we discussed formats. A date format can be used to display a date in a particular way, without changing its value. In Oracle, date formats are also used when you want to enter data and include a time with a date. In Access, a format can be one of the properties of a column.

A sequence in Oracle is a database structure. In Access, it is handled as a datatype. Either method generates a sequential series of numbers that can be automatically placed in a particular column of a table.

An index has no effect on the data in a table. However it can affect the speed of processing performed on that table. Indexes tend to speed up `select` statements, but they can slow down data modification — `insert`, `update`, and `delete` statements.

The Data Dictionary in Oracle contains all the information about how a table or any other database structure is defined. You can use it to retrieve much useful information.

Exercises

1. Goal: Display dates using date formats.

    a. Create a table with one column and one row containing the date October 12, 2015. Then write a `select` statement to display this date in various ways:
    - The date formatted as above
    - The day of the week
    - The Julian date (the number of days since January 1)
    - The quarter of the year
    - The week of the year

Oracle SQL

```
drop table ex0701a;
create table ex0701a
(my_date    date);

insert into ex0701a
values ('12-oct-2015');

commit;

select to_char(my_date, 'month dd, yyyy')
                            as usual_date_format,
       to_char(my_date, 'day') as weekday,
       to_char(my_date, 'ddd') as day_of_year,
       to_char(my_date, 'q') as quarter,
       to_char(my_date, 'ww') as week_of_year
from ex0701a;
```

Access SQL

```
drop table ex0701a;
create table ex0701a
(my_date    datetime);

insert into ex0701a
values (#12-oct-2015#);

select format(my_date, 'mmmm dd, yyyy')
                            as usual_date_format,
       format(my_date, 'dddd') as weekday,
       format(my_date, 'y') as day_of_year,
       format(my_date, 'q') as quarter,
       format(my_date, 'ww') as week_of_year
from ex0701a;
```

b. Run the code in section 7-18 to create the my_days table. Enter significant dates from your life, then display the dates in all the formats shown in exercise 1a.

2. Goal: Enter a time with a date.

  a. Insert a new row into the table ex0701a with the date October 14, 2015, and the time 2:05 p.m.

Oracle SQL

```
insert into ex0701a
values (to_date('14-oct-2015 14:05',
                'dd-mon-yyyy hh24:mi'));
```

Access SQL

```
insert into ex0701a
values (#14-oct-2015 14:05#);
```

---

  b. Add a new row into the table of your life_events. Enter a time with the date.

3. Goal: Find information about the columns of a table from the Data Dictionary.

  a. See section 7-12.

  b. Find the information in the Oracle Data Dictionary about the columns of the tables ex0701a and my_days.

4. Goal: Find information about the creation dates of database objects from the Data Dictionary.

  a. See section 7-15.

  b. Find the creation dates from the Data Dictionary for the tables ex0701a and my_days.

chapter 8

DATA INTEGRITY

This chapter discusses the ways data can be validated before it is entered into the database. Validation is particularly important when many people are entering data and sharing the same database. Validation also ensures that the data meets a certain level of consistency.

In a relational database, *Referential Integrity* is one of the main techniques of data validation. It protects columns that contain codes. For example, a column for gender can only contain the codes M and F. Referential Integrity can enforce that rule.

A `check` constraint is another type of validation. It can check that some statement is true. For example, "Price is less than $100.00." There is always validation on the primary key of a table to preserve its properties. A `not null` constraint is a way to say that the field is required. A `unique` constraint ensures that no two rows contain the same value.

Referential Integrity

Referential Integrity is the main type of data validation within relational databases. It ensures that certain relationships are maintained between the data in one table and the data in another table.

Usually this validation is done when the data is being changed. That is, during the processing of `insert`, `update`, and `delete` statements. These statements will fail if they would change the data in a way that does not conform to the requirements of Referential Integrity.

During massive loads of thousands of rows of data, this validation is usually turned off temporarily. After the load is finished, the validation is turned on again. So what happens if faulty data is entered during these loads? We will not be able to turn on the validation until the data has been fixed. So whenever Referential Integrity is active, we are assured that one table has a certain relationship to another table.

8-1   The concept of Referential Integrity

The drawing below shows the concept of Referential Integrity.

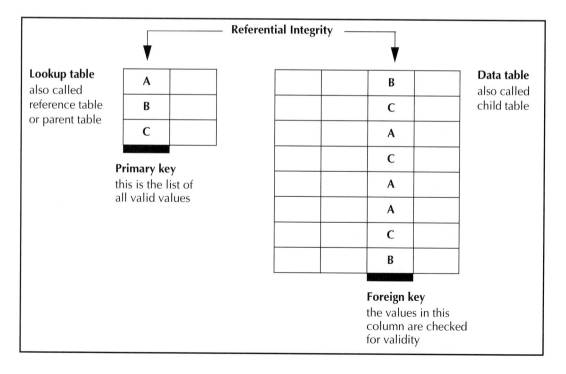

Referential Integrity is a relationship between the data in two columns. These columns are usually in different tables. One column, the primary key, contains a list of all the valid values. The other column, the foreign key, contains data that is validated against this list. The table containing the list of valid values is called a *lookup* table. It is also called a *reference* table or the *parent* table. The other table is sometimes called the *data* table or the *child* table.

The valid values are often a set of codes containing two or three characters. The lookup table contains a list of these codes and their meanings. Sometimes it also contains additional data about them.

The data in both columns is allowed to change. However the rule must be maintained that the foreign key can only contain values that are also in the primary key column. The foreign key can also contain nulls.

The relationship between the data in these two columns has consequences for the way in which the data is allowed to change. In the lookup table, a new value can always be inserted into the primary key, but an `update` or `delete` statement is restricted if it would remove a value that is used in the foreign key.

In the data table, a value can always be deleted or set to null. But any new value introduced with an insert or update must pass validation, otherwise it is rejected.

The two columns often have the same or similar names. The database designers do this to suggest that the columns are related to each other. An index is usually built on each of the columns to keep the database running efficiently.

Before the Referential Integrity relationship can be set up, you must create a primary key, or at least a unique index, in the lookup table. Access strictly enforces this rule, but Oracle allows some exceptions.

8-2 An example of Referential Integrity

In this section we set up a relationship of Referential Integrity between two tables. The `states` table is the lookup table and the `clients` table is the data table. More specifically, we create Referential Integrity between the `state_code` columns of these tables.

The `states` table and the `clients` table are part of an application for a salesman. His sales region consists of three states: California, Oregon, and Washington. He is only allowed to have clients in those states.

In the following example, Referential Integrity is set up using an `alter table` statement. The first line says `alter table`, and then gives the name of the data table, which is the table containing the column with data that will be validated.

The second line says `add constraint`, followed by the name of the constraint. The naming convention used here begins all foreign key constraints with the letters `fk_`, followed by the name of the column that will be validated. This is one of several popular naming conventions.

The third line specifies that this is a foreign key constraint. This is followed by the name of the column to be validated, enclosed in parentheses. The word `references` is followed by the name of the lookup table and then the name of the primary key column enclosed in parentheses. Sometimes the name of the primary key column is omitted and only the name of the lookup table is given.

Task

Set up Referential Integrity. Validate the `state_code` column of the `clients` table.

The `alter table` statement shown below has already been run by the SQLFUN_BUILD_TABLES.SQL script, which created the Referential Integrity relationship. If you run the `alter table` command again, you will get an error. If you want to run this code, you must first delete the relationship by entering

start c:/sqlfun_drop_constraints.sql

After you run this script, you will be able to run the code in the rest of this chapter.

Oracle & Access SQL: Set up Referential Integrity ❶

```
alter table sec0802_clients
add constraint fk_state_code
foreign key (state_code)
   references sec0802_states (state_code);
```

Lookup table (`sec0802_states` table)

```
STATE
CODE    STATE_NAME                              STATE_CAPITAL
-----   ------------------------------          ------------------
CA      CALIFORNIA                              SACRAMENTO
OR      OREGON                                  SALEM
WA      WASHINGTON                              OLYMPIA
```

Data table (`sec0802_clients` table)

```
                                                STATE
CLIENT_ID  CLIENT_NAME                          CODE
---------  ------------------------------       -----
      100  LARRY  COHEN                          CA
      200  ALICE  WILLIAMS                       CA
      300  ROGER  WOLF                           OR
      400  NANCY  KERN                           OR
      500  CATHY  LEE                            WA
      600  STEVEN LAKE                           WA
```

Notes

❶ A primary key has already been created on the `state_code` column of the lookup table. This should be done before the Referential Integrity relationship is established. In the remaining sections of this chapter, the primary key of the lookup table has been created for you.

8-3   Inserts and updates to the data table prevented by RI

This section shows that Referential Integrity provides data validation within a foreign key column of the data table. It prevents a value from being entered into that column if it is not one of the valid values contained in the lookup table.

The SQL in the following example tries to put New York and Massachusetts into the `state_code` column of the `clients` table. These states are not part of the sales region, so they are not included in the `states` table. Referential Integrity rejects these `insert` and `update` statements.

Task

On the `clients` table, write an `insert` and an `update` statement that will be rejected by Referential Integrity.

Oracle & Access SQL

```
insert into sec0802_clients
values (700, 'gail hauser', 'ny');

update sec0802_clients
set state_code = 'ma'
where client_id = 200;
```

Result — An error message ❶

Notes

❶ Access will notify you that an error has occurred and ask you if you want to run the query anyway. Even if you choose Yes, no change is made to the tables.

8-4   Inserts and updates to the data table allowed by RI

This section shows that Referential Integrity allows an `insert` or `update` statement to occur in the foreign key column of the data table as long as it follows the rules. A value can be entered into that column if it is one of the valid values contained in the lookup table.

In the following example, the first two SQL commands are the same as in the previous section, except that the state codes are valid. These states are part of the sales region and they are included in the `states` table. Referential Integrity allows these `insert` and `update` statements.

In the last `insert` statement, the `state_code` is null. This shows that we can enter a null in a foreign key column, even though there is no null in the list of valid values.

Task

On the `clients` table, write an `insert` and an `update` statement that will be allowed by Referential Integrity.

Oracle & Access SQL

```
insert into sec0802_clients
values (700, 'gail hauser', 'or');

update sec0802_clients
set state_code = 'wa'
where client_id = 200;

insert into sec0802_clients
values (800, 'carl logan', null);
```

Beginning table (`sec0802_clients` table)

```
                                         STATE
CLIENT_ID  CLIENT_NAME                   CODE
---------  ----------------------------  -----
      100  LARRY COHEN                   CA
      200  ALICE WILLIAMS                CA
      300  ROGER WOLF                    OR
      400  NANCY KERN                    OR
      500  CATHY LEE                     WA
      600  STEVEN LAKE                   WA
```

Ending table

```
                                         STATE
CLIENT_ID  CLIENT_NAME                   CODE
---------  ----------------------------  ------
      100  LARRY COHEN                   CA
      200  ALICE WILLIAMS                WA
      300  ROGER WOLF                    OR
      400  NANCY KERN                    OR
      500  CATHY LEE                     WA
      600  STEVEN LAKE                   WA
      700  GAIL HAUSER                   OR
      800  CARL LOGAN                    (null)
```

To restore the data to its original form

In Oracle:

```
rollback;
```

In Access, we have to restore the `clients` table to its original condition, shown in the preceding beginning table.

8-5   Updates and deletes to the lookup table prevented by RI

This section shows that Referential Integrity prevents codes from being changed or deleted in the lookup table while those codes are being used in the foreign key column of the data table.

The SQL in the following example tries to change Oregon to Massachusetts and tries to delete California from the `states` table. These states are currently being referred to by rows in the `clients` table, so Referential Integrity rejects these `update` and `delete` statements.

Here we are using RI with the `restrict` option, which is the default and most commonly used option. Later we look at some other ways to set up RI.

Task

On the `states` table, write an `update` and a `delete` statement that will be rejected by Referential Integrity.

Oracle & Access SQL

```
update sec0802_states
set state_code = 'ma'
where state_code = 'or';

delete from sec0802_states
where state_code = 'ca';
```

Result — An error message

8-6   How to delete a code from the lookup table

To delete a value from the primary key of a lookup table, we must first ensure that the value is not being used in the foreign key column by any row of the data table.

In the following example, we want to remove California from the states table. Before we can do this, we must remove it from every row of the clients table. Instead of deleting these clients, we set their state_code values to null.

Task

Delete California from the states table.

Oracle & Access SQL

```
update sec0802_clients
   set state_code = null
where state_code = 'ca';

delete from sec0802_states
where state_code = 'ca';
```

Beginning table 1 (sec0802_states table)

```
STATE
CODE    STATE_NAME                       STATE_CAPITAL
------  -------------------------------  --------------------
CA      CALIFORNIA                       SACRAMENTO
OR      OREGON                           SALEM
WA      WASHINGTON                       OLYMPIA
```

Beginning table 2 (`sec0802_clients` table)

```
                                       STATE
CLIENT_ID CLIENT_NAME                  CODE
--------- ----------------------------- ------
      100 LARRY COHEN                  CA
      200 ALICE WILLIAMS               CA
      300 ROGER WOLF                   OR
      400 NANCY KERN                   OR
      500 CATHY LEE                    WA
      600 STEVEN LAKE                  WA
```

Ending table 1 (`sec0802_states` table)

```
STATE
CODE   STATE_NAME                   STATE_CAPITAL
------ ----------------------------- ------------------
OR     OREGON                       SALEM
WA     WASHINGTON                   OLYMPIA
```

Ending table 2 (`sec0802_clients` table)

```
                                       STATE
CLIENT_ID CLIENT_NAME                  CODE
--------- ----------------------------- ------
      100 LARRY COHEN                  (null)
      200 ALICE WILLIAMS               (null)
      300 ROGER WOLF                   OR
      400 NANCY KERN                   OR
      500 CATHY LEE                    WA
      600 STEVEN LAKE                  WA
```

To restore the data to its original form

In Oracle:

```
rollback;
```

In Access, we have to restore both the `states` and the `clients` tables to their original conditions, shown in the two preceding beginning tables.

8-7   How to change a code in the lookup table

To change a value in the primary key of a lookup table, we use a three-step process. First, we enter the new code into the lookup table. Second, we change all the data in the data table from the old code to the new code. Third, we delete the old code from the lookup table.

In the following example, we want to change the code for California from CA to ZZ. The reason for doing this is to show the process of accomplishing it.

Task

Change the state_code for California to ZZ in both the states table and the clients table.

Oracle & Access SQL

```
insert into sec0802_states
values ('zz', 'california', 'sacramento');

update sec0802_clients
   set state_code = 'zz'
where state_code = 'ca';

delete from sec0802_states
where state_code = 'ca';
```

Beginning table 1 (sec0802_states table)

```
STATE
CODE   STATE_NAME                       STATE_CAPITAL
------ -------------------------------- --------------------
CA     CALIFORNIA                       SACRAMENTO
OR     OREGON                           SALEM
WA     WASHINGTON                       OLYMPIA
```

Beginning table 2 (`sec0802_clients` table)

```
                                       STATE
CLIENT_ID  CLIENT_NAME                 CODE
---------  --------------------------  ------
      100  LARRY  COHEN                 CA
      200  ALICE  WILLIAMS              CA
      300  ROGER  WOLF                  OR
      400  NANCY  KERN                  OR
      500  CATHY  LEE                   WA
      600  STEVEN LAKE                  WA
```

Ending table 1 (`sec0802_states` table)

```
STATE
CODE    STATE_NAME                   STATE_CAPITAL
------  ---------------------------  ----------------
OR      OREGON                       SALEM
WA      WASHINGTON                   OLYMPIA
ZZ      CALIFORNIA                   SACRAMENTO
```

Ending table 2 (`sec0802_clients` table)

```
                                       STATE
CLIENT_ID  CLIENT_NAME                 CODE
---------  --------------------------  ------
      100  LARRY  COHEN                 ZZ
      200  ALICE  WILLIAMS              ZZ
      300  ROGER  WOLF                  OR
      400  NANCY  KERN                  OR
      500  CATHY  LEE                   WA
      600  STEVEN LAKE                  WA
```

8-8   RI as a relationship between the tables

I said before that Referential Integrity is a relationship between the data in two columns, but that is not quite the whole story. It is also a relationship between two tables: the lookup table and the data table. There are two parts to this:

1. We must insert rows into the lookup table before we can insert any rows into the data table.

2. We cannot drop either table until we drop the Referential Integrity relationship.

These are the rules in general, but there are ways to get around them, which we discuss later.

8-9   Setting up RI in the Access GUI

This section shows how to set up Referential Integrity in Access using GUI methods instead of SQL. The tables used here are called `states2` and `clients2`. These are separate copies of the `states` and `clients` tables with Referential Integrity set up in a different way.

Task

Set up Referential Integrity between the `state_code` columns of the `states2` table and the `clients2` table. Use the Access GUI to do this.

Access GUI method

Step 1: Begin at the listing of tables.
Before you follow this procedure, be sure the lookup table has a primary key.

Step 2: Tools → Relationships.
This displays the Relationships panel, which might initially be blank, as shown on the following screen. It is all right if it is not blank.

Step 3: View ➔ Show Table.

Step 4: Choose the tables you want. For this example, choose the SEC0809_STATES2 table. Then choose the SEC0809_CLIENTS2 table. Close the Show Table window.

Step 5: Select the primary key. In this example, choose the STATE_CODE column of the SEC0809_STATES2 table.

Step 6: Hold the mouse down and drag from the primary key to the foreign key, then release the mouse button. In this example, drag from the STATE_CODE column of the SEC0809_STATES2 table to the STATE_CODE column of the SEC0809_CLIENTS2 table. The Edit Relationship window will pop up.

Step 7: Check the Enforce Referential Integrity check box.

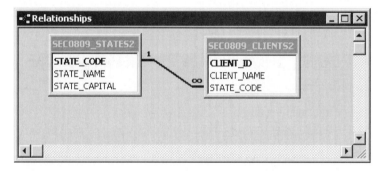

Step 8: Press the Create button.

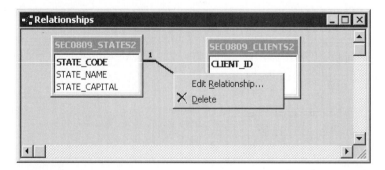

Now RI has been set up.

If at a later time you want to delete or change the relationship, right-click on the line between the two tables.

The Delete Options and Update Options of RI

The previous sections showed you that a delete or an update to the lookup table can be disallowed by RI. This is the most common way RI is set up, but some other options are explained here.

8-10 The three options for deletes and updates to the lookup table

By default, we are not allowed to change or delete values in the primary key of the lookup table, when those values occur in the foreign key of the data table. We discussed this in sections 8-6 and 8-7. Having RI operate this way is called the `restrict` option, because we are restricted from making these changes to the lookup table.

When we set up Referential Integrity, we can choose one of three options for handling deletes from the lookup table. In Access, we can also choose one of three options for handling updates to the lookup table. This gives us nine ways to set up Referential Integrity. The three options are

- `restrict`
  (which is the default if we do not choose the other options)

- `set null`

- `cascade`

In describing RI up to now, I have been describing it with the `restrict` option, because this is the most common form. For some special purposes, we use the `set null` and `cascade` options, but they should always be used carefully.

The `set null` and `cascade` options for deletes say that we can always delete a value from the lookup table. These options for updates say that we can always change a value in the lookup table. Here are the effects of these options on the matching values within the foreign key column of the data table:

`set null`	All the matching values in the foreign key column are automatically changed to null. The rest of the data in the row is unchanged.
`cascade` deletes	The entire row is deleted from the data table when there is a matching value in the foreign key column.
`cascade` updates	All the matching values in the foreign key column are automatically changed to the new value. The rest of the data in the row is unchanged.

Delete options

Oracle supports all three delete options. From an SQL command, Access supports only the `restrict` delete option. The `cascade` delete option is available, but it must be set in the GUI.

Update options

Both Oracle and Access support the `restrict` updates options, which is the default. Access also supports the `cascade` updates option, which must be set in the GUI.

8-11 The delete rule: `set null`

In the following example, the first task sets up Referential Integrity between the `state3` table and the `client3` table using the `set null` option. The second task deletes California from the lookup table. In the foreign key all the references to California are automatically changed to null.

Task 1

Set up Referential Integrity between the `states3` table and the `clients3` table. Use the `set null` option for deletes.

Oracle SQL ❶

```
alter table sec0811_clients3
add constraint fk_state_code3
foreign key (state_code)
  references sec0811_states3 (state_code)
  on delete set null; ❷
```

■ Access does not support this option.

Task 2

Delete California from the `states` table. Do this when Referential Integrity has been set up using the `set null` option.

Oracle SQL

```
delete from sec0811_states3
where state_code = 'ca';
```

■ Access does not support the delete rule `set null`.

Beginning table 1 (`sec0811_states3` table)

```
STATE
CODE     STATE_NAME                      STATE_CAPITAL
------   ------------------------------  ------------------
CA       CALIFORNIA                      SACRAMENTO
OR       OREGON                          SALEM
WA       WASHINGTON                      OLYMPIA
```

Beginning table 2 (`sec0811_clients3` table)

```
                                          STATE
CLIENT_ID CLIENT_NAME                     CODE
--------- ------------------------------  ------
      100 LARRY COHEN                     CA
      200 ALICE WILLIAMS                  CA
      300 ROGER WOLF                      OR
      400 NANCY KERN                      OR
      500 CATHY LEE                       WA
      600 STEVEN LAKE                     WA
```

Ending table 1 (sec0811_states3 table)

```
STATE
CODE    STATE_NAME                          STATE_CAPITAL
------  ----------------------------------  --------------------
OR      OREGON                              SALEM
WA      WASHINGTON                          OLYMPIA
```

Ending table 2 (sec0811_clients3 table)

```
                                           STATE
CLIENT_ID CLIENT_NAME                      CODE
--------- ------------------------------   ------
      100 LARRY COHEN                      (null)  ❸
      200 ALICE WILLIAMS                   (null)  ❸
      300 ROGER WOLF                       OR
      400 NANCY KERN                       OR
      500 CATHY LEE                        WA
      600 STEVEN LAKE                      WA
```

Notes

❶ The `alter table` statement shown below has already been run by the SQLFUN_BUILD_TABLES.SQL script, which created the Referential Integrity relationship. If you run the alter table command again, you will get an error. If you want to run this code, you must first delete the relationship by entering

```
start c:/sqlfun_drop_constraints.sql
```

Running this script drops all the constraints created in this chapter.

❷ This line creates the `set null` option.

❸ The state codes for California are automatically changed to nulls in the foreign key column.

8-12 The delete rule: `cascade`

In the following example, the first task sets up Referential Integrity between the `states4` table and the `clients4` table using the `cascade` option for deletes. The second task deletes California from the lookup table. In the data table all the rows that had `CA` in the foreign key column are deleted.

For emphasis, I want to say this again: It is not the values in the foreign key column that are deleted. It is the entire row of information that gets deleted automatically, so consider the consequences carefully before you set up this option.

Task 1

Set up Referential Integrity between the `states4` table and the `clients4` table. Use the option to have cascading deletes.

Oracle SQL ❶

```
alter table sec0812_clients4
add constraint fk_state_code4
foreign key (state_code)
   references sec0812_states4 (state_code)
   on delete cascade; ❷
```

Access GUI method

Follow the directions in section 8-9 to set up Referential Integrity with the Access GUI. In the Edit Relationships box, check two options:
* Enforce Referential Integrity
* Cascade Delete Related Records

Task 2

Delete California from the `states4` table. Do this when Referential Integrity has been set up using the `cascade` deletes option.

Oracle & Access SQL

```
delete from sec0812_states4
where state_code = 'ca';
```

Beginning table 1 (`sec0812_states4` table)

```
STATE
CODE    STATE_NAME                        STATE_CAPITAL
------  --------------------------------  -------------------
CA      CALIFORNIA                        SACRAMENTO
OR      OREGON                            SALEM
WA      WASHINGTON                        OLYMPIA
```

Beginning table 2 (`sec0812_clients4` table)

```
                                          STATE
CLIENT_ID CLIENT_NAME                     CODE
--------- ------------------------------  ------
      100 LARRY COHEN                     CA
      200 ALICE WILLIAMS                  CA
      300 ROGER WOLF                      OR
      400 NANCY KERN                      OR
      500 CATHY LEE                       WA
      600 STEVEN LAKE                     WA
```

Ending table 1 (`sec0812_states4` table)

```
STATE
CODE    STATE_NAME                        STATE_CAPITAL
------  --------------------------------  -------------------
OR      OREGON                            SALEM
WA      WASHINGTON                        OLYMPIA
```

Ending table 2 (`sec0812_clients4` table) ❸

```
                                      STATE
CLIENT_ID  CLIENT_NAME                CODE
---------  --------------------------  ------
      300  ROGER WOLF                 OR
      400  NANCY KERN                 OR
      500  CATHY LEE                  WA
      600  STEVEN LAKE                WA
```

Notes

❶ The `alter table` statement shown below has already been run by the SQLFUN_BUILD_TABLES.SQL script, which created the Referential Integrity relationship. If you run the alter table command again, you will get an error. If you want to run this code, you must first delete the relationship by entering

`start c:/sqlfun_drop_constraints.sql`

Running this script drops all the constraints created in this chapter.

❷ This line creates the `cascade` option.

❸ All the rows where the state codes were for California are automatically deleted.

8-13 The update rule: `cascade`

In the following example, the first task sets up Referential Integrity between the `state4` table and the `clients4` table using the `cascade` option for updates. The second task changes the abbreviation for California from CA to ZZ within the lookup table. In the data table, all the rows that had CA in the foreign key column now have the new value ZZ. This shows the process of changing codes, even if this example is a bit stretched.

Task 1

Set up Referential Integrity between the `states5` table and the `clients5` table. Use the option to have cascading deletes.

Access GUI method

Follow the directions in section 8-9 to set up Referential Integrity with the Access GUI. In the Edit Relationships box, check two options:
- Enforce Referential Integrity
- Cascade Update Related Fields

Task 2

Delete California from the states5 table. Do this when Referential Integrity has been set up using the cascade updates option.

Access SQL

```
update sec0813_states5
  set state_code = 'zz'
where state_code = 'ca';
```

- Oracle does not support cascaded updates.

Beginning table 1 (sec0813_states5 table)

Beginning table 2 (sec0813_clients5 table)

CLIENT_ID	CLIENT_NAME	STATE_CODE
100	LARRY COHEN	CA
200	ALICE WILLIAM	CA
300	ROGER WOLF	OR
400	NANCY KERN	OR
500	CATHY LEE	WA
600	STEVEN LAKE	WA

Record: 7 of 7

Ending table 1 (sec0813_states5 table)

STATE_CODE	STATE_NAME	STATE_CAPITAL
ZZ	CALIFORNIA	SACRAMENTO
OR	OREGON	SALEM
WA	WASHINGTON	OLYMPIA

Record: 4 of 4

Ending table 4 (sec0813_clients5 table) ❶

CLIENT_ID	CLIENT_NAME	STATE_CODE
100	LARRY COHEN	ZZ
200	ALICE WILLIAMS	ZZ
300	ROGER WOLF	OR
400	NANCY KERN	OR
500	CATHY LEE	WA
600	STEVEN LAKE	WA

Record: 7 of 7

Notes

❶ All the rows in the data table where the state codes were CA are automatically changed to ZZ.

Variations of Referential Integrity

So far when I have described RI to you, the primary key was always a single column and the foreign key was always in a table that was different from the primary key. Some other options are presented in the following sections.

8-14 The two meanings of primary key

The term *primary key* is used with two different meanings. When we are talking about tables in general, we speak about the primary key as the unique identifier of each row. It is the noun or the subject of each row. A table is only allowed to have one primary key, although that key can consist of several columns.

When we are talking about Referential Integrity, we speak about the primary key as the list of valid values, which is contained in the lookup table. A few years ago these were the same. That is, the list of valid values was always the primary key of the lookup table.

In the last few years a new option has become available that makes these two meanings different. The new option is that the list of valid values can be from a column that is different from the primary key of the lookup table. An example of this is shown later.

We cannot use just any column of the lookup table. The column must have a different value in every row and there must be a unique index defined on the column. We discuss unique indexes in section 8-18.

This feature is interesting and it is occasionally useful. But most of the time a lookup table is designed so that its primary key is its list of valid values. So we seldom need to distinguish between the two meanings of primary key.

The following example shows a case where the primary key of the table for the states6 table is different from the primary key for Referential Integrity, the list of valid values. We have two tables, states6 and clients6, with Referential Integrity between them. The state_capital column of the clients6 table is validated from the column of the same name within the states6 table.

Here we see that the `state_code` column is the primary key of the `states6` table. However, the `state_capital` column of the `states6` table provides the list of valid values for the Referential Integrity.

Task

Set up Referential Integrity between the `states6` table and the `clients6` table.

Oracle & Access SQL ❶

```
alter table sec0814_clients6
add constraint fk_state_capital6
foreign key (state_capital)
   references sec0814_states6 (state_capital);
```

Lookup table (`sec0814_states6` table)

STATE CODE	STATE_NAME	STATE_CAPITAL
CA	CALIFORNIA	SACRAMENTO
OR	OREGON	SALEM
WA	WASHINGTON	OLYMPIA

Data table (`sec0814_client6` table)

CLIENT_ID	CLIENT_NAME	STATE_CAPITAL
100	LARRY COHEN	SACRAMENTO
200	ALICE WILLIAMS	SACRAMENTO
300	ROGER WOLF	SALEM
400	NANCY KERN	SALEM
500	CATHY LEE	OLYMPIA
600	STEVEN LAKE	OLYMPIA

Notes

❶ Before this `alter table` is run, a unique index needs to be created on the `state_capital` column of the lookup table, `sec0814_states6`. Here, I have already done this for you.

8-15 Using two or more columns for the primary key

All of our examples so far have had a single column as the primary key. This is by far the most common situation when we are using a lookup table and Referential Integrity. However it is also possible to have several columns in the primary key of the lookup table and within the data table to validate the combination of several columns together.

In fact, this is done in the Lunches database. We have Referential Integrity between the 1_foods table and the 1_lunch_items table. The combination of the supplier_id and product_code columns is validated for every row of the 1_lunch_items table.

Task

Show how Referential Integrity is set up between the 1_foods table and the 1_lunch_items table.

Oracle & Access SQL

```
alter table l_lunch_items
add constraint fk_li_food
foreign key (supplier_id, product_code)
references l_foods (supplier_id, product_code);
```

Lookup table (`l_foods` table)

SUPPLIER ID	PRODUCT CODE	MENU ITEM	DESCRIPTION	PRICE	PRICE INCREASE
ASP	FS	1	FRESH SALAD	$2.00	$0.25
ASP	SP	2	SOUP OF THE DAY	$1.50	(null)
ASP	SW	3	SANDWICH	$3.50	$0.40
CBC	GS	4	GRILLED STEAK	$6.00	$0.70
CBC	SW	5	HAMBURGER	$2.50	$0.30
FRV	BR	6	BROCCOLI	$1.00	$0.05
FRV	FF	7	FRENCH FRIES	$1.50	(null)
JBR	AS	8	SODA	$1.25	$0.25
JBR	VR	9	COFFEE	$0.85	$0.15
VSB	AS	10	DESSERT	$3.00	$0.50

Data table (`l_lunch_items` table)

LUNCH_ID	ITEM_NUMBER	SUPPLIER ID	PRODUCT CODE	QUANTITY
1	1	ASP	FS	1
1	2	ASP	SW	2
1	3	JBR	VR	2
2	1	ASP	SW	2

(and many more)

8-16 The lookup and data tables can be the same table

It is possible for the lookup table and the data table to be the same table. That is, one column of a table is validated against another column from the same table. In fact this occurs within the Lunches database. The l_employees table has an employee_id column and a manager_id column. Each manager_id is required to be a valid employee_id.

Task

Show how Referential Integrity is set up between the employee_id column and the manager_id column of the l_employees table.

Oracle & Access SQL

```
alter table l_employees
add constraint fk_manager_id
foreign key (manager_id)
  references l_employees (employee_id);
```

Lookup table and data table (l_employees table)

EMPLOYEE ID	FIRST NAME	LAST NAME	DEPT CODE	HIRE_DATE	CREDIT LIMIT	PHONE NUMBER	MANAGER ID
201	SUSAN	BROWN	EXE	01-JUN-1998	$30.00	3484	(null)
202	JIM	KERN	SAL	16-AUG-1999	$25.00	8722	201
203	MARTHA	WOODS	SHP	02-FEB-2004	$25.00	7591	201
204	ELLEN	OWENS	SAL	01-JUL-2003	$15.00	6830	202
205	HENRY	PERKINS	SAL	01-MAR-2000	$25.00	5286	202
206	CAROL	ROSE	ACT	(null)	(null)	(null)	(null)
207	DAN	SMITH	SHP	01-DEC-2004	$25.00	2259	203
208	FRED	CAMPBELL	SHP	01-APR-2003	$25.00	1752	203
209	PAULA	JACOBS	MKT	17-MAR-1999	$15.00	3357	201
210	NANCY	HOFFMAN	SAL	16-FEB-2004	$25.00	2974	203

Other Types of Constraints

Some other types of constraints can be placed on one or more columns of data.

8-17 Check constraints

A check constraint ensures that some statement about the data is true for every row of a table. Oracle supports check constraints, but Access does not. Access has *validation rules*, which are somewhat similar. They both validate data when it is being entered or updated. The change to the data is rejected when it does not pass the test.

A constraint always checks all the old data, so we know that all the data in the table passes the test. If the old data does not pass the test, the constraint is rejected. However, a validation rule does not check the old data unless we ask it to, so there may be old data in the table that would not pass the test. That is the main difference.

Another difference is that a check constraint in Oracle is part of Oracle SQL. It is a command that is issued like any other SQL. A validation rule in Access is a property and cannot be set through SQL. It can be set in the GUI, in a macro, or in a module, but not through the SQL window.

Task

In Oracle, set a constraint to check that all the prices in the 1_foods table are less than $10.00. In Access, set a validation rule to do this.

Oracle SQL

```
alter table 1_foods
add constraint foods_max_price
check (price < 10.00);
```

Access GUI

Open the 1_foods table in Design view and highlight the price column. On the Validation Rule line, enter the test you want the data to meet. On the Validation Text line, enter the error message to be displayed if the rule is not met.

8-18 Unique **constraints**

A uniqueness (unique) constraint on a column ensures that every row contains a different value. In other words, no two rows have the same value in that column. Nulls are allowed in the column.

The mechanism that creates a uniqueness constraint is called a *unique index*. It is a type of index. Like any other index, it can make some of the processing in the database more efficient. You can create it by using either the alter table or create index statements. Both methods are shown next.

A uniqueness constraint can be placed on a combination of several columns. Then each one of the columns could have duplicate values, but the combination of columns would have a different value for every row of the table.

Task

Place a uniqueness constraint on the phone_number column of the l_employees table.

Oracle SQL: Method 1

```
alter table l_employees
add constraint unique_emp_phone_num
unique (phone_number);
```

Oracle SQL: Method 2 ❶

```
create unique index ix_phone
on l_employees (phone_number);
```

Access GUI ❷

Open the 1_employees table in Design view, highlight the line for the phone_number column and set the Indexed line to the option that says "Yes (No Duplicates)", as in the screen below.

```
┌──────────────────────────────────────────────────────────────────────────────────┐
│ ▦ L_EMPLOYEES : Table                                                  _ □ ✕        │
├──────────────────────────────────────────────────────────────────────────────────┤
│        Field Name          Data Type                    Description              ▲  │
│ ⑧ EMPLOYEE_ID            Number                                                     │
│   FIRST_NAME             Text                                                        │
│   LAST_NAME              Text                                                        │
│   DEPT_CODE              Text                                                        │
│   HIRE_DATE              Date/Time                                                   │
│   CREDIT_LIMIT           Number                                                      │
│   PHONE_NUMBER           Text                                                        │
│   MANAGER_ID             Number                                                      │
│                                                                                  ▼  │
├──────────────────────────────────────────────────────────────────────────────────┤
│                              Field Properties                                       │
│  ┌ General │ Lookup │                                                               │
│  Field Size          4                                                              │
│  Format                                                                             │
│  Input Mask                                                                         │
│  Caption                                                                            │
│  Default Value                              An index speeds up searches and sorting │
│  Validation Rule                            on the field, but may slow updates.     │
│  Validation Text                            Selecting "Yes - No Duplicates"         │
│  Required            No                     prohibits duplicate values in the       │
│  Allow Zero Length   No                     field. Press F1 for help on indexed     │
│  Indexed             Yes (No Duplicates)  ▼ fields.                                  │
│  Unicode Compression No                                                             │
└──────────────────────────────────────────────────────────────────────────────────┘
```

Notes

❶ If you ran the code for method 1, you will need to drop the constraint before you can run the code for method 2. To do this, use the following code:

```
alter table l_employees
drop constraint unique_emp_phone_num;
```

❷ The method shown can be used to put a uniqueness constraint in one field. To put a uniqueness constraint in a combination of fields, use

```
Table design view → View → Indexes
```

8-19 Not null **constraints**

A not null constraint on a column ensures that there are no nulls in that column. This is another way to say that data is required in that column. A not null constraint can only be placed on a single column.

Oracle SQL

```
alter table l_lunches
add constraint lunches_employee_id_not_null
check (employee_id is not null);
```

Access GUI

Open the l_lunches table in Design view, highlight the employee_id column, and set the Required line to Yes.

8-20 `Primary key` **constraints**

A `primary key` constraint is a combination of both a `unique` constraint and a `not null` constraint. A table is only allowed to have one `primary key` constraint. However it may have several `unique` constraints or `not null` constraints.

Task

Place a `primary key` constraint on the `employee_id` column of the `1_employees` table.

Oracle & Access SQL: View this code, but do not run it

```
alter table 1_employees
add constraint pk_1_employees
primary key (employee_id);
```

Access GUI

Open the `1_employees` table in `Design` view, highlight the `employee_id` column. Click the button on the toolbar that shows a key, as in the following screen.

8-21 Restrictions on the datatype and length of fields

The datatype definition for each column of a table functions as a constraint. That is, it limits the data that can be entered into that column. It limits the datatype of the data and also the length of the data. For example:

1. The value `Jane` cannot be entered into a numeric column.

2. The value `123456789` cannot be entered into a numeric column if the column is restricted to two-digit numbers.

These are restrictions on the data, and therefore they are constraints. However, most discussions of SQL do not list them as constraints.

8-22 Constraints are often coded in the `create table` statement

This section shows some examples of how to code constraints in the `create table` statement. The advantage to doing this is that it puts all the code in one place, which is great after the code has been developed and debugged. When you first develop some code, I suggest you do it in small pieces so that errors are easier to isolate and fix. The following SQL code shows you how to do this, but the l_employees table has already been created, so I do not intend you to run this code.

Oracle SQL: Method 1 — Without naming the constraints

```
create table l_employees
(employee_id    number(3)       primary key
,first_name     varchar2(10)    not null
,last_name      varchar2(10)
,dept_code      varchar2(3)
,hire_date      date
,credit_limit   number(4,2)     check
                                (credit_limit < 50)
,phone_number   varchar2(4)     unique
,manager_id     number(3)       references
                                l_employees(employee_id)
);
```

Oracle SQL: Method 2 — Giving names to the constraints

```
create table 1_employees
(employee_id    number(3)      constraint pk_employees
                               primary key
,first_name     varchar2(10)   constraint nn_f_name
                               check
                               (first_name is not null)
,last_name      varchar2(10)   constraint nn_1_name
                               check
                               (last_name is not null)
,dept_code      varchar2(3)
,hire_date      date
,credit_limit   number(4,2)    constraint max_limit
                               check
                               (credit_limit < 50)
,phone_number   varchar2(4)    constraint unique_phone
                               unique
,manager_id     number(3)      constraint fk_manager
                               references
                               1_employees(employee_id)
);
```

Access SQL: Method 1 — Without naming the constraints

```
create table 1_employees
(employee_id    integer        primary key
,first_name     varchar(10)    not null
,last_name      varchar(10)
,dept_code      varchar(3)
,hire_date      datetime
,credit_limit   money
,phone_number   varchar(4)     unique
,manager_id     integer        references
                               1_employees(employee_id)
);
```

Access SQL: Method 2 — Giving names to the constraints

```
create table 1_employees
(employee_id    integer        constraint pk_employees
                               primary key
,first_name     varchar(10)    constraint nn_f_name
                               not null
,last_name      varchar(10)    constraint nn_l_name
                               not null
,dept_code      varchar(3)
,hire_date      datetime
,credit_limit   money
,phone_number   varchar(4)     constraint unique_phone
                               unique
,manager_id     integer        constraint fk_manager
                               references
                               1_employees(employee_id)

);
```

Summary

Rules can be established about the data that tables can contain. These rules guarantee the validity of the data. This applies to both new data that is being entered and to old data that is already in the table.

Referential Integrity is the most frequently used type of data integrity, although several other types are also available. When we discuss inner joins I will tell you that RI protects the integrity of an inner join and keeps it from losing data.

RI is also considered to be a relationship between tables. It creates a parent table and a child table. We are not allowed to delete the parent table as long as the child table is referring to it.

Exercises

1. Goal: Create a Referential Integrity constraint.

    a. Create a new table, `valid_lunch_dates`, containing all the dates on which a lunch is scheduled. Get this list of valid dates from the `lunch_date` column of the `l_lunches` table. Add one more date to this table: December 15, 2005.

    Create a Referential Integrity constraint between the `valid_lunch_dates` table and the `l_lunches` table. This validates the `lunch_date` value whenever a new row is added to the `l_lunches` table.

    ## Oracle SQL

    ```
    drop table valid_lunch_dates cascade constraints;
    create table valid_lunch_dates as
    select distinct lunch_date
    from l_lunches;

    insert into valid_lunch_dates
    values('15-dec-2005');

    commit;

    alter table valid_lunch_dates
    add constraint pk_valid_dates
    primary key (lunch_date);

    alter table l_lunches
    add constraint fk_lunch_date
    foreign key (lunch_date)
        references valid_lunch_dates (lunch_date);
    ```

Access SQL

```
select distinct lunch_date
into valid_lunch_dates
from l_lunches;

insert into valid_lunch_dates
values(#15-dec-2005#);

alter table valid_lunch_dates
add constraint pk_valid_dates
primary key (lunch_date);

alter table l_lunches
add constraint fk_lunch_date
foreign key (lunch_date)
    references valid_lunch_dates (lunch_date);
```

b. Create a new table, valid_phone_numbers, containing the phone numbers for all the employees. Get this list of valid values from the phone_number column of the l_employees table. Add one more value to this table: 4707.

Create a Referential Integrity constraint between the valid_phone_numbers table and the l_employees table. This validates the phone_number value whenever a new row is added to the l_employees table.

2. Goal: Create a `check` constraint.

   a. Create a `check` constraint on the `quantity` column of the `1_lunch_items` table. Only the numbers 1 or 2 should be allowed in this column

   ### Oracle SQL

   ```
   alter table 1_lunch_items
   add constraint ck_quantity
   check (quantity in (1, 2));
   ```

   Access can do this using the GUI. See section 8-17.

   b. Create a `check` constraint on the `price_increase` column of the `1_foods` table. The `price_increase` should be less than 1/4 of the `price`.

3. Goal: Create a `not null` constraint, which says that a value is required.

   a. In the `1_departments` table, make the `department_name` column a required field.

   ### Oracle SQL

   ```
   alter table 1_departments
   add constraint nn_dept_name
   check (department_name is not null);
   ```

   Access can do this using the GUI. See section 8-19.

   b. In the `1_foods` table, make the `description` column a required field.

chapter 9

Row
Functions

In all the `select` statements we have written so far, the data in the result was an exact copy of the data in some cell of the beginning table. In this chapter, we remove that limitation. Row functions can create new values that do not exist in the original table.

Introduction to Row Functions

Row functions calculate a new value based on the data in a single row of the table. The value can be based on the data in one column or several different columns. Some row functions operate on numbers, and others operate on text or on dates.

9-1   Getting data directly from the beginning table

In all the SQL we have done so far, the data in the result table came directly from the data in the original table. More specifically, the value in each cell of the result table was copied from some cell of the original table. No change at all was made to the value in the cell.

The following conceptual drawing shows this process. Data from a few rows and columns of the beginning table are gathered together to form the result table. All the other data in the beginning table is ignored.

Beginning table

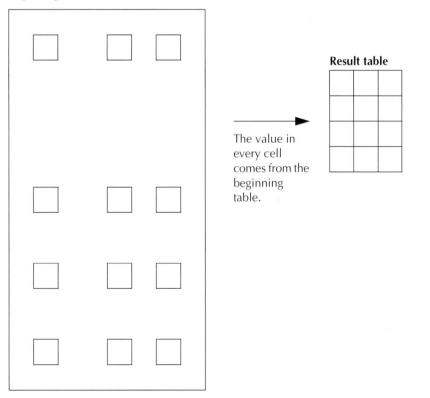

Result table

The value in every cell comes from the beginning table.

9-2   What is a row function?

Row functions calculate or construct a new value that is not in the beginning table. This new value is constructed from the values in one or more cells of the original table. All these cells must be part of a single row within the table.

The following conceptual drawing shows a row function as seen from a point of view that considers one row of the beginning table. A single new value is constructed by the function from the values in one or more cells of the row.

Beginning table

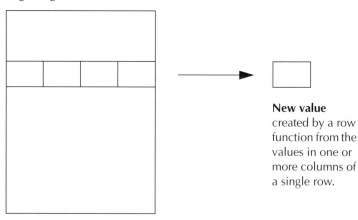

New value
created by a row
function from the
values in one or
more columns of
a single row.

The next conceptual drawing shows a row function as seen from the point of view that considers all the rows of the beginning table. A new value is created for each row. In effect, this adds a new column of data to the beginning table. Then the techniques you have already learned are applied to this enhanced table to create a final report from some of the rows and some of the columns.

Beginning table

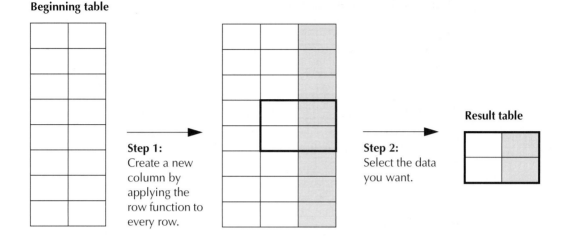

Step 1:
Create a new
column by
applying the
row function to
every row.

Step 2:
Select the data
you want.

Result table

The new values may appear in the result table, they may be used to pick rows from the beginning table, or they may be used to sort the rows of the result table. That is, the row function may be used in the `select` clause, the `where` clause, or the `order by` clause of a `select` statement.

The new column of information is not stored on the disk with the other data of the table. It does not become a permanent part of the table itself. Rather, it is held in memory while the `select` statement is being processed. The memory is released after the `select` statement has finished processing, so the new column of data exists only while one `select` statement is being processed.

More precisely, the processing of the `select` statement occurs as if the new values were all stored in memory. Actually, the computer is allowed to take shortcuts as long as it obtains the correct result. The new values may be calculated for only a few of the rows, if that is sufficient to obtain the result table.

Of course, you can create a new table that stores the new column as data on the disk by using the `create table` statement you learned in section 4-1. An example of this is shown next.

Task

Create a new table that adds a new column to the `1_foods` table. Create the new column by using a row function that adds together the `price` and the `price_increase` columns. Name this column `new_price`.

Oracle SQL

```
column new_price format $0.99 heading 'NEW|PRICE';  ❶

drop table foods_2;
create table foods_2 as
select 1_foods.*,  ❷
       price + price_increase as new_price
from 1_foods;
```

Access SQL

```
select 1_foods.*,  ❷
       price + price_increase as new_price
into foods_2
from 1_foods;
```

Beginning table (`1_foods` table)

```
SUPPLIER  PRODUCT  MENU                              PRICE
ID        CODE     ITEM  DESCRIPTION         PRICE INCREASE
--------  -------  ----- ------------------- -------- --------
ASP       FS          1  FRESH SALAD         $2.00    $0.25
ASP       SP          2  SOUP OF THE DAY     $1.50   (null)
ASP       SW          3  SANDWICH            $3.50    $0.40
CBC       GS          4  GRILLED STEAK       $6.00    $0.70
CBC       SW          5  HAMBURGER           $2.50    $0.30
FRV       BR          6  BROCCOLI            $1.00    $0.05
FRV       FF          7  FRENCH FRIES        $1.50   (null)
JBR       AS          8  SODA                $1.25    $0.25
JBR       VR          9  COFFEE              $0.85    $0.15
VSB       AS         10  DESSERT             $3.00    $0.50
```

New table with a column created by a row function (`1_foods_2` table)

```
SUPPLIER  PRODUCT    MENU                                      PRICE     NEW
ID        CODE       ITEM  DESCRIPTION           PRICE  INCREASE   PRICE
--------  -------   ------  -------------------  -------  --------  ------
ASP       FS           1    FRESH SALAD           $2.00     $0.25   $2.25
ASP       SP           2    SOUP OF THE DAY       $1.50    (null)   (null)  ❸
ASP       SW           3    SANDWICH              $3.50     $0.40   $3.90
CBC       GS           4    GRILLED STEAK         $6.00     $0.70   $6.70
CBC       SW           5    HAMBURGER             $2.50     $0.30   $2.80
FRV       BR           6    BROCCOLI              $1.00     $0.05   $1.05
FRV       FF           7    FRENCH FRIES          $1.50    (null)   (null)  ❸
JBR       AS           8    SODA                  $1.25     $0.25   $1.50
JBR       VR           9    COFFEE                $0.85     $0.15   $1.00
VSB       AS          10    DESSERT               $3.00     $0.50   $3.50
```

Notes

❶ In Oracle we must format the new column using an SQLplus command. I have already included this in the login script, so it is not required here, but there will be no harm done if you run it again. When you create a new column you should tell SQLplus how you want that column to be displayed.

❷ In both Oracle and Access, when we follow `select *` with additional columns, we need to add the table name and a period before the asterisk.

❸ The `new_price` is null when the `price_increase` is null because a null is an unknown value. In general, when a null is added to another value the result is a null.

9-3   An example of a row function in the `select` clause

In the previous section I used a row function to create a new column in the table. This is step 1 in the diagram on page 361. In that example I did not go on to step 2, which would select some data from the new table I created. In this section I combine both steps in a single `select` statement. I use a row function, which defines a new column, and I also select data to display in the final report.

In this example the price increase is added to the price, which creates a new price. This is a function because a new value is obtained. This function uses two columns from the beginning table: `price` and `price_increase`. Other row functions can use a single column or multiple columns.

Task

From the `1_foods` table list the `menu_item`, `description`, and `new_price`. Calculate the `new_price` by adding together the `price` and `price_increase`.

Oracle & Access SQL

```
select menu_item,
       description,
       price + price_increase as new_price ❶
from 1_foods
order by menu_item;
```

Beginning table (1_foods table)

SUPPLIER ID	PRODUCT CODE	MENU ITEM	DESCRIPTION	PRICE	PRICE INCREASE
ASP	FS	1	FRESH SALAD	$2.00	$0.25
ASP	SP	2	SOUP OF THE DAY	$1.50	(null)
ASP	SW	3	SANDWICH	$3.50	$0.40
CBC	GS	4	GRILLED STEAK	$6.00	$0.70
CBC	SW	5	HAMBURGER	$2.50	$0.30
FRV	BR	6	BROCCOLI	$1.00	$0.05
FRV	FF	7	FRENCH FRIES	$1.50	(null)
JBR	AS	8	SODA	$1.25	$0.25
JBR	VR	9	COFFEE	$0.85	$0.15
VSB	AS	10	DESSERT	$3.00	$0.50

Result table

MENU ITEM	DESCRIPTION	NEW PRICE
1	FRESH SALAD	$2.25
2	SOUP OF THE DAY	(null)
3	SANDWICH	$3.90
4	GRILLED STEAK	$6.70
5	HAMBURGER	$2.80
6	BROCCOLI	$1.05
7	FRENCH FRIES	(null)
8	SODA	$1.50
9	COFFEE	$1.00
10	DESSERT	$3.50

Notes

❶ This is the row function.

9-4   An example of a row function used in all the clauses of a `select` statement

This section shows an example of a row function used in several clauses of a `select` statement. In this example it is used in the `select` clause, `where` clause, and `order by` clause. Each time it is used we must write out the entire function. This is not ideal, and the next section shows you how to avoid writing out the function many times.

In this example, the function is fairly simple and writing it several times is not much of a problem. However, when a function is longer and more complex, having several copies of it can create a problem. When small changes are made to one instance of the function and not the others, it can be very difficult to debug.

In the following code, parentheses are put around the function when it is written in the `where` clause and the `order by` clause. These are optional, but I use them because I think it makes the code easier to read.

Task

From the `1_foods` table list the `menu_item`, `description`, and `new_price`. Calculate the `new_price` by adding together the `price` and the `price_increase`. List only the foods where the new price is greater than $2.00. Sort the rows of the result table on the `new_price` column.

Oracle & Access SQL

```
select menu_item,
       description,
       price + price_increase as new_price ❶
from 1_foods
where (price + price_increase) > 2.00 ❷
order by (price + price_increase); ❸
```

Beginning table (1_foods table)

```
SUPPLIER PRODUCT   MENU                                    PRICE
ID       CODE      ITEM DESCRIPTION          PRICE INCREASE
-------- -------   ------- --------------------   -------- --------
ASP      FS           1 FRESH SALAD            $2.00    $0.25
ASP      SP           2 SOUP OF THE DAY        $1.50   (null)
ASP      SW           3 SANDWICH               $3.50    $0.40
CBC      GS           4 GRILLED STEAK          $6.00    $0.70
CBC      SW           5 HAMBURGER              $2.50    $0.30
FRV      BR           6 BROCCOLI               $1.00    $0.05
FRV      FF           7 FRENCH FRIES           $1.50   (null)
JBR      AS           8 SODA                   $1.25    $0.25
JBR      VR           9 COFFEE                 $0.85    $0.15
VSB      AS          10 DESSERT                $3.00    $0.50
```

Result table ❹

```
MENU                         NEW
ITEM DESCRIPTION            PRICE
------- --------------------   ------
      1 FRESH SALAD            $2.25
      5 HAMBURGER              $2.80
     10 DESSERT                $3.50
      3 SANDWICH               $3.90
      4 GRILLED STEAK          $6.70
```

Notes

❶ In the select clause the function is written for the first time.

❷ In the where clause the entire function must be written out again.

❸ In the order by clause the entire function must be written out again.

❹ Rows having a null in the new_price column do not satisfy the condition in the where clause, so they do not appear in the result table.

9-5   Defining a row function in the first step

This section shows you a technique that can be used when the same row function is used in several different clauses of a `select` statement. When this was done in the previous section, the function was written several times. We had no guarantee that the function was exactly the same each time it was used. A typing error could make one instance slightly different from another.

This technique prevents such differences from occurring. It also makes the code easier to write and understand. If the row function is complex, it ensures that all references to the function are defined in exactly the same way. I recommend using this technique in most situations.

The first step of this technique creates a table or view that defines the new column using the row function. The next step is able to use the name of the new column in several places without rewriting the entire definition of the row function.

Task

The task is the same as in the previous section.

Oracle SQL: Step 1 — Create a view ❶

```
create or replace view step_1 as
select menu_item,
       description,
       price + price_increase as new_price ❷
from l_foods;
```

Access SQL: Step 1 — Create a view ❶

Step 1 Part 1: Enter this in the SQL window:

```
select menu_item,
       description,
       price + price_increase as new_price
from l_foods;
```

Step 1 Part 2: Save the query. Name it `step_1`.

Oracle & Access SQL: Step 2 — Use the new view ❷

```
select menu_item,
       description,
       new_price ❸
from step_1
where new_price > 2.00 ❹
order by new_price; ❺
```

Beginning table (1_foods table)

```
SUPPLIER PRODUCT   MENU                                        PRICE
ID       CODE      ITEM DESCRIPTION               PRICE INCREASE
-------- -------   ------- -------------------- -------- --------
ASP      FS            1 FRESH SALAD              $2.00    $0.25
ASP      SP            2 SOUP OF THE DAY          $1.50   (null)
ASP      SW            3 SANDWICH                 $3.50    $0.40
CBC      GS            4 GRILLED STEAK            $6.00    $0.70
CBC      SW            5 HAMBURGER                $2.50    $0.30
FRV      BR            6 BROCCOLI                 $1.00    $0.05
FRV      FF            7 FRENCH FRIES             $1.50   (null)
JBR      AS            8 SODA                     $1.25    $0.25
JBR      VR            9 COFFEE                   $0.85    $0.15
VSB      AS           10 DESSERT                  $3.00    $0.50
```

Result table produced by step 1

```
   MENU                             NEW
   ITEM DESCRIPTION               PRICE
 ------ -------------------- ------
      1 FRESH SALAD              $2.25
      2 SOUP OF THE DAY          (null) ❻
      3 SANDWICH                 $3.90
      4 GRILLED STEAK            $6.70
      5 HAMBURGER                $2.80
      6 BROCCOLI                 $1.05
      7 FRENCH FRIES             (null)
      8 SODA                     $1.50
      9 COFFEE                   $1.00
     10 DESSERT                  $3.50
```

Result table produced by step 2

```
    MENU                              NEW
    ITEM DESCRIPTION                PRICE
  ------- --------------------     ------
        1 FRESH SALAD              $2.25
        5 HAMBURGER                $2.80
       10 DESSERT                  $3.50
        3 SANDWICH                 $3.90
        4 GRILLED STEAK            $6.70
```

Notes

❶ The first step of this technique creates a view that defines the row function and gives a name to the column it creates. Step 1 could have created a table instead of a view, but using a view is usually more efficient.

Note that the row function is written only once with the new technique. However, with the previous technique, it had to be written several times.

❷ The second step is almost the same as the `select` statement in section 9-4. One difference is that the view created in Step 1 is used in the `from` clause. Another difference is that the name of the new column is used in all the clauses instead of writing out the explicit definition of the function.

❸ Here, the new_price column is used in the `select` clause.

❹ Here, the new_price column is used in the `where` clause.

❺ Here, the new_price column is used in the `order by` clause.

❻ A null is an unknown number, so a null added to any other number is a null; at least this is the case for row functions. To prevent a null from occurring here, you can use the `nvl` function in Oracle or the `nz` function in Access. These functions can change the nulls in the price_increase column into zeros. Then the addition will work. I show you how to do this in chapter 10.

Number Functions

Some row functions perform arithmetic on numbers. Others round or truncate numbers.

9-6   Functions on numbers

The row functions for arithmetic do exactly what you expect them to do. An asterisk is used for the multiplication sign, as it is in most computer languages. Null does not mean zero. It means an unknown value. So any row function that operates on a null produces a null as the result.

The following table shows some of the most frequently used functions on numbers. I omitted from this list the trigonometry functions and logarithms. Both Oracle and Access have them. Other, more specialized functions can be found in the technical reference.

Frequently used numerical functions.

Oracle	Access	Description	Examples
ARITHMETIC			
+	+	Addition	Oracle & Access: `3 + 2 = 5` Oracle & Access: `3 + null = null`
−	−	Subtraction	Oracle & Access: `3 − 2 = 1` Oracle & Access: `3 − null = null`
*	*	Multiplication	Oracle & Access: `3 * 2 = 6` Oracle & Access: `3 * null = null`
/	/	Division	Oracle & Access: `10 / 3 = 3.3333` Oracle & Access: `10 / null = null`
power	^	Value raised to an exponent	Oracle: `power(5, 2) = 25` Access: `5^2 = 25`
sqrt	sqr	Square root	Oracle: `sqrt(25) = 5` Access: `sqr(25) = 5`
(can be made)	\	Integer division	Access: `10 \ 3 = 3` Access: `10 \ null = null`
mod	mod	Remainder after division	Oracle: `mod(10, 3) = 1` Access: `10 mod 3 = 1`

More frequently used numerical functions.

Oracle	Access	Description	Examples
SIGN, ROUNDING, AND TRUNCATION			
sign	sgn	Sign indicator (1 if positive, −1 if negative, 0 if zero)	Oracle: `sign(-8) = -1` Access: `sgn(-8) = -1`
abs	abs	Absolute value	Oracle & Access: `abs(-8) = 8`
ceil	(can be made)	Smallest integer larger than or equal to a value	Oracle: `ceil(3.5) = 4`
floor	int	Largest integer less than or equal to a value	Oracle: `floor(3.5) = 3` Access: `int(3.5) = 3`
round	(can be made)	Round to a specified precision	Oracle: `round(3.4567, 2) = 3.46`
trunc	(can be made)	Truncate to a specified precision	Oracle: `trunc(3.4567, 2) = 3.45`

Access has the integer division function, which Oracle does not have. Oracle has more rounding and truncation functions than Access. These "missing" functions, or their equivalents, can all be constructed as shown in the following Notes.

Notes: Examples of constructing the "missing" functions

Getting integer division in Oracle:
    In Oracle, you have **floor (13/3) = 4**
    In Access, you have **13/3 = 4**

Getting `ceil` in Access:
    In Oracle, you have **ceil(3.1) = 4**
    In Access, you have **int(3.1 + .99) = 4**

(Yes, this does need to be adjusted for the precision of the numbers you are dealing with.)

Getting `round` in Access:
    In Oracle, you have **round(3.4567, 2) = 3.46**
    In Access, you have **int(3.4567 * (10 ^ 2) + .5) / (10^2) = 3.46**

Getting `trunc` in Access:
    In Oracle, you have **trunc(3.4567, 2) = 3.45**
    In Access, you have **int(3.4567 * (10^2)) / (10^2) = 3.45**

9-7   How to test a row function

This section shows you one technique for testing a row function. This is a way to discover what a row function does by using it to calculate a value.

The problem with doing calculations in SQL is that everything in SQL must be done in terms of tables. You must begin with a table and end with a table. So how can you multiply two numbers?

You have to start with a table — any table. It does not matter what data is in the table. In Oracle, we have a special table set up for this purpose. It is called the *dual* table. It has only one row and one column. In Access, I have created this table for you. In other Access databases you may have to create this table yourself. When you do this, be sure to put some data in the table. It does not matter what the values are, but they should not be a null.

This technique does not use the data in the beginning table. It only uses the table as a framework to get the `select` statement to process.

Task

Show how to test row functions in Oracle and Access.
As an example, show 3 * 4 = 12.

Oracle & Access SQL ❶

```
select 3 * 4
from dual;
```

Beginning table (dual table)

```
D
-
X
```

Result table

```
     3*4
---------
      12
```

Notes

❶ In Access, you must create the dual table before you can run this code. It can contain a single row and a single column. There must be some data in it, but the content of the data does not matter.

The dual table is used here as an empty vessel. It provides the structure of a table, but no content. This provides a framework to carry other content.

9-8   Another way to test a numeric row function

This section shows you another way to test a function on numbers. In the previous technique, we saw only one specific calculation. One of the significant features of numbers is that they form patterns. Using the previous technique, you could not see the pattern, but with this technique, you can.

This technique uses a table I set up for you containing all the numbers from −10 to +10. The numeric function is calculated on each of these numbers. The advantage is that you get to see how the function behaves over a range of values and the pattern that is created. If you want to see a larger range, you can use another table I set up for you called

`Numbers_0_to_99`

Task

Test the function MOD(X, 3) where X goes from −10 to +10.

Oracle SQL

```
select n,
       mod(n, 3)
from sec0908_test_numbers
order by n;
```

Access SQL

```
select n,
       n mod 3
from sec0908_test_numbers
order by n;
```

Beginning table (`sec0908_test_numbers` table)

```
        N
---------
      -10
       -9
       -8
       -7
       -6
       -5
       -4
       -3
       -2
       -1
        0
        1
        2
        3
        4
        5
        6
        7
        8
        9
       10
```

Result table ❶

```
        N   MOD(N,3)
---------   ---------
      -10         -1
       -9          0
       -8         -2
       -7         -1
       -6          0
       -5         -2
       -4         -1
       -3          0
       -2         -2
       -1         -1
        0          0
        1          1
        2          2
        3          0
        4          1
        5          2
        6          0
        7          1
        8          2
        9          0
       10          1
```

> ### Notes
>
> ❶ The last column shows the pattern created by MOD 3. This pattern is 0, 1, 2, 0 ... on the positive numbers and it is 0, −1,−2, 0 ... on the negative numbers.

Text Functions

Some row functions operate on text. Most of them produce text as output, but a few of them produce numbers.

9-9   Functions on text

The table on the following page shows the row functions on text that are used most often. Other ones can be found in the technical manuals. These row functions operate on both fixed-length and variable-length strings of characters.

The names of some of the Access functions here contain both uppercase and lowercase letters. This is done for readability, not because the names of these functions are case sensitive. It is a convention in Access that if the name is formed from two or more words, then the first letter of each word is capitalized. For instance, the name of the function `StrConv` is a shortened form of "String Conversion." The functions still work if you write them in all lowercase letters, but they are not as easy for people to understand.

Frequently used textual row functions.

Oracle	Access	Description	Examples
FUNCTIONS THAT RESULT IN TEXT			
`concat` or `||`	`&`	Concatenation ❶	Oracle: `concat('sun', 'flower') = 'sunflower'` Oracle: `'sun' || 'flower' = 'sunflower'` Access: `'sun' & 'flower' = 'sunflower'`
`substr`	`Mid`	Substring ❷	Oracle: `substr ('sunflower', 4, 3) = 'flo'` Access: `mid('sunflower', 4, 3) = 'flo'` (starting position = 4, length = 3)
`soundex`	(not available)	Used to compare names that sound similar ❸	Oracle: `where soundex('John') = soundex ('Jon')`
FUNCTIONS THAT CONTROL CAPITALIZATION			
`upper`	`UCase` or `StrConv ( ,1)`	Uppercase ❹	Oracle: `upper ('sunflower') = 'SUNFLOWER'` Access: `ucase('sunflower') = 'SUNFLOWER'` Access: `StrConv('sunflower',1) = 'SUNFLOWER'`
`lower`	`LCase` or `StrConv( ,2)`	Lowercase ❹	Oracle: `lower ('SUNFLOWER') = 'sunflower'` Access: `lcase('SUNFLOWER') = 'sunflower'` Access: `StrConv('SUNFLOWER',2) = 'sunflower'`
`initcap`	`StrConv( ,3)`	Capitalizes the first letter of one or more words. Puts the other letters in lowercase. ❹	Oracle: `initcap ('sunflower') = 'Sunflower'` Access: `StrConv('sunflower', 3) = 'Sunflower'`
FUNCTIONS THAT CONTROL BLANK SPACES			
`ltrim`	`LTrim`	Left trim: remove spaces on left ❺	`ltrim('   hello world   ') = 'hello world   '`
`rtrim`	`RTrim`	Right trim: remove spaces on right ❺	`rtrim('   hello world   ') = '   hello world'`
`trim`	`Trim`	Trim on both the left and right ❺	`trim('   hello world   ') = 'hello world'`
FUNCTIONS THAT RESULT IN NUMBERS			
`length`	`Len`	Number of characters in a text string ❻	Oracle: `length ('sunflower') = 9` Access: `len('sunflower') = 9`
`instr`	`InStr`	Starting position of one string occurring in another ❼	Oracle: `instr ('sunflower', 'low') = 5` Oracle: `instr ('sunflower', 'zzz') = 0` Zero means that the second string does not occur in the first string. Access: `Instr('sunflower', 'low') = 5`

Notes

❶ Concat puts two strings of text together and creates a single string. The second string begins right after the first string ends. If the first string is fixed-length, you may want to trim off the spaces on the right before you concatenate it.

❷ Substr is the opposite of concatenation. It takes characters from the middle of the string, beginning at a starting position and continuing for a specified length. When the length is not specified, the substring goes to the end of the beginning string.

❸ Soundex is used to compare the sounds of two words, to find words that sound alike but are spelled differently. It is used mostly to find people's names when you are not sure how to spell them. The U.S. Census Bureau originally developed this function. It is available in Oracle, but not in Access. It is usually used in the where clause, on both sides of an equal sign.

❹ Upper puts all the letters in uppercase. Lower puts them all in lowercase. Initcap capitalizes the first letter of each word and puts all the other letters in lowercase.

❺ Ltrim deletes all the blank spaces on the left, up to the first non-blank character. Rtrim does the same on the right. Trim deletes all the blank spaces on both the left and the right. These functions are seldom needed when you are working with variable-length character strings. They are used mostly when you are working with fixed-length character strings.

❻ Length gives the total number of characters in the string. For fixed-length strings, it gives the maximum number of characters the string can hold, which is the length of the fixed-length string. When working with fixed-length strings, you may want to trim the beginning and ending blanks from them before taking their lengths.

❼ Instr tests to see if one string is part of another string. If the first string contains the second string, then the starting position is the result. If the first string does not contain the second string, then a zero is the result.

9-10 Combining the first and last names

This section shows you an example that uses text functions. We combine the first name and the last name in a single column, placing one space between the two names.

A single space is then concatenated to the right of the first name. To code that single space, enclose one space within single quotes. Then the last name is concatenated to the end.

Oracle and Access use different signs for concatenation, but they mean the same thing. Access uses the ampersand (&). Oracle uses two double bars (||). On most keyboards the double bar is Shift + Backslash.

Variations of this technique can be used to put the name in other formats such as

Susan W. Brown
Ms. Brown
Brown, Susan W.

Task

List the employee_id and the full name of each employee. Create the full name by combining the first and last names separated by a single space.

Oracle SQL

```
select employee_id,
       first_name || ' ' || last_name as full_name ❶
from l_employees;
```

Access SQL

```
select employee_id,
       first_name & ' ' & last_name as full_name ❷
from l_employees;
```

Beginning table (`1_employees` table)

EMPLOYEE ID	FIRST_NAME	LAST_NAME	DEPT CODE	HIRE_DATE	CREDIT LIMIT	PHONE NUMBER	MANAGER ID
201	SUSAN	BROWN	EXE	01-JUN-1998	$30.00	3484	(null)
202	JIM	KERN	SAL	16-AUG-1999	$25.00	8722	201
203	MARTHA	WOODS	SHP	02-FEB-2004	$25.00	7591	201
204	ELLEN	OWENS	SAL	01-JUL-2003	$15.00	6830	202
205	HENRY	PERKINS	SAL	01-MAR-2000	$25.00	5286	202
206	CAROL	ROSE	ACT	(null)	(null)	(null)	(null)
207	DAN	SMITH	SHP	01-DEC-2004	$25.00	2259	203
208	FRED	CAMPBELL	SHP	01-APR-2003	$25.00	1752	203
209	PAULA	JACOBS	MKT	17-MAR-1999	$15.00	3357	201
210	NANCY	HOFFMAN	SAL	16-FEB-2004	$25.00	2974	203

Result table

EMPLOYEE ID	FULL_NAME
201	SUSAN BROWN
202	JIM KERN
203	MARTHA WOODS
204	ELLEN OWENS
205	HENRY PERKINS
206	CAROL ROSE
207	DAN SMITH
208	FRED CAMPBELL
209	PAULA JACOBS
210	NANCY HOFFMAN

Notes

❶ In Oracle, the concatenation operator is ||, where | is the uppercase symbol on the Backslash key. I always put a space on both sides of the concatenation sign. In the middle of the concatenation, the single space between the names is formed by

single quote — space — single quote

❷ In Access, the concatenation operator is &.

9-11 Separating the first and last names

In the previous section we discussed how to combine the `first_name` and `last_name` to create the `full_name`. In this section we go in the opposite direction. We begin with the `full_name` and divide it into two parts: the `first_name` and the `last_name`.

Finding the position of the space that separates the `first_name` from the `last_name` is the central point of this technique. This is the first step and it can be done with the `instr` function. In the next step the `full_name` column can be divided into two parts: the part before the space and the part after the space, which become the `first_name` and the `last_name` columns, respectively.

In specifying the `last_name`, only two parameters are used: the beginning string and the starting position. The third parameter, which is the length, is not specified. When this is done the substring extends all the way to the end of the beginning string.

Task

The `sec0911` table contains one column, which contains the full name, both the first name and last name separated by a single space. From this table list the full name, the position of the space, the first name, and the last name.

Oracle SQL

```
create or replace view step_1 as ❶
select full_name,
       instr(full_name, ' ') as position_of_space ❷
from sec0911;

select full_name,
       position_of_space,
       substr(full_name, 1, position_of_space - 1)
                                     as first_name, ❸
       substr(full_name, position_of_space + 1)
                                     as last_name ❹
from step_1;
```

Access SQL

Step 1: Enter the following query in the SQL window:

```
select full_name, ❺
       instr(full_name, ' ') as position_of_space ❷
into step_1
from sec0911;
```

Step 2: Save the query. Name it step_1.

```
select full_name,
       position_of_space,
       mid(full_name, 1, position_of_space - 1)
                                   as first_name, ❸
       mid(full_name, position_of_space + 1)
                                   as last_name ❹
from step_1;
```

Beginning table (sec0911 table)

```
FULL_NAME
---------------
SUSAN BROWN
JIM KERN
MARTHA WOODS
ELLEN OWENS
HENRY PERKINS
CAROL ROSE
DAN SMITH
FRED CAMPBELL
PAULA JACOBS
NANCY HOFFMAN
```

Result table

```
                POSITION
FULL_NAME       OF SPACE FIRST_NAME LAST_NAME
--------------- -------- ---------- ----------
SUSAN BROWN            6 SUSAN      BROWN
JIM KERN              4 JIM        KERN
MARTHA WOODS          7 MARTHA     WOODS
ELLEN OWENS           6 ELLEN      OWENS
HENRY PERKINS         6 HENRY      PERKINS
CAROL ROSE            6 CAROL      ROSE
DAN SMITH             4 DAN        SMITH
FRED CAMPBELL         5 FRED       CAMPBELL
PAULA JACOBS          6 PAULA      JACOBS
NANCY HOFFMAN         6 NANCY      HOFFMAN
```

Notes

❶ In Oracle, the first step creates a view that defines the position of the space. Here I use the Oracle command `create or replace view`, which is one way to do a preventative delete.

❷ This is the definition of the position of the space.

❸ The `first_name` begins at the first character of the `full_name`. It extends until the character before the space.

❹ The `last_name` begins at the character after the space. It extends until the end of the `full_name`.

❺ In Access, I chose to have the first step create a new table, rather than a view. This does not create a problem because the amount of data is small.

9-12 Formatting phone numbers

In section 7-5 we formatted the `phone_number` column of the `1_employees` table in Access. In the format we added an area code and the first three digits of the phone number. We could not use the same technique in Oracle because Oracle formats apply only to columns with a date or number datatype.

Now we are ready to format the phone numbers in Oracle by concatenating the `phone_number` with a literal. The same technique also works in Access.

When we use this technique we need to decide how we want to handle nulls in the data. There is one phone number that contains a null. We can exclude it from the result table if we want to by adding a `where` clause to the code:

```
where phone_number is not null;
```

However if we do this, there is a price to pay — the entire row for Carol Rose disappears from the result table, so the listing of the employees is incomplete. We will be able to fix this problem when we discuss unions in chapter 15.

Task

List the employee ID, employee name, and the phone number of all the employees. Format the `phone_number` values to include the area code and the first three digits of the phone number.

Oracle SQL

```
select employee_id,
       first_name,
       last_name,
       '(415) 643-' || phone_number as phone_number2
from 1_employees;
```

Access SQL

```
select employee_id,
       first_name,
       last_name,
       '(415) 643-' & phone_number as phone_number2
from 1_employees;
```

Beginning table (`1_employees` table)

```
EMPLOYEE                      DEPT                   CREDIT PHONE  MANAGER
      ID FIRST_NAME LAST_NAME CODE HIRE_DATE          LIMIT NUMBER      ID
-------- ---------- --------- ---- ----------- ------------- ------ -------
     201 SUSAN      BROWN     EXE  01-JUN-1998       $30.00 3484   (null)
     202 JIM        KERN      SAL  16-AUG-1999       $25.00 8722      201
     203 MARTHA     WOODS     SHP  02-FEB-2004       $25.00 7591      201
     204 ELLEN      OWENS     SAL  01-JUL-2003       $15.00 6830      202
     205 HENRY      PERKINS   SAL  01-MAR-2000       $25.00 5286      202
     206 CAROL      ROSE      ACT  (null)            (null) (null) (null)
     207 DAN        SMITH     SHP  01-DEC-2004       $25.00 2259      203
     208 FRED       CAMPBELL  SHP  01-APR-2003       $25.00 1752      203
     209 PAULA      JACOBS    MKT  17-MAR-1999       $15.00 3357      201
     210 NANCY      HOFFMAN   SAL  16-FEB-2004       $25.00 2974      203
```

Result table

```
EMPLOYEE                        PHONE
     ID FIRST_NAME LAST_NAME    NUMBER
-------- ---------- ----------  ----------------
    201 SUSAN      BROWN        (415) 643-3484
    202 JIM        KERN         (415) 643-8722
    203 MARTHA     WOODS        (415) 643-7591
    204 ELLEN      OWENS        (415) 643-6830
    205 HENRY      PERKINS      (415) 643-5286
    206 CAROL      ROSE         (415) 643-          ❶
    207 DAN        SMITH        (415) 643-2259
    208 FRED       CAMPBELL     (415) 643-1752
    209 PAULA      JACOBS       (415) 643-3357
    210 NANCY      HOFFMAN      (415) 643-2974
```

Notes

❶ This incomplete phone number results from the null in the phone_number column of the beginning table.

Date Functions

Some row functions operate on dates. Functions on dates are different
from the date formats you learned in chapter 7. Date formats change the
appearance of the date without changing its value. Date functions change
the value of the data to another date.

9-13 Functions on dates

This section shows you the date functions that are used most often. Date calculations are usually made in terms of the number of days, rather than months or years, because the number of days in a month or year can vary.

Both Oracle and Access can add a number of days to a date. They can both subtract a number of days from a date. They can both find the number of days between two dates. These are the most important date functions.

Using the table of numbers from 0 to 99, you can add these numbers to any date and create a calendar that is 100 days long. Although you can subtract one date from another date, you cannot add one date to another date.

When you are working with dates, be sure to remember that each date also has a time, even if the time is not being displayed. A fraction can be added to a date to change the time.

In the table on the following page, the Oracle dates are assumed to already be in date format. This assumption works when they are in a column that has a date datatype. If you are writing these dates directly into a `select` statement, the `to_date` function must be used to convert the text string within quotes to a `date` datatype. For example, the first line in the table shows

```
'20-jan-2015' + 3 = '23-jan-2015'
```

To use this function on a column of dates named `date_col`, we would write

```
select date_col + 3
```

To use this function and enter the date directly into the `select` clause, we would write

```
select to_date('20-jan-2015') + 3
```

Frequently used date functions.

Oracle	Access	Description and Examples
date + number	date + number or DateAdd('d',)	Add a number of days to a date. Oracle: '20-jan-2015' + 3 = '23-jan-2015' Access: #20-jan-2015# + 3 = #23-jan-2015# Access: DateAdd('d',3,#01-20-2015#) = #01-23-2015#
date − number	date − number or DateAdd('d',)	Subtract a number of days from a date. Oracle: '20-jan-2015' − 3 = '17-jan-2015' Access: #20-jan-2015# − 3 = #17-jan-2015# Access: DateAdd('d',-3,#01-20-2015#) = #01-17-2015#
date − date	date − date or DateDiff('d', ,)	The number of days between two dates. Oracle: '23-jan-2015' − '20-jan-2015' = 3 Access: #23-jan-2015# − #20-jan-2015# = 3 Access: DateDiff('d', #01-20-2015#,#01-23-2015#) = 3
trunc	DateValue	Sets the date/time to midnight, the beginning of the day. Optionally, may set the date/time to a different starting point such as the beginning of the hour, week, or century. Oracle: trunc('20-jan-2015 5:00 pm') = '20-jan-2015 12:00 am' Access: DateValue(#20-jan-2015 5:00 pm#) = #20-jan-2015#
round	(can be constructed)	Rounds the date/time to midnight, the beginning of the day or optionally to another starting point. Oracle: round('20-jan-2015 5:00 pm') = '21-jan-2015' Access: DateValue(#20-jan-2015 5:00 pm# + .5) = #21-jan-2015#
next_day	(can be constructed)	Date of the next specified weekday. Oracle: next_day ('20-jan-2015', 'mon') = '26-jan-2015' Oracle: next_day ('28-feb-2015', 'wed') = '04-mar-2015'
last_day	(can be constructed)	Date of the last day of the month. Oracle: last_day('20-feb-2016') = '29-feb-2016' Oracle: last_day('20-feb-2015') = '28-feb-2015'
add_months	DateAdd('m',)	Add a number of months to a date. Oracle: add_months('21-jan-2025', 3) = '21-apr-2025' Access: DateAdd('m', 3, #21-jan-2025#) = #21-apr-2025#)
months_between	DateDiff('m',)	Number of months between two dates. Oracle: months_between('21-apr-2025', '21-jan-2025') = 3 Access: DateDiff('m', #21-apr-2025#, #21-jan-2025#) = 3

Notes: Examples of constructing the "missing" functions

Getting `round` in Access:

In Oracle, you have   `round('20-jan-2015 5:00 pm') = '21-jan-2015'`
In Access, you have   `Cdate(Round(#20-jan-2015 5:00pm#)) = #1/21/2015#`

Getting `next_day` in Access:

In Oracle, you have   `next_day('20-jan-2015', 'mon') = '26-jan-2015'`
In Access, the days of the week are numbered from 1 = Sunday to 7 = Saturday
    so 2 = Monday

`#20-jan-2015# + 2 - Weekday(#20-jan-2015#) +`
`iif(2 > Weekday(#20-jan-2015#), 0, 7) = #1/26/2015#`

Getting `last_day` in Access:

In Oracle, you have   `last_day('20-feb-2016') = '29-feb-2016'`
In Access, you have   `Dateserial(Year(#20-feb-2016#),`
      `Month(#20-feb-2016#) + 1, 1) - 1 = #2/29/2016#`

9-14 An example of a date function

This section shows you an example of a date function. This function calculates the number of months each employee has worked for the company as of January 1, 2005. A month is not counted until a full month has been worked.

To count the months in an even way, I have decided to write the code as if all months are 30 days long. First I find the number of days between the person's hire date and January 1, 2005. Then I divide the number of days by 30 and throw away the fraction. This gives me the number of months.

When you are calculating with dates, it is usually best to do your calculation first in terms of the number of days and then, if you desire, convert the answer into weeks, months, or years. This strategy gives you the most control and the most accurate answers.

You might think this would be easier to do using the `months_between` function. However, this function often does not produce precise results. One reason is that the lengths of the months vary. When I tried using it in this example I found that Oracle and Access behave differently, and neither of them was as reliable as working directly with the number of days.

Here is an example of one of the problems with the `months_between` function. Using this function on the computer I found that between February 28 and March 28 there is one month, but between February 28 and March 29 there is less than one month.

Task

List all the employees, their hire dates, and the number of months each person will have worked for the company as of January 1, 2005.

Oracle SQL

```
select first_name,
       last_name,
       hire_date,
       floor((to_date('01-jan-2005') - hire_date)/30) ❶
                          as months_with_the_company

from l_employees;
```

Access SQL

```
select first_name,
       last_name,
       hire_date,
       int((#01-jan-2005# - hire_date)/30)
                          as months_with_the_company
from l_employees;
```

Beginning table (1_employees table)

EMPLOYEE ID	FIRST_NAME	LAST_NAME	DEPT CODE	HIRE_DATE	CREDIT LIMIT	PHONE NUMBER	MANAGER ID
201	SUSAN	BROWN	EXE	01-JUN-1998	$30.00	3484	(null)
202	JIM	KERN	SAL	16-AUG-1999	$25.00	8722	201
203	MARTHA	WOODS	SHP	02-FEB-2004	$25.00	7591	201
204	ELLEN	OWENS	SAL	01-JUL-2003	$15.00	6830	202
205	HENRY	PERKINS	SAL	01-MAR-2000	$25.00	5286	202
206	CAROL	ROSE	ACT	(null)	(null)	(null)	(null)
207	DAN	SMITH	SHP	01-DEC-2004	$25.00	2259	203
208	FRED	CAMPBELL	SHP	01-APR-2003	$25.00	1752	203
209	PAULA	JACOBS	MKT	17-MAR-1999	$15.00	3357	201
210	NANCY	HOFFMAN	SAL	16-FEB-2004	$25.00	2974	203

Result table

```
FIRST_NAME  LAST_NAME   HIRE_DATE     MONTHS_WITH_THE_COMPANY
----------  ----------  -----------   -----------------------
SUSAN       BROWN       01-JUN-1998                        80
JIM         KERN        16-AUG-1999                        65
MARTHA      WOODS       02-FEB-2004                        11
ELLEN       OWENS       01-JUL-2003                        18
HENRY       PERKINS     01-MAR-2000                        58
CAROL       ROSE        (null)        (null)
DAN         SMITH       01-DEC-2004                         1
FRED        CAMPBELL    01-APR-2003                        21
PAULA       JACOBS      17-MAR-1999                        70
NANCY       HOFFMAN     16-FEB-2004                        10
```

Notes

❶ The `to_date` function is used to convert the character string `01-jan-2005` into a date. Subtracting the `hire_date` from this date gives the number of days the employee has worked for the company. Dividing this number by 30 gives the number of months. The `floor` function rounds down to get rid of the fraction.

9-15 Removing the time from a date

Every date in SQL includes a time, even though we do not always see it. Sometimes this can be a problem for us, depending on what we are doing. Sometimes we want to be able to use the date without the time.

This section shows you one way to remove the time from the date. Or rather, it sets all the times to midnight, so all the times have the same value. This technique is presented here because we will need to use it in chapter 11.

Task

List the `l_lunches` table. First, show the times that are in the beginning table. Then show how to remove these times.

Oracle SQL: Show the times in the 1-lunches table

```
select lunch_id,
       lunch_date,
       employee_id,
       to_char(date_entered,
               'dd-mon-yyyy hh:mi am') as date_entered
from 1_lunches;
```

Access SQL: Show the times in the 1-lunches table

```
select lunch_id,
       lunch_date,
       employee_id,
       format(date_entered,
           'dd-mmm-yyyy hh:nn am/pm') as date_entered2
from 1_lunches;
```

Oracle SQL: The trunc function removes the time

```
select lunch_id,
       lunch_date,
       employee_id,
       to_char(trunc(date_entered),
               'dd-mon-yyyy hh:mi am') as date_entered
from 1_lunches;
```

Access SQL: The datevalue function removes the time

```
select lunch_id,
       lunch_date,
       employee_id,
       format(datevalue(date_entered),
           'dd-mmm-yyyy hh:nn am/pm') as date_entered2
from 1_lunches;
```

Beginning table (1_lunches table)

```
           LUNCH         EMPLOYEE
LUNCH_ID   DATE              ID   DATE_ENTERED
---------  ------------  --------  --------------------
        1  16-NOV-2005       201  13-OCT-2005 10:35 AM
        2  16-NOV-2005       207  13-OCT-2005 10:35 AM
        3  16-NOV-2005       203  13-OCT-2005 10:35 AM
        4  16-NOV-2005       204  13-OCT-2005 10:35 AM
        6  16-NOV-2005       202  13-OCT-2005 10:36 AM
        7  16-NOV-2005       210  13-OCT-2005 10:38 AM
        8  25-NOV-2005       201  14-OCT-2005 11:15 AM
        9  25-NOV-2005       208  14-OCT-2005 02:23 PM
       12  25-NOV-2005       204  14-OCT-2005 03:02 PM
       13  25-NOV-2005       207  18-OCT-2005 08:42 AM
       15  25-NOV-2005       205  21-OCT-2005 04:23 PM
       16  05-DEC-2005       201  21-OCT-2005 04:23 PM
       17  05-DEC-2005       210  21-OCT-2005 04:35 PM
       20  05-DEC-2005       205  24-OCT-2005 09:55 AM
       21  05-DEC-2005       203  24-OCT-2005 11:43 AM
       22  05-DEC-2005       208  24-OCT-2005 02:37 PM
```

Result table

```
           LUNCH         EMPLOYEE
LUNCH_ID   DATE              ID   DATE_ENTERED
---------  ------------  --------  --------------------
        1  16-NOV-2005       201  13-OCT-2005 12:00 AM
        2  16-NOV-2005       207  13-OCT-2005 12:00 AM
        3  16-NOV-2005       203  13-OCT-2005 12:00 AM
        4  16-NOV-2005       204  13-OCT-2005 12:00 AM
        6  16-NOV-2005       202  13-OCT-2005 12:00 AM
        7  16-NOV-2005       210  13-OCT-2005 12:00 AM
        8  25-NOV-2005       201  14-OCT-2005 12:00 AM
        9  25-NOV-2005       208  14-OCT-2005 12:00 AM
       12  25-NOV-2005       204  14-OCT-2005 12:00 AM
       13  25-NOV-2005       207  18-OCT-2005 12:00 AM
       15  25-NOV-2005       205  21-OCT-2005 12:00 AM
       16  05-DEC-2005       201  21-OCT-2005 12:00 AM
       17  05-DEC-2005       210  21-OCT-2005 12:00 AM
       20  05-DEC-2005       205  24-OCT-2005 12:00 AM
       21  05-DEC-2005       203  24-OCT-2005 12:00 AM
       22  05-DEC-2005       208  24-OCT-2005 12:00 AM
```

Summary

In this chapter, you learned how to use row functions to create values that are not in the original table. You learned that a wide variety of row functions exist, and that there are many more in the technical manuals that we did not have time to examine.

Exercises

1. Goal: Test some of the row functions with specific values to see what they do.

   People using Access should create a table with one row and one column. Name the table `dual`. Put in any data you like, such as an "A." You can use this table to test the row functions.

   a. Test addition by adding 12 and 34.

   Oracle & Access SQL

   ```
   select 12 + 34
   from dual;
   ```

   ---

   b. Test the row functions shown in the table on the following page. Substitute the values below for "12 + 34" in the code for exercise 1a. The Oracle and Access versions do the same things. Make sure you understand why you get the result that is produced. Do not worry about the column headings.

   In Access, the uppercase letters in these names of the functions are only used to make them easier to read. The uppercase letters are not required.

Purpose	Oracle	Access
Nulls in arithmetic	12 + null	12 + null
Concatenation	'first' || 'second'	'first' & 'second'
Substring	substr('abcdefghij',3,4)	Mid('abcdefghij',3,4)
Length of text	length('abcdefg')	Len('abcdefg')
Starting position, when the second string is part of the first string	instr('abcdefg', 'cd')	InStr('abcdefg','cd')
Starting position, when the second string is not part of the first string	instr('abcdefg','zz')	InStr('abcdefg','zz')
Add days to a date	to_date('07-mar-2011') + 2	#07-mar-2011# + 2
Add months to a date	add_months(to_date('07-mar-2011'),2)	DateAdd('m',2,#07-mar-2011#)
Add years to a date (or 12 months for each year)	add_months(to_date('07-mar-2011'),24)	DateAdd('y',2,#07-mar-2011#)
Find the number of days between two dates	to_date('27-mar-2011') - to_date('07-mar-2011')	#27-mar-2011# - #07-mar-2011#

2. Goal: Test numeric row functions on a series of numbers. A table named `sec0908_test_numbers` contains the integers from −10 to +10. Using this test allows us to see the pattern of numbers that the function creates.

   a. Test division. Divide by 3 all the numbers from −10 to +10. List both the number being divided and the answer.

   ### Oracle & Access SQL

   ```
   select n,
          n/3
   from sec0908_test_numbers
   order by n;
   ```

   b. Test the following functions using the method shown in exercise 2a.

Purpose	Oracle	Access
Addition	n + 100	n + 100
Subtraction	5 − n	5 − n
Multiplication	5 * n	5 * n
Division of N	n / 10	n / 10
Division by N ❶	10 / n	10 / n
Division by N Add the condition: WHERE NOT (N = 0)	10 / n	10 / n
Exponents	power(2, n)	2^n
Square root ❷	sqrt(n)	sqr(n)
Square root Add the condition: WHERE N >= 0	sqrt(n)	sqr(n)
Integer part of division	floor(n/3)	n\3
Remainder after division	mod(n,3)	n mod 3
Sign	sign(n)	sgn(n)
Absolute value	abs(n)	abs(n)

Notes

❶ Oracle handles this differently than Access. Oracle returns an error message and no result table. It refuses to process the query at all. Access produces a result table and calculates a result for all the values of N except when N = 0. It says "#Error" for the value of 10/N when N = 0.

❷ Oracle handles this differently than Access. Oracle returns an error message and no result table. It refuses to process the query at all. Access produces a result table and calculates a result for all the values of N except when N < 0. It says "#Error" for the value of the square root when N < 0.

3. Goal: Use the text functions.

a. See sections 9-10 to 9-12.

b. List the employee ID and the names of all the employees. Display the names in the form "S. BROWN". That is, show only the first letter on the first name, followed by a period, a space, and the last name.

In Oracle, the data is already capitalized. In Access, you will need to change it to uppercase. Name this formatted column `employee_name`. Sort the rows by the `employee_id`.

4. Goal: Use the date functions. Construct and use a table of constants.

a. Find the number of days between December 21, 2020 (winter solstice), and March 21, 2021 (spring equinox). Put both dates in a table of constants, so they both have a datatype of `date`.

Oracle SQL

```
drop table ex0904a;
create table ex0904a
(beg_date      date,
 end_date      date);

insert into ex0904a
values ('21-dec-2020', '21-mar-2021');

commit;

select end_date - beg_date as number_of_days
from ex0904a;
```

Access SQL

```
drop table ex0904a;
create table ex0904a
(beg_date       datetime,
 end_date       datetime);

insert into ex0904a
values (#21-dec-2020#, #21-mar-2021#);

select end_date - beg_date as number_of_days
from ex0904a;
```

b. Find the number of days between July 29, 1969 (man's first landing on the moon), and January 1, 2000.

chapter 10

USING ROW FUNCTIONS

In the last chapter we discussed many of the most commonly used row functions. In this chapter we discuss a few more row functions that are used for special purposes. We also discuss the documentation of row functions and show some of their applications.

Other Functions

A few other row functions also have special purposes.

10-1 Other row functions

Here is an overview of four other types of row functions. We discuss them in more detail in the following sections.

Other row functions.

Oracle	Access	Description and Examples
FUNCTIONS TO IDENTIFY THE USER AND THE DATE		
user	CurrentUser()	Name of the userid for the current session. Oracle: user = 'JPATRICK' Access: CurrentUser() = 'Admin'
sysdate	Now() Date() Time()	The current date and time. Oracle: sysdate = '20-dec-1999' Access: Now() = '12-20-1999 10:30:25 AM' Access: Date() = '12-20-1999' Access: Time() = '10:30:25 AM'
FUNCTIONS TO CHANGE NULLS TO OTHER VALUES		
nvl	nz	Converts nulls to another value. Oracle: nvl(col_1, 0) = 0 if col_1 is null Oracle: nvl(col_1, 0) = col_1 if col_1 is not null Access: nz(col_1, 0) = '0' if col_1 is null Access: nz(col_1, 0) = 'col_1' if col_1 is not null
FUNCTIONS TO CHANGE THE DATATYPE		
to_char	CStr	Converts a number or date to a character string (text). Also used to control the formats of dates in Oracle. Oracle: to_char(7) = '7' Access: CStr(7) = '7'
to_date	CDate	Converts a number or character string to a date. Also used to control the input of dates with a specified format in Oracle. The first date Oracle and Access can handle: Oracle: to_date(1, 'j') = '01-jan-4712 BC Access: CDate(1) = #12/31/1899# A date closer to the present: Oracle: to_date('03/10', 'mm/yy') = '01-mar-2010' Access: CDate('Jan 18, 2010') = #1/18/2010#
to_number	CInt CDbl (others)	Converts a character string to a number. Oracle: to_number('8') = 8 Access: CInt('8') = 8

Other row functions. *(continued)*

Oracle	Access	Description and Examples
FUNCTIONS TO PICK ONE VALUE		
greatest	Not available	Chooses the greatest member of a list. Applies to numbers, text, and dates. 　　Oracle: `greatest(1, 9, 2, 3) = 9`
least	Not available	Chooses the least member of a list. Applies to numbers, text, and dates. 　　Oracle: `least(1, 9, 2, 3) = 1`

10-2　Using functions to identify the user and the date

This section shows you how to use functions to identify the user, the date, and the time. The technique is similar in Oracle and Access, although the details are quite different.

In Oracle, code like this is often used at the beginning of a spool file to identify the session that is being recorded. A spool file, discussed in section 5-7, can save all the commands and results during a session. Access does not support spool files.

In Oracle, the name of the userid is obtained from the User function. This is the name you use when you log on to Oracle. In Access, it is obtained from the `CurrentUser()` function. Unless you have set up special security for Access, the value of this function is set to `Admin`. The opening parenthesis, followed immediately by a closing parenthesis, might seem peculiar. This is an example of a 0-parameter function. The pair of parentheses is retained to show that it is a function, but it does not require any input parameters. In effect, a 0-parameter function is a name for a constant value. Some people call this a *system variable*. Here that constant value depends on the userid you are logged on to.

In Oracle, the date and time are obtained from the `sysdate` function. In Access, they are obtained from the `Now()`, `Date()`, or `Time()` functions. In Oracle, if we want to see the time in addition to the date, we need to format `sysdate` with the `to_char` function. In Access, the time shows up automatically from the default formatting, so we do not need to use the `format` function. We discussed date formats in section 7-1.

Do not confuse the Oracle function `sysdate` with the Access function `Date()`. They both may show only the date and not the time. However, `sysdate` actually contains the time although it is not always shown. `Date()` does not include the time.

In the following code, the `from` clause uses the dual table. In Oracle, this table is already built for us. In Access, we need to build it. This was discussed in section 9-7.

Task

Show how to identify the user, the date, and the time.

Oracle SQL

```
select user,
       to_char(sysdate, 'day month dd, yyyy hh:mi am')
                                      as date_time
from dual;
```

Oracle result table

USER	DATE_TIME
JPATRICK	SUNDAY JULY 08, 2001 06:41 PM

Access SQL

```
select CurrentUser() as user,
       Now() as date_time
from dual;
```

Access result table

10-3   Using functions to change nulls to other values

The `nvl` (Null VaLue) function in Oracle and the `nz` (Non-Zero) function in Access change the nulls in some columns to another value, such as zero. When the original value in the column is not null, no change is made and the value stays the same. The original column can have any datatype — number, text, or date.

In Oracle, the `nvl` function does not change the datatype of the column, so the datatype of the replacement value must be the same as the one the column originally has. This restriction means that nulls in a numeric column can be changed to zero or some other number, but not to text or a date. The nulls in a text column must be replaced with text, or possibly with a string of blanks. The nulls in a date column can only be changed to a date.

In Access, the `nz` function always changes the column to a text datatype. Any data, including numbers and dates, can always be represented as text. The replacement value, which is substituted for nulls, can be any datatype. However, it is changed to text when it is output from the `nz` function.

Task

Show how to replace nulls with other values. Do this with a number column, a text column, and a date column.

Demonstrate two methods of doing this. In one method, the null is replaced with a value that has the same datatype as the column. In the other method, the null is replaced with text.

Oracle SQL: Oracle style —
Replacement value has the same datatype as the column ❶

```
select pkey,
       nvl(num_col,0) as num_col2,
       nvl(text_col, 'zilch') as text_col2,
       nvl(date_col, '01-jan-1900') as date_col2
from sec1003;
```

Access SQL: Oracle style —
Replacement value has the same datatype as the column ❷

```
select pkey,
       nz(num_col,0) as num_col2,
       nz(text_col, 'zilch') as text_col2,
       nz(date_col, #01-jan-1900#) as date_col2
from sec1003;
```

Beginning table (sec1003 table)

```
PKEY    NUM_COL TEXT_COL DATE_COL
-----  --------- -------- -----------
A            1 M         (null)
B            2 (null)    20-JAN-2013
C       (null)   N         21-JAN-2013
```

Result table: Method 1

```
PKEY   NUM_COL2 TEXT_COL DATE_COL2
-----  --------- -------- -----------
A            1 M         01-JAN-1900
B            2 ZILCH     20-JAN-2013
C            0 N         21-JAN-2013
```

Oracle SQL:
Access style — Replacement value is text ❸

```
select pkey,
       nvl(to_char(num_col), 'no number') as num_col2,
       nvl(text_col, 'no text') as text_col2,
       nvl(to_char(date_col), 'no date') as date_col2
from sec1003;
```

Access SQL:
Access style — Replacement value is text ❹

```
select pkey,
       nz(num_col, 'no number') as num_col2,
       nz(text_col, 'no text') as text_col2,
       nz(date_col, 'no date') as date_col2
from sec1003;
```

Result table: Method 2

PKEY	NUM_COL2	TEXT_COL	DATE_COL2
A	1	M	NO DATE
B	2	NO TEXT	20-JAN-2013
C	NO NUMBER	N	21-JAN-2013

Notes

❶ In Oracle, we use the `nvl` function to replace the null values. This example uses zero to replace the nulls in a column of numbers. It uses "zilch," a text string, to replace the nulls in a column of text. It uses January 1, 1900, a date, to replace the nulls in a column of dates. The datatype of the original column is not changed.

❷ In Access, we use the `nz` function to replace the null values. The same replacement values are used as in the Oracle example. The differences are that the name of the function is `nz`, and pound signs are used to enclose the date. In Access, the `nz` function converts all the columns to text, whereas in Oracle, the `nvl` function leaves the datatype of the column unchanged.

❸ In Oracle, if we want to replace the nulls with text, then we must first convert the entire column to text using the `to_char` function. This is an unusual way to write the code in Oracle, but I am doing it here to show that it can be done.

❹ In Access, when you begin with a column of any datatype, you can change the nulls into text strings with the `nz` function.

10-4   Using functions to change the datatype

Functions that change datatypes keep the outer meaning of the data the same while changing the inner representation—the datatype—of the data. For instance, "8" as a character string differs from "8" as a number. They both mean 8 but if you could see the patterns of 1s and 0s inside the computer, you would see one binary pattern for the number and a different binary pattern for the character string.

Why do we care about this difference? One reason is that each row function works only with data that have a particular datatype. For example, consider addition. Addition is defined on numbers, but not on character strings. When 8 and 4 are numbers, then "8 + 4" makes sense, and is equal to the number 12. However, when 8 and 4 are character strings, "8 + 4" does not make sense. It is not equal to anything, and will give us an error message if we use it. At least, so says the theory. Things work a bit differently in practice, as we will see.

Oracle, Access, and most other SQL products do a certain amount of automatic datatype conversion. Some SQL products do more of this than other products. The idea is to make things easier for the user. A novice user might become confused and enraged if the database refuses to add 8 and 4 when they are text. An error message about the datatype might not calm the user. To make things work more smoothly, the 8 and 4 are automatically converted into numbers and then added together. This happens silently, behind the scenes. There is no message to indicate this is occurring.

The following example shows that automatic datatype conversion is used by both Oracle and Access to perform arithmetic on text strings. In this case, Oracle performs all the operations correctly. Access performs subtraction, multiplication, and division correctly, but it has a flaw when it performs addition. Access says that "8 + 4" = 84. Clearly, it is doing concatenation instead of addition. To obtain the correct result, we need to do the datatype conversion ourselves instead of relying on the automatic conversion. To do this we change the text datatype to an integer datatype, using the `cint` (convert to integer) function. This is one example of a time when the conversion must be done using the conversion functions.

Often when I first write some code, I assume that most of the datatype conversions will be done for me automatically. This works 99% of the time. If the results seem strange in some way, I have to debug and fix the code. It is during this process of debugging and fixing that I most often decide to control the datatype conversion myself using a datatype conversion function.

Task

Show the effects of automatic datatype conversion. Perform arithmetic on numbers that are in columns with a text datatype.

Oracle & Access SQL

```
select pkey, ❶
       text_1,
       text_2,
       text_1 + text_2 as text_add, ❷
       text_1 - text_2 as text_subtract,
       text_1 * text_2 as text_multiply,
       text_1 / text_2 as text_divide
from sec1004;
```

Beginning table (sec1004 table)

```
PKEY  TEXT_1  TEXT_2
----  ------  ------
A     8       4
B     33      11
```

Oracle result table — Correct

```
PKEY  TEXT_1  TEXT_2   TEXT_ADD  TEXT_SUBTRACT  TEXT_MULTIPLY  TEXT_DIVIDE
----  ------  ------   --------  -------------  -------------  -----------
A     8       4              12              4             32            2
B     33      11             44             22            363            3
```

Access result table — Addition is incorrect

pkey	text_1	text_2	text_add	text_subtract	text_multiply	text_divide
A	8	4	84	4	32	2
B	33	11	3311	22	363	3

Record: |◄| ◄| [3] |►| |►I| |►*| of 3

Access SQL: Correction

```
select pkey, text_1, text_2,
       cint(text_1) + cint(text_2) as text_add,  ❸
       text_1 - text_2 as text_subtract,
       text_1 * text_2 as text_multiply,
       text_1 / text_2 as text_divide
from sec1004;
```

Access result table — Correct

pkey	text_1	text_2	text_add	text_subtract	text_multiply	text_divide
A	8	4	12	4	32	2
B	33	11	44	22	363	3

Record: |◄| ◄| 3 |► |►I|►*| of 3

Notes

❶ This prints out the primary key and the two text items, so you can show them in the result table. Why is there a primary key? It does not do anything in this example. However, every table should have a primary key and most listings should display it.

❷ The next lines add, subtract, multiply, and divide the two text items. For these operations to make sense, the text must be automatically converted to numbers before the arithmetic can be done.

❸ The cint (convert to integer) function is used to convert the text to integers. Then Access can add them, giving $8 + 4 = 12$.

There is a reason why Access says $8 + 4 = 84$. In many of the early PC computer languages, the plus sign is used with text strings to mean concatenation. For example,

sun + flower = sunflower

Access has decided to preserve this legacy. Some computer code might need to be rewritten if they were to correct this mistake. So there is a reason for it, but I think that it is a bad reason!

Using the Documentation of Row Functions

10-5   Using Expression Builder in Access

In Access, I use the Expression Builder as a reference document to tell me what row functions are available. This is not the only thing that Expression Builder is designed to do, but it is the way that I use it.

In contrast, in Oracle you usually use the printed documentation or the online documentation to find the right row function.

To start the Expression Builder and see the functions, follow these steps:

1. Click Queries.

2. Click New.

3. Highlight Design View.

4. Click OK.

5. Click Close.

6. Right-click on a Field cell or a Criteria cell.

7. Click Build.

8. Double-click the plus sign next to Functions.

9. Click Built-in Functions.

Using the preceding steps to get to Expression Builder.

The Expression Builder opening screen.

10-6   Using the Oracle documentation

The technical reference documentation for Oracle is available from several sources:

- On CD-ROM:

    Online Generic Documentation CD-ROM.

    Personal Oracle CD (for versions before 8.1.6)

- On the Web (use the Search icon at the top of the screen):

    www.oracle.com

    otn.oracle.com

- In books:

    I recommend *Oracle — The Complete Reference* by Kevin Loney and George Koch

These sources are all easy to use. There is a lot of technical documentation, so you will need to know how to approach it. Most of the material that relates to this book is in two manuals, SQL *Reference and SQL*Plus User's Guide and Reference*. You may find it useful to use the Master Index and a search engine called Oracle Information Navigator. These tools appear in several versions of the documentation. For this section I focus on the online Generic Documentation CD-ROM.

To find the meaning of any error messages, you can look up the documentation in two ways. The Error Message section is available on the Internet through a hyperlink on the CD-ROM, or you can go to

List of Books ➜ ERR ➜ Error messages ➜ Contents

Errors are listed by number, with cause and action for each.

Task

Find the reference documentation for the `initcap` function. Use the Online Generic Documentation CD-ROM. Here I am using the online documentation for Oracle9i. Each version is slightly different, so you may not see exactly what is presented here.

Oracle procedure

Step 1: Insert the CD-ROM. If you have AutoStart enabled, it will start automatically. Then click on Browse Documentation. You will see the following screen. Otherwise, open the Doc folder and click on Index.htm to show this screen.

Oracle9*i* Database Online Documentation   Help Feedback
(Release 9.0.1; includes Windows books)

Use these choices to find the most popular reference information:

- List of **books**, including PDF for printing.
- **SQL and PL/SQL** syntax and examples.
- Look up an **error message**.
- **Initialization parameters**.
- **Catalog views / Data dictionary views**.
- Find a short definition in the **Master Glossary**.

Look up a term in the Master Index:

Symbols	Numerals	A	B
C	D	E	F	G	H	I	J
K	L	M	N	O	P	Q	R
S	T	U	V	W	X	Y	Z

Do a search, with results in a tree view showing the matches in each book:

Enter a word or phrase: [   ] [Search]
Search in: [All books ▾]
Display topics: [All matching topics ▾]
☐ Search topic titles, not entire text
☐ Want to see all results on one page? Expand all results in tree view
☐ Overwhelmed by results? Format them into a virtual book

Search requires an Internet connection to Oracle.com and free registration on the Oracle Technology Network. If you do not have Internet access, use the Master Index or List of Books instead.

Tip: Want to find a particular book such as the SQL Reference? Browse the List of Books on the home page.

Step 2: Click the I within the Master Index and find the entry for `initcap`. You will see the following screen:

INITCAP

Syntax

`initcap::=`

→[INITCAP]→(( )→(char)→( ))→

Text description of *initcap*

Purpose

INITCAP returns *char*, with the first letter of each word in uppercase, all other letters in lowercase. Words are delimited by white space or characters that are not alphanumeric.

char can be of any of the datatypes CHAR, VARCHAR2, NCHAR, or NVARCHAR2. The return value is the same datatype as *char*.

Note:

This function does not support CLOB data directly. However, CLOBs can be passed in as arguments through implicit data conversion. Please refer to "Datatype Comparison Rules" for more information.

Example

The following example capitalizes each word in the string:

```
SELECT INITCAP('the soap') "Capitals" FROM DUAL;
```

Creating Patterns of Numbers and Dates

Row functions can be used to create patterns of numbers or dates. These are useful in creating a variety of reports. When you create these patterns, the beginning table is usually a table of numbers. In this book, I have provided you with two tables of numbers: `numbers_0_to_9` and `numbers_0_to_99`.

The technique shown here uses SQL to generate these patterns. SQL is able to do this, but other computer languages are designed to generate patterns and can do so more efficiently. Using another technique, we could generate the pattern of numbers in some other language, create a file, and then load that file into a database table.

Why would you want to create a pattern and put it in a database table? This can be useful in several ways. A pattern of dates can serve as a calendar. Often a pattern is the beginning point for adding other types of data. For instance, we might begin with a calendar and then add to it our plans for each day.

In another application a pattern can help us find flaws or imperfections in some other data. We might have some data that nearly fits into a pattern, but not quite. We might want to show explicitly where the data does not fit the pattern. One way to do this is to generate a perfect pattern and then compare it with the data we have.

10-7   Create a simple pattern of numbers

This section shows you how to create a simple pattern of numbers. The next section shows you how to create a complex pattern of numbers. The idea I want you to get from these two sections is that we can create almost any pattern of numbers.

The example in this section shows how to list all the multiples of three between 50 and 250. The purpose of this is to show you how to create a patterns of numbers. The particular patterns you need may vary. There is no particular significance to this pattern, except that it is easy to create.

The beginning table is the table of `numbers_0_to_99`. I have created this table for you already. In chapter 16, we will discuss how to generate a table like this with as many numbers as you want. For now, 100 numbers are enough to handle.

To get the multiples of three, you multiply all the numbers in the table by three. To create other patterns, you could multiply the numbers in the beginning table by any number, M. Then you could add another number, A. If the numbers in the table are called T, this creates a table of numbers of the form (T * M) + A. You can also take any section from this table by setting a starting point and an ending point. Of course, any series of numbers you can list, you can also save in a new table or view.

Task

List all the numbers that are multiples of three between 50 and 250. To do this, begin with the table of numbers_0_to_99.

Oracle SQL: Step 1

```
create or replace view sec1007 as
select n,
       3 * n as multiple_of_3 ❶
from numbers_0_to_99; ❷
```

Access SQL: Step 1

Step 1 Part 1: Enter this in the SQL window:

```
select n,
       3 * n as multiple_of_3 ❶
from numbers_0_to_99; ❷
```

Step 1 Part 2: Save the query and name it sec1007.

Oracle & Access SQL: Step 2

```
select multiple_of_3
from sec1007
where multiple_of_3 between 50 and 250
order by multiple_of_3;
```

Beginning table (`numbers_0_to_99` table) ❸

```
         N
---------
         0
         1
         2
         3
         4
         5

(and many more)

        97
        98
        99
```

Result table

```
MULTIPLE_OF_3
-------------
           51
           54
           57
           60

(and many more)

          243
          246
          249
```

Notes

❶ This creates a new column called `multiple_of_3`.

❷ The beginning table contains all the numbers from 0 to 99. I have already created this table for you.

❸ The rows of this table are shown in their logical order so that this example is easy to understand. However, the rows in any table are in no particular order. If you display this table without an `order by` clause, the rows may be in a different order. To see them in this order you must include `order by n`.

10-8   Create a complex pattern of numbers

In the previous section we created a simple pattern of numbers. Now I want to show you that you can create a very complex pattern of numbers. The prime numbers are one of the most complex sequences, so we'll use them as an example.

This section shows how to list the prime numbers between 10 and 99. We need to find the numbers that cannot be evenly divided by 2, 3, 5, or 7. This is done in the `where` clause. The `mod` function shows the remainder after division. If we enter

```
mod(x, y) = 0
```

this means that Y divides evenly into X. We want the opposite of that, so we want

```
not (mod(n, 2) = 0)
```

This gives us the numbers that are not divisible by 2. Similar logic is used with 3, 5, and 7.

In Access, this condition is written

```
not ((n mod 2) = 0)
```

Task

List all the prime numbers that are greater than 10 and less than 100.

Oracle SQL

```
select n as prime_number
from numbers_0_to_99
where n > 10
    and not (mod(n, 2) = 0)
    and not (mod(n, 3) = 0)
    and not (mod(n, 5) = 0)
    and not (mod(n, 7) = 0)
order by n;
```

Access SQL

```
select n as prime_number
from numbers_0_to_99
where n > 10
    and not ((n mod 2) = 0)
    and not ((n mod 3) = 0)
    and not ((n mod 5) = 0)
    and not ((n mod 7) = 0)
order by n;
```

Beginning table (numbers_0_to_99 table)

```
        N
---------
        0
        1
        2

(and many more)

       98
       99
```

Result table

```
PRIME_NUMBER
------------
          11
          13
          17
          19
          23

(and many more)

          83
          89
          97
```

10-9   An easy way to solve an algebraic equation

In this section I show you an easy way to solve an algebraic equation. I can hear the groans already. I know, you never wanted to do this again in your life. Well, give me a couple of minutes to show you that there is a much easier way than you learned in school. I'll do all the work and you can watch.

I use three steps to find the solution of the equation in the following task. The first step calculates the value of the function on the left side of the equation for every whole number between 0 and 99. Then I look at these values and I observe that

1. The value of the function at 0 is a negative value.

2. The value of the function at 99 is a positive value.

3. The value of the function changes from negative to positive only once.

4. This change occurs between 90 and 91.

So I have found that this function equals zero somewhere between 90 and 91. Next, I want to refine this solution and make it accurate to two decimal places.

Step 2 generates all the numbers with two decimal places between 90.00 and 90.99. Step 3 calculates the value of the function for each of these numbers. I look at these values and I observe that they change from negative to positive between 90.33 and 90.34, so this is the solution to the equation.

I could repeat this process more times to get additional accuracy.

Task

Find a solution to the equation

$$x^4 - 91x^3 + 66x^2 - 451x - 5913 = 0$$

Find a solution between 0 and 99, if there is one. Make the solution accurate to two decimal places.

Oracle & Access SQL:
Step 1 — Calculate the value of the function between 0 and 99

```
select n,
        (n * n * n * n -91 * n * n * n +66 * n * n
        -451 * n -5913) as value_of_function
from numbers_0_to_99
order by n;
```

Beginning table (numbers_0_to_99 table)

```
        N
---------
        0
        1

(and many more)

       98
       99
```

Result table: Step 1

```
        N VALUE_OF_FUNCTION
--------- -----------------
        0             -5913
        1             -6388

(all negative values)

       89           -933204
       90           -240903
       91            499592
       92           1289907
       93           2131692

(all positive values)

       98           7172097
       99           8358696
```

Step 1 — Conclusion

There is a solution to the equation between 90 and 91.

Oracle SQL: Step 2 — Generate the numbers between 90.00 and 90.99

```
create or replace view sec1009 as
select n,
       90 + (n/100) as m
from numbers_0_to_99;
```

Access SQL: Step 2 — Generate the numbers between 90.00 and 90.99

Step 2 Part1: Enter this query in the SQL window:

```
select n,
       90 + (n/100) as m
from numbers_0_to_99;
```

Step 2 Part 2: Save this query and name it sec1009.

Result table: Step 2

```
        N          M
--------- ---------
        0         90
        1      90.01
        2      90.02

(and many more)

       98      90.98
       99      90.99
```

Oracle & Access SQL:
Step 3 — Calculate the value of the function between 90.00 and 90.99

```
select m,
       (m * m * m * m -91 * m * m * m +66 * m * m
        -451 * m -5913) as value_of_function
from sec1009
order by (m * 100); ❶
```

Beginning table (`sec1009` view)

```
         N         M
--------- ---------
         0        90
         1     90.01
         2     90.02

(and many more)

        97     90.97
        98     90.98
        99     90.99
```

Result table: Step 3

```
         M VALUE_OF_FUNCTION
--------- -----------------
        90          -240903
     90.01        -233739.3
     90.02        -226570.8

(all negative values)

     90.32        -9265.465
     90.33        -1946.697
     90.34         5376.9437
     90.35        12705.458

(all positive values)

     90.98        484299.32
     90.99        491943.17
```

Step 3 — Conclusion

There is a solution to the equation between 90.33 and 90.34.

Notes

❶ Why do I multiply M by 100 in the `order by` clause? I can write `order by m`, which is more logical, in Oracle and Access 2002. However, this does not work in Access 2000. To work around this problem, I multiply M by 100.

10-10 List all the days of one week

This section shows you how to list all seven consecutive days of the week. The purpose is to show that we can create a pattern of dates, just like we can create a pattern of numbers. In fact, any pattern of numbers can also be made into a pattern of dates.

We do this in three steps. The first step creates a table of constants. It contains one column, which is the date on which we want the week to begin. There are several ways to create this table, but I use the method that gives me the most control over the process.

The second step creates a view containing seven consecutive days. We get the beginning date from the table of constants and then add the numbers 0 to 6 to it.

The third step formats these dates in three different ways. The date is actually presented three times with a different format each time.

Task

List all the days for one week beginning February 24, 2010. For each date, also list the day of the week in both abbreviated form and fully spelled out.

Oracle SQL: Step 1 — Create a table of constants

```
drop table sec1010_constants;
create table sec1010_constants
(begin_date    date);

insert into sec1010_constants
values ('24-feb-2010');

commit;
```

Access SQL: Step 1 — Create a table of constants

```
drop table sec1010_constants;
create table sec1010_constants
(begin_date    datetime);

insert into sec1010_constants
values (#24-feb-2010#);
```

Result table: Step 1 (date_constants table)

```
BEGIN_DATE
----------
24-FEB-2010
```

Oracle SQL: Step 2 — Create a view containing seven dates

```
create or replace view sec1010 as
select begin_date + digit as days
from numbers_0_to_9,
     sec1010_constants
where digit < 7;
```

Access SQL: Step 2 — Create a view containing seven dates

Step 2 Part 1: Enter the following query in the SQL window:

```
select begin_date + digit as days
from numbers_0_to_9,
     sec1010_constants
where digit < 7;
```

Step 2 Part 2: Save the query and name it sec1010.

Result table: Step 2 (sec1010 view)

```
DAYS
----------
24-FEB-2010
25-FEB-2010
26-FEB-2010
27-FEB-2010
28-FEB-2010
01-MAR-2010
02-MAR-2010
```

Oracle SQL: Step 3 — List the days formatted in three ways

```
column abbreviated_day format a20;

select days,
       to_char(days, 'dy') as abbreviated_day,
       to_char(days, 'day') as full_day
from sec1010
order by days;
```

Access SQL: Step 3 — List the days formatted in three ways

```
select days,
       format(days, 'ddd') as abbreviated_day,
       format(days, 'dddd') as full_day
from sec1010
order by days;
```

Result table: Step 3

```
DAYS          ABBREVIATED_DAY       FULL_DAY
-----------   -------------------   ---------
24-FEB-2010   WED                   WEDNESDAY
25-FEB-2010   THU                   THURSDAY
26-FEB-2010   FRI                   FRIDAY
27-FEB-2010   SAT                   SATURDAY
28-FEB-2010   SUN                   SUNDAY
01-MAR-2010   MON                   MONDAY
02-MAR-2010   TUE                   TUESDAY
```

10-11   Create a calendar of workdays

In this section we create a more complex pattern of dates. In the previous section we listed several consecutive days. In this section, we only list the days that are between Monday and Friday. We will also use a trick to put one blank line between the weeks.

We use four steps to create this calendar. The first two steps are similar to the technique we used in the previous section. This creates a table containing all the days between a beginning date and an end date. This table also contains a column, n, of whole numbers, which we use later. We create a table, rather than a view, because we want to modify some of these dates in step 3. We would be unable to make these modifications to a view.

In step 3, we delete all the dates on Sundays and we turn all the Saturday dates into nulls. These nulls become the blank lines separating one week from another.

In step 4, we list the dates in two different formats. The trick to positioning the blank lines is `order by n`. Think of N as another column in the result table, but it is hidden. It provides the framework that organizes the rows of the result table. An additional result table in step 4 shows the column that is hidden in the first result table.

Task

Create a calendar showing the workdays, Monday through Friday, for March, April, and May of 2015. List the day of the week in one column and the date in the format `MM/DD/YYYY` in the next column. Leave one blank line between the weeks.

Oracle SQL: Step 1 — Create a table of constants

```
drop table sec1011_boundaries;
create table sec1011_boundaries
(start_date      date,
end_date        date);

insert into sec1011_boundaries
values ('01-mar-2015', '01-jun-2015');

commit;
```

Access SQL: Step 1 — Create a table of constants

```
drop table sec1011_boundaries;
create table sec1011_boundaries
(start_date      datetime,
end_date        datetime);

insert into sec1011_boundaries
values (#01-mar-2015#, #01-jun-2015#);
```

Result table: Step 1

START_DATE	END_DATE
01-MAR-2015	01-JUN-2015

Oracle SQL: Step 2 — Create a table containing all the consecutive days

```
drop table sec1011_calendar;
create table sec1011_calendar as
select n, ❶
        start_date + n as date_1 ❷
from numbers_0_to_99,
    sec1011_boundaries
where start_date + n < end_date;
```

Access SQL: Step 2 — Create a table containing all the consecutive days

```
select n, ❶
        cdate(start_date + n) as date_1 ❷ ❸
into sec1011_calendar
from numbers_0_to_99,
    sec1011_boundaries
where start_date + n < end_date;
```

Result table: Step 2

```
         N DATE_1
--------- -----------
         0 01-MAR-2015
         1 02-MAR-2015
         2 03-MAR-2015
         3 04-MAR-2015
         4 05-MAR-2015
         5 06-MAR-2015
         6 07-MAR-2015
         7 08-MAR-2015
         8 09-MAR-2015

(and many more)

        90 30-MAY-2015
        91 31-MAY-2015
```

Notes

❶ We include the column, n, to use as a framework in step 4.

❷ We name this column date_1 instead of date to avoid the possibility of using a reserved word.

❸ In Access the cdate function is necessary to format this column as dates. Otherwise it appears only as numbers.

Oracle SQL: Step 3

```
delete from sec1011_calendar
where to_char(date_1, 'dy') = 'sun';

update sec1011_calendar
  set date_1 = null
where to_char(date_1, 'dy') = 'sat';

commit;
```

Access SQL: Step 3

```
delete from sec1011_calendar
where format(date_1, 'ddd') = 'sun'; ❹

update sec1011_calendar
  set date_1 = null
where format(date_1, 'ddd') = 'sat'; ❹
```

Result table: Step 3

```
      N DATE_1
------- -----------
      1 02-MAR-2015
      2 03-MAR-2015
      3 04-MAR-2015
      4 05-MAR-2015
      5 06-MAR-2015
      6 (null)
      8 09-MAR-2015

(and many more)

     88 28-MAY-2015
     89 29-MAY-2015
     90 (null)
```

Notes

❹ Another way to write this condition in Access is

```
where weekday(date_1) = 'sun';
```

Oracle SQL: Step 4 — Display the report

```
set null ' '; ❺
column day_of_the_week format a15;

select to_char(date_1, 'day') as day_of_the_week,
       to_char(date_1, 'mm/dd/yyyy') as work_day
from sec1011_calendar
order by n;
```

Access SQL: Step 4 — Display the report

```
select format(date_1, 'dddd') as day_of_the_week,
       format(date_1, 'mm/dd/yyyy') as work_day
from sec1011_calendar
order by n;
```

Result table: Step 4

```
DAY_OF_THE_WEEK WORK_DAY
--------------- ----------
MONDAY          03/02/2015
TUESDAY         03/03/2015
WEDNESDAY       03/04/2015
THURSDAY        03/05/2015
FRIDAY          03/06/2015

MONDAY          03/09/2015
TUESDAY         03/10/2015
WEDNESDAY       03/11/2015
THURSDAY        03/12/2015
FRIDAY          03/13/2015

MONDAY          03/16/2015

(and many more)

FRIDAY          05/22/2015

MONDAY          05/25/2015
TUESDAY         05/26/2015
WEDNESDAY       05/27/2015
THURSDAY        05/28/2015
FRIDAY          05/29/2015
```

Result table: Step 4 — Showing the hidden column, n

```
   N DAY_OF_THE_WEEK WORK_DAY
---- --------------- ----------
   1 MONDAY          03/02/2015
   2 TUESDAY         03/03/2015
   3 WEDNESDAY       03/04/2015
   4 THURSDAY        03/05/2015
   5 FRIDAY          03/06/2015
   6
   8 MONDAY          03/09/2015

(and many more)

  82 FRIDAY          05/22/2015
  83
  85 MONDAY          05/25/2015
  86 TUESDAY         05/26/2015
  87 WEDNESDAY       05/27/2015
  88 THURSDAY        05/28/2015
  89 FRIDAY          05/29/2015
  90
```

Notes

❺ In Oracle, this command makes the nulls appear as spaces. This is the default setting, but we changed it in the login procedure (SQLFUN_LOGIN.SQL). In Access, we did not change the way that nulls are displayed, so they automatically appear as blanks.

10-12   How to find out how many days old you are

Do you know how old you are? How many *days* old? The date functions can tell you very easily. Just enter your birth date in the following code. The integer part of the answer is your age in days.

What does the decimal part of the answer mean? Two meanings are possible. If you know the time you were born and you enter it into the code, the decimal part shows you the fraction of the next day that has already gone by.

If you do not enter a time, the computer sees your birth date with the default time of midnight. It measures this against the current date and the current time, so the decimal represents the current time as of when you are running this code.

Task

Find out how many days old you are.

Oracle SQL

```
select sysdate - to_date('21-mar-1978') as days_old ❶ ❷
from dual;
```

Access SQL

```
select now() - #21-mar-1978# as days_old ❶ ❸
from dual;
```

Result table ❹

```
DAYS_OLD
---------
8509.3539
```

Notes

❶ Use your own birth date.

❷ In Oracle, we must use the `to_date` function to turn the text string `'21-mar-1978'` into a date. We can subtract one date from another, but we cannot subtract a text string from a date.

❸ In Access, enclosing `#21-mar-1978#` in pound signs makes it a date.

❹ Obviously, this number changes every day, so your result will be different from the one shown here.

10-13 How to find the date when you will be 10,000 days old

Do you know on what date you will be 10,000 days old? Again, the date functions can easily tell you. Mark this date on your calendar so you can celebrate it!

Task

Find the date when you will be (or were) 10,000 days old. Use your birth date in the following code.

Oracle SQL

```
select to_date('21-mar-1978') + 10000
                          as celebration_day
from dual;
```

Access SQL

```
select #21-mar-1978# + 10000 as celebration_day
from dual;
```

Result table

```
CELEBRATION
-----------
06-AUG-2005
```

Summary

In this chapter, we discussed the row functions to change the datatype of a column and the null value functions that replace nulls with another value. We discussed the documentation of row functions in both Oracle and Access. We showed how to construct patterns of numbers and specialized calendars, and we also discussed an easy way to solve complex equations.

Exercises

1. Goal: Use the null value function to replace nulls in the data with another value.

   a. List the `employee_id`, `first_name`, `last_name`, and `hire_date` values for all the employees. Where there is a null in the `hire_date` column, use the `nvl` or `nz` function to assign the date January 1, 1900. Keep `hire_date` as the name of the column. (When you replace nulls with a certain value, you often want to use a really absurd value.)

   Oracle SQL

   ```
   select employee_id,
          first_name,
          last_name,
          nvl(hire_date, '01-jan-1900') as hire_date
   from l_employees;
   ```

   Access SQL: Solution 1

   ```
   select employee_id,
          first_name,
          last_name,
          nz(hire_date, '1/1/1900') as hire_date
   from l_employees;
   ```

Access SQL: Solution 2

```
select employee_id,
       first_name,
       last_name,
       nz(hire_date, #01-jan-1900#) as hire_date
from 1_employees;
```

b. List the `employee_id`, `first_name`, `last_name`, and `phone_number` values for all the employees. Where there is a null in the `phone_number` column, assign the value 0000. Keep `phone_number` as the name of the column.

2. Goal: Use SQL to solve an equation in algebra. This uses numeric methods to find the solution to any equation, with as much precision as you want to have.

a. See section 10-9.

b. Find a solution to the following equation between 0 and 99 that is accurate to two decimal places.

$$x^3 - 67x^2 + 5x - 718 = 0$$

3. Goal: Create a calendar of dates with some special features.

a. See section 10-11.

b. Create a calendar showing all the weekends (Saturday and Sunday) for a two-month period after your next birthday. List these dates in a format such as June 5, 2025. In a second column, put the abbreviation of the day, Sat or Sun. Put one blank line between the weeks.

c. Create a table that is a calendar for all the days of your life. Start with the day you were born and enter a row with the date for every day that you plan to be alive. If you plan to live about 110 years, then there will be about 40,000 rows in the table. (Hint: Use the view `numbers_0_to_99999`.)

Only 40,000 rows! That is almost nothing! Database tables often contain millions of rows. Any table with fewer than 100,000 rows is often considered to be small — almost trivial. No wonder we do not get much done in our lives — we live for such a short amount of time!

4. Goal: Calculate with dates.

    a. See section 10-13.

    b. Find the date when the United States will be 100,000 days old. You might want to mark this date on your calendar.

chapter 11

SUMMARIZING
DATA

In the previous chapters, the data in the result table came directly from the beginning table or was a function of a single row of that table. In this chapter, the data in the result table can summarize the data in an entire column of the beginning table. This is done using a column function. The seven types of column functions provide different ways to summarize the data in a column.

In the next chapter, you will see how to control the level of summarization. In this chapter, the summarization always produces a single row in the result table.

Introduction to the Column Functions

The data in a table is summarized using column functions, which examine all the data in a column. Every row of the table is involved. This summarization produces a single row in the result table. The next sections provide an overview of the column functions.

11-1   Summarizing all the data in a column

The conceptual drawing that follows shows the way a column function works when it is applied to the whole table. All the data in a single column is summarized and produces one result. For example, the result might be the sum of all the numbers in the column.

The column can be a row function as well as a column of data stored on the disk. Any of the row functions you studied in chapter 9 can create a new column. A column function can then operate on it.

This summary extends over all the rows in the entire table, which may be hundreds, thousands, or even millions of rows. The data in all these rows is condensed into a single number, text string, or date.

Several different column functions exist, and each one summarizes the data in a different way. One gets the maximum value, one gets the average, one gets the minimum, and there are several others, all listed in section 11-2.

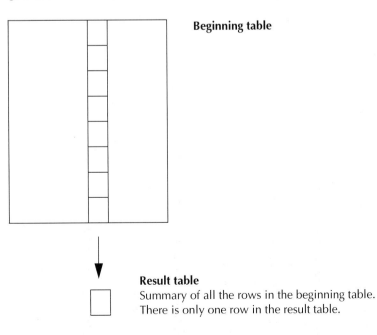

Beginning table

Result table
Summary of all the rows in the beginning table.
There is only one row in the result table.

11-2   A list of the column functions

This section is an overview of the column functions. Each one produces a different type of summarization. They are explained in detail in the next few pages. Column functions are also called *aggregate functions* or *group functions*.

Compared with the row functions, only a few column functions exist — seven main ones, to be exact. Of course, some SQL products extend the list and define other column functions for special purposes. For instance, both Oracle and Access have defined Standard Deviation and Variance. These are not usually considered parts of standard SQL.

Nulls are ignored by all the column functions except one

The column functions ignore nulls in the data. Nulls are treated as if they did not exist. The one exception is the `count(*)` function, which does count nulls and treats them like any other type of data.

Nulls are treated this way because this is how summarization usually deals with unknown values. For example, suppose you have data for 1,000 people, such as which political candidates they like. There are two people who are supposed to be in this sample, but you do not have any data for them yet. Now you are asked to summarize the data. Would you reply that you cannot summarize the data, because you do not have all the data yet? Or would you summarize the data you have for 1,000 people and ignore the two people for whom you do not have any data?

Most people would do the latter: They would summarize the 1,000 pieces of data they have and ignore the two pieces of data they do not have. This process of ignoring the unknown data is exactly what SQL does. When SQL summarizes data, it completely ignores the nulls and treats them as if they were not even there. SQL has not created any new rules here. It has only followed the standard method of summarization.

Overview of the column functions.

Oracle SQL	Access SQL	Meaning
Column functions for text, number, and date columns		
`max`	`max`	Maximum value in the column.
`min`	`min`	Minimum value in the column.
`count(*)`	`count(*)`	Total number of rows in the table.
`count(`*column*`)`	`count(`*column*`)`	Number of rows in the column that are not null.
`count(distinct `*column*`)`	Not available as a column function, but the same result can be achieved by a workaround.	Number of distinct values in the column. Where *column* is the name of a column in the table.
Column functions for numeric columns only		
`sum`	`sum`	Sum of all the values in a column.
`avg`	`avg`	Average of all the values in a column.
`stddev` (two Ds)	`stdev` (one D)	Standard deviation.
`variance`	`var`	Variance.

Examples of column functions.

Column Function	Text Column	Number Column	Date Column
(Data)	Apple	1	25-jan-2055
	Banana	2	null
	Cherry	null	21-jan-2033
	null	2	17-jan-1999
	Peach	3	19-jan-2015
`max`	Peach	3	25-jan-2055
`min`	Apple	1	17-jan-1999
`sum`	n/a	8	n/a
`avg`	n/a	8/4 = 2	n/a
`count(*)`	5	5	5
`count(`*column*`)`	4	4	4
`count(distinct `*column*`)`	4	3	4

Maximum and Minimum

11-3   Finding the maximum and minimum values

This section shows you how to use a column function. It uses the minimum (`min`) and maximum (`max`) column functions, and shows them applied to three columns with the datatypes of text, number, and date.

The datatype of a column determines the sort order that is applied to its data: Text columns are sorted in alphabetic order, number columns are sorted in numeric order, and date columns are sorted in date order. This can affect which values are chosen to be the minimum and maximum values.

When the query does not contain a `where` clause, the column function applies to all the rows in the table. The next section shows the effect of a `where` clause.

The result of a column function is always a single value. In the next chapter, I introduce the `group by` clause. Then the column function will result in more than one value. When you don't have a `group by` clause, the entire table is one group, and therefore you have only one row in the result.

Note that the result table in this example contains only a single row. This single value summarizes all the values in the entire column within all the rows of the table.

Each column of the result table is calculated separately and the row in the result table contains columns that may not be closely related to each other. In the following example, there is no employee named "Susan Woods," but that name appears in the result table. "Susan" is the maximum value in the `first_name` column. "Woods" is maximum value in the `last_name` column. However, "Susan" and "Woods" are not related to each other.

Nulls and column functions

Column functions ignore nulls. So where nulls are placed in the sort order doesn't matter — whether they come first, as in Access, or last, as in Oracle. The maximum or minimum value is not affected by any nulls the column may contain. The maximum and minimum are never a null, unless the entire column is null.

A few people get upset about this. They argue that if a column contains even one null, which is an unknown value, then the maximum or minimum is unknown, so it should be a null. For these people, I make the following points:

1. Summarization always deals with the known data and ignores the unknown data. This approach is part of the process of summarization. It is not a feature that is unique to SQL.

2. If summarization handled nulls in the way these people suggest, then almost all summarized values would be nulls. A single null would be more important than thousands of known values, making summarization itself ineffective. So the process of summarization cannot treat nulls in the way these people suggest. A person can object to all summarization, but that is another matter.

3. The result of every SQL query is based on the data we have right now. We can never obtain some "ultimately perfect" database. We almost never can know every detail we would like to know about any topic.

Task

Find the following:

- The minimum credit limit given to any employee
- The maximum credit limit given to any employee
- The first name of an employee that comes last alphabetically
- The last name of an employee that comes last alphabetically
- The latest date when any of the employees was hired

Oracle & Access SQL

```
select min(credit_limit), ❶
       max(credit_limit),
       max(first_name),
       max(last_name), ❷
       max(hire_date) ❸
from l_employees;
```

Beginning table (1_employees table)

```
EMPLOYEE                       DEPT               CREDIT PHONE   MANAGER
      ID FIRST_NAME LAST_NAME  CODE HIRE_DATE      LIMIT NUMBER       ID
-------- ---------- ---------  ---- ------------ ------- ------  -------
     201 SUSAN      BROWN      EXE  01-JUN-1998  $30.00  3484    (null)
     202 JIM        KERN       SAL  16-AUG-1999  $25.00  8722       201
     203 MARTHA     WOODS      SHP  02-FEB-2004  $25.00  7591       201
     204 ELLEN      OWENS      SAL  01-JUL-2003  $15.00  6830       202
     205 HENRY      PERKINS    SAL  01-MAR-2000  $25.00  5286       202
     206 CAROL      ROSE       ACT  (null)       (null)  (null)  (null)
     207 DAN        SMITH      SHP  01-DEC-2004  $25.00  2259       203
     208 FRED       CAMPBELL   SHP  01-APR-2003  $25.00  1752       203
     209 PAULA      JACOBS     MKT  17-MAR-1999  $15.00  3357       201
     210 NANCY      HOFFMAN    SAL  16-FEB-2004  $25.00  2974       203
```

Result table ❹

```
MIN(CREDIT_LIMIT)  MAX(CREDIT_LIMIT)  MAX(FIRST_  MAX(LAST_N  MAX(HIRE_DA
-----------------  -----------------  ----------  ----------  -----------
          $15.00             $30.00  SUSAN       WOODS       01-DEC-2004
```

Notes

❶ The min function is applied to the credit_limit column, a numeric column. The numeric order is used to decide the minimum value.

❷ The max function is applied to the last_name column, a text column. The alphabetic order is used to decide the maximum value.

❸ The max function is applied to the hire_date column, a date column. The date order is used to decide the maximum value.

❹ The result table contains only one row. Note that in Oracle the column headings for the text and date columns are truncated.

11-4   Using a `where` clause with a column function

When a `where` clause is used in a query that contains a column function, the `where` clause is applied first. The column function is then applied only to the rows that satisfy the `where` condition, not to all the rows of the table.

This section shows the same query we used in the previous section with the addition of a `where` clause. This changes some of the values in the result table.

Task

Perform the same task as in the previous section, but only for some of the rows of the table. For employees 202 to 206, find the following:

- The minimum credit limit given to any employee
- The maximum credit limit given to any employee
- The first name of an employee that comes last alphabetically
- The last name of an employee that comes last alphabetically
- The latest date when any of the employees was hired

Oracle & Access SQL

```
select min(credit_limit),
       max(credit_limit),
       max(first_name),
       max(last_name),
       max(hire_date)
from l_employees
where employee_id between 202 and 206; ❶
```

Beginning table (1_employees table)

```
EMPLOYEE                       DEPT                     CREDIT PHONE   MANAGER
      ID FIRST_NAME LAST_NAME  CODE HIRE_DATE           LIMIT  NUMBER      ID
-------- ---------- ---------- ---- -----------         ------ ------  -------
     201 SUSAN      BROWN      EXE  01-JUN-1998        $30.00  3484    (null)
     202 JIM        KERN       SAL  16-AUG-1999        $25.00  8722       201
     203 MARTHA     WOODS      SHP  02-FEB-2004        $25.00  7591       201
     204 ELLEN      OWENS      SAL  01-JUL-2003        $15.00  6830       202
     205 HENRY      PERKINS    SAL  01-MAR-2000        $25.00  5286       202
     206 CAROL      ROSE       ACT  (null)             (null)  (null)  (null)
     207 DAN        SMITH      SHP  01-DEC-2004        $25.00  2259       203
     208 FRED       CAMPBELL   SHP  01-APR-2003        $25.00  1752       203
     209 PAULA      JACOBS     MKT  17-MAR-1999        $15.00  3357       201
     210 NANCY      HOFFMAN    SAL  16-FEB-2004        $25.00  2974       203
```

First, the where clause is applied to the beginning table ❷

```
EMPLOYEE                       DEPT                     CREDIT PHONE   MANAGER
      ID FIRST_NAME LAST_NAME  CODE HIRE_DATE           LIMIT  NUMBER      ID
-------- ---------- ---------- ---- -----------         ------ ------  -------
     202 JIM        KERN       SAL  16-AUG-1999        $25.00  8722       201
     203 MARTHA     WOODS      SHP  02-FEB-2004        $25.00  7591       201
     204 ELLEN      OWENS      SAL  01-JUL-2003        $15.00  6830       202
     205 HENRY      PERKINS    SAL  01-MAR-2000        $25.00  5286       202
     206 CAROL      ROSE       ACT  (null)             (null)  (null)  (null)
```

Then the column functions are calculated to create the result table

```
MIN(CREDIT_LIMIT)  MAX(CREDIT_LIMIT)  MAX(FIRST_  MAX(LAST_N  MAX(HIRE_DA
-----------------  -----------------  ----------  ----------  -----------
          $15.00             $25.00   MARTHA      WOODS       02-FEB-2004
```

Notes

❶ The where clause limits the scope of the column functions to consider only employees 202 to 206.

❷ The where clause is applied first. In effect, this reduces the number of rows in the beginning table.

11-5   Finding the rows that have the maximum or minimum value

Often, finding the maximum or minimum value in a column is not enough. You want to find more information about the row or rows where the maximum or minimum value occurs.

Several rows may have the minimum or maximum value. In the `l_employees` table, only one row has the maximum value. Asking, "Which row has the maximum value?" is okay, but two rows have the minimum value. So, the question, "Which row has the minimum value?" contains an incorrect assumption that only one such row exists.

Incidentally, you can see that no column function is able to display this additional information. The result table of a column function is always one single row, but the result table in the following example contains three rows.

You can write SQL in two ways to accomplish this goal. These two methods are very similar. In the first method, you run two separate queries. The first `select` statement finds the correct value of the maximum or minimum. In this example, you want to find the minimum credit limit, which is $15.00. You take this value and enter it into the `where` clause of the second query. This method relies on you to transfer the information from the result table of the first query to the SQL code of the second query.

The second method uses a subquery to get the minimum value. A subquery is a `select` statement embedded within another `select` statement. In this case, the inner `select` statement is evaluated first. It obtains the minimum value for the `credit_limit`, which is $15.00. The computer substitutes this result in the outer `select` statement, replacing the inner `select` statement. Then the outer query is evaluated, giving the result table. The benefit of this method is that it uses only one query. It does not rely on the person running the query to transfer information, so it provides a more packaged solution.

Task

Find all the employees who have the minimum credit limit.

Oracle & Access SQL: Method 1 — Step 1 **❶**

```
select min(credit_limit)
from l_employees;
```

Oracle & Access SQL: Method 1 — Step 2 **❷**

```
select employee_id,
       first_name,
       last_name,
       credit_limit
from l_employees
where credit_limit = 15.00 ❸
order by employee_id;
```

Oracle & Access SQL: Method 2 **❹**

```
select employee_id,
       first_name,
       last_name,
       credit_limit
from l_employees
where credit_limit = (select min(credit_limit) ❹
                      from l_employees)
order by employee_id;
```

Beginning table (`1_employees` table)

EMPLOYEE ID	FIRST_NAME	LAST_NAME	DEPT CODE	HIRE_DATE	CREDIT LIMIT	PHONE NUMBER	MANAGER ID
201	SUSAN	BROWN	EXE	01-JUN-1998	$30.00	3484	(null)
202	JIM	KERN	SAL	16-AUG-1999	$25.00	8722	201
203	MARTHA	WOODS	SHP	02-FEB-2004	$25.00	7591	201
204	ELLEN	OWENS	SAL	01-JUL-2003	$15.00	6830	202
205	HENRY	PERKINS	SAL	01-MAR-2000	$25.00	5286	202
206	CAROL	ROSE	ACT	(null)	(null)	(null)	(null)
207	DAN	SMITH	SHP	01-DEC-2004	$25.00	2259	203
208	FRED	CAMPBELL	SHP	01-APR-2003	$25.00	1752	203
209	PAULA	JACOBS	MKT	17-MAR-1999	$15.00	3357	201
210	NANCY	HOFFMAN	SAL	16-FEB-2004	$25.00	2974	203

Result table

EMPLOYEE ID	FIRST_NAME	LAST_NAME	CREDIT LIMIT
204	ELLEN	OWENS	$15.00
209	PAULA	JACOBS	$15.00

Notes

❶ This finds the smallest credit limit of any of the employees. The result is $15.00.

❷ A second query gets additional information about the employees who have the minimum credit limit.

❸ The value "15.00" is obtained from the result of the first query. The dollar sign is dropped. Numbers within SQL code cannot contain dollar signs or commas.

The decimal point and two zeros are optional. They are written here to show that this is a currency value. It could also be written as "15" without the decimal point and zeros.

❹ This is the subquery.

Count

11-6   Counting rows and counting data

SQL has two different methods of counting the data in a column. These methods differ in how they count nulls. Later we discuss a third method of counting that counts the number of different values in the column.

This section shows two varieties of the count column function. The count(*) function counts the number of rows in the table. The count (*col-umn*) function counts the amount of data in a specific column, ignoring all the nulls.

Counting all the rows in a table

The count(*) function counts all the rows in the table. The result is the same as if all the values in any column were counted, including the nulls. This is the only column function that treats nulls the same way it treats other values.

You can think of this function in two ways. If you think of it as counting all the rows in a table, then any nulls in the table do not get involved in this. If you think of it as counting all the values in a column, then all the nulls are included in the count. No matter which column is counted, the result is the same for every column. You are free to think about the function in either way.

Counting all the values in a column, excluding nulls

The count(*column*) function counts all the values in the specified column that are not nulls. It tells you how much data is entered in the column. Clearly, each column can have a different count because each column can contain a different number of nulls. The column can have any datatype — text, number, or date.

Task

Count the number of rows in the 1_employees table. Also, count the number of non-null values in these three columns:

```
last_name
hire_date
manager_id
```

Oracle & Access SQL

```
select count(*), ❶
       count(last_name), ❷
       count(hire_date), ❸
       count(manager_id) ❹
from l_employees;
```

Beginning table (`l_employees` table)

```
EMPLOYEE                          DEPT                      CREDIT PHONE  MANAGER
      ID FIRST_NAME LAST_NAME CODE HIRE_DATE        LIMIT NUMBER      ID
-------- ---------- --------- ---- -----------     ------- ------ -------
     201 SUSAN      BROWN     EXE  01-JUN-1998     $30.00 3484   (null)
     202 JIM        KERN      SAL  16-AUG-1999     $25.00 8722      201
     203 MARTHA     WOODS     SHP  02-FEB-2004     $25.00 7591      201
     204 ELLEN      OWENS     SAL  01-JUL-2003     $15.00 6830      202
     205 HENRY      PERKINS   SAL  01-MAR-2000     $25.00 5286      202
     206 CAROL      ROSE      ACT  (null)          (null) (null) (null)
     207 DAN        SMITH     SHP  01-DEC-2004     $25.00 2259      203
     208 FRED       CAMPBELL  SHP  01-APR-2003     $25.00 1752      203
     209 PAULA      JACOBS    MKT  17-MAR-1999     $15.00 3357      201
     210 NANCY      HOFFMAN   SAL  16-FEB-2004     $25.00 2974      203
```

Result table ❺

```
COUNT(*)  COUNT(LAST_NAME)  COUNT(HIRE_DATE)  COUNT(MANAGER_ID)
--------- ----------------  ----------------  -----------------
      10                10                 9                  8
```

Notes

❶ Count (*) finds the number of rows in the table.

❷ This applies the count (*column*) function to a text column — the last_name column. The result is 10 because there are no nulls in this column.

❸ This applies the count (*column*) function to a date column — the hire_date column. The result is 9 because there is one null in this column.

❹ This applies the count (*column*) function to a column of numbers — the manager_id column. The result is 8 because there are two nulls in this column.

❺ The result table contains only one row.

11-7   Counting to zero

Sometimes you want zeros to appear in your result. When you want this, the way to get it is to apply the `count(`*column*`)` function to a column of nulls. The `count(distinct `*column*`)` function can also create a zero.

No other column function can do this. When any other column function is applied to a column of nulls, the result is a null. The one exception is the `count(*)` function. It counts the number of rows in the table, so it never results in a zero.

Now you are probably thinking that it is unusual for a table to have a column that contains only nulls. That is true. However, in the next chapter we won't be summarizing an entire column at once. Instead, we will divide the rows into several groups and separately summarize each group. A column often contains only nulls for a group of rows.

We use this later, but right now I am trying to show you how each column function works.

Task 1

In Oracle and Access, apply all the column functions to the column that contains only nulls. Show that the `count(`*column*`)` function result in a zero, but the `max`, `min`, `sum`, and `avg` functions result in a null.

Oracle & Access SQL

```
select count(col_2) as count_col,
       count(*) as count_rows,
       max(col_2) as max,
       min(col_2) as min,
       sum(col_2) as sum,
       avg(col_2) as avg
from sec1107;
```

Beginning table (`sec1107` table)

```
PK_1 COL_2
---- ------
A    (null)
B    (null)
C    (null)
D    (null)
E    (null)
```

Result table

COUNT_COL	COUNT_ROWS	MAX	MIN	SUM	AVG
0	5	(null)	(null)	(null)	(null)

Task 2

In Oracle, apply count(distinct *column*) to the column of nulls. Show that this also results in a zero.

Oracle SQL

```
select count(distinct col_2) as count_distinct
from sec1107;
```

- Access does not support count(distinct *column*).

Result table

COUNT_DISTINCT
0

11-8   Counting the number of distinct values in a column

This section shows you how to count the number of different values in a column. Nulls are not counted as values. If the column contains codes, such as the dept_code column, you can use this technique to find out how many different codes are used within that column. Oracle and Access use different methods for this.

In Oracle, the column function count(distinct *column*) produces this result. In Access, this column function does not exist. You can get around this problem by using two steps.

The first step uses `select distinct` to create a table or a view that contains all the distinct values within the column. If there is a null in the column, it is included in the result table produced by `select distinct`. The second step counts the values in this table without counting the null. This gives the correct result.

Task

Find the number of different values in the `manager_id` column of the `1_employees` table.

Oracle SQL ❶

```
select count(distinct manager_id)
from 1_employees;
```

Beginning table (1_employees table)

```
EMPLOYEE                         DEPT                    CREDIT  PHONE   MANAGER
      ID FIRST_NAME LAST_NAME CODE HIRE_DATE        LIMIT   NUMBER       ID
-------- ---------- --------- ---- ------------    -------  ------  -------
     201 SUSAN      BROWN     EXE  01-JUN-1998     $30.00   3484    (null)
     202 JIM        KERN      SAL  16-AUG-1999     $25.00   8722       201
     203 MARTHA     WOODS     SHP  02-FEB-2004     $25.00   7591       201
     204 ELLEN      OWENS     SAL  01-JUL-2003     $15.00   6830       202
     205 HENRY      PERKINS   SAL  01-MAR-2000     $25.00   5286       202
     206 CAROL      ROSE      ACT  (null)          (null)   (null)  (null)
     207 DAN        SMITH     SHP  01-DEC-2004     $25.00   2259       203
     208 FRED       CAMPBELL  SHP  01-APR-2003     $25.00   1752       203
     209 PAULA      JACOBS    MKT  17-MAR-1999     $15.00   3357       201
     210 NANCY      HOFFMAN   SAL  16-FEB-2004     $25.00   2974       203
```

Result table

```
COUNT(DISTINCTMANAGER_ID)
-------------------------
                        3
```

Access SQL (workaround): Step 1 ❷

```
select distinct manager_id ❸
into step1
from l_employees;
```

Access table: Step 1

```
┌─────────────────────────────────┐
│ ⊞ temp_manager : Table  _│□│×│  │
├─────────────────────────────────┤
│          manager_id             │
├───┬─────────────────────────────┤
│ ▶ │                             │
├───┼─────────────────────────┬───┤
│   │                      201│   │
├───┼─────────────────────────┤   │
│   │                      202│   │
├───┼─────────────────────────┤   │
│   │                      203│   │
├───┼─────────────────────────────┤
│ * │                             │
├───┴─────────────────────────────┤
│ Record: Ⅳ ◄       1 ► ►Ⅰ►* │
└─────────────────────────────────┘
```

Access SQL (workaround): Step 2 ❷

```
select count(manager_id) ❹
from step1;
```

Access result table

```
┌─────────────────────────────────┐
│ ▦ Query1 : Select Query  _│□│×│ │
├─────────────────────────────────┤
│            Expr1000             │
├───┬─────────────────────────────┤
│ ▶ │                           3 │
├───┴─────────────────────────────┤
│ Record: Ⅳ ◄      1 ► ►Ⅰ    │
└─────────────────────────────────┘
```

Notes

❶ In Oracle, you can use the count(distinct *column*) function.

❷ In Access, you must write two separate queries and run each one separately.

❸ In Access, the first query creates a table containing all the different values, including the null. If there are several nulls in the manager_id column of the beginning table, there is still only one null in the step1 table. That is, select distinct treats all nulls as though they have the same value, even though they are all unknown values.

❹ In Access, the second query uses the function count (*column*) .

11-9   Counting the number of distinct values in two or more columns

This section shows you how to use `count distinct` to find the number of different values of two or more columns. Here I mean that the columns are taken in combination with each other, so a new combination occurs whenever any one of the columns has a new value.

This combination of the columns into a single unit of data is similar to the way that `select distinct` works with rows. With `select distinct`, two rows are considered identical only when all the columns have the same values.

There is a technical difference between `count distinct` and `select distinct`. `Count distinct` is a column function. Here, `distinct` eliminates duplicate values of a single column. `Select distinct` is an entire `select` statement. Here `distinct` eliminates duplicate rows of the result table.

To get these two structures to work the same way, you need to use a trick: Concatenate all the columns together into a single column before applying `count distinct` to them. The one column that `count distinct` applies to then actually contains the values of all the columns.

A second trick should also be used. A separator should be placed between the columns of the concatenation. The separator is usually a one-character literal. It is often a punctuation character or special character that you know does not appear in the data. If the data might contain any character, you may need to use a separator containing a string of two or three characters. In the following SQL code, an asterisk is used for the separation character.

By using a separator, we prevent the possibility that different values in two columns will produce the same value when they are concatenated. For example:

Column 1	Column 2	Concatenation without a Separator	Concatenation with a Separator
A	BCD	ABCD	A*BCD
AB	CD	ABCD	AB*CD
ABC	D	ABCD	ABC*D

Nulls are counted when the `count distinct` function is applied to two or more columns and a separator is used. Even if there are nulls in all the columns that are concatenated together, it is still counted. The separators are not nulls, so the concatenation is not a null and it is counted.

Column 1	Column 2	Concatenation without a Separator	Concatenation with a Separator
null	null	null	*

In Access, we need to use the same workaround to get `count distinct` that we used in the previous section.

Task

Count the number of distinct combinations of `manager_id` and `credit_limit`.

Oracle SQL

```
select count(distinct (manager_id || '*' || credit_limit))
from l_employees;
```

Beginning table (`l_employees` table)

```
EMPLOYEE                          DEPT                  CREDIT  PHONE   MANAGER
      ID FIRST_NAME  LAST_NAME CODE  HIRE_DATE      LIMIT  NUMBER       ID
-------- ----------  --------- ----  -----------    ------- ------  -------
     201 SUSAN       BROWN     EXE   01-JUN-1998    $30.00  3484    (null)
     202 JIM         KERN      SAL   16-AUG-1999    $25.00  8722       201
     203 MARTHA      WOODS     SHP   02-FEB-2004    $25.00  7591       201
     204 ELLEN       OWENS     SAL   01-JUL-2003    $15.00  6830       202
     205 HENRY       PERKINS   SAL   01-MAR-2000    $25.00  5286       202
     206 CAROL       ROSE      ACT   (null)         (null)  (null)  (null)
     207 DAN         SMITH     SHP   01-DEC-2004    $25.00  2259       203
     208 FRED        CAMPBELL  SHP   01-APR-2003    $25.00  1752       203
     209 PAULA       JACOBS    MKT   17-MAR-1999    $15.00  3357       201
     210 NANCY       HOFFMAN   SAL   16-FEB-2004    $25.00  2974       203
```

Result table

```
COUNT(DISTINCT(MANAGER_ID||'*'||CREDIT_LIMIT))
-----------------------------------------------
                                              7
```

Access SQL (workaround): Step 1 ❶

```
select distinct manager_id,
                credit_limit
into temp_manager_credit
from l_employees;
```

Access temporary table: Step 1

temp_manager_credit... _ □ ×	
manager_id	credit_limit
▸	
	$30.00
201	$15.00
201	$25.00
202	$15.00
202	$25.00
203	$25.00
✱	
Record: ⅠⅠ ◀	1 ▸ ▸Ⅰ ▸

Access SQL (workaround): Step 2

```
select count(*) ❷
from temp_manager_credit;
```

Access result table: Step 2

Query... _ □ ×	
Expr1000	
▸	7
Record: ⅠⅠ ◀	

Notes

❶ This two-step method also works in Oracle, and it avoids the trick of using a separator character.

❷ When you are counting more than one column, use count(*) instead of count (*column*) as you did in section 11-8. The row with the null in both columns is counted.

Sum and Average

11-10   The sum and average functions

This section shows an example using the sum (`sum`) and average (`avg`) column functions. These functions can be applied only to a column of numbers. Text and date columns cannot be used with these functions.

Nulls are ignored by both of these functions. The next section shows how this can sometimes cause a problem for the `sum` function. For the `avg` function, nulls are ignored both in adding up the column and in counting the number of items to set the divisor.

Task

Find the sum and average of all the credit limits in the `l_employees` table.

Oracle & Access SQL

```
select sum(credit_limit), ❶
       avg(credit_limit) ❷
from l_employees;
```

Beginning table (`l_employees` table)

EMPLOYEE ID	FIRST_NAME	LAST_NAME	DEPT CODE	HIRE_DATE	CREDIT LIMIT	PHONE NUMBER	MANAGER ID
201	SUSAN	BROWN	EXE	01-JUN-1998	$30.00	3484	(null)
202	JIM	KERN	SAL	16-AUG-1999	$25.00	8722	201
203	MARTHA	WOODS	SHP	02-FEB-2004	$25.00	7591	201
204	ELLEN	OWENS	SAL	01-JUL-2003	$15.00	6830	202
205	HENRY	PERKINS	SAL	01-MAR-2000	$25.00	5286	202
206	CAROL	ROSE	ACT	(null)	(null)	(null)	(null)
207	DAN	SMITH	SHP	01-DEC-2004	$25.00	2259	203
208	FRED	CAMPBELL	SHP	01-APR-2003	$25.00	1752	203
209	PAULA	JACOBS	MKT	17-MAR-1999	$15.00	3357	201
210	NANCY	HOFFMAN	SAL	16-FEB-2004	$25.00	2974	203

Result table ❸

SUM(CREDIT_LIMIT)	AVG(CREDIT_LIMIT)
210	23.333333

Notes

❶ This is an example of the sum (*column*) function. The result, 210, is the sum of the 9 values in the `credit_limit` column.

❷ This is an example of the avg (*column*) function. It finds the average of the numbers. The result is 210 / 9 = 23.33, where 210 is the sum of the values in the `credit_limit` column and 9 is the number of values in that column, excluding nulls.

❸ The result table contains only one row.

11-11 The problem with addition and how to solve it

SQL has a problem with addition when both of the following conditions exist:

1. Two or more columns are added together.

2. There are nulls in some of those columns.

One of the basic properties of addition is that the order in which you add the numbers does not matter. The sum is always the same. Sometimes addition in SQL violates this property, as the example in this section shows.

The problem is that SQL has two kinds of addition, row addition and column addition. They have different ways of handling nulls. Row addition adds numbers within one row. It is a row function. Row addition handles a null as an unknown value. So, for example

3 + null = null

Column addition adds numbers within one column. It is one of the functions used for summarization. All summarization functions ignore nulls. So, for example

        3
+ null
    ─────
        3

To solve this problem, you need to replace all the nulls with zeros. You can do this by using the row functions `nvl` in Oracle and `nz` in Access. Another method uses the `update` statement to make the change. This method changes the data in the beginning table. If you do not want to change the data permanently, you can do a `rollback` after you perform the calculation.

The following example shows two columns of numbers, and these columns contain some nulls. When all the numbers are added together, you get one result if you add the columns first and you get a different result if you add the rows first.

When the columns are added first, using column addition, you get the result that the sums of the columns are 6 and 15. Adding these together with row addition, you get

6 + 15 = 21

When the rows are added first, using row addition, you get the result that the sums of the rows are 5, null, 8, and null. Adding these together with column addition, you get

$$
\begin{array}{r}
5 \\
+ \text{null} \\
+ \quad 8 \\
+ \text{null} \\
\hline
13
\end{array}
$$

The solution

Several solutions are available. The easiest is to always add the columns first. This works, but it is sometimes tricky to implement. You need to be aware of columns that are defined as row functions of other columns and that information may get hidden.

A better solution is to stay aware of numeric columns in your database that allow nulls. Whenever you use one of these columns, use it with the `nvl` or `nz` function.

Task

Add all the numbers in columns 2 and 3 of the following beginning table. Show that in SQL we get two different answers, depending on the order in which we add the numbers. If we add each of the columns first, the resulting sum is 21. If we add across the rows first, the resulting sum is 13.

   Then show that when the nulls are changed to zeros, the problem with addition is solved: The result is the same whether the columns or the rows are added first.

Oracle & Access SQL: An example of the problem with addition

```
select sum(col_2)+sum(col_3) as columns_added_first, ❶
       sum(col_2 + col_3) as rows_added_first ❷
from sec1111;
```

Beginning table (`sec1111` table)

```
PK_1        COL_2      COL_3
------   ---------  ---------
A               1          4
B          (null)          5
C               2          6
D               3     (null)
```

Result table — Without changing the nulls to zeros ❸

```
COLUMNS_ADDED_FIRST ROWS_ADDED_FIRST
------------------- ----------------
                 21               13
```

Notes

❶ This line adds the columns first.

❷ This line adds the rows first.

❸ This shows that the sums are different.

Explanation

Add columns first

Col_2	Col_3
1	4
null	5
2	6
3	null
——	——

	Col_2	Col_3
Sum	6	15

Then $6 + 15 = 21$.

Add rows first

Col_2	Col_3	Sum
1	4	= 5
null	5	= null
2	6	= 8
3	null	= null

Then $5 + 8 = 13$.

Oracle SQL: Method 1 — Using a row function   CORRECT

```
select sum(nvl(col_2,  0)) + sum(nvl(col_3,  0))  ❹ ❻
                            as columns_added_first,
           sum(nvl(col_2,  0) + nvl(col_3,  0))  ❹
                            as rows_added_first
from sec1111;
```

Access SQL: Method 1 — Using a row function   CORRECT

```
select sum(nz(col_2,  0)) + sum(nz(col_3,  0))  ❺ ❻
                            as columns_added_first,
           sum(nz(col_2,  0) + nz(col_3,  0))  ❺
                            as rows_added_first
from sec1111;
```

Result table — With the nulls changed to zeros ❼

```
COLUMNS_ADDED_FIRST ROWS_ADDED_FIRST
------------------- ----------------
                 21               21
```

Notes

❹ In Oracle, the nvl function is applied to both columns to change the nulls into zeros.

❺ In Access, the nz function is applied to both columns to change the nulls into zeros.

❻ If you remember to always add the columns first, then you do not need to use the nvl or nz functions. This makes the code

```
select sum(col_2) + sum(col_3)
```

In a way, this is the easiest solution. However, sometimes it can leave a trap in your code that someone else may fall into. The next programmer who works on the code might write

```
sum(col_2 + col_3)
```

which would give the wrong answer.

❼ This shows that the sums are the same.

Explanation

Add columns first

Col_2	Col_3
1	4
0	5
2	6
3	0
——	——
Sum 6	15

Then $6 + 15 = 21$.

Add rows first

Col_2	Col_3	Sum
1	4	= 5
0	5	= 5
2	6	= 8
3	0	= 3

Then $5 + 5 + 8 + 3 = 21$.

Oracle SQL: Method 2 — Changing the data temporarily   CORRECT

Step 1: Change the nulls to zeros in one column.

```
update sec1111
  set col_2 = 0
where col_2 is null;
```

Step 2: Change the nulls to zeros in any other columns used in the calculation.

```
update sec1111
  set col_3 = 0
where col_3 is null;
```

Step 3: Run your report.

```
select sum(col_2)+sum(col_3) as columns_added_first,
       sum(col_2 + col_3) as rows_added_first
from sec1111;
```

Step 4: Undo the temporary changes to the data.

```
rollback;
```

In Access, we could use a similar process, but Access does not have a `rollback` statement, so the changes to the data would be permanent.

Other Topics

The next three sections discuss some details that are important in many applications that use summarization.

11-12 Nulls are not always changed to zero

In the previous section, all the nulls were changed to zeros, which is the usual procedure. Ninety percent of the time the nulls in numeric columns are changed to zeros, if their value is changed at all. Sometimes, however, you may want to change the nulls to some other value, perhaps an estimate of what the value will eventually be. This section provides an example of this situation.

In this example, a store receives orders for merchandise that it will ship to customers. At the end of each day, the store wants to know the total value of all the invoices. Each invoice is calculated with the formula

(Price * Quantity) + Tax + Shipping = Invoice

The problem is that sometimes the `tax` or `shipping` columns contain nulls, meaning that it is an unknown amount. In this situation, you need to carefully control how the calculation is performed and how the rows that contain nulls are counted.

There are three choices:

1. Bill all the amounts you know and estimate an amount for the nulls.
2. Bill all the amounts you know and nothing for the nulls.
3. Ignore any invoice with incomplete data.

This section shows the SQL code for the first choice, which is the best one.

Task

Find the total for all the invoices in the following table. Calculate an invoice as

(Price * Quantity) + Tax + Shipping = Invoice

Estimate values for the nulls that occur in the tax and shipping columns by applying these rules:

1. A null in the `tax` column is replaced with: **0.07 * price * quantity**
2. A null in the `shipping` column is replaced with: **0.12 * price * quantity**

Oracle SQL

```
column total_invoices format $999,990.99;

select sum((price * quantity)
            + nvl(tax, 0.07 * price * quantity) ❶
            + nvl(shipping, 0.12 * price * quantity)) ❷
                                    as total_invoices
from sec1112;
```

Access SQL

```
select sum((price * quantity)
            + nz(tax, 0.07 * price * quantity) ❶
            + nz(shipping, 0.12 * price * quantity)) ❷
                                    as total_invoices
from sec1112;
```

Beginning table (sec1112 table)

```
PK_1      PRICE  QUANTITY     TAX SHIPPING
-----  --------  --------  ------- --------
A       $211.00        3   $48.00   $63.00
B       $138.00        7  (null)    $72.00
C       $592.00        1   $51.00   $76.00
D       $329.00        2   $54.00  (null)
```

Result table

```
TOTAL_INVOICES
--------------
    $3,359.58
```

Notes

❶ Change the null in the tax column to an estimate of the tax.

❷ Change the null in the shipping column to an estimate of the shipping charge.

11-13 Counting the number of nulls in a column

How can you count the number of nulls in a column? This goal may seem to be a problem because all the column functions ignore nulls. This section shows the technique. The `where` clause limits the rows to the ones we want to count. Then the `count(*)` function counts them.

Often we are most interested in knowing if a column contains any nulls at all and less interested in getting the exact count.

Task

Find the number of nulls in the `manager_id` column of the `l_employees` table.

Oracle & Access SQL

```
select count(*) as number_of_nulls
from l_employees
where manager_id is null;
```

Beginning table (`l_employees` table)

EMPLOYEE ID	FIRST_NAME	LAST_NAME	DEPT CODE	HIRE_DATE	CREDIT LIMIT	PHONE NUMBER	MANAGER ID
201	SUSAN	BROWN	EXE	01-JUN-1998	$30.00	3484	(null)
202	JIM	KERN	SAL	16-AUG-1999	$25.00	8722	201
203	MARTHA	WOODS	SHP	02-FEB-2004	$25.00	7591	201
204	ELLEN	OWENS	SAL	01-JUL-2003	$15.00	6830	202
205	HENRY	PERKINS	SAL	01-MAR-2000	$25.00	5286	202
206	CAROL	ROSE	ACT	(null)	(null)	(null)	(null)
207	DAN	SMITH	SHP	01-DEC-2004	$25.00	2259	203
208	FRED	CAMPBELL	SHP	01-APR-2003	$25.00	1752	203
209	PAULA	JACOBS	MKT	17-MAR-1999	$15.00	3357	201
210	NANCY	HOFFMAN	SAL	16-FEB-2004	$25.00	2974	203

Result table

NUMBER_OF_NULLS
2

11-14 Counting distinct dates

When you use `count distinct` on a date column, you may not get the result you expect. This happens because the data in a date column may contain a time, which is often not shown. Thus two rows that appear to have the same date may in fact be different because the times are different.

Task

Count the number of different dates in the `date_entered` column of the `1_lunches` table.

Oracle SQL: The problem

```
select count(distinct date_entered) ❶
from 1_lunches;
```

Beginning table (`1_lunches` table) ❷

```
          LUNCH          EMPLOYEE
LUNCH_ID  DATE                 ID  DATE_ENTERE
--------  ------------   --------  -----------
       1  16-NOV-2005         201  13-OCT-2005
       2  16-NOV-2005         207  13-OCT-2005
       3  16-NOV-2005         203  13-OCT-2005
       4  16-NOV-2005         204  13-OCT-2005
       6  16-NOV-2005         202  13-OCT-2005
       7  16-NOV-2005         210  13-OCT-2005
       8  25-NOV-2005         201  14-OCT-2005
       9  25-NOV-2005         208  14-OCT-2005
      12  25-NOV-2005         204  14-OCT-2005
      13  25-NOV-2005         207  18-OCT-2005
      15  25-NOV-2005         205  21-OCT-2005
      16  05-DEC-2005         201  21-OCT-2005
      17  05-DEC-2005         210  21-OCT-2005
      20  05-DEC-2005         205  24-OCT-2005
      21  05-DEC-2005         203  24-OCT-2005
      22  05-DEC-2005         208  24-OCT-2005
```

Result table — The problem ❸

```
COUNT(DISTINCTDATE_ENTERED)
---------------------------
                         16
```

Oracle SQL: The solution

```
select count(distinct trunc(date_entered)) ❹
from l_lunches;
```

Result table — The solution ❺

```
COUNT(DISTINCTTRUNC(DATE_ENTERED))
----------------------------------
                                 5
```

Access SQL: The solution ❻

Step 1:

```
select distinct format(date_entered, 'yyyy-mm-dd') ❼
                                    as date_entered2
into temp_date
from l_lunches;
```

Step 2:

```
select count(date_entered2)
from temp_date;
```

Beginning table (l_lunches table as shown in Access) ❽

LUNCH_ID	LUNCH_DATE	EMPLOYEE_ID	DATE_ENTERED
1	11/16/2005	201	10/13/2005 10:35:24 AM
2	11/16/2005	207	10/13/2005 10:35:39 AM
3	11/16/2005	203	10/13/2005 10:35:45 AM
4	11/16/2005	204	10/13/2005 10:35:58 AM
6	11/16/2005	202	10/13/2005 10:36:41 AM
7	11/16/2005	210	10/13/2005 10:38:52 AM
8	11/25/2005	201	10/14/2005 11:15:37 AM
9	11/25/2005	208	10/14/2005 2:23:36 PM
12	11/25/2005	204	10/14/2005 3:02:53 PM
13	11/25/2005	207	10/18/2005 8:42:11 AM
15	11/25/2005	205	10/21/2005 4:23:50 PM
16	12/5/2005	201	10/21/2005 4:23:59 PM
17	12/5/2005	210	10/21/2005 4:35:26 PM
20	12/5/2005	205	10/24/2005 9:55:27 AM
21	12/5/2005	203	10/24/2005 11:43:13 AM
22	12/5/2005	208	10/24/2005 2:37:32 PM

Record: 17 of 17

Access result table: Step 1

temp_date : Table
date_entered2
2005-10-13
2005-10-14
2005-10-18
2005-10-21
2005-10-24
▶
Record: I◄ ◄   6 ▶

Result table: Step 2

Query1 : Select Qu...
Expr1000
▶   5
Record: I◄ ◄   1 ▶

Notes

❶ You need to be careful when you use `count distinct` with a date field. You need to remember that a date always includes a time.

❷ Only the dates are shown in this listing of the `l_lunches` table. The times are not shown, even though they are actually in the data.

❸ The result shows there are 16 different values in this column. The date in each row is different because the times are different.

❹ The solution is to apply the `trunc` function to the date column. This truncates the time and leaves only the date.

❺ Now we get the answer we expected.

❻ Because Access does not support `count distinct`, you must use the workaround given in section 11-9.

❼ Here the `format` function is used to remove the time from the data in the `date_entered` column. There are other ways to achieve the same thing. In Oracle you can use the `trunc` function and in Access you can use the `DateValue` function.

❽ In Access the default date format does show the time, so the problem described in this section is less likely to happen.

Summary

In this chapter we discussed the column functions, which are used to summarize the data in a table. There are seven column functions and we discussed each one in detail.

Exercises

1. Goal: Use the `min` function.

   a. See sections 11-3 and 11-5.

   b. Find the price of the least expensive food in the `1_foods` table. Then find all the foods with that minimum price.

2. Goal: Use the `count` function.

   a. See section 11-6.

   b. Count the number of rows in the `1_lunch_items` table.

3. Goal: Use `count distinct` to find all the combinations of two columns.

   a. See section 11-9.

   b. Within the `1_lunch_items` table, count the number of different combinations of the `supplier_id` column and the `product_code` column. (Access does not directly support `count distinct`, so you will need to use the workaround shown in section 11-9.)

4. Goal: Use the `sum` function and use it with the `nvl` function.

   a. See sections 11-10 and 11-11.

   b. Find the sum of all the prices and all the price increases of foods in the `1_foods` table. Do this in two ways:

   1. Add the columns first.
   2. Add the rows first.

   (Hint: Use the `nvl` function to change the nulls into zeros.)

chapter 12

CONTROLLING
THE LEVEL OF
SUMMARIZATION

In chapter 11 we summarized all the data in a column of a table. The result was a single value. In this chapter we divide the rows of the table into *groups*, which are nonoverlapping sets of rows. Each group is summarized separately, resulting in a summary value for each of the groups.

At our discretion, we can either summarize a column into a single value or divide it into 100 pieces and summarize each piece. This gives us control over the level of detail we want to see.

Dividing a Table into Groups of Rows and Summarizing Each Group

You can divide the rows of a table into separate groups. The `group by` clause in a `select` statement can do this. Then, the column functions summarize each group. This allows you to control the level of summarization and detail.

12-1   Summary of groups of data within a column

This section shows a conceptual drawing of the way a column function works when it is applied to groups of rows within a table. Each row of the table is assigned to a group. Each row can be part of only a single group.

The column function produces a summary of each group of rows, which is a single value for each group. The result of the column function has one row for every group of rows in the beginning table.

The number of groups that the beginning table is divided into determines how detailed and fine-grained the summarization is. At one extreme, each row of the beginning table can be a separate group. Then no summarization occurs at all. At the other extreme, all the rows of the beginning table can be put into a single group. This was the case when we summarized the entire table in the previous chapter. Then all the data within the column is condensed down to a single value — a single number, text item, or date.

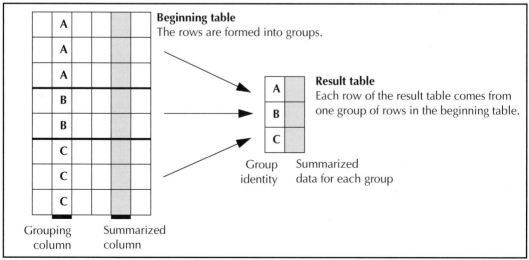

Grouping the rows of a table, then summarizing each group.

12-2   The group by **clause**

The example in this section shows how you can control the level of summarization using a group by clause. In this example a single column is used in the group by clause. This is the simplest case.

Each group is formed from all the rows of the table with the same value in the grouping column, so each row of the table is placed in a group and no row is in more than one group.

The columns are then summarized separately for each group. The result table contains one row for each group along with the summarized data for that group.

All the rows with a null in the grouping column are placed within a single group called the *null group*. The null group is similar to the Other category that is often used when data is summarized. This may seem a little unusual because nulls are unknown values and normally we do not consider one null to be equal to another. But what would the alternative be? It would not work well if SQL formed a separate group from each null value. Each of these groups would contain only one row. There would be too many groups with only a single row and the summarization would not work well. Therefore the only effective solution is to form a single group from all the rows with a null in the grouping column.

We often say that every table should have a primary key, although we allow some exceptions. However, in this example you could not put a primary key on the manager_id column. Because of the null group, there is a null value in this column and a primary key column must not contain a null. You often cannot put a primary key on the result table of a grouped query.

Task

For each manager_id, list the number of employees each one manages. Also list the range of their employees' credit limits by showing the minimum and maximum. Omit employee 202.

Oracle & Access SQL

```
select manager_id, ❸
        count(employee_id) as number_of_employees,
        min(credit_limit) as minimum_credit,
        max(credit_limit) as maximum_credit
from l_employees
where not (employee_id = 202) ❶
group by manager_id ❷
order by manager_id;
```

Beginning table (l_employees table)

EMPLOYEE ID	FIRST_NAME	LAST_NAME	DEPT CODE	HIRE_DATE	CREDIT LIMIT	PHONE NUMBER	MANAGER ID
201	SUSAN	BROWN	EXE	01-JUN-1998	$30.00	3484	(null)
202	JIM	KERN	SAL	16-AUG-1999	$25.00	8722	201
203	MARTHA	WOODS	SHP	02-FEB-2004	$25.00	7591	201
204	ELLEN	OWENS	SAL	01-JUL-2003	$15.00	6830	202
205	HENRY	PERKINS	SAL	01-MAR-2000	$25.00	5286	202
206	CAROL	ROSE	ACT	(null)	(null)	(null)	(null)
207	DAN	SMITH	SHP	01-DEC-2004	$25.00	2259	203
208	FRED	CAMPBELL	SHP	01-APR-2003	$25.00	1752	203
209	PAULA	JACOBS	MKT	17-MAR-1999	$15.00	3357	201
210	NANCY	HOFFMAN	SAL	16-FEB-2004	$25.00	2974	203

First the where clause is applied and the row for employee_id = 202 is removed ❹

EMPLOYEE ID	FIRST_NAME	LAST_NAME	DEPT CODE	HIRE_DATE	CREDIT LIMIT	PHONE NUMBER	MANAGER ID
201	SUSAN	BROWN	EXE	01-JUN-1998	$30.00	3484	(null)
203	MARTHA	WOODS	SHP	02-FEB-2004	$25.00	7591	201
204	ELLEN	OWENS	SAL	01-JUL-2003	$15.00	6830	202
205	HENRY	PERKINS	SAL	01-MAR-2000	$25.00	5286	202
206	CAROL	ROSE	ACT	(null)	(null)	(null)	(null)
207	DAN	SMITH	SHP	01-DEC-2004	$25.00	2259	203
208	FRED	CAMPBELL	SHP	01-APR-2003	$25.00	1752	203
209	PAULA	JACOBS	MKT	17-MAR-1999	$15.00	3357	201
210	NANCY	HOFFMAN	SAL	16-FEB-2004	$25.00	2974	203

Then the rows of the table are divided into groups that have the same value in the `manager_id` column ❺

EMPLOYEE ID	FIRST_NAME	LAST_NAME	DEPT CODE	HIRE_DATE	CREDIT LIMIT	PHONE NUMBER	MANAGER ID
203	MARTHA	WOODS	SHP	02-FEB-2004	$25.00	7591	201
209	PAULA	JACOBS	MKT	17-MAR-1999	$15.00	3357	201
204	ELLEN	OWENS	SAL	01-JUL-2003	$15.00	6830	202
205	HENRY	PERKINS	SAL	01-MAR-2000	$25.00	5286	202
207	DAN	SMITH	SHP	01-DEC-2004	$25.00	2259	203
208	FRED	CAMPBELL	SHP	01-APR-2003	$25.00	1752	203
210	NANCY	HOFFMAN	SAL	16-FEB-2004	$25.00	2974	203
201	SUSAN	BROWN	EXE	01-JUN-1998	$30.00	3484	(null)
206	CAROL	ROSE	ACT	(null)	(null)	(null)	(null)

Result table ❻

MANAGER ID	NUMBER_OF_EMPLOYEES	MINIMUM_CREDIT	MAXIMUM_CREDIT
201	2	$15.00	$25.00
202	2	$15.00	$25.00
203	3	$25.00	$25.00
(null)	2	$30.00	$30.00

Notes

❶ ❹ First, the `where` clause is applied to the rows of the beginning table. It eliminates some of the rows. In this example, employee 202 is deleted from further consideration.

❷ ❺ Second, the remaining rows of the table are divided into groups by their value in the `manager_id` column. This creates four groups:

- The two rows with a `manager_id` of 201.
- The two rows with a `manager_id` of 202.
- The three rows with a `manager_id` of 203.
- The two rows with a null value in the `manager_id` column.

❸ ❻ Third, the column functions summarize the data in each of the groups. They produce one row in the result table for each of the groups.

The result table is usually structured to identify each group and then give summary information about that group. It does not need to be structured this way, but that is usually the most logical way to present the data. To achieve this, the `select` clause lists the grouping column(s) first, followed by column functions. The `select` clause here is organized that way.

Last, the `order by` clause sorts the rows of the result table into a logical order. Usually the `order by` clause contains the same columns as the `group by` clause.

12-3   Groups formed on two or more columns

This section shows a `group by` clause that uses two grouping columns. Each group is formed from all the rows that have identical values in both of these columns. If two rows have different values in either of these columns, then they belong to different groups. The groups are the same regardless of the order in which the columns are listed in the `group by` clause.

A `group by` clause can list any number of columns. When a new column is added to the `group by` clause, each prior group may split into two or more new groups.

Drill down is a term that is used to describe the process of beginning with a high level of summarization and progressing to finer levels of detail. You can compare the result table of this section with the one from the previous section to see an example of a drill down.

The usual SQL technique behind a drill down is to add another column to the `group by` clause. This further divides each of the groups of rows. The same column is also added to the `select` clause and the `order by` clause. In the following example, the `dept_code` column is added to these clauses. I highlighted this change in the code.

Task

From the code in section 12-2, drill down by adding the department code. Omit employee 202.

Oracle & Access SQL

```
select manager_id, ❸
       dept_code,
       count(employee_id) as number_of_employees,
       min(credit_limit) as minimum_credit,
       max(credit_limit) as maximum_credit
from l_employees
where not (employee_id = 202) ❶
group by manager_id, ❷
         dept_code
order by manager_id, ❹
         dept_code;
```

Beginning table (1_employees table)

EMPLOYEE ID	FIRST_NAME	LAST_NAME	DEPT CODE	HIRE_DATE	CREDIT LIMIT	PHONE NUMBER	MANAGER ID
201	SUSAN	BROWN	EXE	01-JUN-1998	$30.00	3484	(null)
202	JIM	KERN	SAL	16-AUG-1999	$25.00	8722	201
203	MARTHA	WOODS	SHP	02-FEB-2004	$25.00	7591	201
204	ELLEN	OWENS	SAL	01-JUL-2003	$15.00	6830	202
205	HENRY	PERKINS	SAL	01-MAR-2000	$25.00	5286	202
206	CAROL	ROSE	ACT	(null)	(null)	(null)	(null)
207	DAN	SMITH	SHP	01-DEC-2004	$25.00	2259	203
208	FRED	CAMPBELL	SHP	01-APR-2003	$25.00	1752	203
209	PAULA	JACOBS	MKT	17-MAR-1999	$15.00	3357	201
210	NANCY	HOFFMAN	SAL	16-FEB-2004	$25.00	2974	203

First the `where` clause is applied and the row for `employee_id` = 202 is removed ❺

EMPLOYEE ID	FIRST_NAME	LAST_NAME	DEPT CODE	HIRE_DATE	CREDIT LIMIT	PHONE NUMBER	MANAGER ID
201	SUSAN	BROWN	EXE	01-JUN-1998	$30.00	3484	(null)
203	MARTHA	WOODS	SHP	02-FEB-2004	$25.00	7591	201
204	ELLEN	OWENS	SAL	01-JUL-2003	$15.00	6830	202
205	HENRY	PERKINS	SAL	01-MAR-2000	$25.00	5286	202
206	CAROL	ROSE	ACT	(null)	(null)	(null)	(null)
207	DAN	SMITH	SHP	01-DEC-2004	$25.00	2259	203
208	FRED	CAMPBELL	SHP	01-APR-2003	$25.00	1752	203
209	PAULA	JACOBS	MKT	17-MAR-1999	$15.00	3357	201
210	NANCY	HOFFMAN	SAL	16-FEB-2004	$25.00	2974	203

Then the rows of the table are divided into groups that have the same values in both the `manager_id` and `dept_code` columns ❻

EMPLOYEE ID	FIRST_NAME	LAST_NAME	DEPT CODE	HIRE_DATE	CREDIT LIMIT	PHONE NUMBER	MANAGER ID
203	MARTHA	WOODS	SHP	02-FEB-2004	$25.00	7591	201
209	PAULA	JACOBS	MKT	17-MAR-1999	$15.00	3357	201
204	ELLEN	OWENS	SAL	01-JUL-2003	$15.00	6830	202
205	HENRY	PERKINS	SAL	01-MAR-2000	$25.00	5286	202
207	DAN	SMITH	SHP	01-DEC-2004	$25.00	2259	203
208	FRED	CAMPBELL	SHP	01-APR-2003	$25.00	1752	203
210	NANCY	HOFFMAN	SAL	16-FEB-2004	$25.00	2974	203
201	SUSAN	BROWN	EXE	01-JUN-1998	$30.00	3484	(null)
206	CAROL	ROSE	ACT	(null)	(null)	(null)	(null)

Result table

```
MANAGER DEPT
     ID CODE NUMBER_OF_EMPLOYEES MINIMUM_CREDIT MAXIMUM_CREDIT
------- ---- -------------------- -------------- --------------
    201 MKT                     1         $15.00         $15.00
    201 SHP                     1         $25.00         $25.00
    202 SAL                     2         $15.00         $25.00
    203 SAL                     1         $25.00         $25.00
    203 SHP                     2         $25.00         $25.00
 (null) ACT                     1 (null)          (null)
 (null) EXE                     1         $30.00         $30.00
```

Notes

❶ ❺ The where clause is applied first. In this example it eliminates the row for employee 202 from further consideration.

❷ ❻ Groups of rows are formed that have identical values in both the manager_id and dept_code columns.

❸   Then the column functions in the select clause are evaluated separately for each group. The result table contains one row for each group. The department code is added to the select clause to fully identify each group in the listing of the result table.

❹   As a last step, the rows of the result table are sorted on the two columns used to create the groups. Although the order of these columns does not matter in the group by clause, it does matter in the order by clause. Because the manager_id is listed first in the order by clause, the primary sort is done on that column.

12-4   Null groups when there are two or more grouping columns

This section shows what happens when the rows of a table are grouped on two or more columns and several of those columns contain nulls. In this situation, the nulls are handled as if "null" was a specific value, like any other value. That is, if two nulls occur within a single grouping column, they are handled as if they have the same value and they are placed within the same group. If they occur in different grouping columns, they are handled separately, as any other values would be. Actually, this occurred in the previous section, but this section emphasizes the point.

In effect, this can create several Other categories within the summarization, but all the nulls are not placed into a single Other category. That is how the process is sometimes described, and that description is wrong. It is correct only when there is a single grouping column.

A null in the data is handled in two different ways within a grouped summarization. A null in a grouping column is handled as if it is a specific value and it is placed in a null group. However, a null in a column that is being summarized is ignored by the column functions that do the summarization.

In the following example, the groups are formed on `col_2` and `col_3`. Both of these columns contain nulls. There are five separate groups that contain a null group in one of the two grouping columns. In the result table, each of these groups creates a separate row. In effect, this gives five Other categories.

Then the data in `col_4` and `col_5` are summarized for each of the groups. When the data is summarized with the `count(*)` function, we could think that the nulls are being counted, although it is really the rows that are being counted for each group. When the data is summarized with the `count(column)` function, the nulls are completely ignored.

Within this example we can see that nulls in grouping columns are handled differently from nulls in summarized columns.

Task

Group the following table on the two columns, col_2 and col_3. For each group of rows, calculate
1. The number of rows in the group
2. The number of rows that have data in column col_4
3. The number of rows that have data in column col_5

Oracle & Access SQL

```
select col_2, ❶
       col_3, ❶
       count(*),
       count(col_4),
       count(col_5)
from sec1204
group by col_2,
         col_3 ❷
order by col_2,
         col_3;
```

Beginning table (sec1204 table) divided into groups

PK_1	COL_2	COL_3	COL_4	COL_5
1	A	Y	M	(null)
2	A	Y	(null)	(null)
3	A	Z	M	(null)
4	A	Z	(null)	(null)
5	A	(null)	M	(null)
6	A	(null)	(null)	(null)
7	B	Y	M	(null)
8	B	Y	(null)	(null)
9	B	Z	M	(null)
10	B	Z	(null)	(null)
11	B	(null)	M	(null)
12	B	(null)	(null)	(null)
13	(null)	Y	M	(null)
14	(null)	Y	(null)	(null)
15	(null)	Z	M	(null)
16	(null)	Z	(null)	(null)
17	(null)	(null)	M	(null)
18	(null)	(null)	(null)	(null)

Result table ❸

COL_2	COL_3	COUNT(*)	COUNT(COL_4)	COUNT(COL_5)
A	Y	2	1	0
A	Z	2	1	0
A	(null)	2	1	0
B	Y	2	1	0
B	Z	2	1	0
B	(null)	2	1	0
(null)	Y	2	1	0
(null)	Z	2	1	0
(null)	(null)	2	1	0

This is what does *not* happen when the beginning table (`sec1204` table) is divided into groups. Here all the rows with a null in either grouping column form a single group. If SQL worked this way, there would be only one Other category

PK_1	COL_2	COL_3	COL_4	COL_5
1	A	Y	M	(null)
2	A	Y	(null)	(null)
3	A	Z	M	(null)
4	A	Z	(null)	(null)
7	B	Y	M	(null)
8	B	Y	(null)	(null)
9	B	Z	M	(null)
10	B	Z	(null)	(null)
5	A	(null)	M	(null) ❹
6	A	(null)	(null)	(null)
11	B	(null)	M	(null)
12	B	(null)	(null)	(null)
13	(null)	Y	M	(null)
14	(null)	Y	(null)	(null)
15	(null)	Z	M	(null)
16	(null)	Z	(null)	(null)
17	(null)	(null)	M	(null)
18	(null)	(null)	(null)	(null)

Notes

❶ `Col_2` and `col_3` are used to group the data from the beginning table. They are listed in the `select` clause so that the result table makes sense.

❷ The `group by` clause lists both `col_2` and `col_3`.

❸ The highlighted rows in the result table show the five separate null groups. In more general terms, these are five separate Other categories.

❹ This is what does not happen. SQL does not form a single group out of all the rows that have a null in one of the grouping columns.

12-5 Summarized data cannot be mixed with nonsummarized data in the same `select` statement

A `select` statement cannot list both summarized data and detail data because the output of a `select` statement must be like a table. I have been calling this the Result table. It must have columns and rows. In particular, each of the columns must have the same number of rows.

The example in this section shows a `select` statement that does not work and produces an error message. This error occurs because this `select` statement is mixing summarized data with detail data.

The second and third columns of the `select` clause are detail data. They are `first_name` and `last_name`. No column functions are applied to these columns and they are not listed in the `group by` clause. That is why they yield detail data. If the `select` clause listed only these columns, the result table would have 10 rows. Each row of the result table would come from a single row in the beginning table. The result table would be similar to the following:

```
FIRST_NAME      LAST_NAME
----------      ---------

(10 rows of detail data)
```

The first and fourth columns of the `select` clause are summarized data. The first column is `manager_id`. This column is also listed in the `group by` clause, so it is a grouping column, which is summarized data. The fourth column uses the `max` column function, so it is also summarized data. If the select clause listed only these columns, the result table would have four rows. Each of these rows would summarize all the rows with a particular manager_id. There are four different values in the manager_id column, so the result table would be similar to the following:

```
MANAGER_ID      MAX(CREDIT_LIMIT)
----------      ----------------

(4 rows of summarized data)
```

These two tables cannot be combined to form a single table because the columns contain different numbers of rows. For this reason, you are not allowed to mix summarized data and detail data in the same select statement.

Error messages

This section also shows that the error messages produced by Oracle and Access do not always tell you specifically what the error is or how to fix it. This is a problem with almost all computer software, not just Oracle and Access. It is very difficult for any type of computer software to tell you what the problems are in your code. Often when the computer detects a problem, it is genuinely confused, so it gives you a confused error message. It may point to the wrong location of the error — often the error actually occurs on the line above or below where the error message says it occurs. The error message may say that one thing is wrong, when the problem is something else entirely. The one thing you can count on is that when an error message appears, there is actually an error of some sort somewhere in your code. This is one of the basic problems you must learn to deal with any type of computer programming.

The error messages shown in this section illustrate another difficulty. These error messages are specific to the problem and they do indicate accurately where the error first occurs. However, they are worded in a manner that is difficult to understand.

How to solve the problem

At times, you will attempt to mix summarized data with detail data. It happens to everyone, even me. You will receive the error messages shown here. The question is, how do you move on and deal with the problem?

On a technical level, there are two main techniques you can use. The one you choose depends on what you are trying to do. The next two sections show these techniques with the SQL code used in this section. The techniques are as follows:

1. Add more columns to the group by clause. Add all the columns that contain detail data.

2. Separate your query into two separate select statements, one for summarized data and the other for detail data.

Task

Show the error that occurs when a summarized column and a nonsummarized column both occur within the same select statement.

Oracle & Access SQL: This contains an error

```
select manager_id, ❶
       first_name, ❷
       last_name, ❷
       max(credit_limit) ❸
from l_employees
group by manager_id
order by manager_id;
```

Beginning table (l_employees table)

EMPLOYEE ID	FIRST_NAME	LAST_NAME	DEPT CODE	HIRE_DATE	CREDIT LIMIT	PHONE NUMBER	MANAGER ID
201	SUSAN	BROWN	EXE	01-JUN-1998	$30.00	3484	(null)
202	JIM	KERN	SAL	16-AUG-1999	$25.00	8722	201
203	MARTHA	WOODS	SHP	02-FEB-2004	$25.00	7591	201
204	ELLEN	OWENS	SAL	01-JUL-2003	$15.00	6830	202
205	HENRY	PERKINS	SAL	01-MAR-2000	$25.00	5286	202
206	CAROL	ROSE	ACT	(null)	(null)	(null)	(null)
207	DAN	SMITH	SHP	01-DEC-2004	$25.00	2259	203
208	FRED	CAMPBELL	SHP	01-APR-2003	$25.00	1752	203
209	PAULA	JACOBS	MKT	17-MAR-1999	$15.00	3357	201
210	NANCY	HOFFMAN	SAL	16-FEB-2004	$25.00	2974	203

Oracle error message ❹

```
      FIRST_NAME,
      *
ERROR at line 2:
ORA-00979: not a GROUP BY expression
```

Access error message ❺

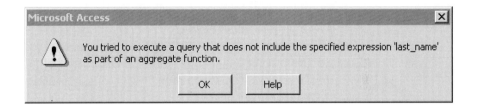

Notes

❶ The `manager_id` column is a grouping column because it is listed in the `group by` clause.

❷ The `first_name` and `last_name` columns are detail data. They are not summarized.

❸ The `maximum_credit_limit` column is summarized data because it applies a column function.

❹ In Oracle the asterisk under `first_name` indicates that this is the location of the first error. The message, "not a GROUP BY expression," is meant to suggest that you should put `first_name` in the `group by` clause.

Sometimes Oracle displays a more cryptic message, "not a single-group group function," to indicate that you are trying to mix summarized data with detail data.

❺ In Access, the error message can also be confusing.

12-6   Solution 1: Add more columns to the `group by` clause

This section shows one technique for dealing with the error that occurred in the SQL code of section 12-5. In this technique, all the columns of the `select` clause that are not column functions are placed in the `group by` clause.

This technique works, in the sense that it produces SQL code that runs. However, it may or may not produce the result you want. It can add many more groups to your result, which can affect the level of summarization.

In this example several new groups have been formed by adding the `first_name` and `last_name` columns to the `group by` clause. In fact a separate group has been created for each employee, because there are no two employees with the same name. Each of these groups has only one row, so the column function `max(credit_limit)` produces the same result as simply listing the `credit_limit` column. It is up to you to decide if this is the result you want.

Task

Show one technique to deal with the error in the SQL code of section 12-5. This technique adds more columns to the `group by` clause. (I highlighted the changes to the code.)

Oracle & Access SQL

```
select manager_id,
       first_name, ❶
       last_name, ❶
       max(credit_limit)
from l_employees
group by manager_id,
         first_name, ❷
         last_name ❷
order by manager_id;
```

Beginning table (`1_employees` table)

```
EMPLOYEE                        DEPT               CREDIT  PHONE   MANAGER
     ID FIRST_NAME  LAST_NAME  CODE  HIRE_DATE     LIMIT   NUMBER       ID
-------- ----------  ---------  ----  ------------  -------  ------  -------
    201 SUSAN       BROWN      EXE   01-JUN-1998   $30.00  3484    (null)
    202 JIM         KERN       SAL   16-AUG-1999   $25.00  8722       201
    203 MARTHA      WOODS      SHP   02-FEB-2004   $25.00  7591       201
    204 ELLEN       OWENS      SAL   01-JUL-2003   $15.00  6830       202
    205 HENRY       PERKINS    SAL   01-MAR-2000   $25.00  5286       202
    206 CAROL       ROSE       ACT   (null)        (null)  (null)  (null)
    207 DAN         SMITH      SHP   01-DEC-2004   $25.00  2259       203
    208 FRED        CAMPBELL   SHP   01-APR-2003   $25.00  1752       203
    209 PAULA       JACOBS     MKT   17-MAR-1999   $15.00  3357       201
    210 NANCY       HOFFMAN    SAL   16-FEB-2004   $25.00  2974       203
```

Result table

```
MANAGER
     ID FIRST_NAME  LAST_NAME  MAX(CREDIT_LIMIT)
------- ----------  ----------  -----------------
    201 JIM         KERN                       25
    201 MARTHA      WOODS                      25
    201 PAULA       JACOBS                     15
    202 ELLEN       OWENS                      15
    202 HENRY       PERKINS                    25
    203 DAN         SMITH                      25
    203 FRED        CAMPBELL                   25
    203 NANCY       HOFFMAN                    25
 (null) CAROL       ROSE        (null)
 (null) SUSAN       BROWN                      30
```

Notes

❶ First_name and last_name were detail data in the `select` statement in the previous section. Here they are summarized data because they appear in the `group by` clause.

❷ First_name and last_name are added to the `group by` clause.

12-7   Solution 2: Divide the query into two separate `select` statements

This section shows another technique for dealing with the error that occurred in the SQL code of section 12-5. In this technique, the query is divided into two separate `select` statements, one statement for summarized data and one for detail data.

In the statement for summarized data all the columns of detail data are removed from the `select` clause. No other clause needs to be changed. In the statement for the detail data all the column functions are removed and the `group by` clause is removed. This gets both of the `select` statements to run and produce results. Then it is up to you to decide how to put those results together to express your meaning.

Task

Show another technique to deal with the error in the SQL code of section 12-5. This technique divides the `select` statement into two separate select statements — one for summarized data and one for detail data.

Oracle & Access SQL: Statement 1 — For summarized data

```
select manager_id,
       max(credit_limit)
from l_employees
group by manager_id
order by manager_id;
```

Beginning table (`l_employees` table)

EMPLOYEE ID	FIRST_NAME	LAST_NAME	DEPT CODE	HIRE_DATE	CREDIT LIMIT	PHONE NUMBER	MANAGER ID
201	SUSAN	BROWN	EXE	01-JUN-1998	$30.00	3484	(null)
202	JIM	KERN	SAL	16-AUG-1999	$25.00	8722	201
203	MARTHA	WOODS	SHP	02-FEB-2004	$25.00	7591	201
204	ELLEN	OWENS	SAL	01-JUL-2003	$15.00	6830	202
205	HENRY	PERKINS	SAL	01-MAR-2000	$25.00	5286	202
206	CAROL	ROSE	ACT	(null)	(null)	(null)	(null)
207	DAN	SMITH	SHP	01-DEC-2004	$25.00	2259	203
208	FRED	CAMPBELL	SHP	01-APR-2003	$25.00	1752	203
209	PAULA	JACOBS	MKT	17-MAR-1999	$15.00	3357	201
210	NANCY	HOFFMAN	SAL	16-FEB-2004	$25.00	2974	203

Result table

```
MANAGER
     ID MAX(CREDIT_LIMIT)
------- -----------------
    201                25
    202                25
    203                25
(null)                 30
```

Oracle & Access SQL: Statement 2 — For detail data

```
select manager_id,
       first_name,
       last_name
from l_employees
order by manager_id;
```

Result table

```
MANAGER
     ID FIRST_NAME LAST_NAME
------- ---------- ----------
    201 JIM        KERN
    201 MARTHA     WOODS
    201 PAULA      JACOBS
    202 ELLEN      OWENS
    202 HENRY      PERKINS
    203 DAN        SMITH
    203 FRED       CAMPBELL
    203 NANCY      HOFFMAN
(null)  SUSAN      BROWN
(null)  CAROL      ROSE
```

12-8   How to create a report with subtotals and a grand total

A common type of report shows details and also has subtotals and a grand total. How can SQL produce a report like this? The previous sections have stated that you cannot get both detail data and summarized data from a single select statement, so it will take more than a single select statement to produce such a report.

The usual way to produce a report like this is to have SQL work together with another layer of reporting software. SQL supplies the detail data sorted in the correct order. The other layer of software takes care of the control breaks (where the subtotals are placed), the subtotals, and the grand total.

This arrangement, having SQL work together with another layer of software, goes back to the idea of using SQL as part of a back-end data server. The plan is for SQL to deal with the information level while the other layer of software deals with the presentation level.

What can you use for this other layer of software? There are many options. Oracle SQLplus can create a report with totals and subtotals. Access can also, using its reports. Another option is a software package called Crystal Reports.

12-9   Counting to zero, part 2

This is part two of a series. We want to count the number of lunches each employee will attend and list all the employees, even the two who are not attending any lunches. For those two, we want to put a zero in the `number_of_lunches` column. We will achieve this goal in chapter 14. Right now we are building up to it.

Section 11-7 is part one of this series. There we showed that the `count(column)` function is capable of counting to zero. In this part we use the `1_lunches` table and that column function to count the number of lunches for each employee who is listed in that table. This is a good first try that gets most of the answer.

When we examine the result table we see some success and also that some improvement is needed. The success is that it counts the number of lunches for the employees who are attending at least one lunch. The changes we want to make are to list the two employees who are not attending any lunches and to list the names of all the employees.

Task

From the `1_lunches` table, count the number of lunches each employee will attend.

Oracle & Access SQL

```
select employee_id,
       count(lunch_id) as number_of_lunches
from 1_lunches
group by employee_id
order by employee_id;
```

Beginning table (`l_lunches` table)

```
            LUNCH       EMPLOYEE
LUNCH_ID DATE               ID DATE_ENTERE
-------- ------------ -------- -----------
       1 16-NOV-2005       201 13-OCT-2005
       2 16-NOV-2005       207 13-OCT-2005
       3 16-NOV-2005       203 13-OCT-2005
       4 16-NOV-2005       204 13-OCT-2005
       6 16-NOV-2005       202 13-OCT-2005
       7 16-NOV-2005       210 13-OCT-2005
       8 25-NOV-2005       201 14-OCT-2005
       9 25-NOV-2005       208 14-OCT-2005
      12 25-NOV-2005       204 14-OCT-2005
      13 25-NOV-2005       207 18-OCT-2005
      15 25-NOV-2005       205 21-OCT-2005
      16 05-DEC-2005       201 21-OCT-2005
      17 05-DEC-2005       210 21-OCT-2005
      20 05-DEC-2005       205 24-OCT-2005
      21 05-DEC-2005       203 24-OCT-2005
      22 05-DEC-2005       208 24-OCT-2005
```

Result table ❶

```
EMPLOYEE
      ID NUMBER_OF_LUNCHES
-------- -----------------
     201                 3
     202                 1
     203                 2
     204                 2
     205                 2
     207                 2
     208                 2
     210                 2
```

Notes

❶ There are no rows for employees 206 or 209.

12-10 Counting to zero, part 3

To get to the final result of this "Counting to zero" series, you need to use two techniques: summarization and outer join. Because we have talked about summarization in this chapter, I want you to see the summarization part of the solution, so for now I am giving you the outer join part. In chapter 14, I show you how to create it yourself. This outer join adds two rows to the `l_lunches` table, one for employee 206 and one for employee 209. These rows have a null in the `lunch_id` and `lunch_date` columns.

The one thing that is a bit tricky in the summarization is the `group by` clause. You might think it is enough to have just the `employee_id` column in this clause because that is what really forms the groups. However, then we would be mixing summarized data (`employee_id` and `number_of_lunches`) with detail data (`first_name` and `last_name`), which we are not allowed to do.

You might say that we know that there is only one first name and one last name for each employee ID because `employee_id` is the primary key of the `l_employees` table. There is some validity to that point, but that level of intelligence is not built into SQL.

The computer does not know that there is only one first name and one last name for each employee ID, or at least it is not thinking about that fact when it processes this `select` statement. SQL requires you to put `first_name` and `last_name` into the `group by` clause. Then all the columns in the `select` clause are summarized data.

Task

Count the number of lunches each employee will attend. List the employee IDs and names of all the employees.

Oracle & Access SQL

```
select employee_id,
       first_name, ❶
       last_name, ❶
       count(lunch_id) as number_of_lunches
from sec1210
group by employee_id,
         first_name,
         last_name
order by employee_id;
```

Beginning view (`sec1210 view`)

```
EMPLOYEE                                        LUNCH
      ID FIRST_NAME LAST_NAME   LUNCH_ID DATE
-------- ---------- ---------- ---------- ------------
     201 SUSAN      BROWN               1 16-NOV-2005
     201 SUSAN      BROWN               8 25-NOV-2005
     201 SUSAN      BROWN              16 05-DEC-2005
     202 JIM        KERN                6 16-NOV-2005
     203 MARTHA     WOODS               3 16-NOV-2005
     203 MARTHA     WOODS              21 05-DEC-2005
     204 ELLEN      OWENS              12 25-NOV-2005
     205 HENRY      PERKINS            15 25-NOV-2005
     205 HENRY      PERKINS            20 05-DEC-2005
     206 CAROL      ROSE         (null)     (null)        ❷
     207 DAN        SMITH               2 16-NOV-2005
     207 DAN        SMITH               4 16-NOV-2005
     207 DAN        SMITH              13 25-NOV-2005
     208 FRED       CAMPBELL            9 25-NOV-2005
     208 FRED       CAMPBELL           22 05-DEC-2005
     209 PAULA      JACOBS       (null)     (null)        ❷
     210 NANCY      HOFFMAN             7 16-NOV-2005
     210 NANCY      HOFFMAN            17 05-DEC-2005
```

Result table

```
EMPLOYEE FIRST      LAST
      ID NAME       NAME       NUMBER_OF_LUNCHES
-------- ---------- ---------- -----------------
     201 SUSAN      BROWN                      3
     202 JIM        KERN                       1
     203 MARTHA     WOODS                      2
     204 ELLEN      OWENS                      2
     205 HENRY      PERKINS                    2
     206 CAROL      ROSE                       0  ❸
     207 DAN        SMITH                      2
     208 FRED       CAMPBELL                   2
     209 PAULA      JACOBS                     0  ❸
     210 NANCY      HOFFMAN                    2
```

Notes

❶ We must add the `first_name` and `last_name` to the `group by` clause.

❷ These new rows are created by an outer join.

❸ All the employees are shown. A zero is created for the two people who are not attending any lunches.

Eliminating Some of the Summarized Data

After data has been summarized, it is possible to eliminate some of the rows of the result. This is done with the `having` clause of a `select` statement. We might do this if we only want to see the largest categories or the most relevant portion of the data.

Often by the time data is grouped and summarized, the result table is only a few pages long and we do not object to looking at the whole thing. In that case, we do not need a `having` clause.

When there are many groups in the summarization, the `having` clause can be a convenient way to focus on the ones we are most interested in.

12-11 The `having` clause

There is one more clause in the `select` statement that we have not yet discussed: the `having` clause. When the result table contains data that are grouped and summarized, the `having` clause can eliminate some of the groups from the result table. The groups are still formed and all the calculations and summarizations are done, but they are deleted at the end of the process.

The example in this section shows a query with a `having` clause that eliminates the foods for which fewer than 10 servings have been ordered.

For the data shown here, only a few rows are eliminated from the result table. The `having` clause is usually used with a larger amount of data. For instance, out of 100 employees, most of them would only attend one lunch. The `having` clause can help you find the few people who are attending two or more lunches. This clause is often used to find exceptions in the data.

The `having` clause is always used with a `group by` clause, but a `group by` clause is often used alone. As the following code shows, the `having` clause is written directly after the `group by` clause and before the `order by` clause.

Task

From the 1_lunch_items table list the supplier ID and product code (these identify a food) of all the foods for which 10 servings or more have been ordered.

Oracle & Access SQL

```
select supplier_id,
       product_code,
       sum(quantity) as total_servings
from 1_lunch_items
group by supplier_id,
         product_code
having sum(quantity) >= 10 ❶
order by supplier_id,
         product_code;
```

Beginning table (1_lunch_items table) ❷

LUNCH_ID	ITEM_NUMBER	SUPPLIER ID	PRODUCT CODE	QUANTITY
1	1	ASP	FS	1
1	2	ASP	SW	2
1	3	JBR	VR	2
2	1	ASP	SW	2
2	2	FRV	FF	1
2	3	JBR	VR	2
2	4	VSB	AS	1
3	1	ASP	FS	1
3	2	CBC	GS	1
3	3	FRV	FF	1
3	4	JBR	VR	1
3	5	JBR	AS	1

(and many more rows)

Result table before the `having` clause is applied

```
SUPPLIER  PRODUCT
ID        CODE     TOTAL_SERVINGS
--------  -------  --------------
ASP       FS                    9
ASP       SP                   11
ASP       SW                    7
CBC       GS                   10
CBC       SW                    5
FRV       FF                   10
JBR       AS                   11
JBR       VR                   17
VSB       AS                    6
```

Result table after the `having` clause is applied ❸

```
SUPPLIER  PRODUCT
ID        CODE     TOTAL_SERVINGS
--------  -------  --------------
ASP       SP                   11
CBC       GS                   10
FRV       FF                   10
JBR       AS                   11
JBR       VR                   17
```

Notes

❶ This is the `having` clause. You often write a column function within this clause.

❷ The rows of the beginning table are grouped and processed in the same way, as if the `having` clause were not present.

❸ The `having` clause eliminates rows from the result table.

12-12 The `having` clause contrasted with the `where` clause

The `having` clause is similar to the `where` clause in the following ways:

1.   They both eliminate data from the result table.

2.   They both set conditions that some data will pass and other data will not pass.

3.   A null in the data can never satisfy a condition in either a `having` clause or a `where` clause. The only exception occurs with the `is null` condition.

The `having` clause is different from the `where` clause in the following ways:

1.   The `where` clause can only eliminate rows from the beginning table, the raw data, before any other processing occurs.

2.   The `having` clause can eliminate data that have been grouped and summarized, after most of the processing has already taken place.

3.   The `where` clause cannot use column functions in the conditions it sets.

4.   The `having` clause can use column functions in its conditions.

12-13 The whole process of the `select` statement on a single table

Here is a summary of the entire process that a `select` statement describes when it operates on a single table. All six clauses of the `select` statement are shown here. This is an idealized model of the processing. The computer is allowed to use shortcuts in its processing as long as it gets the same result that this idealized model would produce.

Step 1: The `from` clause chooses the beginning table.

Step 2: The row functions are calculated. In effect, this adds new columns to the beginning table.

Step 3: The `where` clause chooses which rows of data to process from the table. Any rows that do not satisfy its condition are eliminated.

Step 4: The `select` clause chooses which columns of data to process and list in the result table. The process also includes other columns used in the `group by`, `having`, and `order by` clauses. Any other columns are eliminated.

Step 5: The `group by` clause separates the rows into different groups.

Step 6: The column functions summarize the data in each group.

Step 7: The `having` clause chooses which rows of summarized data to put in the result table.

Step 8: The `order by` clause chooses which columns are used to sort the rows of the result table for its presentation.

12-14   The `having` clause does not add any more power to the `select` statement

The `having` clause is sometimes convenient to use, but it is never required. At best it can save us one step, one SQL statement. To eliminate a `having` clause use the following procedure:

Step 1: Create a view or a table from all the data after it is grouped and summarized. Do not include the `having` clause.

Step 2: Write a `select` statement from that view. In this `select` statement a `where` clause can be used to do the same work that the `having` clause did before.

Task

Show an example of replacing a `having` clause with a two-step process. Rewrite the SQL code of section 12-11 and eliminate the `having` clause.

Oracle SQL:
Step 1 — Create a view from the grouped and summarized data

```
create or replace view sec1214 as
select supplier_id,
       product_code,
       sum(quantity) as total_servings
from l_lunch_items
group by supplier_id,
         product_code;
```

Access SQL:
Step 1 — Create a view from the grouped and summarized data

Step 1 Part 1: Enter this `select` statement in the SQL window:

```
select supplier_id,
       product_code,
       sum(quantity) as total_servings
from l_lunch_items
group by supplier_id,
         product_code;
```

Step 1 Part 2: Save this query. Name it `sec1214`.

Beginning table (`l_lunch_items` table)

LUNCH_ID	ITEM_NUMBER	SUPPLIER ID	PRODUCT CODE	QUANTITY
1	1	ASP	FS	1
1	2	ASP	SW	2
1	3	JBR	VR	2
2	1	ASP	SW	2
2	2	FRV	FF	1
2	3	JBR	VR	2
2	4	VSB	AS	1
3	1	ASP	FS	1
3	2	CBC	GS	1
3	3	FRV	FF	1
3	4	JBR	VR	1
3	5	JBR	AS	1

(and many more rows)

View created by step 1

```
SUPPLIER PRODUCT
ID       CODE    TOTAL_SERVINGS
-------- ------- --------------
ASP      FS                   9
ASP      SP                  11
ASP      SW                   7
CBC      GS                  10
CBC      SW                   5
FRV      FF                  10
JBR      AS                  11
JBR      VR                  17
VSB      AS                   6
```

Oracle & Access SQL: Step 2

```
select *
from sec1214
where total_servings >= 10 ❶
order by supplier_id,
         product_code;
```

Result table from step 2

```
SUPPLIER PRODUCT
ID       CODE    TOTAL_SERVINGS
-------- ------- --------------
ASP      SP                  11
CBC      GS                  10
FRV      FF                  10
JBR      AS                  11
JBR      VR                  17
```

Notes

❶ This where clause does the same work that the having clause is doing in section 12-11.

12-15   Use a `where` clause instead of a `having` clause to eliminate raw data

When the condition in a `having` clause does not involve a column function, it is better to write that condition in a `where` clause. The code produces the same result either way. However, the process is more efficient for the computer when a `where` clause is used because the data is eliminated earlier in the process. The result is obtained faster and costs less.

In theory, it should not make a difference whether we code a condition in the `where` clause or in the `having` clause. People should specify only the result. The optimizer is responsible for determining the most efficient way to obtain the result. However, optimizers are not always perfect and most do not even attempt to make a change of this type.

The code in this section shows an example of a `having` clause that can be replaced by a `where` clause.

Task

For each `manager_id` between 201 and 203, show the number of employees the manager supervises.

Oracle & Access SQL: Using a `having` clause

```
select manager_id,
       count(*)
from l_employees
group by manager_id
having manager_id between 201 and 203; ❶
```

Oracle & Access SQL:
Gets the same result more efficiently by using a `where` clause

```
select manager_id,
       count(*)
from l_employees
where manager_id between 201 and 203 ❷
group by manager_id;
```

Beginning table (`1_employees`)

```
EMPLOYEE                        DEPT                    CREDIT  PHONE   MANAGER
      ID FIRST_NAME LAST_NAME  CODE HIRE_DATE           LIMIT  NUMBER       ID
-------- ---------- ---------  ---- ------------       -------  ------  -------
     201 SUSAN      BROWN      EXE  01-JUN-1998        $30.00  3484    (null)
     202 JIM        KERN       SAL  16-AUG-1999        $25.00  8722       201
     203 MARTHA     WOODS      SHP  02-FEB-2004        $25.00  7591       201
     204 ELLEN      OWENS      SAL  01-JUL-2003        $15.00  6830       202
     205 HENRY      PERKINS    SAL  01-MAR-2000        $25.00  5286       202
     206 CAROL      ROSE       ACT  (null)             (null)  (null)  (null)
     207 DAN        SMITH      SHP  01-DEC-2004        $25.00  2259       203
     208 FRED       CAMPBELL   SHP  01-APR-2003        $25.00  1752       203
     209 PAULA      JACOBS     MKT  17-MAR-1999        $15.00  3357       201
     210 NANCY      HOFFMAN    SAL  16-FEB-2004        $25.00  2974       203
```

Result table — Both `select` statements give the same result

```
MANAGER
     ID  COUNT(*)
------- ---------
    201         3
    202         2
    203         3
```

Notes

❶ This shows a condition limiting the data written in the `having` clause.

❷ This shows the same condition written in the `where` clause.

Restrictions on Summarization

Several restrictions are placed on grouped summarization. We may write code that seems perfectly logical, yet the computer cannot process it. There is always a way to work around these restrictions by dividing the process into a series of steps.

The official specification of SQL places several restrictions on what can be done in a grouped summarization. These restrictions are not absolute limitations. They only restrict how much we can do in a single `select` statement, so the solution is to use two or more `select` statements.

Many SQL products have removed some of these restrictions. I usually ignore these restrictions when I first write code. If it does not work, I divide it into simpler steps until it does work.

12-16 Three restrictions on grouped summarization

The three main restrictions on grouped summarization are shown here. The next sections show how to get around each of these restrictions.

1. Only a column can be listed in a `group by` clause, not a function.

2. The word `distinct` can be used only once in a `select` clause.

3. You cannot apply one column function to another column function.

12-17 How to work around restriction 1

This section shows you how to work around the restriction that we cannot use a row function in a `group by` clause. The first step creates a view with a new column in it to use in the `group by` clause. The second step is a `select` statement using that view. A variation of this procedure uses a table in place of a view.

Task

Show how to divide the following problem SQL statement into two steps so that it will run. (Actually the problem SQL does run in Oracle and similar code also runs in Access.)

Oracle SQL: Problem SQL

```
select to_char(lunch_date, 'yyyy-mm') as lunch_month,
       count(employee_id) as number_of_lunches
from l_lunches
group by to_char(lunch_date, 'yyyy-mm') ❶
order by to_char(lunch_date, 'yyyy-mm');
```

Oracle SQL: Step 1 — Create a view ❷

```
create or replace view sec1217 as
select to_char(lunch_date, 'yyyy-mm') as lunch_month,
       employee_id
from l_lunches;
```

Access SQL: Step 1 — Create a view ❷

Step 1 Part 1: Enter this code in the SQL window:

```
select format(lunch_date, 'yyyy-mm') as lunch_month,
       employee_id
from l_lunches;
```

Step 1 Part 2: Save the query. Name it `sec1217`.

Beginning table

```
          LUNCH        EMPLOYEE
LUNCH_ID DATE          ID DATE_ENTERE
-------- ------------ -------- -----------
       1 16-NOV-2005      201 13-OCT-2005
       2 16-NOV-2005      207 13-OCT-2005
       3 16-NOV-2005      203 13-OCT-2005
       4 16-NOV-2005      204 13-OCT-2005
       6 16-NOV-2005      202 13-OCT-2005
       7 16-NOV-2005      210 13-OCT-2005
       8 25-NOV-2005      201 14-OCT-2005
       9 25-NOV-2005      208 14-OCT-2005
      12 25-NOV-2005      204 14-OCT-2005
      13 25-NOV-2005      207 18-OCT-2005
      15 25-NOV-2005      205 21-OCT-2005
      16 05-DEC-2005      201 21-OCT-2005
      17 05-DEC-2005      210 21-OCT-2005
      20 05-DEC-2005      205 24-OCT-2005
      21 05-DEC-2005      203 24-OCT-2005
      22 05-DEC-2005      208 24-OCT-2005
```

View created (`sec1217` view)

```
        EMPLOYEE
LUNCH_M       ID
------- --------
2005-11      201
2005-11      207
2005-11      203
2005-11      204
2005-11      202
2005-11      210
2005-11      201
2005-11      208
2005-11      204
2005-11      207
2005-11      205
2005-12      201
2005-12      210
2005-12      205
2005-12      203
2005-12      208
```

Oracle & Access SQL: Step 2

```
select lunch_month,
       count(employee_id) as number_of_lunches
from sec1217
group by lunch_month ❸
order by lunch_month;
```

Result table

```
LUNCH_M NUMBER_OF_LUNCHES
------- -----------------
2005-11                11
2005-12                 5
```

Notes

❶ The `group by` clause contains a `to_char` function.

❷ If this technique doesn't work, try creating a table instead of a view in step 1.

❸ This `group by` clause contains a column.

12-18 How to work around restriction 2

This section shows how to work around the restriction that the word `distinct` can only be used once in a `select` statement.

Task

Show how to divide the following problem SQL into a series of steps that will run. (Actually the problem SQL does run in both Oracle and Access, but it might not run in some other SQL products.)

Here I only show the Oracle SQL. The Access SQL is very similar, except that you create a view with the GUI as discussed in section 4-2.

Problem SQL

```
select count(distinct last_name),
       count(distinct credit_limit),
       count(distinct manager_id)
from 1_employees;
```

Oracle SQL: Step 1 — Create a view using `distinct` once

```
create or replace view sec1218a as
select count(distinct last_name) as number_of_last_names
from 1_employees;
```

Beginning table (1_employees table)

EMPLOYEE ID	FIRST_NAME	LAST_NAME	DEPT CODE	HIRE_DATE	CREDIT LIMIT	PHONE NUMBER	MANAGER ID
201	SUSAN	BROWN	EXE	01-JUN-1998	$30.00	3484	(null)
202	JIM	KERN	SAL	16-AUG-1999	$25.00	8722	201
203	MARTHA	WOODS	SHP	02-FEB-2004	$25.00	7591	201
204	ELLEN	OWENS	SAL	01-JUL-2003	$15.00	6830	202
205	HENRY	PERKINS	SAL	01-MAR-2000	$25.00	5286	202
206	CAROL	ROSE	ACT	(null)	(null)	(null)	(null)
207	DAN	SMITH	SHP	01-DEC-2004	$25.00	2259	203
208	FRED	CAMPBELL	SHP	01-APR-2003	$25.00	1752	203
209	PAULA	JACOBS	MKT	17-MAR-1999	$15.00	3357	201
210	NANCY	HOFFMAN	SAL	16-FEB-2004	$25.00	2974	203

View created (`sec1218a` view)

```
NUMBER_OF_LAST_NAMES
-------------------
                 10
```

Oracle SQL: Step 2 — Create a view using `distinct` once

```
create or replace view sec1218b as
select count(distinct credit_limit)
                    as number_of_credit_limits
from l_employees;
```

View created (`sec1218b` view)

```
NUMBER_OF_CREDIT_LIMITS
----------------------
                     3
```

Oracle SQL: Step 3 — Create a view using `distinct` once

```
create or replace view sec1218c as
select count(distinct manager_id) as number_of_manager_ids
from l_employees;
```

View created (`sec1218c` view)

```
NUMBER_OF_MANAGER_IDS
--------------------
                   3
```

Oracle SQL: Step 4 — List all the views together

```
select number_of_last_names,
       number_of_credit_limits,
       number_of_manager_ids
from sec1218a,
     sec1218b,
     sec1218c;
```

Result table

```
NUMBER_OF_LAST_NAMES NUMBER_OF_CREDIT_LIMITS NUMBER_OF_MANAGER_IDS
-------------------- ----------------------- --------------------
                 10                       3                    3
```

12-19   How to work around restriction 3

This section shows you how to work around the restriction that we cannot apply a column function to another column function. The code in the following example does not run in either Oracle or Access.

The problem with using a column function embedded within another column function is that to make it work we would need to be able to write two `group by` statements, one for each column function. However, that is not allowed.

Task

Show how to divide the following problem SQL into a series of steps that will run. The problem area is highlighted.

Problem SQL

```
select supplier_id,
       product_code
       max(sum(quantity))
from l_lunch_items
group by supplier_id,
         product_code;
```

Oracle SQL: Step 1 — Create a view using one column function

```
create or replace view sec1219 as
select supplier_id,
       product_code,
       sum(quantity) as total_quantity
from l_lunch_items
group by supplier_id,
         product_code;
```

Access SQL: Step 1 — Create a view using one column function

Step 1 Part 1: Enter this in the SQL window:

```
select supplier_id,
       product_code,
       sum(quantity) as total_quantity
from l_lunch items
group by supplier_id,
         product_code;
```

Step 1 Part 2: Save the query. Name it `sec1219`.

Beginning table (`1_lunch_items` table)

```
                            SUPPLIER  PRODUCT
  LUNCH_ID  ITEM_NUMBER  ID        CODE     QUANTITY
  --------  -----------  --------  -------  ---------
         1            1  ASP       FS              1
         1            2  ASP       SW              2
         1            3  JBR       VR              2
         2            1  ASP       SW              2
         2            2  FRV       FF              1
         2            3  JBR       VR              2
         2            4  VSB       AS              1
         3            1  ASP       FS              1
         3            2  CBC       GS              1
         3            3  FRV       FF              1
         3            4  JBR       VR              1
         3            5  JBR       AS              1

(and many more rows)
```

View created in step 1 (`sec1219` view)

```
SUPPLIER  PRODUCT
ID        CODE     TOTAL_QUANTITY
--------  -------  --------------
ASP       FS                    9
ASP       SP                   11
ASP       SW                    7
CBC       GS                   10
CBC       SW                    5
FRV       FF                   10
JBR       AS                   11
JBR       VR                   17
VSB       AS                    6
```

Oracle & Access SQL: Step 2 —
Apply the other column function to the view created in step 1

```
select max(total_quantity)
from sec1219;
```

Result table of step 2

```
MAX(TOTAL_QUANTITY)
------------------
                17
```

Oracle & Access SQL: Step 3 — Finish the report ❶

```
select supplier_id,
       product_code,
       total_quantity
from sec1219
where total_quantity = 17;
```

Result table of step 3

```
SUPPLIER PRODUCT
ID       CODE    TOTAL_QUANTITY
-------- ------- --------------
JBR      VR                  17
```

Notes

❶ In Access, you will get an error message when you run this code. The problem is that Access thinks the field `total_quantity` should have no more than one digit because it is defined from the field `quantity`, which is allowed to have only one digit. So Access thinks there is an error when you say `where total_quantity = 17`, because 17 has two digits. I consider this to be a bug in Access.

To get this code to work, you first need to expand the datatype of the quantity column to allow larger numbers. You can do this with the code

```
alter table l_lunch_items
alter column quantity byte;
```

This allows `total_quantity` to be any number that will fit within the `byte` datatype (any number up to 255).

Summary

In this chapter we discussed the `group by` clause, the `having` clause, and how to work around the restrictions that some SQL products have on grouped summarization. The `group by` clause places the rows into separate groups, each of which is summarized. This controls the level of summarization.

Exercises

1. Goal: Use a `group by` clause.

   a. From the `1_foods` table, list each `supplier_id` and the number of foods provided by that supplier. Sort the rows by the `supplier_id`.

Oracle & Access SQL

```
select supplier_id,
       count(product_code) as number_of_foods_on_menu
from 1_foods
group by supplier_id
order by supplier_id;
```

   b. From the `1_employees` table, count the number of employees who work in each department. Sort the rows of the result table by the `dept_code`.

   c. Modify the code you wrote for exercise 1b to count the employees by both `dept_code` and `credit_limit`.

   That is, from the `1_employees` table, list all the different combinations of `dept_code` and `credit_limit`. Count the number of employees who are in each of these categories. Sort the rows by `dept_code` and then by `credit_limit`.

2. Goal: Group on a date column and use only part of the information in that date.

a. Count the number of lunches entered into the `1_lunches` table on each date entered. (Step 1 changes the date to a text field with the date formatted the way you want to see it in the result. Step 2 summarizes the lunches using the date field you created in step 1.)

Oracle SQL: Step 1

```
create or replace view ex1202a as
select lunch_id,
       to_char(date_entered, 'yyyy-mm-dd') as date_entered_2
from 1_lunches;
```

Access SQL: Step 1

Step 1 Part 1: Enter this query in the SQL window:

```
select lunch_id,
       format(date_entered, 'yyyy-mm-dd') as date_entered_2
from 1_lunches;
```

Step 1 Part 2: Save the query. Name it ex1202a.

Oracle & Access SQL: Step 2

```
select date_entered_2 as date_entered,
       count(lunch_id) as number_of_lunches_entered
from ex1202a
group by date_entered_2;
```

b. From the `1_lunches` table, count the number of lunches served each day. (The date a lunch is served is the `lunch_date`. Hint: This is similar to the problem solved in section 12-17, but you must modify the date format to include the day.)

c. From the `1_employees` table, count the number of employees hired in each year. (Hint: Format the `hire_date` showing only the year.)

3. Goal: Use a `having` clause.

a. The table `ex1203a` contains the numbers from 1 to 1,000. A few of the numbers occur several times in the table and a few numbers are missing. Find all the numbers that are less than 200 and that occur more than once. Sort these numbers from the greatest to the least.

Here is what this table looks like:

ex1203a table

N
1
2
3
3
4
6
etc
1000

Oracle & Access SQL

```
select n,
       count(*) as number_of_occurrences
from ex1203a
where n < 200
group by n
having count(*) > 1
order by n desc;
```

b. The table `ex1203b` contains the first name, last name, and state of people who want to receive a free magazine. Some people have signed up more than once.

List all three columns of the `ex1203b` table and a count of the number of times each row occurs. List only the people from California, Oregon, or Washington who are in the table more than once. Put these names in alphabetical order by last name. If two people have the same last name, then sort them by the first name. (Hint: Count the number of times each row occurs and put all three columns in the `group by` clause.)

4.   Goal: Work with an outer join to count to zero.

a. See sections 12-9 and 12-10.

b. The table `ex1204b` contains two columns: `complete_set` and `N`. The `complete_set` column contains all the numbers from 1 to 1,000. The `N` column contains the numbers from the `ex1203a` table. In the following discussion I will refer to these tables using the short names 3a and 4b.

Table 4b is an outer join. We have not discussed outer joins yet so I will tell you what the rows look like. There are only three types of rows and I will give you an example of each. You need to know that the 3a table is missing the number 5 and contains the number 3 twice. The 4b table contains the rows shown here:

ex1204b table

complete_set	N	
1	1	❶
2	2	
3	3	
3	3	❷
4	4	
5	null	❸
6	6	

❶ Most numbers occur only once in the 3a table. For each of these numbers, there is one row in the 4b table with the same number in both columns. Examples are 1, 2, 4, and 6.

❷ If a number occurs several times in the 3a table, then it occurs the same number of times in the 4b table. Again, both columns of the 4b table are equal. For example, the number 3 occurs twice in the 3a table and there are two rows in the 4b table with a 3 in both columns.

❸ When a number is missing from the 3a table, then the 4b table has a row with the missing number in the `complete_set` column and a null in the `N` column. An example is 5.

Task: From the 4b table, list all the numbers that do not occur in the 3a table. That is, list all the rows of the 4b table that have a null in the `N` column.

c. From the 4b table, begin by listing all the numbers in the `complete_set` column and the number of times that number appears in the N column. Most numbers will have a count of one. All of the numbers you got in the result table of exercise 4b should have a count of zero.

Then add the following `having` clause:

```
having count(n) = 0
```

so that only the rows with a count of zero will appear in the result table. This is another way of showing which numbers are missing from the 3a table.

d. Modify the code you wrote in exercise 4c. Change the `having` clause to the following:

```
having not (count(n) = 1)
```

The result table shows all the numbers that are missing from the 3a table. It also shows all the numbers that occur in the table more than once and how many times they occur.

(This exercise is a bit tricky. I have solved it for you in chapter 14, section 11, but you can try it yourself first.)

chapter 13

INNER JOINS

So far, we have obtained data from one table or view, sometimes adding a table of constants. In the next four chapters we discuss seven different ways to combine two tables. On a conceptual level, the tables are combined first, which creates a single table. Then the techniques we have discussed so far are applied to get a final report from that table.

This chapter discusses inner joins, the most common way to combine two tables.

Introduction to Joins

An inner join combines the data from two or more tables. The result of this is a single table that is often quite large. The techniques you have learned in previous chapters are then used to extract a small amount of data from this large table.

An inner join used to just be called a *join* and many people still speak this way. But now the terminology is changing. *Outer joins* have become an official part of SQL. To distinguish what we used to call a join from an outer join, we now use the term *inner join*. We discuss outer joins in the next chapter.

13-1   A query can use data from several tables

Often, several different tables are used together in a `select` statement. This is necessary when the data you need does not all reside in one table or view. On a conceptual level this process has two steps: First, the separate tables are combined into a single table. Then the `select` statement operates on this table using any of the techniques we have discussed so far.

The following diagram shows these two steps. In the first step, four separate tables of data are combined together to form a single table that can be very large. It may contain several copies of the four beginning tables in different permutations and combinations. One row of any of the beginning tables can be matched with many combinations of rows from the other tables.

In the second step, a report is extracted from the single table. It gathers a few of the rows and a few of the columns of the table, applies row functions and column functions to them, and sorts the result.

The single table that combines all the data might exist only in theory. It might never be formed physically within the computer, either in memory or on the disk. It might be too large for the computer to handle. However, the final report that is produced must be the same as if this table were formed. The computer is allowed to take shortcuts in the process, as long as they do not affect the result.

The two steps shown here may be coded in SQL as a single `select` statement, or each step can be a separate `select` statement. There are many different ways to write the SQL statements, but the process is always fundamentally the same as the one shown in the following diagram.

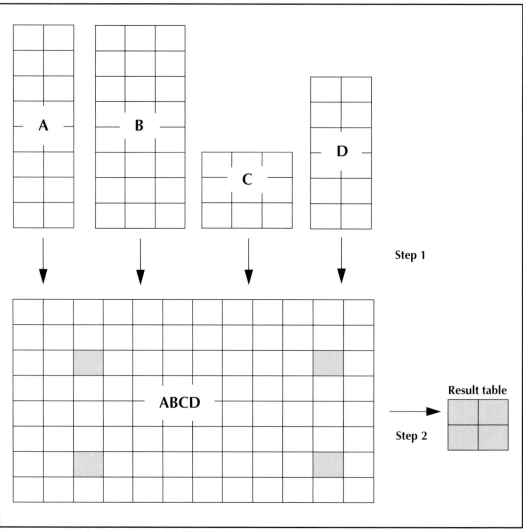

A query can use data from several tables.

In this model, in step 1 all the tables are joined at once into a single large table. Then, in step 2, we extract a small amount of information from this large table using the techniques described in the previous chapters.

13-2   The best approach is to join two tables at a time

You can combine several tables at one time, as shown in the previous section. However, this process often becomes difficult to control and it is prone to errors.

Often, the best technique is to combine the beginning tables two at a time. The first step of this process combines two of the tables and each step after that adds one additional table.

The following diagram shows this process with four beginning tables. This shows the way the SQL code can be written. Each step in the diagram is a separate SQL statement and the process is written as a series of three SQL statements, each of which creates a table or view. Creating views is usually more efficient.

Step 1a combines tables A and B. This can be coded as one `select` statement and saved as a view.

Step 1b combines the result of step 1 with table C. This can also be coded as a `select` statement and saved as a view.

Step 1c combines the result of step 2 with table D. The view this creates combines the data from all four of the beginning tables. Together, the three steps of this process are equivalent to the first step of the diagram in the previous section.

Step 2 extracts a small amount of data using all the techniques we have discussed so far.

You can understand a join of several tables as a series of steps that each join two tables at a time. The presentation in the next few chapters is focused on the process of combining just two tables.

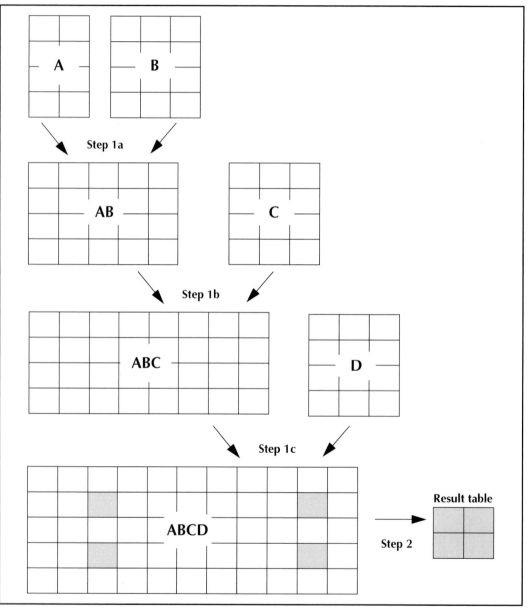

Combining tables two at a time.

A query can use data from several tables. In this model, in step 1 the tables are joined two at a time to form a single large table. Then, in step 2, we extract a small amount of information from this large table.

Inner Joins of Two Tables

The most common way to combine two tables is with an inner join. An inner join strictly enforces the join condition. Any row without a matching row in the other table is dropped from the result. Because of this, an inner join may lose information.

13-3   A one-to-one relationship

This section shows a model case of combining two tables with an inner join. This shows the technique that is always used, but avoids the complexities, which we discuss later. For now, just focus on this simple example.

Rows from one table are matched with rows from the other table. There are no hidden links between the two tables. The data in the tables determines how to combine the rows. One column is chosen from each table. When these columns have the same value, the rows are combined.

The data

In the example that follows, the fruit number column (`f_num`) is chosen from the `fruits` table and the color number column (`c_num`) is chosen from the `colors` table. These are sometimes called the *matching columns*. A row of the `fruits` table is matched with a row of the `colors` table when the matching columns have the same value. The apple is matched with red because both the matching columns contain a 1. The banana is matched with yellow because both matching columns contain a 2, and so on.

Each row of the `fruits` table matches with one and only one row of the `colors` table. Likewise, each row of the `colors` table matches with one and only one row of the `fruits` table. This is sometimes called a *one-to-one relationship* between the two tables. It is a special condition that can occur only when both tables have the same number of rows. (Some people use the term one-to-one relationship with a slightly different meaning, but that is another story.)

The data in the chosen columns creates this relationship. The tables are seemingly being "zipped together" by the values of the data in the matching columns. Note that the color red occurs in rows 1 and 3 of the `colors` table. This is allowed; there is no rule that every row has to be a different color.

Task

Join the `fruits` table and the `colors` table with an inner join. Match the `f_num` column of the `fruits` table with the `c_num` column of the `colors` table. Combine a row of the `fruits` table with a row of the `colors` table when the values in these matching columns are equal. Because of the data in the beginning tables, this creates a one-to-one relationship between the two beginning tables.

Oracle & Access SQL — Explained on page 529

```
select a.fruit,
       a.f_num,
       b.c_num,
       b.color
from sec1303_fruits a,
     sec1303_colors b
where a.f_num = b.c_num
order by a.fruit;
```

Beginning table 1 sec1303_fruits table		Relationship f_num = c_num	Beginning table 2 sec1303_colors table	

FRUIT	F_NUM		C_NUM	COLOR
APPLE	1	<-------------->	1	RED
BANANA	2	<-------------->	2	YELLOW
CHERRY	3	<-------------->	3	RED
GRAPE	4	<-------------->	4	PURPLE
ORANGE	5	<-------------->	5	ORANGE

Result table

FRUIT	F_NUM	C_NUM	COLOR
APPLE	1	1	RED
BANANA	2	2	YELLOW
CHERRY	3	3	RED
GRAPE	4	4	PURPLE
ORANGE	5	5	ORANGE

The SQL for this inner join

The SQL statement in this example needs some explanation. The `from` clause lists both beginning tables. It also assigns a *table alias* to each table. This is an alternative name or short name for the table, which only applies within the context of a single `select` statement. The `fruits` table is assigned the table alias `a` and the `colors` table is assigned the table alias `b`. The table alias follows the name of the table. A comma separates the entry for the first table from the one for the second table.

When table aliases have been assigned in the `from` clause, they can be used in all the other clauses of the `select` statement. When there is more than one beginning table, it is a good idea to identify the table to which each column belongs. This is done whenever the column is used throughout the `select` statement. To do this, write the table alias and a period before the name of each column. For example, in the first line of the following code, `a.fruit` means the `fruit` column from the `fruits` table.

The `select` clause in this code includes all the columns of both beginning tables. I want to show you how the two tables join together, which is step 1 in the diagram on page 524. At this time, I am not doing any selection from this data, which is step 2 in this same diagram. In section 13-16 I show how both steps can be combined in a single `select` statement.

The `where` clause contains the *join condition*, which is a statement. When that statement is true, a row from one table is matched with a row from the other table. Here the join condition is that the fruit number (`f_num`) column of the `fruits` table is equal to the color number (`c_num`) column of the `colors` table. This is written as follows:

```
a.f_num = b.c_num
```

In every row of the result table, we see that the fruit number column has the same value as the color number column because of the join condition we have used. With a more complex join condition, they might not always have the same value.

The `order by` clause is not usually included as part of the join, but I wrote it here so that the rows of the result table would be in a logical order.

13-4   A many-to-one relationship

The next five sections, including this one, all use the same SQL statement as the previous section. What differs is the data in the beginning tables. The changing data gives us an opportunity to discuss other aspects of this inner join.

In this section a strawberry has now been added to the `fruits` table. The row of the `strawberry` has a 1 in the `f_num` column, which matches with the 1 in the `c_num` column for the color red.

The result shows that there is a red apple and a red strawberry. So, two rows of the `fruits` table are matched with a single row of the `colors` table.

In effect, the row 1 RED is duplicated within the result table. It occurs twice in the result table, even though it occurs only once in the beginning `colors` table.

This section shows a *many-to-one relationship* between the two tables. Some colors are matched with many fruits. In this context, *many* means more than one. However, each fruit is matched with only one color.

Task

Join the `fruits` table and the `colors` table with an inner join. Use the same join condition as the previous section. The data here shows a many-to-one relationship between the tables.

Oracle & Access SQL

```
select a.fruit,
       a.f_num,
       b.c_num,
       b.color
from sec1304_fruits a,
     sec1304_colors b
where a.f_num = b.c_num
order by a.fruit;
```

Beginning tables

sec1304_fruits table   **sec1304_colors table**

FRUIT	F_NUM
APPLE	1
BANANA	2
CHERRY	3
GRAPE	4
ORANGE	5
STRAWBERRY	1

C_NUM	COLOR
1	RED
2	YELLOW
3	RED
4	PURPLE
5	ORANGE

Result table

FRUIT	F_NUM	C_NUM	COLOR
APPLE	1	1	RED
BANANA	2	2	YELLOW
CHERRY	3	3	RED
GRAPE	4	4	PURPLE
ORANGE	5	5	ORANGE
STRAWBERRY	1	1	RED

13-5   A one-to-many relationship

In this section the color green has been added to the `colors` table and the strawberry has been temporarily removed. The color `green` has 1 as its color number (`c_num`), which is the same as the color number value for `red`.

This is an example of a *one-to-many relationship*. It is the same as the previous section, except the roles of the tables are reversed. Here some fruits match with many colors, although each color is matched with only one fruit.

The result table shows that the `apple` row in the beginning `fruits` table is matched with both the `red` and `green` rows of the `colors` table. This results in a red apple and a green apple. The `apple` row occurs once in the beginning tables, but twice in the result table.

This shows that inner joins are symmetric. The principles work the same way regardless of the order of the tables.

Task

Join the `fruits` table and the `colors` table with an inner join. Use the same join condition as in the previous sections.

Oracle & Access SQL

```
select a.fruit,
       a.f_num,
       b.c_num,
       b.color
from sec1305_fruits a,
     sec1305_colors b
where a.f_num = b.c_num
order by a.fruit;
```

Beginning tables

sec1305_fruits table

FRUIT	F_NUM
APPLE	1
BANANA	2
CHERRY	3
GRAPE	4
ORANGE	5

sec1305_colors table

C_NUM	COLOR
1	RED
1	GREEN
2	YELLOW
3	RED
4	PURPLE
5	ORANGE

Result table

FRUIT	F_NUM	C_NUM	COLOR
APPLE	1	1	RED
APPLE	1	1	GREEN
BANANA	2	2	YELLOW
CHERRY	3	3	RED
GRAPE	4	4	PURPLE
ORANGE	5	5	ORANGE

13-6   A many-to-many relationship

In this section we combine the changes in the last two sections. Here we have both the strawberry in the `fruits` table and green in the `colors` table. The `strawberry` has a 1 in the fruit number (`f_num`) column and `green` has a 1 in the color number (`c_num`) column.

This is an example of a *many-to-many relationship* between the tables. Here, two fruits, the apple and the strawberry, have a 1 in the matching column of the `fruits` table. Also two colors, red and green, have a 1 in the matching column of the `colors` table.

The result table shows all the possible combinations and permutations of these matches. There is a red apple, a green apple, a red strawberry, and a green strawberry.

If there were 10 fruits and 10 colors that all matched, these would create 100 rows in the result table, so you can see that the result table can easily become very large.

Task

Join the `fruits` table and the `colors` table with an inner join. Use the same join condition as in the previous sections.

Oracle & Access SQL

```
select a.fruit,
       a.f_num,
       b.c_num,
       b.color
from sec1306_fruits a,
     sec1306_colors b
where a.f_num = b.c_num
order by a.fruit;
```

Beginning tables
sec1306_fruits table   sec1306_colors table

FRUIT	F_NUM		C_NUM	COLOR
-----------	-----		-----	------
APPLE	1		1	RED
BANANA	2		1	GREEN
CHERRY	3		2	YELLOW
GRAPE	4		3	RED
ORANGE	5		4	PURPLE
STRAWBERRY	1		4	GREEN
			5	ORANGE

Result table ❶

FRUIT	F_NUM	C_NUM	COLOR
APPLE	1	1	RED
APPLE	1	1	GREEN
BANANA	2	2	YELLOW
CHERRY	3	3	RED
GRAPE	4	4	PURPLE
GRAPE	4	4	GREEN
ORANGE	5	5	ORANGE
STRAWBERRY	1	1	RED
STRAWBERRY	1	1	GREEN

Notes

❶ The result of a join includes all the possible combinations of rows from the first table and second table that satisfy the join condition. So here we have a red apple, a green apple, a red strawberry, and a green strawberry.

In this example I have kept the tables small. However, when you are handling larger tables, you may be surprised at the number of rows in the result table. For instance, if the beginning tables each contain 100 rows, the result table could contain 10,000 rows.

13-7   Unmatched rows are dropped

This section shows that rows are dropped if they do not have a matching row in the other table — they do not appear in the result table. This situation occurs whether the rows are in the first table or the second table.

The only rows that appear in the result tables are those that have a matching row in the other table. It is somewhat like a dance where you must bring your partner — singles are not allowed. This feature distinguishes an inner join. Outer joins, discussed in the next chapter, provide an alternative and restore some of the rows that have been dropped.

The inner join applies a strict interpretation to the join condition. All the rows of the result table must satisfy the join condition. This requires a matching pair of rows with one coming from each beginning table.

With an inner join, many rows from the beginning tables can be dropped, so information that is in the beginning tables may not be in the result table. That is, information may be lost. There is no warning message when this occurs.

In the beginning tables that follow, the highlighted rows are the ones dropped from the result table.

Task

Join the `fruits` table and the `colors` table with an inner join with the join condition used in the previous sections. The data here shows that rows in beginning tables may not appear at all in the result table.

Oracle & Access SQL

```
select a.fruit,
       a.f_num,
       b.c_num,
       b.color
from sec1307_fruits a,
     sec1307_colors b
where a.f_num = b.c_num
order by a.fruit;
```

Beginning tables

`sec1307_fruits` table   **`sec1307_colors` table**

```
FRUIT            F_NUM                    C_NUM COLOR
----------   ---------                ---------  ---------
APPLE            1                          1  RED
BANANA           2                          2  YELLOW
CHERRY           3  ❶                       1  GREEN
GRAPE            4  ❶                       5  ORANGE
ORANGE           5                          6  WHITE  ❶
STRAWBERRY       1
```

Result table

```
FRUIT            F_NUM       C_NUM COLOR
----------   ---------   ---------  ---------
APPLE            1           1  GREEN
APPLE            1           1  RED
BANANA           2           2  YELLOW
ORANGE           5           5  ORANGE
STRAWBERRY       1           1  GREEN
STRAWBERRY       1           1  RED
```

Notes

❶ These rows do not have a matching row in the other table, so they disappear from the result table.

13-8   Rows with a null in the matching column are dropped

This section shows a detail from the previous section. If there is a null in one of the matching columns, then the entire row that contains that null will be dropped from the result table. This is because a null can never satisfy any join condition in the `where` clause that combines two tables together.

In the following data, the kiwi has a null in the matching column. The color brown also has a null in the matching column. The join condition says the values in the two matching columns must be equal before a pair of rows can be combined in the result table.

However, a null is an unknown value and the two nulls are not considered to be equal, so both these rows are dropped from the result table.

Task

Join the `fruits` table and the `colors` table with an inner join using the join condition from the previous sections. Note that there is no brown kiwi in the result table.

Oracle & Access SQL

```
select a.fruit,
       a.f_num,
       b.c_num,
       b.color
from sec1308_fruits a,
     sec1308_colors b
where a.f_num = b.c_num
order by a.fruit;
```

Beginning tables

sec1308_fruits table   **sec1308_colors table**

FRUIT	F_NUM
APPLE	1
BANANA	2
CHERRY	3
GRAPE	4
ORANGE	5
KIWI	(null)

C_NUM	COLOR
1	RED
2	YELLOW
3	RED
4	PURPLE
5	ORANGE
(null)	BROWN

Result table

FRUIT	F_NUM	C_NUM	COLOR
APPLE	1	1	RED
BANANA	2	2	YELLOW
CHERRY	3	3	RED
GRAPE	4	4	PURPLE
ORANGE	5	5	ORANGE

13-9   Five ways to write the SQL for an inner join

This section shows five variations of the SQL code used in the previous sections. There is no difference in what these variations do, in terms of the result tables they produce. They are just different ways to write the same code. Which one you choose is just a matter of style and what you find easiest to read and understand.

Variation 1 is the one I usually like best. Each table alias is a single letter and the names of all the columns are spelled out.

Variation 2 is similar, except that `select *` is used instead of spelling out the names of the columns. This emphasizes that all the columns from both tables are being included. It is also easier to write than variation 1 when the tables have many columns. Note that the table alias must precede the asterisk. In the `select` clause `a.*` means "all the columns of the `fruits` table" and `b.*` means "all the columns of the `colors` table."

Variation 3 uses table aliases that are longer than a single letter, allowing them to be more descriptive of the beginning table they stand for.

Variation 4 does not use table aliases. The `from` clause lists the beginning tables, but it does not assign table aliases to them. Within the other clauses of the `select` statement, the full name of each table is written before each column. So, instead of

Table_Alias.Column_Name

we write

Table_Name.Column_Name

Variation 5 also does not use any table aliases. It makes use of the fact that there is no column in the first table with exactly the same name as any column in the second table. When this is true, the computer is able to figure out which table each column belongs to, just from the column name itself, so we are not required to identify the table. The computer can understand this SQL code, but it is kinder to the other people who may read it if we identify the beginning table of each column. I always try to write my code so that both computers and people can easily understand. I do not recommend using this variation.

Task

Show five ways of writing the SQL for the inner join used in the previous sections.

Oracle & Access SQL: Variation 1 — This is the best solution

```
select a.fruit,
       a.f_num,
       b.c_num,
       b.color
from sec1304_fruits a,
     sec1304_colors b
where a.f_num = b.c_num
order by a.fruit;
```

Oracle & Access SQL: Variation 2

```
select a.*,
       b.*
from sec1304_fruits a,
     sec1304_colors b
where a.f_num = b.c_num
order by a.fruit;
```

Oracle & Access SQL: Variation 3

```
select fru.fruit,
       fru.f_num,
       col.c_num,
       col.color
from sec1304_fruits fru,
     sec1304_colors col
where fru.f_num = col.c_num
order by fru.fruit;
```

Oracle & Access SQL: Variation 4

```
select sec1304_fruits.fruit,
       sec1304_fruits.f_num,
       sec1304_colors.c_num,
       sec1304_colors.color
from sec1304_fruits,
     sec1304_colors
where sec1304_fruits.f_num = sec1304_colors.c_num
order by sec1304_fruits.fruit;
```

Oracle & Access SQL: Variation 5
Fine for computers, confusing for people — Not recommended

```
select fruit,
       f_num,
       c_num,
       color
from sec1304_fruits,
     sec1304_colors
where f_num = c_num
order by fruit;
```

Variations of the Join Condition

The preceding examples all showed the most common type of join condition: using just one matching column from each table and requiring the two matching columns to have the same value. This section shows examples of the many other types of inner join conditions.

13-10 A join using two or more matching columns

This section shows an example of a join condition that uses two matching columns from each table. This contrasts with the previous sections, which used a single column from each table to form the inner join. The same principle shown here can be used to join tables on any number of columns.

Here, a color is matched with a fruit only when both sets of matching columns have the same values:

fruits.f_num_1 = colors.c_num_1

and

fruits.f_num_2 = colors.c_num_2

The first row of the `fruits` table matches with the first row of the `colors` table, giving a red apple. This match occurs because the first column of each row has the value 1 and the second column of each row has the value 5. However, the first row of the `fruits` table does not match with the second row of the `colors` table. That is, no yellow apple exists because the second columns of these rows have different values — the `fruits` table has the value 5 and the `colors` table has the value 6.

Task

Join the `fruits` table and the `colors` table with an inner join. Use a join condition that matches rows when the first two columns of each table are equal.

Oracle & Access SQL

```
select a.f_num_1, ❶
       a.f_num_2,
       a.fruit,
       b.c_num_1,
       b.c_num_2,
       b.color
from sec1310_fruits a,
     sec1310_colors b
where a.f_num_1 = b.c_num_1 ❷
  and a.f_num_2 = b.c_num_2
order by a.fruit; ❸
```

Beginning tables

sec1310_fruits table

F_NUM_1	F_NUM_2	FRUIT
1	5	APPLE
1	6	BANANA
2	5	CHERRY
2	6	GRAPE
2	7	ORANGE

sec1310_colors table

C_NUM_1	C_NUM_2	COLOR
1	5	RED
1	6	YELLOW
2	5	RED
2	6	PURPLE
2	7	ORANGE

Result table

F_NUM_1	F_NUM_2	FRUIT	C_NUM_1	C_NUM_2	COLOR
1	5	APPLE	1	5	RED
1	6	BANANA	1	6	YELLOW
2	5	CHERRY	2	5	RED
2	6	GRAPE	2	6	PURPLE
2	7	ORANGE	2	7	ORANGE

Notes

❶ All the columns are listed from both tables.

❷ The join condition is written in the where clause. Here there are two conditions combined together with the word and.

❸ The order by clause is not really part of the join, but it is included here to make the result table easier to read.

13-11 A join using between to match on a range of values

This section shows an example of using the between condition in a join, rather than a condition of equality. Three columns are involved in this join condition, and the value in one column must lie between the values in the other two.

In this example, test scores between 90 and 100 get an A, those between 80 and 89 get a B, and so on. The grade ranges must not overlap.

Task

Assign grades to students by placing their individual test scores within one of the grading ranges.

Oracle & Access SQL

```
select a.student_name, ❶
       a.test_score,
       b.letter_grade
from sec1311_student_scores a,
     sec1311_grade_ranges b
where a.test_score between b.beginning_score
                      and b.ending_score ❷
order by a.student_name; ❸
```

Beginning tables

sec1311_student_scores table

STUDENT_NAME	TEST_SCORE
CATHY	85
FRED	60
JOHN	95
MEG	92

sec1311_grade_ranges table ❹

BEGINNING SCORE	ENDING SCORE	LETTER GRADE
90	100	A
80	89	B
70	79	C
60	69	D
0	59	F

Result table

STUDENT_NAME	TEST_SCORE	LETTER_GRADE
CATHY	85	B
FRED	60	D
JOHN	95	A
MEG	92	A

Notes

❶ Here, only three columns are listed in the `select` clause because that is enough to understand this join and that is all I wanted in the result.

❷ The join condition is written in the `where` clause. Note that this condition uses `between`. The test score is placed `between` the beginning score and the ending score.

❸ The `order by` clause makes the result table easier to read. It is not part of the join.

❹ You must set up the grade ranges so there are no overlaps. Each score must correspond to only one letter grade.

13-12   A join using the greater than condition

This section shows an example of using a *greater than* condition to form a join, rather than an equality. Variations of this type of join can use

- Less than

- Less than or equal

- Greater than or equal

In this example, each row of one table is paired with many rows of the other table. For example, row 6 from the `bigger_numbers` table is matched with rows 1 to 5 from the `smaller_numbers` table.

Task

Join the `bigger_numbers` table with the `smaller_numbers` table. Create a join condition that pairs each bigger number with all the smaller numbers that are less than it.

Oracle & Access SQL

```
select a.*, ❶
       b.*
from sec1312_bigger_numbers a,
     sec1312_smaller_numbers b
where a.larger_number > b.smaller_number ❷
order by a.larger_number, ❸
         b.smaller_number;
```

Beginning tables

`sec1312_bigger_numbers` table   **`sec1312_smaller_numbers` table**

LARGER_NUMBER	WORD
1	ONE
2	TWO
3	THREE
4	FOUR
5	FIVE
6	SIX ❹

SMALLER_NUMBER	WORD
1	ONE
2	TWO
3	THREE
4	FOUR
5	FIVE
6	SIX

Result table

LARGER_NUMBER	WORD	SMALLER_NUMBER	WORD
2	TWO	1	ONE
3	THREE	1	ONE
3	THREE	2	TWO
4	FOUR	1	ONE
4	FOUR	2	TWO
4	FOUR	3	THREE
5	FIVE	1	ONE
5	FIVE	2	TWO
5	FIVE	3	THREE
5	FIVE	4	FOUR
6	SIX	1	ONE ❹
6	SIX	2	TWO ❹
6	SIX	3	THREE ❹
6	SIX	4	FOUR ❹
6	SIX	5	FIVE ❹

Notes

❶ All the columns are listed from both tables.

❷ The `where` clause contains the join condition, which says that one column is greater than another column.

❸ The `order by` clause makes the result table easier to read.

❹ The one row, 6, in the `bigger_numbers` table, combines with each row of the `smaller_numbers` table and generates five rows within the result table.

13-13   A join using a row function

This section shows a row function being used to create a join condition. In the following example, the values of two columns are added together. Each of the beginning tables contains one of these columns. Rows from the two beginning tables are joined together whenever the sum is equal to six.

Oracle & Access SQL

```
select a.fruit,
       a.f_num,
       b.c_num,
       b.color
from sec1306_fruits a,
     sec1306_colors b
where a.f_num + b.c_num = 6
order by a.fruit;
```

Beginning tables

sec1306_fruits table   **sec1306_colors table**

FRUIT	F_NUM
APPLE	1
BANANA	2
CHERRY	3
GRAPE	4
ORANGE	5
STRAWBERRY	1

C_NUM	COLOR
1	RED
1	GREEN
2	YELLOW
3	RED
4	PURPLE
4	GREEN
5	ORANGE

Result table

FRUIT	F_NUM	C_NUM	COLOR
APPLE	1	5	ORANGE
BANANA	2	4	PURPLE
BANANA	2	4	GREEN
CHERRY	3	3	RED
GRAPE	4	2	YELLOW
ORANGE	5	1	RED
ORANGE	5	1	GREEN
STRAWBERRY	1	5	ORANGE

13-14 Writing the join condition in the `from` clause

This section shows a new way of writing the join of the `fruits` table with the `colors` table. This method of writing a join is part of the new SQL standard, called SQL-92. This syntax places the join condition within the `from` clause, rather than in the `where` clause. The older syntax is still valid, and will remain valid in the future. Access and Oracle9i support this newer syntax, but Oracle8 does not.

The newer syntax writes the join condition in an `on` clause within the `from` clause. This allows the `where` clause to be focused on the rows of data we want to use for the final report. It does not need to handle the join condition.

There is no comma after the `a`, which is the table alias for the first table. Instead of this comma, the words `inner join` are placed between the two tables.

Task

Show the syntax for joining two tables in the `from` clause. Join the `fruits` table and the `colors` table as we have done before.

Oracle & Access SQL: Older syntax ❶

```
select a.fruit,
       a.f_num,
       b.c_num,
       b.color
from sec1306_fruits a, ❷
     sec1306_colors b
where a.f_num = b.c_num ❸
order by a.fruit;
```

Oracle 9i & Access SQL: New syntax ➍

```
select a.fruit,
       a.f_num,
       b.c_num,
       b.color
from sec1306_fruits a, ➎
     inner join sec1306_colors b
     on a.f_num = b.c_num ➏
order by a.fruit;
```

■ Oracle8 does not support the new syntax.

Beginning tables

sec1306_fruits table

FRUIT	F_NUM
APPLE	1
BANANA	2
CHERRY	3
GRAPE	4
ORANGE	5
STRAWBERRY	1

Record: 7

sec1306_colors table

C_NUM	COLOR
1	RED
1	GREEN
2	YELLOW
3	RED
4	PURPLE
4	GREEN
5	ORANGE

Record: 8

Result table

Query1 : Select Query

fruit	f_num	c_num	color
APPLE	1	1	RED
APPLE	1	1	GREEN
BANANA	2	2	YELLOW
CHERRY	3	3	RED
GRAPE	4	4	PURPLE
GRAPE	4	4	GREEN
ORANGE	5	5	ORANGE
STRAWBERRY	1	1	RED
STRAWBERRY	1	1	GREEN

Record: 9 of 9

Notes

❶ The older syntax is valid in both Oracle and Access.

❷ The `from` clause lists the tables and assigns aliases (short names) to the tables. There is a comma between the names of the tables.

❸ The join condition is written in the `where` clause.

❹ The newer syntax is valid in Access and in Oracle9i.

❺ The `from` clause specifies that this is an inner join, in addition to listing the tables and assigning the aliases. There is no comma between the names of the tables.

❻ The join condition is written within the `from` clause. The word `on` precedes the join condition.

Applications of Joins

Now let's look at a few applications of inner joins.

13-15   Lookup tables

A lookup table is also known as a *table of codes*. It is a table that contains a set of codes and their meanings. In the `Lunches` database, the `l_departments` table is a lookup table because it contains a row for each valid department code and the full name of that department. Because this is a typical lookup table, let's look at it while I explain more about this type of table.

An example of a lookup table (`l_departments` table)

```
DEPT
CODE  DEPARTMENT_NAME
----  ------------------
ACT   ACCOUNTING
EXE   EXECUTIVE
MKT   MARKETING
PER   PERSONNEL
SAL   SALES
SHP   SHIPPING
```

A lookup table often has only two columns: a column of the codes and a column of their meanings. There can be additional columns of information that, when present, contain further information about the code. For example in the `l_departments` table, additional columns could include department budget, department staff level, or department manager.

The column of codes is the primary key of the table. This column contains a row for each code that is a valid value. Referential Integrity, a form of data validation, is set up between the lookup table and any other table that uses the code. In this example, the first column, `dept_code`, of the `l_departments` table is the list of all the valid values of the department code.

The `l_employees` table also contains a `dept_code` column, and a data validation rule is applied to that column. Whenever a new row is inserted into the `l_employees` table, the value in the `dept_code` column must be one of the valid values. Otherwise the row is rejected and we get an error message.

The same data validation rule also applies to updates. In a row that already exists in the `l_employees` table, we can change the value of the `dept_code` column to any valid value. If we try to change it to an invalid value, the update is rejected and we get an error message.

There is a many-to-one relationship between a lookup table and another table that makes use of its codes. In our example, a code can occur only once in the `l_departments` table, which is the lookup table, but the code can occur many times in the `l_employees` table, which uses the codes.

Lookup tables are often used in database design to make the database self-documenting. The very large tables in a database use codes to save disk space and to validate the data. The lookup tables provide the meanings of those codes and a complete list of all their valid values.

Inner joins and lookup tables

An inner join can be used to look up the meanings of the codes from a lookup table. The example below shows the department name for each employee. The `l_employees` table contains only the `dept_code` column. The `department_name` column is looked up from the `l_departments` table.

When we use an inner join we must remember that some of the rows of data could be dropped. We need to sit down and analyze this in detail to see if anything important may have been lost. In the following example, we want all the employees to appear in the result table. An employee will be dropped if there is no matching row in the `l_departments` table. In this example, no employees are dropped because the `dept_code` column of the `l_employees` table

1. Has Referential Integrity with the `l_departments` table.

2. Contains no nulls.

Referential Integrity assures us that every value within the `dept_code` column of the `l_employees` table has a matching row in the `l_departments` table, so no employee will be dropped.

Task

For each employee show the `employee_id`, `first_name`, `last_name`, `dept_code`, and the `department_name`. Sort the rows by the `employee_id`. Use an inner join to get the `department_name` from the `l_departments` table.

Oracle & Access SQL

```
select a.employee_id,
       a.first_name,
       a.last_name,
       a.dept_code,
       b.department_name
from l_employees a,
     l_departments b
where a.dept_code = b.dept_code
order by a.employee_id;
```

Beginning table 1 (`1_employees` table)

EMPLOYEE ID	FIRST_NAME	LAST_NAME	DEPT CODE	HIRE_DATE	CREDIT LIMIT	PHONE NUMBER	MANAGER ID
201	SUSAN	BROWN	EXE	01-JUN-1998	$30.00	3484	(null)
202	JIM	KERN	SAL	16-AUG-1999	$25.00	8722	201
203	MARTHA	WOODS	SHP	02-FEB-2004	$25.00	7591	201
204	ELLEN	OWENS	SAL	01-JUL-2003	$15.00	6830	202
205	HENRY	PERKINS	SAL	01-MAR-2000	$25.00	5286	202
206	CAROL	ROSE	ACT	(null)	(null)	(null)	(null)
207	DAN	SMITH	SHP	01-DEC-2004	$25.00	2259	203
208	FRED	CAMPBELL	SHP	01-APR-2003	$25.00	1752	203
209	PAULA	JACOBS	MKT	17-MAR-1999	$15.00	3357	201
210	NANCY	HOFFMAN	SAL	16-FEB-2004	$25.00	2974	203

Beginning table 2 (`1_departments` table)

DEPT CODE	DEPARTMENT_NAME
ACT	ACCOUNTING
EXE	EXECUTIVE
MKT	MARKETING
PER	PERSONNEL
SAL	SALES
SHP	SHIPPING

Result table

EMPLOYEE ID	FIRST_NAME	LAST_NAME	DEPT CODE	DEPARTMENT_NAME
201	SUSAN	BROWN	EXE	EXECUTIVE
202	JIM	KERN	SAL	SALES
203	MARTHA	WOODS	SHP	SHIPPING
204	ELLEN	OWENS	SAL	SALES
205	HENRY	PERKINS	SAL	SALES
206	CAROL	ROSE	ACT	ACCOUNTING
207	DAN	SMITH	SHP	SHIPPING
208	FRED	CAMPBELL	SHP	SHIPPING
209	PAULA	JACOBS	MKT	MARKETING
210	NANCY	HOFFMAN	SAL	SALES

13-16   Combining a join and selection of data

The SQL code in section 13-15 combined the inner join and the selection of data from that join. A `select` statement often does both of these things.

Now, I want to show you that there are two steps going on here, even though we wrote only one SQL statement. The first step forms the inner join of the `1_employees` table and the `1_departments` table. This creates a table or view that contains all the columns of both tables: eight columns from the `1_employees` table and two from the `1_departments` table, for a total of 10 columns.

In the second step only part of that data is selected to be in the result table. In this case, five of the columns are retained and the other five are dropped.

Each of these steps can have a `where` clause. In step 1 the `where` clause is the join condition used to combine the two tables. In step 2 the `where` clause selects the rows we want to appear in the result table. When both steps are combined into a single `select` statement, the `where` clause performs both of these roles.

Task

Modify the SQL in section 13-15 so that only employees 201 to 205 appear in the result table. This is an example of a `where` clause that performs two roles.

Then rewrite this SQL to show the two separate steps: the inner join and the selection of data.

Oracle & Access SQL

```
select a.employee_id,
       a.first_name,
       a.last_name,
       a.dept_code,
       b.department_name
from 1_employees a,
     1_departments b
where a.dept_code = b.dept_code ❶
  and a.employee_id < 206 ❷
order by a.employee_id;
```

Oracle SQL: Step 1 — Create the inner join of the tables

```
create or replace view sec1316 as
select a.*,
       b.dept_code as dept_code2,
       b.department_name
from l_employees a,
     l_departments b
where a.dept_code = b.dept_code; ❸
```

Access SQL: Step 1 — Create the inner join of the tables

Step 1 Part 1: Enter this query in the SQL window:

```
select a.*,
       b.dept_code as dept_code2,
       b.department_name
from l_employees a,
     l_departments b
where a.dept_code = b.dept_code; ❸
```

Step 1 Part 2: Save the query. Name it sec1316.

Step 1 result table (sec1316 view)

EMPLOYEE ID	FIRST_NAME	LAST_NAME	DEPT CODE	HIRE_DATE	CREDIT LIMIT	PHONE NUMBER	MANAGER ID	DEP	DEPARTMENT NAME
201	SUSAN	BROWN	EXE	01-JUN-1998	$30.00	3484	(null)	EXE	EXECUTIVE
202	JIM	KERN	SAL	16-AUG-1999	$25.00	8722	201	SAL	SALES
203	MARTHA	WOODS	SHP	02-FEB-2004	$25.00	7591	201	SHP	SHIPPING
204	ELLEN	OWENS	SAL	01-JUL-2003	$15.00	6830	202	SAL	SALES
205	HENRY	PERKINS	SAL	01-MAR-2000	$25.00	5286	202	SAL	SALES
206	CAROL	ROSE	ACT	(null)	(null)	(null)	(null)	ACT	ACCOUNTING
207	DAN	SMITH	SHP	01-DEC-2004	$25.00	2259	203	SHP	SHIPPING
208	FRED	CAMPBELL	SHP	01-APR-2003	$25.00	1752	203	SHP	SHIPPING
209	PAULA	JACOBS	MKT	17-MAR-1999	$15.00	3357	201	MKT	MARKETING
210	NANCY	HOFFMAN	SAL	16-FEB-2004	$25.00	2974	203	SAL	SALES

Oracle & Access SQL:
Step 2 — Select part of the data from the `sec1316` table

```
select employee_id,
       first_name,
       last_name,
       dept_code,
       department_name
from sec1316
where employee_id < 206 ❹
order by employee_id;
```

Step 2 result table

```
EMPLOYEE                        DEPT
      ID FIRST_NAME LAST_NAME   CODE DEPARTMENT_NAME
-------- ---------- ----------  ---- ----------------
     201 SUSAN      BROWN       EXE  EXECUTIVE
     202 JIM        KERN        SAL  SALES
     203 MARTHA     WOODS       SHP  SHIPPING
     204 ELLEN      OWENS       SAL  SALES
     205 HENRY      PERKINS     SAL  SALES
```

Notes

❶ This is the join condition, which refers to both tables.

❷ This is a selection condition, which refers to only one table.

❸ In step 1, this is the join condition, which combines the two tables.

❹ In step 2, this is the selection condition, which selects the rows for the result table.

13-17 Using a join with summarization

The example in this section shows all six clauses of the `select` statement
and an inner join, all working together. The `where` clause contains a join
condition and also a condition that selects the data for the result table. The
`group by` clause needs to contain three columns of data to make every column a summarized column.

Task

List all the employees who are attending more than one lunch, except employee
208. Show the following columns: `employee_id`, `first_name`, `last_name`,
and `number_of_lunches`.

Oracle & Access SQL

```
select a.employee_id,
       a.first_name,
       a.last_name,
       count(*) as number_of_lunches
from l_employees a,
     l_lunches b
where a.employee_id = b.employee_id
  and not (a.employee_id = 208)
group by a.employee_id,
         a.first_name,
         a.last_name
having count(*) > 1
order by a.employee_id;
```

Result table

```
EMPLOYEE
     ID FIRST_NAME LAST_NAME  NUMBER_OF_LUNCHES
-------- ---------- ---------- -----------------
    201 SUSAN      BROWN                      3
    203 MARTHA     WOODS                      2
    204 ELLEN      OWENS                      2
    205 HENRY      PERKINS                    2
    207 DAN        SMITH                      2
    210 NANCY      HOFFMAN                    2
```

13-18 How to find the columns of the primary key from the Data Dictionary

In section 5-17 I showed you how to find the columns of the primary key of a table using two steps. I promised to show you how to do it in a single step, and now that you understand an inner join I can fulfill that promise.

Task

Find all the columns in the primary key of the 1_foods table.

Oracle SQL: Two-step method

```
select table_name,
       constraint_type,
       constraint_name
from user_constraints
where table_name = '1_foods';


select *
from user_cons_columns
where table_name = '1_foods';
```

Oracle SQL: One-step method using an inner join

```
select b.column_name,
       b.position
from user_constraints a, ❶
     user_cons_columns b
where a.table_name = b.table_name ❷
  and a.constraint_name = b.constraint_name
  and a.table_name = '1_foods' ❸
  and a.constraint_type = 'p'; ❹
```

Result table ❺

```
COLUMN_NAME                              POSITION
--------------------------------------   ---------
SUPPLIER_ID                                      1
PRODUCT_CODE                                     2
```

Notes

❶ Both Data Dictionary tables are used in the `from` clause.

❷ The first two lines of the `where` clause join the two tables.

❸ This line gives the name of the table. We want to find whether this table has a primary key. If so, this code will show which columns are part of that key.

❹ A constraint type of `'p'` is a primary key constraint. The other values of this column are
   r — Referential Integrity constraint
   u — Uniqueness constraint
   c — Check contstraint

❺ The primary key of the `l_foods` table has these two columns.

13-19 Combining three or more tables with inner joins

You can combine three or more tables with inner joins. You can join several tables together all at the same time, as I do in this section, or you can join the tables together two at a time in a series of steps.

When you combine several tables at once, the `where` clause can become quite long and complex. You must be sure to put all the join conditions into the where clause and relate each table to every other table.

When you combine several tables together with inner joins, you need to keep in mind that some of the information from the beginning tables may be dropped. The rows of the result table will only be the perfectly matched combinations of rows from all the beginning tables. In other words, if four tables are being joined, a matching row from each of those four tables is required to produce one row in the result table. If any of these rows is missing, data will be dropped.

Sometimes that is not a problem, because that is exactly what you want to happen. At other times, it is a problem.

Task

Show information about all the lunches ordered by people in the shipping department. Show the employee ID, names of the employees, the lunch date, and the descriptions and quantities of the foods they will eat. Sort the result by the `employee_id` and the `lunch_date` columns. To do this you need to join four tables.

Oracle & Access SQL

```
select a.employee_id,
       a.first_name,
       a.last_name,
       b.lunch_date,
       d.description,
       c.quantity
from l_employees a, ❶
     l_lunches b,
     l_lunch_items c,
     l_foods d
where a.employee_id = b.employee_id ❷
  and b.lunch_id = c.lunch_id
  and c.supplier_id = d.supplier_id
  and c.product_code = d.product_code
  and a.dept_code = 'shp' ❸
order by a.employee_id,
         b.lunch_date;
```

Result table

```
EMPLOYEE FIRST       LAST        LUNCH
      ID NAME        NAME        DATE          DESCRIPTION         QUANTITY
-------- ---------- ----------- ------------   ------------------  ---------
     203 MARTHA      WOODS       16-NOV-2005   FRESH SALAD                1
     203 MARTHA      WOODS       16-NOV-2005   GRILLED STEAK              1
     203 MARTHA      WOODS       16-NOV-2005   COFFEE                     1
     203 MARTHA      WOODS       16-NOV-2005   SODA                       1
     203 MARTHA      WOODS       16-NOV-2005   FRENCH FRIES               1
     203 MARTHA      WOODS       05-DEC-2005   SOUP OF THE DAY            1
     203 MARTHA      WOODS       05-DEC-2005   DESSERT                    1
     203 MARTHA      WOODS       05-DEC-2005   COFFEE                     2
     203 MARTHA      WOODS       05-DEC-2005   GRILLED STEAK              1
     207 DAN         SMITH       16-NOV-2005   SANDWICH                   2
     207 DAN         SMITH       16-NOV-2005   FRENCH FRIES               1
     207 DAN         SMITH       16-NOV-2005   COFFEE                     2
     207 DAN         SMITH       16-NOV-2005   DESSERT                    1
     207 DAN         SMITH       25-NOV-2005   SOUP OF THE DAY            2
     207 DAN         SMITH       25-NOV-2005   SANDWICH                   2
     207 DAN         SMITH       25-NOV-2005   SODA                       1
     207 DAN         SMITH       25-NOV-2005   FRENCH FRIES               1
     208 FRED        CAMPBELL    25-NOV-2005   FRESH SALAD                1
     208 FRED        CAMPBELL    25-NOV-2005   SOUP OF THE DAY            1
     208 FRED        CAMPBELL    25-NOV-2005   HAMBURGER                  2
     208 FRED        CAMPBELL    25-NOV-2005   FRENCH FRIES               1
     208 FRED        CAMPBELL    25-NOV-2005   COFFEE                     1
     208 FRED        CAMPBELL    25-NOV-2005   SODA                       1
     208 FRED        CAMPBELL    05-DEC-2005   FRESH SALAD                1
     208 FRED        CAMPBELL    05-DEC-2005   GRILLED STEAK              1
     208 FRED        CAMPBELL    05-DEC-2005   FRENCH FRIES               1
     208 FRED        CAMPBELL    05-DEC-2005   COFFEE                     1
     208 FRED        CAMPBELL    05-DEC-2005   SODA                       1
```

Notes

❶ The `from` clause must list all the tables being joined, even if no column from the table appears in the `select` clause.

❷ The first four lines of the `where` clause make up the join condition that relates each table to all of the other tables.

❸ The last line of the `where` clause limits the data that appear in the final result table. It is not part of the join condition.

Summary

Two tables, A and B, can be combined with an inner join. This creates another table that has all the columns from both table A and table B. One row from table A is combined with one row from table B whenever the join condition is satisfied.

When table A is joined with table B, this creates a much larger table. Your final result is selected from the columns and rows of this larger table.

An inner join can lose information because it drops any row that does not have a matching row in the other table. There is no warning message when this occurs.

Exercises

1. Goal: Use a lookup table and a row function.

    a. See section 13-15.

    b. For every type of food in the `1_foods` table, list the following:
    - The full name of the supplier from the `1_suppliers` table
    - The description of the food
    - The `price` plus the `price_increase`; name it `total_price`

    When the price increase is null, assume that 10 cents will be added to the price. Sort this information by the total price.

    (Hint: Use the null value function on the `price_increase` column to change the nulls to 10 cents. In Oracle, use the `nvl` function. In Access, use `nz`.)

2. Goal: Use a lookup table and grouped summarization.

    a. See section 13-17.

    b. From the `l_lunch_items` table, list the following:
    - The description of the food from the `l_foods` table
    - The total quantity of servings of that food in all the lunches

    Sort the rows by the `description` column.

    c. Modify the code you wrote for exercise 2b to show only the number of servings used in the lunch on November 16, 2005.

3. Goal: Use an inner join to find the intersection of two sets.

    a. Tables `ex1303a` and `ex1303b` contain lists of numbers. Find the numbers that are on both lists.

    Oracle & Access SQL

    ```
    select a.n
    from ex1303a a,
         ex1303b b
    where a.n = b.n
    order by a.n;
    ```

    ---

    b. Find the numbers that are in both the tables `ex1303a` and `ex1303c`.

    c. Find the numbers that are in all three lists `ex1303a`, `ex1303b`, and `ex1303c`.

    Use a method that combines all three tables in one join.

chapter 14

OUTER JOINS

An inner join may drop some of the rows from the beginning tables. An outer join puts back some of those rows. There are three types of outer joins, each type adding back a different set of the dropped rows.

Introduction to Outer Joins

Inner joins often drop some of the rows of the beginning tables if they do not have a matching row in the other table. If we want to keep these unmatched rows instead of dropping them, we need to use an outer join.

14-1 Outer joins are derived from inner joins

An outer join is derived from an inner join by adding back some of the rows that the inner join dropped from the beginning tables. Each of the three types of outer joins adds back a different set of rows. However, all three types of outer joins begin by forming the inner join.

Most of this discussion of outer joins is based on two tables named `twos` and `threes`. The `twos` table contains a column of numbers that consists of all the multiples of two up to 20, with the addition of one null. This table also contains a column of words that describe the numbers and the null.

The `threes` table is similar, except that it contains the multiples of three up to 20. The joins will be done on the columns of numbers. The columns of words are there to show that the tables have columns other than those used in the joins. Often, many such columns exist. We always join these tables on the columns of numbers, matching the number column from the `twos` table with the number column from the `threes` table.

In both tables, the number column contains a null and the word column for that row does not contain a null. It contains a word with four letters: N, U, L, and L. These are meant to be a description of what is in the number column.

The inner join of these tables contains three rows — 6, 12, and 18. All the other rows of the beginning tables are dropped from the result table.

Task

Show the inner join of the `twos` table and the `threes` table. Make a list of the rows of the beginning tables that are dropped from the result table.

Oracle & Access SQL

```
select a.*,
       b.*
from twos a,
     threes b
where a.number_2 = b.number_3
order by a.number_2;
```

Beginning tables
twos table   ### threes table

```
NUMBER_2 WORD_2                       NUMBER_3 WORD_3
-------- ---------------              -------- --------------
       2 TWO                                 3 THREE
       4 FOUR                                6 SIX
       6 SIX                                 9 NINE
       8 EIGHT                              12 TWELVE
      10 TEN                                15 FIFTEEN
      12 TWELVE                             18 EIGHTEEN
      14 FOURTEEN                    (null)    NULL
      16 SIXTEEN
      18 EIGHTEEN
      20 TWENTY
(null)    NULL
```

Result table (inner join)

```
NUMBER_2 WORD_2                NUMBER_3 WORD_3
-------- ---------------       -------- --------------
       6 SIX                          6 SIX
      12 TWELVE                      12 TWELVE
      18 EIGHTEEN                    18 EIGHTEEN
```

Rows dropped from the twos table   ## Rows dropped from the threes table

```
NUMBER_2       WORD_2                 NUMBER_3       WORD_3
------------   ---------------        ------------   ---------------
         2 TWO                                 3 THREE
         4 FOUR                                9 NINE
         8 EIGHT                              15 FIFTEEN
        10 TEN                         (null)    NULL
        14 FOURTEEN
        16 SIXTEEN
        20 TWENTY
(null)       NULL
```

14-2   The three types of outer joins

There are three types of outer joins: the left outer join, the right outer join, and the full outer join. They all begin with the inner join, and then they add back some of the rows that have been dropped.

The left outer join adds back all the rows that are dropped from the first table. Nulls are placed in the columns that come from the other table. For instance, in the first row of the following table, the row 2 TWO is added back to the result table. The columns for the matching row of the threes table, number_3 and word_3, are set to null.

The right outer join adds back all the rows that are dropped from the second table. In all the rows that are added back, the columns for the matching rows of the twos table are set to null.

The full outer join adds back all the rows dropped from both tables.

Task

For the twos table and the threes table, show the results of the three types of outer joins.

Result table — Left outer join (has all the rows from the first table)

NUMBER_2	WORD_2	NUMBER_3	WORD_3
2	TWO	(null)	(null)
4	FOUR	(null)	(null)
6	SIX	6	SIX
8	EIGHT	(null)	(null)
10	TEN	(null)	(null)
12	TWELVE	12	TWELVE
14	FOURTEEN	(null)	(null)
16	SIXTEEN	(null)	(null)
18	EIGHTEEN	18	EIGHTEEN
20	TWENTY	(null)	(null)
(null)	NULL	(null)	(null)

Result table — Right outer join (has all the rows from the second table)

```
NUMBER_2 WORD_2           NUMBER_3 WORD_3
-------- ---------------  -------- ---------------
(null)   (null)                  3 THREE
       6 SIX                     6 SIX
(null)   (null)                  9 NINE
      12 TWELVE                 12 TWELVE
(null)   (null)                 15 FIFTEEN
      18 EIGHTEEN               18 EIGHTEEN
(null)   (null)           (null)   NULL
```

Result table — Full outer join (has all the rows from both tables)

```
NUMBER_2 WORD_2           NUMBER_3 WORD_3
-------- ---------------  -------- ---------------
       2 TWO              (null)   (null)
(null)   (null)                  3 THREE
       4 FOUR             (null)   (null)
       6 SIX                     6 SIX
       8 EIGHT            (null)   (null)
(null)   (null)                  9 NINE
      10 TEN              (null)   (null)
      12 TWELVE                 12 TWELVE
      14 FOURTEEN         (null)   (null)
(null)   (null)                 15 FIFTEEN
      16 SIXTEEN          (null)   (null)
      18 EIGHTEEN               18 EIGHTEEN
      20 TWENTY           (null)   (null)
(null)   NULL             (null)   (null)
(null)   (null)           (null)   NULL
```

14-3   The left outer join

Both Oracle and Access can produce a left outer join. The result tables are exactly the same. However, they write the SQL code in different ways. Oracle uses the older syntax for writing joins, which places the join condition in the `where` clause. Access uses the new syntax for writing joins, which places the join condition in the `from` clause.

Oracle implemented the left outer join before it became part of the SQL standard. There was no agreement on how to write this type of join, so Oracle developed its own syntax for it. Access was developed after Oracle. By the time Access was developed the left outer join had become part of the new SQL standard, SQL-92, so Access used the notation from that standard. Oracle9i supports both ways of writing outer joins.

A left outer join keeps all of the rows from the first table, but has only the rows from the second table that match with a row from the first table.

In the following example, the rows of the result table are sorted on the number column from the first table to put them in a logical order. In Oracle, the null is sorted at the end of the table. In Access, it is sorted at the beginning. The order by clause in this example is not needed to join the two tables together. It is used here to display the rows of the result in a logical order.

Task

Show the syntax to write a left outer join in Oracle and in Access.

Oracle SQL

```
select a.*,
       b.*
from twos a,
     threes b
where a.number_2 = b.number_3  (+)  ❶
order by a.number_2;  ❷
```

Oracle9i & Access SQL

```
select a.*,
       b.*
from twos a
     left outer join  threes b  ❸
     on  a.number_2 = b.number_3  ❹
order by a.number_2;
```

Beginning tables
twos table   ### threes table

```
NUMBER_2 WORD_2                          NUMBER_3 WORD_3
-------- ---------------                 -------- --------------
       2 TWO                                    3 THREE
       4 FOUR                                   6 SIX
       6 SIX                                    9 NINE
       8 EIGHT                                 12 TWELVE
      10 TEN                                   15 FIFTEEN
      12 TWELVE                               18 EIGHTEEN
      14 FOURTEEN                      (null)    NULL
      16 SIXTEEN
      18 EIGHTEEN
      20 TWENTY
(null)    NULL
```

Result table — Left outer join

```
NUMBER_2 WORD_2            NUMBER_3 WORD_3
-------- ---------------   -------- ---------------
       2 TWO               (null)    (null)
       4 FOUR              (null)    (null)
       6 SIX                      6 SIX
       8 EIGHT             (null)    (null)
      10 TEN               (null)    (null)
      12 TWELVE                  12 TWELVE
      14 FOURTEEN          (null)    (null)
      16 SIXTEEN           (null)    (null)
      18 EIGHTEEN                18 EIGHTEEN
      20 TWENTY            (null)    (null)
(null)    NULL            (null)    (null)
```

Notes

❶ In Oracle, the join condition is written in the where clause. A plus sign in parentheses, (+), is written to the right of the join condition. This specifies a left outer join. When several clauses are in the join condition, the plus sign must be written to the right of each of them.

Putting the plus sign on the right might not seem to make sense to write a left outer join. One way to think about this is that the plus sign is written on the side where the nulls are added to the incomplete rows that are added back.

❷ The order by clause puts the rows in a logical order. It is not required in a left outer join.

❸ In Access, "left outer join" is written in the from clause. The word "outer" is optional, so you can also write "left join" here.

❹ In Access, the join condition is written in the on subclause of the from clause.

14-4   The right outer join

The right outer join is similar to the left outer join, except it is the reverse: The rows dropped from the second table are added back instead of the rows from the first table. The syntax is also similar. The difference between the syntax for Oracle and Access is the same for both the left and right outer joins.

A right outer join keeps all of the rows from the second table, but has only the rows from the first table that match with a row from the second table.

Task

Show the syntax to write a right outer join in Oracle and in Access.

Oracle SQL

```
select a.*,
       b.*
from twos a,
     threes b
where a.number_2 (+) = b.number_3 ❶
order by b.number_3; ❷
```

Oracle9i & Access SQL

```
select a.*,
       b.*
from twos a
     right outer join threes b ❸
     on a.number_2 = b.number_3 ❹
order by b.number_3;
```

Beginning tables
twos table   **threes table**

```
NUMBER_2 WORD_2                    NUMBER_3 WORD_3
-------- ---------------          -------- -------------
       2 TWO                             3 THREE
       4 FOUR                            6 SIX
       6 SIX                             9 NINE
       8 EIGHT                          12 TWELVE
      10 TEN                            15 FIFTEEN
      12 TWELVE                         18 EIGHTEEN
      14 FOURTEEN              (null)      NULL
      16 SIXTEEN
      18 EIGHTEEN
      20 TWENTY
(null)    NULL
```

Result table — Right outer join

```
NUMBER_2 WORD_2              NUMBER_3 WORD_3
-------- ---------------     -------- ---------------
(null)    (null)                   3 THREE
       6 SIX                       6 SIX
(null)    (null)                   9 NINE
      12 TWELVE                   12 TWELVE
(null)    (null)                  15 FIFTEEN
      18 EIGHTEEN                 18 EIGHTEEN
(null)    (null)             (null)    NULL
```

Notes

❶ In Oracle, the join condition is written in the `where` clause. A plus sign in parenthesis, `(+)`, is written to the left of the equal sign. This specifies a right outer join. When several clauses are in the join condition, the plus sign must be written on the left side of each of them.

❷ The `order by` clause puts the rows in a logical order. It is not required in a right outer join.

❸ In Access, "right outer join" is written in the `from` clause. The word "outer" is optional, so you can also write "right join" here.

❹ In Access, the join condition is written in the `on` subclause of the `from` clause.

14-5   The full outer join

The full outer join adds back all the rows dropped from both tables by the inner join. It keeps all the rows from both tables and makes as many matches as the data and the join condition allow.

Oracle9i has direct support for the full outer join. That is, you can do it with a single command. However, in Access and previous versions of Oracle, you must construct it yourself.

You can create a full outer join by writing a `union` of the left outer join and the right outer join. The next two sections of this chapter tell you as much as you need to know about the `union` to understand it when it is used in a full outer join. For now, you can think of it as a way to combine a left outer join and a right outer join. We discuss the `union` in more detail in the next chapter.

The SQL may look complicated, but it is only

- Left outer join
- `union`
- Right outer join

The order of the left and right outer joins does not matter and can be reversed. So, the full outer join can also be written

- Right outer join
- `union`
- Left outer join

Task

Show the syntax to write a full outer join in Oracle and in Access.

574   SQL FUNDAMENTALS

Oracle SQL

```
select a.*,
       b.*
from twos a,
     threes b
where a.number_2 = b.number_3 (+)
union
select c.*,
       d.*
from twos c,
     threes d
where c.number_2 (+) = d.number_3;
```

Oracle9i SQL ❶

```
select a.*,
       b.*
from twos a
     full outer join threes b
     on a.number_2 = b.number_3;
```

Oracle9i & Access SQL

```
select a.*,
       b.*
from twos a
     left outer join threes b
     on a.number_2 = b.number_3
union
select c.*,
       d.*
from twos c
     right outer join threes d
     on c.number_2 = d.number_3;
```

Beginning tables — Twos table and threes table, shown in the previous sections

Result table — Full outer join ❷

```
 NUMBER_2  WORD_2             NUMBER_3  WORD_3
---------  ----------------  ---------  ----------------
        2  TWO                (null)    (null)
 (null)    (null)                    3  THREE
        4  FOUR               (null)    (null)
        6  SIX                       6  SIX
        8  EIGHT              (null)    (null)
 (null)    (null)                    9  NINE
       10  TEN                (null)    (null)
       12  TWELVE                   12  TWELVE
       14  FOURTEEN           (null)    (null)
 (null)    (null)                   15  FIFTEEN
       16  SIXTEEN            (null)    (null)
       18  EIGHTEEN                 18  EIGHTEEN
       20  TWENTY             (null)    (null)
 (null)    NULL               (null)    (null)
 (null)    (null)             (null)    NULL
```

Notes

❶ This shows that Oracle9i has direct support for a full outer join.

❷ I have put the rows of this table in a logical order so you can see what is going on. When you run the code you will probably see the rows in a different order.

14-6   An introduction to the union

This section introduces the union because we have used it in creating a full outer join. At this time, I limit the discussion to its use in this context. The next chapter discusses the union in more detail.

A union of two tables adds the rows of one table to the other table, and the two beginning tables are combined to form a single table, as shown in the following diagram. The rows of the two tables must be identical or nearly identical in structure, so that they can all fit together within the framework of a single table. This means that they must have the same number of columns and the datatypes of these columns must be in the same order. Otherwise, a union cannot be formed.

Duplicate rows are eliminated from a union. If two rows have the same values in every column, the union keeps only one of them and drops the other one. This action is taken whether both rows come from the same table or whether they come from different tables.

The union of tables is defined corresponds closely to the way a union of sets is defined in mathematics. In a union of sets no duplicates are allowed. This is why the duplicate rows are eliminated from a union of tables.

You have formed a union of two tables before, in previous exercises. The method used there was to insert the rows from one table into the other table and then to use select distinct to eliminate the duplicate rows.

When a union is written within SQL code, the word union is placed between two select statements. Each select statement stands for a table — the result table it produces.

In the case of a full outer join, the union is placed between the select statements for the left outer join and the right outer join. These two tables always have the same number of columns and the datatypes of those columns are always in the same order, so the union can always be formed.

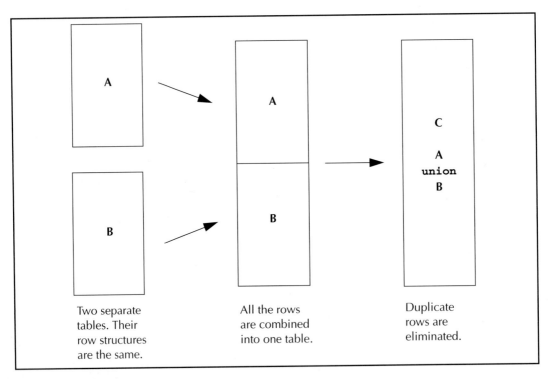

Two separate tables. Their row structures are the same.

All the rows are combined into one table.

Duplicate rows are eliminated.

The process of forming a union.

Task 1

Show how to write a union in SQL. Show the `select` statement for the preceding diagram. Write the `select` statement so that its result table is table C in the diagram.

Oracle & Access SQL: `Select` statment for the preceding diagram

```
select *
from A
union
select *
from B;
```

Task 2

Show another way to write the SQL for the preceding diagram. Write this SQL to create table C as a new table.

Oracle & Access SQL: Step 1

```
insert into B
   select *
   from A;
```

Oracle SQL: Step 2

```
create table C as
   select distinct *
   from B;
```

Access SQL: Step 2

```
select distinct *
into C
from B;
```

Notes

This is a model of the SQL code for the diagram. This SQL does not actually run.

14-7   An example of a `union` of two tables with matching columns

This section shows an example of a `union`. The two beginning tables have the same structure. That is, they both have three columns and the datatypes of these columns in order are as follows:

- Numeric
- Text
- Date/time

These are the three main types of columns that are used in relational databases. This example shows they can all be used in a `union`.

The result table contains all the rows from both beginning tables. We can call these rows 1 through 7. Rows 1 and 2 come only from the first beginning table. Rows 6 and 7 come only from the second beginning table. Rows 3, 4, and 5 come from both beginning tables; however, only a single copy of these rows is kept in the result table, because the duplicate copies of rows are eliminated.

Look at the column headings of the result table. The first `select` statement sets them. The column headings of the first beginning table are used, unless a column alias is assigned. The `word_1` column in this example is assigned to the column alias `text_1`.

The `order by` clause is the last line and it is placed after the second `select` statement. A `union` can have only one `order by` clause, and it must be the last line of the `union`. This clause sorts all the rows of the `union` into a designated order.

After you examine this example of a `union`, turn back to section 14-2 and look at the tables for the three types of outer joins. Can you see how the full outer join is the result of a `union` between the left outer join and the right outer join?

Task

Show an example of a `select` statement that uses a `union`.

Oracle & Access SQL

```
select a.number_1, ❶
       a.word_1 as text_1, ❷
       a.date_1
from sec1407_first a
union ❸
select b.number_2, ❹
       b.word_2,
       b.date_2
from sec1407_second b
order by number_1; ❺
```

Beginning tables

`sec1407_first` table

NUMBER_1	WORD_1	DATE_1
1	ONE	01-DEC-2001
2	TWO	02-DEC-2002
3	THREE	03-DEC-2003
4	FOUR	04-DEC-2004
5	FIVE	05-DEC-2005

`sec1407_second` table

NUMBER_2	WORD_2	DATE_2
3	THREE	03-DEC-2003
4	FOUR	04-DEC-2004
5	FIVE	05-DEC-2005
6	SIX	06-DEC-2006
7	SEVEN	07-DEC-2007

Result table ❻

NUMBER_1	TEXT_1	DATE_1
1	ONE	01-DEC-2001
2	TWO	02-DEC-2002
3	THREE	03-DEC-2003
4	FOUR	04-DEC-2004
5	FIVE	05-DEC-2005
6	SIX	06-DEC-2006
7	SEVEN	07-DEC-2007

Notes

❶ The first `select` statement lists three columns. It determines the heading for the columns. It cannot have an `order by` clause.

❷ In a `union`, a column alias is assigned within the first `select` statement. Aliases cannot be assigned in the second `select` statement.

❸ The word `union` is placed between the two `select` statements.

❹ The second `select` statement must have the same number of columns as the first `select` statement and the datatypes of the matching columns must be compatible.

❺ The `order by` clause is placed at the end of the `union`.

❻ Even though both beginning tables have rows 3, 4, and 5, the result table contains only a single copy of these rows. This shows that duplicate rows are eliminated.

Applications of Outer Joins

The following sections provide some applications of outer joins.

14-8   Counting to zero, part 4

This section shows the full SQL solution in our continuing discussion of how to count the number of lunches each employee will attend. The new aspect shown here is the outer join between the `l_employees` table and the `l_lunches` table.

Task

Show the number of lunches each employee will attend.

Oracle SQL

```
select a.employee_id,
       a.first_name,
       a.last_name,
       count(b.lunch_id) as number_of_lunches ❶
from 1_employees a,
     1_lunches b
where a.employee_id = b.employee_id (+)
group by a.employee_id,
         a.first_name,
         a.last_name
order by a.employee_id;
```

Oracle9i & Access SQL

```
select a.employee_id,
       a.first_name,
       a.last_name,
       count(b.lunch_id) as number_of_lunches ❶
from 1_employees a
     left outer join 1_lunches b
     on a.employee_id = b.employee_id
group by a.employee_id,
         a.first_name,
         a.last_name
order by a.employee_id;
```

Beginning table 1 (1_employees table)

EMPLOYEE ID	FIRST_NAME	LAST_NAME	DEPT CODE	HIRE_DATE	CREDIT LIMIT	PHONE NUMBER	MANAGER ID
201	SUSAN	BROWN	EXE	01-JUN-1998	$30.00	3484	(null)
202	JIM	KERN	SAL	16-AUG-1999	$25.00	8722	201
203	MARTHA	WOODS	SHP	02-FEB-2004	$25.00	7591	201
204	ELLEN	OWENS	SAL	01-JUL-2003	$15.00	6830	202
205	HENRY	PERKINS	SAL	01-MAR-2000	$25.00	5286	202
206	CAROL	ROSE	ACT	(null)	(null)	(null)	(null)
207	DAN	SMITH	SHP	01-DEC-2004	$25.00	2259	203
208	FRED	CAMPBELL	SHP	01-APR-2003	$25.00	1752	203
209	PAULA	JACOBS	MKT	17-MAR-1999	$15.00	3357	201
210	NANCY	HOFFMAN	SAL	16-FEB-2004	$25.00	2974	203

Beginning table 2 (1_lunches table)

LUNCH_ID	LUNCH DATE	EMPLOYEE ID	DATE_ENTERE
1	16-NOV-2005	201	13-OCT-2005
2	16-NOV-2005	207	13-OCT-2005
3	16-NOV-2005	203	13-OCT-2005
4	16-NOV-2005	204	13-OCT-2005
6	16-NOV-2005	202	13-OCT-2005
7	16-NOV-2005	210	13-OCT-2005
8	25-NOV-2005	201	14-OCT-2005
9	25-NOV-2005	208	14-OCT-2005
12	25-NOV-2005	204	14-OCT-2005
13	25-NOV-2005	207	18-OCT-2005
15	25-NOV-2005	205	21-OCT-2005
16	05-DEC-2005	201	21-OCT-2005
17	05-DEC-2005	210	21-OCT-2005
20	05-DEC-2005	205	24-OCT-2005
21	05-DEC-2005	203	24-OCT-2005
22	05-DEC-2005	208	24-OCT-2005

Result table

EMPLOYEE_ID	FIRST_NAME	LAST_NAME	NUMBER_OF_LUNCHES
201	SUSAN	BROWN	3
202	JIM	KERN	1
203	MARTHA	WOODS	2
204	ELLEN	OWENS	2
205	HENRY	PERKINS	2
206	CAROL	ROSE	0
207	DAN	SMITH	2
208	FRED	CAMPBELL	2
209	PAULA	JACOBS	0
210	NANCY	HOFFMAN	2

Notes

❶ Here the count (*column*) function is being applied to the lunch_id column from the 1_lunches table. Why did I choose this column? To get the zeros, I could have used any column from the 1_lunches table, because the outer join sets all the columns to nulls when an employee is not attending any lunches.

14-9   Combining an outer join with a selection of the data

The SQL code in the previous section combined two steps into a single `select` statement. In theory, the first step creates the outer join of the two beginning tables. The result of this step is a table that has all the columns from both tables and all the rows that the outer join creates.

The second step selects some of the data from this table, groups it, and summarizes it. This creates the result table.

The following example solves the same problem as in the previous section, but shows each of these steps separately. When the problem is more complex than the one shown here, this method of coding is easier to create and less prone to errors.

Task 1

Create an outer join of the `1_employees` table and the `1_lunches` table. Retain all the rows of data from both tables.

Oracle SQL

```
create table sec1409 as
select a.*,
       b.lunch_id,
       b.lunch_date,
       b.employee_id as employee_id2,
       b.date_entered
from 1_employees a,
     1_lunches b
where a.employee_id = b.employee_id (+);
```

Oracle9i & Access SQL

```
select a.*,
       b.lunch_id,
       b.lunch_date,
       b.employee_id as employee_id2,
       b.date_entered
into sec1409
from l_employees a
     left outer join l_lunches b
     on a.employee_id = b.employee_id;
```

Beginning tables
The l_employees table and the l_lunches table are shown in the previous section.

Result table
Sec1409 table, except for the last column, date_entered, which does not fit here.

EMP ID	FIRST NAME	LAST NAME	DEPT CODE	HIRE_DATE	CREDIT LIMIT	PHONE NUMBER	MANAGER ID	LUNCH ID	LUNCH DATE	EMP ID2
201	SUSAN	BROWN	EXE	01-JUN-1998	$30.00	3484	(null)	1	16-NOV-2005	201
201	SUSAN	BROWN	EXE	01-JUN-1998	$30.00	3484	(null)	8	25-NOV-2005	201
201	SUSAN	BROWN	EXE	01-JUN-1998	$30.00	3484	(null)	16	05-DEC-2005	201
202	JIM	KERN	SAL	16-AUG-1999	$25.00	8722	201	6	16-NOV-2005	202
203	MARTHA	WOODS	SHP	02-FEB-2004	$25.00	7591	201	3	16-NOV-2005	203
203	MARTHA	WOODS	SHP	02-FEB-2004	$25.00	7591	201	21	05-DEC-2005	203
204	ELLEN	OWENS	SAL	01-JUL-2003	$15.00	6830	202	4	16-NOV-2005	204
204	ELLEN	OWENS	SAL	01-JUL-2003	$15.00	6830	202	12	25-NOV-2005	204
205	HENRY	PERKINS	SAL	01-MAR-2000	$25.00	5286	202	15	25-NOV-2005	205
205	HENRY	PERKINS	SAL	01-MAR-2000	$25.00	5286	202	20	05-DEC-2005	205
206	CAROL	ROSE	ACT	(null)	(null)	(null)	(null)	(null)	(null)	(null)
207	DAN	SMITH	SHP	01-DEC-2004	$25.00	2259	203	2	16-NOV-2005	207
207	DAN	SMITH	SHP	01-DEC-2004	$25.00	2259	203	13	25-NOV-2005	207
208	FRED	CAMPBELL	SHP	01-APR-2003	$25.00	1752	203	9	25-NOV-2005	208
208	FRED	CAMPBELL	SHP	01-APR-2003	$25.00	1752	203	22	05-DEC-2005	208
209	PAULA	JACOBS	MKT	17-MAR-1999	$15.00	3357	201	(null)	(null)	(null)
210	NANCY	HOFFMAN	SAL	16-FEB-2004	$25.00	2974	203	7	16-NOV-2005	210
210	NANCY	HOFFMAN	SAL	16-FEB-2004	$25.00	2974	203	17	05-DEC-2005	210

Task 2

Show the number of lunches each employee will attend. Start with the sec1409 table. Then select these columns: employee_id, first_name, and last_name. Group this data and summarize it to count the number of lunches each employee will attend.

This code is almost identical to the SQL in section 12-10.

Oracle & Access SQL

```
select employee_id,
       first_name,
       last_name,
       count(lunch_id) as number_of_lunches
from sec1409
group by employee_id,
         first_name,
         last_name
order by employee_id;
```

Result table

```
EMPLOYEE
      ID FIRST_NAME LAST_NAME  NUMBER_OF_LUNCHES
-------- ---------- ---------- -----------------
     201 SUSAN      BROWN                      3
     202 JIM        KERN                       1
     203 MARTHA     WOODS                      2
     204 ELLEN      OWENS                      2
     205 HENRY      PERKINS                    2
     206 CAROL      ROSE                       0
     207 DAN        SMITH                      2
     208 FRED       CAMPBELL                   2
     209 PAULA      JACOBS                     0
     210 NANCY      HOFFMAN                    2
```

14-10 A full outer join in sorted order

This section shows a full outer join of the `twos` table with the `threes` table. The rows of the result table are sorted into their logical order. This order may not seem surprising to you, but a trick is required to achieve it.

The difficulty in sorting the rows of a full outer join is that they need to be sorted on a combination of the two columns, `number_2` and `number_3`. If it is sorted on a single column, all the rows that contain a null in that column are sorted together. In Oracle, all of these rows go to the bottom. In Access, they all go to the top. Both the `number_2` column and the `number_3` column contain many nulls because this is a full outer join. Sorting on either of these columns does not give us the result we want.

The trick is to use a row function that combines the values of the `number_2` and `number_3` columns. In Oracle, we can use the `nvl` (null value) function:

NVL(number_2, number_3)

In Access, we can use the `nz` (non-zero) function and multiply the result by one:

NZ(number_2, number_3) * 1

The resulting value from both of these functions is as follows:

number_2   if it is not null

number_3   if `number_2` is null, even if `number_3` is a null

In Access, we multiply the `nz` function by one to convert it into a number. Otherwise, it would be a text field and would sort the rows in alphabetic order rather than numeric order. Because a `union` requires the columns of each `select` statement to match, these functions must be placed within each of the `select` statements.

Task

Create a full outer join of the `twos` table and the `threes` table. Create a column that will sort the rows in numeric order.

Oracle SQL

```
select a.*,
       b.*, ❶
       nvl(a.number_2,b.number_3) as sort_order  ❷
from twos a,
     threes b
where a.number_2 = b.number_3 (+)
union  ❸
select c.*,
       d.*, ❹
       nvl(c.number_2,d.number_3)  ❺
from twos c,
     threes d
where c.number_2 (+) = d.number_3
order by sort_order;  ❻
```

Access SQL

```
select a.*,
       b.*,
       nz(a.number_2,b.number_3) * 1 as sort_order  ❼
from twos a
     left outer join threes b
     on a.number_2 = b.number_3
union
select c.*,
       d.*,
       nz(c.number_2,d.number_3) * 1
from twos c
     right outer join threes d
     on c.number_2 = d.number_3
order by sort_order;
```

Beginning tables
twos table   **threes table**

```
NUMBER_2 WORD_2                    NUMBER_3 WORD_3
-------- ---------------          -------- ---------------
       2 TWO                             3 THREE
       4 FOUR                            6 SIX
       6 SIX                             9 NINE
       8 EIGHT                          12 TWELVE
      10 TEN                            15 FIFTEEN
      12 TWELVE                         18 EIGHTEEN
      14 FOURTEEN               (null)    NULL
      16 SIXTEEN
      18 EIGHTEEN
      20 TWENTY
(null)    NULL
```

Result table ❷

```
NUMBER_2 WORD_2            NUMBER_3 WORD_3            SORT_ORDER
-------- ---------------   -------- ---------------   ----------
       2 TWO               (null)     (null)                   2
(null)     (null)                 3 THREE                      3
       4 FOUR              (null)     (null)                   4
       6 SIX                      6 SIX                         6
       8 EIGHT             (null)     (null)                   8
(null)     (null)                 9 NINE                       9
      10 TEN               (null)     (null)                  10
      12 TWELVE                  12 TWELVE                     12
      14 FOURTEEN          (null)     (null)                  14
(null)     (null)                15 FIFTEEN                    15
      16 SIXTEEN           (null)     (null)                  16
      18 EIGHTEEN                18 EIGHTEEN                   18
      20 TWENTY            (null)     (null)                  20
(null)     NULL            (null)     (null)            (null)
(null)     (null)          (null)     NULL              (null)
```

Notes

❶ The first `select` statement is a left outer join. It includes all the columns of both tables and an additional column to determine the sort order.

❷ The null value function, `nvl`, is used in Oracle to determine the sort order. This is equal to the `number_2` column, except if that column contains a null, in which case it is equal to the `number_3` column. The column alias `sort_order` is given to this column.

❸ Here is the `union`, which is used to form the full outer join.

❹ The second `select` statement is the right outer join.

❺ The `nvl` function to create the `sort_order` column must be included in the second `select` statement.

❻ The full outer join, which is formed with a `union`, is sorted by the `sort_order` column.

❼ In Access, the `nz` function is multiplied by one to give it a numeric datatype.

❽ Often the `sort_order` column is not displayed. This makes the sort order just "naturally appear." To use this trick, you could create a view from the `select` statement in this section, and then not list the `sort_order` column, but still use it for sorting.

14-11   Finding the defects in a pattern

This section provides an answer to exercise 4 in chapter 12. The idea is that we will find all the defects in a pattern by comparing it to a perfect pattern. Usually, we would have to create the perfect pattern ourselves, but here it is given to us as the table `numbers_1_to_1000`. The pattern containing defects is table `ex1203a`.

The SQL does an outer join between these tables, keeping all the rows of the perfect pattern and listing the columns from both tables. If a number, such as 5, is missing from the `ex1203a` table, the join shows it by producing the row `<5, null>`. If a number is repeated several times in the `ex1203a` table, it is also repeated that many times in the join. An example is that 3 occurs twice in the `ex1203a` table, and the outer join contains the row `<3, 3>` twice.

Then the SQL groups the rows of the join, making a separate group for each number. It counts each group on the column that comes from the defective table. Most numbers have a count of 1. When these are eliminated, only the defects are shown in the result table.

Task

We have a table `ex1203a` that contains the numbers from 1 to 1,000. A few numbers are missing and a few numbers are repeated. Find all the missing numbers and all the repeated numbers. Count the number of times each of these numbers occurs. For the missing numbers, count that they occur zero times.

Oracle SQL

```
select a.n,
       b.n,
       count(b.n)
from numbers_1_to_1000 a,
     ex1203a b
where a.n = b.n (+)
group by a.n,
         b.n
having not (count(b.n) = 1)
order by a.n;
```

Oracle9i & Access SQL

```
select a.n,
       b.n,
       count(b.n)
from numbers_1_to_1000 a
     left outer join ex1203a b
     on a.n = b.n
group by a.n,
         b.n
having not (count(b.n) = 1)
order by a.n;
```

Beginning table (ex1203a table)

```
        N
---------
        1
        2
        3
        3
        4
        6
        7
        8
        9
       10
       11
       12
       13
       13
       13
       13
       14
(and many more)
```

Result table

```
        N           N COUNT(B.N)
--------- --------- ----------
        3         3          2
        5 (null)             0
       13        13          4
       48        48          4
       67        67          2
       72        72          3
      103       103          2
      113       113          5
      123 (null)             0
      148       148          4
      167       167          2
      172       172          3
      248       248          2
      267       267          2
      275 (null)             0
      367 (null)             0
      460 (null)             0
      503       503          2
      548       548          2
      555 (null)             0
      619 (null)             0
      713       713          2
      748       748          2
      778 (null)             0
      821 (null)             0
      872       872          2
      913       913          2
      972       972          2
      998 (null)             0
```

14-12 Comparing tables using two or more columns

This section shows you how to compare two tables that contain two or more columns by finding the rows in one table that do not exist in another table. This can be done in several ways.

The technique shown here lists all the columns from both tables. It forms a left outer join between the first table and the second table. This join retains all the rows in the first table, and when the second table does not have a matching row, nulls are placed in the columns of the second table.

The second part of this technique selects all the rows that have a null in a column of the second table. This shows the rows of the first table that do not exist in the second table.

You can also do this process in two steps. It may be easier to understand that way. In the first step, form the left outer join and examine the results. In the second step, select the rows that have a null in one of the columns of the second table.

Task

Find the rows in the sec1412a table that do not exist in the sec1412b table.

Oracle SQL

```
select a.first_col,
       a.second_col,
       b.first_col,
       b.second_col
from sec1412a a,
     sec1412b b
where a.first_col = b.first_col (+)
  and a.second_col = b.second_col (+)
  and b.first_col is null ❶
order by a.first_col,
         a.second_col;
```

Oracle9i & Access SQL

```
select a.first_col,
       a.second_col,
       b.first_col,
       b.second_col
from sec1412a a
     left outer join sec1412b b
     on a.first_col = b.first_col
     and a.second_col = b.second_col
where b.first_col is null ❶
order by a.first_col,
         a.second_col;
```

Beginning table 1 (sec1412a table)

FIRST_COL	SECOND_COL
11101	22201
11101	22202
11101	22203
11102	22201
11102	22202
11102	22203
11103	22201
11103	22202
11103	22203
11104	22201
11104	22202
11104	22203
11105	22201
11105	22202
11105	22203

Beginning table 2 (`sec1412b` table)

```
FIRST_COL          SECOND_COL
---------------    -----------
11101              22201
11101              22202
11101              22203
11102              22201
11102              22203
11103              22202
11103              22203
11104              22201
11104              22202
11105              22201
11105              22202
11105              22203
```

Result table

```
FIRST_COL          SECOND_COL          FIRST_COL          SECOND_COL
---------------    ----------------    ----------------   ------------
11102              22202               (null)             (null)
11103              22201               (null)             (null)
11104              22203               (null)             (null)
```

Notes

❶ Eliminate this `where` condition if you want to perform the process in two steps. That creates the first step, which forms the left outer join. In the second step, apply this `where` condition.

14-13 Comparing two different full outer joins

People sometimes talk as if there were only one way to form a full outer join between two tables. However, there are many ways to create the join. Every join condition you can write can be used to form a different full outer join. In this section we compare two full outer joins of the same tables to see how they are similar and how they are different. For this example, we return to the `fruits` and `colors` tables from chapter 13.

Task

Use the two tables `sec1307_fruits` and `sec1307_colors`. Form the full outer join of these table using the join condition

f_num = c_num

Then form the full outer join using the join condition

fruit = color

Examine the result tables. State what is similar and what is different about these full outer joins.

Oracle SQL

First full outer join:

```
select a.*,
       b.*
from sec1307_fruits a,
     sec1307_colors b
where a.f_num = b.c_num (+)
union
select a.*,
       b.*
from sec1307_fruits a,
     sec1307_colors b
where a.f_num (+) = b.c_num;
```

Second full outer join:

```
select a.*,
       b.*
from sec1307_fruits a,
     sec1307_colors b
where a.fruit = b.color (+)
union
select a.*,
       b.*
from sec1307_fruits a,
     sec1307_colors b
where a.fruit (+) = b.color;
```

Access SQL

First full outer join:

```
select a.*,
       b.*
from sec1307_fruits a
     left outer join sec1307_colors b
     on a.f_num = b.c_num
union
select a.*,
       b.*
from sec1307_fruits a
     right outer join sec1307_colors b
     on a.f_num  = b.c_num;
```

Second full outer join:

```
select a.*,
       b.*
from sec1307_fruits a
     left outer join sec1307_colors b
     on a.fruit = b.color
union
select a.*,
       b.*
from sec1307_fruits a
     right outer join sec1307_colors b
     on a.fruit = b.color;
```

Beginning tables
sec1307_fruits table   sec1307_colors table

FRUIT	F_NUM		C_NUM	COLOR
APPLE	1		1	RED
BANANA	2		2	YELLOW
CHERRY	3		1	GREEN
GRAPE	4		5	ORANGE
ORANGE	5		6	WHITE
STRAWBERRY	1			

First full outer join using the join condition: f_num = c_num

FRUIT	F_NUM	C_NUM	COLOR
APPLE	1	1	GREEN
APPLE	1	1	RED
BANANA	2	2	YELLOW
CHERRY	3	(null)	(null)
GRAPE	4	(null)	(null)
ORANGE	5	5	ORANGE
STRAWBERRY	1	1	GREEN
STRAWBERRY	1	1	RED
(null)	(null)	6	WHITE

Second full outer join using the join condition: fruit = color

FRUIT	F_NUM	C_NUM	COLOR
APPLE	1	(null)	(null)
BANANA	2	(null)	(null)
CHERRY	3	(null)	(null)
GRAPE	4	(null)	(null)
ORANGE	5	5	ORANGE
STRAWBERRY	1	(null)	(null)
(null)	(null)	1	GREEN
(null)	(null)	1	RED
(null)	(null)	2	YELLOW
(null)	(null)	6	WHITE

Similarities between the two full outer joins

1. They both contain all the rows from the beginning tables.

2. They both contain all the columns from the beginning tables.

Differences between the two full outer joins

1. Different rows are related to each other by the join conditions. In the first full outer join:

   - 4 fruits match with at least one color

   - 2 fruits did not match with any color

   - 4 colors matched with at least one fruit

   - 1 color did not match with any fruit

   In the second full outer join:

   - 1 fruit matched with a color

   - 5 fruits did not match with any color

   - 1 color matched with a fruit

   - 4 colors did not match with any fruit

2. Different rows were duplicated. In the first full outer join, there are two apples and two strawberries because the join condition matched them with more than one color. In the second full outer join, no rows are duplicated.

Summary

There are three types of outer joins:

Type of Outer Join	Effect on First Table	Effect on Second Table
Left outer join	Keeps all the rows	Keeps only the matching rows
Right outer join	Keeps only the matching rows	Keeps all the rows
Full outer join	Keeps all the rows	Keeps all the rows

Exercises

1. Goal: Find rows that are not matched. (They are dropped from an inner join.)

   a. Find out if there are any foods that have not been ordered. List the supplier ID, product code, and description of these foods. Sort them by the columns of the primary key from the `l_foods` table. Those columns are `supplier_id` and `product_code`.

   ## Oracle SQL

   ```
   select a.supplier_id,
          a.product_code,
          a.description
   from l_foods a,
        l_lunch_items b
   where a.supplier_id = b.supplier_id (+)
     and a.product_code = b.product_code (+)
     and b.supplier_id is null
   order by a.supplier_id,
            a.product_code;
   ```

   ## Oracle9i & Access SQL

   ```
   select a.supplier_id,
          a.product_code,
          a.description
   from l_foods a
        left outer join l_lunch_items b
        on a.supplier_id = b.supplier_id
        and a.product_code = b.product_code
   where b.supplier_id is null
   order by a.supplier_id,
            a.product_code;
   ```

b. Are there any employees who are not attending any of the lunches? If so, who are they? List the employee ID, first name, and last name of these employees. Sort them on the `employee_id`.

c. List the suppliers that are not supplying any food on the current menu. List the supplier ID and the supplier name. Sort on the `supplier_id`.

2. Goal: Use an outer join with the `count` and `sum` column functions.

a. See section 14-8.

b. Count the number of foods supplied by each supplier. List all the suppliers. Show the supplier ID, supplier name, and the number of foods from each supplier. Sort the rows on the `supplier_id`.

c. Count the number of employees who work in each department. List all the departments. Show the department code, department name, and the number of employees. Sort on the `dept_code`.

d. Count the number of servings of each food in all the lunches in the `l_lunch_items` table. Show all of the foods, supplier ID, product code, description, and the number of servings in all of the lunches.

(Hint: Add up the quantities. Use the `sum` column function. You will get a null in the count. Use the `nvl` or `nz` function to change this null to a zero.)

3. Goal: Create a full outer join and put the rows into a logical order.

a. See section 14-10.

b. Create the full outer join of the `sec1407_first` table and the `sec1407_second` table. Join the rows when both tables have the same value in their first column, that is:

`sec1407_first.number_1 = sec1407_second.number_2`

Show all the columns of both tables and create a column to put the rows into a sort order based on the values of the number columns.

chapter 15

UNION AND
UNION ALL

The union was introduced in the last chapter because it was needed to code a full outer join. In this chapter we discuss the union in detail. Union and union all provide two more ways to combine tables.

Unions

A `union` of tables combines the rows of two tables together in a single table without making any changes to those rows. For all the rows to fit into one table, the rows of both tables must have the same structure. That is, they must have the same number of columns and the datatypes of corresponding columns must be the same.

15-1   The difference between a `union` and a join

A `union` and a join are similar in that they are both ways of combining two tables to form another table. However, they do this combining in very different ways. The geometry is different, as shown in the following diagram.

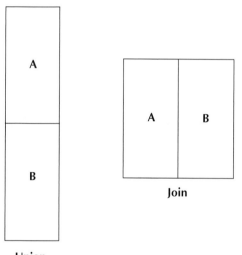

The differing geometry of a `union` and a join.

In a `union`, the rows of one table must fit into the other table. The number of columns in the result table is the same as the number in both of the beginning tables. No new columns are added. The rows of all the tables have the same sequence of datatypes for their columns.

In a join, the rows of one table may be very different from the rows of the other table. The result table can contain columns from both the first and second tables. It can contain all the columns of the first table and all the columns of the second table.

In a union, the maximum number of rows is the *sum* of the number of rows in the two tables. In a join, the maximum number of rows is the *product* of them.

Neither a join nor a union automatically gets a primary key. If you want to create a primary key for them, you must use an alter table statement. We did this in section 6-6.

Task

Show an example of the difference between a union and a join. Here, we use the same tables we used in chapter 14.

Oracle & Access SQL — For a union

```
select number_1,
       word_1,
       date_1
from sec1407_first
union
select number_2,
       word_2,
       date_2
from sec1407_second
order by number_1;
```

Beginning tables
sec1407_first table　　　　　　　　　　**sec1407_second table**

NUMBER_1	WORD_1	DATE_1	NUMBER_2	WORD_2	DATE_2
1	ONE	01-DEC-2001	3	THREE	03-DEC-2003
2	TWO	02-DEC-2002	4	FOUR	04-DEC-2004
3	THREE	03-DEC-2003	5	FIVE	05-DEC-2005
4	FOUR	04-DEC-2004	6	SIX	06-DEC-2006
5	FIVE	05-DEC-2005	7	SEVEN	07-DEC-2007

Result table — A `union`

```
NUMBER_1 WORD_1      DATE_1
-------- ----------  -----------
       1 ONE         01-DEC-2001
       2 TWO         02-DEC-2002
       3 THREE       03-DEC-2003
       4 FOUR        04-DEC-2004
       5 FIVE        05-DEC-2005
       6 SIX         06-DEC-2006
       7 SEVEN       07-DEC-2007
```

Oracle & Access SQL — For an inner join

```
select a.*,
       b.*
from sec1407_first a,
     sec1407_second b
where a.number_1 = b.number_2
order by a.number_1;
```

Result table — An inner join

NUMBER_1	WORD_1	DATE_1	NUMBER_2	WORD_2	DATE_2
3	THREE	03-DEC-2003	3	THREE	03-DEC-2003
4	FOUR	04-DEC-2004	4	FOUR	04-DEC-2004
5	FIVE	05-DEC-2005	5	FIVE	05-DEC-2005

15-2   Union all

`Union all` is another way to combine tables. It is very similar to a `union`. The only difference is that duplicate rows are not eliminated and the rows are not automatically sorted. In a `union` the rows get sorted as part of the process of eliminating duplicate rows.

A `union all` requires less computing resources than a `union`, so use it when you can, particularly when you are handling large tables. In most situations you should use a `union`. The situations when you should use `union all` are:

1. You know you have duplicate rows and you want to keep them.

2. You know there cannot be any duplicate rows.

3. You do not care whether there are any duplicate rows.

The rules that apply to a `union` also apply to `union all`, so as I discuss the details of a `union`, I am usually discussing them both.

In the following example, the `union all` has two identical rows numbered 3. As the previous section shows, a `union` has one of these rows. Except for duplicate rows, the result tables of the `union` and the `union all` are the same.

Task

Show an example of a `union all`.

Oracle & Access SQL — For a `union all`

```
select number_1,
       word_1,
       date_1
from sec1407_first
union all
select number_2,
       word_2,
       date_2
from sec1407_second
order by number_1;
```

Beginning tables
sec1407_first table   **sec1407_second table**

NUMBER_1	WORD_1	DATE_1
1	ONE	01-DEC-2001
2	TWO	02-DEC-2002
3	THREE	03-DEC-2003
4	FOUR	04-DEC-2004
5	FIVE	05-DEC-2005

NUMBER_2	WORD_2	DATE_2
3	THREE	03-DEC-2003
4	FOUR	04-DEC-2004
5	FIVE	05-DEC-2005
6	SIX	06-DEC-2006
7	SEVEN	07-DEC-2007

Result table — Showing a union all

NUMBER_1	WORD_1	DATE_1
1	ONE	01-DEC-2001
2	TWO	02-DEC-2002
3	THREE	03-DEC-2003
3	THREE	03-DEC-2003
4	FOUR	04-DEC-2004
4	FOUR	04-DEC-2004
5	FIVE	05-DEC-2005
5	FIVE	05-DEC-2005
6	SIX	06-DEC-2006
7	SEVEN	07-DEC-2007

15-3   The `select` statements within a `union`

The `select` statements within a `union` can be quite complex. They are allowed to contain all six clauses, except for the `order by` clause. They are allowed to contain row functions, grouped summarization, inner joins, and outer joins.

If we want to assign a new name to a column—a column alias—then we must do this in the first `select` clause within the `union`.

In the following example, the first `select` statement contains an inner join and grouped summarization. It contains all five clauses of the `select` statement that it can use: `select`, `from`, `where`, `group by`, and `having`. The `select` clause lists three columns: the first two are text and the third is a number. That sets the structure of the rows of the result table. The rows from the second `select` statement must have the same structure. The first `select` clause also assigns the column alias `number_of_lunches`.

The second `select` statement may seem to be entirely different. It is as simple as it can be. The `select` clause contains literals and the dual table is used in the `from` clause. The `order by` clause is not part of the second `select` statement, it is part of the `union`. The `select` clause does have three columns with the datatypes: text, text, and number. That is as similar as it needs to be to the first `select` statement.

Some people consider this to be a sneaky way to put more data into the result table.

Task

From the `l_lunches` table, count the number of lunches each employee will attend. Get the last name and first name of each employee from the `l_employees` table using an inner join. Do not try to include employees who are not attending any lunches. Use a `union` to include a row showing that you will not attend any of the lunches.

Oracle & Access SQL

```
select a.last_name,
       a.first_name,
       count(b.lunch_id) as number_of_lunches
from l_employees a,
     l_lunches b
where a.employee_id = b.employee_id
group by a.first_name,
         a.last_name
having count(b.lunch_id) < 5
union all ❶
select 'patrick',
       'john',
       0
from dual
order by last_name;
```

Beginning tables — The l_lunches table and the l_employees table from the Lunches database

Result table

```
LAST_NAME   FIRST_NAME NUMBER_OF_LUNCHES
----------  ---------- -----------------
BROWN       SUSAN                      3
CAMPBELL    FRED                       2
HOFFMAN     NANCY                      2
KERN        JIM                        1
OWENS       ELLEN                      2
PATRICK     JOHN                       0
PERKINS     HENRY                      2
SMITH       DAN                        2
WOODS       MARTHA                     2
```

Notes

❶ Here I am using a union all instead of a union because I already know that there are no duplicate rows.

15-4   The order by **clause in a** union

A union can have only one order by clause and it must be placed at the end of the statement. It provides the sort order for all the rows of the union from both select statements.

There are some choices about what kind of items we can sort by. There is also some confusion here. The order by clause in a union can seem to be a bit temperamental. In some SQL products you may have to try several options before you find one that works. In some circumstances we may find that only some of these options work. Here is a list of possibilities to try:

1. A column name from the first select clause

2. A column alias from the first select clause

3. A number that is the position of the column within the union

The first two options are preferred because they make the code easier to read and understand. They are shown in task 1 and task 2. Task 3 shows that in Access we can specify which table the column name or column alias comes from. The third option, shown in task 4, almost always works, even when the first two options do not.

Task 1

Show a `union` that uses a column name in its `order by` clause.

Oracle & Access SQL

```
select number_1,
       word_1,
       date_1
from sec1407_first
union
select *
from sec1407_second
order by word_1;
```

Beginning tables
sec1407_first table   **sec1407_second table**

NUMBER_1	WORD_1	DATE_1
1	ONE	01-DEC-2001
2	TWO	02-DEC-2002
3	THREE	03-DEC-2003
4	FOUR	04-DEC-2004
5	FIVE	05-DEC-2005

NUMBER_2	WORD_2	DATE_2
3	THREE	03-DEC-2003
4	FOUR	04-DEC-2004
5	FIVE	05-DEC-2005
6	SIX	06-DEC-2006
7	SEVEN	07-DEC-2007

Result table — Sorted on the second column

NUMBER_1	WORD_1	DATE_1
5	FIVE	05-DEC-2005
4	FOUR	04-DEC-2004
1	ONE	01-DEC-2001
7	SEVEN	07-DEC-2007
6	SIX	06-DEC-2006
3	THREE	03-DEC-2003
2	TWO	02-DEC-2002

Task 2

Show a union that uses a column alias in its order by clause.

Oracle & Access SQL

```
select number_1,
       word_1 as text_1,
       date_1
from sec1407_first
union
select *
from sec1407_second
order by text_1;
```

Beginning tables — Same as in task 1

Result table — Same as in task 1

Task 3

Show that in Access we can use a table alias in an order by clause of a union.

Access SQL

```
select a.number_1,
       a.word_1,
       a.date_1
from sec1407_first a
union
select *
from sec1407_second
order by a.word_1;
```

- Oracle does not support using a table alias in an order by clause of a union.

Beginning tables — Same as in task 1

Access result table

number_1	word_1	date_1
5	Five	12/5/2005
4	Four	12/4/2004
1	One	12/1/2001
7	Seven	12/7/2007
6	Six	12/6/2006
3	Three	12/3/2003
2	Two	12/2/2002

Record: 7 of 7

Task 4

Show a union that uses a column number in its order by clause.

Oracle & Access SQL

```
select *
from sec1407_first
union
select *
from sec1407_second
order by 2; ❶
```

Beginning tables — Same as in task 1

Result table — Same as in task 1

Notes

❶ This says to sort the rows of the result table on its second column.

15-5   Creating a table or view that includes a `union`

A few years ago, in the earlier versions of SQL, people were not allowed to create a view that contained a `union`. This restriction no longer applies to most SQL products, so we do not need to worry about it. If you have inherited some SQL code written years ago, you may find that code had to work around this restriction.

Although this feature is available now, it does not work perfectly in most SQL products. It can still give you a few surprises. The following examples show you how to create a table and a view that includes a `union`. The notes discuss the surprises I found.

Task 1

Create a view in Oracle that includes a `union`.

Oracle SQL: Create a view — Do not include an `order by` clause ❶

```
create or replace view sec1505a as
select *
from sec1407_first
union
select *
from sec1407_second;
```

Beginning tables — `Sec1407_first` table and `sec1407_second` table. See preceding listing.

Result view (`sec1505a` view)

```
NUMBER_1 WORD_1      DATE_1
--------- ---------- -----------
       1 ONE        01-DEC-2001
       2 TWO        02-DEC-2002
       3 THREE      03-DEC-2003
       4 FOUR       04-DEC-2004
       5 FIVE       05-DEC-2005
       6 SIX        06-DEC-2006
       7 SEVEN      07-DEC-2007
```

Task 2

Create a table in Oracle that includes a union.

Oracle SQL: Create a table

```
create table sec1505b as
select *
from sec1407_first
union
select *
from sec1407_second;
```

Result table — Same as in task 1

Task 3

Create a view in Access that includes a union.

Access SQL: Create a view — It is OK to include an order by clause ❷

Step 1: Enter this query in the SQL window:

```
select *
from sec1407_first
union
select *
from sec1407_second
order by 2;
```

Step 2: Save the query. Name it sec1505a.

Task 4

Create a table in Access that includes a union.

Access SQL: Create a table from the saved query ❸

```
select *
into sec1505b
from sec1505a;
```

Notes

❶ In recent versions of Oracle, when we define a view, we are usually allowed to include an `order by` clause. However, this does not work well when the view also includes a `union`. There are two problems:

1. Sometimes the `order by` clause causes an error in the context of a `create view` statement, even though it would run without the `create view`. Because of this error, the view is not created.

2. Even when the `order by` clause is included in the definition of the view, it is not used to sort the rows of the view. It is simply ignored.

❷ In Access, we can use an `order by` clause when we create a saved query (view). It works as we expect it to and there are no problems that I know of.

❸ In Access, we cannot directly create a table from a `union` query. The workaround is to first create a saved query containing the `union` and then create a table from the saved query.

15-6   Automatic datatype conversion in a `union`

The result table of a `union` contains all the rows from both beginning tables. Each column of this result table has one specific datatype, like any column of any other table. Does this mean that we can only form a `union` when both beginning tables have columns with exactly the same datatypes in all their columns? No.

Text

First, consider text columns. Suppose the first column of one beginning table contains text strings that are 10 characters long. Suppose the first column of the other beginning table contains text strings that are 20 characters long. I am speaking about the first columns because it is convenient, but I mean any matching set of columns from each table. The small difference in the datatype of these columns means that the data from them cannot be put into a single column so a `union` cannot be formed.

However, Oracle resolves this difference and makes the `union` possible. In the process of forming a `union`, Oracle will automatically convert the data of the first table from 10-character text strings into 20-character text strings. Then all the data has precisely the same datatype, so all the data can be put into a single column. This permits the `union`.

When two columns of text strings have different lengths, this difference in their datatypes is resolved by making the length of all the data equal to the length of the longest column. This is the shortest possible length to use without losing any part of the data.

Numbers

Next, consider numeric columns. Suppose the first column of one beginning table contains numbers that are 2 digits long and the first column of the other beginning table contains numbers that are 7 digits long. Because these datatypes are different, we cannot put all of the data into a single column. We cannot form a `union`.

However, Oracle resolves this difference and makes the `union` possible. In the process of forming a `union`, Oracle will automatically convert all of the numbers of both tables to 24-digit numbers. Then all the data has precisely the same datatype, so all the data can be put into a single column. This permits the `union`.

When two columns of numbers have different lengths, this difference in their datatypes is resolved by giving all the numbers the maximum length allowed to any number. In the version of Oracle I am currently using, the maximum length of a number is 24 digits. In other versions of Oracle the maximum length may be different.

Dates

Last, consider date columns. There is only one datatype for dates, so all columns of dates have precisely the same datatype.

Compatability

Because of this automatic datatype conversion, we say that any two columns of text are compatible and any two columns of numbers are compatible. By extension, we also say that any two columns of dates are compatible. In conclusion, we can always form a `union` of two tables if they have the same number of columns and the matching columns from each table are compatible.

Task

Show an example of automatic datatype conversion taking place in a `union`.

Oracle SQL

```
create or replace view sec1506_union as
select number_n7 as number_col,
       text_t7 as text_column
from sec1506_first
union
select number_n2,
       text_t2
from sec1506_second;
```

Access SQL

Step 1: Enter this query in the SQL window:

```
select number_n7 as number_col,
       text_t7 as text_column
from sec1506_first
union
select number_n2,
       text_t2
from sec1506_second;
```

Step 2: Use the GUI to save the query. Name it `sec1506_union`.

Beginning tables

sec1506_first table   **sec1506_second table**

NUMBER_N7	TEXT_T7		NUMBER_N2	TEXT_T2
1111111	AAAAAAA		33	CC
2222222	BBBBBBB		44	DD
3333333	CCCCCCC		55	EE
4444444	DDDDDDD		66	FF
5555555	EEEEEEE		77	GG

Result table

```
NUMBER_COL TEXT_COLUMN
------------- -----------
         33 CC
         44 DD
         55 EE
         66 FF
         77 GG
    1111111 AAAAAAA
    2222222 BBBBBBB
    3333333 CCCCCCC
    4444444 DDDDDDD
    5555555 EEEEEEE
```

Unconventional Unions

It is common knowledge that we can only create a union of two tables if they have the same number of columns and the datatypes of the matching columns are compatible. That common knowledge is wrong! It is only true on the most detailed (trivial) level. On the broader level of handling information, it is false. In the next two sections I break both of these rules.

I end up with the opinion that I can perform a union of any two tables. The one limitation on this is that the columns of the result have some consistent meaning and they must make sense.

15-7   A `union` of tables with different datatypes

This section shows a `union` that matches a numeric column with a text column. Some people think this cannot be done.

The reason it can be done is that the data in all types of columns can be converted to text. When all the columns have been converted to text, they all fit together in a `union`. I use a row function to explicitly convert the datatype of each column to text, rather than relying on automatic datatype conversion.

In the following example, numeric data is changed into text data so that it can be combined in the `union` with other text data. The `to_char` function in Oracle changes numeric data and date/time data to text data.

Task

Show how to use datatype conversion functions in a `union`.

Oracle SQL

```
create view sec1507_union as
select to_char(number_n7) as first_column,
       text_t7 as second_column
from sec1506_first
union
select text_t2,
       to_char(number_n2)
from sec1506_second;
```

Access SQL

Step 1: Enter this query in the SQL window:

```
select format (number_n7) as first_column,
       text_t7 as second_column
from sec1506_first
union
select text_t2,
       format (number_n2)
from sec1506_second;
```

Step 2: Use the GUI to save the query. Name it sec1507_union.

Beginning tables
sec1506_first table   ### sec1506_second table

NUMBER_N7	TEXT_T7
1111111	AAAAAAA
2222222	BBBBBBB
3333333	CCCCCCC
4444444	DDDDDDD
5555555	EEEEEEE

NUMBER_N2	TEXT_T2
33	CC
44	DD
55	EE
66	FF
77	GG

Created view (sec1507_union view)

FIRST_COLUMN	SECOND_COLUMN
1111111	AAAAAAA
2222222	BBBBBBB
3333333	CCCCCCC
4444444	DDDDDDD
5555555	EEEEEEE
CC	33
DD	44
EE	55
FF	66
GG	77

15-8   A union of two tables with different numbers of columns

This section shows a union of two tables that have different numbers of columns. Some people think this cannot be done. It can be done because we can add extra columns to one table to give both tables the same number of columns.

In the following example, I do a union of a table that has two columns with a table that has three columns. To do this I add a column of nulls to the first table. Both tables have three columns when the union is performed.

Task

Show how to form a union of two tables that have different numbers of columns.

Oracle8i SQL — Workaround

```
select a.number_col,
       a.text_col,
       a.date_col
from sec1508_first a
union
select b.number_col,
       b.text_col,
       to_date(null) ❶
from sec1508_second b;
```

Oracle9i & Access SQL

```
select a.number_col,
       a.text_col,
       a.date_col
from sec1508_first a
union
select b.number_col,
       b.text_col,
       null ❷
from sec1508_second b;
```

Beginning tables

sec1508_first table   **sec1508_second table**

```
NUMBER_COL TEXT_COL DATE_COL          NUMBER_COL TEXT_COL
---------- -------- -----------       ---------- --------
   1111111 AAAAAAA  01-DEC-2015          3333333 CCCCCCC
   2222222 BBBBBBB  02-DEC-2015          4444444 DDDDDDD
   3333333 CCCCCCC  03-DEC-2015          5555555 EEEEEEE
   4444444 DDDDDDD  04-DEC-2015          6666666 FFFFFFF
   5555555 EEEEEEE  05-DEC-2015          7777777 GGGGGGG
```

Result table

```
NUMBER_COL TEXT_COL DATE_COL
---------- -------- -----------
   1111111 AAAAAAA  01-DEC-2015
   2222222 BBBBBBB  02-DEC-2015
   3333333 CCCCCCC  03-DEC-2015
   3333333 CCCCCCC  (null)
   4444444 DDDDDDD  04-DEC-2015
   4444444 DDDDDDD  (null)
   5555555 EEEEEEE  05-DEC-2015
   5555555 EEEEEEE  (null)
   6666666 FFFFFFF  (null)
   7777777 GGGGGGG  (null)
```

Notes

❶ Oracle8i requires this null to be formatted with the `to_date` function to make it compatible with the dates in column 3 of the first `select` statement. This is a workaround for a bug in Oracle8i. Whether a null is in a text, number, or date column, they should all work the same way. We should not be required to put a format on a null. Oracle9i has fixed this problem.

❷ Oracle9i and Access do not require any formatting of the null.

Applications of a Union

A union has some very useful applications. It gives us a lot of power that we have not had until now. Two analogies come to mind when I think of the applications of a union. The first is the saying from ancient Rome, "Divide and conquer." We are able to divide the rows of a table into separate groups, apply a different type of processing to each group, and then use a union to put all the rows back into one table.

The other analogy is "management by exception." This contrasts with "management by handling all the details," which has the problem that we can be overwhelmed by the volume of details. We are able to isolate the exceptional cases and flag them so we can see and handle the special circumstances they present. Using a union, we can merge these exceptional cases with the majority of the data to again create a unified view of all the data.

15-9   Determining if two tables are identical

When two tables have the same number of columns and rows, they might appear to be identical, but perhaps one of the cells has a different value in one table than in the other. How can we be certain about this?

One way is to form the union of the two tables. This method works if the tables have primary keys or if you know that they do not have any duplicate rows, which is the case for most tables.

If the two tables are identical, the union will have the same number of rows as the beginning tables. All the rows of the second table will be eliminated as duplicates. If they are not identical, the union will have more rows.

If there is a difference, this technique does not help us find out what it is. We have other ways of finding that information. This technique only determines whether there is a difference.

Task

Test whether two tables are identical. We already know that these tables have the same number of columns and that the datatypes of those columns are compatible.

Oracle & Access SQL:
Step 1 — Determine if the tables have the same number of rows

```
select count(*) from l_foods;
select count(*) from sec1509_foods;
```

Beginning table 1 (`1_foods` table)

```
SUPPLIER PRODUCT    MENU                                          PRICE
ID       CODE       ITEM DESCRIPTION                   PRICE   INCREASE
-------- -------    ------- ----------------------   --------  --------
ASP      FS            1 FRESH SALAD                   $2.00     $0.25
ASP      SP            2 SOUP OF THE DAY               $1.50    (null)
ASP      SW            3 SANDWICH                      $3.50     $0.40
CBC      GS            4 GRILLED STEAK                 $6.00     $0.70
CBC      SW            5 HAMBURGER                     $2.50     $0.30
FRV      BR            6 BROCCOLI                      $1.00     $0.05
FRV      FF            7 FRENCH FRIES                  $1.50    (null)
JBR      AS            8 SODA                          $1.25     $0.25
JBR      VR            9 COFFEE                        $0.85     $0.15
VSB      AS           10 DESSERT                       $3.00     $0.50
```

Beginning table 2 (`sec1509_foods` table)

```
SUPPLIER PRODUCT    MENU                                          PRICE
ID       CODE       ITEM DESCRIPTION                   PRICE   INCREASE
-------- -------    ------- ----------------------   --------  --------
ASP      FS            1 FRESH SALAD                   $2.00     $0.25
ASP      SP            2 SOUP OF THE DAY               $1.50    (null)
ASP      SW            3 SANDWICH                      $3.50     $0.40
CBC      GS            4 GRILLED STEAK                 $6.00     $0.70
CBC      SW            5 HAMBURGER                     $2.50     $0.30
FRV      BR            6 BROCCOLI                      $1.00     $0.05
FRV      FF            7 FRENCH FRIES                  $1.50    (null)
JBR      AS            8 SODA                          $1.25     $0.25
JBR      VR            9 COFFEE                        $0.85     $0.15
VSB      AS           10 DESSERT                       $3.00     $0.50
```

The result table is the same for both `select` statements in step 1.
This shows that both tables have the same number of rows.

```
COUNT(*)
---------
       10
```

Oracle SQL:
Step 2 — Create a view that is the union of both tables

```
create or replace view sec1509_union as
select * from 1_foods
union
select * from sec1509_foods;
```

Access SQL:
Step 2 — Create a view that is the union of both tables

Step 2 Part 1: Enter this query in the SQL window:

```
select * from 1_foods
union
select * from sec1509_foods;
```

Step 2 Part 2: Save this query. Name it sec1509_union.

Oracle & Access SQL:
Step 3 — Count the number of rows in the view

```
select count(*) from sec1509_union;
```

Result table

```
COUNT(*)
---------
       10
```

Conclusion

The tables are identical.

15-10 Using a literal in a union to identify the source of the data

In this section we add a new column to each of the beginning tables using a literal. That column identifies the table that the data comes from. After we perform the union, the source of each row of data is identified.

If both tables contain an identical row, the duplicate is not eliminated. Rather, it is shown to come from both tables. This might be what we want to happen.

The new column ensures that no row from the first table can be identical to a row from the second table, so we may as well use a union all instead of a union.

Task

Show a select statement that uses a union with literals to identify the source of each row.

Oracle & Access SQL

```
select number_1, ❶
       word_1,
       date_1,
       'from the first table' as source_of_the_data ❷
from sec1407_first
union all
select number_2, ❸
       word_2,
       date_2,
       'from the second table' ❹
from sec1407_second
order by number_1;
```

Beginning tables

sec1407_first table   **sec1407_second table**

NUMBER_1	WORD_1	DATE_1
1	ONE	01-DEC-2001
2	TWO	02-DEC-2002
3	THREE	03-DEC-2003
4	FOUR	04-DEC-2004
5	FIVE	05-DEC-2005

NUMBER_2	WORD_2	DATE_2
3	THREE	03-DEC-2003
4	FOUR	04-DEC-2004
5	FIVE	05-DEC-2005
6	SIX	06-DEC-2006
7	SEVEN	07-DEC-2007

Result table

NUMBER_1	WORD_1	DATE_1	SOURCE_OF_THE_DATA
1	ONE	01-DEC-2001	FROM THE FIRST TABLE
2	TWO	02-DEC-2002	FROM THE FIRST TABLE
3	THREE	03-DEC-2003	FROM THE FIRST TABLE
3	THREE	03-DEC-2003	FROM THE SECOND TABLE
4	FOUR	04-DEC-2004	FROM THE FIRST TABLE
4	FOUR	04-DEC-2004	FROM THE SECOND TABLE
5	FIVE	05-DEC-2005	FROM THE FIRST TABLE
5	FIVE	05-DEC-2005	FROM THE SECOND TABLE
6	SIX	06-DEC-2006	FROM THE SECOND TABLE
7	SEVEN	07-DEC-2007	FROM THE SECOND TABLE

Notes

❶ The first `select` statement lists the rows from the first table. It attaches a literal to each of these rows.

❷ The literal is text placed within quotation marks. A column alias gives this column a name. Every row of the first table has the same value in this new column.

❸ The second `select` statement lists the rows from the second table. It attaches a different literal to each of these rows.

❹ This is the text that is added to each row of the second table.

15-11 Attaching messages to flag exceptions, warnings, and errors

This section shows you how to attach messages to rows of data. The rows of a table are divided into two groups: a small group that will be flagged with a message and a much larger group that will receive no message.

This technique is useful for finding exceptional conditions in the data and for attaching warning messages and error messages.

The `where` clauses in the two `select` statements divide the rows of data into two groups. One group receives a message and the other group gets a blank space instead of a message. Then the `union` puts all these rows back into a single table.

When we divide the rows into two separate groups, it is important to remember that SQL uses three-valued logic. It is not enough to use a condition, A, in one `where` clause and its opposite, NOT A, in the other. We must always consider the possibility that there are nulls in the data and handle that case.

Task

List the foods and their prices. Add the message "expensive item" to the foods that cost more than $2.00. List the foods in alphabetical order.

Oracle & Access SQL

```
select description,
       price,
       'expensive item' as message
from l_foods
where price > 2.00
union all
select description,
       price,
       ' '
from l_foods
where not (price > 2.00)
   or price is null
order by description;
```

Beginning table (`1_foods` table)

```
SUPPLIER PRODUCT   MENU                                     PRICE
ID       CODE      ITEM DESCRIPTION           PRICE INCREASE
-------- -------   ------- -------------------- -------- --------
ASP      FS         1 FRESH SALAD            $2.00    $0.25
ASP      SP         2 SOUP OF THE DAY        $1.50   (null)
ASP      SW         3 SANDWICH               $3.50    $0.40
CBC      GS         4 GRILLED STEAK          $6.00    $0.70
CBC      SW         5 HAMBURGER              $2.50    $0.30
FRV      BR         6 BROCCOLI               $1.00    $0.05
FRV      FF         7 FRENCH FRIES           $1.50   (null)
JBR      AS         8 SODA                   $1.25    $0.25
JBR      VR         9 COFFEE                 $0.85    $0.15
VSB      AS        10 DESSERT                $3.00    $0.50
```

Result table

```
DESCRIPTION          PRICE MESSAGE
-------------------- -------- --------------
BROCCOLI             $1.00
COFFEE               $0.85
DESSERT              $3.00 EXPENSIVE ITEM
FRENCH FRIES         $1.50
FRESH SALAD          $2.00
GRILLED STEAK        $6.00 EXPENSIVE ITEM
HAMBURGER            $2.50 EXPENSIVE ITEM
SANDWICH             $3.50 EXPENSIVE ITEM
SODA                 $1.25
SOUP OF THE DAY      $1.50
```

15-12 Dividing data from one column into two different columns

This section shows you how to divide one column of data into two or more columns. This technique can be useful in making some types of data stand out or in sorting the data into several categories.

This technique is similar to the ones we have used before. The `where` clauses of the `select` statements divide the rows of the beginning table into separate groups. Then the data is listed in the desired column and a blank is placed in the other columns. A `union` puts all these pieces back together.

Task

Divide the `cost` column from the beginning table into two columns: `debits` and `credits`.

Oracle8i SQL — Workaround

```
-- SQLplus command to show nulls as blanks
set null ' ';  ❶

select item,
       to_number(null) as debits,  ❷
       cost as credits
from sec1512_finances
where cost > 0
union all
select item,
       cost,
       to_number(null)  ❷
from sec1512_finances
where cost < 0
   or cost is null
order by item;
```

Oracle9i & Access SQL

```
select item,
       null as debits,  ❸
       cost as credits
from sec1512_finances
where cost > 0
union all
select item,
       cost,
       null  ❸
from sec1512_finances
where cost < 0
   or cost is null
order by item;
```

Beginning table (`sec1512_finances` table)

```
ITEM                             COST
------------------------  -----------
SAMSONITE SUITCASE            -$248.13
RENT FOR APRIL                 $700.00
OPERA TICKET                  -$145.00
LUNCH                          -$15.62
DEBT REPAID BY JIM              $20.00
CAR REPAIR                    -$622.98
HAIRCUT                        -$22.00
BIRTHDAY GIFT FROM MOM         $200.00
```

Result table

```
ITEM                        DEBITS   CREDITS
------------------------  --------  --------
BIRTHDAY GIFT FROM MOM                $200.00
CAR REPAIR                -$622.98
DEBT REPAID BY JIM                     $20.00
HAIRCUT                    -$22.00
LUNCH                      -$15.62
OPERA TICKET              -$145.00
RENT FOR APRIL                        $700.00
SAMSONITE SUITCASE       -$248.13
```

Notes

❶ In Oracle, we want the nulls to appear as spaces in this example. In Access, they already appear this way. To reset Oracle to our normal setting, use

```
set null '(null)';
```

❷ In Oracle8i, we need to say that the null will be part of a numeric column. We format it this way with the `to_number` function. This technique works around a problem in Oracle8i. Oracle9i has fixed this problem.

❸ In Oracle9i and Access, it is not necessary to specify the format of the nulls.

15-13 Applying two functions to different parts of the data

This section shows you how to apply several different calculations to the data in different rows. First, we use the `where` clauses in the `select` statements to divide the rows into groups. We make a separate group for each calculation and perform the calculations on all the rows within each group. Then we use a `union` to combine all the groups again.

Task

Show how to make two different calculations, depending on the data in a row. Increase the price of all foods costing more than $2.00 by 5%. Increase the price of all other foods by 10%. Ignore the existing `price_increase` column.

Oracle & Access SQL

```
select menu_item,
       description,
       price + (price * .05) as new_price
from l_foods
where price > 2.00
   or price is null
union all
select menu_item,
       description,
       price + (price * .10)
from l_foods
where price <= 2.00
order by menu_item;
```

Beginning table (1_foods table)

SUPPLIER ID	PRODUCT CODE	MENU ITEM	DESCRIPTION	PRICE	PRICE INCREASE
ASP	FS	1	FRESH SALAD	$2.00	$0.25
ASP	SP	2	SOUP OF THE DAY	$1.50	
ASP	SW	3	SANDWICH	$3.50	$0.40
CBC	GS	4	GRILLED STEAK	$6.00	$0.70
CBC	SW	5	HAMBURGER	$2.50	$0.30
FRV	BR	6	BROCCOLI	$1.00	$0.05
FRV	FF	7	FRENCH FRIES	$1.50	
JBR	AS	8	SODA	$1.25	$0.25
JBR	VR	9	COFFEE	$0.85	$0.15
VSB	AS	10	DESSERT	$3.00	$0.50

Result table

MENU ITEM	DESCRIPTION	NEW PRICE
1	FRESH SALAD	$2.20
2	SOUP OF THE DAY	$1.65
3	SANDWICH	$3.68
4	GRILLED STEAK	$6.30
5	HAMBURGER	$2.63
6	BROCCOLI	$1.10
7	FRENCH FRIES	$1.65
8	SODA	$1.38
9	COFFEE	$0.94
10	DESSERT	$3.15

15-14   A union of three or more tables

You can code a union of as many tables as you wish, as many as 10 or more. The union operation works the same way. If you want to use column aliases, you must assign them in the first select statement. The code may be long, but it is not complex.

Task

List the letters from 'a' to 'g'. Do this as a union of seven tables.

Oracle & Access SQL

```
select 'a' as letters
from dual
union
select 'b'
from dual
union
select 'c'
from dual
union
select 'd'
from dual
union
select 'e'
from dual
union
select 'f'
from dual
union
select 'g'
from dual
order by 1;
```

Beginning table

```
DUMMY
-------
X
```

Result table

```
LETTERS
-------
A
B
C
D
E
F
G
```

Set Intersection and Set Difference in Oracle

Oracle has created extensions to standard SQL that provide direct support for finding the intersection and difference between two tables. These operations can be done in any brand of SQL, but the Oracle extensions make them easier. These methods provide a good way to compare two tables to determine which rows are identical and which rows are different.

15-15 Set intersection

The intersection of two tables consists of all the rows that are identical in both tables. In Oracle, we can find the intersection of two tables with the `intersect` operation. This works much like a `union` in that the word goes between two `select` statements. These `select` statements define the tables that we are intersecting.

You can perform the same operation in other brands of SQL by writing an inner join of the tables, listing all the rows that are identical in both tables. This method is shown in the Access code.

Task

Find the intersection of two tables. That is, find all the rows that occur in both tables.

Oracle SQL ❶

```
select number_1,
       word_1,
       date_1
from sec1407_first
intersect
select number_2,
       word_2,
       date_2
from sec1407_second
order by number_1;
```

■ Access does not support this method.

Access SQL ❷

```
select a.number_1,
       a.word_1,
       a.date_1
from sec1407_first a,
     sec1407_second b
where a.number_1 = b.number_2
  and a.word_1 = b.word_2
  and a.date_1 = b.date_2
order by a.number_1;
```

Beginning tables

sec1407_first table   sec1407_second table

NUMBER_1	WORD_1	DATE_1		NUMBER_2	WORD_2	DATE_2
1	ONE	01-DEC-2001		3	THREE	03-DEC-2003
2	TWO	02-DEC-2002		4	FOUR	04-DEC-2004
3	THREE	03-DEC-2003		5	FIVE	05-DEC-2005
4	FOUR	04-DEC-2004		6	SIX	06-DEC-2006
5	FIVE	05-DEC-2005		7	SEVEN	07-DEC-2007

Result table

NUMBER_1	WORD_1	DATE_1
3	THREE	03-DEC-2003
4	FOUR	04-DEC-2004
5	FIVE	05-DEC-2005

Notes

❶ This method works even when there are nulls in several of the columns.

❷ This method works only when there are no nulls in any of the columns. To compare tables that contain nulls, one method is to temporarily change all the nulls to some other value, doing a `rollback` at the end to return them to nulls. Another method is to change the join condition on each column to include the possibility of nulls. Using this method, instead of writing

```
a.column1 = b.column1
```

we would write

```
(a.column1 = b.column1
or (a.column1 is null and b.column1 is null))
```

15-16 Set difference

Oracle supports the `minus` operation to find all the rows in one table that are not present in another table. The word `minus` is placed between two `select` statements, similar to the way the word `union` is placed.

This is a very nice feature that Oracle has created. It is not part of standard SQL. Rather, it is an extension to standard SQL that Oracle has added. Few, if any, other types of SQL have a feature like this.

Clearly, this operation is one-sided. That is, it makes a difference which table is the first table and which one is second. To find all the differences between two tables, A and B, we must look at both

```
A minus B
```

and

```
B minus A
```

Another way to produce this result uses an outer join. The Access code shows this technique.

Task

Find all the rows that are in one table and not in the other table. Do this both ways to find all the differences between the two tables.

Oracle SQL: Step 1 ⊙

```
select number_1,
       word_1,
       date_1
from sec1407_first
minus
select number_2,
       word_2,
       date_2
from sec1407_second
order by number_1;
```

- Access does not support the `minus` operation.

Access SQL: Step 1 ❷

```
select a.number_1,
       a.word_1,
       a.date_1
from sec1407_first a
     left outer join sec1407_second b
     on a.number_1 = b.number_2
     and a.word_1 = b.word_2
     and a.date_1 = b.date_2
where b.number_2 is null
order by a.number_1;
```

Beginning tables
sec1407_first table   **sec1407_second table**

```
NUMBER_1 WORD_1     DATE_1            NUMBER_2 WORD_2     DATE_2
-------- ---------- -----------       -------- ---------- -----------
       1 ONE        01-DEC-2001              3 THREE      03-DEC-2003
       2 TWO        02-DEC-2002              4 FOUR       04-DEC-2004
       3 THREE      03-DEC-2003              5 FIVE       05-DEC-2005
       4 FOUR       04-DEC-2004              6 SIX        06-DEC-2006
       5 FIVE       05-DEC-2005              7 SEVEN      07-DEC-2007
```

Result table — Step 1

```
NUMBER_1 WORD_1     DATE_1
-------- ---------- -----------
       1 ONE        01-DEC-2001
       2 TWO        02-DEC-2002
```

Oracle SQL: Step 2 ❶

```
select number_2,
       word_2,
       date_2
from sec1407_second
minus
select number_1,
       word_1,
       date_1
from sec1407_first
order by number_2;
```

- Access does not support the minus operation.

Access SQL: Step 2 ❷

```
select b.number_2,
       b.word_2,
       b.date_2
from sec1407_first a
     right outer join sec1407_second b
     on a.number_1 = b.number_2
     and a.word_1 = b.word_2
     and a.date_1 = b.date_2
where a.number_1 is null
order by b.number_2;
```

Result table — Step 2

```
NUMBER_2 WORD_2      DATE_2
-------- ---------- -----------
       6 SIX         06-DEC-2006
       7 SEVEN       07-DEC-2007
```

Notes

❶ This method works even when there are nulls in several of the columns.

❷ This method works only when there are no nulls in any of the columns. To compare tables that contain nulls, one method is to temporarily change all the nulls to some other value, doing a `rollback` at the end to return them to nulls. Another method is to change the join condition on each column to include the possibility of nulls. Using this method, instead of writing

```
a.column1 = b.column1
```

we would write

```
(a.column1 = b.column1
or (a.column1 is null and b.column1 is null))
```

Summary

In this chapter we discussed `union` and `union all`. The idea of a `union` is very simple, but the ways it can be applied are very powerful. Unfortunately, many of the graphical (GUI) tools that generate SQL do not support the `union`, which is one of their major failings.

In many SQL products, the `union` is not yet an industrial-strength operation. In particular, its `order by` clause may be weak. If you are writing a `union` query with an `order by` clause, you may have to try several variations of the `order by` clause before you find one that works.

Oracle has added two special operations, extensions to SQL that are similar to `union`: `intersect` and `minus`.

Exercises

1. Goal: Form a `union` of two tables having different numbers of columns. Identify which rows come from each table. Flag the most expensive items, and divide the debits and credits into two separate columns.

    a. See sections 15-8, 15-10, 15-11, and 15-12.

    Bob and Sue are thinking about getting married. As a first step they have decided to keep track of their daily expenses in a single database. Bob's expenses currently are in the table `ex1501_bob`. It has one column: `cost`. Sue's expenses are currently in the table `ex1501_sue`. It has three columns: `item`, `price`, and `date_purchased`. Both tables use positive numbers for credits and negative numbers for debits.

    b. Use a `union` to list all the rows from these two tables.

    (Hints: match the `cost` column of Bob's table with the `price` column of Sue's table. It is easier to put Sue's table as the first `select` statement in the `union` because its columns are more specific. In Oracle8i, you will need to use `to_date(null)` for Bob's column of nulls that matches with Sue's `date_purchased` column. Use `union all` so you do not eliminate duplicate rows.)

c. Modify the code of exercise 1b to identify which rows came from Bob and which rows came from Sue. Name the new column `person`. Create a view, which you will use in exercise 1d.

d. Create a new view from the one you made in exercise 1c. Put a new column called `message` on all the rows where the price is greater than $50.00.

(Hint: Prices are shown as negative numbers. So "price is greater than $50" can be expressed as `price <-50`.)

e. Use the view you created in exercise 1d. Show the credits and debits in separate columns. Sort the rows by `date_purchased`. Show the nulls as blanks.

(Hint: In Oracle8i, use `to_number(null)`, instead of `NULL`, in the `credit` and `debit` columns.)

2. Goal: Compare two tables to see if they are identical. If they are not identical, find the differences.

a. See sections 15-9, 15-15, and 15-16.

b. The table `ex1502_lunch_items` is very similar to the `l_lunch_items` table. Determine if they are identical. If they are different, find the differences.

(Hint: This is easier to do in Oracle. If you code this in Access, you can use the fact that there are no nulls in any column of either table.)

chapter 16

CROSS JOINS AND SELF JOINS

This chapter finishes the discussion of techniques used to join two tables. You will not use these techniques very often, but knowing them will add depth to your understanding of all joins. They will also enable you to get results that would be almost impossible to obtain otherwise.

A cross join is used to define an inner join. It is also important in detecting errors in your code. Cross joins of small tables are acceptable and useful at times, but cross joins of large tables should be avoided.

A self join involves joining a table with itself. This is necessary when you need information from several rows of the same table at the same time.

Cross Joins

A *cross join* is another way to combine two tables. It should only be used with small tables.

Cross joins are important to understand because they provide the foundation for both inner and outer joins. The properties of inner joins are derived from the properties of cross products.

16-1 Definition of a cross join

This section shows an example of a cross join, which is also called a *cross product* and a *Cartesian product*. A cross join matches every row of the first table with every row of the second table, which results in all possible combinations. Cross joins often generate a lot of data, so they should be used infrequently and with great care.

The number of columns and rows in a cross join are as follows:

Columns in cross join = Sum of the number of columns in the beginning tables. (Add)

Rows in cross join = Product of the number of rows in the beginning tables. (Multiply)

In the following example, the cross join is written by putting both of the beginning tables in the `from` clause. This may look similar to an inner join. The difference is that there is no join condition. There is also no `where` clause, which would contain the join condition.

The first table has four rows and the second table has five, so the result table has 20 rows.

Task

Show an example of a cross join.

Oracle & Access SQL ❶

```
select a.*,
       b.*
from sec1601_first a,
     sec1601_second b;
```

Beginning tables
sec1601_first table
sec1601_second table

FCOL_1	FCOL_2
1	A
2	B
3	C
4	D

SCOL_1	SCOL_2	SCOL_3
25	VV	05-AUG-2025
26	WW	06-SEP-2026
27	XX	07-OCT-2027
28	YY	08-NOV-2028
29	ZZ	09-DEC-2029

Result table

FCOL_1	FCOL_2	SCOL_1	SCOL_2	SCOL_3
1	A	25	VV	05-AUG-2025
2	B	25	VV	05-AUG-2025
3	C	25	VV	05-AUG-2025
4	D	25	VV	05-AUG-2025
1	A	26	WW	06-SEP-2026
2	B	26	WW	06-SEP-2026
3	C	26	WW	06-SEP-2026
4	D	26	WW	06-SEP-2026
1	A	27	XX	07-OCT-2027
2	B	27	XX	07-OCT-2027
3	C	27	XX	07-OCT-2027
4	D	27	XX	07-OCT-2027
1	A	28	YY	08-NOV-2028
2	B	28	YY	08-NOV-2028
3	C	28	YY	08-NOV-2028
4	D	28	YY	08-NOV-2028
1	A	29	ZZ	09-DEC-2029
2	B	29	ZZ	09-DEC-2029
3	C	29	ZZ	09-DEC-2029
4	D	29	ZZ	09-DEC-2029

Notes

❶ There is no where clause. That is how a cross join is coded.

16-2   Why are cross joins important?

A cross join is such a simple concept that people sometimes ask, "What is their purpose? What are they good for?"

As the following sections show, cross joins are important for several reasons:

1. The definition of an inner join is based on a cross join.

2. Sometimes errors show up as cross joins.

3. A cross join of small tables can be used to show all combinations.

4. We need to avoid cross joins of large tables.

16-3   An inner join is derived from a cross join

A inner join is defined from a cross join. Here is the exact definition of the process that creates an inner join of two tables:

1. Create the cross join of the beginning tables.

2. Evaluate the join condition for each row of the cross join. The join condition is a statement. (Some people prefer to call it an *expression* or a *logical expression*.) For every row of the cross join, that statement will be either True, False, or Unknown.

3. Keep only the rows that evaluate to True.

4. Remove the evaluation column.

Task

Show each step of the process to create an inner join of the `fruits` and `colors` tables. Use the join condition `f_num = c_num`.

Oracle & Access SQL

```
select a.*,
       b.*
from sec1603_fruits a,
     sec1603_colors b
where a.f_num = b.c_num;
```

Beginning tables
sec1603_fruits table   sec1603_colors table

```
FRUIT           F_NUM            C_NUM COLOR
----------   ---------       --------- ---------
APPLE               1               1 RED
BANANA              2               2 YELLOW
STRAWBERRY          1               1 GREEN
GRAPE               4               5 WHITE
KIWI        (null)       (null)       BROWN
```

5 rows   5 rows

Step 1 — Form the cross join of the two tables

```
FRUIT           F_NUM       C_NUM COLOR
----------   ---------   --------- ----------
APPLE               1           1 RED
APPLE               1           1 GREEN
APPLE               1           2 YELLOW
APPLE               1           5 WHITE
APPLE               1 (null)       BROWN
BANANA              2           1 RED
BANANA              2           1 GREEN
BANANA              2           2 YELLOW
BANANA              2           5 WHITE
BANANA              2 (null)       BROWN
GRAPE               4           1 RED
GRAPE               4           1 GREEN
GRAPE               4           2 YELLOW
GRAPE               4           5 WHITE
GRAPE               4 (null)       BROWN
KIWI        (null)           1 RED
KIWI        (null)           1 GREEN
KIWI        (null)           2 YELLOW
KIWI        (null)           5 WHITE
KIWI        (null)   (null)       BROWN
STRAWBERRY          1           1 RED
STRAWBERRY          1           1 GREEN
STRAWBERRY          1           2 YELLOW
STRAWBERRY          1           5 WHITE
STRAWBERRY          1 (null)       BROWN
```

25 rows

Step 2 — Evaluate the join condition in each row of the cross join

Assign an evaluation to each row: True, False, or Unknown.
Here, the join condition is `f_num = c_num`.

FRUIT	F_NUM	C_NUM	COLOR	EVALUATION
APPLE	1	1	GREEN	TRUE
APPLE	1	1	RED	TRUE
APPLE	1	2	YELLOW	FALSE
APPLE	1	5	WHITE	FALSE
APPLE	1	(null)	BROWN	UNKNOWN
BANANA	2	1	GREEN	FALSE
BANANA	2	1	RED	FALSE
BANANA	2	2	YELLOW	TRUE
BANANA	2	5	WHITE	FALSE
BANANA	2	(null)	BROWN	UNKNOWN
GRAPE	4	1	GREEN	FALSE
GRAPE	4	1	RED	FALSE
GRAPE	4	2	YELLOW	FALSE
GRAPE	4	5	WHITE	FALSE
GRAPE	4	(null)	BROWN	UNKNOWN
KIWI	(null)	1	GREEN	UNKNOWN
KIWI	(null)	1	RED	UNKNOWN
KIWI	(null)	2	YELLOW	UNKNOWN
KIWI	(null)	5	WHITE	UNKNOWN
KIWI	(null)	(null)	BROWN	UNKNOWN
STRAWBERRY	1	1	GREEN	TRUE
STRAWBERRY	1	1	RED	TRUE
STRAWBERRY	1	2	YELLOW	FALSE
STRAWBERRY	1	5	WHITE	FALSE
STRAWBERRY	1	(null)	BROWN	UNKNOWN

Step 3 — Keep only the rows that evaluate as True

FRUIT	F_NUM	C_NUM	COLOR	EVALUATION
APPLE	1	1	RED	TRUE
APPLE	1	1	GREEN	TRUE
BANANA	2	2	YELLOW	TRUE
STRAWBERRY	1	1	RED	TRUE
STRAWBERRY	1	1	GREEN	TRUE

Step 4 — Remove the evaluation. This is the inner join

```
FRUIT            F_NUM      C_NUM COLOR
----------  ---------  --------- ----------
APPLE                1          1 RED
APPLE                1          1 GREEN
BANANA               2          2 YELLOW
STRAWBERRY           1          1 RED
STRAWBERRY           1          1 GREEN
```

16-4   The properties of an inner join

This section shows you how the properties of an inner join, which we discussed in chapter 13, are derived from the definition of an inner join given in the previous section.

- **An inner join contains all valid combinations of rows. Each row of one table can match with many rows of the other table.**

This occurs because the first step of forming an inner join is to form a cross join. The cross join creates all possible combinations of the rows. Every possible combination that passes the validity test of the succeeding steps becomes part of the inner join.

- **Rows are dropped from the join if there is no matching row in the other table.**

In step 2 of the definition in the previous section, for each row of the cross join, the statement of the join condition was evaluated. If there is no matching row in the other table, the this evaluation is never True. It is always False or Unknown.

In step 3 we only keep the rows of the cross join that evaluate to True. This drops all the rows from one of the beginning tables that do not have a match in the other beginning table.

- **Rows are dropped from the join if any matching column(s) contains a null.**

In step 2, the join condition statement always evaluates to Unknown if any of the matching columns contains a null because a null is always handled as an unknown value when we evaluate row functions.

In step 3, all of these rows of the cross join are dropped.

- **Inner joins are symmetric. The order in which the tables are joined does not matter. Expressed mathematically:**
  $$A \times B = B \times A$$
  and $\quad (A \times B) \times C = A \times (B \times C)$

The symmetry of inner joins occurs because each of the steps in the definition is symmetric.

In step 1, the cross join is symmetric. That is, "A cross join B" is equal to "B cross join A." This is because a cross join creates all possible combinations of the rows. It does not consider the order of the tables.

Step 2 evaluates the join condition statement. It does not know or care which table came first.

Step 3 drops all the rows of the cross join that do not evaluate to True. This has no reference to the order of the tables.

Step 4 drops the evaluation column. The order of the tables plays no role here.

16-5 An error in the join condition can appear to be a cross join

One frequent type of error that occurs in SQL is omission of one of the join conditions within the `where` clause. The result of this often resembles a cross product. You may see the data you expected, but then see it repeated many times. For example, if you were expecting to have 100 rows in the result, you may find that you have 2,000, with each of the rows you wanted repeated 20 times.

If you see this, do not panic. Just examine your `where` clause carefully to be sure it contains all the conditions it needs. Sometimes you might not be sure if a condition is needed or not. It may seem redundant and unnecessary. Putting extra conditions in the `where` clause may cause more processing to occur, but at least the results are accurate. Putting too few conditions in the `where` clause can produce the wrong results. When in doubt, add extra conditions to the `where` clause.

As you write SQL, you should pay attention to the size of your tables and know approximately how much data to expect. If your results do not meet your expectations, you can search for possible coding errors.

In the following example, there is a mistake in the first version of the SQL. The join between the `l_lunch_items` table and the `l_foods` table is incorrect. This join should match on two columns, `supplier_id` and `product_code`, but the condition that the product codes are equal has been left out of the `where` clause.

The effect of the mistake in this example is subtle. When we look at the result table, we might notice that the values in the `supplier_id` column are repeated several times. That gives us a hint that there could be an error.

The repetition is due to a cross join, which occurs because we have left one of the join conditions out of the `where` clause. To confirm our suspicions, we could ask how many items are expected in lunch 2. By looking at the `l_lunch_items` table, we would find that there should be four items in this lunch, but the result table lists eight items, so we know there is an error somewhere.

The first thing I would do in this situation would be to review all the join conditions in the `where` clause. In this case, that would solve the problem.

The effect of the error is that when someone orders one item from a supplier, they get all the items offered by that supplier.

Task

Show an example of SQL that contains an error. Leave one of the join conditions out of the `where` clause. Show how we might detect this error.

For lunch 2, list the `lunch_id`, `supplier_id`, `product_code`, `description`, `price`, and `quantity` columns. Use the `l_foods` table and the `l_lunch_items` table.

Oracle & Access SQL: Join is wrong

```
select a.lunch_id,
       b.supplier_id,
       b.product_code,
       b.description,
       b.price,
       a.quantity
from l_lunch_items a,
     l_foods b
where a.supplier_id = b.supplier_id
  and a.lunch_id = 2;
```

Incorrect result table

```
            SUPPLIER  PRODUCT
LUNCH_ID    ID        CODE     DESCRIPTION              PRICE     QUANTITY
---------   --------  -------  --------------------     --------  ---------
        2   ASP       FS       FRESH SALAD              $2.00            2
        2   ASP       SP       SOUP OF THE DAY          $1.50            2
        2   ASP       SW       SANDWICH                 $3.50            2
        2   FRV       BR       BROCCOLI                 $1.00            1
        2   FRV       FF       FRENCH FRIES             $1.50            1
        2   JBR       AS       SODA                     $1.25            2
        2   JBR       VR       COFFEE                   $0.85            2
        2   VSB       AS       DESSERT                  $3.00            1
```

Oracle & Access SQL: Join is correct

```
select a.lunch_id,
       b.supplier_id,
       b.product_code,
       b.description,
       b.price,
       a.quantity
from 1_lunch_items a,
     1_foods b
where a.supplier_id = b.supplier_id
  and a.product_code = b.product_code
  and a.lunch_id = 2;
```

Correct result table

```
            SUPPLIER  PRODUCT
LUNCH_ID    ID        CODE     DESCRIPTION              PRICE     QUANTITY
--------    --------  -------  --------------------     -----------  ---------
        2   ASP       SW       SANDWICH                 $3.50            2
        2   FRV       FF       FRENCH FRIES             $1.50            1
        2   JBR       VR       COFFEE                   $0.85            2
        2   VSB       AS       DESSERT                  $3.00            1
```

16-6   Using a cross join to list all the possible combinations

Sometimes we might want to list all the possible combinations of several factors. This occurs mostly when we are trying to analyze a complex situation or when we just want to be sure we have considered all the possibilities.

For example, suppose I have decided to buy a new car. I plan to spend some time shopping for it, so I get exactly the one I want. I know that salesmen are going to try to get me to make a purchase before I have completed all my shopping, so I want to set up a framework, a checklist, for myself.

I have decided to look at four types of cars: Ford, Toyota, Volkswagen, and Chevy. I want to look at three colors: white, red, and green. I could make two lists:

Car Type
Ford
Toyota
Volkswagen
Chevy

Color
White
Red
Green

Then I could arrange the options as a two-dimensional grid:

	White	Red	Green
Ford			
Toyota			
Volkswagen			
Chevy			

Or I could use a cross join to create a table of all the combinations. This table has 12 rows. The first few are as follows:

Car Type	Color
Ford	White
Ford	Red
Ford	Green
Toyota	White
Toyota	Red

It might seem that the two-dimensional layout is the easiest to use. It is more compact than the format generated by the cross join. The problem is that it is limited to handling only two factors and it cannot easily handle additional factors. In contrast, the cross join layout is able to handle any number of factors without any changes.

For example, suppose I also decide to look at two-door cars and four-door cars. I want to add this factor into my shopping. With the cross join approach, this is easy to do.

I get 24 rows in the table I create with the cross join. The first few are as follows:

Car Type	Color	Doors
Ford	White	2
Ford	White	4
Ford	Red	2
Ford	Red	4
Ford	Green	2

Task

Use a cross join to list all the combinations of the following factors: car_type and color.

Oracle & Access SQL

```
select a.car_type,
       b.color
from sec1606_car_types a,
     sec1606_colors b
order by a.car_type,
         b.color;
```

Beginning tables
sec1606_car_types table   **sec1606_colors table**

CAR_TYPE		COLOR
----------		-------
FORD		WHITE
TOYOTA		RED
VOLKSWAGEN		GREEN
CHEVY		

Result table

CAR_TYPE	COLOR
----------	----------
CHEVY	GREEN
CHEVY	RED
CHEVY	WHITE
FORD	GREEN
FORD	RED
FORD	WHITE
TOYOTA	GREEN
TOYOTA	RED
TOYOTA	WHITE
VOLKSWAGEN	GREEN
VOLKSWAGEN	RED
VOLKSWAGEN	WHITE

16-7   Avoid a cross join of large tables

Never perform a cross join of two large tables! This can bring even a large computer to its knees. It can use up a large amount of the computer's resources and cost a lot of money. It probably will not give you anything useful anyway.

There have been a few times in my career as a programmer when I considered doing a cross join on some large tables. Usually I was searching for something, I had been working on a problem for several days, and using a cross join seemed to be the only solution.

In every one of those cases, after a bit more thought, I was able to avoid the cross join or at least limit it to a few small tables. Before you do a cross join take a good look at the tables you are going to join. If there are any rows you can eliminate from these tables, you should do so. I have always found that I only needed a small part of the entire table.

If you first create new tables that have only a few rows of the original large table, then it is okay to perform a cross join on those small tables.

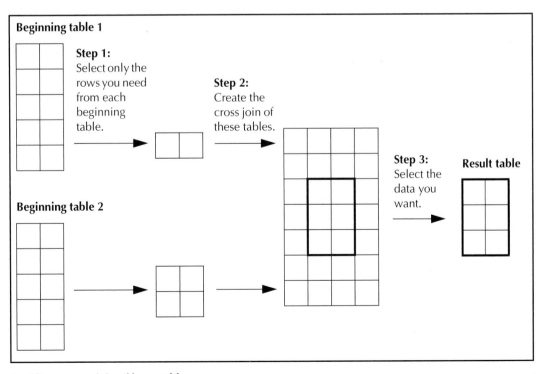

Avoiding a cross join of large tables.

Self Joins

A self join is any inner or outer join in which a table is joined with itself. Many database designers consider self joins to be confusing and unintuitive, so they try to avoid them. Most databases are designed so that self joins are rarely needed for everyday tasks. However, using a self join can provide information that cannot be obtained in any other way.

16-8   Why join a table with itself

It does not seem to make sense to join a table with itself

When we work on a problem, one of the first things we decide is which tables are needed. To make this decision, we think about the tables as containing certain kinds of information — one table contains information about food, another table contains information about employees. Joining a table with itself seems to just give us two copies of the same thing. It doesn't seem to give us any more information, so it does not seem to make any sense.

Why it does make sense

All databases, Oracle and Access included, process one row of a table at a time. You can access all the columns within a row, but only within one row. If we need information from two different rows at the same time, then it is necessary to join the table with itself.

How it is done

We can think about a self join as if we have two separate tables. They just happen to be identical. In the `from` clause the table is listed twice. The two copies are distinguished by giving each one a separate table alias.

We only need to have one copy of the table stored on the disk. The computer software is able to behave as if we had two separate copies of it. If we are using a view instead of a table, that view only needs to be defined once.

In the following example, the beginning table contains a G and an H in column 1 (`col_1`). They are in different rows, so the computer cannot use both of them at the same time. However, in the result table of the cross join, there are two rows containing both G and H. From this table the computer can use both G and H at the same time.

Within the SQL, we see that the same table is listed twice in the `from` clause. Each time it is listed we give it a different table alias. The first table alias is A and the second one is B.

Task

Form a cross join of a table with itself.

Oracle & Access SQL

```
select a.col_1,
       a.col_2,
       b.col_1 as col_3,
       b.col_2 as col_4
from sec1608 a,
     sec1608 b;
```

Beginning table (`sec1608` table)

COL_1	COL_2
G	1
H	2
I	3
J	4

Result table (Cross join of the `sec1608` table with itself)

COL_1	COL_2	COL_3	COL_4	
G	1	G	1	
H	2	G	1	❶
I	3	G	1	
J	4	G	1	
G	1	H	2	❶
H	2	H	2	
I	3	H	2	
J	4	H	2	
G	1	I	3	
H	2	I	3	
I	3	I	3	
J	4	I	3	
G	1	J	4	
H	2	J	4	
I	3	J	4	
J	4	J	4	

Notes

❶ These two lines both include G and H.

16-9   An example of a self join

This section shows you an example of a self join. We want to list information about the employee and the manager on the same row of a report. The problem is that the information about the manager is in a different row from the information about the employee. So, we need to use two different rows of the table at the same time. We might picture the situation like this:

Employee ID	Last Name	Phone	Manager ID
XXXXX	XXXXX	XXXXX	⬭	employee information
⬭	XXXXX	XXXXX		manager information

Next, we change the picture above to a different form. The next depiction shows two tables being joined. They are placed side by side and the join condition is shown. The join condition is that the value in the Manager ID column of the first table equals the value in the Employee ID column of the second table. These two tables just happen to be identical. That is what makes this a self join. Now all the information we need is in a single row.

Employee Information table (emp):
First copy of 1_employees table

Employee ID	Last Name	Phone	Manager ID
XXXXX	XXXXX	XXXXX	⬭

Manager Information table (boss):
Second copy of 1_employees table

Employee ID	Last Name	Phone	Manager ID
⬭	XXXXX	XXXXX	

In the SQL, the `l_employees` table is joined to itself. The first copy is given the table alias `emp`, meaning that employee information is taken from this copy of the table. The second copy is given the table alias `boss`, meaning that manager information is taken from this copy of the table. The computer only needs a single copy of the table, but it acts as if it has two separate copies.

The preceding depiction shows that the join condition is

```
emp.manager_id = boss.employee_id
```

A left outer join is used because we want to include all the employees, even those who do not currently have a manager.

Task

From the `l_employees` table, list the employee ID, last name, and phone number of each employee with the name and phone number of their manager. Include a row for each employee, even those who do not have a manager. Sort the rows by the `employee_id` column.

Oracle SQL

```
select emp.employee_id,
       emp.last_name,
       emp.phone_number,
       boss.last_name as manager_name,
       boss.phone_number as manager_phone
from l_employees emp,
     l_employees boss
where emp.manager_id = boss.employee_id (+)
order by emp.employee_id;
```

Oracle9i & Access SQL

```
select emp.employee_id,
       emp.last_name,
       emp.phone_number,
       boss.last_name as manager_name,
       boss.phone_number as manager_phone
from 1_employees emp
     left outer join 1_employees boss
     on emp.manager_id = boss.employee_id
order by emp.employee_id;
```

Beginning table (1_employees table)

EMPLOYEE ID	FIRST_NAME	LAST_NAME	DEPT CODE	HIRE_DATE	CREDIT LIMIT	PHONE NUMBER	MANAGER ID
201	SUSAN	BROWN	EXE	01-JUN-1998	$30.00	3484	(null)
202	JIM	KERN	SAL	16-AUG-1999	$25.00	8722	201
203	MARTHA	WOODS	SHP	02-FEB-2004	$25.00	7591	201
204	ELLEN	OWENS	SAL	01-JUL-2003	$15.00	6830	202
205	HENRY	PERKINS	SAL	01-MAR-2000	$25.00	5286	202
206	CAROL	ROSE	ACT	(null)	(null)	(null)	(null)
207	DAN	SMITH	SHP	01-DEC-2004	$25.00	2259	203
208	FRED	CAMPBELL	SHP	01-APR-2003	$25.00	1752	203
209	PAULA	JACOBS	MKT	17-MAR-1999	$15.00	3357	201
210	NANCY	HOFFMAN	SAL	16-FEB-2004	$25.00	2974	203

Result table

EMPLOYEE ID	LAST_NAME	PHONE NUMBER	MANAGER_NAME	MANAGER_PHONE
201	BROWN	3484	(null)	(null)
202	KERN	8722	BROWN	3484
203	WOODS	7591	BROWN	3484
204	OWENS	6830	KERN	8722
205	PERKINS	5286	KERN	8722
206	ROSE	(null)	(null)	(null)
207	SMITH	2259	WOODS	7591
208	CAMPBELL	1752	WOODS	7591
209	JACOBS	3357	BROWN	3484
210	HOFFMAN	2974	WOODS	7591

16-10   Generating the numbers from 0 to 999

This section shows you how to create a table containing all the numbers from 0 to 999. To do this we will use both a self join and a cross join. We will cross join a table with itself. With this technique, you can create as many numbers as you want.

First, we create a table of all the digits, all the numbers from 0 to 9. Then, we create another table from this by using a `select` statement.

We have already been using a table of numbers from 0 to 99. I created this table for you. Here you will see how to create a table like this for yourself whenever you want one.

In the first step, a table is created to contain all the digits. Oracle and Access must use their own datatypes, `number` for Oracle and `smallint` for Access. Otherwise, the SQL is the same. At this point, the table contains no data.

In the second step, the data is put into the table. There are only 10 records, so this is easy. The SQL is exactly the same in Oracle and Access.

In the third step, this table of digits is used to create a new table containing the numbers from 0 to 999. The table, `numbers_0_to_9`, is cross joined with itself. You can see this self join in the `from` clause, which lists the table three times. The first copy of the table is given the table alias `a`, the second copy is given the table alias `b`, and the third copy is given the table alias `c`. The result of this join is every combination of three digits.

The `select` clause turns each combination of three digits into a single, three-digit number. It multiplies the first digit by 100, and the second digit by 10. Then it adds up all the numbers to get a single three-digit number. For example,

three digits: 3,   4,   5

become one number: $(3 \times 100) + (4 \times 10) + 5 = 345$

This much of the third step is the same in both Oracle and Access. However, they differ in their techniques to save these results in a table.

Task

Create a table with all the numbers from 0 to 999. First, create a table of the numbers from 0 to 9. Then cross join it with itself.

Oracle SQL: Step 1 — Create a table to contain all 10 digits

```
drop table numbers_0_to_9
create table numbers_0_to_9
(digit     number(1));
```

Access SQL: Step 1 — Create a table to contain all 10 digits

```
drop table numbers_0_to_9
create table numbers_0_to_9
(digit     smallint);
```

Oracle & Access SQL: Step 2 — Put data in the table

```
insert into numbers_0_to_9 values (0);
insert into numbers_0_to_9 values (1);
insert into numbers_0_to_9 values (2);
insert into numbers_0_to_9 values (3);
insert into numbers_0_to_9 values (4);
insert into numbers_0_to_9 values (5);
insert into numbers_0_to_9 values (6);
insert into numbers_0_to_9 values (7);
insert into numbers_0_to_9 values (8);
insert into numbers_0_to_9 values (9);
```

Created table (numbers_0_to_9 table)

```
    DIGIT
---------
        0
        1
        2
        3
        4
        5
        6
        7
        8
        9
```

Oracle SQL: Step 3 — Create a table of numbers from 0 to 999

```
drop table numbers_0_to_999
create table numbers_0_to_999 as
select ((a.digit * 100) + (b.digit * 10) + c.digit) as n
from numbers_0_to_9 a,
     numbers_0_to_9 b,
     numbers_0_to_9 c;
```

Access SQL: Step 3 — Create a table of numbers from 0 to 999

```
drop table numbers_0_to_999
select ((a.digit * 100) + (b.digit * 10) + c.digit) as n
into numbers_0_to_999
from numbers_0_to_9 a,
     numbers_0_to_9 b,
     numbers_0_to_9 c;
```

Created table (numbers_0_to_999 table)

```
          N
---------
          0
          1
etc
        999
```

16-11 Numbering the lines of a report in Oracle and Access

Sometimes you have a report in which the lines are sorted in a particular order. You may want to number these lines in the order in which they appear. To do this, you can create a new column that contains the line numbers.

Both Oracle and Access have special features to help you do this, but these features work differently.

The Oracle method

1. Create a new view from the beginning `select` statement. Oracle allows us to keep the `order by` clause in a view.

2. Use `rownum` to add a column of line numbers.

The Access method

1. Create a new table from the beginning `select` statement. Access allows us to keep the `order by` clause.

2. Add a new column with the `alter table` command. Give the new column the datatype `counter`. This assigns the numbers automatically.

Task

The following `select` statement creates a report. All the lines of the report are sorted in a particular order. We want to number the lines of this report sequentially, beginning with the number one.

```
select price,
        description
from 1_foods
where price > 1.75
order by price,
        description;
```

Beginning report

```
     PRICE DESCRIPTION
----------- ---------------
     $2.00 FRESH SALAD
     $2.50 HAMBURGER
     $3.00 DESSERT
     $3.50 SANDWICH
     $6.00 GRILLED STEAK
```

Oracle SQL:
Step 1 — Create a view that includes an `order by` clause

```
create or replace view sec1611 as
select price,
        description
from 1_foods
where price > 1.75
order by price,
        description;
```

Oracle SQL:
Step 2 — Use `rownum` to create the line numbers

```
select rownum as line_number,
       a.*
from sec1611 a
order by rownum;
```

Access SQL:
Step 1 — Create a table that includes an `order by` clause

```
select price,
       description
into sec1611
from l_foods
where price > 1.75
order by price,
         description;
```

Access SQL: Step 2 — Add a column of line numbers ❶

```
alter table sec1611
add column line_number counter;
```

Result table

```
LINE_NUMBER       PRICE DESCRIPTION
----------- ----------- ----------------
          1      $2.00 FRESH SALAD
          2      $2.50 HAMBURGER
          3      $3.00 DESSERT
          4      $3.50 SANDWICH
          5      $6.00 GRILLED STEAK
```

Notes

❶ In Access, this code will make the line numbers the last column.

Summary

In this chapter we discussed cross joins and self joins. A cross join of two tables contains all possible combinations of a row from one table with a row from the other table. To code a cross join, you write an inner join with no join condition and no `where` clause.

Cross joins are useful in several ways. They help us understand inner joins with more precision. If you get a cross join in a result table that you did not intend, then you might have left one of the join conditions out of the `where` clause. You should avoid performing a cross join of large tables, but sometimes it is useful to create a cross join of small tables.

A self join is a join of a table with itself that allows you to access information from several rows of the table at the same time.

Exercises

1. Goal: Use a cross join to list all combinations.

    a. See section 16-6.

    b. Use a cross join to create a table having all combinations of
    Ice cream: chocolate, vanilla, coffee, strawberry
    Sauce: hot fudge, butterscotch, chocolate
    Nuts: peanuts, pecans, almonds, no nuts
    Cherry: cherry, no cherry

    First you need to create a table for each of these lists of options. (Hint: You will get 96 rows.)

2. Goal: Use a self join.

    a. See section 16-9.

    b. Determine if any employee is working for a manager who was hired after that employee was hired. Show the `employee_id`, `first_name`, and `hire_date` of both the employee and the manager.

    c. List the lunch IDs of the lunches that include both coffee and dessert. First create a view containing the `lunch_id` and `description` for all the orders of either coffee or dessert. Then join this view with itself to find all the lunches that include both items.

COMBINING TABLES IN A PRODUCTION DATABASE

Congratulations! If you have read this far, you have finished all the topics that I cover in detail. The last four chapters of this book round out the discussion and place that material in context. The viewpoint changes here to a broader perspective and less detail.

Chapter 17 discusses some of the challenges in combining tables within a production-sized system, which is a much larger system than those we have discussed until now.

Chapter 18 discusses the `if-then-else` functions, parameter queries, and subqueries. These are important topics that I have not covered yet because they did not fit into the framework of our discussion so far.

Chapter 19 discusses the multiuser environment. Most databases are shared environments that many people use at the same time. This environment is set up by the DBAs, but you can work more effectively if you understand how it is done.

Chapter 20 discusses the design of SQL and what the language is attempting to achieve. It also discusses forms and reports, which have become the way many people interact with a database.

Methods of Joining Three or More Tables

When you need to join three or more tables for a query, the method I recommend is to use a series of steps and combine the tables two at a time. The first step combines two of the tables and saves the result as a view. The next step combines that view with one more table and creates another view. This is repeated as many times as necessary.

This method gives you maximum control. It is less prone to errors than other methods. If errors do occur, they are easier to find and fix. If your query takes a long time to run, you can time and monitor each step individually.

To keep this process as efficient as possible for the computer, particularly if you run some of the steps individually, you should select the data you want as early in the process as possible. The idea is to keep the size of your tables as small as possible so the computer does not have to handle a lot of rows that you will later discard.

That is my recommendation, but there is another school of thought. Some people like to write a single `select` statement that joins all their tables and selects all their data at the same time.

17-1   Joining several tables in a series of steps

Here is an example of code that joins two tables at a time in a series of steps. This is the technique I recommend.

Task

For the lunch on November 16, 2005, list all the foods served, the quantities, the total price of each food, and who will be eating the lunches. The price increases will be in effect and 10 cents will be added to the price when the price increase is null. List the following columns:

```
employee_id
first_name
last_name
food
quantity
total_price
```

Oracle SQL

```
create or replace view sec1701a as
select a.employee_id,
       a.first_name,
       a.last_name,
       b.lunch_id
from l_employees a,
     l_lunches b
where a.employee_id = b.employee_id
  and b.lunch_date = '16-nov-2005';


create or replace view sec1701b as
select a.*,
       b.supplier_id,
       b.product_code,
       b.quantity
from sec1701a a,
     l_lunch_items b
where a.lunch_id = b.lunch_id;


create or replace view sec1701c as
select a.*,
       b.description as food,
       b.price+nvl(b.price_increase,.10) as new_price
from sec1701b a,
     l_foods b
where a.supplier_id = b.supplier_id
  and a.product_code = b.product_code;


select employee_id,
       first_name,
       last_name,
       food,
       quantity,
       new_price * quantity as total_price
from sec1701c
order by employee_id,
         food;
```

Access SQL

The Access code is very similar, and I encourage you to write your own. Remember that Access does not have `create view`, so you have to create saved queries using the GUI.

Result table

EMPLOYEE ID	FIRST NAME	LAST NAME	FOOD	QUANTITY	TOTAL_PRICE
201	SUSAN	BROWN	COFFEE	2	$2.00
201	SUSAN	BROWN	FRESH SALAD	1	$2.25
201	SUSAN	BROWN	SANDWICH	2	$7.80
202	JIM	KERN	COFFEE	2	$2.00
202	JIM	KERN	DESSERT	1	$3.50
202	JIM	KERN	FRENCH FRIES	1	$1.60
202	JIM	KERN	GRILLED STEAK	1	$6.70
202	JIM	KERN	SOUP OF THE DAY	1	$1.60
203	MARTHA	WOODS	COFFEE	1	$1.00
203	MARTHA	WOODS	FRENCH FRIES	1	$1.60
203	MARTHA	WOODS	FRESH SALAD	1	$2.25
203	MARTHA	WOODS	GRILLED STEAK	1	$6.70
203	MARTHA	WOODS	SODA	1	$1.50
204	ELLEN	OWENS	FRENCH FRIES	1	$1.60
204	ELLEN	OWENS	HAMBURGER	2	$5.60
204	ELLEN	OWENS	SODA	2	$3.00
204	ELLEN	OWENS	SOUP OF THE DAY	2	$3.20
207	DAN	SMITH	COFFEE	2	$2.00
207	DAN	SMITH	DESSERT	1	$3.50
207	DAN	SMITH	FRENCH FRIES	1	$1.60
207	DAN	SMITH	SANDWICH	2	$7.80
210	NANCY	HOFFMAN	COFFEE	1	$1.00
210	NANCY	HOFFMAN	DESSERT	1	$3.50
210	NANCY	HOFFMAN	FRESH SALAD	1	$2.25
210	NANCY	HOFFMAN	GRILLED STEAK	1	$6.70
210	NANCY	HOFFMAN	SOUP OF THE DAY	1	$1.60

17-2   Joining several tables at once in the `where` clause

This section shows all the tables being joined within one `select` statement. This is a style of coding that I do not recommend, because it can get too complex.

Task

The task here is the same as section 17-1.

Oracle SQL

```
select a.employee_id,
       a.first_name,
       a.last_name,
       d.description as food,
       c.quantity,
       ((d.price + nvl(d.price_increase,.10))
          * c.quantity)                   as total_price
from l_employees a,
     l_lunches b,
     l_lunch_items c,
     l_foods d
where a.employee_id = b.employee_id
  and b.lunch_date = '16-nov-2005'
  and b.lunch_id = c.lunch_id
  and c.supplier_id = d.supplier_id
  and c.product_code = d.product_code
order by a.employee_id,
         d.description;
```

Access SQL

For Access, just change the `nvl` function to an nz function and enclose the date in pound signs.

17-3   Joining several tables at once in the `from` clause

This is a variation of the code in section 17-2. The difference here is that the join condition is written in the `from` clause rather than the `where` clause. Note that with this new syntax, the syntax itself forces you to join two tables at a time. This is done in a nesting arrangement, which you can see in the code.

Task

The task here is the same as section 17-1.

Oracle8i SQL

Oracle8i does not support writing a join condition in the `from` clause.

Oracle9i SQL

```
select a.employee_id,
       a.first_name,
       a.last_name,
       d.description as food,
       c.quantity,
       ((d.price + nvl(d.price_increase,.10))
       * c.quantity)                     as total_price
from ((l_employees a
     inner join l_lunches b
     on a.employee_id = b.employee_id)
        inner join l_lunch_items c
        on b.lunch_id = c.lunch_id)
           inner join l_foods d
           on c.supplier_id = d.supplier_id
           and c.product_code = d.product_code
where b.lunch_date = '16-nov-2005'
order by a.employee_id,
         d.description;
```

Access SQL

```
select a.employee_id,
       a.first_name,
       a.last_name,
       d.description as food,
       c.quantity,
       ((d.price + nz(d.price_increase,.10))
          * c.quantity)                as total_price
from ((1_employees a
      inner join 1_lunches b
      on a.employee_id = b.employee_id)
         inner join 1_lunch_items c
         on b.lunch_id = c.lunch_id)
            inner join 1_foods d
            on c.supplier_id = d.supplier_id
            and c.product_code = d.product_code
where b.lunch_date = #16-nov-2005#
order by a.employee_id,
         d.description;
```

Result table — Same as in section 17-1

Losing Information

One of the things we need to think carefully about when we join several tables together is what data might be lost in the process. Inner joins, left outer joins, and right outer joins can all lose information. Only a full outer join always preserves all the information.

17-4   Be careful with an inner join

An inner join can lose more data than any other type of join. A row from one of the beginning tables is lost unless there is a matching row in *every* other table. If any of the tables has a null in a column used in the join condition, then some data may be lost. The only time we can be certain an inner join will not lose any information is when Referential Integrity protects the join condition between the tables. The more tables you use in an inner join, the greater the chance of losing data.

Some aspects of inner joins do make them easy to use. When we use an inner join we do not need to be concerned about which table comes first and which comes second. The same result is produced either way. This is sometimes expressed as

A inner join B = B inner join A

Also, when we combine three or more tables with inner joins, the order in which we combine them does not matter. The result is always the same. This is sometimes expressed as

(A inner join B) inner join C = A inner join (B inner join C)

17-5   Be careful with a left and right outer join

A left and right outer join restores some of the information lost by an inner join, but it does not restore all of the lost data. Of course, a left outer join and a right outer join are the same thing except for the order of the tables, so I am talking about one type of join here, not two different types. This means that we can turn all right outer joins into left outer joins by changing the order of the tables.

A left (or right) outer join of two tables is fairly straightforward and easy to understand. However, things get trickier when we use left outer joins to combine three or more tables. The order in which we combine the tables can make a difference — which two tables are joined first, which one is third, which one is fourth, and so on. This subtle difference can cause errors that are not easy to detect.

17-6   A full outer join preserves all the information

A full outer join does not lose any information. It keeps all the information in all of the tables. This is nice from the perspective of the application programmer. On the other hand, it requires more computing resources, so use it only when you need to.

Full outer joins also have the nice properties of inner joins. We do not need to be concerned about which table comes first and which one comes second. That is,

A full outer join B = B full outer join A

Also, when we combine three or more tables with full outer joins, the order in which we combine them does not matter. The result is always the same. That is,

(A full outer join B) full outer join C = A full outer join (B full outer join C)

17-7 A full outer join of several tables

Because full outer joins preserve all of the information, why don't we use them all of the time? Some people do. This can be a good practice, particularly when you are working with several small tables that are often not completely consistent with each other.

In general, we are discouraged from using full outer joins all the time, particularly when we are working with large tables. Why? A full outer join requires more computer resources to process than an inner join. Sometimes people are trying to protect the computer when they tell you not to use a full outer join.

When I am developing new code and working with tables I am not completely familiar with, I use a full outer join whenever I think I might need one. When I create code that will run frequently — every day, every week, or even once a month, then I try to use inner joins whenever I can.

People sometimes ask me how to combine three or more tables with full outer joins. If you do it as a series of steps, it is simple and easy to do. The following task shows an example of how to do this. If you try to do it all in one `select` statement, it will be quite difficult.

Task

Join three tables: `l_employees`, `l_departments`, and `l_lunches`. Join all the tables with full outer joins.

The point here is the technique of writing the SQL code, so I won't show you the beginning tables and result table.

Oracle SQL

```
/* step 1: create a full outer join from two of the tables
*/


create or replace view sec1707a as
select a.*,
       b.lunch_id,
       b.lunch_date,
       b.date_entered
from l_employees a,
     l_lunches b
where a.employee_id = b.employee_id (+)
union
select a.*,
       b.lunch_id,
       b.lunch_date,
       b.date_entered
from l_employees a,
     l_lunches b
where a.employee_id (+) = b.employee_id;




/* step 2: create a full outer join from the results of
step 1 and the third table
*/


create or replace view sec1707b as
select a.*,
       b.department_name
from sec1707a a,
     l_departments b
where a.dept_code = b.dept_code (+)
union
select a.*,
       b.department_name
from sec1707a a,
     l_departments b
where a.dept_code (+) = b.dept_code;
```

Access SQL

Step 1: Enter this code in the SQL window:

```
select a.*,
       b.lunch_id,
       b.lunch_date,
       b.date_entered
from l_employees a
     left outer join l_lunches b
     on a.employee_id = b.employee_id
union
select a.*,
       b.lunch_id,
       b.lunch_date,
       b.date_entered
from l_employees a
     right outer join l_lunches b
     on where a.employee_id = b.employee_id;
```

Step 2: Save this query. Name it sec1707a.
Step 3: Enter this query in the SQL window:

```
select a.*,
       b.department_name
from sec1707a a,
     l_departments b
where a.dept_code = b.dept_code (+)
union
select a.*,
       b.department_name
from sec1707a a,
     l_departments b
where a.dept_code (+) = b.dept_code;
```

Step 4: Save this query. Name it sec1707b.

Caring About the Efficiency of Your Computer

If you are going to combine several large tables together, you should be aware of the effect this might have on your computer. If you are running on your own computer, your query might take a long time to run. Some queries can run for several hours.

If you are running on a computer you share, a long-running query can affect the other people using the computer and it can cost a lot of money.

17-8   Monitor your queries

It is a good idea to monitor your queries in some way, particularly when you are handling several large tables. I consider a table to be large when it has more than 100,000 rows.

It is good to have an approximate idea of the number of rows of the beginning tables, the number of rows you expect in the result, and how long you expect the query to run. If you expected a result in less than two minutes and your query has been running for more than 20 minutes, you might want to stop the processing and examine your code.

In many shops you can also monitor the cost of your queries. This is an approximate measure of the amount of computer resources required to process the query. Do not try to be too precise about the cost, because the accounting procedures that produce the cost are usually not very accurate.

Sometimes you might want to ask for help from another programmer or your DBA. The next sections may also give you some hints.

17-9   Use the indexes

One way to improve the efficiency of your queries is to use the indexes that the database has. You need to find out which columns have indexes on them. Try to use those columns in your join conditions and when you place selection conditions in the `where` clause. Most databases already have indexes on all the columns intended for use in join conditions.

Here is one of my experiences involving indexes. Once I was writing some queries at a large company and every time I wrote a query using a particular table, the query would time out. When a query times out, this means that the query has processed in the computer for the maximum time allowed, which was about an hour at that shop. So when I submitted one of these queries, it would run for an hour, then I would get an error message from the operating system, no result table, and a bill for $3,000.

I investigated this by going to the Data Dictionary and looking for the indexes on the table. I found that an index was missing. I told the DBA, and within two days the index was built. Then my queries ran in just a few minutes.

17-10   Select the data you want early in the process

Another way to improve the efficiency of your queries is to select the data you want early in the process. Make the beginning tables as small as possible before you join them. In other words, don't ask the computer to handle rows of data that you know you will not use.

This is fairly simple to do if you organize your code as a series of steps. Just put steps at the beginning that eliminate some of the rows from each beginning table.

If the optimizer always worked perfectly, it would do this for you automatically. But most optimizers are not that smart yet, so it is worthwhile for you to try doing it yourself.

17-11   Use a table to save summarized data

Sometimes we may develop a small amount of data, perhaps a few thousand rows, from several tables that are much larger, and using a query that runs for an hour. If we anticipate using this information several times or if we intend to do some complex manipulations on it, then we might want to save it in a table rather than a view.

If we saved it as a view, the information would need to be created afresh each time we wanted to use it. By saving it in a table we know that it only needs to be created once.

We did this at a company I worked for. The company had more than 10,000 employees and an accounting system that kept track of every penny each person spent. There were 2,000,000 rows of data generated each month. Once a month we would summarize these expenses into 500 categories and save the data in a table. Then we would run all the monthly budgeting reports from the summarized data in that table, instead of running them from the raw data.

17-12   Try several ways of writing the SQL

Suppose you have a long-running query that is scheduled to process regularly — daily, weekly, or even monthly. You might try to write the SQL in several different ways to see if you can find one way that is more efficient than the others. For instance, you might try combining the tables in a different order, or you might try using a subquery instead of a join. This type of experimentation is not worth doing if the query is only run occasionally, but it can pay off when the query is run many times.

Standardizing the Way That Tables Are Joined

You should seldom have to invent ways to join tables. You should just follow the pattern that has already been set up by the designers of the database. If a view has been created that joins all the tables together, then you can use that view to get information as if it were a single table.

17-13 The joins are part of the database design

Usually the people who design the database tables also design a way for those tables to be joined. You should almost always follow their design. You should not have to guess or make things up yourself. However, this information is not always communicated very clearly.

Sometimes the names of the columns suggest how to make the join. All the columns with identical names should be joined. Sometimes you can look at code other people have written to see what join conditions they used. Your DBA may be able to help. Rarely will it be worthwhile to try to find the documents from the database design team. Occasionally, the database may have changed and evolved, which could mean that you will need to use a different join condition.

17-14 A view can standardize the way tables are joined

If the tables in a database are fairly small, we can set up one view that combines the data from all of the tables. Then anyone who wants information from the database can select it from this one view. It is as if the whole database were one table. The following example creates a view like this for the `Lunches` database.

If the database contains several large tables, we usually do not combine them into a single view because that could consume too much of the computer's resources. However, we might create a few views that combine two or three of the tables at a time.

The view created in this section contains all the employees, even the ones who are not attending any of the lunches. It also contains all the foods, even the one that has not been ordered. However, it contains only the departments that have employees in them and only the suppliers that are supplying foods on the current menu.

Task

Create a single view that combines all the tables of the Lunches database. Name this view all_lunches.

Oracle SQL

```
create or replace view sec1714a as
select a.*,
       b.department_name
from l_employees a,
     l_departments b
where a.dept_code = b.dept_code;


create or replace view sec1714b as
select a.*,
       b.business_name,
       b.business_start_date,
       b.lunch_budget,
       b.owner_name
from sec1714a a,
     l_constants b;


create or replace view sec1714c as
select a.*,
       b.lunch_id,
       b.lunch_date,
       b.date_entered
from sec1714b a,
     l_lunches b
where a.employee_id = b.employee_id (+);
```

```
create or replace view sec1714d as
select a.*,
       b.supplier_name
from l_foods a,
     l_suppliers b
where a.supplier_id = b.supplier_id (+);


create or replace view sec1714e as
select a.*,
       b.lunch_id,
       b.item_number,
       b.quantity
from sec1714d a,
     l_lunch_items b
where a.supplier_id = b.supplier_id (+)
  and a.product_code = b.product_code (+);


create or replace view all_lunches as
select a.*,
       b.supplier_id,
       b.product_code,
       b.menu_item,
       b.description,
       b.price,
       b.price_increase,
       b.supplier_name,
       b.item_number,
       b.quantity
from sec1714c a,
     sec1714e b
where a.lunch_id = b.lunch_id (+)
union
select a.*,
       b.supplier_id,
       b.product_code,
       b.menu_item,
       b.description,
       b.price,
       b.price_increase,
       b.supplier_name,
       b.item_number,
       b.quantity
from sec1714c a,
     sec1714e b
where a.lunch_id (+) = b.lunch_id;
```

Access SQL

Step 1: Enter this query in the SQL window:

```
select a.*,
       b.department_name
from l_employees a,
     l_departments b
where a.dept_code = b.dept_code;
```

Step 2: Save the query. Name it sec1714a.
Step 3: Enter this query in the SQL window:

```
select a.*,
       b.business_name,
       b.business_start_date,
       b.lunch_budget,
       b.owner_name
from sec1714a a,
     l_constants b;
```

Step 4: Save the query. Name it sec1714b.
Step 5: Enter this query in the SQL window:

```
select a.*,
       b.lunch_id,
       b.lunch_date,
       b.date_entered
from sec1714b a
     left outer join l_lunches b
     on a.employee_id = b.employee_id;
```

Step 6: Save the query. Name it sec1714c.
Step 7: Enter this query in the SQL window:

```
select a.*,
       b.supplier_name
from l_foods a
     left outer join l_suppliers b
     on a.supplier_id = b.supplier_id;
```

Step 8: Save the query. Name it sec1714d.
Step 9: Enter this query in the SQL window:

```
select a.*,
       b.lunch_id,
       b.item_number,
       b.quantity
from sec1714d a
     left outer join l_lunch_items b
     on a.supplier_id = b.supplier_id
        and a.product_code = b.product_code;
```

Step 10: Save the query. Name it sec1714e.
Step 11: Enter this query into the SQL window:

```
select a.*,
       b.supplier_id,
       b.product_code,
       b.menu_item,
       b.description,
       b.price,
       b.price_increase,
       b.supplier_name,
       b.item_number,
       b.quantity
from sec1714c a
     left outer join sec1714e b
     on a.lunch_id = b.lunch_id
union
select a.*,
       b.supplier_id,
       b.product_code,
       b.menu_item,
       b.description,
       b.price,
       b.price_increase,
       b.supplier_name,
       b.item_number,
       b.quantity
from sec1714c a
     right outer join sec1714e b
     on a.lunch_id = b.lunch_id;
```

Step 10: Save the query. Name it all_lunches.

Result table — The result table has 25 columns and 74 rows

17-15   Ad hoc reporting

Sometimes a database is called on to do things that it was never designed to do. Sometimes a business needs to respond to unforeseen changes. Maybe the currency rate has changed. Maybe congress is considering a new law and we need to estimate how it will affect the business. At such times the database can be looked on as a resource, a vast collection of data. People try to use the database to fill their immediate needs, even if it was not designed for that purpose. This is always a bit unreliable, but it can provide some information.

An ad hoc report is meant to run only once. The database can be used in some very creative ways. One of the features of a relational database that is supposed to help with ad hoc reporting is that it is possible to join tables together in ways that the designers never imagined.

Summary

When you are combining several tables it is important to do it carefully and in a way that is easy to debug. I think the best approach is usually to use a series of steps that combine two tables at a time. Carefully follow the way the tables in the database were designed to be joined with each other and watch out for the effects of nulls in the data.

The tables may be combined in many ways. You can use an inner join, three types of outer join, `union`, cross join, or self join. All the reporting that comes later depends on the way the tables have been combined, so it is important to make sure it has been done correctly. Because the data in the tables changes, it is important to write code that can deal with any data that could be put into the tables, not just the data that is there right now.

The two major problems when combining several tables are loss of data and using excessive computer resources. Loss of data can occur if the tables are not combined correctly. This is sometimes difficult to detect. The data just seems to disappear. It requires careful checking to make sure that you are getting all the data you think you should have.

Databases have often been accused of requiring excessive computer resources. It is hard to know if that is true or not. However, certainly if a query is to be run daily, we should pay attention to the amount of resources it consumes. Sometimes a small change can make a query run much more efficiently.

chapter 18

If-Then-Else and Subqueries

This chapter discusses three important topics that do not fit into the framework of the rest of the book. The first section discusses `if-then-else` logic. Oracle implements this with the `decode` function. Access uses the Immediate If (`iif`) function. These functions do not introduce any new power into SQL, but they make some queries easier to write.

The second topic is parameter queries. This type of query asks you some questions before it runs. For example, it might ask, "What are the beginning and ending dates?" The answers you provide are used to modify the SQL, so the result is tailored to your needs.

The last topic is subqueries. When one query is written inside another query, it is called a subquery. This was once considered to be the most important feature of SQL, but now its use has diminished and it is only used occasionally.

If-Then-Else Logic

The original design of SQL intentionally omitted the `if-then-else` and `goto` constructs. They were considered to add too much complexity. The objective was to keep the SQL language very simple and straightforward.

Sometimes people say that the `decode` function in Oracle introduces `if-then-else` logic into SQL. The examples in this section show what they mean by this statement. They imply that this makes SQL more powerful and capable of doing new things.

Actually, everything that can be done using this function can also be done using a `union`. No new capabilities are added. However, the `decode` function does make many SQL statements easier to write.

In Access, the Immediate If (`iif`) function can do everything that the `decode` function can do. In fact, it can do a little bit more.

18-1   The `decode` function in Oracle

The `decode` function is an extension that Oracle has added to standard SQL. It names some specific values that will be turned into other values. It performs a series of tests to determine whether the data in the column is equal to one of a few specific values. If one of these values is matched, it places a new value in the column. Otherwise, if none of the specific values is matched, it places a default value (else-value) in the column.

This is based on a series of tests for an Equal condition. It can also test for a Less Than or Greater Than condition by using a trick with the `sign` function that I show you in section 18-3.

Oracle syntax

```
DECODE(tested_value,
       if_1, then_1,
       if_2, then_2,
       ...
       default_value)
```

where

tested_value = a column of a table or a row function.

If tested_value equals if_1, then the decode function equals then_1.

If tested_value equals if_2, then the decode function equals then_2.

And so on.

If tested_value is not equal to any of the if values, then the decode function equals the last value, in the default_value position.

The if value, the then value, and the default_value may be:

A literal (of any data type)

A null

A column

A row function, using one or several columns in a single row

Task 1

Show an example using the decode function in Oracle. Substitute carrots for broccoli in the menu of lunch foods.

Oracle SQL

```
-- Override a value in one column.
select decode(description, ❶
              'broccoli', 'carrots', ❷
              description) as new_menu, ❸
       price
from l_foods;
```

Beginning table (1_foods table)

SUPPLIER ID	PRODUCT CODE	MENU ITEM	DESCRIPTION	PRICE	PRICE INCREASE
ASP	FS	1	FRESH SALAD	$2.00	$0.25
ASP	SP	2	SOUP OF THE DAY	$1.50	(null)
ASP	SW	3	SANDWICH	$3.50	$0.40
CBC	GS	4	GRILLED STEAK	$6.00	$0.70
CBC	SW	5	HAMBURGER	$2.50	$0.30
FRV	BR	6	BROCCOLI	$1.00	$0.05
FRV	FF	7	FRENCH FRIES	$1.50	(null)
JBR	AS	8	SODA	$1.25	$0.25
JBR	VR	9	COFFEE	$0.85	$0.15
VSB	AS	10	DESSERT	$3.00	$0.50

Result table

NEW_MENU	PRICE	
FRESH SALAD	$2.00	
SOUP OF THE DAY	$1.50	
SANDWICH	$3.50	
GRILLED STEAK	$6.00	
HAMBURGER	$2.50	
CARROTS	$1.00	❹
FRENCH FRIES	$1.50	
SODA	$1.25	
COFFEE	$0.85	
DESSERT	$3.00	

Notes

❶ The change is based on the data in the `description` column.

❷ If the value in the `description` column is `broccoli`, then change it to `carrots`.

❸ Otherwise, if the value in the `description` column is not `broccoli`, the value of this function is equal to the value in the `description` column.

❹ This is the row that was changed.

Task 2

The decode function in task 1 changed the value in a single column. To change several columns, we must use a separate decode function for each column. In addition to the changes we made in task 1, change the price of the carrots to $1.20.

Oracle SQL

```
-- Override the values in two columns.
select decode(description,
              'broccoli', 'carrots',
              description) as new_menu,
       decode(description, ❶
              'broccoli', 1.20, ❷
              price) as price ❸
from l_foods;
```

Result table

```
NEW_MENU                 PRICE
-------------------- --------
FRESH SALAD              $2.00
SOUP OF THE DAY          $1.50
SANDWICH                 $3.50
GRILLED STEAK            $6.00
HAMBURGER                $2.50
CARROTS                  $1.20 ❹
FRENCH FRIES             $1.50
SODA                     $1.25
COFFEE                   $ .85
DESSERT                  $3.00
```

Notes

❶ To determine which row will receive the changed value, we test the description column, because we only want to change one price of one item.

❷ If the description column is equal to broccoli, then we change the price to $1.20. You might think that because we want to change the price of the carrots, we should use carrots in this test, but the data comes from the beginning table, and there the value is broccoli.

❸ Otherwise, for all rows except the one for broccoli, the value of this function is equal to the value in the price column.

❹ This is the row that has been changed. Only the value in the result table is changed. The value in the beginning table is not changed.

18-2   The Immediate If (`iif`) function in Access

The Immediate If (`iif`) function is used to create an `if-then-else` condition in Access. This is an extension to standard SQL that Access has added. It tests a statement to determine whether it is true or false. It assigns one value to the function if the statement is true. It assigns a different value if the statement is false.

The condition used in the test can be any SQL condition, including

- Equal
- Less than
- Greater than
- In
- Between
- Like
- Is null

The `iif` function handles nulls with the "is null" condition. This is more precise than the `decode` function, which handles nulls with the "equal to" condition.

Access syntax

`iif(true_or_false_expression, true_value, false_value)`

where

> `true_or_false_expression` is any expression resulting in a value of True or False.

In Access, False is the value 0 and True is any other value (−1 is often used).

> If `true_or_false_expression` is True, then the `iif` function equals `true_value`.

> If `true_or_false_expression` is False, then the `iif` function equals `false_value`.

> If `true_or_false_expression` is Unknown, then the `iif` function equals `false_value`.

Task 1

Show an example of an SQL statement using the `iif` function. Substitute carrots for broccoli in the menu of lunch foods.

Access SQL

```
select iif(description = 'broccoli', 'carrots',
           description) as new_menu,
       price
from l_foods;
```

Beginning table (`l_foods` table)

SUPPLIER_ID	PRODUCT_CO|	MENU_ITEM	DESCRIPTION	PRICE	PRICE_INCREASE
Asp	Fs	1	Fresh Salad	$2.00	$0.25
Asp	Sp	2	Soup Of The Da	$1.50	
Asp	Sw	3	Sandwich	$3.50	$0.40
Cbc	Gs	4	Grilled Steak	$6.00	$0.70
Cbc	Sw	5	Hamburger	$2.50	$0.30
Frv	Br	6	Broccoli	$1.00	$0.05
Frv	Ff	7	French Fries	$1.50	
Jbr	As	8	Soda	$1.25	$0.25
Jbr	Vr	9	Coffee	$0.85	$0.15
Vsb	As	10	Dessert	$3.00	$0.50
				$0.00	$0.00

Record: 11 of 11

Result table

new_menu	price
Fresh Salad	$2.00
Soup Of The Day	$1.50
Sandwich	$3.50
Grilled Steak	$6.00
Hamburger	$2.50
Carrots	$1.00
French Fries	$1.50
Soda	$1.25
Coffee	$0.85
Dessert	$3.00
	$0.00

Record: 11

Task 2

In addition to the changes you made in task 1, change the price of the carrots to $1.20.

Access SQL

```
select iif(description = 'broccoli', 'carrots',
            description) as new_menu,
        iif(description = 'broccoli', 1.20, a.price) ❶
                          as price
from 1_foods a;
```

Result table

new_menu	price
Fresh Salad	$2.00
Soup Of The Day	$1.50
Sandwich	$3.50
Grilled Steak	$6.00
Hamburger	$2.50
Carrots	$1.20
French Fries	$1.50
Soda	$1.25
Coffee	$0.85
Dessert	$3.00

Record: 11

Notes

❶ In Access, I write "a.price" to say it is a column from the beginning table and distinguish it from the column alias price. The "a" is a table alias for the 1_foods table.

18-3   Attaching messages to rows

The `decode` and `iif` functions can be used to attach messages to certain rows. These messages might convey information, flag exceptions, issue warnings, or show errors. This can also be done with a `union`.

The task of this section is the same as in section 15-11 in which the SQL code was written with a `union`. Here it is written using the `decode` and `iif` functions.

Which way of writing the code is best? In this example the Access code using the `iif` function gets my vote. It is the easiest to understand. It does not use tricks, while all the other solutions involve some sort of trick. If some other programmer needs to modify it, it will be easier to modify and there will be less chance of making an error.

Task

List the foods and their prices. Add the message "expensive item" to the foods that cost more than $2.00. List the foods in alphabetical order.

Oracle SQL — Using `decode`

```
select description,
       price,
       decode(sign(price - 2.00), ❶
                    +1, 'expensive item',
                     0, '   ',
                    -1, '   ',
                    null, '   ') as message
from l_foods
order by description;
```

Access SQL — Using `iif`

```
select description,
       price,
       iif (price > 2.00, 'expensive item', '   ')
                                              as message
from l_foods
order by description;
```

Beginning table (1_foods table)

```
SUPPLIER PRODUCT   MENU                                        PRICE
ID       CODE      ITEM DESCRIPTION              PRICE INCREASE
-------- -------   ------- -------------------- ----------- --------
ASP      FS            1 FRESH SALAD             $2.00    $0.25
ASP      SP            2 SOUP OF THE DAY         $1.50   (null)
ASP      SW            3 SANDWICH                $3.50    $0.40
CBC      GS            4 GRILLED STEAK           $6.00    $0.70
CBC      SW            5 HAMBURGER               $2.50    $0.30
FRV      BR            6 BROCCOLI                $1.00    $0.05
FRV      FF            7 FRENCH FRIES            $1.50   (null)
JBR      AS            8 SODA                    $1.25    $0.25
JBR      VR            9 COFFEE                  $0.85    $0.15
VSB      AS           10 DESSERT                 $3.00    $0.50
```

Result table

```
DESCRIPTION              PRICE MESSAGE
-------------------- ----------- --------------
BROCCOLI                  $1.00
COFFEE                    $0.85
DESSERT                   $3.00 EXPENSIVE ITEM
FRENCH FRIES              $1.50
FRESH SALAD               $2.00
GRILLED STEAK             $6.00 EXPENSIVE ITEM
HAMBURGER                 $2.50 EXPENSIVE ITEM
SANDWICH                  $3.50 EXPENSIVE ITEM
SODA                      $1.25
SOUP OF THE DAY           $1.50
```

Notes

❶ In Oracle, the sign function allows decode to cover a range of values, rather than just a few specific values. This is a trick. We take the price and subtract $2.00 from it. Then we test the result to see if it is positive or negative. The result is positive when the price is greater than $2.00.

The value of the sign function is +1 for all positive numbers. It is −1 for all negative numbers. Otherwise, it is 0 or null. In this example, the sign function creates a +1 when the price is more than $2.00, a 0 when the price is equal to $2.00, a −1 when the price is less than $2.00, and a null when the price is null.

This trick reduces a range of values to four distinct possibilities.

18-4   Dividing data from one column into two different columns

The decode and iif functions can be used to divide the data in one column into two columns. This is done to make the information easier for people to absorb. The task in this section is the same as in section 15-12, where the SQL was written using a union.

Task

Divide the cost column from the beginning table into two columns: debits and credits.

Oracle SQL — Using decode

```
set null '  '; ❶

select item,
       decode (sign(cost),
                    +1, null, ❷
                     0, null,
                    -1, cost,
                    null, null) as debits,
       decode (sign(cost),
                    +1, cost,
                     0, cost,
                    -1, null, ❸
                    null, null) as credits
from sec1512_finances
order by item;
```

Access SQL — Using iif

```
select item,
       iif(cost < 0, cost, '  ') as debits,
       iif(cost >=0, '  ', cost) as credits
from sec1512_finances
order by item;
```

Beginning table (`sec1512_finances` table)

ITEM	COST
SAMSONITE SUITCASE	-$248.13
RENT FOR APRIL	$700.00
OPERA TICKET	-$145.00
LUNCH	-$15.62
DEBT REPAID BY JIM	$20.00
CAR REPAIR	-$622.98
HAIRCUT	-$22.00
BIRTHDAY GIFT FROM MOM	$200.00

Result table

ITEM	DEBITS	CREDITS
BIRTHDAY GIFT FROM MOM		$200.00
CAR REPAIR	-$622.98	
DEBT REPAID BY JIM		$20.00
HAIRCUT	-$22.00	
LUNCH	-$15.62	
OPERA TICKET	-$145.00	
RENT FOR APRIL		$700.00
SAMSONITE SUITCASE	-$248.13	

Notes

❶ In Oracle, this command tells SQLplus to display nulls as blank spaces. After running this query, you may want to see the nulls as (null) again. If you do, you can use this command:

```
set null '(null)';
```

❷ In Oracle, the datatype of the decode function is determined by the datatype of the first value the function might assume. This is the datatype of the third parameter. In this example we want the debits column to be numeric, so we need to make the value assigned to +1 numeric, even though it is a null. This is done by applying the to_number function to the null.

❸ In Oracle, the null here cannot be replaced with a space enclosed in single quotes because the credits column is numeric, as cost is a number. We are not allowed to enter text values into a numeric column.

18-5   Applying two functions to different parts of the data

The decode and iif functions can be used to apply one function to part of the data and another function to the rest of the data. The task in this section is the same as in section 15-13, where the SQL code was written using a union.

Task

Increase the price of all foods costing more than $2.00 by 5%. Increase the price of all other foods by 10%. Ignore the price_increase column.

Oracle SQL — Using decode

```
select menu_item,
       description,
       decode (sign(price - 2.00),
                    +1, price * 1.05),
                     0, price * 1.10),
                    -1, price * 1.10),
                    null, null)          as new_price
from l_foods
order by menu_item;
```

Access SQL — Using iif

```
select description,
       iif(price > 2.00, price * 1.05, price * 1.10)
                                                as new_price
from l_foods;
```

Beginning table (`1_foods` table)

```
SUPPLIER PRODUCT   MENU                                           PRICE
ID       CODE      ITEM DESCRIPTION                  PRICE    INCREASE
-------- -------   ------- -------------------- ----------- --------
ASP      FS            1 FRESH SALAD                  $2.00     $0.25
ASP      SP            2 SOUP OF THE DAY              $1.50
ASP      SW            3 SANDWICH                     $3.50     $0.40
CBC      GS            4 GRILLED STEAK                $6.00     $0.70
CBC      SW            5 HAMBURGER                    $2.50     $0.30
FRV      BR            6 BROCCOLI                     $1.00     $0.05
FRV      FF            7 FRENCH FRIES                 $1.50
JBR      AS            8 SODA                         $1.25     $0.25
JBR      VR            9 COFFEE                       $0.85     $0.15
VSB      AS           10 DESSERT                      $3.00     $0.50
```

Result table

```
   MENU                               NEW
   ITEM DESCRIPTION                  PRICE
------- -------------------- --------
      1 FRESH SALAD                  $2.20
      2 SOUP OF THE DAY              $1.65
      3 SANDWICH                     $3.68
      4 GRILLED STEAK                $6.30
      5 HAMBURGER                    $2.63
      6 BROCCOLI                     $1.10
      7 FRENCH FRIES                 $1.65
      8 SODA                         $1.38
      9 COFFEE                        $.94
     10 DESSERT                      $3.15
```

Parameter Queries

There are no variables in SQL. Everything about an SQL query must be specific — the literal values, the column names, and the table names. The state of the data can be an unknown, because the data may be constantly changing, but there are no unknowns within an SQL query or command.

In this chapter, I discuss two methods that take a step toward introducing variables into SQL — parameter queries and subqueries. We have already discussed another method, using a table of constants. In that method, many of the literal values are put as data into a table instead of being coded directly into the SQL. Often a table of constants has only one row.

In a parameter query, the variables do not belong to the SQL itself, rather they belong to the environment that people use to submit SQL queries. In Oracle, this environment is SQLplus. In Access, it is in the GUI layer, before the SQL query is sent to the JET database engine for processing.

You usually write a parameter query for an end user to run. At runtime, the end user is asked to provide specific values for all the variables. These values are placed into the SQL statement before it is sent to the DBMS.

18-6   A parameter query in Oracle

A parameter query in Oracle is a `select` statement that contains variables. These variables begin with an ampersand, such as `&employee_id`. When SQLplus finds a variable beginning with `&`, it asks you for the value of the variable. It substitutes the value you give to the variable into the `select` statement, so that the select statement no longer contains any variables. Then it sends that statement to the SQL level for processing.

In this section, you cannot type the commands directly into SQLplus. To write a parameter query in Oracle, you must write it in Notepad and save it as a file. This is called an Oracle script file. To run this file, enter "start" within SQLplus, followed by the name of the file. An example of this follows.

Parameter queries are used to make the SQL code more flexible. The person running the code can enter the values they need. Oracle allows you to use parameters with all types of SQL statements.

Task

Write an Oracle script file containing a parameter query. Make the query prompt for a value of the `employee_id` number and have it return the row for that employee from the `l_employees` table.

Step 1: Create a file using Notepad

Save this code in a file named c:\temp\sec1806.sql.

```
set echo off; ❶

set scan on; ❷
set define on;

select *
from l_employees
where employee_id = &employee_num; ❸

-- Return SQLplus to the standard settings ❹
set scan off;
set define off;
set echo on;
```

Step 2: Oracle SQLplus — Run the parameter query

```
start c:\temp\sec1806.sql ❺
```

Prompt from the computer ❻

```
Enter value for employee_num: 210
```

Result table

EMPLOYEE ID	FIRST NAME	LAST NAME	DEPT CODE	HIRE_DATE	CREDIT LIMIT	PHONE NUMBER	MANAGER ID
210	NANCY	HOFFMAN	SAL	16-FEB-2004	$25.00	2974	203

Notes

❶ This prevents detail messages from appearing on the screen. They are irrelevant in this context.

❷ The next two lines set up the SQLplus environment to accept parameter queries. The set scan on tells SQLplus to scan SQL statements for variables, which begin with an ampersand. The set define on allows SQLplus to define variables.

❸ &employee_num is a variable. SQLplus will ask you what value you want this variable to have.

❹ These commands return the SQLplus environment to its original state.

❺ This runs the parameter query.

❻ The computer asks you for information, and you enter the number 210.

18-7   Using a parameter more than once in Oracle

In an Oracle script file, we may want to use the same variable several times. To do this, we begin the name of the variable with two ampersands (&&) the first time it occurs. When SQLplus encounters a variable beginning with &&, it asks for a value of the variable and remembers the value you have given to that variable. Then it will use that value whenever it finds the variable again.

Task

Write an Oracle script file containing a parameter query. Have the query prompt for a value of the employee_id number and have it return all the rows for that employee from the l_employees table and the l_lunches table.

Step 1: Create a file using Notepad

Save this code in a file named c:\temp\sec1807.sql.

```
set echo off;

set scan on;
set define on;

select *
from l_employees
where employee_id = &&employee_num;  ❶

select *
from l_lunches
where employee_id = &employee_num;  ❷

-- Return SQLplus to the standard settings
undefine employee_num;  ❸
set scan off;
set define off;
set echo on;
```

Step 2: Oracle SQLplus — Run the parameter query

```
start c:\temp\sec1807.sql
```

Prompt from the computer

```
Enter value for employee_num: 210
```

Result table

```
EMPLOYEE FIRST       LAST      DEPT                        CREDIT  PHONE   MANAGER
     ID NAME        NAME      CODE   HIRE_DATE            LIMIT  NUMBER       ID
-------- --------   --------  ------ ------------      --------  ------  -------
     210 NANCY      HOFFMAN   SAL    16-FEB-2004        $25.00  2974         203

1 row selected.

           LUNCH            EMPLOYEE
 LUNCH_ID  DATE                  ID DATE_ENTERE
--------- ------------     -------- -----------
        7 16-NOV-2005          210 13-OCT-2005
       17 05-DEC-2005          210 21-OCT-2005
```

Notes

❶ &&employee_num prompts for the value, remembers it, and uses this value whenever it encounters &employee_num again.

❷ The value of &employee_num has already been set, so you will not be prompted for the value of this variable.

❸ This resets the SQLplus environment so that the value of the &employee_num variable is no longer defined. Notice that in this statement there is no & before the name of the variable.

18-8   More ways to define parameters in Oracle

There are two other ways to define a parameter in an Oracle script file. One way uses the define command. The word define is followed by the name of the variable, then an equal (=) sign, then the value of the variable. This is useful if you want to have variables in your code to keep it flexible, but you do not want to be prompted for the variable at runtime. I use this method in the script file sqlfun_build_tables.sql.

The other way to define a parameter prompts you for its value. It allows you to write the message asking for the value of the variable. This requires two commands, `prompt` and `accept`. The word `prompt` is followed by the message without single quotes. This is the message the person running the query will answer. The `accept` command creates a variable and gives it a value. The word `accept` is followed by the name of the variable without an ampersand, and this is followed by the datatype of the variable. The datatype can be `number`, `char`, or `date`. Use `char` for text items.

Step 1: Create a file using Notepad

Save this code in a file named c:\temp\sec1808.sql.

```
set echo off;

set scan on;
set define on;

define table = l_employees; ❶

prompt Enter a valid Employee ID number; ❷
accept employee_num number; ❸

prompt Enter a Department code;
accept depart_code char; ❹

select *
from &table ❺
where employee_id = &employee_num;

select *
from &table
where dept_code = '&depart_code'; ❻

-- Return SQLplus to the standard settings
undefine table;
undefine employee_num;
undefine depart_code;
set scan off;
set define off;
set echo on;
```

Step 2: Oracle SQLplus — Run the parameter query

```
start c:\temp\sec1808.sql
```

Prompt from the computer

```
Enter a valid Employee ID number
210
Enter a Department code
sal
```

Result table

EMPLOYEE ID	FIRST NAME	LAST NAME	DEPT CODE	HIRE_DATE	CREDIT LIMIT	PHONE NUMBER	MANAGER ID
210	NANCY	HOFFMAN	SAL	16-FEB-2004	$25.00	2974	203

1 row selected.

EMPLOYEE ID	FIRST NAME	LAST NAME	DEPT CODE	HIRE_DATE	CREDIT LIMIT	PHONE NUMBER	MANAGER ID
202	JIM	KERN	SAL	16-AUG-1999	$25.00	8722	201
204	ELLEN	OWENS	SAL	01-JUL-2003	$15.00	6830	202
205	HENRY	PERKINS	SAL	01-MAR-2000	$25.00	5286	202
210	NANCY	HOFFMAN	SAL	16-FEB-2004	$25.00	2974	203

Notes

❶ This `define` command creates a variable called `table` and gives it the value `l_employees`. Notice that there is no ampersand at the beginning of the word `table` when the variable is defined. However, there is an ampersand in `&table` when the variable is used.

❷ This `prompt` command displays the message "Enter a valid Employee ID number". It does not have single quotes around the message. If you use single quotes, they will appear in the message. The message is case sensitive.

❸ This `accept` command takes the value that has been entered and assigns it to the variable `employee_num`. The variable is defined as a numeric datatype.

❹ This `accept` command takes the value that has been entered and assigns it to the variable `depart_code`. The variable is defined as a text datatype.

❺ This line uses the `&table` variable, the value of which has already been set by the `define` command.

❻ This line uses the `&depart_code` variable, the value of which has already been set by the `accept` command. Notice that single quotes are placed around the variable. These are required because it is a text item. Without the quotes, after substitution, this line would read: **where dept_code = sal**

This would result in an error message. With the quotes, after substitution, this line reads: **where dept_code = 'sal'**

This is correct code.

18-9   A parameter query in Access

Access automatically prompts you for the value of any variable it does not recognize. It is tuned to prompt for parameter values. You may have encountered this already. If you misspell the name of a column, it prompts you to enter a value for that column. Usually, that is not what you want to do. This can create some strange error messages.

When you want to create a parameter query in Access, it is easy to do. Access is always ready to accept parameters.

Task

Write a procedure in Access that will ask for an employee ID number. After the user enters this number, the procedure finds the information about that employee in the `l_employees` table.

Access SQL — Using `iif`

```
select *
from l_employees
where dept_code = [Enter a valid Department Code]; ❶
```

Prompt for information

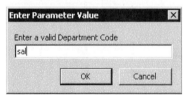

Result table

EMPLOYEE_ID	FIRST_NAME	LAST_NAME	DEPT_CODE	HIRE_DATE	CREDIT_LIMIT	PHONE_NUMB	MANAGER_ID
202	Jim	Kern	Sal	8/16/1999	$25.00	8722	201
204	Ellen	Owens	Sal	7/1/2003	$15.00	6830	202
205	Henry	Perkins	Sal	3/1/2000	$25.00	5286	202
210	Nancy	Hoffman	Sal	2/16/2004	$25.00	2974	203
					$0.00		

Record: I◄ ◄ | 5 ► ►I ►* of 5

Notes

❶ The text within the square brackets indicates a single parameter. The actual text is used to prompt for the information. This technique will work even without the square brackets, as long as the text contains no spaces

18-10   A query in Access with two parameters

When there are two or more parameters within a query in Access, the same value is placed in all the parameters with the same name. If you want to put different values in two parameters, you must give them different names. The name of a parameter comes from the text that it prompts for.

Task

Ask the person running the query for a beginning date and an ending date. Then show the rows from the l_employees table for all the people hired between those two dates.

Access SQL — Incorrect

```
select *
from l_employees
where hire_date between [date] and [date]
order by hire_date;
```

   With this code, there will be only one prompt for date. The same value will be placed into both parameters. The query returns only the rows for the people hired on that one date.

Access SQL — Correct

```
select *
from l_employees
where hire_date between [Enter beginning date]
                   and [Enter ending date]
order by hire_date;
```

18-11   Limitations on parameters in Access

In Access, you can only use a parameter in a query to hold the place for a specific value, such as "102," "Bob," or "March 4, 1906." You cannot use a parameter in the place of a column name or a table name. In contrast, Oracle allows you to use a parameter for any word within a query.

Within an Oracle script file, the same parameter can be used in several related queries. You cannot do this in Access, because the SQL window only allows you to enter one query at a time.

Subqueries

A `select` statement that is embedded within another `select` statement is called a *subquery*. In the following sections I discuss several variations on this idea. Most of the time you do not have to use subqueries. There are still a few places where you have to use them, and you may have to understand code that was written ten years ago when outer joins were not available and inner joins were less efficient than they are today.

18-12 Introduction to subqueries

When SQL was first created, people thought that subqueries would be the most important feature of the language. One style of coding SQL makes extensive use of subqueries. This style can be found in older code. Some people still write code this way, but this style has now fallen out of favor.

It has largely been replaced by a style that prefers to use joins, when there is a choice. There are three reasons for this change. One reason is that the processing of joins has become much more efficient. Originally it was thought that subqueries would always process much more quickly than joins. In the past few years many improvements have been made to the Optimizer that make joins more efficient. Now joins are often just as efficient as subqueries, and sometimes even more efficient.

The second reason is that outer joins have now become a standard part of the language. The early SQL standards, SQL-86 and SQL-89, did not include outer joins. Subqueries were used to write them. Now most products support outer joins and they are included in the newest standard, SQL-92. Now we can write an outer join without using a subquery.

The third reason is that code written with many subqueries is difficult to understand and maintain. Code written with joins is often easier to understand and modify when changes are needed, and other people can work with the code more easily.

Task

Show an example of a subquery. List the foods that cost less than the average price of all the items on the menu. List the descriptions and prices of these foods. Sort the rows in ascending order on the `description` column.

Oracle & Access SQL

```
select a.description,
       a.price
from 1_foods a
where a.price < (select avg(b.price)
                 from 1_foods b)
order by a.description;
```

Beginning table (1_foods table)

```
SUPPLIER PRODUCT   MENU                                            PRICE
ID       CODE      ITEM DESCRIPTION                PRICE INCREASE
-------- -------   ------- -------------------- ----------- --------
ASP      FS             1 FRESH SALAD               $2.00    $0.25
ASP      SP             2 SOUP OF THE DAY           $1.50   (null)
ASP      SW             3 SANDWICH                  $3.50    $0.40
CBC      GS             4 GRILLED STEAK             $6.00    $0.70
CBC      SW             5 HAMBURGER                 $2.50    $0.30
FRV      BR             6 BROCCOLI                  $1.00    $0.05
FRV      FF             7 FRENCH FRIES              $1.50   (null)
JBR      AS             8 SODA                      $1.25    $0.25
JBR      VR             9 COFFEE                    $0.85    $0.15
VSB      AS            10 DESSERT                   $3.00    $0.50
```

How the computer processes this query

Step 1: The subquery is processed first.

```
select avg(b.price)
from 1_foods b;
```

Result table: Step 1

```
AVG(B.PRICE)
-----------
       2.31
```

Step 2: The result is placed in the outer query.

```
select a.description,
       a.price
from l_foods a
where a.price < 2.31
order by a.description;
```

Step 3: The outer query is processed.

Result table

```
DESCRIPTION                    PRICE
-------------------- -----------
BROCCOLI                       $1.00
COFFEE                         $0.85
FRENCH FRIES                   $1.50
FRESH SALAD                    $2.00
SODA                           $1.25
SOUP OF THE DAY                $1.50
```

18-13 Subqueries that result in a list of values

Some subqueries result in a single value and others return a list of values. Those are the only options. A subquery is not allowed to return any more values than that. For example, it cannot return a table with several rows and several columns. The reason is that the result of the subquery must fit into the statement of the outer query. Within the context of an SQL statement, only a single value or a list of values can make sense.

This section shows a subquery that results in a list of values. To make this list work with the syntax of the outer join, the condition in the where clause must be

```
    IN
or  NOT IN
```

Task 1

Find all the rows from the twos table where the number_2 column matches a value in the number_3 column of the threes table.

Oracle & Access SQL: Using the `in` condition

```
select number_2,
       word_2
from twos
where number_2 in (select number_3 ❶
                   from threes);
```

Beginning tables

twos table

```
NUMBER_2 WORD_2
-------- -----------
       2 TWO
       4 FOUR
       6 SIX
       8 EIGHT
      10 TEN
      12 TWELVE
      14 FOURTEEN
      16 SIXTEEN
      18 EIGHTEEN
      20 TWENTY
 (null)    NULL
```

threes table

```
NUMBER_3 WORD_3
-------- -----------
       3 THREE
       6 SIX
       9 NINE
      12 TWELVE
      15 FIFTEEN
      18 EIGHTEEN
 (null)    NULL
```

Result table ❷

```
NUMBER_2 WORD_2
-------- ---------------
       6 SIX
      12 TWELVE
      18 EIGHTEEN
```

Notes

❶ The result of this subquery is the list (3, 6, 9, 12, 15, 18, null). When this list is substituted in the main query, the `select` statement is

```
select number_2,
       word_2
from twos
where number_2 in (3, 6, 9, 12, 15, 18, null);
```

❷ The result of this subquery is the same as an inner join.

Task 2

Find all the rows from the `twos` table where the `number_2` column does not match any value in the `number_3` column of the `threes` table.

Oracle & Access SQL: Using the `not in` condition

```
select number_2,
       word_2
from twos
where number_2 not in (select number_3 ❶
                       from threes
                       where number_3 is not null);
```

Result table ❷

```
NUMBER_2 WORD_2
-------- -------------
       2 TWO
       4 FOUR
       8 EIGHT
      10 TEN
      14 FOURTEEN
      16 SIXTEEN
      20 TWENTY
```

Notes

❶ The result of this subquery is the list (3, 6, 9, 12, 15, 18). The null has been removed because the `not in` condition is used (see section 18-15). When this list is substituted in the main query, the `select` statement is:

```
select number_2,
       word_2
from twos
where number_2 not in (3, 6, 9, 12, 15, 18);
```

❷ The row with a null in the `number_2` column does not appear in the result table.

18-14   Subqueries that result in a single value

This section shows a subquery that results in a single value. One way to ensure that there is only one value is to use a column function such as `max` or `sum`. Here, the condition in the `where` clause can be any of the following:

```
= (equal)
<> (not equal)
< (less than) or <= (less than or equal)
> (greater than) or >= (greater than or equal)
IN
NOT IN
BETWEEN
```

Task 1

Find the row of the `twos` table where the `number_2` column is equal to the maximum value in the `number_3` column of the `threes` table.

Oracle & Access SQL: Using the Equal condition

```
select number_2,
       word_2
from twos
where number_2 = (select max(number_3) ❶
                  from threes);
```

Beginning tables — Same as in the previous section

Result table

```
NUMBER_2 WORD_2
-------- ----------------
      18 EIGHTEEN
```

Notes

❶ This subquery results in the value 18. When this value is substituted in the main query, the `select` statement is

```
select number_2,
       word_2
from twos
where number_2 = 18;
```

Task 2

Find all the rows of the `twos` table where the `number_2` column is not equal to the maximum value in the `number_3` column of the `threes` table.

Oracle & Access SQL: Using the Not Equal condition

```
select number_2,
       word_2
from twos
where number_2 <> (select max(number_3) ❶
                   from threes);
```

Result table ❷

```
NUMBER_2 WORD_2
-------- -----------
       2 TWO
       4 FOUR
       6 SIX
       8 EIGHT
      10 TEN
      12 TWELVE
      14 FOURTEEN
      16 SIXTEEN
      20 TWENTY
```

Notes

❶ This subquery results in the value 18.

❷ The row with a null in the `number_2` column does not appear in the result table.

18-15 Avoid using `not in` with nulls

If you use a subquery that generates a list of values and the subquery is used in a `where` clause with the `not in` condition, then you need to make sure that the subquery excludes nulls from its list.

The SQL code for task 2 shows that no rows are selected when both of the following conditions apply: The result of a subquery is a list that includes a null, and the list is used with a `not in` condition. This makes sense because a null is an unknown value. There are not any rows that we can say are definitely not in a list, when the list contains an unknown value. The following example shows how this works.

Task 1

Find all the rows of the `twos` table where the `number_2` column is equal to one of the values in the `number_3` column of the `threes` table. This SQL code shows that the `in` condition is not affected by nulls.

Oracle & Access SQL

```
select number_2,
       word_2
from twos
where number_2 in (select number_3 ❶
                   from threes);
```

Result table

```
NUMBER_2 WORD_2
-------- --------------
       6 SIX
      12 TWELVE
      18 EIGHTEEN
```

Task 2

Find all the rows of the `twos` table where the `number_2` column is not equal to any of the values in the `number_3` column of the `threes` table. You need to be careful here because the `number_3` column contains a null. The SQL code here shows that nulls are critical when you are using the `not in` condition with a subquery.

Oracle & Access SQL: Incorrect

```
select number_2,
       word_2
from twos
where number_2 not in (select number_3 ❷
                              from threes);
```

Result — The query runs, but there is no data in the result

Oracle & Access SQL: Correct

```
select number_2,
       word_2
from twos
where number_2 not in (select number_3 ❸
                              from threes
                              where number_3 is not null);
```

Result table

```
NUMBER_2 WORD_2
--------- ---------------
       2 TWO
       4 FOUR
       8 EIGHT
      10 TEN
      14 FOURTEEN
      16 SIXTEEN
      20 TWENTY
```

Notes

❶ This subquery results in the list (3, 6, 9, 12, 18, null). The null in this list does not cause a problem when it is used with an in condition.

❷ This subquery results in the list (3, 6, 9, 12, 18, null). The null in this list causes a major problem when it is used with a not in condition. The query runs, but it produces a message that says "no rows selected".

❸ This subquery results in the list (3, 6, 9, 12, 18). The null is removed by the where condition in the subquery. This list works with a not in condition.

Applications of Subqueries

The sections that follow show you some of the ways in which subqueries are most useful. You often have to use them in update statements, to compare tables, or to select the most current data from your tables.

18-16   Subqueries used in an update command

Often you may be given several changes to make in the data of a large table. If you use an update statement to make these changes, you will need to use a subquery. In fact, you will need to use two subqueries: one in the set clause and one in the where clause.

The subquery in the set clause gives new values to the column that is being changed. The subquery in the where clause specifies which rows to change. Without this second subquery, every value in the column is changed. Many of these values are set to null.

Task

Apply the updates given in the table below to change the manager_id column of the l_employees table.

Beginning table to be updated (l_employees table)

EMPLOYEE ID	FIRST NAME	LAST NAME	DEPT CODE	HIRE_DATE	CREDIT LIMIT	PHONE NUMBER	MANAGER ID
201	SUSAN	BROWN	EXE	01-JUN-1998	$30.00	3484	(null)
202	JIM	KERN	SAL	16-AUG-1999	$25.00	8722	201
203	MARTHA	WOODS	SHP	02-FEB-2004	$25.00	7591	201
204	ELLEN	OWENS	SAL	01-JUL-2003	$15.00	6830	202
205	HENRY	PERKINS	SAL	01-MAR-2000	$25.00	5286	202
206	CAROL	ROSE	ACT	(null)	(null)	(null)	(null)
207	DAN	SMITH	SHP	01-DEC-2004	$25.00	2259	203
208	FRED	CAMPBELL	SHP	01-APR-2003	$25.00	1752	203
209	PAULA	JACOBS	MKT	17-MAR-1999	$15.00	3357	201
210	NANCY	HOFFMAN	SAL	16-FEB-2004	$25.00	2974	203

Beginning table of updates (`sec1816_changes` table)

```
EMP_ID NEW_MANAGER
--------- -----------
      206         204
      207         204
      209         205
      210         205
```

Oracle & Access SQL: Incorrect

```
update l_employees a
set a.manager_id = (select b.new_manager
                    from sec1816_changes b
                    where a.employee_id = b.emp_id);
```

Result table — Incorrect

EMPLOYEE ID	FIRST NAME	LAST NAME	DEPT CODE	HIRE_DATE	CREDIT LIMIT	PHONE NUMBER	MANAGER ID
201	SUSAN	BROWN	EXE	01-JUN-1998	$30.00	3484	(null) ❶
202	JIM	KERN	SAL	16-AUG-1999	$25.00	8722	(null) ❶
203	MARTHA	WOODS	SHP	02-FEB-2004	$25.00	7591	(null) ❶
204	ELLEN	OWENS	SAL	01-JUL-2003	$15.00	6830	(null) ❶
205	HENRY	PERKINS	SAL	01-MAR-2000	$25.00	5286	(null) ❶
206	CAROL	ROSE	ACT	(null)	(null)	(null)	204
207	DAN	SMITH	SHP	01-DEC-2004	$25.00	2259	204
208	FRED	CAMPBELL	SHP	01-APR-2003	$25.00	1752	(null) ❶
209	PAULA	JACOBS	MKT	17-MAR-1999	$15.00	3357	205
210	NANCY	HOFFMAN	SAL	16-FEB-2004	$25.00	2974	205

Notes

❶ The incorrect SQL code placed nulls in the `manager_id` column of these rows.

Oracle recovery:

```
rollback;
```

Access recovery:

Do not make these changes permanent.

Oracle & Access SQL: Correct

```
update l_employees a
set a.manager_id = (select b.new_manager
                    from sec1816_changes b
                    where a.employee_id = b.emp_id)
    where a.employee_id in (select c.emp_id ❶
                    from sec1816_changes c);
```

Result table

EMPLOYEE ID	FIRST NAME	LAST NAME	DEPT CODE	HIRE_DATE	CREDIT LIMIT	PHONE NUMBER	MANAGER ID	
201	SUSAN	BROWN	EXE	01-JUN-1998	$30.00	3484	(null)	
202	JIM	KERN	SAL	16-AUG-1999	$25.00	8722	201	
203	MARTHA	WOODS	SHP	02-FEB-2004	$25.00	7591	201	
204	ELLEN	OWENS	SAL	01-JUL-2003	$15.00	6830	202	
205	HENRY	PERKINS	SAL	01-MAR-2000	$25.00	5286	202	
206	CAROL	ROSE	ACT	(null)	(null)	(null)	204	❷
207	DAN	SMITH	SHP	01-DEC-2004	$25.00	2259	204	❷
208	FRED	CAMPBELL	SHP	01-APR-2003	$25.00	1752	203	
209	PAULA	JACOBS	MKT	17-MAR-1999	$15.00	3357	205	❷
210	NANCY	HOFFMAN	SAL	16-FEB-2004	$25.00	2974	205	❷

Notes

❶ A second subquery is required to specify which rows to change.

❷ Changes are made only to the desired rows.

18-17   Finding the difference between two tables

This section shows you how to find the differences between two tables. This method uses a subquery to remove all the rows that are identical in the two tables, so only the rows that are different remain. Two tricks are involved in this process.

The first trick concatenates all the columns of a table to form a single value. A separator is placed between the columns. We used a similar trick in section 11-9. This is necessary because a subquery is able to compare one list of single values with another, but it cannot compare rows of values.

The second trick is to use two SQL queries. Each query finds all the rows in one table that are not present in the other table. So two queries are needed to find all the rows that do not match.

Task 1

Find all the rows of the `sec1407_first` table that are not identical to any row of the `sec1407_second` table.

Oracle & Access SQL

```
select *
from sec1407_first
where (number_1||'*'||word_1||'*'||date_1)
    not in (select (number_2||'*'||word_2||'*'||date_2)
                from sec1407_second);
```

Beginning tables

`sec1407_first` table   **`sec1407_second` table**

NUMBER_1	WORD_1	DATE_1
1	ONE	01-DEC-2001
2	TWO	02-DEC-2002
3	THREE	03-DEC-2003
4	FOUR	04-DEC-2004
5	FIVE	05-DEC-2005

NUMBER_2	WORD_2	DATE_2
3	THREE	03-DEC-2003
4	FOUR	04-DEC-2004
5	FIVE	05-DEC-2005
6	SIX	06-DEC-2006
7	SEVEN	07-DEC-2007

Result table

NUMBER_1	WORD_1	DATE_1
1	ONE	01-DEC-2001
2	TWO	02-DEC-2002

Task 2

Find all the rows of the `sec1407_second` table that are not identical to any row of the `sec1407_first` table.

Oracle & Access SQL

```
select *
from sec1407_second
where (number_2||'*'||word_2||'*'||date_2)
    not in (select (number_1||'*'||word_1||'*'||date_1)
            from sec1407_first);
```

Result table

```
NUMBER_2   WORD_2      DATE_2
---------  ----------  -----------
        6  SIX         06-DEC-2006
        7  SEVEN       07-DEC-2007
```

18-18   Using the most current data

Sometimes you may need to use a subquery to get the most current data out of a table. Some tables contain historic data as well as current data.

I had to do this when I was working with a table that received new data every month. The old data was retained in the table. It would have been a cleaner database design if the current data had been kept separate from the historic data, but in this case the database tables were not designed that way. I could not change the design. I had to code around it.

I used a subquery to make sure the most current data was being used. My SQL code looked something like this:

```
select ...
from historic_data
where data_date = (select max(data_date)
                   from historic_data)
```

Older Features of Subqueries

I suggest you do not use the features shown in the following sections. You need to understand them because they may be used in code that you inherit. They show an older way of using SQL that is rarely used today.

18-19 Correlated subqueries

A correlated subquery is a subquery that contains a reference to the table in the outer query. Because of this, a correlated subquery cannot be evaluated before the outer query. In the following SQL code, the twos table is named in the from clause of the outer query. The threes table is named in the from clause of the subquery. However, the where clause of the subquery references both the twos table and the threes table.

Because of this reference, the subquery cannot be evaluated separately from the outer query. They must be evaluated together. This is a complex process and you may want to skip this section unless you need to know it.

Step 1: A row is obtained from the twos table, which is the table of the outer select statement. This could be any row, but we suppose it is the row for the number 2. Next, the number 2 is placed into the subselect, resulting in

```
(select b.number_3
 from threes b
 where 2 = b.number_3)
```

This results in no values, so a list containing no values is plugged into the outer select statement, which becomes

```
select a.number_2,
       a.word_2
from twos a
where a.number_2 = null
order by a.number_2;
```

This select results in no values, so the number 2 does not become part of the final result table.

Step 2: Another row is obtained from the `twos` table. This could be any row, but we suppose it is the row for the number 6. Next, the number 6 is placed into the subselect, resulting in

```
(select b.number_3
 from threes b
 where 6 = b.number_3)
```

The result table of this subselect is the number 6, so the value 6 is plugged into the outer `select` statement, which becomes

```
select a.number_2,
       a.word_2
from twos a
where a.number_2 = 6
order by a.number_2;
```

This `select` results in the number 6, which comes from the `twos` table. So the number 6 does become part of the final result table.

Step 3 through Step 10,000: This process is repeated for every rc v of the `twos` table, however many there are.

Task

Use a correlated subquery to find all the rows of the `twos` table that match with a row of the `threes` table. Use the `number` columns of both tables to do the match.

Oracle & Access SQL

```
select a.number_2,
       a.word_2
from twos a
where a.number_2 = (select b.number_3
                    from threes b
                    where a.number_2 = b.number_3)
order by a.number_2;
```

Result table

```
NUMBER_2 WORD_2
--------- ---------------
       6 SIX
      12 TWELVE
      18 EIGHTEEN
```

18-20 Subqueries using `exists`

The word `exists` can be used in the `where` clause with a subquery. This is always a correlated subquery. As shown earlier, the process of evaluating this query goes through a separate step for every row of the table in the outer query. A row of the outer query becomes part of the result table only if there is at least one row when the subquery is evaluated.

Task

Use a correlated subquery with `exists` to find all the rows of the `twos` table that match with a row of the `threes` table. Use the `number` columns of both tables to do the match.

Oracle & Access SQL

```
select a.number_2,
       a.word_2
from twos a
where exists (select b.number_3
                from threes b
                where a.number_2 = b.number_3)
order by a.number_2;
```

Result table

```
NUMBER_2 WORD_2
--------- ----------------
       6 SIX
      12 TWELVE
      18 EIGHTEEN
```

18-21   Using a subquery to write an outer join

It used to be that if you wanted to use an outer join you had to write it yourself using a subquery with `not exists`. You would not write code like this today. The following example shows you how this used to be done. We will form a left outer join of the `twos` table and the `threes` table.

There are two `select` statements that are combined with a `union`. The first `select` statement forms the inner join of the two tables. The second `select` statement adds back all the rows from the `twos` table that were dropped by the inner join.

Task

Form the left outer join of the `twos` table and the `threes` table. Show how this code used to be written before outer joins were included in SQL.

Oracle & Access SQL

```
select a.number_2, ❶
       a.word_2,
       b.number_3,
       b.word_3
from twos a,
     threes b
where a.number_2 = b.number_3
union all ❷
select a.number_2, ❸
       a.word_2,
       null, ❹
       null
from twos a
where not exists (select b.number_3 ❺
                  from threes b
                  where a.number_2 = b.number_3)
order by 1;
```

Result table

```
NUMBER_2 WORD_2              NUMBER_3 WORD_3
-------- ---------------     -------- ---------------
       2 TWO                 (null)   (null)
       4 FOUR                (null)   (null)
       6 SIX                        6 SIX
       8 EIGHT               (null)   (null)
      10 TEN                 (null)   (null)
      12 TWELVE                    12 TWELVE
      14 FOURTEEN            (null)   (null)
      16 SIXTEEN             (null)   (null)
      18 EIGHTEEN                  18 EIGHTEEN
      20 TWENTY              (null)   (null)
(null)    NULL               (null)   (null)
```

Notes

❶ This `select` is an inner join of the `twos` table and the `threes` table.

❷ A `union all` can be used instead of `union` because no rows from the first `select` will be duplicated by a row of the second `select`.

❸ This `select` lists the rows from the `twos` table that were dropped by the inner join.

❹ In Oracle8i, replace this null with `to_number (null)`. Oracle requires the null to be declared as a numeric datatype. This is a workaround for a problem in Oracle8i. Oracle9i has fixed this problem.

❺ A `not exists` is used with a correlated subquery to find the rows of the `twos` table that were dropped by the outer join.

18-22 Nested subqueries

The SQL language allows you to nest subqueries 15 levels deep, but you should never do this. I could not even bring myself to make an example for you to see. It is acceptable to have one or two levels of subqueries. Beyond that, the code is almost impossible to understand, change, and maintain. If you find code like this, I recommend that you rewrite it.

18-23   Subqueries can be used in limited locations

It is sometimes said that subqueries can act as variables. However, they are not very good variables because they have a limitation: They can only be used in the `where` clause and the `having` clause. For instance, they cannot be used in the `select` clause as a variable name for a column. They cannot be used in the `from` clause as a variable name for a table.

18-24   Many subqueries can also be written as a join

The subqueries in the previous sections could also be written as joins. See chapters 13 and 14 if you would like to compare the two methods. In most cases I recommend you use joins because the code they produce is easier to understand, maintain, and change.

If a query is run frequently, such as every day, the performance of the query might be the most important issue. In some cases a subquery will run faster than a join. In other cases, the join will run faster. You may have to code a query both ways and test them to see which is faster.

Summary

If-then-else logic is available in both Oracle and Access. This can provide an easier way to write some queries. However, all these queries can also be written with a `union`. The tasks performed in this chapter using if-then-else logic are the same tasks performed in chapter 15 using the union.

A parameter query can ask questions at the time it is run. Then it places the answers within the SQL. This gives your queries much more flexibility. It allows the people who run the queries to specify more precisely what they want the queries to do.

Subqueries occur when one `select` statement is embedded within another one. They were used extensively in the early days of SQL, before the processing of joins became efficient. Now they are used much less. The SQL language still contains many complex features to support subqueries, even though these features are rarely used today. Many subqueries can also be written as joins or outer joins and that is usually a better way to write them.

chapter 19

THE
MULTIUSER
ENVIRONMENT

One of the most important features of a database is its ability to coordinate the work of many people who are all using its data at the same time. Many people can change the data and many other people can run queries simultaneously. Each person can work independently, as if he or she is working alone. The database coordinates all the work and prevents conflicts.

In this chapter I only discuss Oracle so we can cover more material more quickly. Access also has a way to implement many of these same concepts and to set up a secure multiuser environment. However, many of the details are different, so it would be too complex to discuss both products at the same time.

This chapter is an introduction to this topic. It covers the most important points. If you need more detail, you can refer to the Oracle or Access technical reference manuals.

Database Configurations

A database can be set up and configured in many ways. It can be set up to be used by a single person, or it can be set up for thousands of people to use with computers located in many different places. This configuration is performed by the DBAs. As an end user or application programmer, you simply use the computers you are given and many of the details of the configuration are hidden from you. However, it is my experience that the details are never completely hidden and understanding some of the basics of the configuration is important for everybody using the database.

19-1   The single-user environment

So far in this book we have not discussed how the computer and database are configured. That is what we discuss in this chapter. When you use SQL, you may have pictured yourself working alone on your own computer. In this configuration the database belongs to you, it runs on your own personal computer, and you are the only user.

This is one way a database can be set up. It is the default configuration for Access. For Oracle it is rare to run this way, but it is possible. In fact, you probably have run Oracle with this configuration as you studied this book. The following drawing shows a single-user configuration.

Bob

One person working alone on his own computer. So far, this is the configuration we have been working with throughout this book.

19-2   The multiuser environment

In a multiuser configuration many people use the database at the same time. The database is on a server. Each user has his or her own personal computer. A network connects all the PCs to the server. Most of this chapter discusses issues involved in this configuration.

Usually the database is installed on a userid that belongs to the application, rather than to a particular user. Each user has his or her own userid. All of these userids are installed on the same server.

Most of SQL works the same in this configuration as it does in the single-user configuration. The main difference is in the names of the tables. To refer to a table that belongs to a different userid, we use the format

`Owner_Name.Table_Name`

For example, suppose the `Lunches` database has been installed on a userid named "Lunches". And suppose I am logged onto a different userid named "John". If I want to list all the data in the `l_employees` table, I would write

```
select *
from lunches.l_employees;
```

Similarly, I could refer to any table that belonged to another user, if I had permission to do so. The following drawing shows a multiuser configuration.

Several people working together using a database on a shared server. This configuration is often used in medium-sized companies.

19-3   The distributed environment

In the previous configuration the database resided on a single server. Sometimes the database can be distributed across several servers connected in a network. The servers are often in diverse locations. Perhaps one is in London, another is in San Francisco, and a third is in Tokyo. This is a complex configuration and it can have many variations. We discuss it only briefly in this section.

The distribution of data can take several forms. Usually some tables are on one server and other tables are on another server. In Access, we use *linked tables*. In Oracle, the servers are connected together on the software level using *database links*. Again, the table names show this difference. In Oracle, the format of the table names is

```
Owner_Name.Table_Name@Database_Link
```

The server that you are logged onto is called your *local server*. Any other server is called a *remote server*. If you have the right permissions, you can access all the data in the distributed database this way. Database links allow you to handle a distributed database as if it were a single integrated database.

However, there is a serious problem: A query can be very inefficient if it is getting a lot of data from a remote server. Moving a large amount of data across the network can be very slow. There are two solutions to this problem.

One solution is to design your queries so they only bring small amounts of data across the network. This requires careful design and programming, which can be a lot of work.

Another solution makes local copies of many of the tables that are on the remote servers. In Oracle, these are called *snapshots* or *materialized views*. In Access, they are called *replicas* and the process is called *replication*. These copies are often set up to be read-only, but they can also be set up to be updateable so you can do an `insert`, `update`, or `delete` to modify the data.

This solves one problem, but it creates another. When you have two copies of the same table, they may start to diverge. So you have the problem of synchronization and setting a refresh rate.

Designing a distributed database is complex because you must consider the network, the number of servers, the distribution of the data, which tables to replicate, and how often to synchronize them. The following drawing shows a distributed database.

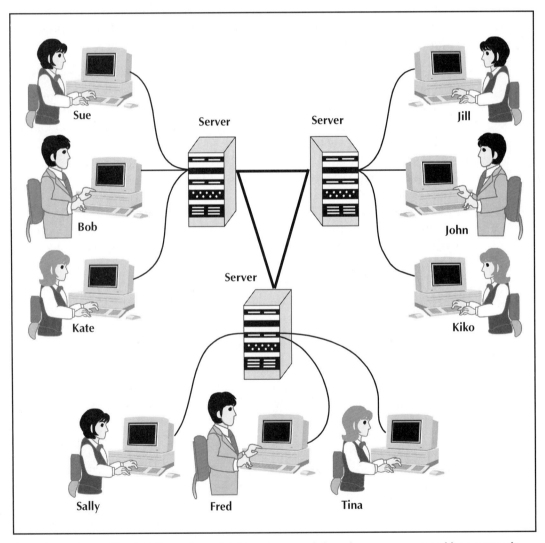

Several people working together using a database on several shared servers connected by a network. This configuration is often used in large companies.

19-4   Connecting via the Internet

So far, the descriptions of the multiuser configuration and the distributed database configuration showed a network connecting all the pieces. Recently, databases have started to develop the ability to use the Internet as an alternative to using a dedicated network. Also, an Internet browser can be used as a tool to work with a database. In Oracle, the products Oracle Portal and Application Server are examples of this. This is a topic that is currently evolving and the products are improving all the time.

Operating in a Multiuser Environment

When you work in a multiuser environment, you often need to use tables you do not own. These tables may be in a remote location. You might develop your own names for them, called *synonyms*, or you might find that many of these complexities are hidden from you. Sometimes when a table is in a remote location, you will work with a local version of it called a snapshot.

19-5   How to use a table you do not own

So far you have owned all the tables you have used. When you create a table, view, or other database object, you are the owner of it. This gives you the exclusive right to use it, change it, or delete it. You can also share it with other people by giving them permission to use it. There are many different levels of permission you can grant to others, which we discuss later in this chapter.

When you have permission to use a table you do not own, you can refer to it by writing the owner name before the table name, in the following format:

```
owner_name.table_name
```

This section provides an example of using a such a table name. Usually when Oracle is installed, a demonstration userid is set up called `scott` and a table called `emp` is created on it. You will list all the data in this table. First, I must show you how to set this up. By the way, Scott was one of the programmers who helped develop Oracle, and Tiger was his cat.

Task

In Oracle, list all the data in the table emp owned by scott. Before you can do this, you will need to log on as scott and give yourself permission to use this table.

Oracle setup

Step 1: Log on to the userid scott. The password is tiger. If you are already logged on to another userid, you can connect to scott by entering

```
connect scott/tiger;
```

Step 2: Give yourself permission to run a select statement with the emp table. In this code replace sqlfun with the name of your userid.

```
grant select on emp to sqlfun;
```

Step 3: Leave userid scott and reconnect to your own userid. In this code replace sqlfun with your userid and replace puppy with your password.

```
connect sqlfun/puppy;
```

Oracle SQL

```
select *
from scott.emp; ❶
```

Result table ❷

```
EMPNO ENAME      JOB          MGR HIREDATE        SAL    COMM DEPTNO
----- ---------- ---------- ------- --------- --------- ------ ------
 7369 SMITH      CLERK         7902 17-DEC-80   $800.00 (null)     20
 7499 ALLEN      SALESMAN      7698 20-FEB-81  $1600.00   $300     30
 7521 WARD       SALESMAN      7698 22-FEB-81  $1250.00   $500     30
 7566 JONES      MANAGER       7839 02-APR-81  $2975.00 (null)     20
 7654 MARTIN     SALESMAN      7698 28-SEP-81  $1250.00  $1400     30
 7698 BLAKE      MANAGER       7839 01-MAY-81  $2850.00 (null)     30
 7782 CLARK      MANAGER       7839 09-JUN-81  $2450.00 (null)     10
 7788 SCOTT      ANALYST       7566 09-DEC-82  $3000.00 (null)     20
 7839 KING       PRESIDENT   (null) 17-NOV-81  $5000.00 (null)     10
 7844 TURNER     SALESMAN      7698 08-SEP-81  $1500.00     $0     30
 7876 ADAMS      CLERK         7788 12-JAN-83  $1100.00 (null)     20
 7900 JAMES      CLERK         7698 03-DEC-81   $950.00 (null)     30
 7902 FORD       ANALYST       7566 03-DEC-81  $3000.00 (null)     20
 7934 MILLER     CLERK         7782 23-JAN-82  $1300.00 (null)     10
```

Notes

❶ The emp table is owned by `scott`.

❷ The SQL_LOGIN.SQL file set the column formats. This adds the dollar signs to the `SAL` and `COMM` columns and does other formatting. The column formats continue to work within the SQLplus session even though we have logged on and off of another Oracle userid.

19-6   Synonyms

In Oracle, a synonym is an alternate name for a table or view. It can also be an alternate name for many other types of database objects, such as a sequence or snapshot. A synonym is a database object. It is permanent until you drop it. This contrasts with a table alias, which is also an alternate name for a table or view. However, a table alias exists only within the scope of a single `select` statement. It vanishes when the `select` statement has finished running.

A synonym can be private or public. A private synonym can be used only by the userid that created it or owns it. A public synonym can be used by anyone on any userid.

Synonyms are often used in a multiuser configuration or a distributed database configuration. They are used to make the names of the tables or other database objects simpler and easier to remember. Synonyms can hide the owner name or the name of the database link. They can create the illusion that you are working in a single-user configuration by hiding the complex names of objects in the other configurations.

Task 1

Create a synonym for the `l_employees` table on the `lunches` userid of the `denver` server. Give it the name `d_employees`.

Oracle SQL ❶

```
create synonym d_employees
for lunches.employees@denver;
```

Notes

❶ You can run this code and create the synonym, but you will not be able to use it unless you happen to have a remote server named `denver`.

Task 2

Create a synonym for the emp table owned by scott. Give this synonym the name emp. You already have permission to use a select statement with this table. A synonym will allow you to use a simpler name for this table, as if it were your own table.

Then list all the data in this table using the synonym in the select statement.

```
create synonym emp
for scott.emp;

select *
from emp; ❶
```

Result table ❷

```
EMPNO ENAME      JOB            MGR HIREDATE         SAL   COMM DEPTNO
----- ---------- --------- ------- --------- --------- ------ ------
 7369 SMITH      CLERK        7902 17-DEC-80   $800.00 (null)     20
 7499 ALLEN      SALESMAN     7698 20-FEB-81  $1600.00   $300     30
 7521 WARD       SALESMAN     7698 22-FEB-81  $1250.00   $500     30
 7566 JONES      MANAGER      7839 02-APR-81  $2975.00 (null)     20
 7654 MARTIN     SALESMAN     7698 28-SEP-81  $1250.00  $1400     30
 7698 BLAKE      MANAGER      7839 01-MAY-81  $2850.00 (null)     30
 7782 CLARK      MANAGER      7839 09-JUN-81  $2450.00 (null)     10
 7788 SCOTT      ANALYST      7566 09-DEC-82  $3000.00 (null)     20
 7839 KING       PRESIDENT (null)  17-NOV-81  $5000.00 (null)     10
 7844 TURNER     SALESMAN     7698 08-SEP-81  $1500.00     $0     30
 7876 ADAMS      CLERK        7788 12-JAN-83  $1100.00 (null)     20
 7900 JAMES      CLERK        7698 03-DEC-81   $950.00 (null)     30
 7902 FORD       ANALYST      7566 03-DEC-81  $3000.00 (null)     20
 7934 MILLER     CLERK        7782 23-JAN-82  $1300.00 (null)     10
```

Notes

❶ emp is a synonym for scott.emp, which is the emp table owned by scott.

❷ This is the same table we listed in the previous section.

19-7   Snapshots

A snapshot is a copy of a table made at a particular time. To an end user, it might appear exactly like a table. A snapshot is frequently used in a distributed database to create a local copy of a remote table. This speeds up the processing of queries that use that table, because it saves the time of transferring the data across the network. A snapshot is also called a *materialized view* or a *replica*.

Snapshots are used mostly to "tune" a database and get it to perform more quickly. Only DBAs create snapshots, but you need to know what they are because you might use them.

A snapshot can be set up in a number of different ways. Most snapshots are read-only. This means they can be used in queries, but you cannot modify the data. Updateable snapshots allow you to make changes to the data by using `insert`, `update`, and `delete`. However, updateable snapshots are more complex and they are used less frequently.

A major issue with any snapshot is how often it is refreshed. It needs to be synchronized with the table it has copied. When you are using snapshots, you will need to be aware of the timing of this synchronization. The data you see may not be completely current, and when you change the data, people at other locations may not see those changes immediately.

Task

Create a snapshot and use it in a query. You will need DBA authority to perform this task. You can do this on your own computer, but you will not be able to do it on a computer you share with others at work or school.

Oracle setup

```
connect system/manager;

create snapshot local_employees
as
select * from l_employees;

grant select on local_employees to public;

connect sqlfun/puppy;
```

Oracle SQL

```
select *
from system.local_employees;
```

Result table

EMPLOYEE ID	FIRST NAME	LAST NAME	DEPT CODE	HIRE_DATE	CREDIT LIMIT	PHONE NUMBER	MANAGER ID
201	SUSAN	BROWN	EXE	01-JUN-98	$30.00	3484	(null)
202	JIM	KERN	SAL	16-AUG-99	$25.00	8722	201
203	MARTHA	WOODS	SHP	02-FEB-04	$25.00	7591	201
204	ELLEN	OWENS	SAL	01-JUL-03	$15.00	6830	202
205	HENRY	PERKINS	SAL	01-MAR-00	$25.00	5286	202
206	CAROL	ROSE	ACT	(null)	(null)	(null)	(null)
207	DAN	SMITH	SHP	01-DEC-04	$25.00	2259	203
208	FRED	CAMPBELL	SHP	01-APR-03	$25.00	1752	203
209	PAULA	JACOBS	MKT	17-MAR-99	$15.00	3357	201
210	NANCY	HOFFMAN	SAL	16-FEB-04	$25.00	2974	203

Security and Privileges

When many people are working with the same database, there are usually restrictions on which data each person is allowed to change. There are also restrictions on what data they can access. These rules are often defined for a group of people, such as for the payroll department, and each person within that department is given the privileges of that group.

19-8   Identifying the user

Each user should have his or her own userid and password. You must use them to identify yourself when you log on to the database. From a computer's point of view, a human is a userid. That is the basis for the security of the database. This may seem obvious, but Access, for instance, does not usually require you to log on to the database.

Sometimes a computer is set up so that the userid and password you supply when you log on to the operating system are automatically passed to Oracle. These replace the userid and password for the Oracle login.

19-9   Privileges

When you create a table, view, or other database object on your userid, you are the owner of that object and you are the only person who can use it (although DBAs can access anything in the database). You can allow other people to use your table by granting them the privilege to use it in a `select` statement, or you can grant them the privilege to use an `insert` statement, `update`, `delete`, or any combination of these. Using a view, you can limit their access to certain rows and certain columns. You can also revoke privileges any time you wish.

The privileges you can grant are very fine-grained. That means you have a high degree of control. You can be very specific about what you allow people to do and what you do not allow.

You can grant a privilege to one particular userid or grant it to the public. When you grant a privilege to the public, you are granting it to every userid.

Up to now, we have discussed object privileges. There are also system privileges that a DBA can grant to a userid to control the operations that it can do. For example there is a Create Table privilege. Without it, you cannot create a table. There is also a Connect privilege. Without it, you cannot log on to the userid.

Why would someone set up a userid and not allow anyone to log on to it? This is a common practice for an application userid. For example, suppose we set up the Lunches database so that three people, Bob, Jill, and Mary, can use it. Suppose that we do not want any of these people to own the database. They are just allowed to use it.

We would set up three individual userids for Bob, Jill, and Mary. We would also set up an application userid for the Lunches database. It would own all the tables, views, and other database objects of the application. No one would be allowed to log on directly to the Lunches userid. People could only log on to their individual userids and use the privileges they have been granted to the Lunches database.

Task 1

Grant to scott the privilege to insert new rows into the l_lunches table.

Oracle SQL

```
grant insert on l_lunches to scott;
```

Task 2

Revoke the privilege granted in task 1.

Oracle SQL

```
revoke insert on l_lunches from scott;
```

Task 3

Allow anyone to use the `l_employees` table in a `select` statement.

Oracle SQL

```
grant select on l_employees to public;
```

19-10 Roles

Privileges can control access to the database, but they are difficult to manage because they are so fine-grained. A privilege usually authorizes one userid to perform one operation. In many applications there are thousands of privileges that must be granted. That can be a lot of work!

Roles provide a more organized way to manage privileges. A role is a set of privileges and it has a name. To use a role, you first create it and give it a name. DBA authority is required to create a role, so you will need to use the `system` userid. If you are not running your own copy of Oracle, you may not be allowed to create a role.

After the role is created, you grant a set of privileges to the role. When you grant the role to a userid, it gets all the privileges assigned to the role. This makes it easy to assign the same set of privileges to many userids.

Task 1

Create a role named `dept_role`.

Oracle SQL ❶

```
connect system/manager;

create role dept_role;
```

Task 2

Grant to the dept_role the privilege to run a select, insert, update, or delete statement on the dept table owned by scott. Grant this role to the userid sqlfun.

Oracle SQL

```
connect scott/tiger; ❷

grant select, insert, update, delete
on dept to dept_role;

grant dept_role to sqlfun; ❸
```

Task 3

From the userid sqlfun, display all the rows and columns of the dept table owned by scott.

Oracle SQL

```
connect sqlfun/puppy; ❹

select *
from scott.dept;
```

Result table

```
DEPTNO DNAME          LOC
------ -------------- --------------
    10 ACCOUNTING     NEW YORK
    20 RESEARCH       DALLAS
    30 SALES          CHICAGO
    40 OPERATIONS     BOSTON
```

Notes

❶ Connect to the system userid. This has DBA authority, which is needed to create a role. The role created here has no privileges yet. It only has a name.

❷ Connect to the scott userid and grant privileges to the role.

❸ Grant all the privileges of the role to the sqlfun userid.

❹ Connect to the sqlfun userid and view the dept_table that belongs to scott. You are allowed to view this table because scott has given you permission to do so.

Several People Using the Same Table at the Same Time

Several people can use the same table at the same time. If one person changes the data, only that person can see the changes until they are committed. Several people can change data in the table as long as they are changing different rows. A problem occurs only when two people try to change the same row at the same time. Oracle handles this problem by making some changes wait until the other changes have been committed or rolled back.

When you are sharing a database with many other people, you should keep your transactions short and commit frequently because your uncommitted changes could be causing someone else to wait.

19-11 One person changing data while another person is looking at it

Suppose there are two userids, B and C, that are using a table at the same time. Suppose B is making changes to the data in the table, while C is only looking at the table.

Before B does a `commit` or `rollback`, if they both look at the table, they will see different data in it. B will see the data with all the changes, but C will not see any of the changes.

After the `commit` or `rollback`, they will both see the same data in the table.

This only applies to making changes to the data in the table, which you might do using the `insert`, `update`, or `delete` commands. Changes to the structure of the table, such as using the `alter table` command, are committed immediately and cannot be rolled back.

How to run two Oracle sessions at the same time

Until now when you ran Oracle, you opened a single Oracle session. For the next few sections you will run two Oracle sessions simultaneously so you can see how the actions of one userid can affect the other userid. You will see both sessions side by side on your computer screen. Here is how to set this up:

1. Log on to your Oracle userid as you usually do, beginning at the Start button. The userid I use is called `sqlfun`, but yours might have a different name.

2. Using your mouse, move the pointer to the right edge of the screen. The mouse pointer will change to a double arrow. Hold down the mouse button and drag the edge to the center of the screen.

3. Log on to the `scott` Oracle userid, beginning at the Start button. The password is `tiger`.

4. Arrange your screen so it shows two windows: `sqlfun` on the left half of the screen and `scott` on the right. If `scott` opened on top of `sqlfun`, then drag it to the right side of the screen using the title bar at the top of the window. Make sure both scrollbars are showing.

These windows behave like any other two windows. Only one of these userids will be active at a time. That is, only one will have the focus of the Windows operating system. You can tell which one is active by the colors of the title bars. To change this focus, click the mouse in the window you want to activate.

Result screen — Two Oracle sessions with different userids are open at the same time
`sqlfun`   `scott`

```
Oracle SQL*Plus                _ □ ×    Oracle SQL*Plus                _ □ ×
File Edit Search Options Help           File Edit Search Options Help
SQL> set serveroutput on;               SQL> set serveroutput on;
SQL>                                    SQL>
SQL> rem                                SQL> rem
SQL> rem Allow blank lines within SQL statement  SQL> rem Allow blank lines within SQL statement
SQL> rem (This option is new. It may not run in  SQL> rem (This option is new. It may not run in
SQL> rem get an error message for this command.  SQL> rem get an error message for this command.
SQL> set sqlblanklines on;              SQL> set sqlblanklines on;
SQL>                                    SQL>
SQL> rem                                SQL> rem
SQL> rem Convert all text of SQL statements to   SQL> rem Convert all text of SQL statements to
SQL> rem This includes literals (values inside   SQL> rem This includes literals (values inside
SQL> set sqlcase upper;                 SQL> set sqlcase upper;
SQL>                                    SQL>
SQL> rem                                SQL> rem
SQL> rem Use spaces in the output, instead of t  SQL> rem Use spaces in the output, instead of t
SQL> rem This makes it easier to copy the outpu  SQL> rem This makes it easier to copy the outpu
SQL> set tab off;                       SQL> set tab off;
SQL>                                    SQL>
SQL> rem                                SQL> rem
SQL> rem determine what editor to use   SQL> rem determine what editor to use
SQL> define_editor = "notepad";         SQL> define_editor = "notepad";
SQL>                                    SQL>
SQL>                                    SQL>
SQL> set echo off;                      SQL> set echo off;


.   *****************************************   .   *****************************************
.   *                                          .   *
.   *      The SQLplus environment is now set   .   *      The SQLplus environment is now set
.   *                                          .   *
.   *****************************************   .   *****************************************

SQL> |                                  SQL> |
```

Task 1

Show that both userids see the same data in the dept table owned by scott.

Oracle SQL

In sqlfun:

select *
from scott.dept;

In scott:

select *
from dept;

Result screen
sqlfun   **scott**

```
Oracle SQL*Plus                            _ □ ×    Oracle SQL*Plus                            _ □ ×
File  Edit  Search  Options  Help                   File  Edit  Search  Options  Help
SQL>                                           ▲    SQL>                                           ▲
SQL> rem                                            SQL> rem
SQL> rem Use spaces in the output, instead of t     SQL> rem Use spaces in the output, instead of t
SQL> rem This makes it easier to copy the outpu     SQL> rem This makes it easier to copy the outpu
SQL> set tab off;                                   SQL> set tab off;
SQL>                                                SQL>
SQL> rem                                            SQL> rem
SQL> rem determine what editor to use               SQL> rem determine what editor to use
SQL> define_editor = "notepad";                     SQL> define_editor = "notepad";
SQL>                                                SQL>
SQL>                                                SQL>
SQL> set echo off;                                  SQL> set echo off;


.    *********************************************    .    *********************************************
.    *                                               .    *
.    *       The SQLplus environment is now set       .    *       The SQLplus environment is now set
.    *                                               .    *
.    *********************************************    .    *********************************************


SQL> select *                                       SQL> select *
  2  from scott.dept;                                  2  from dept;

DEPTNO DNAME          LOC                            DEPTNO DNAME          LOC
------ -------------- -------------                  ------ -------------- -------------
    10 ACCOUNTING     NEW YORK                           10 ACCOUNTING     NEW YORK
    20 RESEARCH       DALLAS                             20 RESEARCH       DALLAS
    30 SALES          CHICAGO                            30 SALES          CHICAGO
    40 OPERATIONS     BOSTON                             40 OPERATIONS     BOSTON

4 rows selected.                                    4 rows selected.

SQL>                                                SQL> |
◄ |                                          ► |    ◄ |                                          ► |
```

Task 2

Using `sqlfun`, make a change to the data in the table. Add a new department named `planning` located in `san francisco`. Do not `commit` or `rollback` this change. Then look at the data in the table from both userids. You will notice that `sqlfun` sees the new row, and `scott` does not.

Oracle SQL

In `sqlfun`:

```
insert into scott.dept
values (50, 'planning', 'san francisco');

select *
from scott.dept;
```

In `scott`:

```
select *
from dept;
```

Result screen

`sqlfun`   **`scott`**

```
SQL> select *
  2  from scott.dept;

DEPTNO DNAME          LOC
------ -------------- -------------
    10 ACCOUNTING     NEW YORK
    20 RESEARCH       DALLAS
    30 SALES          CHICAGO
    40 OPERATIONS     BOSTON

4 rows selected.

SQL> insert into scott.dept
  2  values (50, 'planning', 'san francisco');

1 row created.

SQL>
SQL> select *
  2  from scott.dept;

DEPTNO DNAME          LOC
------ -------------- -------------
    10 ACCOUNTING     NEW YORK
    20 RESEARCH       DALLAS
    30 SALES          CHICAGO
    40 OPERATIONS     BOSTON
    50 PLANNING       SAN FRANCISCO

5 rows selected.

SQL>
```

```
      *****************************************
      *
      *       The SQLplus environment is now set
      *
      *****************************************

SQL> select *
  2  from dept;

DEPTNO DNAME          LOC
------ -------------- -------------
    10 ACCOUNTING     NEW YORK
    20 RESEARCH       DALLAS
    30 SALES          CHICAGO
    40 OPERATIONS     BOSTON

4 rows selected.

SQL> select *
  2  from dept;

DEPTNO DNAME          LOC
------ -------------- -------------
    10 ACCOUNTING     NEW YORK
    20 RESEARCH       DALLAS
    30 SALES          CHICAGO
    40 OPERATIONS     BOSTON

4 rows selected.

SQL>
```

Task 3

Using `sqlfun`, `commit` the changes. Then look at the data in the table from both userids. Now both `sqlfun` and `scott` see the same data.

Oracle SQL

In `sqlfun`:

commit;

select *
from scott.dept;

In `scott`:

select *
from dept;

Result screen
sqlfun   **scott**

```
Oracle SQL*Plus                    _ □ x     Oracle SQL*Plus                    _ □ x
File  Edit  Search  Options  Help          File  Edit  Search  Options  Help

SQL>                                             10 ACCOUNTING    NEW YORK
SQL> select *                                    20 RESEARCH      DALLAS
  2  from scott.dept;                            30 SALES         CHICAGO
                                                 40 OPERATIONS    BOSTON
DEPTNO DNAME           LOC
------ -------------- -------------         4 rows selected.
    10 ACCOUNTING      NEW YORK
    20 RESEARCH        DALLAS             SQL> select *
    30 SALES           CHICAGO             2  from dept;
    40 OPERATIONS      BOSTON
    50 PLANNING        SAN FRANCISCO      DEPTNO DNAME           LOC
                                          ------ -------------- -------------
5 rows selected.                              10 ACCOUNTING      NEW YORK
                                              20 RESEARCH        DALLAS
SQL> commit;                                  30 SALES           CHICAGO
                                              40 OPERATIONS      BOSTON
Commit complete.
                                          4 rows selected.
SQL>
SQL> select *                             SQL> select *
  2  from scott.dept;                       2  from dept;

DEPTNO DNAME           LOC                 DEPTNO DNAME           LOC
------ -------------- -------------        ------ -------------- -------------
    10 ACCOUNTING      NEW YORK                10 ACCOUNTING      NEW YORK
    20 RESEARCH        DALLAS                  20 RESEARCH        DALLAS
    30 SALES           CHICAGO                 30 SALES           CHICAGO
    40 OPERATIONS      BOSTON                  40 OPERATIONS      BOSTON
    50 PLANNING        SAN FRANCISCO           50 PLANNING        SAN FRANCISCO

5 rows selected.                          5 rows selected.

SQL>                                      SQL>
```

19-12 Two people changing different rows in the same table

Suppose there are two userids, B and C, that are both changing the data in the same table at the same. Suppose they are changing different rows of the table. They can `insert`, `update`, or `delete` rows. But for now, we suppose that they never both make changes to the same row.

Before either person commits the changes, they each see only their own changes. After B commits, B will see only B's changes, but C will see all the changes of both B and C.

After they both commit, they will both see all the updates.

Task 1

Using `sqlfun`, change the location of department 20 to `austin`. Using `scott`, delete the `planning` department. Do not `commit` either change. Then look at the data in the table from both userids. Notice that each userid sees only its own changes.

Oracle SQL

In `sqlfun`:

```
update scott.dept
set loc = 'austin'
where deptno = 20;
```

In `scott`:

```
delete from dept
where deptno = 50;

select *
from dept;
```

In `sqlfun`:

```
select *
from scott.dept;
```

Result screen
sqlfun   scott

```
┌─ Oracle SQL*Plus ──────────────────── _ □ × ┐ ┌─ Oracle SQL*Plus ──────────────────── _ □ × ┐
│ File  Edit  Search  Options  Help           │ │ File  Edit  Search  Options  Help           │
│ SQL>                                      ▲  │ │ 4 rows selected.                          ▲  │
│ SQL> select *                                │ │                                              │
│   2  from scott.dept;                        │ │ SQL> select *                                │
│                                              │ │   2  from dept;                              │
│ DEPTNO DNAME          LOC                    │ │                                              │
│ ------ -------------- -------------          │ │ DEPTNO DNAME          LOC                    │
│     10 ACCOUNTING     NEW YORK               │ │ ------ -------------- -------------          │
│     20 RESEARCH       DALLAS                 │ │     10 ACCOUNTING     NEW YORK               │
│     30 SALES          CHICAGO                │ │     20 RESEARCH       DALLAS                 │
│     40 OPERATIONS     BOSTON                 │ │     30 SALES          CHICAGO                │
│     50 PLANNING       SAN FRANCISCO          │ │     40 OPERATIONS     BOSTON                 │
│                                              │ │     50 PLANNING       SAN FRANCISCO          │
│ 5 rows selected.                             │ │                                              │
│                                              │ │ 5 rows selected.                             │
│ SQL> update scott.dept                       │ │                                              │
│   2  set loc = 'austin'                      │ │ SQL> delete from dept                        │
│   3  where deptno = 20;                      │ │   2  where deptno = 50;                      │
│                                              │ │                                              │
│ 1 row updated.                               │ │ 1 row deleted.                               │
│                                              │ │                                              │
│ SQL> select *                                │ │ SQL>                                         │
│   2  from scott.dept;                        │ │ SQL> select *                                │
│                                              │ │   2  from dept;                              │
│ DEPTNO DNAME          LOC                    │ │                                              │
│ ------ -------------- -------------          │ │ DEPTNO DNAME          LOC                    │
│     10 ACCOUNTING     NEW YORK               │ │ ------ -------------- -------------          │
│     20 RESEARCH       AUSTIN                 │ │     10 ACCOUNTING     NEW YORK               │
│     30 SALES          CHICAGO                │ │     20 RESEARCH       DALLAS                 │
│     40 OPERATIONS     BOSTON                 │ │     30 SALES          CHICAGO                │
│     50 PLANNING       SAN FRANCISCO          │ │     40 OPERATIONS     BOSTON                 │
│                                              │ │                                              │
│ 5 rows selected.                             │ │ 4 rows selected.                             │
│                                              │ │                                              │
│ SQL>                                      ▼  │ │ SQL> |                                     ▼  │
│ ◄ |                                       ►  │ │ ◄ |                                       ►  │
└──────────────────────────────────────────── ┘ └──────────────────────────────────────────── ┘
```

Task 2

Using `sqlfun`, `commit` the changes. Then look at the data in the table from both userids. Notice that `sqlfun` sees only its changes, and `scott` sees all the changes.

Oracle SQL

In `sqlfun`:

```
commit;

select *
from scott.dept;
```

In `scott`:

```
select *
from dept;
```

Result screen

sqlfun   **scott**

```
Oracle SQL*Plus                                    _ □ X    Oracle SQL*Plus                                    _ □ X
File  Edit  Search  Options  Help                          File  Edit  Search  Options  Help
1 row updated.                                             5 rows selected.

SQL> select *                                              SQL> delete from dept
  2  from scott.dept;                                        2   where deptno = 50;

DEPTNO DNAME           LOC                                  1 row deleted.
------ --------------- -------------
    10 ACCOUNTING      NEW YORK                             SQL>
    20 RESEARCH        AUSTIN                               SQL> select *
    30 SALES           CHICAGO                                2  from dept;
    40 OPERATIONS      BOSTON
    50 PLANNING        SAN FRANCISCO                         DEPTNO DNAME           LOC
                                                             ------ --------------- -------------
5 rows selected.                                                10 ACCOUNTING      NEW YORK
                                                                20 RESEARCH        DALLAS
SQL> commit;                                                    30 SALES           CHICAGO
                                                                40 OPERATIONS      BOSTON
Commit complete.
                                                           4 rows selected.
SQL>
SQL> select *                                              SQL> select *
  2  from scott.dept;                                        2  from dept;

DEPTNO DNAME           LOC                                  DEPTNO DNAME           LOC
------ --------------- -------------                        ------ --------------- -------------
    10 ACCOUNTING      NEW YORK                                 10 ACCOUNTING      NEW YORK
    20 RESEARCH        AUSTIN                                   20 RESEARCH        AUSTIN
    30 SALES           CHICAGO                                  30 SALES           CHICAGO
    40 OPERATIONS      BOSTON                                   40 OPERATIONS      BOSTON
    50 PLANNING        SAN FRANCISCO
                                                           4 rows selected.
5 rows selected.
                                                           SQL>
SQL>
```

Task 3

Using scott, commit the changes. Then look at the data in the table from both userids. Now both userids see the same data.

Oracle SQL

In scott:

commit;

select *
from dept;

In sqlfun:

select *
from scott.dept;

Result screen

sqlfun   **scott**

19-13 Two people changing the same row in a table

Suppose there are two userids, B and C, that are both changing the data in the same row of the same table at the same time. They can `update` or `delete` the row.

The first change is accepted by the database. However, the second change is not accepted until the first change is either committed or rolled back. The person who entered the second change has to wait until the row is released. Meanwhile, his terminal is frozen.

Task 1

Using `sqlfun`, change the name of department 30 to `marketing`. Then, using `scott`, change the location of department 30 to `denver`. You will notice that scott's change cannot be completed until after `sqlfun` has committed its change to department 30. After both changes have been committed, both userids see the same data.

Oracle SQL

In `sqlfun`:

```
update scott.dept
set dname = 'marketing'
where deptno = 30;

select *
from scott.dept;
```

In `scott`:

```
update dept
set loc = 'denver'
where deptno = 30;
```

Now the Oracle session for `scott` freezes. It will not respond to any command he enters. His `update` command remains pending until `sqlfun` commits its changes to the row. There is no SQL prompt.

In sqlfun:

commit;

Now the Oracle session for scott revives. It makes the change to the row and shows a confirming message, "1 row updated." The SQL prompt is displayed again.

In scott:

select *
from dept;

commit;

In sqlfun:

select *
from scott.dept;

Result screen
sqlfun   scott

```
 Oracle SQL*Plus                    _ □ ×        Oracle SQL*Plus                    _ □ ×
 File  Edit  Search  Options  Help             File  Edit  Search  Options  Help
   3   where deptno = 30;                      DEPTNO DNAME          LOC
                                               ------ -------------- -------------
1 row updated.                                     10 ACCOUNTING     NEW YORK
                                                   20 RESEARCH       AUSTIN
SQL>                                               30 SALES          CHICAGO
SQL> select *                                      40 OPERATIONS     BOSTON
  2  from scott.dept;
                                               4 rows selected.
DEPTNO DNAME          LOC
------ -------------- -------------            SQL> update dept
    10 ACCOUNTING     NEW YORK                   2  set loc = 'denver'
    20 RESEARCH       AUSTIN                      3  where deptno = 30;
    30 MARKETING      CHICAGO
    40 OPERATIONS     BOSTON                   1 row updated.

4 rows selected.                               SQL> select *
                                                 2  from dept;
SQL> commit;
                                               DEPTNO DNAME          LOC
Commit complete.                               ------ -------------- -------------
                                                   10 ACCOUNTING     NEW YORK
SQL> select *                                      20 RESEARCH       AUSTIN
  2  from scott.dept;                              30 MARKETING      DENVER
                                                   40 OPERATIONS     BOSTON
DEPTNO DNAME          LOC
------ -------------- -------------            4 rows selected.
    10 ACCOUNTING     NEW YORK
    20 RESEARCH       AUSTIN                    SQL>
    30 MARKETING      DENVER                    SQL> commit;
    40 OPERATIONS     BOSTON
                                               Commit complete.
4 rows selected.
                                               SQL>
SQL>
```

Locks

Locks and rollback segments are the mechanisms that are used to coordinate the work of all the people who are using the database at the same time. The details can get quite complex, but usually you do not need to think about these things because the database takes care of them automatically.

19-14 Row locks

Oracle uses row locks. A lock is put on a row when the data in that row has been changed by an `insert`, `update`, or `delete` statement. Each row is locked separately from any other row. The lock is released by a `commit` or `rollback`. These locks are placed on the uncommitted rows of a table to prevent other people from modifying them before the changes are finalized.

Some brands of SQL do not use row locks. They place locks on blocks of rows instead of individual rows. The number of rows in a block depends on many factors, but for this discussion let's suppose there are four rows in a block. If userid B makes a change to one row, all four rows in its block are locked until a `commit` or `rollback` is done. This means that userid C cannot make changes to any of these four rows while they are locked.

19-15 `Rollback` **segments**

When the data in a row is changed with an `insert`, `update`, or `delete` statement, the new data in the row is written into the database even before the row is committed. The old data in the row is written to a `rollback` segment.

If a transaction is committed that has changed several rows, the locks are released and the data in the `rollback` segment is no longer needed. However, if the transaction is rolled back, then the old values are obtained from the `rollback` segment and they are written back into the database.

If another user looks at a row before it is committed, the old value of the row is retrieved from the `rollback` segment.

19-16 Table locks

If many changes are going to be made to the rows in a table, sometimes we lock the whole table instead of the individual rows. This is much easier and more efficient for the computer.

Table locks are also acquired by `insert`, `update`, and `delete` in addition to the row locks. The table locks prevent the `alter table` and `drop table` commands.

19-17 Types of locks

There are five types of table locks:

- Row Share (RS)

- Row Exclusive (RX)

- Share (S)

- Share Row Exclusive (SRX)

- Exclusive (X)

Each type of lock permits certain types of commands and does not permit others. They are listed here from the most permissive to the most restrictive. The point here is that the details of locking can become quite complex. Usually you do not need to worry about these details.

By contrast, there is only one type of row lock. So row locking is fairly easy to understand.

19-18 `Select for update`

The `select` statement can be used to place locks on some rows. This reserves the rows so that you are the only person who can change or delete them. When you want to release the rows, you can issue a `commit` or `rollback` command. This allows other people to make changes to them.

Task 1

Using sqlfun, place row locks on the rows with employee numbers 10 and 20 in the dept table owned by scott.

Oracle SQL

In sqlfun:

```
select *
from scott.dept
where deptno in (10, 20)
for update;
```

Result screen

sqlfun   scott

Task 2

Using scott, make a change to the row for department 10. Change the location to albany. You will see that Oracle waits for the row to be released.

Oracle SQL

In scott:

```
update dept
set loc = 'albany'
where deptno = 10;
```

Result screen ❶

sqlfun   scott

```
Oracle SQL*Plus                                  _□X     Oracle SQL*Plus                                     _□X
File  Edit  Search  Options  Help                        File  Edit  Search  Options  Help
SQL>                                                     SQL>
SQL>                                                     SQL>
SQL>                                                     SQL>
SQL>                                                     SQL>
SQL>                                                     SQL>
SQL>                                                     SQL>
SQL>                                                     SQL>
SQL>                                                     SQL>
SQL>                                                     SQL>
SQL>                                                     SQL>
SQL>                                                     SQL>
SQL>                                                     SQL>
SQL>                                                     SQL>
SQL>                                                     SQL>
SQL>                                                     SQL>
SQL>                                                     SQL>
SQL>                                                     SQL>
SQL>                                                     SQL>
SQL>                                                     SQL>
SQL>                                                     SQL>
SQL> select *                                            SQL>
  2  from scott.dept                                     SQL>
  3  where deptno in (10, 20)                            SQL>
  4  for update;                                         SQL>
                                                         SQL>
DEPTNO DNAME          LOC                                SQL>
------ -------------- -------------                      SQL>
    10 ACCOUNTING     NEW YORK                           SQL>
    20 RESEARCH       DALLAS                             SQL>
                                                         SQL> update dept
2 rows selected.                                           2  set loc = 'albany'
                                                           3  where deptno = 10;
SQL>
```

Notes

❶ Scott does not receive an SQL prompt. His change has to wait until the lock is released on row 10.

Task 3

Using sqlfun, release the locks on the two rows by doing a commit. This returns the SQL prompt to scott. Then using scott, commit the change and list all the rows and columns of the table.

Oracle SQL

In sqlfun:

commit;

In scott:

commit;

select * from dept;

Result screen

sqlfun   **scott**

Oracle SQL*Plus	Oracle SQL*Plus
File Edit Search Options Help	File Edit Search Options Help

```
SQL>                                  SQL>
SQL>                                  SQL>
SQL>                                  SQL>
SQL>                                  SQL>
SQL>                                  SQL>
SQL>                                  SQL>
SQL>                                  SQL>
SQL>                                  SQL>
SQL>                                  SQL>
SQL>                                  SQL>
SQL>                                  SQL>
SQL>                                  SQL>
SQL>                                  SQL> update dept
SQL>                                    2   set loc = 'albany'
SQL>                                    3   where deptno = 10;
SQL>
SQL>                                  1 row updated.
SQL> select *
  2   from scott.dept                 SQL> commit;
  3   where deptno in (10, 20)
  4   for update;                     Commit complete.

DEPTNO DNAME          LOC             SQL> select * from dept;
------ -------------- ------------
    10 ACCOUNTING     NEW YORK        DEPTNO DNAME          LOC
    20 RESEARCH       AUSTIN          ------ -------------- -------------
                                          10 ACCOUNTING     ALBANY
2 rows selected.                          20 RESEARCH       AUSTIN
                                          30 MARKETING      DENVER
SQL> commit;                              40 OPERATIONS     BOSTON

Commit complete.                      4 rows selected.

SQL>                                  SQL>
```

19-19   Stability while running a `select` statement

Two people cannot change the same row at the same time. Row locks and table locks coordinate all the changes to the data and they prevent this. Occasionally, you have to wait for a row to be released. That is the price you must pay for this level of coordination.

That completely solves one problem, but there are two other problems of coordination that must also be addressed. Picture that the data in the database is constantly being changed, usually at a slow rate. In that environment, the problems are as follows:

- How can a `select` statement run on a consistent set of data?

- How can a transaction run on a consistent set of data?

Oracle automatically provides for a `select` statement. Oracle runs a `select` statement as if the data does not change from the time it begins until the time it ends. If any data changes during that time, the old value of the data is written to a `rollback` segment and the `select` statement uses the value of the data at the time the `select` statement began. This ensures that the results of any `select` statement are produced from a consistent set of data as it was at one moment of time.

The next section discusses how the data can be stabilized during a transaction, which involves setting the isolation level.

19-20   Stability while running a transaction

A transaction may include several `select` statements in addition to several changes to the data. It is a single unit of work within a database. It may take several minutes to complete a transaction and during that time the data in the database may be changing. Oracle is able to hold the data stable during the entire transaction so that all the data is held as it was at a single point in time, when the transaction began.

A lot of computer resources may be required to stabilize the data during an entire transaction. This is available only on request — it is not the default. To make this request, set the transaction isolation level. Oracle supports three transaction isolation levels:

- Read-committed
- Read-only
- Serializable

The read-committed isolation level is the default. It stabilizes the data during the processing of any one SQL statement — `select`, `insert`, `update`, or `delete` — but it does not keep the data stable for the entire duration of a transaction.

The read-only isolation level keeps the data stable during several `select` statements. However, it does not allow changes to be made to the data within the transaction.

The serializable isolation level stabilizes the data during the entire transaction, which can include `select`, `insert`, `update`, and `delete` statements. The serializable isolation level is more expensive to use because it requires a greater amount of computer resources. The read-only isolation level provides a less expensive alternative.

To set the isolation level to read-only, the command is

```
set transaction isolation level read only;
```

This must be the first command in a transaction. That means the command before it ends the previous transaction by doing a `commit` or a `rollback`.

Additional computer resources are required to have transaction-level consistency, so you should talk to your DBA if you are planning to use the read-only or serializable isolation levels.

Task 1

Using `sqlfun`, start a transaction at the read-only isolation level. Then list all the columns and rows of the `dept` table owned by `scott`.

Oracle SQL

In sqlfun:

commit; ❶

set transaction read only;

select * from scott.dept;

Result screen
sqlfun   **scott**

```
Oracle SQL*Plus                          _ □ ×    Oracle SQL*Plus                          _ □ ×
File  Edit  Search  Options  Help                  File  Edit  Search  Options  Help
SQL>                                               SQL>
SQL>                                               SQL>
SQL>                                               SQL>
SQL>                                               SQL>
SQL>                                               SQL>
SQL>                                               SQL>
SQL>                                               SQL>
SQL>                                               SQL>
SQL>                                               SQL>
SQL>                                               SQL>
SQL>                                               SQL>
SQL>                                               SQL>
SQL>                                               SQL>
SQL> commit;                                       SQL>
                                                   SQL>
Commit complete.                                   SQL>
                                                   SQL>
SQL> set transaction read only;                    SQL>
                                                   SQL>
Transaction set.                                   SQL>
                                                   SQL>
SQL> select * from scott.dept;                     SQL>
                                                   SQL>
DEPTNO DNAME          LOC                           SQL>
------ -------------- -------------                 SQL>
    10 ACCOUNTING     ALBANY                        SQL>
    20 RESEARCH       AUSTIN                        SQL>
    30 MARKETING      DENVER                        SQL>
    40 OPERATIONS     BOSTON                        SQL>
                                                   SQL>
4 rows selected.                                   SQL>
                                                   SQL>
SQL>                                               SQL> |
```

Notes

❶ This commit statement ensures that the next statement occurs at the beginning of a transaction.

Task 2

Using scott, make a change to the data in the dept table and commit it. Change the location of the accounting department to new york. Then list all the columns and rows of the table. You will see that the changes have been made.

Oracle SQL

In scott:

```
update dept
set loc = 'new york'
where deptno = 10;

commit;

select * from dept;
```

Result screen

sqlfun   **scott**

```
Oracle SQL*Plus                        _ □ ×     Oracle SQL*Plus                        _ □ ×
File  Edit  Search  Options  Help                File  Edit  Search  Options  Help
SQL>                                             SQL>
SQL>                                             SQL>
SQL>                                             SQL>
SQL>                                             SQL>
SQL>                                             SQL>
SQL>                                             SQL>
SQL>                                             SQL>
SQL>                                             SQL>
SQL>                                             SQL>
SQL>                                             SQL>
SQL>                                             SQL>
SQL>                                             SQL> update dept
SQL>                                                2   set loc = 'new york'
SQL>                                                3   where deptno = 10;
SQL>
SQL> commit;                                     1 row updated.

Commit complete.                                 SQL>
                                                 SQL> commit;
SQL> set transaction read only;
                                                 Commit complete.
Transaction set.
                                                 SQL>
SQL> select * from scott.dept;                   SQL> select * from dept;

DEPTNO DNAME           LOC                        DEPTNO DNAME           LOC
------ --------------- --------------             ------ --------------- --------------
    10 ACCOUNTING      ALBANY                         10 ACCOUNTING      NEW YORK
    20 RESEARCH        AUSTIN                         20 RESEARCH        AUSTIN
    30 MARKETING       DENVER                         30 MARKETING       DENVER
    40 OPERATIONS      BOSTON                         40 OPERATIONS      BOSTON

4 rows selected.                                 4 rows selected.

SQL> |                                           SQL>
```

Task 3

Using `sqlfun`, list the `dept` table again. The data will not show the change made by `scott`. Then issue a `commit` command to release the resources that are holding a stable image of the data. After the `commit`, `sqlfun` will see `scott`'s changes.

Oracle SQL

In `sqlfun`:

```
select * from scott.dept;

commit;

select * from scott.dept;
```

Result screen
sqlfun   **scott**

Conclusion

For `sqlfun` the data in the table was held steady even though `scott` made a change to the data and committed his change. This stabilization occurred because the isolation level was set to read-only.

The Data Dictionary and the Multiuser Environment

You can find all the information about your multiuser environment in the Data Dictionary.

19-21 ALL **versus** USER

The names of the tables in the Oracle Data Dictionary begin with ALL, USER, or DBA. Most tables have all three versions. To see what this means, consider an example:

Table Name	Information in the Data Dictionary Table
USER_TABLES	Information about all the tables you own. That is, all the tables created on your userid.
ALL_TABLES	Information about all the tables you own and all the tables on other userids that you have been granted the privilege to use.
DBA_TABLES	Information about all the tables in the database. To use this table you must have DBA privileges. If you have Oracle installed on your home computer, you can use this table from userid = system. The password is manager.

19-22 How to find the tables you want in the Data Dictionary

In the Data Dictionary you can find information about the multiuser environment — synonyms, snapshots, privileges, and roles. You will have to look in several tables. Use the dictionary table to find the names of the tables you want. Here is how to get started.

Task

Find the names of the Data Dictionary tables containing information about synonyms.

Oracle SQL

```
select *
from dictionary
where table_name like '%syn%';
```

Result table

TABLE_NAME	COMMENTS
ALL_SYNONYMS	All synonyms accessible to the user
USER_SYNONYMS	The user's private synonyms
SYN	Synonym for USER_SYNONYMS

19-23   How to find the meaning of the columns

Once you know the name of a Data Dictionary table, you can find the meaning of all of its columns using the `dict_columns` table.

Task

Find the meanings of all the columns of the `all_synonyms` table.

Oracle SQL

```
select *
from dict_columns
where table_name = 'all_synonyms';
```

Result table

TABLE_NAME	COLUMN_NAME	COMMENTS
ALL_SYNONYMS	OWNER	Owner of the synonym
ALL_SYNONYMS	SYNONYM_NAME	Name of the synonym
ALL_SYNONYMS	TABLE_OWNER	Owner of the object referenced by the synonym
ALL_SYNONYMS	TABLE_NAME	Name of the object referenced by the synonym
ALL_SYNONYMS	DB_LINK	Name of the database link referenced in a remote synonym

How to Create a Shared Application

A shared application usually has a userid of its own, which is separate from the userids that belong to the people who work with it. Usually a shared application is installed on a network of computers with a client/server configuration. Here, we set it up on a single computer because that is what we have available.

19-24 Creating the Lunches database as a shared application

In this section I show you how to set up a shared application. We set up the Lunches database so many people can use it at the same time. A userid is set up for the application, which is separate from any of the userids of the people using the application. We will name this userid lunches. The shared tables are all created on this userid and they will belong to it.

We also give everyone permission to use the tables — to run select, insert, update, and delete statements with them. And we set up synonyms so people can refer to them with simple names, which do not explicitly show that the tables are on the lunches userid.

Task 1

Prepare to create a new userid named lunches. First, check if this userid already exists. Then check the names of the tablespaces on your system.

Oracle SQL: Prepare to create a new userid

If you are not already logged onto system:

```
connect system;
```

(the password is manager)
From system:

```
select username
from dba_users;
```

The result is a list of all the userids currently on your system. Make sure you do not have a userid named `lunches`. If you do have this userid, use the command

drop user lunches cascade;

Then check the names of your tablespaces.

select tablespace_name
from dba_tablespaces;

Result table ❶

```
TABLESPACE_NAME
------------------------
SYSTEM  ❷
RBS  ❸
USERS  ❹
TEMP  ❺
TOOLS
INDX  ❻
DRSYS
```

Notes

❶ The tablespace names on your system may be different. Oracle sometimes changes these names from one version to the next. However, the names are usually similar enough that you can easily guess how they correspond to the names shown here.

❷ The `SYSTEM` tablespace contains the Data Dictionary and other parts of the DBMS. It is best to reserve this for Oracle and not put any of your data into this space.

❸ The `RBS` tablespace is used for the `rollback` segments.

❹ The `USERS` tablespace is where you should build your tables.

❺ The `TEMP` tablespace is a workspace Oracle uses for sorting and searching the data.

❻ The `INDX` tablespace is where you should build your indexes.

Task 2

Create a userid for the `lunches` application.

Oracle SQL: Create a new userid

```
create user lunches identified by hunger ❶
default tablespace users ❷
temporary tablespace temp; ❸

grant resource, connect to lunches; ❹
```

Notes

❶ This creates a new userid named `lunches`. Its password is `hunger`.

❷ The name of a tablespace is `users`. Adjust this for your system.

❸ The name of a tablespace is `temp`. Adjust this for your system.

❹ The new userid cannot function without these privileges.

Task 3

Copy the tables of the `Lunches` database to the new userid. Here I only show you the code to move the `l_employees` table. Moving all the other tables is similar.

Oracle SQL: Move the tables to the new userid ❶

Fromuserid: `system`:

```
create table lunches.employees as
select *
from sqlfun.l_employees; ❷
```

Notes

❶ To move the tables of the `Lunches` database, you need to move each of the seven tables, one at a time.

❷ Use the name of your userid in place of `sqlfun`.

Task 4

Allow every userid to use the Lunches application. Grant them permission to use a select, insert, update, or delete statement on the l_employees table on the lunches userid. Also set up a public synonym so they can all refer to this table as

l_employees

instead of

lunches.employees

Oracle SQL: Grant privileges and set up synonyms

```
connect lunches;
```

The password is hunger.

```
grant select, insert, update, delete
on employees to public; ❶
```

```
connect system;
```

The password is manager.

```
create public synonym l_employees
for lunches.employees; ❷
```

Notes

❶ This allows any userid to use a select, insert, update, or delete command on the employees table belonging to the lunches userid.

❷ This allows any userid to refer to the employees table as l_employees. You may need to issue this command from the system userid, some versions of Oracle require this.

Task 5

Test that `scott` can use the `l_employees` table.

Oracle SQL: Test

```
connect scott;
```

The password is `tiger`.

```
select *
from l_employees;
```

Result table

EMPLOYEE ID	FIRST NAME	LAST NAME	DEPT CODE	HIRE_DATE	CREDIT LIMIT	PHONE NUMBER	MANAGER ID
201	SUSAN	BROWN	EXE	01-JUN-1998	$30.00	3484	(null)
202	JIM	KERN	SAL	16-AUG-1999	$25.00	8722	201
203	MARTHA	WOODS	SHP	02-FEB-2004	$25.00	7591	201
204	ELLEN	OWENS	SAL	01-JUL-2003	$15.00	6830	202
205	HENRY	PERKINS	SAL	01-MAR-2000	$25.00	5286	202
206	CAROL	ROSE	ACT	(null)	(null)	(null)	(null)
207	DAN	SMITH	SHP	01-DEC-2004	$25.00	2259	203
208	FRED	CAMPBELL	SHP	01-APR-2003	$25.00	1752	203
209	PAULA	JACOBS	MKT	17-MAR-1999	$15.00	3357	201
210	NANCY	HOFFMAN	SAL	16-FEB-2004	$25.00	2974	203

Summary

A database has the ability to coordinate the work of 1,000 people or more, all working with the same data at the same time. It prevents two people from changing the same row at the same time. It stabilizes the data while a `select` command is running, still allowing the underlying data to be changed. It can also stabilize the data for the duration of an entire transaction.

When a database is shared by many people, it is important to know what privileges you have and what synonyms have been set up for you to use.

chapter 20

THE DESIGN OF SQL

SQL lies at the heart of most information systems today. The main objective of SQL is to find the correct information for you. It relies on other software to present that information to you in a polished manner. A variety of software can provide that polish.

SQL is often used with software that can produce forms and reports. A form displays one record at a time. Data in a single row can be entered, viewed, changed, or deleted. Most people find this easier than entering SQL commands.

A report displays many records. It is always based on a query. It cleans up the result table, puts in page numbers, column headings, totals, and adds other elements that make the report easier to read.

Original SQL Design Objectives

In the early 1970s people were devising ways to handle very large amounts of information. Solving that problem was the original motivation that led to relational databases and SQL. Essential aims of the design are to make the handling of information as simple as possible and to make the information accessible to a large number of people.

20-1   Do one thing and do it well

SQL was designed to handle a large amount of information and to coordinate the use of that information by a group of people. That is all it was designed to do. It was never intended to be a complete application in itself or to replace other types of software. It was designed to be an information repository and to work in cooperation with other types of software. It was designed to do one thing and do it well.

Until now in this book I have focused the discussion on SQL itself. I have invited you to imagine that the database is already built and you are sitting alone at a computer trying to get some information out of it or perhaps making a few modifications to the data. I have invited you to imagine that you are the only person using the database, that it belongs to you, and that SQL is the only software you will use. That has been a useful illusion for teaching you SQL, but in the real world you will usually be sharing the database with many other people. SQL will provide an important part of what you need, but it may leave a few gaps for you to fill with other tools.

20-2   Focus on information

SQL makes a distinction between the *information level* and the *presentation level*. Within that dichotomy, SQL focuses primarily on the information level and leaves the presentation level to other software. This is not meant to suggest that the presentation is less important than the information. The presentation may be very important, but it is not what SQL is designed to do well.

For example, SQL does not put page numbers on a report. It might produce a report of 100 pages without any page numbers. If you want page numbers on the report, and I would want them, you might pull the report into Microsoft Word. There you could choose between several types of page numbers, in several sizes and typefaces, placed on the page in a variety of ways. It is important to have these options and to use them. However, it is not the job of SQL to give them to you.

SQL is designed to work hand-in-hand with other programming languages such as Java, COBOL, and Visual Basic. The idea is that SQL will provide some specialized services and these other languages will do all the other things that need to be done. Some of those other things are:

- Presenting the data in a polished form

- Interacting with the end user

- Interfacing and integrating with other programming systems

- Providing complex rules for data validation

In fact, when we used SQL in this book, we always had another level of software between SQL and us. When we used Oracle, we reached SQL through SQLplus. Another language that is frequently used with Oracle is PL/SQL. When we used Access, we reached the JET engine, which processes SQL, through GUI screens that actually communicate with JET using a language called Data Access Objects (DAO). Another language that can be used to communicate with Jet SQL is ActiveX Data Objects (ADO).

20-3   Keep it simple

SQL is designed to avoid the things that make many computer languages complex. Because of this, sometimes programmers feel that SQL is missing some important parts. It does not have all the things that programmers are used to having in a computer language. In particular, SQL does not have

- Variables

- Loops or `goto` statements

- `If-then-else` statements

- Mixing of detail data with summarized data

- An object model with objects, properties, events, and methods

This is not a mistake. The design of SQL intentionally avoids these things. The idea is to keep the handling of information as simple as possible.

These structures have the potential to lead to excessive complexity, so they are not included in SQL.

The issue we discussed in the previous section is also a part of the strategy to keep the design simple. That is, SQL is intended to do one thing well — handle information. It is not intended to do other things, and that is a major part of what keeps it simple.

Variables, loops, and the other things listed are available in most programming languages. Because SQL is designed to work along with one of these languages, there is no reason to also have these things within SQL itself. If you need a variable or a loop, then you can get it from the other programming language.

As SQL has evolved over a few decades, an effort has been made to make it still simpler. When SQL was first developed it was designed so that subqueries would be used extensively. The original design allowed subqueries to be nested 15 levels deep. This produced code that was hard to understand and maintain even if you had written it yourself.

In the past few years outer joins have become an official part of SQL. To a large extent, an outer join can be used to replace a subquery. This makes the code much easier to understand and maintain, taking SQL one step further toward its goal of being simple.

20-4   Coordinate people to work together

One of the strengths of SQL is that it allows a large group of people to work together using current information. People at all levels of an organization can work on the same project. In this aspect, SQL is a tool for coordinating a large workforce and getting everyone to pull in the same direction, as we discussed in chapter 19.

In the world today, databases lie at the heart of most large businesses and government agencies. The database plays a role in coordinating the people as well as providing a store of information.

Newer Interfaces

When SQL was first designed, the idea was that everybody from vice presidents to secretaries would write `select` queries. That would be the way they would interact with the database. However, experience has shown that most vice-presidents do not want to write their own `select` queries, so new interfaces are needed.

Forms provide a universal language that everyone feels comfortable with. They are used a lot in business and government, so forms were adopted as a front end to databases. Forms deal primarily with data at the lowest level of detail.

Reports provide formatting to make larger collections of information easier to read. Web tools are in the process of being integrated into many databases so that forms and reports can be accessed over the Internet. Databases also interface with programming languages such as Java or Visual Basic to provide a bridge to other software applications.

20-5   Forms

Forms can be used to enter, modify, and delete data and to find individual records in a database. This is equivalent to writing an `insert`, `update`, `delete`, or `select` statement in SQL. Forms usually handle one row at a time. Some forms show a few records together. An example of a form is shown here.

20-6   Reports

While forms handle individual records, reports handle many records at a time. The example on the following three pages shows the detail of every lunch, along with subtotals and a grand total. It has a title for the report, a date when the report was run, page numbers, and the data in the first three columns is not repeated on every line.

20-7   Web tools

Oracle and Access are currently developing the ability to use forms and reports over the Internet. This is one of the main features added to the new versions of both products. Several different approaches are being developed. No solution has yet been accepted as standard.

Employee Lunches

Employee ID	First Name	Lunch Date	Description	Quantity	Total Price
201	Susan	Nov 16, 2005	Sandwich	2	$7.00
			Coffee	2	$1.70
			Fresh Salad	1	$2.00
		Summary for 'Lunch Date' = Nov 16, 2005 (3 detail records)			
		Sum		5	*$10.70*
201	Susan	Nov 25, 2005	Fresh Salad	1	$2.00
			Grilled Steak	1	$6.00
			Soda	1	$1.25
		Summary for 'Lunch Date' = Nov 25, 2005 (3 detail records)			
		Sum		3	*$9.25*
201	Susan	Dec 05, 2005	Hamburger	1	$2.50
			Soda	1	$1.25
			Sandwich	1	$3.50
			Fresh Salad	1	$2.00
			Coffee	1	$0.85
		Summary for 'Lunch Date' = Dec 05, 2005 (5 detail records)			
		Sum		5	*$10.10*
Summary for 'Employee ID' = 201 (11 detail records)					
Sum				13	*$30.05*
202	Jim	Nov 16, 2005	Soup Of The Day	1	$1.50
			Grilled Steak	1	$6.00
			French Fries	1	$1.50
			Coffee	2	$1.70
			Dessert	1	$3.00
		Summary for 'Lunch Date' = Nov 16, 2005 (5 detail records)			
		Sum		6	*$13.70*
Summary for 'Employee ID' = 202 (5 detail records)					
Sum				6	*$13.70*
203	Martha	Nov 16, 2005	Fresh Salad	1	$2.00
			Coffee	1	$0.85
			Soda	1	$1.25
			French Fries	1	$1.50
			Grilled Steak	1	$6.00
		Summary for 'Lunch Date' = Nov 16, 2005 (5 detail records)			
		Sum		5	*$11.60*
203	Martha	Dec 05, 2005	Soup Of The Day	1	$1.50
			Grilled Steak	1	$6.00
			Coffee	2	$1.70
			Dessert	1	$3.00

Employee ID	First Name	Lunch Date	Description	Quantity	Total Price
		Summary for 'Lunch Date' = Dec 05, 2005 (4 detail records)			
		Sum		5	$12.20
Summary for 'Employee ID' = 203 (9 detail records)					
Sum				10	$23.80
204	Ellen	Nov 16, 2005	Hamburger	2	$5.00
			French Fries	1	$1.50
			Soup Of The Day	2	$3.00
			Soda	2	$2.50
		Summary for 'Lunch Date' = Nov 16, 2005 (4 detail records)			
		Sum		7	$12.00
204	Ellen	Nov 25, 2005	Fresh Salad	1	$2.00
			Grilled Steak	1	$6.00
			Coffee	2	$1.70
			Dessert	1	$3.00
		Summary for 'Lunch Date' = Nov 25, 2005 (4 detail records)			
		Sum		5	$12.70
Summary for 'Employee ID' = 204 (8 detail records)					
Sum				12	$24.70
205	Henry	Nov 25, 2005	Soda	2	$2.50
			Soup Of The Day	1	$1.50
			Grilled Steak	1	$6.00
			French Fries	1	$1.50
		Summary for 'Lunch Date' = Nov 25, 2005 (4 detail records)			
		Sum		5	$11.50
205	Henry	Dec 05, 2005	Fresh Salad	1	$2.00
			Soup Of The Day	1	$1.50
			Grilled Steak	1	$6.00
			French Fries	1	$1.50
			Soda	1	$1.25
		Summary for 'Lunch Date' = Dec 05, 2005 (5 detail records)			
		Sum		5	$12.25
Summary for 'Employee ID' = 205 (9 detail records)					
Sum				10	$23.75
207	Dan	Nov 16, 2005	French Fries	1	$1.50
			Coffee	2	$1.70
			Sandwich	2	$7.00
			Dessert	1	$3.00
		Summary for 'Lunch Date' = Nov 16, 2005 (4 detail records)			
		Sum		6	$13.20
207	Dan	Nov 25, 2005	Soup Of The Day	2	$3.00
			Sandwich	2	$7.00
			French Fries	1	$1.50

Employee ID	First Name	Lunch Date	Description	Quantity	Total Price
207	Dan	Nov 25, 2005	Soda	1	$1.25

Summary for 'Lunch Date' = Nov 25, 2005 (4 detail records)

| | | | **Sum** | 6 | *$12.75* |

Summary for 'Employee ID' = 207 (8 detail records)

| **Sum** | | | | 12 | *$25.95* |

208	Fred	Nov 25 2005	Hamburger	2	$5.00
			Coffee	1	$0.85
			French Fries	1	$1.50
			Fresh Salad	1	$2.00
			Soup Of The Day	1	$1.50
			Soda	1	$1.25

Summary for 'Lunch Date' = Nov 25, 2005 (6 detail records)

| | | | **Sum** | 7 | *$12.10* |

208	Fred	Dec 05, 2005	Fresh Salad	1	$2.00
			Grilled Steak	1	$6.00
			French Fries	1	$1.50
			Soda	1	$1.25
			Coffee	1	$0.85

Summary for 'Lunch Date' = Dec 05, 2005 (5 detail records)

| | | | **Sum** | 5 | *$11.60* |

Summary for 'Employee ID' = 208 (11 detail records)

| **Sum** | | | | 12 | *$23.70* |

210	Nancy	Nov 16, 2005	Fresh Salad	1	$2.00
			Dessert	1	$3.00
			Coffee	1	$0.85
			Soup Of The Day	1	$1.50
			Grilled Steak	1	$6.00

Summary for 'Lunch Date' = Nov 16, 2005 (5 detail records)

| | | | **Sum** | 5 | *$13.35* |

210	Nancy	Dec 05, 2005	Dessert	1	$3.00
			Soup Of The Day	1	$1.50
			Grilled Steak	1	$6.00
			French Fries	1	$1.50
			Coffee	2	$1.70

Summary for 'Lunch Date' = Dec 05, 2005 (5 detail records)

| | | | **Sum** | 6 | *$13.70* |

Summary for 'Employee ID' = 210 (10 detail records)

| **Sum** | | | | 11 | *$27.05* |

| ***Grand Total*** | | | | 86 | *$192.70* |

Typical Applications

20-8   Smaller databases

SQL and relational databases were originally developed to handle very large amounts of data. It was considered overkill to use them for smaller amounts of data. It used to be said that if you used a relational database for your address book, it would be like using a bulldozer to crack a peanut.

Today, SQL and relational databases are being used for much smaller databases, such as for a lawyer's office. I even use a database to balance my checkbook and organize my address book. Once you start thinking in terms of representing information in tables, you see how you can use this framework to organize many things, big or small. One of the leading SQL products for developing smaller databases is Access.

20-9   OLTP

Online transaction processing (OLTP) systems focus mostly on inputting data. There may also be a few small reports. Often, OLTP systems use forms and handle only a few records at a time.

There is no "typical" OLTP system. Every application is different. But here is a sketch of one such system:

- 25,000,000 rows of data

- 200 users who can simultaneously enter and retrieve data

- Two-second response time on most transactions

20-10   Data warehouses

Data warehouses emphasize the collection and analysis of even larger amounts of data. These systems often focus on reports that perform a detailed analysis of the data.

Again, there is no "typical" data warehouse system, but here is a sketch of one such system:

- 500,000,000 rows of data
- One report is run at a time to analyze the data
- Three hours is a typical time to run a report

Summary

SQL was originally designed to be simple and easy to use. It was designed to do one thing well — handle information. Another layer of software in another programming language would handle other tasks.

It turned out that SQL was not quite simple enough for nonprogrammers to use. Today most people who use databases interact with them through forms and reports. The new trend is for people to be able to use those forms and reports over the Internet.

OBTAINING AND
INSTALLING
ORACLE

This appendix discusses the following:

1. Which version of Oracle to use

2. How to obtain Oracle

3. How to install Oracle

4. How to create a new userid

5. How to install the tables used in this book

Getting Current Information

The information in this appendix is subject to change because, from time to time, Oracle Corporation changes its policies and the way it markets its products. To obtain the most current information, please visit the Web site for this book, *www.sqlfun.com*.

Which Product Should You Get?

To run the examples of SQL code in this book on your computer at home, you will need Personal Oracle, which is also called Oracle Personal Edition. You can also use the Enterprise Edition. The version number of Oracle is often included in the name. The current version is 9i so this product is called Oracle9i.

If you have Oracle at work or at school, you might have a different product or version. All the examples should run there too, so use the version you have available. The reason I recommend the Personal Edition is because it requires less disk space and memory from the computer.

When you order the software, you must get the version that matches your operating system. There are different versions for Windows 98, Windows 2000, Windows XP, and Linux. Oracle is not available for Windows Me or for the Macintosh. If you have Windows 98, you may need to get Oracle8i.

You can get a trial version of Oracle that gives you a license to use it for 30 days for prototyping and development. This is much less expensive than buying a fully licensed version. There are two ways to obtain Oracle: You can download it over the Internet for free, or you can order it on a CD-ROM for about $40.

Downloading Oracle from the Internet

This download is practical if you have a broadband connection to the Internet. Otherwise it can take many hours. If you have a 56k modem, you will probably want to start it in the evening before you go to bed and check on it in the morning. You need to have an ISP that can hold a long connection. You will need to register with Oracle Technology Network (OTN) before you can start the download, but that is free. They will need your name, address, and some other information.

Directions to register

1. Go to *otn.oracle.com*.

2. Click on Membership.

3. Sign up for a new account — it is free.

4. You will get a confirmation by e-mail.

Directions to download

1. Go to *otn.oracle.com*.

2. Click on Downloads.

3. You should read the Software Download FAQ.

4. In the Select a Product box, choose 9i Database or 8i Personal Edition.

5. Choose the version for your operating system. For instance, Oracle9i Database Enterprise Edition for Windows NT/2000. (In version 9i the Personal Edition is packaged together with the Enterprise Edition. In version 8i they are packaged separately)

6. Read and accept the Eligibility Export Restrictions and the Oracle Technology License Agreement.

7. Follow the remaining directions on the Web page.

Ordering Oracle on a CD

1. Go to *www.oracle.com*.

2. Click on Store.

3. Click on the CD Pack tab.

4. Choose Oracle9i CD Pack for your operating system.

5. Go through the checkout process. A credit card is required.

Installing Oracle

Check the system requirements

Oracle requires a fairly strong computer. Each version of Oracle has different system requirements. Here are some typical requirements:

	Minimum	Recommended
CPU	Pentium 133	Pentium 200
RAM	64 MB	128 MB
Disk space	800 MB on an uncompressed drive	1000 MB on an uncompressed drive

Installation procedure

The following directions might be all you need, though you might have received more detailed instructions with your copy of Oracle. The instructions below are for installation on Windows 2000.

1. Turn off your computer. Then turn it on again. It is best to have nothing running. If you are installing on Windows NT or Windows 2000, be sure to log on as the administrator or to a userid that has the privileges of an administrator.

2. Put the CD in the drive. If you have AutoStart turned on, you will get a screen that says "Oracle9i Server." You will have three options:

   Install/Deinstall Products
   Explore CD
   Browse Documentation

3. If you do not have AutoStart turned on, you can get to the beginning screen with

   Start ➜ Run ➜ D:\autorun\autorun.exe

   where D is the CD drive.

4. Choose Browse Documentation.

5. Choose Documentation.

6. Print the Installation Instructions Quick Tour. This is probably all the information you will need. Follow these instructions.

7. If you do need more information, you can find it in the Database Installation Guide.

Your initial userids and passwords

After Oracle is installed, you will have these userids and passwords:

Userid	Password	Notes
scott	tiger	Ordinary user
system	manager	Has DBA authority

Setting Up to Run the Examples in This Book

There are a few more steps you need to do before you are ready to run the examples in this book. Follow each of these next steps.

Create a `temp` directory on your C drive

This book often uses the c:\temp directory. Please create it if you don't already have one. Copy into it all the files from the CD-ROM.

Log on to SQLplus with userid `system`

To get to the logon screen, use

Start ➔ Programs ➔ Oracle ➔ Application Development ➔ SQL Plus

Then enter

    User Name: `system`

    Password: `manager`

    Host String: (leave blank)

Oracle should start and give you an SQL> prompt. If it doesn't, look for a Start Database option somewhere under

Start ➜ Programs ➜ Oracle

Start the database and then try again to log on.

Verify that Oracle is running correctly

To verify that Oracle is running, you will ask it to name the userid you are logged on to. At the SQL prompt, enter

```
select user from dual;
```

and press the Enter key.

The response should be as follows:

```
USER
-----------
SYSTEM
```

Verify the names of your tablespaces

In some versions, Oracle changes the names of the tablespaces it installs. You need these names to set up a new userid and install the tables for this book, so you need to check the names of the tablespaces you have.

At the SQL prompt, enter

```
select tablespace_name from dba_tablespaces;
```

and press Enter.

The usual response is as follows:

```
TABLESPACE_NAME
------------------
SYSTEM
RBS
USERS
TEMP
TOOLS
INDX
DRSYS
```

In case your tablespace names are different, find the closest match you have for USERS, TEMP, and INDX. Substitute the names you have in the steps that follow. For example, your names might be USER_DATA instead of USERS, and INDEX_DATA instead of INDX.

Setting Up a New Userid

If you are working on your own computer, I recommend that you set up a new userid to work with this book. If you are working on a shared computer at work or at school, you may not be able to do this.

In the following code, I will create the new userid sqlfun and give it a password of puppy. You can use a different name and password. The password must begin with a letter, not a number.

At the SQL prompt, enter

```
create user sqlfun identified by puppy
temporary tablespace temp
default tablespace users;
```

Oracle should respond, "User created." Then enter

```
grant resource, connect to sqlfun;
```

Oracle should respond, "Grant succeeded."

Log on to your new userid

If you are currently logged on to `system`, enter

```
connect sqlfun/puppy;
```

Oracle should respond, "Connected."

If you are logging on afresh, follow the directions above for logging on to `system`, but use your new userid and password.

Installing the Tables Used in This Book

All the tables used in this book are created in one Oracle script file that is on the CD in this book. You only need to run this procedure once. Oracle will permanently store all these tables, so you will have them any time you log on.

If you are working on your own computer and you have tablespaces named `USER` and `INDX`, run the command

```
start c:\temp\oracle\sqlfun_build_tables.sql
```

This assigns tablespace names as it builds the tables. Otherwise, accept the default tablespace names by running the command

```
start c:\temp\oracle\sqlfun_build_tables2.sql
```

Another option allows you to assign different tablespace names. I discuss it at the end of this appendix.

When you run the above code, you will see this initial message:

```
*************************************************
*                                               *
* Build the tables for SQL Fundamentals         *
*                                               *
* Version 1: Assigns the tablespace names       *
*                                               *
* Press ENTER to continue.                      *
* Press CTRL + C to exit.                        *
*************************************************
```

Press Enter and the tables will be built.

Check that the tables loaded correctly

You should see the following reports on your screen:

```
OBJECT_TYPE             COUNT(*)
------------------      ---------
INDEX                         20
SEQUENCE                       2
TABLE                         85
VIEW                          11
```

```
CONSTRAINT_TYPE                        COUNT(*)
-------------------------------------  ---------
CHECK CONSTRAINT                               2
PRIMARY KEY CONSTRAINT                        18
REFERENTIAL INTEGRITY CONSTRAINT               6
UNIQUENESS CONSTRAINT                          2
```

You might have to scroll up the screen to see the first one. If the numbers match the ones above, then the load worked correctly. In that case, you are now ready to run the code in this book. See appendix B for some tips on using Oracle.

If your load did not work correctly, look at the log file

c:\temp\sqlfun_build_tables.txt

Search the file for "ERROR". Some error messages are expected. These follow a DROP statement, such as DROP TABLE, DROP SEQUENCE, DROP CONSTRAINT, or DROP VIEW. These expected errors look as follows:

```
SQL> drop table l_employees cascade constraints;
DROP TABLE L_EMPLOYEES CASCADE CONSTRAINTS
            *
ERROR at line 1:
ORA-00942: table or view does not exist
```

You will need to find an error that is different from this. Then find someone to help you with it.

Disaster recovery

In case you create the Oracle tables on a production ID, you can drop all the tables and other database objects created by the sqlfun_build_tables.sql file. To do this enter:

```
start d:\oracle\droptables\sqlfun_drop_tables.sql
```

where D is the letter identifying your CD-ROM drive.

How to Build the Tables and
Assign Other Tablespace Names

Here is a procedure you can use to build the tables and assign the tablespaces if you are working on your own computer and your tablespaces have names other than USERS and INDX.

Modify the code of the Build Tables script before you run it. Edit the file

```
c:\temp\oracle\sqlfun_build_tables.sql
```

Change two lines near the top of the file. Currently these lines say:

```
define users = users;
define indx = indx;
```

If your tablespace names are USER_DATA and INDEX_DATA, you should change these lines to:

```
define users = user_data;
define indx = index_data;
```

Then run this file. Enter:

```
start c:\temp\oracle\sqlfun_build_tables.sql
```

This builds all the tables with the tablespace names you designate.

appendix B

TIPS ON USING ORACLE

This appendix contains a sample session that shows you how to use Oracle. This demonstration shows you all the tricks you need to know. I begin by showing you how to log on and run the login script. Then I show you how to enter a query, run it, print the result, log off, and examine the spool file. After the session, I show you several other techniques you can use.

Starting Oracle

Step 1: Start ➜ Programs ➜ Oracle ➜ Application Development ➜ SQLplus.

This is what you will see:

```
┌─────────────────────────────────────────────┐
│ Log On                                        │
│                                               │
│                                               │
│   User Name:     ┌───────────────────────┐    │
│                  └───────────────────────┘    │
│                                               │
│   Password:      ┌───────────────────────┐    │
│                  └───────────────────────┘    │
│                                               │
│   Host String:   ┌───────────────────────┐    │
│                  └───────────────────────┘    │
│                                               │
│      ┌──────────────┐    ┌──────────────┐     │
│      │     OK       │    │   Cancel     │     │
│      └──────────────┘    └──────────────┘     │
└─────────────────────────────────────────────┘
```

Step 2: Enter the User Name (userid) and Password you set up when you installed Oracle. If you followed my suggestions in appendix A, enter User Name = sqlfun and Password = puppy. Leave the Host String blank. If you didn't set up a special ID for this book, then use User Name = scott and Password = tiger.

Here are the messages you will see (or something like this):

```
 Oracle SQL*Plus
 File  Edit  Search  Options  Help

SQL*Plus: Release 8.1.6.0.0 - Production on Sat Sep 22 02:25:07 2001

(c) Copyright 1999 Oracle Corporation.  All rights reserved.


Connected to:
Oracle8i Enterprise Edition Release 8.1.6.0.0 - Production
With the Partitioning option
JServer Release 8.1.6.0.0 - Production

SQL>
```

Step 3: Run the SQL login script. You will need to do this every time you log on to Oracle. This sets up the Oracle environment in the standard way I am using in this book. These settings are not preserved from one session to another.

After the SQL prompt, enter

```
start c:\temp\sqlfun_login.sql
```

If you have installed the login script in a different location, adjust the full path name above.

You will get the following information message:

```
*************************************************************************
*                                                                       *
* Set up the SQL*Plus environment for SQL Fundamentals                  *
*                                                                       *
* Press ENTER to continue.                                              *
* Press CNTL + C to exit.                                               *
*************************************************************************
```

Press Enter to continue.

After the login script runs, this is the message you will receive:

```
*************************************************************************
*                                                                       *
*      The SQLplus environment is now set up for you to run             *
*      the examples and exercises for SQL FUNDAMENTALS                  *
*                                                                       *
*************************************************************************
```

Now you have finished logging on. You can enter SQL commands at the SQL prompt.

Entering a Query

Step 1: Open a Notepad session. I prefer to enter SQL code into Notepad and then paste it into Oracle because it is easier to edit the code in Notepad. Since the SQL I write at first is rarely perfect, I plan ahead to be able to edit it. To open Notepad

Start → Programs → Accessories → Notepad

Step 2: Within Notepad, enter an SQL query such as

```
select first_name
from l_employees;
```

Press Enter after you enter the semicolon, so the cursor is at the beginning of a new line. This prevents some error messages.

Step 3: Copy this SQL by highlighting all of the lines and then pressing CTRL+C.

Step 4: Go back to Oracle SQLplus by clicking on that window and paste the SQL into it by pressing CTRL+V. You might need to press Enter to run the query. Here is the result:

```
SQL> select first_name
  2  from l_employees;

FIRST
NAME
--------
SUSAN
JIM
MARTHA
ELLEN
HENRY
CAROL
DAN
FRED
PAULA
NANCY

10 rows selected.

SQL>
```

The "2" under the first SQL prompt means that this is the second line of the code. The SQLplus environment contains a line editor, which generates these numbers. I prefer to use Notepad to edit my SQL code, so I do not use this line editor.

If you get stuck in the line editor and it just keeps generating more numbers, then it thinks you are still entering a query. To get out, enter a semicolon and press Enter.

Step 5: Next, improve the query by adding the `last_name` column. To do this, go to Notepad and change the code to

```
select first_name,
       last_name,
from 1_employees;
```

Step 6: Copy this code into Oracle SQLplus and run it. You will receive an error message, as in the following screen:

```
SQL> select first_name,
  2          last_name,
  3  from 1_employees;
FROM L_EMPLOYEES
     *
ERROR at line 3:
ORA-00936: missing expression
```

In theory, the asterisk in the message should identify where the error is. Oracle is saying that the error occurs with the word FROM. However, the error here is actually caused by the comma after `last_name` on line 2.

In most software products the error messages are imprecise. SQL is no better or worse than any other type of software in this regard. The problem is that the computer is genuinely confused by the error, it does not understand what you mean, and it is doing its best to point out where the error might be. However, the computer is behaving like a bewildered four-year old child, so you cannot rely on the error message it gives you.

Step 7: Go back to Notepad and correct the error. You need to remove the comma after `last_name`. Now the code is:

```
select first_name,
       last_name
from 1_employees;
```

Step 8: Copy the code from Notepad into Oracle SQLplus and run it. This time you receive the result you wanted.

```
SQL> select first_name,
  2          last_name
  3  from 1_employees;

FIRST      LAST
NAME       NAME
---------- ----------
SUSAN      BROWN
JIM        KERN
MARTHA     WOODS
ELLEN      OWENS
HENRY      PERKINS
CAROL      ROSE
DAN        SMITH
FRED       CAMPBELL
PAULA      JACOBS
NANCY      HOFFMAN

10 rows selected.

SQL>
```

Step 9: Now print your result. You cannot print directly from Oracle SQL-plus, so you must use another method. Place the mouse at the upper left corner of the area you want to print and drag it to the bottom right corner, highlighting the entire area. Copy it with CTRL+C. Open a new Notepad session, paste your text in it and use Notepad to print it.

Step 10: Save the code you wrote. Since your code is already in Notepad, you can save it as a text file. That way it is completely under your control.

Step 11: Close your Oracle session. Enter EXIT at the SQL prompt.

Step 12: Examine your spool file. After you exit from your Oracle session, you can open the spool file. This file captures all the SQL you entered and all of the responses from Oracle — in short, everything that occurred during the session. The name of the spool file I set up for you is

`c:\temp\sqlfun_last_session.txt`

If you look at this file before you close your Oracle session, the file might not be complete. Each time you begin an Oracle session, a new spool file will be started, which replaces the old spool file. So if you want to keep your spool file, you need to rename it at the end of the session.

Other Ways to Edit Your SQL Code

If you don't like entering your code into Notepad, there are two other methods you can use:

1. Cut and paste the code within SQLplus.

2. Use the SQLplus line editor.

Starting point

The following discussion assumes that you have already entered the following query into the SQLplus environment:

```
select first_name
from 1_employees;
```

Using the cut-and-paste method

First, highlight all the code up to and including the first line you want to change. In this case, you need to put a comma at the end of the first line and add a new line after that, so only the first line is highlighted. Then use CTRL+C to copy the highlighted code. Press CTRL+V to copy it to the SQL prompt. Add the comma to the end of the line. Then add the new line last_name as you did in the first example. Copy the rest of the code, and run it as usual.

Using the **SQLplus line editor**

SQLplus contains a line editor. Its commands are `list`, `change`, `delete`, `append`, and `input`. Here is an example of how to use it:

```
SQL> list 1
  1* select first_name
SQL> change /name/name,/
  1* select first_name,
SQL> input last_name
SQL> list
  1  select first_name,
  2  last_name
  3* from l_employees
SQL>
```

Explanation

Entry	What It Does
`list 1`	Lists line one, the line you want to change. SQLplus shows you that line
`change /name/name,/`	Puts a comma after name
`input last_name`	Adds a new line containing `last_name`
`list`	Lists the entire SQL statement except the ending semicolon, which has been automatically deleted

To run the code, enter a forward slash (/) at the SQL prompt and press Enter.

Error Messages Are Sometimes Correct

This is an example of an error message where Oracle correctly identifies the error.

```
SQL> select first_name,
  2            last_name
  3  from l_employes;
FROM L_EMPLOYES
     *
ERROR at line 3:
ORA-00942: table or view does not exist


SQL>
```

The problem is that I misspelled the name of the table. Oracle identifies this error by printing the line that contains the error and putting an asterisk under the word that is in error. The message, "table or view does not exist", suggests that I misspelled the name of the table. So it is not necessary to look up the error message ORA-00942.

Using the Scrollbars

I have set up the SQLplus environment for you as if it were a giant sheet of paper. It is about 1,000 lines long and 1,000 characters wide. You can use the scrollbars to see the portion that does not appear on the screen.

Occasionally, on some computers, the bottom scrollbar does not work. If this happens to you, here is a trick to get it to work:

Options → Environment

Make a change to the value in the Buffer Width. If the Buffer Width is 999, then change it to 998. If it is 998, then change it to 999.

This trick makes no sense at all, so do not try to understand it. However it usually makes the bottom scrollbar work correctly.

If Oracle Does Not Respond

Occasionally you might find that nothing happens when you type commands into SQLplus. There is no response at all. This occurs sometimes when you return to Oracle after working in some other application. The problem is that the SQLplus window is not selected and does not have the focus. Within the Windows operating system, only one window has the focus at a time. To solve this, click once in the SQLplus window.

Installing the LOGIN Script

If you install the LOGIN script, it will run automatically each time you begin an Oracle session. The following steps show you how to install it.

Step 1: Find the folder that contains the file SQLPLUSW.EXE. This folder will have a name similar to:

```
c:\oracle\ora81\bin
```

Step 2: Copy the file SQLFUN_LOGIN.SQL to that folder.

Step 3: If the folder contains a file named LOGIN.SQL, then delete it.

Step 4: Rename SQLFUN_LOGIN.SQL to LOGIN.SQL in that folder.

Running All the SQL for a Chapter

You can run all the Oracle SQL for a chapter at one time and then look at the spool file to see the results. For example, to run the code for chapter 2, you can enter

```
start c:\temp\chapters\ch02.sql
```

This runs the SQL for all the examples in the chapter and it creates a spool file named

```
c:\temp\oracle02.txt
```

All the code from chapters 2 to 18 can be run this way, except the following:

- Chapter 6, sections 15, 16 and exercise 2a
- Chapter 18, sections 6, 7, and 8

For those sections, see the directions in the text.

TIPS ON USING ACCESS

Here is a sample session that shows you how to use Access. I begin by showing you how to start the program. Then I show you how to enter a query, run it, and print the result.

You Can Use Access 2000 or 2002

The CD-ROM for this book contains two versions of the Access database. One file is in Access 2000 format and the other is in Access 2002 format. They are in different folders and have different names. Each version contains all the tables you need from this book. In appendix A, I asked you to copy both versions to your c:\temp directory.

Starting Access

There are several ways to open Access. The way I recommend is to right-click on the Start button. Click Explore. Then find the database you want to open, which will have the file type of MDB, and double-click on it. It usually opens to the Tables tab, but if it doesn't, just click that tab. Another way to open it is

Start ➔ Programs ➔ Microsoft Access

If you get a message that the database is read-only, you will need to make some corrections and start again. You need the database to be read-write in order to enter SQL queries. If you find that it is read-only, there are two major things to check.

The most common cause is that the read-only property is set. To change this, go to Explorer and locate the Access database file, which has a file type of MDB, and click on it. Select the Properties option and uncheck the check box that says Read-Only. Then click Apply.

SQLFUN.mdb Properties	? X

General

SQLFUN.mdb

Type of file:	Microsoft Access Application
Opens with:	Microsoft Access for Window Change...
Location:	C:\Temp
Size:	1.27 MB (1,335,296 bytes)
Size on disk:	1.27 MB (1,335,296 bytes)
Created:	Saturday, September 01, 2001, 10:53:30 AM
Modified:	Tuesday, September 25, 2001, 5:31:04 PM
Accessed:	Today, September 27, 2001
Attributes:	☑ Read-only ☐ Hidden ☑ Archive

OK   Cancel   Apply

Another reason some Access databases are read-only is that they are on a read-only disk drive. This occurs in the computer labs of many schools where the teacher has placed some files on a server for the students to copy. To use the database, you must copy the Access database file onto your local read-write drive. This is usually the C drive. When you have successfully started Access, you will see something like this:

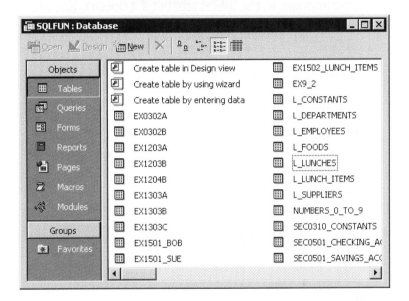

Entering an SQL Query

Step 1: In the preceding screen, the Tables tab was pressed, under Objects. Now press the Queries tab and you will see something like this:

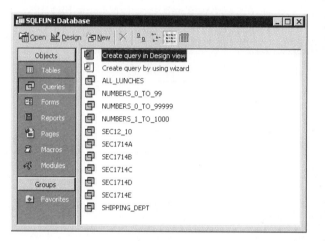

Step 2: Double-click on "Create query in Design View" and here is what you see:

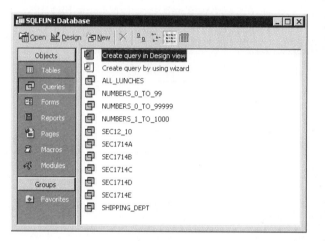

Step 3: The previous screen is for entering a query using the GUI, but we want to enter it with SQL, so press the Close button on the Show Table screen. Then you will see something like this:

Step 4: Press either the SQL button on the toolbar or go to the View menu and choose SQL View. This brings up the following SQL window:

Step 5: At this point, open Notepad and enter your query. I recommend that you enter your query into Notepad, rather than directly into Access, so you have more control over it. Access reformats a query when it is saved, but in Notepad your query will retain the format you give it. Notepad provides an easy way to edit your queries and also to print them.

Within Notepad, enter a query such as

```
select first_name,
        last_name
from 1_employees;
```

and paste it into the Query screen.

Step 6: To run the query, press the toolbar button with the red exclamation point. Another method is to go to the Query menu and choose Run. You will see the following result table:

first_name	last_name
Susan	Brown
Jim	Kern
Martha	Woods
Ellen	Owens
Henry	Perkins
Carol	Rose
Dan	Smith
Fred	Campbell
Paula	Jacobs
Nancy	Hoffman

Record: 11

Step 7: If you want to return to the SQL window after you have run the query, go to the View menu and choose SQL View. Your code will be displayed there.

Dealing with Errors

Some of the error messages in Access are very helpful and others are less so. First, I give you an example of an error message that identifies the error correctly. I enter the following code, where the table name is misspelled:

```
select first_name,
        last_name
from 1_employes;
```

This is the error message I receive:

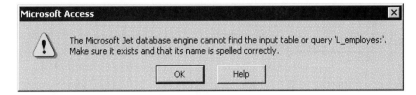

This message is helpful and specific. It tells me that the name of the table is spelled incorrectly. To correct the error, I press OK, make the correction, and run my query again.

Next I show you an error message that might confuse you. Once you understand it, this message is quite useful. However, on the surface it does not tell you what you need to know. I enter the following code, where the last name is misspelled:

```
select first_name,
       last_nme
from l_employees;
```

This is the error message I receive:

This error message is prompting me to enter a value for `last_nme`. But the problem is that `last_name` is misspelled. So my response to this error message is to press the Cancel button, correct the spelling of `last_name`, and run the query again.

For people who want to know more about this particular error message, here is an explanation: Access assumes that anything it does not recognize is a parameter, which is a type of variable value that is entered when the query is run. In this case, Access is asking you for the value of `last_nme`. If you responded to the message by entering "Smith", Access would replace `last_nme` in the query with `Smith`, which is equivalent to placing the literal `Smith` in the query. The result table would like this:

first_name	last_nme
Susan	Smith
Jim	Smith
Martha	Smith
Ellen	Smith
Henry	Smith
Carol	Smith
Dan	Smith
Fred	Smith
Paula	Smith
Nancy	Smith

Record: 11

Printing

You can print your result tables directly from Access by using

File → Print

The one thing you cannot print this way is your SQL code. That is one of the reasons you should put your SQL code into Notepad. You can print it from there.

DIAGRAM OF
THE LUNCHES
DATABASE

This appendix contains a diagram of the Lunches database that shows all the tables in the database and how they are related to each other. It contains a list of the join conditions to use when you are obtaining data from more than one table. The data validation rules are also shown here.

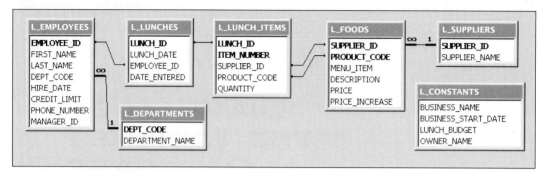

Diagram of the Lunches database.

The columns of the primary key are shown in bold.

The names of all the tables in the Lunches database begin with the prefix l_. This prefix shows that these tables are related and that they are all parts of a single system.

The lines between the tables show the join conditions.

The lines containing a "1" and an infinity sign show join conditions which are also Referential Integrity constraints.

Join Conditions

The relationships between the tables.

Tables to Be Joined	SQL Code Showing the Join Condition (The join condition is shown in the where clause.)

l_employees
l_departments
	``
	select a.*,
	       b.*
	from l_employees a,
	     l_departments b
	where a.dept_code = b.dept_code;
	``

l_employees
l_lunches
	``
	select a.*,
	       b.*
	from l_employees a,
	     l_lunches b
	where a.employee_id = b.employee_id;
	``

l_lunches
l_lunch_items
	``
	select a.*,
	       b.*
	from l_lunches a,
	     l_lunch_items b
	where a.lunch_id = b.lunch_id;
	``

The relationships between the tables. *(continued)*

Tables to Be Joined	SQL Code Showing the Join Condition (The join condition is shown in the `where` clause.)
| `l_lunch_items`<br>`l_foods` | ```
select a.*,
       b.*
from l_lunch_items a,
     l_foods b
where a.supplier_id = b.supplier_id
  and a.product_code = b.product_code;
``` |
| `l_foods`<br>`l_suppliers` | ```
select a.*,
       b.*
from l_foods a,
     l_suppliers b
where a.supplier_id = b.supplier_id;
``` |
| `l_constants`<br>Any other table | ```
select a.*,
       b.*
from l_constants a
     any_other_table b;
```<br>(No join condition is needed between the `l_constants` table and any other table because this table contains only one row.) |

Data Validation Rules

Table	Column	Validation Rule
Validation Rule 1: Referential Integrity Constraint		
`l_employees`	`dept_code`	Data is checked. It must have a valid value.
`l_departments`	`dept_code`	List of all the valid values.
Validation Rule 2: Referential Integrity Constraint		
`l_foods`	`supplier_id`	Data is checked. It must have a valid value.
`l_suppliers`	`supplier_id`	List of all the valid values.
Validation Rule 3: Uniqueness Constraint		
`l_employees`	`phone_number`	Each employee must have a distinct phone number.
Validation Rule 4: Not Null Constraint		
`l_lunches`	`employee_id`	`employee_id` is a required field.
Validation Rule 5: Check Constraint		
`l_foods`	`price`	The price must be less than $10.00.
```

INDEX

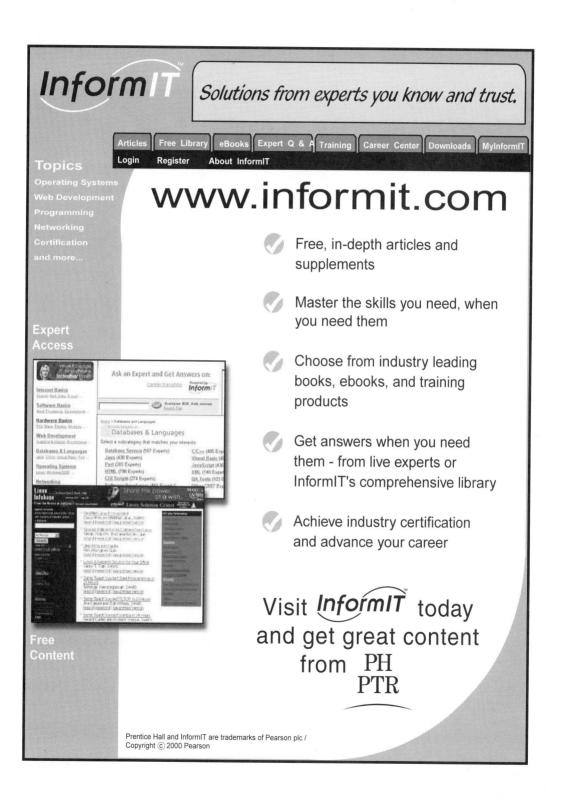

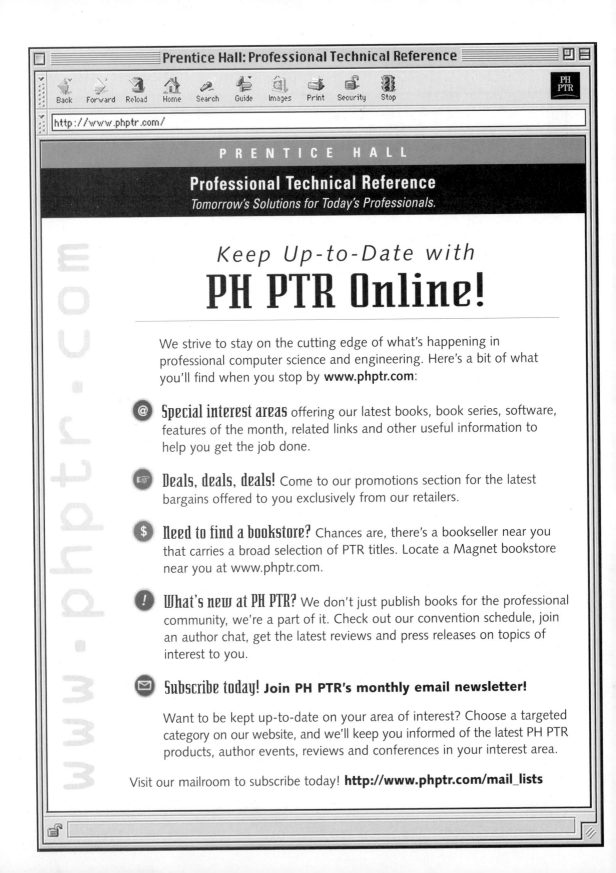

ABOUT THE CD-ROM

The CD-ROM included with SQL *Fundamentals, 2nd Edition* contains all the tables of data used in this book. It also contains the SQL for the examples in the chapters. The data is available in both Oracle® and Access® formats. The appendices in this book give you full instructions for using this software. The graphic at the bottom of this page shows the relationship of all the tables found in the Lunches database.

The CD-ROM can be used on Microsoft® Windows® 98/NT®/2000/XP. The Oracle portion can also be used on UNIX® and Linux®. The Access portion can also be used on Microsoft Windows Me.

License Agreement

Use of the software accompanying SQL *Fundamentals, 2nd Edition* is subject to the terms of the License Agreement and Limited Warranty, found on the previous page.

Technical Support

Prentice Hall does not offer technical support for any of the programs on the CD-ROM. However, if the CD-ROM is damaged, you may obtain a replacement copy by sending an e-mail that describes the problem to: disc_exchange@prenhall.com.

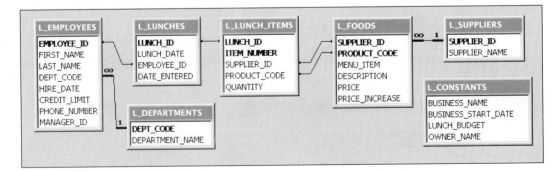

Diagram of the Lunches database.